Rural Guatemala, 1760–1940

Rural Guatemala

1760–1940

David McCreery

Stanford University Press
Stanford, California

Stanford University Press
Stanford, California
© 1994 by the Board of Trustees
of the Leland Stanford Junior University
Printed in the United States of America

CIP data appear at the end of the book

Stanford University Press publications are distributed exclusively by Stanford University Press within the United States, Canada, Mexico, and Central America; they are distributed exclusively by Cambridge University Press throughout the rest of the world.

Acknowledgments

Above all, I thank my family, my wife, Angela, and my children, Shimby and Elizabeth Carmen. Without their love and help this book would never have been written.

Over the years a number of funding agencies have supported my research on rural Guatemala: the Fulbright-Hays Faculty Research Abroad Program (1980–81), the Social Science Research Council (1981), the Fulbright Program (1986–87), and the Georgia State University Research Enhancement Fund (1990).

Portions of the material in this book appeared first in the following articles and are used here with permission: "Debt Servitude in Rural Guatemala, 1876–1936," *Hispanic American Historical Review* 63, no. 4 (Nov. 1983): 26–37; "An Odious Feudalism: *Mandamientos* and Commercial Agriculture in Guatemala, 1861–1920," *Latin American Perspectives*, 13, no. 1 (Winter 1986): 99–117; "Land, Labor, and Violence in Highland Guatemala: San Juan Ixcoy (Huehuetenango), 1890–1940," *The Americas* 45, no. 2 (Oct. 1988): 237–49; "State Power, Indigenous Communities, and Land in Nineteenth Century Guatemala," in C. Smith, ed., *Indian Communities and the State: Guatemala, 1540–1988* (Austin, Tex., 1989), 96–115; "Hegemony and Repression in Rural Guatemala," *Peasant Studies* 17, no. 3 (Spring 1990): 157–77; and "A Terrible Scourge: Guatemala in the Influenza Pandemic of 1918–19," in F. van Hartsvelt, ed., *The Influenza Pandemic of 1918–1919: The Urban Impact in the Western World* (Lewiston, N.Y., 1992), 161–83.

Both in Guatemala and in the United States many persons helped me with this project, including the several directors and the staff of the Archivo General de Centro América, especially Don Gregorio Conchoa, the staff of the Archivo Histórico Arquidiocesano, Bill Sweezy, Steve Elliott and the staff of the Centro de Investigaciones Regionales de Centro América, and Jane Hobson and the staff of the Georgia State Inter-Library Loan office. I have discussed the project in all or part innumerable times with anyone who would listen and with many more people than I can remember, but particularly helpful were observations by Angela McCreery, Carol Smith, George Lovell, Lowell Gudmundson, Lee Woodward, Robert Carmack, Jim Handy, John Watanabe, David Stoll, Victor Pereira, Ben Paul, and Steve Webre. Chris Lutz read and commented on the entire manuscript, a particularly unselfish piece of work from someone known for his help to all those interested in Central America. Tod Little, Wade Kit, and Blake Pattridge read parts of the manuscripts and commented on these when I taught at Tulane University in the fall of 1990. And Lee Woodward, E. Bradford Burns, and Murdo MacLeod repeatedly have written letters for me to support my efforts to obtain research funding.

Shirley Taylor did an enormous amount of work editing the manuscript, and I thank her, even if I did not always agree with her.

Finally, the faculty and the several chairs—particularly Gary Fink and Tim Crimmins—of the History Department and various administrators at Georgia State University have strongly supported my research and writing. I am very grateful, and I hope this book meets their expectations.

D.McC.
Goiânia–Go.
Brazil
December 1993

Contents

Maps and Tables

Maps

Tables

Rural Guatemala, 1760–1940

east of the Elbe, slaves in the U.S. South, or the highland Indians of Guatemala. Thus, far from bringing homogeneity, the expansion of capitalism on a world scale generated "a complex hierarchical system controlled by the capitalist mode of production, but including a vast array of subsidiary regions that exhibited different combinations of the capitalist mode with other modes."[8] Instead of being a sort of pre-history of capitalism, primitive accumulation proved to be an ongoing and self-reproducing historical process, a parallel and associated, and, in the more functionalist variants, necessary part of the continuation of capitalist profitability.[9] Such an understanding assumes some form of world economic system from the sixteenth century, a system dominated first by merchant wealth and then by industrial capital originating chiefly in the North Atlantic "core."[10] By the nineteenth century almost all the world, whether voluntarily or involuntarily, was part of an international complex structured by the economic, political, ideological, and military power of a small number of North Atlantic capitalist nation states.

The intent here is to examine the history of the process of primitive accumulation in rural Guatemala for the two centuries from the Bourbon Reforms to the 1940's. Prior to this period the Spanish state and its local representatives exploited Guatemala's indigenous population chiefly through tributary or tax mechanisms. Despite the introduction of new tools and plants and animals and beneath a gloss of religious and political change, the rural population largely continued to create and inhabit its own socioeconomic and political spaces and to suffer only limited outside interference on a day-to-day basis. Commercial production impinged hardly at all on much of the countryside, and even that declined after 1800 with the collapse of the indigo trade and the onset of political chaos following independence. Freed from the attentions of the state and the economic elites, Indian "traditional" culture came for a brief period to full fruition. After 1860, the onset of large-scale coffee production carried with it unprecedented demands on the rural indigenous population for land and labor. Because of the Indians' resistance to the appropriation of their labor and resources and because coffee cultivation in Guatemala depended on labor extracted only seasonally from the villages, the communities and the noncapitalist forms that for centuries had dominated production relations within the communities and between the communities and the commercial producers persisted. Far from obliterating preexisting forms or spreading capitalist relations to the countryside, the new crop of coffee generalized, strengthened, and perpetuated noncapitalist modes of exploitation. Over time, however, the effects of Liberal ideology, cash wages, land loss, population growth, and socioeconomic differentiation among the villagers undercut the viability of the Indian communities and pushed more and more of the population into the labor market as "semiproletariats" or free labor.

In studying these and related historical changes, it is essential to keep in mind that those who make history are not Althusserian "bearers of class positions" but are simply individuals, groups, and classes living and making decisions and choices in a world of limited alternatives and imperfect knowledge. As people struggle to make their own history, they rarely do so as they "should," as they might wish, or as later observers may imagine would have been in their best interests. Peoples and societies almost always hold and act on contradictory ideas and understandings, and they proceed not on the basis of their actual situation but rather on what they perceive that situation to be. Most historians today understand the dangers of judging the past in the context of current values and prejudices, but it is equally dangerous to seek to enforce upon history and historical actors a rationality or a consistency of thought or action patently absent from our own experience. Similarly, there is almost literally a world of distance between the airy castles of theory and the grime and chaos of the piles of documents from which historians attempt to extract history.

One victim of this chasm has been the concept of "modes of production." Much debated and written about in the 1970's and early 1980's, modes of production proved at best a clumsy tool for constructing history. Forms derived from theory rarely coincided with "the real world" as revealed in artifacts, documents, and testimony. One response was to generate an ever proliferating number of "modes of production" based upon evident empirical differences, but this proved so unsatisfactory that even many former enthusiasts became disenchanted, dismissing the entire undertaking as "name creating" and an excess of youth.[11] Others retreated into the sort of abstract theory, unintentionally parodied in Hindess and Hirst's *Pre-Capitalist Modes of Production*, that absolved the writer of any obligation to link rationalist constructs to human experience. A few attempted to write structural Marxist history, with largely unreadable results.[12] Simply piling up facts is no better. History never emerges voluntarily from the sources, nor does empiricism substitute for analysis.

So we are left with the possibility of admitting the vacuousness of seeking to reduce history to abstract structures while recognizing the utility of illuminating ideas and relations with theoretical constructs such as "modes of production" and "socioeconomic formation" and "determination in the last instance." In the chapters that follow, theory informs questions and suggests likely causes and connections, and empirical evidence tests theory, or rather hypotheses derived from theory. Neither predetermines what will be found. The result should be the history of the struggles of people to construct their own history, even if this turns out to be not as they, or we, or theory, would have it.

At this point, and following from the above, it is necessary to make clear my use of "peasant," a term that has been much abused in the last two decades. In the present context, I speak of peasants as persons and families who gain most of their livelihood from subsistence agriculture but also occasionally enter the cash economy to buy or sell, whether food, handicraft items, or labor power. In most cases this involvement is voluntary in the sense that the seller or buyer is motivated only by the need or the desire to obtain something via the market. In other instances, and Guatemala's history reveals a number, subsistence producers are coerced involuntarily into the market, by systems of forced wage labor (in Guatemala, *repartimientos* or *mandamientos*) or through the forced purchase or sale of goods (*repartimientos de efectos* or *mercancías*). To this extent the peasant is part of a larger social, economic, and political system usually structured to extract rent, labor, and product from him on exploitative terms. It follows that there can be no "peasant mode of production." Rather, "peasant" is an empirical category the inhabitants of which exhibit varying characteristics depending upon the interaction of different sets of production relations, including those of subsistence agriculture, petty commodity production,[13] and wage labor. Before 1940, and apart from a very few "wild" Indians in the northern El Petén region and a small number of fully proletarianized day laborers and *colonos*, almost all the rural poor of Guatemala fell into this category.

The present study follows "economic time"–that is, it embraces what one might call an extended nineteenth century, running from the 1760's to 1940, during which the development and fruition of a new international economic order brought a dramatic increase in the degree of integration of local production, markets, and populations into the world economy. The period has a strong unity, but the history is far from uniform across time or region. The expansion of capitalism on a world scale, the attempt of capitalists and the states they dominated to create a universal market and sources of supply, and the impact of these efforts on and within the noncapitalist areas of the rest of the world provoked highly uneven results. Capitalism ebbed and flowed,[14] the result of new means of communications, changes in technology and the demands these engendered, and the periodic accumulation crises labeled "business cycles." For Guatemala this meant that over the course of the long nineteenth century large landowners and peasants in different parts of the country were drawn or forced into the commercial economy at different times, just as some later on found themselves abandoned as new crops and areas took precedence. Amatitlán, for example, prospered after 1840 as the leading producer of cochineal but fell behind Antigua in the 1850's because of local problems with plant and human diseases. When the export economy began to shift to coffee in the 1860's the landowners of Amatitlán planted trees in large numbers, only to lose out again to the better-suited lands of the western piedmont and the Alta Verapaz. Entrepreneurs experimenting with new crops or seeking to expand export production shifted their interests about the country, disrupting, sometimes destroying, and not always replacing, existing agricultural patterns. The priest at Cubulco-Joyabaj, in the Verapaz, for example, during the 1840's converted Indian community lands to cochineal only to find that he could not compete with Antigua and Amatitlán. In the 1860's landowners on the south coast tore up flourishing cacao plantations to plant cotton that soon succumbed to diseases, and then coffee trees that withered and died in the heat. In time, the cash economy of Guatemala moved toward a dependence on the export production of coffee,[15] but this did not occur smoothly or without fits and starts, and the end result showed wide regional and class differences.

The Country

The colonial Captaincy General of Guatemala encompassed most of what is today Central America and included also much of Soconusco and Chiapas in present-day southern Mexico. For the purposes of this book, however, and even when treating the last years of the colony, "Guatemala" will refer only to the area that is included in the modern republic (see Map 1). This is no way meant to be a comprehensive treatment of Guatemala's agrarian history. It focuses rather on the parts of the countryside that were most involved at a given moment in the commercial and export economies, as well as on areas that were linked to these by demands of market and supply. In the late colonial period, for example, the cash economy centered on the region south and east of the new capital city of Guatemala. This involved modest levels of indigo and tobacco production and the supply of grain, animals, and handicraft commodities to the capital and to the flourishing indigo-growing districts of El Salvador and Sonsonate to the south. The collapse of the indigo trade after 1800 threw Guatemala's cash economy into depression, a depression aggravated by the political upheaval attendant on independence. Slowly out of this wreckage a small but profitable trade developed around Amatitlán and Antigua producing and exporting the beautiful red dye cochineal, or *grana*. Experiments with this crop began in the late 1810's and 1820's; the industry peaked in the late 1840's and early 1850's, but competition from other growers and the popularity of the new aniline dyes brought crisis and decay after 1860. The waning prospects of cochineal prompted export elites to shift their attentions to new crops, the most successful of which was coffee. While over the next half-century coffee production came to center chiefly in the western piedmont and the upper Verapaz, it drew into commercial and export circuits Guatemalan land and labor resources on an unprecedented, indeed revolutionary, scale.

A study of two hundred years of the economic and social history of a complex nation has to limit itself not only to a few areas or regions but also to a small number of groups or classes, and to only certain of their activities. In this book I am concerned chiefly with the relations between landowner-planter elites and indigenous communities that resulted from their efforts to define, control, and make use of land and labor. Interwoven in these struggles were the activities of the rural, poor *ladinos*. In late colonial Guatemala the term ladino was largely indistinguishable from the more commonly used *casta* and referred to anyone who was not Indian but was not evidently white. *Mulatto* also indicated persons of mixed origins, whether or not they had or seemed to have black ancestry. And *creole* generally applied to the descendants of immigrant white Europeans, though it might be used too for the offspring of African blacks born in the New World. Over the course of the nineteenth century the peculiar local usage of mulatto disappeared and creole largely ceased to have relevance. Ladino became detached from blood or race to become a term for anyone, of whatever racial constitution or phenotypical appearance, who showed what seemed to be the most important characteristics of

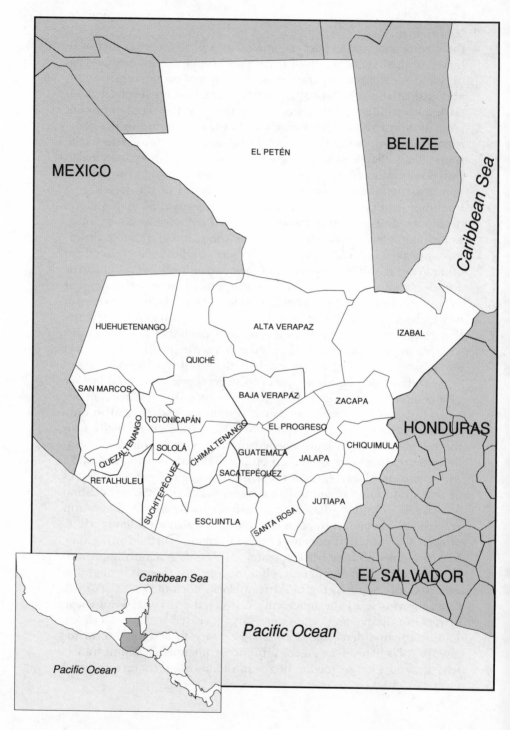

Map 1. Guatemala

"European" or "national" culture, such as speaking Spanish and wearing non-Indian clothing. Theoretically, someone born an Indian could become a ladino by adopting the proper cultural traits, but because racist overtones lingered, he or she could gain recognition as a ladino, as opposed to a "redressed" Indian, only by leaving the community of origin and appearing in the new status in a new setting. Ladino populations historically were strongest in the eastern part of the country, but with the onset of large-scale coffee production thousands migrated to the western piedmont and highlands. There they took up intermediary roles in labor recruitment and control, as shopkeepers and petty officials, and as small commercial producers of coffee and food crops. Separated from their home communities and alienated by relations of race and power both from the indigenous population that surrounded them and from the elites they served, the rural and small-town ladinos of the west were from the outset a marginal population.

State and Society

The key to export success and elite prosperity in nineteenth-century Guatemala lay in control of the state, and, through the state, also of land and labor. To achieve such control, and, indeed, to function effectively at all, any state must have hegemony, that is, the ability to guarantee at least some degree of compliance with a policy or goal of the national government in all the sovereign territory.[16] It is necessary to differentiate political from ideological hegemony. Political hegemony rests directly on the threat or use of force or coercion; ideological hegemony implies the achievement of policy ends based on willing, or apparently willing, compliance. Ideological hegemony depends on shared ideas and values. This split is possible, and in preindustrial or peasant-based societies is usual, because ideological hegemony is not the exclusive or even the normal property of the elites or the state they control. It resides instead in civil society:

The term "civil society" connotes the other organizations in a social formation which are neither part of the processes of material production in the economy, nor part of state-funded organizations, but which are relatively long-lasting institutions supported and run by people outside of the other two major spheres. A major component of civil society so defined would be religious institutions and organizations, apart from entirely state-funded and state-controlled religious organizations.[17]

The institutions of the civil society of Guatemala's indigenous population during the nineteenth century were the product of a long history of struggle and found their embodiment in "custom," the final arbiter of what was acceptable and valuable, socially and morally correct. In illiterate and largely unschooled societies not only is custom rarely under the control of "ideological state apparatuses" but it commonly remains quite beyond the ken of most of the state's representatives. It may not, and indeed it rarely does, share in all the values, goals, and orientations of the elite-dominated "national" culture. By language, moral assumptions, and socially esteemed activities, the masses typically are a "race wholly apart."[18] This was, and still is, particularly true for rural Guatemala, with its Europeanized and ladino elites as against an indigenous majority and given the great differences that exist between the Indian communities themselves. Where political and ideological hegemony coincide, as is typical of modern, industrial societies, these reinforce each other and the power of the state, allowing that institution to maintain the illusion that it operates in the general interest. Where ideological hegemony is lacking, the state if it is to assert control must rely on threatened or real force, on political hegemony. Few modern peasantries anywhere have expected the state to share their values or to be anything but oppressive, exploitative, and immoral.

With this in mind, if the history that follows here can be said to have a "hero" it is the Indian, not so much as an individual but as part of a community formed by centuries of struggle and structured by custom. It does no service to the Indians of Guatemala, however, or to any oppressed people, to romanticize their attitudes and actions or in some way to create a history that may be attractive to the researcher but is patently illogical, to "discover," for example, rebellion and defiance where acquiescence and evasion prevailed. Oppressed people have no obligation to act in ways that outside observers find interesting or appropriate. They seek instead to protect themselves and their families, to survive and to keep intact as much of their world as possible. It is the intent here to locate Indians at the center of their history, not just as objects, victims, or symbols but as actors. At the same time, it is necessary to recognize that no group more so than the peasantry, and particularly if it is a racially and culturally oppressed peasantry, makes its history under conditions over which it has so little influence or knowledge. Their relations with the elites and the state have been almost entirely those of reaction and avoidance. Peasants typically resist superordinate demands for land or labor or taxes with various ingenious if only sometimes effective tactics and stratagems. But the willingness and ability of any segment of the peasantry to understand, define, and defend its immediate interests, even if perhaps ignorant of the larger context, may be a serious impediment to state designs and elite schemes.

To say that Guatemala's Indians routinely obstructed efforts to maintain or increase levels of exploitation is not to argue that they always and in every instance manifested a clear class or ethnic consciousness or a consistent awareness of who the enemy was or where or how to carry out the most effective forms of opposition. Most evident was the division already noted between poor ladinos and Indians, which was exacerbated in the late nineteenth century by the increase in the cultivation of coffee. Equally important, if less often noted, have been the divisions within and among the indigenous communities themselves. Anthropologists and historians from the 1930's have tended to treat the colonial *pueblo de indios* (Indian town)[19] and the municipality after independence as the irreducible building blocks of indigenous social organization. According to the standard scheme, a "cargo system" of interlocking religious and civil offices held these "closed corporate peasant communities" together, mediating contacts with a threatening and exploitative outside world and regulating or "burning off" sources of internal tensions in the manner of a social and economic thermostat.[20] We now know from recent research that there was a good deal more cleavage and conflict within those communities, more than was previously recognized or admitted. There were divisions along lines of family-clan, wealth, religion, and microregionalism. At the same time that racism or cultural prejudice kept ladinos and Indians apart, cultural differences, long histories of land conflict, and government policies set one town against another, undercutting the development of a single "Indian" consciousness. Throughout the nineteenth century the indigenous population of Mesoamerica on the whole failed to develop an operative consciousness that extended beyond the community at any but the ephemeral and destructive levels of messianic religion and *caudillaje* (bossism). Even these instances remained rare and ineffective as organizing forces in Guatemala's western highlands and upper Verapaz. The towns fought each other and the state alone.

Political History

Guatemala, as the term here applies, in 1760 consisted of the northern districts of the Captaincy General of Guatemala, an area that embraced nearly half of the colony's population, in 1770 approximately 350,000 out of a total of some 720,000, and much more of its wealth.[21] In the capital, Santiago de los Caballeros de Guatemala (La Antigua) until an earthquake destroyed the town in 1773 and Nueva Guatemala de la Asunción (Guatemala City) thereafter, Spanish bureaucrats ruled the colony and collected taxes, and Spanish merchants controlled both imports and a rising export of indigo grown in El Salvador and Sonsonate. Creole elites competed with limited success for office and trade, and many owned large but generally poorly capitalized haciendas, located chiefly around the capital and in the *Oriente*. The trade in indigo and the supply of food and clothing to the indigo plantations integrated the cash economy of much of the northern part of the colony, but locusts, war, and competition damaged the dye industry after 1800, throwing the region into crisis. While much of the Spanish Empire moved toward independence, creole discontent in Guatemala remained weak and unfocused, dampened by a precarious economic situation and unrest among the rural Indian population. A strong Captain General easily held it in check. The break with Spain, when it came, was imposed upon the region by the Mexican Empire. "Absolute independence" in 1823 resulted from the collapse of Iturbide's experiment and the withdrawal of Mexican forces, not from a nationalist uprising. The ex-colony now reconstituted itself as the United Provinces of Central America, but in reality local elites ruled the towns, regions, and states of the isthmus much as they wished, and conflict soon proved endemic.

Most of the original supporters of independence could be classified as one sort or another of Enlightenment liberal.[22] When the reforms they enacted failed to produce the anticipated results and, worse still, provoked widespread popular unrest in the countryside, a number split off in the mid-1820's to form a Conservative party. The Conservatives intended to resuscitate what they saw as the proven political, economic, and social policies and institutions of the Empire. A new Liberal party gathered together those who believed that reforms had not yet gone far enough. Under Mariano Gálvez the Liberals dominated the Guatemalan state in the early 1830's, but the changes they tried to institute provoked first astonishment and then anger among poor ladinos and Indians alike. A widespread outbreak of cholera, seen by many as God's judgment on the Liberals, stoked rural discontent and helped to provoke a massive peasant uprising in 1837 led by the young Rafael Carrera. This "War of the Mountain" toppled the Liberals from office and brought to power a Conservative government, and by the late 1840's the new regime had crystallized into a dictatorship of Carrera.

Carrera reinstated the Spanish Laws of the Indies as they pertained to Indians, allowed the return of the religious orders expelled by the Liberals and renewed church control over matters such as marriage and birth registration, and put restrictions on the foreign colonization companies whose massive land concessions had agitated the countryside. Apart from these changes, and to the Indians' and poor rural ladinos' great relief, the new national leadership for the most part left the population of the countryside to its own devices. Banditry persisted, rebellions flared occasionally, and the country fought a series of foreign wars, but for the mass of the population life was more tranquil than it had been at any time for almost a century. The new export crop of cochineal made few demands on peasant lands or labor. The rural population was able to consolidate community economic and social structures, and its numbers increased steadily, perhaps for the first time since the Conquest (see Appendix A). Carrera's Dictatorship of Thirty Years also brought the elites a welcome social and political peace, and for a time, cochineal provided a modest prosperity.[23] By the 1850's and 1860's, however, many of the elites had begun to take note of the evidence that Guatemala not only was not developing as they had anticipated but was, indeed, showing signs of falling behind the rest of the Americas. When cochineal faltered, planters and merchants turned to coffee, and with the new crop came increased demands for the state to take a more active role both in helping to mobilize needed factors of production and in providing required infrastructure. The Conservative leadership, either incapable or unwilling, did little.

A new generation of Liberals replaced the Conservatives in the wake of the Revolution of 1871. Under Manuel García Granados and, after him, General Justo Rufino Barrios, the new regime put in place a number of changes now known in Guatemalan history as La Reforma. These bridled the church and stripped it of its property, promoted roads, railroads, and telegraphs, opened land to coffee, and later bananas, and forced more and more Indians out of their villages and into labor on the new coffee plantations (*fincas*). Barrios, and the other "order and progress" dictators who succeeded him, presided over almost three decades of expanding exports and the rapid growth of the national product. Politics was constitutional and democratic in form but authoritarian and elite-dominated in practice, and the rural population suffered in the name of development the progressive erosion of their customary rights and freedoms as well as of their means of subsistence. The coffee collapse of 1898 and the following two decades of stagnation in the export sector brought the rural population no relief, however, for the growers, assisted by the iron rule of Manuel Estrada Cabrera, sought to alleviate their own distress by squeezing the workers all the more.

In the wake of a massive earthquake in 1917, the 1918–19 worldwide influenza pandemic, and still another world coffee crisis in 1919–20, a popular uprising brought down Estrada Cabrera. For the next decade a series of generally more democratic but corrupt and unstable governments presided over an unprecedented public debate about political, social, and economic issues and about what direction the country should take. The coffee economy rebounded strongly after 1923 only to collapse again in 1928 following a record harvest in Brazil, which presaged for Guatemala the 1929 world crash and Depression. The crisis prompted Guatemala's elites to come together again in self-defense behind another nineteenth century–style neo-Liberal dictator, President General Jorge Ubico. The motorcycle-riding caudillo obligingly built roads, issued laws on public probity, repressed worker discontent in the cities and the countryside, and shot "communists." Guatemala's coffee producers managed to weather the 1930's remarkably well, and without being forced to face the wrenching changes of import substitution or the humiliations of populism. But by the early 1940's Ubico's lack of attention to the interests of a small but growing urban middle class, along with the disruption brought by world war and the general decline in prestige of the sort of pseudo-fascist dictatorships that he represented, suggested that problems lay ahead. These burst forth in the 1944 Revolution.[24]

Part I

Guatemala Before Coffee, 1760–1860's

Chapter 1

State, Society, and Agriculture

Agriculture has always been considered the most necessary
and the richest source of wealth for a state.
                "Apuntamientos sobre la agricultura y comercio
                        del Reino de Guatemala," 1810

The economy of late colonial Guatemala rested on agriculture. It
was the chief source of wealth for the elites and the state and of
subsistence for the mass of the population, but these groups extracted
a product from the soil by very different means. The rural Indians and
casta or ladino peasantry wrested their living as direct producers of
food and handicrafts for their own use and for sale in the few urban
markets available or to areas of export production. When the Spanish conquerors failed to find the mineral wealth they had anticipated,
those who did not drift off to more promising frontiers also came to
depend upon agriculture, not primarily as producers but by the extortion from the indigenous population of commodities such as cacao
and cotton for resale and export, and by taxes and rents. Only gradually, and usually only when depression forced them out of the cities,
did the elites extend sheep and cattle ranches and mixed haciendas
into the interior, chiefly to the south and east of the capital.[1] Poor
communications, competition from the Indian communities, and lack
of markets discouraged them from taking up agriculture in all but the
most depressed of times. The dominant characteristic of most of rural
Guatemala during the colonial period was precisely the failure of the
Spanish and better-off ladinos to penetrate the countryside as large-
scale landowners and agricultural producers. Their route to riches, or
even to a modest prosperity, generally lay elsewhere.

The State

Wealth above all depended upon access to and use of the political
power that resided in the state, whether to gain lucrative contracts and

import privileges, to evade duties or fines, or to obtain land and labor on favorable terms. It followed that agriculture in nineteenth-century Guatemala was inextricably linked to the changing structure, composition, and programs of the state. But the state manifested a number of internal conflicts, even apart from the fundamental contradiction between those with power and the majority of the population. One of these tended to set the Spanish colonial regime against local Spanish and creole elites over the distribution of what monies and goods could be extracted from the indigenous population.[2] The severity of the exploitation of the Indians increased when and where the interests of the Crown and the local elites coincided in this purpose, as, for example, with the system of repartimientos de efectos or mercancías. Because the Crown underpaid most of its functionaries, it found it necessary much of the time to overlook the governor-merchant alliances that squeezed a profit from the Indians through such forced trade.[3] Demands upon the population were less intense and the Crown more likely to champion the cause of the Indians where contradictions between the state and local elites appeared. In labor repartimientos, for example, if employers cheated the Indians at every turn and commonly abused them, the Crown in Central America depended on tribute revenues[4] and sought reasonable treatment and the payment of adequate wages for its subjects. There was a conflict, too, between the *hacendados* who preferred large landholdings worked by cheap labor and the merchants of the capital who foresaw better markets if land were redistributed into small properties and the population converted from semi-bound Indians and poor ladinos into a prosperous peasantry and a wage-earning work force.[5]

Whereas the Hapsburgs had left the villages largely to their own devices as long as they paid their taxes and gave at least outward obedience to the dictates of the church, the Bourbons after 1750 moved aggressively to intervene in community life. Not only did the Bourbon state overhaul land and labor laws in efforts to stimulate commercial production, but also it sought more direct control over community resources such as the capitals of the *cajas de la comunidad* (community chests) and the *cofradías* (religious brotherhoods). Repeatedly, the Crown and Crown officials *"hecharon la mano"* ("dipped the hand") in village reserves to meet real or imagined state emergencies. This provoked conflict not only with the communities but also with local elites who were themselves intent on dipping into these funds. The Bourbons converted Indian tribute from kind to coin in 1747, and beginning in the 1780's they sought with limited success to raise the amount the Indians paid under this tax.[6] In 1812 the state attempted to replace the personal service and food supplies by which the Indians supported their priests with money fees at "Spanish" levels for the administration of sacraments.[7] Such efforts ran up against both a general shortage of money in the colony and a strong resistance within the indigenous population to what they viewed as yet another scheme to overturn custom for the purpose of increasing levels of exploitation. The merchants of the Guatemala City Consulado de Comercio understood this well enough: "It is true that the Indians are very attached to what they call 'custom'; because things always get worse, they prefer the evil they know to the good they cannot imagine or believe possible."[8]

For reasons not altogether of their own making, however, the Bourbons and their reforms had little success in rural Guatemala. The falling off after 1800 of the cash and export economy together with the increasingly chaotic condition of Spanish administration made it nearly impossible to collect taxes.[9] The nationalization of church loans in 1804 and the "patriotic loan" that followed it were the last even partly successful efforts to extract large amounts of revenue from the colony.[10] Highland villages openly defied the efforts of state agents to collect the new, higher tribute. The raising of an Indian "king" at Totonicapán in 1820[11] was only the culmination of more than two decades of growing opposition among the general population to the centralizing and standardizing tendencies and to the increased fiscal demands of the Bourbon state. As elsewhere in much of Latin America, the Bourbon Reforms in Guatemala in the end worked to dismember and delegitimize the old Hapsburg system without managing to implant a new regime sanctioned by custom before state control began to break down in the early 1800's.

The Bourbons did little to assist agriculture in Guatemala. The grandest scheme, the credit and the labor reforms of the 1780's that were supposed to encourage indigo (*añil*) production in El Salvador and Sonsonate, benefited only a few well-connected planters and drove many of the small growers (*poquiteros*) out of production.[12] The state was chiefly concerned with taking revenue out of Guatemala, or at least using the monies generated there to bolster colonial administration and defense, and it had few funds available to assist rural development. At best, Bourbon incentives amounted to limited tax concessions or small prizes. For example, the tax holiday promised in

1803 to those who would grow sugar cane, coffee, indigo, and cacao in the wake of a devastating locust invasion applied only to increases in production, not to acreage already under cultivation.[13] The conversion of *aguardiente* (1753) and tobacco (1765) into government monopolies (*estancos*) certainly led to reduced production of these crops.[14] The Sociedad Económica de Amigos del País (Economic Society of Friends of the Country) and the Consulado de Comercio sponsored contests on "developmental" possibilities, published information on likely new crops and improved techniques in newspapers and pamphlets, and lobbied for road and port development.[15] But the Bourbon drain of specie from the economy, the determination of many merchants to export their profits abroad, and the absence of a significant mining sector in the economy [16] left little capital available for experimentation. With these burdens, aggravated by the disruptions resulting from the war in Europe and the unpredictable policies of the Spanish state, most landowners and communities thought not of innovation but of survival.

Commercial agriculture fell into a depression early in the nineteenth century, from which it was unable to extract itself for several decades. Observers lamented:

1804—They have sold not just the cheese but the cow that produced it; not only the egg but the chicken; not just the corn and the sugar but the ox that works the fields, the mule or the horse that helps them.

1810—Today, unfortunately, extreme misery and need afflict us inside the Capital and out.

1818—A melancholy picture confronts me. . . . Failures in agriculture, industry, and commerce are inevitable because everything is far away, the road in ruin, and transport expensive as a result. . . . The poverty of your vassals is evident.[17]

Stagnation and decline persisted into the early 1820's, but the hopes of the independent state nevertheless were bright. A government commission in 1825 optimistically reported an improved situation over the last years of the colony. Compared with the five years before independence, trade was said to have doubled recently and exports and prices for indigo were up, and new products such as vanilla and cochineal were finding export markets. Other crops that would do well included coffee, cotton, cacao, and tobacco; they only needed serious attention to be turned into valuable items of commerce. Cattle and sheep production could be expanded, and in the rural areas waited mines "without doubt the richest in the world." [18] But after a brief economic revival sparked by indigo and cochineal exports, the economy foundered, a victim not only of competition from other dye producers in international markets but also of the social and political conflicts that soon erupted in Central America. Of the early 1830's one writer commented, "The country only produces small quantities of two or three exportable items, lacks commercial relations with foreign markets, has no good roads or ports or maritime transport . . . and the state has no income to use to develop the country's economy."[19] The next decade saw only limited improvement: "Political disturbances have paralyzed business," the governor of Amatitlán reported.[20] Increased British imports hurt the artisan weaving industry and weakened local markets for raw materials and dye products.[21] Without agriculture there were no taxes, and without taxes, the state could not function: "The uncertainties resulting from the revolutions have forced capitalists to suspend all business of agriculture and commerce and for this reason there is nothing in the public treasury."[22] Not until the late 1840's and early 1850's did the economy and agriculture revive, and even then they remained at levels well below those of the late eighteenth century.[23]

Independence removed the Spanish Crown's control of Guatemalan politics and the restraints this had imposed not only on the exploitation of the mass of the population but also on intra-elite conflict. The region fell into three decades of experiment and civil war. An English traveler at the time observed, "The Liberals . . . abruptly freed from a thraldom which they had borne for ages . . . seize upon every new thing with avidity; plunge into schemes of which they understand nothing; and, in their zeal to overthrow all existing institutions, forget to separate the good from the bad."[24] One of the goals of the Bourbon Reforms, for example, had been to transform the indigenous population from a captive of custom and special legislation into a free peasantry that could contribute actively and on an equal basis to economic modernization and the expansion of commercial agriculture.[25] In the words of the translation of the decree ending tribute:

> Now there is no one
> Who has thought to say
> That we are not Spaniards
> all of us . . .[26]

This sort of innovation had found little support outside the Consulado, but the effects of independence appeared to resolve the question of the indigenous population's status in the favor of reform. The Constitution of 1825 declared that no distinctions "other than those of virtue and talent" existed among Guatemala's citizens, and new laws abolished tribute and ended a variety of petty taxes and duties that had been levied on the Indian communities.[27] Depending on one's perspective, the newly independent government either freed the Indians from the bondage of colonial paternalism or stripped them of their colonial protections. Not all the Indians were happy with such changes: in 1826 the inhabitants of Patulul protested, "The Spanish government never treated us as badly as does this so-called 'Liberal' government."[28] With the state near collapse, violence ravaged the countryside; crops were destroyed and trade and established social relations fell apart. The Indians of San Pedro Carchá in the upper Verapaz complained: "Everyone is fighting in Quezaltenango, in Chiquimula, in Salamá; because the town has no life, no one wants to work but instead they flee to the mountains. . . . Everywhere there is conflict and war."[29]

Until they split apart in the conflicts of the mid-1820's, most of the first generation of independence leaders shared the eighteenth-century liberal expectation that the removing of the Spanish hand would release the economic energies of the nation and bring prosperity to all.[30] But to an even greater extent than the late colonial regime, the new state was impoverished and its possibilities limited. As the participant and historian Alejandro Marure explained, "Of the taxes that remain, only four were designated for the expenses of the [the Central American] government: gunpowder, the mails, import duties, and tobacco [and] the States found themselves in the same situation, because the income from the stamped paper, alcohol sales, local trade levies, and similar minor taxes that they were allowed did not meet their needs."[31] An English agent reported an 1825 budget of 806,888 pesos income and 878,828 pesos expenses, 627,828 pesos of that for the military.[32] As the struggles among the elites for political control escalated and the factions hardened their positions, the Liberal party pushed ahead with reforms, but with no more success than the Bourbons had had.[33] Poverty limited the government to the familiar role of making available information on new crop opportunities and of offering modest prizes and tax concessions.[34] In 1831 the Gálvez government exempted cochineal from all taxes, and in 1835 it promised prizes to those who cultivated and harvested coffee.[35] The Liberals also sought to improve roads and bridges,[36] but travelers' accounts suggest a singular lack of success. The North American diplomat John L.

Stephens reported of the main road to the Atlantic port of Izabal: "At every step the mules sank to their fetlocks in mud. . . . As we advanced, the shade of the trees became thicker, the holes larger and deeper, and roots, rising two or three feet above the ground, crossed the path in every direction. . . . For five long hours we were dragged through mudholes, squeezed in gulleys, knocked against trees, and tumbled over roots."[37]

By the late 1830's Liberal innovations, aggravated by the effects of an outbreak of cholera, had provoked peasant revolts in the Oriente and in the western highlands. The government fell and a Conservative regime dominated by the mixed-blood caudillo Rafael Carrera took power, intent on rescuing the country and the people from the damage brought on by Liberal policies.[38] "Under the pretext of poorly understood 'equality,'" the newspaper *El Tiempo* declared, "the Indians whom the old laws protected because of their lack of education have been abandoned and exposed to all manner of vexations without having anyone to defend them or to seek their well-being." Worse, the indigenous population had "lost the habit of respect." They were refusing to pay taxes except for the tithe, and attacked the few castas living among them saying that Carrera had given them permission to "do as they would with the ladinos."[39] To restore order, the Conservatives reimposed colonial custom, reviving Catholicism as the state religion, providing interpreters in the courts, setting up a Junta Protectora de los Indios (Indian Protection Council), appointing a special land judge for Indian disputes, and, in general, reinstating the colonial Laws of the Indies as these applied to the indigenous population.[40] In reality, however, Carrera and the Conservatives forces brought few immediate changes to the countryside. The government was too impoverished and, up until the 1850's, too harassed by foreign wars and internal revolts and banditry to give much attention to day-to-day conditions in the rural communities. In the words of the governor of Escuintla, the people continued to give themselves over to "vagrancy, theft, and other crimes."[41] Although the Conservatives reinstated the Consulado and renegotiated the immigration concessions that had so irritated the population of the Oriente, it pursued essentially the same rural development policies of prizes and temporary exemptions as had the Liberals, only on an even more limited scale.[42]

Under both the Bourbons and the republic, agricultural development took place largely independent of government efforts to promote growth and diversification, and not infrequently, as in the case of grana after 1830, in the teeth of violence and chaos unleashed by political contests. Why did state efforts prove so ineffective? Political leaders of all stripes addressed first the interests of state revenues and merchant profits. Agriculture, if it concerned them at all, was a secondary matter, as was all too evident from the operation of the tobacco monopoly, the manipulation of the indigo and cattle trade, and the Consulado's road and port construction policies. Local elites had unrealistically high expectations both of the rewards to be obtained from greater submission to the dictates of free trade and of what Guatemala might be able to produce for this trade. Many were ignorant of their own countryside and of world markets and the competition they could expect to encounter there. The Bourbons had assumed that simply removing the pernicious influence of Hapsburg policies would foster development; depending on their personal interests, the creole elites who led after 1821 were certain that they would prosper if they could but escape the control of Spain, or of Guatemala, or of Guatemala City. Guatemala was held back, they agreed, only by old failed policies and external circumstances. Most did not understand, as many of the first generation of foreign investors and promoters did not, that the country was merely one among a rapidly growing number of producers of the new tropical raw materials, and one without, at least before the mid-nineteenth century, any particular advantage.

The Church and Agriculture

From the late colonial period on, there had been increasing conflict between the secular state and the Catholic church over the rights and powers of the church and over the revenues they both sought to extract from the general population. The Bourbon Crown consciously and systematically encroached on church prerogatives, and the post-independence Liberal regimes expanded these policies, lowering the taxes paid to the church, secularizing many fee-receiving activities previously enjoyed by the clergy, and confiscating the resources of the regular orders. The Conservatives by no means reversed all these innovations after 1839.[43] Elite resentment against the church tended to focus not on land, as it did in other areas of the former empire, but on what the landowners and merchants saw as the diversion of excessive amounts of Indian labor and monies to the local priest and the church hierarchy.[44] For the hacendados this was doubly aggravating because the Guatemalan church, unlike the church in some of the other parts of the colonies, lent relatively little money to agriculture. This is evident in the pattern of loans made from the interest and capital of *capellanías*.[45] Capellanías, or chantries, were gifts to the church from the faithful for the purpose of funding masses for the souls of the deceased, or for dowries for women entering convents, or for the support of good works (*obras pias*) such as orphanages and hospitals. They should not be confused with loans made from church funds, although church records did not always make the distinction clear, treating both as credits due. Such confusion in the past has been responsible in part for the church's reputation as a major agricultural lender. Occasionally the founder of a chantry handed over a gift of money or property, but more frequently the pious donor executed a lien against a piece of rural or urban property equal to the value of the pledge. Owners, heirs, or purchasers subsequently paid interest, usually calculated at 5 percent, on the value of the lien, unless and until they redeemed its capital value. Since little cash was available in capital-starved Guatemala and those who could put their hands on money had other uses for it than turning it over to the church, chantries tended to pass with properties from owner to owner and from generation to generation. The church spent the money it received from capellanías on the masses and good works designated, but it also lent at interest any surplus available above its immediate requirements. Although many chantries had fallen into default, the church by the end of the colonial period claimed rights to some fifteen hundred, representing a total capital of approximately 1,800,000 pesos.[46] More than half of these rested on rural properties.

In Guatemala there was no Juzgado de Capellanías (Court of Chantries), and therefore those who sought loans from the chantry income applied to the Cabildo Eclesiástico (Ecclesiastical Council) of the Archbishop. Loans usually carried a term of two years and an interest rate of 6 percent. It is clear from marginal notations on the contracts, however, that church officials routinely extended outstanding notes indefinitely as long as the borrowers kept interest current. Because the church sought first of all a return on its capital and cared less about acquiring landed property, its lawyers moved to embargo or foreclose on houses or farms only as a last resort. But by regularly rolling over unpaid notes the church greatly reduced the availability of new, lendable funds.

Records rarely indicate the specific purpose for which an applicant sought money. The most frequent reason given was "for my uses."[47] The church, in any event, was less interested in the ends to which the money would be put than in the security that was offered. Those putting up guarantees of urban property, import-export commodities, or a vendible office almost without exception received precedence over those who offered rural property. Borrowers who could guarantee a single large loan were preferred to those who were seeking smaller amounts, and sometimes they obtained better terms. Because some persons certainly borrowed against haciendas for consumption or commercial uses, while others, knowing the preferences of church lawyers, pledged their urban holdings as collateral for capital to develop haciendas and *labores* (medium-sized farms), the actual uses to which chantry funds went are far from clear. For the purposes of analysis, however, we shall assume that all loans that a borrower claimed to be for investment in haciendas or other agricultural enterprises, and all loans for which borrowers offered rural properties as collateral were "agricultural." As Table 1.1 shows, in only three of the twenty-five two-year periods between 1761 and 1820 for which information is available did loans for agricultural purposes exceed 50 percent of the total loans granted. Usually they were much less.

Records for the difficult 1820's and 1830's consist almost entirely of renegotiated extensions and the assumption of outstanding loans by the inheritors and purchasers of properties. In all, and in comparison, for example, with the Juzgado de Capellanías in New Spain, which regularly lent tens of thousands of pesos a year and at Independence reported an estimated "active" capital of four million pesos,[48] there was never much church money to be had in Guatemala. And although agricultural loans as a percentage rose, the overall amount of funds available declined from the 1760's to the 1820's, reflecting an economy unsettled by the 1773 earthquake that destroyed the capital and much church wealth, the drain on local resources resulting from Bourbon reforms and wartime demands, and the agricultural crises after the turn of the century. But by the 1850's and 1860's, when the church and the economy had in part recovered and the Cabildo again had disposable funds, the pattern of church loans was much as it had been a half-century earlier.[49] Loan contracts were still usually for two years at 6 percent against urban property, and applicants continued to give little indication of their intended use for the money, although evidence suggests that commerce received preference to the risks of cochineal.

Thus, the church through the Cabildo Eclesiástico, and to a lesser

TABLE 1.1
Loans from Capellanía Funds, 1761–1820
(two-year totals in pesos)

Years	Total loans	Loans for agriculture	Years	Total loans	Loans for agriculture
1761–62	$42,581	$ 895	1791–92	na	
1763–64	$40,832	$5,453	1793–94	$ 7,820	$2,000
1765–66	$30,865	$ 220	1795–96	$17,658	$4,175
1767–68	$13,358	$2,000	1797–98	$11,263	$ 0
1769–70	na		1799–1800	na	
1771–72	$25,454	$6,720	...		
1773–74	$29,332	$1,477	1802–3	$13,800	$ 500
1775–76	$ 8,350	$1,800	1804–5	$ 4,777	$2,000
1777–78	$16,530	$1,950	...		
1779–80	$13,700	$7,800	1809–10	$ 8,400	$3,000
1781–82	$21,067	$1,400	1811–12	$ 8,662	$1,400
1783–84	$12,245	$ 0	1813–14	$ 3,508	$3,000
1785–86	$21,457	$2,000	1815–16	$ 5,454	$3,366
1787–88	$ 7,520	$ 0	1817–18	$13,716	$1,828
1789–90	$ 4,366	$ 0	1819–20	$ 9,225	$1,000

SOURCE: AHA, Diezmos (*sic*) tomo 6 nos. 40 and 42, tomo 5 no. 52, tomo 4 no. 55, and tomo 3 no. 74.

extent through the lending practices of the convents and monasteries,[50] gathered interest on chantries that burdened chiefly agricultural properties and re-lent most of this for commercial or urban real estate purchase, repair, and speculation. At the same time, various taxes paid to the church also tended to shift resources from rural to urban areas.[51] Rather than financing agriculture, therefore, church loan and tax policies worked in quite the opposite direction, transferring resources from the countryside to the capital and draining money from the rural economy into commerce and the towns.

Capital

If not from the church, where might hacendados, communities, or small farmers seek capital? Not from the mining sector, which in Guatemala remained backward and impoverished.[52] And for merchants with liquid funds, profits were better and more secure in the import-export trade, in contraband, and in officeholding, or the financing of officeholding, than in the countryside. They might buy land for security, prestige, or diversification, but apart from interest in a few very limited areas suitable for market or export production, for example, indigo in El Salvador–Sonsonate or sugar and food production in the immediate area of the capital, merchants in the late colonial period did not invest heavily in agriculture or divert money from commerce to any but their own properties. Estate inventories and descriptions of the rural areas by travelers and Crown officials make it clear that agriculture was severely undercapitalized at all levels. The United States Minister to Central America, for example, reported shortly after independence that in traveling three hundred leagues one would not see twenty ploughs.[53]

Aside from the church and the merchant houses, potential sources of capital for agriculture were limited and scattered. One possibility was the cajas de la comunidad, the village reserve funds accumulated from the revenues of a small tax paid by local inhabitants or from the product of community-owned land or animals.[54] In the unstable environment of the last years of the colony, towns generally tried to preserve caja funds to help meet tribute demands or to deal with local disasters,[55] but loans to individuals from cajas monies could be a profitable way for the village to invest funds not immediately needed, and this also helped to keep the money out of the hands of ever-impecunious Crown agents. Records are not available of small loans within communities but typical of the larger sort was that obtained in 1778 by Antonio López Peñalvez, who borrowed 2,000 pesos from "the towns of Sacatepéquez."[56] In 1805 the cajas of the various districts of Guatemala reported thirteen separate loans outstanding totaling 40,975 pesos, and most borrowers appeared current on their interest.[57] A decade and a half later the situation had deteriorated markedly. A detailed list from 1820 recorded some 92,444 pesos in loans from caja funds for all Central America, but the impact of events in the intervening years was readily evident. Not only were most of the loans now long overdue, but borrowers had fallen behind in their interest payments and the cajas' capital was lost or effectively paralyzed. A typical case was that of Rafael Ferrer, who owed the towns of San Salvador, Comayagua, and Totonicapán 10,000 pesos; the legal proceedings attending his bankruptcy assigned this debt twenty-first place, meaning that the communities had little hope of collecting it.[58] The cajas in the late colonial period had at best a very limited amount of capital to lend outside the communities, and even this diminished rapidly after the turn of the century as the economy declined and borrowers fell into default.

Cofradías, or religious confraternities, also lent money on occasion. The members of these brotherhoods accumulated funds to celebrate the saints by cultivating or renting land or raising animals, by forced (*derramas*) or voluntary contributions from community inhabitants, and from commercial activities. Sometimes they sought to increase this capital by lending out all, or part of it, at interest. Except in very rare instances, however, the amount of money available from this source was small, and the members and particularly the officers of the cofradías tended to monopolize it for themselves.[59] Indeed, the so-called "capital" reported to the archbishops by many cofradías during the ecclesiastics' periodic visits often existed only on paper. The money itself long ago had been disbursed among members and their families, who paid yearly interest on the sums in the manner of the chantries. Occasionally small surpluses did become available to be lent to outsiders, but these transactions were not centralized and only scattered and incomplete records remain.[60]

To help finance its European wars, the Spanish crown after 1804 extended to the empire the *consolidación* (nationalization or consolidation) of all loans due the church, of all the principals of outstanding chantries and obras pias, and of all debts due the cajas and the cofradías.[61] The law required borrowers to pay the state without delay the balance of what they owed on loans and pledges, though these were, in many cases, decades or even centuries old. The Crown guaranteed the original creditors 5 percent interest on the amounts it received. The application of the policy was uneven, and records were haphazardly kept or have been lost or destroyed, and in a number of cases debtors only redeemed a portion of what they owed, but it is clear that consolidation wiped out the savings of at least some communities and cofradías and nearly ruined those of others. Altogether the measure drained more than a million pesos from the colony's economy, hurting not just the villages but haciendas and commerce as well.[62] With Napoleon's invasion of Spain and the collapse of the Spanish state after 1808, the church and the villages could hardly have received very much of their promised interest. Furthermore, the disturbances preceding independence and the wars that followed meant that many of those who had borrowed money from the cofradías and the cajas but had somehow escaped the consolidation were now unable or unwilling to repay what they owed. There was little the towns could do. In 1843, for example, the cofradía of Las Animas of San Martín Jilotepeque complained that José María Dardón owed them various sums dating back more than forty years and totaling over 2,000 pesos, plus overdue interest. Now he was offering only 500 pesos cash to cancel the debt, and the local priest was recommending that the cofradía accept this as the best that it could expect under the circumstances.[63]

Natural Hazards

Agricultural production in all areas of Guatemala, whether for subsistence or for market, faced not only the problems resulting from primitive technology and shortages of capital, and increasingly from political conflict, but also a variety of natural hazards. Pests, particularly locusts, repeatedly ravaged crops. A traveler described encountering a cloud of these flying insects on the Pacific coast:

It is melancholy to see a swarm of these locusts drifting on the breeze, high above, descending and falling, of a sudden, on a smiling corn field, where the rich green stalks are just shooting into maturity and budding with fruit. . . . You may come upon part of the road where their fat, loathsome, yellow bodies are piled over one another, on every leaf, branch, stalk, and on the road itself. Your horses crush hundreds at every step.[64]

The plague of locusts that hit Guatemala at the turn of the century proved to be particularly fierce and destructive. Reports reached the colony in 1801 that an extraordinary swarm of locusts had formed at Leon in Nicaragua and was working its way north, devastating the indigo fields of El Salvador and Sonsonate. The following year, as the locust season approached, the Audiencia organized the governors of the south coast districts to fight the invasion. The state and the communities mobilized thousands of workers to dig trenches to bury the eggs and young "hoppers." Desperate farmers sounded trumpets, set off rockets, and lighted bonfires in hopes of driving the insects away, but their efforts were of little use. In a few hours the locusts would devour the plantings of whole communities. In Suchitepéquez alone, and just among the ladinos, the collector of tithes estimated that the locusts in 1802 destroyed thousands of acres of cotton, corn, and beans. Governors forced the people back into the fields to make second plantings of corn in the hopes of avoiding disastrous food shortages, and the lowland districts, which usually produced large surpluses of corn, now imported it from the highlands. But the plague did not limit itself to the lowlands, extending its damage as far as the Verapaz and the Cuchumatán Mountains.[65]

Rain—too much or too little—could be equally ruinous.[66] Except for a few places along the Motagua River and around lakes where irrigation was practical, agriculture in Guatemala depended almost entirely on natural rainfall. A rainy season that usually began in April–May and ended in October–November set the rhythm of planting and harvest. Serious droughts afflicted much of the colony in 1746, 1752, 1803, 1810, 1822, 1824–25, 1840, 1842–44, and 1860,[67] and the pleas of towns for exemptions or reduction of tribute reveal dozens of more localized calamities, often aggravated by unusually cold or hot weather and by outbreaks of disease.[68] A very wet season could be equally disastrous. An official in the mid-eighteenth century described the results of a particularly powerful storm:

The Los Esclavos River [on the Pacific coastal plain] rose and overflowed its course, destroying everything in its path: in the town of Nancinta what the river did not take of the corn plantings are flooded; from the haciendas of the cofradías of Chiquimulilla the river took two hundred head of cattle; Pasaco lost its plantings, and when the river arrived at the sea it flooded the fisheries and the salt pans; of all the corn, cotton, and banana plantings in the area, none remain. Great hunger is anticipated (unless God wills otherwise).[69]

Problems of food cost and food supply haunted both the authorities and the Indians throughout the late colonial–early national period. In the areas adjacent to indigo production, pronounced shifts in patterns of land use drove food prices up before 1800. The *Gaceta de Guatemala* reported in 1797, "The increase in indigo wiped out the cattle industry and greatly reduced the production of corn, rice, beans, etc., and hardly anyone plants wheat any more."[70] It is more difficult to determine whether, and to what extent, food prices increased in any general or systematic way in these years, or whether scarcities became more common, more severe, or more prolonged. Guatemala had no public granary (*alhondiga*), and in most years the church farmed the tithes, so that the two most common sources of quantitative material used to study food prices in other areas of the Empire are not available for Guatemala.[71] The colony evidently experienced repeated bad years, but we do not know whether these were significantly worse than, for example, a century earlier.

TABLE 1.2
Corn Prices as Reflected in Diezmo Sales, 1792–1809
(in *reales* per *fanega*)

Year	Huehuetenango	Las Mesas/Canales	Year	Huehuetenango	Las Mesas/Canales
1792		7–20	1801		17–36
1793		7–24	1802		7–10
1794	12–16	17–25	1803		8–18
1795	24–32	10–15	1804	8–36	
1796	24–32	9.5–36	1805	6–15	
1797		18	1806	8–24	
1798		6–13	1807	12–24	
1799		13.5–29	1808	18–24	
1800		10–13	1809	36–48	

SOURCE: AHA, Diezmos, tomo 1 no. 48, tomo 2 no. 53, and tomo 3 no. 52.
NOTE: A fanega of grain equals approximately 1.6 bushels.

Lacking reliable price series, it is possible to select figures and comments from among scattered sources that appear to support almost any argument.[72] From the 1790's to the early 1800's, however, price series for a few areas and for limited time spans can be reconstructed from *diezmo* (tithe) figures, as Table 1.2 shows.[73] What these suggest rather than any escalating crisis is considerable variability over time within the same region and between regions, a pattern typical of poorly capitalized agriculture vulnerable to the vagaries of nature and hampered by inadequate and expensive communications. Because the lure of the Guatemala City market drew supplies from a wide area, prices tended to stabilize there at levels only slightly higher than those of rural districts not suffering shortages.[74] Travelers after Independence generally found prices low and a variety of food items available.[75] However, and whether because of the impacts of the conversion of land in nearby areas to cochineal or because of turmoil and fighting, the corn prices in the capital do appear to have increased noticeably by the 1850's, from an average of 15 *reales* circa 1795–1805 to 22 reales by mid-century.[76]

Whether such increases in grain prices were also true in the countryside is not clear. Food availability and cost were always more uneven in the rural areas than in the capital. Isolated areas in the high Cuchumatanes, for example, that had to depend on quite localized production suffered violent oscillations of supply and price from year to year and season to season. Reports of grain shortages and editorials decrying the backward condition of local food agriculture, and of the Indians chiefly responsible for producing it, together with government efforts to encourage plantings, and extraordinary measures such as buying grain and distributing it to the poor, indicate that the cycles of abundance and dearth continued in the nineteenth century much as they had in the past.[77] Political chaos and roving bands of soldiers and bandits after 1821 complicated the supply situation. Although travelers did occasionally report shortages of food, in other instances they commented that corn was so cheap that it had no fixed price and was not worth the cost of transporting it to Guatemala City.[78] Access to food and its price at a given time continued to depend upon where, and, of course, who, you were.

Population

At the base of the economic, and social-political, pyramid of late colonial rural Guatemala stood a mass of Indians, "mulattoes," and ladinos, who together formed more than 80 percent of the population of the colony. Incomplete figures from the 1770's give the approximate distribution and ratios between Indians and non-Indians for the different regions of the colony, as indicated in Table 1.3. The "Indian" of the late eighteenth and early nineteenth century was, of course, not the pre-Conquest survivor anthropologists hoped to find when they took up ethnographic research in the 1930's nor was he or she entirely or simply a creation of the Spanish colonial regime.[79]

TABLE 1.3
Indian and Non-Indian Population Circa 1770, by Jurisdiction

Jurisdiction	Indians	Percent of total	Non-Indians	Percent of total
Sololá	20,295	98%	467	2%
Totonicapán	31,936	96	1,238	4
Verapaz	30,231	90	3,399	10
Corregimiento "del Valle"	68,737	89	8,502	11
Chimaltenango	na	na	na	na
S Antonio Suchitepéquez	14,311	88	1,893	12
Quezaltenango	14,019	79	3,787	21
Chiquimula/Acasaguastlán	29,843	69	13,224	31
Escuintla/Guazacapán	12,678	61	8,204	39
TOTAL	222,050	84.5%	40,714	14.5%

SOURCE: Solórzano Fonseca, "Comunidades indígenas," p. 94.

Individuals and groups even among conquered peoples tend to retain or develop an ability to define and act on interests independent of those that are imposed upon them. The Maya throughout Mesoamerica showed themselves particularly resistant to Spanish pressures, whether in their residential patterns, economic activities, language, or religion.[80] The Indian of late colonial Guatemala was a product of the interaction of Spanish culture, or at least the part of it that was transmitted to what was left of the area's indigenous population, with the aspects of indigenous culture that had been preserved, recreated, synthesized, and modified over the course of several hundred years of history. Indian culture was at the same time general over wide areas and highly particular to each community or region. Like all cultures, it was a construct, the outcome in this case of centuries of struggle.[81] That the contest may appear to have been unequal, weighted unfairly on the side of the conqueror, made it no less a struggle. The "Indian," and the "traditional" Indian culture that emerged from this dialectic and came to full fruition in the middle of the nineteenth century, were perhaps the most characteristic and enduring product of Guatemala's colonial history.

The Indian population dominated the western highlands and the isolated upper Verapaz; non-Indians were more numerous in the warm lowlands south and east of the capital. By the end of the colonial period non-Indians made up perhaps a quarter of all rural inhabitants.[82] Archbishop Pedro Cortés y Larraz on his tireless rounds of visits in the 1760's and 1770's complained unceasingly of a profusion of degraded "Spanish," castas, and mulattoes who lived in promiscuity and "excess liberty" in the "bush," on haciendas, and in unregulated and illegal rural settlements (valles) beyond the supervision of church or state: "An unknown number of persons from many parishes who never think of mass or the Christian doctrine or of the sacraments live there; their idea is to hide themselves from the priests and all civilization and religion with no one knowing who they are or where they are."[83] By 1804, although many of these "people of broken color" still lived dispersed or in valles, many also had illegally penetrated the indigenous communities (see Table 1.4). The assiduousness with which most castas and poor Spaniards sought to avoid census takers and other state agents suggests a disproportionate undercounting of these populations, particularly outside the urban areas. Nevertheless, the Crown's prohibitions against ladinos residing in Indian villages, which were supposed to protect the inhabitants from the deleterious influ-

TABLE 1.4

Non-Indian Population by Residence, 1804

Jurisdiction	In Indian towns	Forced settlements	Valles/haciendas
Sololá	1,134	1,067	27
Totonicapán	4,964		
Verapaz	1,499		1,269
Sacatepéquez (del Valle)	n.a.		
Chimaltenango	2,313		
Suchitepéquez	2,520	1,431	1,107
Quezaltenango	6,516		
Chiquimula	16,673		5,900
Escuintla	3,438	2,079	2,408
TOTALS	39,057	4,577	10,711 = 54,345

SOURCE: AGCA, A1 2646 22150.

ences of mixed-blood "vagrants" and "mulattoes," clearly had broken down.[84] This was not a new phenomenon. According to the comments of the compiler of the 1804 census, "Almost all the ladinos living in the Indian towns have been there a long time, some for fifty or more years."[85] These non-Indians invaded the communities, taking advantage of the ignorance or fear of the indigenous population and seeking access to the resources the villages controlled. Some forced their way on to community lands and into local government and others worked as intermediaries in trade between the villages and the capital, as mule drivers, and as artisans. A few kept small inns on the main routes or were priests or officials or had connections with such persons.[86] Many, to judge from the numerous vagrancy laws and regulations, fell into drunkenness, idleness, and crime, and they were accused of corrupting the Indians into the same habits.[87]

The problem for the rural castas, and the danger for society in general, was the difficulty the castas were said to have in gaining secure access to employment or land: "The man who has no property possesses nothing, and he who possesses nothing has nothing to lose, and he who has nothing to lose has no country; for this reason this group is the most to be feared in any period of popular unrest."[88] Whereas Spanish-creole settlements might aspire to town status and the right this gave to *ejidos*, or community lands, and the Indian villages enjoyed rights to land that the Crown itself admitted predated the Conquest, ladinos who lived in the illegal valles found it more difficult, if not always impossible, to acquire title to land.[89] They could buy it if they had the money, but few did.[90] Some rented land, but, as one observer commented, their situation was not always good: "These [were] unhappy men, hounded from pillar to post and always persecuted, seeking only someone who will rent them a piece of land under the harsh condition of personal servitude as well as rent."[91] The census of 1804 indicated 1,006 "Spanish" and 2,531 ladino renters, which must have been a substantial undercounting. Others simply and precariously (*precarista* is the Spanish word for squatter) squatted on Crown land, on private property, or on the lands of the Indian villages.[92]

The land problem rested not with Spanish law, which did not bar casta settlements from town status or property, but with the custom of the Guatemala elites who resisted granting legal status to mixed-blood settlements.[93] From this the Guatemalan historian Severo Martínez Peláez has argued that the castas suffered an "agrarian block" that was the result of an undeclared but well-understood conspiracy between the local representatives of the state and the hacendados to bar casta access to land in order to assure landowners a supply of cheap labor.[94] The ladinos certainly faced difficulties in acquiring land, but the conspiracy theory also presumes that most of the hacienda work force was ladino rather than Indian, and evidence contradicts this. Many Indians also lived and worked on the large properties. They sought refuge there from pressures for taxes and forced labor and gained access to the land denied them in their communities. Julio Pinto Soria has pointed out that the problem for the rural castas was not precisely an "agrarian block," if by that is meant a lack of land that drove them into wage labor; the existence of a number of valles and the sort of rental arrangements noted in the 1804 census show that land was available.[95] Rather, the problem was the uncertain situation in which those without the means to buy land or to establish a legal claim to state lands found themselves. As squatters on state or private property they had few rights and few means of protecting themselves or the fruit of their work. They had no incentive to improve their living conditions or cultivations. The situation of renters was better, but owners could expel them or increase rent demands with few impediments.[96] One of the changes brought by independence was the better possibility of regularizing the status of the ladino valles by converting them into legal municipalities under new, liberalized regulations.[97] The structure of economic and class power in Guatemala remained largely unchanged, however. Moreover, the postindependence period saw a political convergence of the large landowners with the merchants, now cut off from Salvadorian indigo and more dependent than before on local production. This guaranteed that the situation of most rural ladinos remained one of poverty, oppression, and insecurity.

The Regions of Guatemala

Because this study focuses on the area included in present-day Guatemala, we shall not deal with Chiapas-Soconusco nor shall we treat in detail the much more important, in these years, indigo districts of El Salvador and Sonsonate. The indigo region enjoyed considerable administrative autonomy within the Captaincy General. For example, the 1784 finance and labor regulations that were meant to promote the crop applied specifically to El Salvador–Sonsonate and not to Guatemala.[98] Indigo nevertheless had importance outside the area in which it grew. Miles Wortman has argued that "as high prices stimulated indigo production . . . the Guatemalan highlands and the Honduran and Nicaraguan tablelands were drawn into the network, supplying grain, cloth, and meat for the growing laboring population of the indigo regions. . . . Central America was more integrated than at any other time in its history."[99] Yet in 1803 the newspaper *Gaceta de Guatemala*, which presumably had a reasonably clear idea of the condition of trade, in referring to the indigo area reported that "each town is turned in upon itself and hardly trades with even those in the surrounding area."[100] Indigo exports increased steadily from the early 1770's until almost the end of the century (see Table 1.5), and with the success of the crop growers in El Salvador–Sonsonate turned away from mixed agriculture to monoculture, with the result that local food costs increased.[101] For a time a new market opened that attracted food, cloth, and artisan handicraft producers from other regions: corn from Guazacapán-Escuintla, cattle from Honduras, cotton cloth from the Verapaz, and wool fabrics woven and transported to market by the Indians of the western highlands. But by 1800, and certainly after the locust invasion of 1801–2, this was all but over. Most of the small producers of indigo, who at one time were responsible for more than half the total output, had been ruined by drought and locusts, unstable and falling prices, competition from the large growers, and monopolization of profits by Guatemala City merchants. One effect was greatly to reduce secondary markets in the indigo areas, and the continued fall in dye exports after 1800 wrecked what demand remained. The

TABLE 1.5
Indigo Exports, Captaincy General of Guatemala, 1772–1818
(five-year averages)

Years	Pounds	Years	Pounds	Years	Pounds
1772–76	561,000	1797–1801	1,006,000	1813–14	339,903
1777–81	834,000	1802–4	637,227	1815–16	394,790
1782–86	884,000	...		1817–18	332,200
1787–91	1,016,000	1809–10	736,695		
1792–96	1,035,000	1811–12	493,450		

SOURCES: R. Smith, "Indigo," pp. 197–98, 201–2; Wortman, *Government*, p. 187; Woodward, *Class Privilege*, p. 40.

indigo towns fell into a stagnation that limited trade to a local orbit, and mixed agriculture reasserted itself.[102]

The Central Valleys

The key event for the history of the central part of the colony in the last years of empire was the shift of the capital from Santiago to La Hermita valley in 1776.[103] The earthquake of 1773 and the resulting transfer of the center of government meant the loss of hundreds of thousands of pesos in urban property values, a particularly hard blow to the church, which was the chief mortgage holder.[104] Forced work on the construction of the new city ruined many artisans and put heavy demands on the Indian communities in the vicinity.[105] The move also reoriented the whole market economy, which had centered on the capital. For those suppliers who had always been far removed, such as the wheat producers of the western highlands and the cacao growers of the Pacific coast, the shift meant little, but in the immediate area of La Hermita valley dramatic change resulted.[106] New haciendas sprang up in the Valle de las Mesas and in the Sierra de Canales and existing ones took on added life and value. Towns feeling the competition for land complained: "Almost from Pinula to Santa Rosa and all the land beyond is large haciendas."[107] Properties such as de Arrivillaga, San Nicolás, Guillen, Villalobos, Fraijanes, Barcena[s], Naranjo, and Uriondo, together with other large and medium-sized holdings, sold corn, wheat, cattle and horses, cheese, chickens, eggs, and firewood to the city.[108] These haciendas were worked by a mixed labor force of resident colonos, renters, and black slaves, along with seasonal crews of indebted workers and labor drafted from neighboring Indian communities. A few properties, such as La Companía, which belonged to the Dominicans after 1767, Anís, and Nuestra Señora de Guadalupe, specialized in sugar production, which they undertook with black slaves because the law forbade this work to Indians.[109] Ladino and Indian small producers also supplied wood, food, and handicraft manufactures to the capital, as did some of the indigenous communities.[110] The villages also exported workers, not simply in repartimientos but also as more or less voluntary wage labor labeled variously *peseros* (paid a peso a week), *meseros* (contracted by the month), *luneros* (worked from Monday to Monday), and *gañanes* (free workers).

Labor pressures on the Indian towns in the area of the new capital, aggravated by ladino incursions into their now increasingly valuable land, prompted growing numbers of the inhabitants to move. Some found a new life, though at the price of a loss of personal freedom, as renters or colonos on the haciendas.[111] Others, at the price of insecurity, became squatters on Crown or private land. A church official reported: "Many people in this kingdom live outside the towns, and it might even be the majority but not less than a third, and it would certainly be more than half if one added to the number of those in illegal Indian settlements those at the salt pans, on the haciendas, and in the valles."[112] Others kept on the move, forming, together with landless ladinos, the group known as *escoteros* (casual workers) that Archbishop Pedro Cortés y Larraz reported seeing or hearing about on many properties.[113] Worsened by the effects of recurrent epidemics after 1780, this drain of population from the communities made it difficult for towns to meet tribute and repartimiento demands and increased the pressures on those inhabitants who remained, prompting yet more to seek to escape. By 1816, for example, the governor of Sacatepéquez was arguing that because of such losses of population most of the towns of his district desperately needed a recount and a reduction in the amounts of tribute required of them; at roughly the same time, the haciendas in the nearby Sierra de Canales were gaining population.[114] While village leaders sought the return of the emigrants or at least wanted them to pay the taxes and the labor service they owed the town, hacendados, always short of workers, hid runaway Indians and protected castas from the authorities. Repeated efforts in the late colonial period to bring together scattered populations into *reducciones* or *congregaciones* (forced settlements) under state and church supervision, or somehow to enforce taxes and repartimientos on these, were seldom effective. Crown officials burned houses and illegal settlements and rounded up individuals and families, but the Indians and castas simply melted back into the bush at the first opportunity.[115]

The resistance to concentration was not always only the product, as the Archbishop and secular authorities claimed to believe, of a desire to live in promiscuity and vice, nor was it necessarily entirely an effort to evade the exactions of state and church. Such settlement patterns also resulted from the predominant mode of mobile, swidden agriculture practiced by rural Indians and poor ladinos alike. Even the Archbishop admitted, "The lands are poor and it is necessary to shift cultivation every year or frequently, and the Indians by custom live on the land they are planting."[116] Often the unauthorized Indian settlements (*pajuides*) were, as the inhabitants repeatedly attempted to explain to the skeptical Archbishop, temporary encampments set up to exploit better-quality land than what was available near the village or to take advantage of ecological differences to grow, for example, tropical products in the hot country. In other cases, Indian resistance to concentration in towns found its origins in claims to land or need of access to religious sites abandoned earlier under the pressures of forced settlement schemes.[117]

The Western Highlands

From the edges of the plains of Chimaltenango through the Sierra de los Cuchumatánes the western *altiplano* was above all the domain of the Indian.[118] The general poverty of the region and the watchfulness of the regular orders charged with missionizing the Indians limited Spanish and ladino intrusion here and contributed to the survival into the nineteenth century of a large and relatively culturally intact indigenous population.[119] Pockets of ladino activity did exist. For example, a few large haciendas bobbed in the sea of Indians, as Table 1.6 demonstrates. Properties closer to the capital raised wheat with colono labor and renters and depended on repartimiento labor drafts to harvest the crop and carry it to Santiago or, later, to Nueva Guatemala. The activities of these haciendas provoked almost continual conflict with their Indian neighbors. Not only were there disagreements over land, wages, and working conditions, but also, because the villages often were themselves cash producers of wheat, they resisted being forced to supply cheap labor and transport to their landed rivals.[120] Haciendas farther to the west raised cattle, horses, and sheep for wool that they sold in town markets, and they rented land to Indians and poor ladinos

TABLE 1.6
Major Haciendas in the Western Highlands, Circa 1800

Jurisdiction	Municipality	Name	Owner
Huehuetenango/ Totonicapán	Chiantla	Moscoso-Chancol	familia Barrutia
	Huehuetenango	Guayla-Xetena	Cura Mig. Muñoz
	Cuilco	Canibal	José Cosio
	San Cris. Toto.	Urbina	Urbina
Sololá	Sololá	Argueta	Dña María Morales
Quiché	Quiché	Chiché	Mariano Barrutia
	Joyabaj	Chuacorral-Tululché	Mariano Barrutia

SOURCE: AGCA, A3.15 352 7308 and 7309.
NOTE: Only properties claiming 200 or more animals are listed; many gave no numbers.

for subsistence agriculture and pasture. A number of smaller Spanish and ladino-owned properties, sometimes called haciendas but more properly labores or even *rancherías* (small, private holdings) clustered between Quezaltenango and Salcajá, and along a Huehuetenango–Malacatán–San Marcos axis.[121] They competed for land among themselves and with neighboring Indian towns and sought orders from the state to force reluctant communities to supply them with workers, though generally with less success than the larger properties.[122] Ladino squatters and small holders also inhabited a handful of valles intermixed among the highland Indian towns, including San Carlos Sija, Chinique, Salcajá, and San Antonio Bobos (Sibilia).[123] The people who lived in these settlements existed at a material level little different from that of their Indian neighbors.[124] Indeed, there was little incentive for the ordinary ladino to seek his fortune in this area where scant profit was to be had and where not only the Indians but the church and the state made the outsider's existence precarious.

The dominant settlement pattern for the indigenous population of the western highlands was the pueblo de índios, the corporate Indian town.[125] The inhabitants were chiefly farmers and artisans who by the eighteenth century traded among themselves in a system of local and regional markets and with the Spanish on the open market or through the notorious and illegal repartimientos de efectos or mercancías. The repartimientos de efectos, sometimes confused by writers with labor repartimientos, operated in at least three different forms in late colonial Guatemala.[126] The most common sort involved a government official, usually a district governor, working in conjunction with a merchant supplying the capital, who forced the Indians under his administration to buy "Spanish" goods from him at monopoly prices. Critics complained that such repartimientos were "violent and tyrannical, and useful only to enrich the governors, and to drive the Indians deeper and deeper into poverty, forcing them violently to buy things they do not need, and at exorbitant prices."[127] Undoubtedly there were instances of silk stockings foisted upon shoeless Indians and books upon illiterates, but a review of repartimiento records shows that the more common items in the highland Guatemala trade were iron tools, locally made cloth and clothing, and animals. The prices, if high, were not in most cases blatantly extortionate. Governors and their allies answered attacks on the repartimientos by arguing that the Indians could not afford these goods without the "credit" the system provided; they complained, too, that they suffered losses in the trade, although few seem to have found this a reason to abandon it. A second type of repartimiento of goods required the Indians to deliver valuable commodities, such as cacao in the late sixteenth and early seventeenth centuries, for which they were paid below-market prices.[128] This form seems to have been rare in the Bourbon years because the Indians could be made to produce few items of interest to the elites. Finally, the governors' agents sometimes brought to the villages quantities of raw cotton or wool, with orders that this be spun into thread or woven into cloth.[129] Payment for the labor involved was below free wage levels, and it was not unheard of for officials to short-weight the raw materials, so that the Indians had to buy more to make up the amount of final product required. Such spinning and weaving repartimientos generally fell most directly on the women, and it was usually they who protested abuses.[130] For the most part, the indigenous population tolerated repartimientos of goods as long as they did not exceed "custom," what they expected and could manage, but overly rapacious officials could and did provoke open resistance and even revolt.[131] Moreover, although Indian *justicias* (officials of the towns) and the Spanish priests sometimes cooperated with the governor to exploit the village through the repartimientos, quite as often they defended the community, appealing excessive demands to the Audiencia and the Archbishop.[132] This defense might be rooted in concern for the well-being of their charges or in the fear that someone else might gain control of whatever wealth could be extracted from the town.

Overall, highland Indian communities in the last years of the colony accumulated little in the way of surplus above their immediate needs. Given access to adequate amounts of reasonably good quality land, slash-and-burn *milpa* (subsistence) agriculture could be very productive, particularly relative to capital requirements. By the late colonial period, however, two sets of circumstances already were at work to limit its productivity. In the central valleys and in the districts west and northwest of Lake Atitlán Spanish and ladino land intrusions and the erosion resulting from decades, or even centuries, of overgrazing and overcropping had created in some localities conditions of genuine land shortage.[133] Renewed, if still uneven, population growth after 1750 exacerbated the situation (see Appendix A). Even where land and population pressures had not yet become a problem, Indians saw little point in producing more than they needed for material and ritual purposes given the enthusiasm with which Crown and church agents latched on to any resource that looked to be available. Similarly, there was little incentive to be a "rich" Indian and much less to be seen as such. It is hard to imagine, for example, that Archbishop Cortés y Larraz did not understand the irony of his comment when he wrote, "It may be that these Indians are rich and they are said to be; but since all Indians appear the same, you cannot know or find out (no one can) what they do with the money they make from selling their products."[134]

Apart from a few towns favorably situated to supply food or wood to the capital, most villages lacked the communications or transport facilities necessary to participate profitably in the cash economy. Their involvement in market trade remained limited to barter or to petty commerce in local markets or to an occasional purchase made with laboriously accumulated and hoarded silver or to forced exchanges purposely devised to drain them of wealth. The Crown's shift of tribute payment to money in 1747 and its attempts to raise rates in the turn-of-the-century "equalization" reforms aggravated shortages of cash and capital in the villages and forced growing numbers of people to go out in search of wage work or trade in the money economy.[135] These communities resisted repeated efforts by the church to make them substitute cash payments for the long-standing system of supporting the Catholic priests by personal service and food.[136] Altogether, the combination of secular state taxes, church charges and fees, and repartimientos de efectos extracted from the indigenous populations much of the liquid wealth they managed to generate and was a strong incentive, too, for the Indians to dispose of what remained as quickly as possible in drink and ritual custom. As much as the need to re-inforce social solidarity and to level community differences, this was the motive for the elaboration of the region's well-known civil-religious "cargo" systems.[137] Of course, once in place, the cargo systems—and different observers have found it useful to emphasize one aspect or the other—might serve at the same time the purposes of the village and as yet another vehicle by which elites and outsiders exploited the Indians.[138]

The Oriente

The eastern part of the country, particularly the Montaña region, Chiquimula, and the valleys running off the Motagua River, was a land of small, hard-scrabble ladino farms and valles interspersed with a few surviving Indian communities and large but for the most part not very productive haciendas.[139] A few municipalities, like Asunción Mita, boasted a dozen properties each possessing 700–800 cattle, dozens of horses and mules, and commercial plantings of sugar, but more typical of the impoverished countryside was the wealth reported to the tax collector in the 1790's by a sample of the inhabitants of the valle of Xanco, in the jurisdiction of the town of San Juan Hermita, where no one had a hundred cattle and no one harvested 100 pesos' worth of cheese. The epidemics that followed the Conquest had de-stroyed much of the original population.[140] Over the years, Spaniards, poor ladinos, and castas moved in, attracted by the temperate climate, pockets of fertile land, markets in the indigo fields of El Salvador,[141] a relative absence of state control, and the presence of weakened Indian communities from which land and labor might be pried. Of these im-migrants, a few were able to put together what were by local standards substantial haciendas, especially on the eastern approaches to the new capital and along the banks of the Motagua and Guastatoya, where irrigation supported sugar, tobacco, and some indigo, as well as the ladino rural staples of corn and cattle. But development of the region was hampered by labor shortages, droughts and plagues, and diffi-cult communications. Technology was so rudimentary that a sugar mill boasting a set of iron, rather than the more usual wooden, rollers, gave name to a settlement. Those who failed to prosper vegetated away the decades in the many isolated dwellings and settlements that studded the low mountains of the region, paying taxes of one or two cheeses each a year, or nothing at all, and drinking up the product of their small cane fields as illegal alcohol. Impoverished castas and elites alike

complained bitterly that the decayed Indian towns of the region controlled large areas of land that they did not use but that they refused
to rent or sell.[142] By the end of the colonial period the region was relatively heavily populated, and the inhabitants constituted the largest
ladino population of rural Guatemala,[143] but most were poor and with
little likelihood that their situation would soon improve. Only under
exceptional and usually short-lived circumstances could the Oriente's
products compete with cattle from Honduras, cacao from the Pacific
coast, or the indigo of El Salvador–Sonsonate.

The Verapaz

The conditions that would split the Verapaz into two separate departments a hundred years later already were evident in the last decades of the colony.[144] While relatively strong, landholding Indian
towns and Indian cofradías with extensive cattle holdings survived at
Rabinal (including San Miguel Chicaj) and Cubulco, the district capital
of Salamá had lost most of its ejidos and much of its Indian character. The inhabitants now rented land where they could and migrated
to work for wages on Spanish and church-owned haciendas.[145] Community claims and the power of the Dominicans blocked ladino penetration of the central valley, but castas, Spaniards, and Indians lived,
or so the peripatetic Archbishop Cortés y Larraz observed, in undif-
ferentiated confusion in the southern valles of Los Ramones, Urran,
Saltán and Chivac, and El Chol: "Here gather the fugitives from many
towns, and it is impossible to find out where they come from. Even
if you try you can find out nothing about who they are, because they
often change their names and deny their origins, lying and hiding
their past; they come and go as they fancy, producing all manner of
confusion and disorder."[146] Most were "of little consideration," and
they were getting poorer as increasing numbers pressed against available land.[147] In this confusion the dominant economic force was the
Dominican order. The Guatemala City and the Cobán convents owned
a number of large haciendas, including San José near Cubulco, San
Nicolás above San Miguel, and the huge sugar plantation San Jeronimo, of more than 50,000 acres, east of Salamá.[148] There was probably
no agricultural operation in eighteenth-century Guatemala to match
San Jeronimo, with its 1,000 workers, including 700 African slaves,
producing 15,000 pounds of sugar a month for the Guatemala City
market and for conversion into alcohol.[149]

By contrast, the upper part of the Verapaz remained almost entirely

Indian, but even more than the south it was under the firm economic and ideological grip of the Dominicans, inheritors of Bartolome de las Casas's "Land of True Peace." Their monopoly of the profits of a modest cotton and cattle trade discouraged the immigration of castas and ladinos and preserved the resources and structures of the villages comparatively intact. Around San Pedro Carchá and Cobán and to the north and east a large population cultivated corn, and in the adjacent lowlands they grew tropical products.[150] The church organized the inhabitants of Cobán into cofradías. Members wove the cotton that they planted in the hot country or obtained from Cahabón into thread and cloth and carried these products to the capital, to the Pacific coast, and to El Salvador and Sonsonate.[151]

Runaway black slaves, chiefly from Belize,[152] and free blacks and mulattoes of obscure origin dotted the lower reaches of rivers that emptied from the Verapaz and the Oriente into the Caribbean. The state recruited a few of them to garrison the forts at Omoa in Honduras and at San Felipe, on the Rio Dulce at the mouth of Lake Izabal.[153] Most, however, lived at a subsistence level along the coast, in almost total isolation from the interior and the central government. Of all the regions of Guatemala, the northern coast was the least populated, the most difficult to transit, and the most disease-infested, and for centuries it had blocked ready access to the Atlantic world.

The Pacific Coast

Export agriculture first returned high profits for the Conquerors in the cacao groves of "Sapotitlán" and Suchitepéquez on the Pacific coast.[154] Instead of working the groves directly they forced Indian producers to give up large quantities of cacao as taxes and tribute.[155] These pressures, together with the diseases introduced by the Conquest, devastated the local population as well as the gangs of highland Indians brought forcibly to the coast to work the groves or driven there in search of cacao with which to pay their tribute. Resistance from elites based in the highlands who saw their labor force dwindling and from the Crown that justly feared for its tribute revenues ended labor drafts for cacao. Competition from the inferior but cheaper cacao of Guayaquil and Nueva Granada drove the local product out of the important Mexican market, and the industry collapsed.[156] Mulattoes and castas muscled into dying Indian towns and took over the groves, but few prospered. Ladino-owned haciendas given over chiefly to fattening yearling cattle brought from Soconusco emerged. The owners loosed animals on nearby communities, trying to destroy what remained of the settlements so that they could claim the land as that of "extinguished" towns: at Don García, for example, the inhabitants complained that a hacendado's cattle ate not only their corn and cotton plantings but their thatched church as well.[157] Whole villages disappeared, and the forest threatened to overrun the few that survived. In 1766 the governor of Suchitepéquez reported:

There remain only twelve useful towns and the rest are on the verge of collapse: San Juan Naguapa, completely abandoned; San Miguel with a population of eight to ten Indians from elsewhere; Santo Tomás with a few more; San Francisco Zapotitlán, not more than thirty individuals, some of them lepers; Santuario de la Santisima Virgen de Candelaria de San Lorenzo, may have a dozen Indians; San Martín has perhaps thirty; San Felipe about the same; San Luís de la Real Corona, a single Indian; Santa Catarina Retalhuleu, about thirty.[158]

But diseases and parasites limited the development of the cattle industry in the area, and the south coast was unable to compete successfully at this with Honduras. When in the eighteenth century landowners attempted to develop indigo, the population resisted forced labor, and the crop did not prosper.[159]

South and east along the coast the economy of the district of Escuintla-Guazacapán approximated a poor version of El Salvador–Sonsonate. Large but weakly capitalized properties produced indigo, sugar, and cattle. They shared the countryside with decayed Indian towns, casta settlements, and coastal fishing villages and saltworks.[160] The owners here also sought labor repartimientos to expand production, but the few surviving Indian communities could support only limited drafts, and, though exceptions abounded, the Crown now generally enforced the laws banning coerced labor that took Indians from the highlands to the hot country. Many "Indian" towns of Escuintla-Guazacapán in fact contained predominantly casta and mulatto populations imperfectly hidden behind a facade of Indian officials, maintained to ensure legal recognition and access to land. State agents and landowners attempted repeatedly but with little success to force the castas into labor drafts. Along the coast, fishing villages and salt pans supported an unknown population absolutely beyond the purview of state or church: "The abandon in which many of these people live is evident in the fact that although there are many fisheries and haciendas in this parish [Guazacapán], the priest has nothing to do with them and does not consider them his parishioners."[161]

The decadence of the coast and recommendations for its revival were staple topics of eighteenth- and early nineteenth-century observers and officials.[162] There was general agreement that the area suffered above all from a shortage of available workers. Other than the laziness commonly ascribed to all Indians and the general perversity assumed of all the mulattoes, memorialists disagreed on the exact cause of the region's sparse and, it was said, poor-quality population. Archbishop Cortés y Larraz laid the blame on the diseases common to the region, the invasion and extortions of the castas, and the depredations of the governors.[163] Guatemala City merchants, on the other hand, saw the problem as resulting from the excessive demands of the church itself. The Consulado's "Apuntamientos," for example, detailed what it said were the quite extraordinary labor requirements of the cofradías and the priest of the main town of San Antonio Suchitepéquez.[164] By 1800 most of the workers in the towns, on the cattle ranches, in the cacao groves, and on the indigo plantations of the coast were either *forasteros* (outsiders)—Indians who had come temporarily from the highlands to earn tribute money or to evade tribute and labor demands of their home communities—or a shifting and indeterminate number of mulattoes and castas.[165] The few surviving local Indians lived off rents, subsistence agriculture, day labor, and officeholding.

The Bourbons and the postindependence Liberal and Conservative states largely failed in their efforts to promote commercial and export agriculture. Their first interest always was revenue for their immediate political survival; long-term development took a distant second place. Too, ill-founded hope and an imperfect understanding of their own limitations and of international conditions prompted unrealistic expectations. The indigo boom evaporated by the turn of the century and with it the limited commercial integration of the colony the crop had provoked, and the situation deteriorated after 1821. Cochineal financed a small-scale state and elite, but it had little impact on the country as a whole. Left largely to their own devices, the Indians and castas not drawn into rebuilding the capital or enticed into the grana fields of Amatitlán enjoyed an autonomy unrivaled since the sixteenth century.

Chapter 2

Land

They go from place to place always planting in new areas.
AGCA-ST, Alta Verapaz 1/11

L and in the colony of Guatemala belonged by right of conquest to the king and to those of his subjects to whom he gave or sold it, but at the same time the Crown recognized that land belonged also to the local indigenous population by natural right and as a consequence of prior occupation.[1] Grappling with this apparent contradiction, government lawyers argued that the state had ownership rights only to "unoccupied land" (*terrenos baldíos* or *realengas*),[2] not to the legitimate possessions of those individuals, corporations, or communities, or their descendants, that had existed before the arrival of the Spanish, "the ancient lords of the lands of America before their conquest."[3] Moreover, although by law Spaniards, creoles, and castas were required to possess a legal, written title or risk losing what they imagined or claimed they owned,[4] there could be no question that the indigenous population, by virtue of possession "from time immemorial" and regardless of whether or not they had papers upon which to base their claims, had full rights to their community lands. But there were still problems and complications. What, for example, constituted "unoccupied"? Unoccupied before the arrival of Spanish diseases? Before or after the Conquest? As a result of resettlements? In the eighteenth century? What, in any event, was acceptable evidence of occupation? What exactly constituted "community" land or lands? And, notwithstanding the assurances of the Crown's attorney, there was in late colonial Guatemala, as in most societies, some disjunction between law and reality. Conflicting interests within the state, as well as between the groups represented in the state and the mass of the population and between and within the villages themselves, had at least as much to do with the nature of land ownership as did the law.

Land Law

As the Spanish conquerors swept across the Caribbean and invaded
the mainland in the sixteenth century, the Crown moved aggressively
to assert control and promote development of New World resources.
One of the first priorities in Indian-dominated colonies such as Guatemala was to protect the lands and other resources of the indigenous
populations from the designs of its more rapacious subjects. This acknowledged both humanitarian and Christian purposes and the importance to the state of Indian tribute. Without adequate and stable
access to productive resources the Indians would find it difficult or impossible to pay their taxes and church fees, as they themselves argued
successfully in innumerable law suits, protests, and petitions. The land
situation nevertheless quickly became confused. Villages and haciendas, for example, made use of land to which they had no legal right.
In such cases, from the Crown's point of view the land ought either to
be paid for and titled if realenga, or if it had been usurped, returned
to its proper owners. Accurate measurements and clear titles would
reduce the near constant conflicts over land among the villages and
between villages and private owners, which drained Indian resources
to no purpose useful for the state.[5] Given, too, "the many expenses"
of the king, the sale of land and the regulation of titles were attractive sources of revenue.[6] Not surprisingly, therefore, the state over
the course of the colonial period repeatedly found fault with existing
documents and required new measurements and sales or "composition," that is, the payment of a fee to regularize possession of illegally
held land.[7] Individuals and towns sometimes took the opportunities
that such revisions presented to grab land from their less aggressive
or aware neighbors, while in other areas the latest decree might be
ignored or specifically not applied. As a result, each round of sales,
measurements, and titling rather than clearing up problems generated more conflicts and more confusion, and more potential income
for the state. This was perhaps not accidental.

In 1754 the Crown issued yet another set of instructions and regulations for the "granting, sale, and composition" of public lands.[8] The
decree identified as its chief purpose the increase of state revenues.
But it also warned that in the pursuit of these revenues Indians were
not to be perturbed in the possession and use of the communal lands
they had held "from time immemorial": "Do not oppress the Indians

or make any changes," the decree advised, "continuing them in possession of what is theirs, returning to them what has been usurped,
and granting them more land if their population warrants it." As the
new law applied to private landowners, if they did not have a title but
could demonstrate effective and undisputed possession of a tract for
thirty years, had not acquired it by fraud or violence, and were not
violating the rights of an indigenous community or a neighbor's legally
titled property, they could qualify for "moderated composition." Moderated composition was the right to buy the land at half its assessed
value and without auction competition. Of those who could not show
uninterrupted possession for the required time or were not making
active use of their land, the regulations demanded measurement or
remeasurement and valuation of the area claimed and its composition
or sale at public auction. To limit abuses and speed the processes of
land titling and sale, the Crown subsequently published a number of
additional instructions and explanations for the 1754 decree, and it
repeated these on frequent occasions, but there is no evidence that
this did much to straighten out the colony's tangled land situation.[9]

Existing patterns of land ownership and use came under increasing
attack in the last years of the colony. It was an article of faith of the
Bourbon state, and one taken over and canonized by the nineteenth-
century Liberals, that private property was more efficient than communal ownership and that breaking up village lands into privately
owned plots would lead to more and faster agricultural development.[10]
No one, it was said, had security of tenure under communal ownership.
The inhabitants of the villages were at the mercy of Indian officials or
of local caciques who might take away plots and redistribute them at
will, or so the ladino lawmakers imagined or argued. The individual
cultivator could have no incentive to improve or invest in the land
or to plant permanent crops: "While communal lands appear to be
the patrimony of all, in fact only a minority controls them and even
these only undertake shifting cultivation, because permanent crops
are not possible where there is no indisputable property." [11] Such an
interpretation of usages in the indigenous villages ignored or underestimated the power of custom and the readiness of the populations
to rise against local tyranny, but the power of local elites sometimes
did allow them to accumulate land at the expense of their fellows or
to force the general population to provide them cheap labor for personal profit.[12] Communal ownership and rotating cultivation might
also, and depending on the specific situation, limit the possibilities or

rationality for long-term capital investment or development. As a result, the term "common lands" sometimes concealed vast differences and inequalities in access to and use of land within the community.

The Guatemalan merchants' Consulado de Comercio argued in 1810, in consonance with many other would-be reformers in the empire, that the solution was land reform: "The lands of the Indians taken by Spaniards ought to be returned to them. And these ought to be divided fairly among the Indians without special treatment for anyone."[13] The Liberal-dominated Spanish Cortes agreed, ordering in 1812 that Indian villages were to distribute up to half their community lands as plots of private property "to married Indians and those of twenty-five or more years."[14] The following year the colonial state expanded this to include baldíos and realengas, providing that "all public lands except the ejidos necessary to the towns will be converted into private property."[15] King Ferdinand VII's return in 1814 and his sweeping aside of the Cortes' reforms gave these laws little opportunity to take hold. The 1820 revolution revived the decrees of the earlier period, but independence soon put into question all Spanish legislation.[16]

The terms "común" or "common lands" or "ejidos" as generally used in documents and references of this period were in fact too vague to be very helpful in clarifying patterns of rural land possession and use. Whereas, for example, Spanish laws defined a legal town ejido as one square league, or approximately 38.75 caballerías,[17] centered on the church or plaza, by the end of the colonial period custom and history had created a quite different situation in much of Guatemala. Of the Escuintla-Guazacapán region a subdelegate reported that although most towns had no titles or documents and generally recognized ejidos of only eight to ten caballerías each, some claimed as much as two leagues in all directions.[18] Inequalities and anomalies abounded. La Gomera, for example, with 200 inhabitants claimed 900 caballerías of community lands, while neighboring Don García (present-day La Democracia), with a much larger population, had no ejidos at all and only a small amount of purchased land. In the adjacent district of Suchitepéquez the corregidor found that the town of San Antonio Suchitepéquez, with 122 tribute payers, claimed more than sixteen square leagues; its annex San Gabriel, with 127 tributaries, sought to control some twenty leagues. Both resisted outsiders' efforts to settle in the area or sometimes even to rent land.[19] Other villages, such as San Sebastián, with 596 tributaries, had no community land.[20] Few towns

TABLE 2.1
Community Land, District of Suchitepéquez, 1812

Town	Land possessed/claimed in caballerías	Title?
Cuyotenango	34+	1734
S. Sebastián Quezaltenango	none	lost in fire
S. Andrés Villaseca	?	a "stay"
S. Francisco Zapotitlán	98+	1746
Santiago Zambo	very little	no title
S. Bernadino	private property	no title
Samayac	don't know	illegible
S. Antonio Retalhuleu	don't know	no title
Mazatenango	don't know	no title
S. Domingo Retalhuleu	rent from San Antonio Suchitepéquez	
S. Lorenzo el Real	don't know	documents from 1588
S. Antonio Suchitepéquez	don't know	illegible
S. Pablo Jocopilas	private property	no title

SOURCE: AGCA-ST, Suchitepéquez, 3/2; AGCA, A3.30 2578 37864.

possessed legal title to the common land they claimed, as an 1812 report made clear (see Table 2.1). However, even if a legal square league of ejido were allowed for each legitimate community in Suchitepéquez, one judge pointed out, there would still be more than 700 square leagues of untitled state land available for sale in the district.

The situation in the highlands was little different from that on the coast. In Totonicapán, for example, the town of Santa María Chiquimula, with a population of fifteen to sixteen thousand, had only scant ejidos and for at least a century had had to rent land from nearby San Antonio Ilotenango, a town that had fewer than five hundred inhabitants but controlled more than eight hundred caballerías.[21] In the Verapaz, Cobán claimed in 1785 never to have marked its boundaries "for love of its neighbors, who also have no fixed borders." Local officials, when questioned by the authorities, suggested that the town's plantings extended eight days' walk to the north, twelve to the northeast, three to the southwest, seven to the south, and ten to the west.[22] Summing up the situation of all of rural Guatemala shortly after independence, a surveyor explained that, whatever the government might think and whatever might be the law, irregularity and inequality prevailed among community lands.[23]

The overthrow of Spanish rule in 1821 resulted in a flurry of new land laws notable both for their ineffectualness and for the hostility they engendered. Comprehensive regulations issued by the National Assembly in 1825, and repeated and expanded in 1829 when the Liberals returned to power, set the agenda for the independent state.[24] Echoing the short-lived Cortes, the Assembly asserted that "the small number of private landowners is one of the causes for the backwardness of agriculture." The infant state claimed the right inherited from the Spanish Crown to the ownership of all untitled or improperly possessed land—usually called *baldío* after independence—in the national territory, and it proposed to convert this as rapidly as possible into private property. Towns would be allowed to retain their "ejidos and common pastures," but ominously the laws failed to guarantee even the colonial minimum square league. Within six months each community was to draw up and forward to the central government a summary of all communal, group or corporate, and individual properties in its jurisdiction, and all baldío. This would serve as the basis for registration and orderly alienation of public lands. Although the new laws provided that the state might add to the ejidos of a town where this was necessary, the emphasis of Liberal policy was on titling land as individual private property. The intent, too, was to force the land into productive use. Anyone who obtained title but subsequently did not cultivate or make productive use of a piece of land risked losing it. Additional regulations issued after 1830 modified the 1825 and 1829 laws to guarantee the possessions of the many Indian communities that failed to register within the allotted times, to extend repeatedly the opportunity to register, and, finally, to allow moderated composition for those that had missed all the deadlines.[25] Few towns sought to regularize their situation under the 1825 and 1829 regulations, and most of those that did saw their efforts founder in the political confusion and violence of the time. Even under the most favorable of circumstances the reform of an institution as deeply rooted in history and tradition as land tenure would have been difficult; to attempt it in the midst of the civil wars that racked Guatemala from the 1820's to the 1840's was suicidal.[26] It is perhaps the best example of the inability of this first generation of Liberals to reconcile theory with reality. Together with other unpopular innovations, Liberal land policy accomplished the unlikely feat of bringing many of the large owners and merchants together with the indigenous population in opposition to the state.

To encourage efficient use of land the government in 1832 replaced the colonial tithe with a tax of four reales per caballería (*contribución territorial*) on all property, whether cultivated or not.[27] In response, claimants registered almost 37,000 caballerías with the state. As of February 1836 this included 10,317 caballerías for Guatemala, 8,815 caballerías for Chiquimula, 4,954 caballerías for Sacatepéquez, 4,661 caballerías for Totonicapán, 3,196 caballerías for Quezaltenango, 2,454 caballerías for Sololá, and 2,138 caballerías for the Verapaz.[28] These figures clearly represented a vast undercounting of landholding in rural Guatemala, although exactly how vast remains uncertain because no one had the least idea of the quantity of baldío or even the total area of the republic. Most indigenous communities, for example, did not register at all, and the few that did generally declared that they did not know the size of their common lands and had no title. Most private owners, too, not to mention thousands of small squatters, failed to list their holdings or understated the size of those they did. All but a few of those who registered claimed to have titles to their properties, but it is not likely that all of these would have passed the scrutiny of the courts. And few paid the tax. Even with the small amount of property registered, tax returns should have amounted to 18,000–20,000 pesos a year, but with chaos rapidly enveloping the countryside, collections never exceeded 2,000 pesos.[29] By comparison, after the Conservative government revived the tithe in 1839 and there followed some measure of peace and of cooperation from the rural population, income exceeded 20,000 pesos by 1859.[30]

Rural indigenous communities might simply ignore new or different taxes,[31] but two laws issued in 1836 much more directly threatened communal property. Article 25 of the 1829 land ordinance had provided that "all the inhabitants [*vecinos*] of the towns may make use of the ejidos and their own properties without special privileges or being made to pay rent." Taken with other laws that now provided full membership for ladinos in mixed-race towns and town governments,[32] this provision greatly weakened Indian control over even those villages in which they predominated. Then, in April 1836 the National Assembly announced that "the government may authorize the municipalities to sell their ejidos and the lands and properties of the cofradías."[33] In theory, the towns had always had the right to dispose of ejido land, but because of requirements imposed by the colonial regime, as well as Indian dominance of village government, such sales had been difficult and uncommon. The intent of the new law was, obviously, to reverse such colonial protectionism, as was made clear in the provision that anyone who in the past had acquired land directly from Indians or from the indigenous communities (a transaction that before 1821 almost certainly would have been illegal) could now regularize this possession by paying the national government 10 percent of the value of the property.

In August 1836 the Liberals went further, declaring "All ejidos will be converted into private property. . . . In the future the government will not grant land for ejidos either to existing towns or to those that may be established."[34] With this law the state moved from possibilities and ideological pronouncements to an apparent open attack on community ejidos. The government would appoint survey commissions to settle boundary disputes and measure existing community lands, which then would be divided into individually owned and titled plots.[35] The dissatisfaction provoked by this innovation contributed to the outbreak of the Carrera revolt the following year,[36] but the law had little actual effect on village lands. From a footnote in the standard collection of laws for this period stating that the government did not revoke the August 1836 decree until 1852, the assumption has been that it resulted in large-scale losses for the communities.[37] It is true that the law was not rescinded until 1852, but the National Assembly suspended its application in November 1837 in response to growing rural unrest: "The laws that currently exist regarding land, property, and possession are cause for discontent among the towns and individuals." More to the point, the independent state in the decree now specifically subscribed to the colonial guarantee that "towns are taken to include an ejido of a square league . . . as well as such lands as they have purchased from the state."[38]

The second 1836 law had only limited impact, but it was not entirely without result. For example, the government surveyor Valerio Rivas pointed out how the decree aggravated land problems in one area of the central highlands. The governor of Totonicapán, Rivas reported, "made himself owner and lord of [community] land," selling or renting it to whomever he wished without attention to existing possession or custom and jailing those who complained; he moved his cattle in and built a sugar mill on the Indians' lands.[39] The ladinos of Tecpán Guatemala similarly took advantage of the law to "strip the Indians of their lands," and the ladino-dominated municipal government of San Martín Jilotepeque seized land from the Indians' cofradías.[40] Additional research would no doubt turn up more examples. But the August 1836 law remained in effect for too short a time, and the conditions of the state and the countryside were too chaotic, for it to have a major impact on land. Its chief result was political. As the government attorney noted, "Mistrust has captured the hearts of the Indians."[41]

Perhaps not surprisingly, given that many Conservatives were, or aspired to be, landowners, the new government that took over from the Liberals in 1839 did not immediately or greatly alter existing land laws, but it made no particular effort to enforce them either. Carrera sometimes intervened in land disputes on the side of the communities, and his 1844 Guadalupe Agreement with the Conservatives provided for a special land judge to protect the interests of the Indian and ladino peasantry. But neither Carrera nor the judge was very active in the Indians' interests after the mid-1840's.[42] In 1840, 1845, and again in 1850, the Conservative government called on those who possessed baldíos without the proper title to register the land with the state.[43] It was no more successful than the Liberals had been. When the state eventually revoked the offensive August 1836 land law, it made it clear that this action did not invalidate legitimate sales that had taken place under the law.[44] Only in 1863 did the Conservative-dominated Assembly attempt to write a new land law, a proposal that, in any event, would have made only minor changes on the 1825 and 1829 Liberal laws. The draft confirmed the communities in possession of a square league of ejido, as well as property bought from the state or from individuals and land held in "undisputed and uninterrupted possession," and it allowed them to organize and use the land as they wished, though not, apparently, to sell it. The new regulations were of such little concern to the regime, however, that the Assembly misplaced the draft and only rediscovered it in 1870, and then the body failed to enact it before the Liberals returned to power the following year.[45]

Under the postindependence states as under the Bourbons, conflicting interests of the state, merchants, and Spanish and creole landowners, together with regional differences and economic cycles, pulled policy and the enforcement of policy in different directions. At the center of much conflict was the question of what was or was not baldío, state-owned land. The state had an interest in clearing up the evident confusion, both for control and for revenue. It was in the interest of the communities, on the other hand, to perpetuate the "confusion" so that they could absorb more land and avoid taxes. More broadly, a great deal of conflict arose out of differing ideas of what in fact constituted adequate title. The state and the hacendados emphasized the paper process, which they controlled; most Indians would have agreed with those of Suchitepéquez who explained to the governor that the land they used did not belong to the king but had been given them by God.[46] God, of course, did not collect taxes or hail village leaders into court to examine community titles.

Measurement and Titling

The effectiveness of land laws in clearing up possession or owner-ship disputes and resolving boundary conflicts depended in large part on the competence and interests of public authorities and on the accu-racy of the information upon which they based their decisions. Notions of the geography and topography of the countryside were extremely vague in nineteenth-century Guatemala. There were no general agri-cultural censuses until almost the last decade of the century, there was little mapping, and until 1877 there was no central registry of land transactions or titles. Because of inadequate and confused docu-mentation land sales often took place *ad corpus*—that is, although the boundaries of the property might be more or less clearly described, the seller gave no guarantee as to area. Boundary markers sometimes could not be found, or had been moved or destroyed. Also, because different owners might have different names for these markers or be-cause they had changed over time, disputes not uncommonly broke out over the proper identification of a given point mentioned in title documents. Papers commonly disappeared in the confusion and civil wars after 1821.[47] A litigant in the 1830's, for example, complained that twice in the same year rebels had occupied Antigua and burned the municipal building, destroying his papers.[48] Towns and individuals pawned land documents as surety for loans and then failed to pay off the debt or neglected to retrieve the titles; some papers simply van-ished, destroyed in house fires or mislaid by lawyers or heirs.[49] There could be deliberate sabotage, too, as when papers sent to court mys-teriously disappeared, or when a lawyer or judge "lent" papers to the opposition who, not surprisingly, then refused to return them. Inter-ested parties routinely lied to surveyors and state officials, concealed evidence, and altered documents. One dispute, between the town of Mataquescuintla and a neighboring hacienda, dragged on for decades, in part, the landowner protested, because the official in charge of the measurements took bribes, concocted documents, and incited the

Indians against him.[50] In a conflict between two haciendas that came to light in the 1770's and continued for more than a century, a judge complained that not only had at least one of the owners obviously forged some of his papers, but "neither [of the measurements] is any good."[51]

The subdelegates who surveyed land under the late Bourbons were usually junior military officers with at best a limited knowledge of mathematics and measurement techniques and little enthusiasm for the work. After independence there was no formal training available for surveyors until the 1870's.[52] Some surveyors were honest and skilled, but many others were clearly incompetent, corrupt, or simply lazy.[53] Required by law, for example, to measure property boundaries with a chain of a prescribed length, surveyors routinely substituted irregular instruments or simply took visual bearings and estimated distances and areas, claiming that the boundary lines were too "broken" to traverse. When the government supervisor of surveys (*revisor*) detected such derelictions, he usually rejected the measurement and ordered the work to be done again, but by then the town or hacienda might be out the money and unable to raise more or to recover what it already had paid the first surveyor. The leaders of one town, for example, found in the 1780's that because of a surveyor's failures several of the documents key to their suit against a neighboring hacienda were worthless, and, furthermore, the person responsible had gone bankrupt and could not repay the money they had given him.[54] Remeasurements sometimes led to bizarre and even deadly results. In 1865 a remeasurement of the ejidos of Quezaltepeque, Chiquimula, coincided in not a single line and at very few marker points (*mojones*) with a late-eighteenth-century map of the community; the government threw out both surveys as worthless.[55] Dozens of Indians died at Parraché on the south coast during the 1850's in battles over a point where the measurements of the lands of Santa Catarina Ixtahuacán, San Francisco Zapotitlán, and Zunil overlapped.[56] In another case, litigants complained that, because of incompetence or malice, a surveyor working for Santo Tomás Chichicastenango had "invaded" land belonging to San Miguel Totonicapán, Lemoa, Quiché, Sololá, and the hacienda Tululché.[57] A judge summed up the frustration many must have felt: "We have here a modern measurement and a remeasurement [of the same property] done by supposedly qualified engineers but that are in complete disagreement. . . . It makes even the most uninitiated wonder about the honesty of one or the other."[58]

Competent or not, surveyors faced working conditions that were difficult, and sometimes dangerous. Often they were forced to live in the bush for extended periods or to spend weeks in the most desolate villages, and they always had the problem of whether or not, and when, they would be paid. But perhaps their most constant concern was that they might be attacked by one of the parties in a measurement dispute. Assaults on surveyors were common, particularly in the years between the end of the colony and the consolidation of state power in the 1870's. The surveyor Ignacio Rivas, for example, was roughed up at Mataquescuintla in the mid-1820's, became embroiled in Santa María Chiquimula's problems in the early 1830's, and found himself again in peril in San Francisco el Alto in 1838, where the governor jailed him.[59] Again and again the state had to turn out troops to protect surveyors, a costly business and one for which soldiers could not always be spared during the years of political turmoil and banditry.[60] Usually surveyors had to work alone, depending for protection on their own diplomatic skills or on a well-timed retreat. Under the circumstances, it is hardly surprising that they might seek to find measurements with which the Indians were "happy," rather than necessarily ones that were "mathematically perfected," however lamentable the consequences.[61]

The Ejidos

By the end of the colonial period the term ejido or ejidos tended to be used interchangeably with tierras comunales or común. All these terms applied broadly to all the lands that a village and its inhabitants possessed or claimed or made use of. The ejidos might in fact include a legal ejido, and even between 1825 and 1837 when the law did not specify a square league, both the towns and government representatives took this to be the standard. If the community did not already possess such a legal ejido, the state was under some obligation to attempt to provide one, and in subsequent remeasurements this area generally did not need to be composed or otherwise purchased again, and often it was exempt from taxes.[62] There were towns that did not possess even a league, however, either because neighboring communities and private properties hemmed them in or because they had at some past time lost the land.[63] Depending on local custom, the ejido might be open to the use of all town residents for wood and water or pasture and cultivation without restriction apart from that of not infringing on the rights and activities of others. Or the municipal government might allocate or rent parcels and rights. Because the preferred location for an ejido was directly surrounding the village, its usefulness depended on the location of the town and the quality of the land in the area. Where a natural disaster or political conflict forced the transfer of a community from one site to another or when the state for political or religious reasons brought various populations together, this raised again the question of what was "abandoned" land and who might claim it.[64] Much of the movement and dispersal of populations that troubled public authorities was the result of Indian attempts to make use of land distant from where they lived but to which they had traditional claims.

A second category of village land was land that was purchased by or for the community, from terrenos baldíos, at public auction, by private contract, or through the mechanisms of composition. Although no general statistics are available, it is evident from the land records of specific towns that the practice was common, particularly for villages that were subject to ladino pressures or where land shortages had begun to manifest themselves. The town of San Andrés Semetabaj, for instance, bought land from its neighbor Panajachel, San Pedro Sacatepéquez (San Marcos) bought the hacienda Vasquez from its ladino owner and divided it among the townspeople, and Cantel, after decades of disputes, bought part of the hacienda Urbina.[65] Villa Nueva, on the other hand, possessed at independence only the five caballerías that village inhabitants had acquired from the Crown after the 1763 flooding of their original site; none of the surrounding haciendas would sell land to the town, and there was no baldío available in the area.[66] Other villages similarly hemmed in went farther afield: Zaragoza, in Chimaltenango, for example, bought sixteen caballerías in the distant piedmont.[67]

Towns also used the mechanisms of composition and moderated composition to regularize title to land they possessed illegally. The Spanish historian Francisco Solano has detailed a number of compositions in Guatemala during the half-century after 1750, many involving indigenous communities (see Table 2.2).[68] Other records make it clear that this is but a small sample of such transactions. A typical example was that of the village of Santiago Atitlán, which in 1751 applied to have its community lands measured and titled. A survey found 99.50 caballerías of generally poor quality land valued at four to twelve reales a caballería. The Audiencia ruled that the town might receive title to its legal square league of ejido and compose the rest at six reales per caba-

TABLE 2.2
"Composiciones" by Indian Communities, 1750–1799

Year	Community	Quantity in caballerías	Paid per caballería in reales
1750	Joyabaj	207	12 reales
	Comalapa	17.2	
	Esquipulas	9	
	Ermita (indios)	7	
1751	Amatitlán (S. Cris.)	131	28
	Amatitlán (S. Juan)	49.3	8
	Sta. Catalina (?)	?	
1772	Salamá (indios)	18.5	48
1773	Cubulco (indios)	152	32
1774	Zacapa (indios)	18	
1777	Quezaltepeque (indios)	19	32
	S. Pedro Sac. (?)	32	80
1778	Zunil	28	
1780	Mixco (indios)	11	40
1785	Parramos	15	
1789	Sacapulas	113	28
	Comapa (indios)	30	40
1791	S. Martín Jilotepeque	70	24
1794	S. Luís Salcajá (indios)	?	
1799	Gualan (indios)	23	80

SOURCES: Solano, *Tierra y sociedad*, follows, p. 115; Solano, *Los Mayas*, pp. 125–26 n. 207.

llería. Atitlán agreed but failed to follow through, and not until thirty years later, and threatened with the loss of all the land, did it finally make the necessary payments and take out the required documents.[69] In 1754 the subdelegate for Chiquimula measured 635 caballerías to Jocotán. Deducting an ejido of one square league left 597 caballerías of *excesos*, which the surveyor valued at four reales a caballería. The Audiencia, citing moderated composition, allowed Jocotán to buy this at half price.[70]

Until the twentieth century, the sale or composition of state lands generally followed procedures established in the colonial period. A would-be buyer applied to the governor of the appropriate district or department for permission to buy a specific parcel of land, giving the approximate size and location of the tract and usually identifying it by a locally recognized toponym. This application (*denuncia*) was advertised in the government gazette and on posters in nearby towns, to allow other possible claimants the opportunity to make their case. Assuming that the denuncia encountered no opposition, the interested party then paid to have the land measured by a government-approved surveyor and valued by local experts familiar with agriculture and land prices in the area. Unless composition or moderated composition applied, the state then sold the parcel at public auction, with first preference, bids being equal, to the person who originally sought it, or to the current possessor, or to communities in need of land. If someone other than the initial applicant bought the property, he or she had to repay measurement costs and reimburse any squatters for the value of existing "improvements."

Base prices for the auctions varied over time and with the quality of the land involved. The 1825 land law, for example, put the minimum at twelve reales to four pesos a caballería; the 1829 law, taking into account the effects of recent violence, stipulated a maximum of twelve reales; a June 9, 1830, decree reportedly again raised prices, this time to twelve reales to twenty pesos a caballería.[71] It is unlikely that before mid-century bid prices often approached the higher values, apart from a few areas favorable for the new crop of cochineal or for small quantities actively sought by a community. The law also empowered the state to grant to individuals and towns land at reduced costs or free of cost. This most commonly occurred when the government sought to reward individuals or to favor needy or politically troublesome communities. In the 1850's, for example, when the government attorney ruled that Santo Tomás Chichicastenango might buy some 412 caballerías in moderated composition, Carrera intervened with an order to give this to the town without cost, perhaps in the hope that it would curb the maxeños's notorious aggressions against their neighbors.[72] In 1829 the state limited the size of tracts that could be sold to an individual to five caballerías or less, but two years later it lifted this restriction.[73] Other than the villages and a series of ill-fated foreign immigration companies, however, there were few bidders in these years for large tracts of undeveloped land.

Towns did buy or compose land in the years from the end of the colony to the 1860's, but, again, comprehensive figures are lacking. Typical was the case of Zunil, which in 1833 protested the sale of land to a hacienda at Patio de Bolas in the nearby piedmont. The village claimed to have titled the tract itself by a recent purchase from baldíos. Although it turned out that Zunil's rights actually applied to a nearby but different parcel, the state nevertheless reopened the auction, and the town outbid the private individual, paying 28 pesos per caballería for slightly more than eighteen caballerías.[74] There were other similar examples: Concepción Chiquirichapa in 1841 bought more than eight caballerías of public land for twelve reales per caballería; Santa Lucía Cotzumalguapa composed 120 caballerías in 1830 for the same price; San Pedro Sacatepéquez (San Marcos) acquired baldío to fill in areas between the town and the parcels earlier cut from the hacienda Vasquez; Patzicía took funds from the community caja to buy land from private owners; Jacaltenango bought the hacienda San José Montenegro; Jutiapa in 1846 also acquired land from a neighboring estate; Santa Clara la Laguna bought a tract in the piedmont from a ladino and in turn gave 66 caballerías to San Juan la Laguna; Salamá used moderated composition to expand its ejidos; and San Pedro Yepocapa bought at auction, and over the bid of the ladino town of Zaragosa, some 40 caballerías at Yucales for twelve pesos each.[75] Land sales of all types brought the government 2,497 pesos in 1833–34 and 12,675 pesos the following year as production of cochineal began to take hold, but the upsurge of political violence and the cholera epidemic that spread after 1836 soon weakened the market. By 1839 income from the sale of baldío fell to only 1,817 pesos.[76]

In addition to an ejido and to tracts bought by the municipality, village common lands might also include areas that originally had been purchased or otherwise acquired by individuals, families, or groups within the community but had over time come to be regarded as village land. Clan (*parcialidad*) properties, for example, may have existed fairly widely in the nineteenth century, but their significance largely escaped the Spanish and republican officials who surveyed and categorized land. The subtleties of indigenous classifications tended to disappear in the broad categories of "tierras comunales" or "ejidos," and the Indians did not always hasten to explain to outsiders the peculiarities of the local situation. Thus, only in areas where the institution of corporate clans survived in a particularly vigorous form did landholding by parcialidades make its way into the records. Examples include Aguacatán-Chalchitán, some of the communities around Cobán, and, particularly, the towns of the Totonicapán region and the adjacent Quiché.[77] For Sacapulas the ethnohistorians James Hill and John Monaghan found that the local population needed to "educate" Bourbon officials when it seemed to the town's advantage to make the state understand the difference between the ejido and the properties of the clans.[78] As a result, measurements and maps of Sacapulas's community lands from the 1790's clearly indicated both the size and location of the holdings of each of the town's parcialidades as well as, and apart from, the square league of town ejido centered on the church. One hundred years later, however, although witnesses and the surveyor occasionally still spoke in terms of clans, the official map of the town showed only "community lands" with no internal distinctions.[79] Over time, the land-holding functions of groups below the level of the village, and above that of the immediate family, tended to be weakened and then obliterated by the effects of population growth, erosion, declining availability of resources, ignorance and neglect by the state and the priest, and the shift toward private property promoted by the Liberal regimes.

Traditionally, cofradías also controlled land, which they rented out or used to pasture animals to pay for the support of religious festivals.[80] As pressures on community resources mounted in the nineteenth century questions arose of who actually owned these properties. A struggle not uncommonly developed that might pit the local priest against the cofradías, the cofradías against town officials, and these officials against various secular state agents and representatives of the church hierarchy.[81] The priest typically argued that, in view of the economic crisis and mounting political chaos, only by taking direct control of the land and animals of the cofradía could he guarantee that the members would not lose, squander, or steal the "saints' property" and thus would be able to meet their obligations to the cult.[82] The Indians had always resisted attempts by the priests to intervene in what they saw as their affair, and as the state weakened they became more belligerent: "One does not know," a priest complained, "what the Indians have today, because even if you ask them they will not tell you."[83]

Town officials often entered the fray too, claiming that because the land or animals of the cofradías had been acquired with money or goods of the community, these properly belonged to the entire village, and they as community leaders had the right and obligation to determine their use and disposition.[84] For example, the Indian and ladino officials of Chiquimulilla complained in 1860 that their priest was attempting to usurp their land. In the past century, they said, their ancestors had bought the parcels of La Placeta, Pantaleón, Michatoya, and Teconala. Now the priest was claiming that these were cofradía properties and was seeking to take control of them and to rent the land out to pay for "the celebration of the images." He was even trying to charge the villagers themselves rent. This was community not cofradía property, the officials protested. Documents perhaps not available at the time make it clear that in 1744 the cofradías had purchased at least some of the tracts in question and had had this ownership confirmed in a lawsuit with a neighboring hacienda in the 1780's. Confusingly, however, the state in 1837 also had issued a stay in the name of the town guaranteeing possession. Efforts by the Carrera regime to enforce a Solomonic decision that would have given half of the disputed area to the community and half to the "cofradías," meaning to the control of the priest, came to nought; it had similar luck with a suggestion that everyone should pay rent. The dispute fades from the records with the state's attorney and the officials of Chiquimulilla arrayed against the district governor, the priest, and the archbishop and with no solution in sight.[85]

Towns also claimed or used large amounts of land based on possession "from time immemorial," even though, at least from the perspective of the colonial and republican state, they had scant legal right to the land. In the Oriente the goal of the towns and the haciendas alike was to gain access to the few pockets of good land scattered among the low, barren hills and along the rivers. This required and prompted broad claims.[86] For the communities of the western highlands and the upper Verapaz, on the other hand, broad definitions of "común" or "ejidos" grew out of the advantages of access to lands in both the hot country and the cold country. Except for a few cases of towns that exploited very high parts of the Cuchumatán Mountains (the *paramo*) or the coastal salt flats, land in the western part of the country and to the north fell into two broad folk classifications: "la costa" or hot-country land, including the southern and northern slopes of the mountains (boca costa), broad plains down to the Pacific (*costa grande*), the northern jungles, and the intermountain and river valleys of the highlands itself, and the altiplano, the cold-country land above four or five thousand feet. The common pattern was for the inhabitants of the highland towns to work the cold-country ejidos surrounding their village more or less year-round. Corn here took four to six months to mature. It was this environment that the leaders of Todos Santos Cuchumatán described in 1813 with the exaggeration typical of land cases: "Our town has absolutely nowhere to cultivate . . . because the icy conditions do not let us plant anywhere. . . . Frosts happen all the time."[87] To offset such problems, inhabitants of the highland towns would go for a few weeks at a time to the lowlands, to plant and harvest corn, which matured there in only sixty to ninety days (*milpas de segundo* or *de fuego*), and to work plots of tropical crops.

By the early nineteenth century the Pacific piedmont and plain was littered with the ejidos of decayed and disappeared communities[88] and with tracts of unclaimed baldío potentially open to highland migrants. Despite sometimes heated conflicts over specific parcels there generally was sufficient land available on the "coast" for highland communities to gain access to what they needed under reasonable conditions, whether by rent, purchase, or squatting. Where the highlands fell off into the northern jungles and savannas no one at the national level had the least idea who farmed what or where.[89] Gradually, as Archbishop Cortés y Larraz discovered, temporary and sometimes permanent settlements grew up on or near these lowland plantings, colonies of the highland towns that generally maintained the costume and customs of the home community and acknowledged political and religious subordination to that village.[90] In other cases the population was mixed. A priest described, for example, the origins of Santo Domingo Retalhuleu in Suchitepéquez: "A little while ago there began to appear in this area the huts of ladinos who came at the time of the cotton harvest, but over time more and more of them have remained and taken in Indians and other ladinos."[91]

Two types of communities typically found it more difficult than most to gain secure access to land—the casta settlements and the communities that grew out of clusters of hacienda workers. Most casta valles that failed to gain legal recognition in the colonial period, or obtained it only in the last years of the colony or after independence, were short of land, victims of population growth and three centuries of hacienda and community expansion. Although new laws eased the requirements of municipal status, there often remained little public land in the vicinity of ladino settlements from which to form ejidos, and there was equally little chance that the villagers could meet the costs of buying land from private owners. Valles too poor to buy land or to compose what they possessed were left to squat on public or private land, in the promiscuous abandon that so exercised Archbishop Cortés y Larraz. Only a few settlements of this sort managed to establish a permanent presence. The Indians of Don García in Escuintla, for example, protested in 1812 that as an indigenous population they had the right to control the village's ejidos but that local castas forced them to pay rent. Upon investigation it appeared that the ancestors of both groups had migrated to the region in the seventeenth century to work in the indigo mill of one Juan García. When this enterprise failed, the owner defaulted on capellanías owed the Convent of Santa Catarina. The ladinos living on the property then bought the land from the sisters in 1708, or so their descendants now claimed. What in fact they had promised was to pay rent to the convent equal to the amount of the interest on the existing capellanías. They could not have been very punctual in this, for by 1799 they owed some 3,600 pesos in back rent. The government attorney ruled that neither group qualified for an ejido but that existing custom might continue, with the exception that, since the mulattoes had said they wished to live in equality with the Indians, they, too, were now to pay rent.[92]

Other cases suggest similar patterns. The nearby town of La Gomera, for example, guarded titles to ten "sites, mills, and ranches" obtained originally in the seventeenth century by purchases made by "various settlers of the town." These separate properties had gradually merged into communal lands, a form of possession the state repeatedly confirmed in order to stabilize and support the mulatto militia members who guarded the south coast against pirates.[93] When the Audiencia raised San Carlos Sija and Salcajá in Quezaltenango to municipalities during the 1770's there was no public land near either town from which to form ejidos.[94] The inhabitants of the ladino town of Zaragosa, in Chimaltenango, explained to the Audiencia in the same years that their common land originally had belonged to Francisco Argueta; his descendants had divided and redivided it among themselves over the years and had intermarried, "until becoming confused as to our ancestry" they agreed to hold it in common. Fifty years later Zaragosa's population had doubled and its lands were worn out, so the inhabitants had to rent from the neighboring Indian community of Chimaltenango and also buy land on the distant boca costa.[95]

The second group of land-short communities in the nineteenth century, those that had had their beginnings in clusters of resident workers on haciendas, were perhaps even harder pressed. The governor of Guatemala pointed this out in supporting Sanarate's 1865 request for an ejido and added that the situation was common to many settlements in the region; they were independent but were without land.[96] The village of Palencia, for example, struggled first against the Dominicans who owned the hacienda Palencia and then with the landowner who bought the property from the state after 1829.[97] San Jeronimo in the Verapaz fought for most of the nineteenth century to free itself from the hacienda San Jeronimo. Declared independent in 1822 and raised to municipal status in 1836, San Jeronimo remained locked in conflict for half a century with the hacienda over ownership of house sites and even of the religious articles in the church.

They had to go long distances to find community agricultural lands.[98] Haciendas as well as existing communities usually controlled not only the best land but the water resources in a given area, so that, even if a settlement of workers or former workers gained municipal independence, it seldom could find an ejido. Useful baldío was rarely available, and already developed land was expensive, if, indeed, the hacienda was willing to sell it.[99]

Haciendas

The privately owned properties that held land in rural Guatemala were of various sizes, uses, and forms of possession. Archbishop Cortés y Larraz, in his famous survey carried out in the late 1760's and early 1770's, noted some 380 "haciendas," mainly in the Oriente and along the south coast,[100] but the majority of these were isolated, largely undeveloped, and unprofitable tracts of land that counted little in the commercial economy. By the standards usually associated with Latin American latifundia, they were not particularly large. A sample of the average size of rural properties registered for the 1830's land tax ranges from 2.66 caballerías in Totonicapán to 112.53 caballerías in Escuintla (see Table 2.3). Even these figures were deceptive, because a typical jurisdiction included only a few large properties and many more of below average size. Probably, also, fewer of the small properties registered. Most of the haciendas in the Oriente produced cattle and corn, and sugar cane if water was available, and remained weakly capitalized: "Although [the] haciendas are large, apart from a few they are in reality quite poor." [101] Local markets, already limited by the relative absence of urban or mining centers, declined after 1800 and collapsed in the wake of independence. The rise of cochineal in the early 1830's and after 1840 in the area west of the capital provided some very limited stimulus to adjacent districts, but the economy remained sluggish.[102]

Haciendas that had grown in size in the sixteenth and early seventeenth centuries were now saddled with debts and worn-out land. Histories of the haciendas Lo de Pereira, near Mataquescuintla, and Sapayuca, in the municipality of Jalpatagua, neither of which appears in the 1830's registration, show how a property could grow in size even while it stagnated or declined in value.[103] In 1608 Lo de Pereira measured one *sitio de estancia* (a square league) plus six caballerías;

TABLE 2.3
Average Size of Some Registered Rural Private Properties
by Municipio, 1835

Jurisdiction	Size (in caballerías)
Totonicapán	2.66
S. Juan Sacatepéquez	9.98
Huehuetenango	15.40
Esquipulas	18.00
Salamá	36.20
San Marcos	41.70
Chiquimulilla	43.29
Jalapa	60.73
Escuintla	112.53

SOURCE: AHA, Cartas, Matrículas de Tierras, 1832–35.

subsequent owners added another four caballerías and retitled the property in 1718; in 1731 they paid off a capellanía of 1,600 pesos to the convent of Santa Catarina, and in 1755 they sold the hacienda for the sum of 10,000 pesos (4,000 pesos for another capellanía and 6,000 pesos in cash). The new owners added 12.5 caballerías from Crown land. Late in the century they again sold the property, now totaling slightly more than 50 caballerías, this time for 13,000 pesos, but only 1,360 pesos of this was cash and most was a mortgage granted by the seller for an indefinite period and at a below market interest rate.

In the case of Sapayuca, Alferez Pedro Almengor in 1669 sold the property to Gregorio de León Mortalla for an undetermined price but including a debt of 2,000 pesos to the Monastery La Merced. "Because the owner had abandoned it," the Mercederians sold the property in 1729 to Captain Miguel Fernandez de Córdoba "without a title" for the recognition of a 1,000-peso capellanía; by 1730 de Córdoba had found the title, but a remeasurement discovered only 40 caballerías instead of the 53 the document indicated, a result of invasions by neighboring property owners or inaccurate earlier surveys, or both. The hacienda sold in 1745 for 500 pesos cash and the 1,000-peso debt to La Merced and then again for the same price to Tadeo Piñol before 1799, when he received confirmation from the Audiencia.

In the western highlands the dominant activities of the larger ladino holdings were wheat growing for those near the capital and livestock, chiefly sheep, raising on those more distant. A few of the properties were large, and some made extensive use of baldíos and even community lands when they could, but even these ran small numbers of animals (see Table 2.4).[104] The best known of the livestock properties in the West was the hacienda Moscoso-Chancol, enormous by local standards. It had title to 363 caballerías on the plains above Chiantla.[105] Although estimates of the sheep on the property placed the number as high as 30,000, a mid-eighteenth-century inventory found slightly more than 9,000, a number that rose to 10,335 by 1817 and to 11,404 in 1829.[106] If less than sometimes imagined, this figure was still very high for Guatemala. The property was said to be worth at least 50,000 pesos but rented in 1815 for only 500 pesos a year and sold at auction for 15,000 pesos in early 1834.[107] Far from encroaching on its neighbors, Moscoso-Chancol was under constant pressure from nearby Indian towns, which sought to assert control over the hacienda's population of renters and shepherds and disputed boundaries and encroached on land claimed by the hacienda.[108] Other well-known properties in the altiplano, such as Chiché, Chuacorral-Tululché-Portuguese, Argueta, Veinte Palos, Urbina, and Sucún, by all evidence returned scant profits, struggled constantly to survive, and had little opportunity or incentive to expand. Besides raising wheat or sheep, these haciendas leased tracts of land for corn and pasture to poor ladinos and nearby Indian communities, although as the state broke down most owners counted themselves lucky when they could collect this rent.

The late colonial–early national period was not one of hacienda expansion in Guatemala. Francisco de Solano's list of compositions,

TABLE 2.4

Livestock Haciendas in the Western Highlands, Circa 1800

Jurisdiction	Number of haciendas	Average number of animals per hacienda
Salcajá	5	133
Momostenango	2	71
San Carlos Sija	3	92
Huehuetenango	10	175
Chiantla	2	6,150
Malacatán	11	90
Cuilco	2	500

SOURCE: AGCA, A3.5 352 07308, 07309, and 07318; A3.5 1155 20488.

for example, shows the acquisition by individuals of small amounts of property, chiefly in the Canales Mountains and north of the capital around San Raymundo, but no large-scale land grabbing and very little titling by names recognizable as belonging to the elite. The best-known properties were already formed, and land, aside from a few favored pockets, was of little value. Where the owners added land they did so largely by purchase and composition, not by violence or extralegal usurpation.[109] Indeed, it was common for existing properties to come apart as a result of divisions at inheritance and bankruptcies.[110] Before 1800 there was a good deal of interest in properties in El Salvador– Sonsonate, but with the decline of indigo, land in this area was not so attractive an investment. Established landowners or would-be land-owning elites found even less attractive the idea of pouring scarce funds into acquiring, enlarging, or modernizing properties in the less favored areas of the colony. Owners did a considerable amount of speculative buying and selling, and they encroached casually on neighbors and nearby Indian and ladino communities, and they sued each other over land, but notary documents, sales and titling records, and legal cases make it clear that such activities were of limited economic importance and not nearly so profitable as commerce and officehold-ing.[111] Land acquisition reflected imperatives of diversification, social prestige, and security against the fluctuations of trade more than any serious effort to found or develop wealth based on rural property.

In addition, debts, in the form of capellanías, obras pías, and loans, pressed on many of the landowners. The Consulado de Comercio criticized the hacendados: "Because of the way they operate, they are always going into debt; indeed, it seems that they study carefully how to lose what they have." [112] A random sample of hacienda sales from the last years of the colony suggests the relative weight of capellanía debts alone, often amounting to a third to a half or more of the sale price (see Table 2.5). A tally compiled in 1810 of the more substantial hacien-das along the south coast from Don García to the Sonsonate border included some two hundred properties, of which fewer than twenty-five had a liquid value of 5,000 pesos or more after debts.[113] The heirs of Miguel Asturias owned haciendas worth more than 150,000 pesos, and the Juarros family or Tadeo Piñol possessed properties in several districts estimated at tens of thousands of pesos; but the most valuable "estate" in the valle of Santa Rosa was put at 570 pesos after debts and the most valuable in Zacualpa was worth only 1,341 pesos. Large debts relative to the value of properties allowed speculators to acquire them

TABLE 2.5
Hacienda Sales, 1765–1808

Date	Property	Price in pesos	Price less capellanía debts
1765	Concepción	1,500	300
1767	a "piece"		100
1770	crop land	2,550	550
1775	*labor*	800	300
1782	Santiago	2,362	1,362
1786	*labor*	1,500	500
1791	La Sabana Grande	2,000	500
1796	San Jacinto	1,000	400
1804	Los Ocotes	20,500	13,500
1808	Obraje Quemado	1,800	1,000

SOURCE: AGCA, Protocolos, and AHA records.

with little cash outlay,[114] but this did not bode well for profitability and almost guaranteed undercapitalization, frequent defaults, and a rapid turnover in ownership, with a consequent lack of attention to developing the property. With the decay of the economy after the turn of the century, some indebted owners simply gave up and handed the haciendas over to their creditors, much as others had done a century earlier.[115]

With the exception of the cochineal areas, rural land prices generally stagnated or fell in the one hundred years after 1760. Not all properties declined in value, of course, and prices probably began to move upward again after 1850, but to judge from sale and resale prices recorded in notary records, the overall trend was down (see Table 2.6). More generally, land was of little value compared with the worth of improvements, tools and equipment, and animals on a property. An inventory of the famous hacienda Villalobos, for example, taken around the turn of the century, put its value at slightly more than 22,000 pesos—including 5,409 pesos for the house and furniture, 7,559 pesos for the animals, and only 2,015 for the land.[116] For several reasons, however, we cannot make a systematic evaluation of land values or changes in real prices over time. Those involved in such transactions routinely understated the value of properties to avoid or reduce taxes; furthermore, documents, and probably not entirely out of carelessness, tended to be vague as to the amounts of land involved, making it difficult to compare sales and resales of the same property.

TABLE 2.6
Hacienda Prices, 1764–1868
(in pesos)

Hacienda	Original sale price	Resale price
Lo de Ayarsa	21,000 (1769)	8,000 (1834)
Chiquiquitán	9,217 (1770)	1,400 (1835)
La Ahumada	1,100 (1796)	630 (1840)
Obraje Quemado	1,800 (1796)	1,800 (1808)
Cimarron	2,500 (1800)	470 (1859)
Punian	38,000 (1808)	9,000 (circa 1850)
Villalobos	23,000 (1808)	23,000 (1868)
Yspanguarte	9,250 (1843)	5,589 (1864)
Sansur	4,000 (1844)	406 (1854)

SOURCE: AGCA, Protocolos.

Evidently the traffic in agricultural land was not an object of great concern to the late colonial or newly independent state nor one over which they exerted much control.

The political turmoil after 1821, following on several decades of economic decline, made conditions for rural property deteriorate even more sharply. Travelers reported abandoned and neglected haciendas and properties that could not be sold for the price of the equipment. Owners and renters suffered the effects of repeated attacks and sackings.[117] Creditors lost. In 1832 the hacienda Choacorral, near Guatemala City, had a book value of 16,550 pesos but also carried a debt of 12,572 pesos in capellanías, and under present conditions was said not to be worth even this; two partners acquired it by agreeing to pay half of the interest on the capellanías.[118] Political refugees abandoned properties, records disappeared, and the legal and judicial system broke down. Those with political power took advantage of the confused situation to profit from dubious land transactions. Rafael Carrera, operating in the name of his wife, and in company with Tomás Larraondo, also working under his wife's name, put together the hacienda Trapiche Grande of more than a thousand caballerías taken from a number of towns on the Suchitepéquez coast.[119] Despite its size, the hacienda was of little immediate value.[120] After Carrera's death, Doña Juana Mayorga sued successfully for the return of a property the dictator had extorted from her.[121] Other government officials similarly used their positions to take advantage of communities and private individuals.[122] Beyond the immediate area of the capital, however, and aside from the cochineal-growing area around Antigua-Amatitlán, rural Guatemala stagnated in the half-century after 1800.

Sharing the countryside with the communities and the haciendas were hundreds of small private properties. These ranged from substantial labores and holdings of several caballerías that produced corn and animals for market to obscure subsistence plots tucked into the folds of the mountains and worked by Indians, castas, and poor Spaniards. We know from dozens of eyewitness accounts and offhand comments in other documents that such properties existed, but they remain almost invisible in available systematic records. Few of the owners took out or registered titles, engaged in lawsuits, received labor drafts, left capellanías or obras pias, paid taxes, or otherwise interacted with the state and church bureaucracies. Most ran a dozen or so cattle and a few horses and earned perhaps 50–100 pesos a year from the sale of corn, cheese, and sugar. Many, the governors reported, "had absolutely nothing." [123] The 1804 census listed some 1,200 ladino and an equal number of Spanish rural property owners but did not indicate what or how much they owned or on what basis "ownership" was determined. This count certainly underestimated their numbers, as did also the 1832–35 land tax survey, which included approximately 700 individual claimants of properties of all sizes. Because of the costs and complications of buying and legally titling land, and of defending that title, most ladino small holders must have been at least technically squatters, whether on Crown baldíos, on the common lands of indigenous communities, or on the fringes of large privately owned properties. Others paid rent in kind or labor when the reputed owners of the land they used could enforce this. Many worked part of the year for wages on the haciendas or at occupations such as mule driving and petty trade or crossed over into cattle theft and the illegal alcohol traffic or raised and sold tobacco outside the state monopoly. Undoubtedly, as one writer recently argued, "The economy of mestizo small producers was much more important at the beginning of the nineteenth century than has been recognized," [124] but also, at least for the moment, its participants and the type and extent of their activities remain uncertain and obscured to outsiders, as they intended they should be.

Church Property

Apart from cofradía properties, over which it exercised at best limited influence, the church had some measure of control over two, or possibly three, other sorts of rural property. Most obvious were those that belonged to the secular branch, usually acquired as a result of the loan and chantry activities of the Cabildo Eclesiástico, and the haciendas and mills of the regular orders. Land escheated to the Cabildo when owners could not or would not pay what they owed. An instance of this, from the late eighteenth century, involved the hacienda Pueblo Nuevo in Guazacapán, whose owner died in 1782 nine years behind in interest payments on capellanías; when the widow failed to pay, the church foreclosed and had the property put up for auction. In 1800 the church initiated an action against Policarpio Landero for a debt of 4,491 pesos, plus 1,116 pesos in past-due interest; the land and equipment were worth no more than 4,000 pesos, and Landero managed to strip the property of animals before he abandoned it, leaving the Cabildo with a loss.[125] The Cabildo made it a practice to sell, or at least rent as soon as possible, the rural properties it acquired by default, since abandoned properties were an open invitation to squatters, as the church knew from experience. The owner of the hacienda La Sabana Grande, near Guazacapán, fled the property early in the eighteenth century rather than pay the interest on capellanías, and for years the church could find no one to take it. Eventually squatters invaded the hacienda and forced the church in 1786 to sell it to them on favorable terms.[126] Since chantries were not loans from church funds but pledges or gifts of the faithful, even selling or renting a property for less than the nominal charges against it was a net benefit to the church treasury, but when owners defaulted on loans the loss was real. It was partly for this reason, and given the generally depressed state of agriculture, that the Cabildo made few loans against rural properties and, as a result, came into possession of relatively few of these.

The regular orders and the women's convents, on the other hand, owned and operated, or rented out, a number of valuable rural properties, which they had come into possession of by gifts of the faithful or from persons who took orders, sometimes by purchase, and in lieu of unpaid debts and capellanías. The whole subject of the wealth and the economic activities of the monastic orders in Guatemala has been so little examined that at this point one can draw only a few very preliminary conclusions about their importance in rural life. The Dominicans were the richest order in the colony and controlled the largest assembly of agricultural holdings. One source suggests that, together with the income from the parishes they administered, the Dominican-held haciendas and sugar mills returned the order a million pesos between 1775 and 1808.[127] A partial listing of Dominican agricultural holdings would include Cerro Redondo (150 caballerías) in the Oriente, Palencia (97 caballerías) also east of the capital, De Batres in the suburbs of Guatemala City, and La Compañía (31 caballerías) near Amatitlán; in the Verapaz the Dominicans owned San Jeronimo (473 caballerías), Santa Barbara, Santa Catalina, Llano Grande, Chuacul, and San Nicolás, and in Quiché, the hacienda Tululché-Chiché (182 caballerías) and a number of smaller properties.[128] The possessions of the Jesuits, Franciscans, Mercederians, and San Felipe Neri, less important orders in Guatemala, were much more modest, typically no more than a hacienda or two of limited value. The institutions of the female religious orders owned an undetermined but apparently substantial amount of agricultural property.[129] Obras pias, for example, hospitals and orphanages, also had rural properties.[130]

The Liberals expelled the regular orders in 1829 and confiscated their possessions, and in the early 1830's the government sold these. The only record of these transactions presently available is that published in Lorenzo Montufar's *Reseña historica de Centro América*, an accounting that scattered references in notary records and land title documents make clear was representative but incomplete.[131] The famous sugar hacienda San Jeronimo sold for an astounding 253,526 pesos, making it by far the single most valuable agricultural property in the country, and Palencia brought 28,075 pesos, but most of the other rural properties went for quite modest prices: Cerro Redondo sold for 11,416 pesos, including animals and equipment, Tululché-Chiché in the highlands brought only 409 pesos, San Nicolás in the Verapaz sold for 6,278 pesos, and Ixpanguazate was worth only recognition of 4,000 pesos in capellanías and 3,706 pesos cash. Other properties apparently disappeared into private hands by less open routes, but the evidence is fragmentary.

Although writers generally have accepted that after 1839 "most [of the orders' ex-properties] were restored to the original owners," this was not the case.[132] Elites proved reluctant to give up the bargains they had gained, and Carrera specifically opposed blanket restoration.[133] Church propagandists warned repeatedly of the dire consequences certain to befall a country and a government that failed to return to the orders what was theirs, but the admonitions had little effect.[134] The biggest prize of all, San Jeronimo, remained in the hands of the descendants of Marshall Bennett until almost the end of the century, perhaps, the church carped, because these were foreign hands and the state feared diplomatic intervention.[135] The Dominicans regained Palencia in 1848 only after an extended lobbying campaign and then under clear restrictions that forbade selling or renting it and guaranteed the rights of the families living there.[136] Several of the orders' ex-properties had been broken into lots and auctioned off in the mid-1830's, including the land of the sugar plantations La Compañía and Anís; because much of this was in cochineal production by the 1840's, it was too profitable for its new owners to imagine giving up.[137] The Jesuits managed to acquire the hacienda Las Nubes near Guatemala City, and San Felipe Neri made use of, although it claimed not to own, El Incienso, also close by the capital, but none of the orders ever regained even the limited position in agriculture they had enjoyed before 1829. When the Liberals in 1873 again nationalized church possessions, they found few rural properties.[138]

One additional category of church-related property was that owned by members of the secular clergy, or by their close relatives, in or near the parishes they served. Some of this they acquired legitimately, but it was not unheard of for a priest to take advantage of his special position to take land from the community. One such priest was Presbítero Ponciano Garrote Bueno, who during thirty years in the parish of San Lorenzo Mazatenango–San Gabriel, Suchitepéquez, aggressively developed and expanded various forms of exploitation and abuse for his own profit.[139] In addition to the usual practices of overcharging for his services, misappropriating money from the cofradías and the community caja, demanding extraordinary amounts of food and service, and physically assaulting Indians, Ponciano, in cooperation with his brother Manuel, actively extorted land and labor from the towns to develop their hacienda San Rafael. One scheme involved taking on the guardianship of orphans and minors and stealing the property they were to inherit, and the brothers loosed cattle on the plantings of Indian neighbors in order to force them to sell or rent their land at low prices. Ponciano must have had friends in high places, for he and his brother prospered, weathering repeated protests by villagers and Spanish civil officials alike. After independence Manuel Garrote (there is no mention of Ponciano, who perhaps by this time had died) became involved in a scheme to separate Suchitepéquez from Guatemala and join it to Mexico. When this failed, he fled the country, and the state auctioned his properties for 15,000 pesos, a substantial sum given the uncertainty of the times and depressed land prices.[140] The rapacity and longevity of the Garrote Buenos was exceptional, but hundreds of complaints preserved in the church's records make it clear that other priests also took advantage of their positions to acquire land at the expense of the indigenous communities.

Rental Relations

"What a strange phenomenon," remarked the *Gaceta de Guatemala* in the 1790's, "that where there exists land enough to occupy all the workers of Spain" poor castas had to seek land to rent.[141] Rent relations in fact crisscrossed the economic and social life of nineteenth-century rural Guatemala, and not just among the Spanish and mulattoes. The Dominicans rented land to their own black slaves on Chiché and San Jeronimo.[142] Among the inhabitants of the indigenous villages custom varied, but rent there, too, was common. Indians might, for example, and depending on their situation and needs, rent land from corporate groups such as the cofradías or clans or from individual Indian, Spanish, or casta property owners in or outside the community. It was only an apparent contradiction—and leaving aside problems of communications and the quality and utility of specific tracts—that Guatemala in the early nineteenth century had both a surplus of land relative to the size of its population and a multiplicity of rent relations. Whereas the state reckoned large areas of the countryside as baldío because of the absence of legal title, local populations commonly recognized, and sought to make others recognize, rights of possession and control over much of this, whether such rights were said to rest on ancient documents, on locally accepted custom, on longtime occupation, on fraud, ignorance, and confusion, or on threats of violence.[143] The Indians of Santa Catarina Ixtahuacán, for example, paid rent for decades to hacienda Chocolá until a remeasurement showed that Chocolá had no right to the area.[144] And in 1851 one Pedro Moratalla sought a 75 percent rent increase from the families occupying a tract of land near Chinautla, north of the capital, which he said he owned. When they resisted he moved to evict them. It soon became clear, however, that he had no title nor any right to the rent he had been collecting for several years. The Guatemala City government noted that such usurpations were common and warned that the uprisings in the 1830's had originated in precisely this sort of "lack of justice and abuses." [145]

Under the colonial "laws of Castile," renters enjoyed certain legal rights, which the Liberals recognized and enforced after independence. Owners, for example, could not deny renters the renewal of customary arrangements so long as they met their obligations nor could they expel the renters because of political differences, no small concession given the conflicts of the 1820's and 1830's.[146] For all their reputed concern for the peasantry, it was the Conservatives, under pressure from uprisings in the late 1840's, who abolished such customary rights, ruling in 1849 that "owners of haciendas may expel from their properties any resident they do not wish to remain there; in the event of resistance, public authorities will assist the owner." [147]

Probably the most common rental relationship in the countryside, apart from the arrangements within some of the indigenous communities, was the leasing of hacienda land either by residents of the property itself or by outsiders. It is difficult to recover information on this because most of the contracts were verbal, and to render such agreements as do survive into terms that make sense to a modern reader is often impossible. What is one to understand, for example, of the information that a renter is to pay two "nets" of corn for each *labor* cultivated? Rental payments took various forms, including cash and labor rent and sharecropping, and actual instances usually involved a combination of several of these. Whereas colonos of Cerro Redondo in 1810 seem to have been charged only cash rent, each ladino family on the hacienda Palencia in 1829 had to pay annual rents of four reales for each head of cattle pastured, one *fanega* of corn for each ten *cuerdas* cultivated, eight days' labor a year on the hacienda, or the payment of one peso, and all taxes due the priest.[148] They described this as "the harshest slavery," and the charges do seem high, particularly the pasturage costs for animals that were themselves not worth more than a few pesos each. A number of the Indians of the town of San Juan Sacatepéquez, north of Guatemala City, in 1841 contracted to rent thirty cuerdas each from the property Las Trojes, for cultivation and as a source for *ocote* (pitch pine), firewood, and pasture. For this each gave each year four fanegas of corn, a peso, and a chicken, *faena* (unpaid Sunday "cleanup" work), seasonal harvest labor paid at one peso a week, additional labor, as needed, at the customary wage, and women's labor as cooks, as needed, at two reales a week and food.[149] Whether such arrangements proved burdensome probably depended on how the landowner interpreted the labor requirements. Haciendas undoubtedly sought to rachet up rents where possible, and the ladino and Indian renters cited custom and resisted. In general, however, there is little evidence of extortionate demands during these years. Land was readily available for rent, and the rural population had the confidence and the ability to defend its interests, by violent means if necessary.

In some areas where the population had outgrown or threatened to outstrip available resources and where village lands were hemmed in by the ejidos of neighboring towns or by haciendas, communities as a corporate group rented land. The residents of Salamá, for example, leased land from haciendas across much of the lower Verapaz, as did the Indians of San Agustín Acasaguastlán.[150] Chiquimulilla rented land from neighboring haciendas owned by Tadeo Piñol, a transaction to which Piñol agreed, or so he claimed, only to stop the Indians from continuing to steal his animals.[151] Perhaps most notorious in the late colony were the problems of Santa María Chiquimula, in the highland department of Totonicapán. The population was large and growing, but the inhabitants were impoverished by the insufficiency and poor quality of the land available to them. From at least the early eighteenth century the community had had to rent land in the Verapaz at Cobán, Cahabón, Salamá, and Cubulco, from towns on the south coast, and from San Pedro Jocopilas and Sacapulas; the town of Santa Cruz del Quiché "enslaved" Santa María, a priest reported, demanding "exorbitant rents" for desperately needed corn land. But it was with nearby San Antonio Ilotenango that the chiquimulas had their most serious and persistent problems. In return for the use of land belonging to that town, they gave Ilotenango 120 pesos a year, supplied the materials and labor to rebuild the town's church and municipal buildings, and paid any taxes levied on Ilotenango. The town harassed the chiquimulas with a constant stream of petty demands: "They charge us even for the water our sheep drink." Town officials of Ilotenango lived in a drunken stupor funded by the chiquimulas' money, arbitrarily beat and jailed them and confiscated their plantings, and forced them to do civil and religious service in Ilotenango. Not surprisingly, violence flared repeatedly between the towns in the half-century after independence. Santa María's *principales* despaired: "Each day we are worse off, submerged in misfortune and misery, poorer and more ignorant," but there was no public land available in the area and no easy solution to the town's problem.[152]

Before 1821 the leasing or renting of Indian community lands to ladinos from outside the village without the specific sanction of the state was usually illegal. The practice nevertheless seems to have been fairly common, particularly in the ladino-dominated Oriente.[153] Where such rental relations did receive state approval they usually took the form of *censo enfiteusis*, a long-term lease requiring an annual payment to the town of 2 or 3 percent of the estimated value of the land; renters from outside the community paid the higher rate. Contracts commonly ran for nine years and could be renewed. Renters had the right, subject to the approval of the municipality, to sell to third parties both the unexpired term of their lease, their so-called *dominio útil* (use rights), and any standing crops or improvements they had made. Poor castas and elites alike also worked out illegal but profitable accommodations with local officials and Crown agents to use town and cofradía lands. Although censo contracts by definition recognized community ownership, renters schemed unceasingly to convert possession into property rights. At Quezaltepeque, for example, a ladino from outside the town illegally purchased a small piece of property from a local Indian, and then by threats or bribes gained permission to lease adjoining ejido lands. Not only did he fail to pay the agreed-upon rent, but in 1769 he sold out to one Pedro Ximenez, who now claimed not rental but property rights to the ejido land. Ximenez also forced private owners to sell him town lots, and he invaded the lands of Indian minors who were unable to defend themselves. The leaders of Quetzaltepeque took him to court and eventually won a favorable decision, but meanwhile Ximenez's cattle and pigs roamed untended in the Indians' plantings and the resulting food shortages drove people from the town.[154]

Tecpán Guatemala confronted a similar problem a century later but on a wider scale. According to the governor of Chimaltenango, ladinos had been "buying" small plots in Tecpán's ejidos since the colonial period, "and from these many small pieces they formed large plantations and pastures, considering themselves owners and lords of this land and controlling the ejidos." What they had "bought" was no more than use rights to land held in censo, but "because of carelessness or ignorance or bad faith" they were attempting to convert possession into property. Ignoring the underlying lease contracts, they claimed that thirty years' possession gave them ownership under the 1825 and 1829 land laws. The state's attorney, while arguing the superior utility of private property, rejected the renters' arguments and sustained the community in the ownership of its ejidos.[155] If the ladinos' effort failed in this instance, rent relations often did provide an opening wedge into communities' lands. Castas and hacendados sought to enlarge and to reinforce this opening after 1821 with appeals that unfavorably contrasted the "inefficiency" of Indian subsistence agriculture to their own market production. Not all local Indian leadership was as aware or vigilant, or as resistant, apparently, to bribery and threats as was that of Quezaltepeque and Tecpán. The Indians of Mixco remembered in the early 1870's that the town had lost its community's lands to ladinos a generation before because their ancestors "had thought that they were without rights" and had failed to complain when the ladinos converted rented land into private property.[156]

As Quezaltepeque's experience demonstrated, almost anytime a community rented land to Spaniards or castas problems erupted, especially over the damage the ladinos' cattle caused Indian agriculture. Spanish law prescribed a distance of at least half a league between cattle ranches and Indian plantings, but this provision was not always observed before 1821, and it was largely ignored thereafter.[157] The activities of the Garrote Bueno brothers showed how cattle could be one of a landowner's chief offensive weapons. They not only "cleared" nearby properties for grazing but helped to destroy the Indians' livelihood, forcing them to seek wage labor. The Indians constantly protested cattle damage and fought back, fencing their plantings and confiscating or killing intrusive animals, but many towns, particularly those on the south coast, had few sources of income except the rental of land to the haciendas. Conflict there was endemic.[158] The leaders of San Francisco Zapotitlán, for example, in 1801 approached the governor of Suchitepéquez asking his help in finding someone to lease an unused portion of the community's lands. The town had fallen "into almost total decadence," they said, and could not pay the priest or other village expenses. The governor arranged a contract between San Francisco and the hacienda owner, Luís Valladares of Cuyotenango, who had similar agreements with other decayed towns in the area. The results were not what San Francisco had anticipated. Valladares stopped paying rent after three or four years, the town protested, and his cattle were destroying the town's corn, cotton, and cacao plantings. Now he was claiming ownership of the tract. The landowner dismissed San Francisco's complaints, saying that there was hardly a town there at all. He blamed the accusations on the priest of Samayac, who, he said, was stirring the town up to drive out competition to his own cattle hacienda. The governor ordered the community to abide by the contract.[159] The law may have been on the side of the indigenous population, but particularly in those parts of the countryside that were attractive to cattle raisers the balance of power was largely against the communities. After 1821 the Indian farmers had fewer and fewer real chances of recourse.

Chapter 3

Labor

Laziness dominates them, and they know nothing of avarice.
AGCA, A3.21.3 5678 325

From the days of the Conquest, landowners and state representatives in Guatemala complained both of a shortage of available
workers and of the poor quality of those to be found.[1] Guatemala
did not lack population, at least not after this began to rebound in
the eighteenth century,[2] but the Indians and castas in the countryside
resisted working for the landowners and the state for the wages and
under the conditions that the elites sought to impose upon them. As
long as the rural population had access to land or to other resources
adequate to assure its survival, most inhabitants of the communities
and valles shunned steady wage labor on the haciendas and in the
mills. If hard pressed, they would work to meet immediate cash obligations, but when they had enough money they would leave. The
shifting of the capital after 1773 and the expansion of haciendas to
supply Nueva Guatemala, the indigo boom in El Salvador–Sonsonate
and the secondary markets this created, and an expanding traffic with
the north coast put the indigenous communities in the center of the
colony and the Oriente under increasing pressure in the second half
of the eighteenth century. Demands for labor subsided after the turn
of the century, but the availability of the means to coerce labor, and
the assumption of the need for coercion, persisted. As the commercial
economy ebbed and revived and planters turned to new crops and
new areas in the century following 1760, Guatemala witnessed a complex and fluid struggle between the indigenous and the other rural
populations, on the one hand, and economic and political elites, on
the other, over the control of labor power. Who would decide how and
where and to what purpose this work would be set in motion, and who
would appropriate what portion of labor's product?

The Indian as Laborer

Most Spaniards, creoles, and ladinos assumed the Indian to be lazy, stupid, dirty, and too much attached to his own, largely incomprehensible, customs. Such generalizations usually preceded efforts to make the indigenous population do something it was resisting, whether to attend church, wear shoes, or provide cheap labor for the elites or the state. The predominant, if not always openly asserted, opinion was that the Indian resisted "Spanish" values because he was not quite human, or, at least was so backward that he could not understand his own best interest. An English traveler summed up the ladino opinion of the Indian as "a sort of animated vegetation that requires nothing for its support but what the terraqueous globe, in its spontaneous liberality affords; some maize, some chile-pepper and the pure spring water are all the meat and drink he wishes for."[3] Most annoying was his apparent lack of drive to accumulate material goods: "His necessities are satisfied by a small amount of simple food and a bit of clothing, and he aspires to nothing else because he has no other needs."[4] For most ladinos, such an astonishing lack of acquisitive interests could only be an innate character defect and evident proof of inherent inferiority; other writers blamed it on centuries of crushing exploitation: "Who would not give themselves over to 'laziness' when it is their only escape or consolation and their only revenge against useless forced labor?"[5] If a few were willing to admit that the Indian worked hard when offered an effective incentive, and others saw the resistance as something that might be eroded by education, the majority could only think in terms of force, at least for the moment: "For now they need blows."[6]

Employers argued that it would be useless to try to attract additional labor by raising wages.[7] Indians were not so ignorant or bound by custom that they did not understand or pursue the possibility of better wages,[8] but because most labored for cash only to pay such fixed or limited costs as tribute, church fees, and cofradía expenses, higher wages meant less work. Preindustrial populations with fixed or traditional cash requirements and an intact subsistence economy generally will work for wages only to the point where they have satisfied their money needs, and they will then abandon the labor market, regardless of the wages and conditions offered.[9] This behavior was reinforced in a population caught in the toils of a system of domination that constantly invented and refined mechanisms to extract from them any surplus above the minimum necessary for their immediate survival. The Bourbon reforms that shifted tribute payments to money and, in some cases, raised these, together with the parallel attempts to convert church dues to money, increased the need for cash in the communities and obliged more and more Indians to seek wage labor, and for longer periods. These shifts accentuated the contradiction never resolved in the colonial period between, on the one hand, the employers who generally sought to depress wages and to cheat the Indians of these where possible, and, on the other, a state and a church and a merchant class that saw in better wages the opportunity for increased tax and fee levies and better markets.

To the description of the Indian as "lazy, stupid, dirty," and given to his own habits, most Guatemalan elites would have added "drunken." Certainly drinking to excess was the vice most commonly reported to Archbishop Pedro Cortés y Larraz by his priests and observed by him in his visits, although it was one that was hardly limited to the indigenous population.[10] The Archbishop felt that it contributed also to a host of other sins and abuses—fornication, wife beating, and murder, and the Indians' and poor castas' traditional reluctance or inability to work on *San Lunes*, the Monday after a Sunday of heavy drinking. Besides the damage it did to the Indians, alcohol diverted resources from the coffers of the state and the church. From the Indians' point of view, ritual drunkenness was pleasing to the saints and a satisfying social affair, and it also made good sense to consume any community surplus in activities such as cofradías and local celebrations rather than allow Crown officials or local ladinos to implement yet another scheme to appropriate it for themselves. After centuries of royal orders that sought fruitlessly to ban the manufacture and sale of aguardiente in the colony, the Crown in 1753 made the traffic a state monopoly,[11] both to gain some measure of control over the use and misuse of alcohol and to tap its revenue possibilities. In 1781 the government prohibited the sale of distilled alcohol in Indian villages. On several occasions the Audiencia attempted also to regulate the sale of the less potent but more prevalent *chicha* (fermented fruit juice).[12] None of this had much effect. Indeed, the imposition of monopoly may have increased the problem, for not only did the poor now drink more clandestine alcohol of questionable quality, but the ladinos who purchased from the state the right to operate taverns in the villages sought by all means to increase their sales. In Mixco, near Guatemala City, for example, local leaders complained that outsiders had set up stills in the town and were inducing the inhabitants to waste their money and to pawn their clothing and tools for drink.[13] The governor of Chimaltenango reported that in San Sebastián El Texar the "workers . . . fail to turn up for their jobs, arrive home without their pay, and mistreat their families. The drink shop is a central reason for the decline of religion and political life."[14] The cofradías complained that the monopoly cut into the profits they made brewing and selling illegal alcohol at fiestas.[15] Town officials and district governors tended to oppose taverns in their jurisdictions, and local populations rioted against these establishments, for the contradictory reasons that they were an evil influence on the community and that they competed with local contraband alcohol.[16]

The independent governments after 1821 continued to bemoan the deleterious effects of alcohol on the population: "The tavern operators imagine that a license to sell alcohol gives them the right to turn everyone into drunks. Unhappy towns where there is not a food store, a primary school or any other of the institutions necessary for society nevertheless have a tavern."[17] But the government kept the monopoly system because as an impoverished state caught up in civil wars it could ill afford to give up any regular source of income.[18] As the Liberal regime struggled to remain afloat financially in the late 1820's and the 1830's, drink shops multiplied.[19] A few men built fortunes on the trade.[20] Confronted with a growing rural unrest provoked in part by the liquor monopoly, the government in 1837 agreed to limit aguardiente sales to towns where it generated at least 1,000 pesos a year in tax revenues and to remove the posts entirely from any community willing to pay this amount as a direct tax.[21] The Carrera government kept the monopoly system after 1839, although it revived, but failed to enforce, a colonial ban on the sale of rum in Indian communities.[22] Ending the monopoly would not end drinking or drunkenness, the regime argued, so these "terrible but necessary establishments" would remain.[23] Travelers reported taverns thronged with drunken Indians and ladinos alike, and employers complained of the problems these institutions provoked.[24] A century after the visit of Archbishop Cortés y Larraz, the priest of the Indian town of San Francisco el Alto complained to his archbishop saying the presence of the drink shop in the village made religious activities almost impossible. The tavern was open day and night, on Sundays and religious holidays, and was a source of constant noise and disorder near the church. Its proprietor ignored the rules about hours and illegally accepted clothing and tools for drink. In common with all the towns in the region, the priest said, "no one goes to church, but everyone goes to the tavern."[25]

Slave Labor and Free Labor

Neither slavery nor free labor was as important as repartimientos to the commercial economy of late colonial Guatemala. Although Indian slavery in Guatemala ended with the New Laws, black slavery persisted until shortly after independence.[26] Black slavery failed to develop as an important source of labor, however, because of the availability of Indian workers and the cost of bringing in blacks, as well as elite fears of servile revolt.[27] After 1760 few slaves reached Guatemala, and even Bourbon Reforms that freed up the traffic sparked little interest. The number of slaves held on agricultural properties appears to have declined in these years,[28] replaced by repartimiento drafts and indebted casta and Indian workers. There were slaves in urban service and artisan occupations, and others were employed as foremen and skilled workers on rural haciendas,[29] but the largest number labored at fieldwork prohibited to the Indians, chiefly sugar production and, in some instances, indigo. The Dominicans, for example, used many black slaves on their plantations, more than 700 on the San Jeronimo property alone.[30] And the most common slave bought in the colony in these years was a young adult born on San Jeronimo. Males and females appear in the records in about the same number, apparently confirming the predominance of a creole population. Prices stayed fairly stable from 1750 to the early 1800's, but declined after 1810: a prime (15–25-year-old) male sold at the turn of the century for about 150 pesos; a woman fetched closer to 200, perhaps because of a demand for female domestic servants.[31]

The material working and living conditions of the slaves appear not to have differed markedly from those of Indian wage or repartimiento laborers.[32] On the plantation Arrivillaga, for example, the owner reported in 1793 that both black and Indian workers ate meat, cheese, or beans and tortillas three times a day and dressed in locally made clothing. The black slaves worked from eight to eleven in the morning and then again from four to six in the evening, or from six in the morning to five or six in the evening, "depending on the season." The Indian or casta wage laborers generally worked by the task, typically starting earlier and finishing in the early afternoon. On San Jeronimo the slaves cultivated sugar cane in the mornings and their own food plots in the afternoon. Descriptions of slave conditions furnished by owners must, of course, be approached with much caution, but black slaves in late colonial Guatemala worked together with Indian and casta wage laborers and with repartimiento drafts on plantations and haciendas at the same types of tasks, apart from sugar and indigo processing, and apparently under more or less the same conditions. Because there was more cost and risk in employing black slaves than with free castas or repartimientos, there was little incentive for the system to expand beyond those areas closed by law to indigenous workers. When independence brought an end to the idea of "prohibited work" for Indians, little impeded putting an end to slavery. The Liberals abolished it in 1824. In the following years the Caribbean coast of Guatemala became a refuge for runaway slaves from Belize, whom the government consistently refused to return.

Free labor in the strict sense of a proletariat divorced from ownership in the means of production and dependent on the sale of its labor power hardly existed in turn-of-the-century Guatemala. By the last years of the colony there was a growing urban, and largely casta, lower plebe, slightingly referred to by those above them as *leperos* (lepers) or *cacos* (bums). Apart from domestic service to a small number of elite families, only a few artisan handicraft industries and retail shops offered regular urban employment, and even these limited opportunities suffered serious blows from increased contraband in the eighteenth century, the opening of commerce by the Bourbons, and free trade after 1821.[33] The result was widespread unemployment and misery among the urban poor, a problem the state treated as one for the police. Governments before and after independence repeatedly passed laws outlawing "vagrancy," "because laziness and idleness are the root of all manner of vice and opposed to the true doctrines of religion, the common well-being and the state and government of the republic."[34] The principal object of such statutes was social control in the towns, but a secondary prospect was the mobilization of workers for industry and agriculture. As the new Liberal regime explained in 1829, "Agriculture, font of all wealth in the country, finds itself in total abandon, not because there are not workers but because of the indolence and vices of these workers [therefore]: (1) All individuals without a known source of income or who are not practicing their mechanical trades are required to find work on haciendas and labores."[35] The new state was scarcely in a position to enforce such a law, and in 1837, desperately backpedaling from earlier reforms, the Liberals specifically abandoned vagrancy laws as a means to recruit agricultural labor.[36] The Conservatives revived them a decade later as the new export of cochineal peaked. To regulate "the employment of agricultural workers" and to end fraud by those who took wage advances and failed to work them off, the government enacted a requirement of "good conduct" certificates for all rural workers.[37] There is no evidence that the measure went into effect. Whether or not the towns and the countryside were as awash in vagrants as these laws, and some horrified observers, suggested, vagrancy statutes had little impact on the supply of workers for agriculture during the century after 1750.

Meanwhile, as had long been their custom, many among the rural population did seek wage labor on haciendas and plantations for part of each year. The governor of Suchitepéquez, for example, reported in 1792 that Indians came from the highlands in groups "to earn their tribute" on the haciendas on the coast.[38] After 1773 Indians and castas filtered into the Sierra de Canales to work on the grain haciendas developing there. By the last years of the colony the population of many towns in the lower Verapaz could not survive without wage labor. Seasonal migrants worked on haciendas near Tocoy and around the Acasaguastlanes, and others journeyed forty leagues to Antigua and Amatitlán in search of employment. Most of this work proceeded on the basis of verbal contracts, with the landowner or hacienda administrator making an advance of money or goods (*habilitación*) to the laborer who promised to work this off at an agreed-upon rate by day or by task.[39] At mid-century the governor of Sacatepéquez sought to codify custom:

All men as well as women must be made to comply with the work agreements for which they have received wage advances from employers in this department and others. If they receive money from two individuals, the first has preference, and they are not to receive a second advance until they have worked off the first; the secretary of the municipality will keep a record of who has received advances, the amount of money involved, and the number of days worked agreed upon."[40]

Such workers came, the landowners explained, "of their own free will and without obligation . . . to seek advances from the employers."[41] This was just as well, since the hacendados' control over free labor was very limited, regulations notwithstanding. A common complaint was that "every employer has to pay out huge amounts of money in advances to his workers, and then they lose this when the workers disappear."[42]

Most wage laborers returned to their villages or valles after working off all or part of what they owed, but a few stayed to become resident colonos or renters on the haciendas.[43] A person who did not have access to enough land in the home community, for example, or one with personal or money problems, might ask to be taken on as a colono. The custom was for the hacienda to pay the tribute and church fees of its colonos and renters, and also to give them advances against future wages and sometimes credit for purchases of food and clothing. It was in the landowners' self-interest to shield their colonos from the demands of their former villages or the state or past employers. As a result, haciendas were a not unattractive refuge for those pressed by civil or religious authority.[44] Archbishop Cortés y Larraz again and again deplored the growth of a large, uncontrolled, and "ladinoizing" Indian and casta population resident on the large rural properties. All too often colonos got mixed up in drunken brawls, robbery and assault, and the kidnapping of women from nearby towns, and then escaped back to the safety of the hacienda.[45] An investigation by the Audiencia in 1802 found many south coast properties to be inhabited by casta and Indian criminals and fugitives—on one hacienda alone from "Tecpán Guatemala, Cobán, Comitán, Cotzal, Cubulco, Santa Lucía Cotzumalguapa, Salcajá, Santa Ana, Quezaltenango, Nebaj, Santa Ana Mixtan, San Cristóbal Verapaz, San Jeronimo Verapaz," and various Soconusco towns.[46]

Most villages needed these emigrant populations to help meet the state's tax and labor demands and did not easily give up their claims to them.[47] The owner of the huge livestock hacienda Moscoso-Chancol successfully challenged the efforts of Indian towns in the area to apply to his property a 1779 Audiencia order calling for all "dispersed Indians" to return to their communities. He argued that his shepherds had lived on the hacienda for generations and without them the property would lose its value "in three days."[48] But in another case, on the south coast, Luís Valladares was unable in 1802 to prevent Indian officials of Mazatenango from forcing some of his colonos back to the town.[49] Poor rural castas who had little to secure them to impoverished plots or isolated valles or Indians at odds with their community might find colono status, with its access to wage advances and credit and some protection from the more arbitrary demands of other landowners and the state, a relatively attractive option.

Repartimientos

Most of the Indians in eighteenth- and early nineteenth-century Guatemala who engaged in wage labor outside their community did so as a result of repartimientos or, as they came increasingly to be called after 1800, mandamientos. Forms of coerced labor that might be labeled proto-repartimientos existed in sixteenth-century Guatemala, but a royal cedula of 1601 formally erected the system of labor repartimientos in the Captaincy General, and a 1609 decree regulated its operation.[50] In the 1660's abuses prompted a major investigation and minor reforms, and it is on the material gathered for that occasion, together with what Thomas Gage had to say about the drafts, that most writers base descriptions of forced wage labor in the colony. But by 1760 a century of history and custom had introduced major changes. Above all, the Crown had lost control of repartimientos. This became apparent in 1759 when local officials and employers ignored a royal order halting the drafts.[51] An inquiry the following year into the advisability of raising repartimiento wages to compensate for recent increases in food prices likewise came to nought.[52] It could hardly have been a surprise, then, that when a new president of the Audiencia, Fernando Alonzo Heredia, took over in August 1761, one of his first actions was to move to regain state authority over repartimientos. The drafts, he reminded what must have been a startled group of local landowners, existed above all "for the well-being of the Indians, to avoid the laziness to which they [had] a propensity."[53] He intended to overhaul the system for the "conservation and relief" of the King's Indians. Because repartimientos had become so disorganized, no one had a clear idea of how much labor was being asked of the indigenous population, altogether or in any of the separate communities. President Heredia suspended repartimientos and required that all existing orders be returned to him to be reviewed, and reissued, modified, or canceled as necessary.

After 1761 only the Audiencia issued repartimientos.[54] Anyone wishing to make use of drafted workers had to apply in writing to the court, detailing the number of Indians he needed, what work they would do and where, and from which towns they should come. The formula also included a promise to treat the Indians well and to "pay them personally and in silver" for the labor and for travel time to and from the property. The usual wage was one to one and a half reales a day. Depending on local custom, the employer might also pay a one-time tax of a quarter to a half real per head to the state or village.[55] Usually he paid all wages for the workers in advance to the officials of the community, who were responsible for mobilizing the necessary men and making certain that they arrived at the property on time.

By law, a person, not a piece of property, received the right to a repartimiento draft, so that if the hacienda changed hands and the new owner wanted to make use of forced wage labor, he had to re-apply.[56] It is therefore sometimes possible to trace part of the repartimiento history of a specific property. For example, in 1776 Juan Antonio Gutierrez leased the hacienda Sucún from the cofradías of Sololá, and he asked the Audiencia for twenty Indians from Tecpán Guatemala, ten from Santa Apolonia, and "others" from San Andrés Semetabaj. The Crown responded that because these towns fell within the thirty-league radius from which the Audiencia was drawing labor to build the new capital and because the Indians themselves had not yet completed their plantings, he could make use of repartimiento workers from these villages only for the current harvest. In 1778 he re-applied. After checking population figures the Audiencia allowed him to draw ten laborers from Tecpán Guatemala, ten from Santa Apolonia, and ten from San Andrés Semetabaj on a continuing basis. By the 1790's José Cirilio Solórzano owned or rented Sucún. He obtained from the Audiencia an order for a much larger number of workers, including one quarter of the available populations of Santo Tomás Chichicastenango, Concepción, San Andrés Semetabaj, Panajachel, and San Antonio and Santa Catarina Palopó. The Indians of the two Palopós protested, saying that in the past they had been made to work on the hacienda and had suffered illness and abuse from the owner's foreman. After an investigation the Audiencia suspended the repartimiento from at least one of the towns. Doña María Gertrudis Croquer y Muñoz, wife of the ex-governor of Sololá, bought Sucún sometime before 1802. In that year she applied for a repartimiento draft to harvest wheat and carry it to the capital. The Audiencia granted her the one-quarter part of Chichicastenango, San Andrés Semetabaj, Concepción, and Santa Catarina and San Antonio Palopó, but the Indians of these last towns continued to resist going.[57]

Whatever the law, custom in fact tended to attach the labor of certain communities to specific properties. The "right" to this labor then passed from owner to owner without the knowledge, or at least the intervention, of the state.[58] Also, whereas in other areas of Spanish America employers received repartimientos on a weekly or monthly

TABLE 3.1
Number of Repartimiento Drafts, 1760–1809
(by five-year periods)

Years	Number of drafts	Years	Number of drafts
1760–64	11	1785–89	20
1765–69	26	1790–94	27
1770–74	40	1795–99	35
1775–79	55	1800–1804	37
1780–84	25	1805–9	3

SOURCE: AGCA, A3 223-27.

basis, in late colonial Guatemala an assignment was permanent, unless specifically qualified. Indians worked weekly, seasonally, or "as needed," depending on the requirements of the employer and the specific wording of the order. Thus, any falling off in the number of repartimiento orders issued would not necessarily indicate the declining importance of forced drafts or a shifting toward free labor.[59] More probably it would mean that all employers who wished to use forced wage labor had the necessary orders or that the populations of available towns were fully allocated. As Table 3.1 indicates, there was in any event no noticeable slackening in the number of repartimiento orders issued in Guatemala until the early 1800's, in the aftermath of the fight against the locusts and as the economy slowed.

When the Audiencia received a repartimiento request the first step was for the official of the court known as the Fiscal Protector de los Indios (Protector of the Indians) to check the population of the town or towns involved and to determine whether or not there existed any labor orders against them. The state rarely took censuses as such but relied instead for population information on counts drawn up for tribute collection (*padrones*). In Bourbon Guatemala, tribute generally fell on all males aged eighteen to fifty not otherwise exempted, roughly the group also liable for repartimientos.[60] By law and custom, not more than a quarter of a town's tribute population could be taken at one time for labor drafts, and this less a variety of exempted persons. Tribute counts were seldom accurate to begin with, however, and quickly fell out of date, and the state was slow to revise them.[61] During the 1760's and 1770's the Fiscal Protector seems to have made a good faith effort to check populations and existing repartimiento loads, but by the 1790's the Audiencia for the most part was granting drafts with the proviso, "if it fits in the one-quarter part"; or it would order a town to supply "what remained of the one-quarter part," without making it clear who would determine this or how.[62] Furthermore, the Audiencia increasingly delegated to the governors of the highland districts the power to supply landowners labor "as needed," usually on a seasonal basis—another symptom of the breakdown of the recentralization effected in the 1760's.[63] Communities resisted repartimientos usually by arguing that they could not furnish the workers ordered owing to village needs, to confused or overlapping orders, or to recent population losses. Any labor the Indians eventually supplied, and to whom, was a matter of constant negotiation and renegotiation among the community, the state, and the would-be employers. It must rarely have corresponded closely to what was on paper.

Towns were particularly resistant to demands for drafts of women, sometimes requested as cooks to prepare food for free laborers or repartimiento gangs. Although the Audiencia was solicitous of their moral well-being and made certain that they had proper chaperons, it was not always so careful with the physical safety of these women.[64] In 1799 the Indian officials of Zacapa protested that women sent to cook for the garrisons on the coast and along the Rio Motagua "rarely returned." Most of them died of disease before completing the required three months of service, and because they could not take their children, these died of neglect. San Pablo repeated Zacapa's lament, claiming that of seven women ordered to the coast recently five had died. The Fiscal Protector supported these complaints, pointing out that in other instances the state had sent mulattas "in need of correction" as cooks.[65] But the drafting of Indian women continued.

According to the law, rural castas and Indians living dispersed in the countryside also could be called for service in repartimientos, but efforts to do this rarely succeeded. As a frustrated hacendado explained, "Because for ladinos the lowest thing imaginable is to be forced to go to work on repartimiento drafts, they absolutely will not obey orders to do this."[66] In 1805, for example, the owner of hacienda San Nicolás near Escuintla received an order granting him an unspecified number of Indians from among the 200 living "in the wilderness of Tepestenango," but no help in rounding them up.[67] Scattered settlement patterns and the resistance of hacienda owners to allowing anyone from the outside access to their workers, together with the absence of obvious community leadership structures in the valles, made it difficult to cite or mobilize scattered populations of ladinos or Indians for forced wage labor. The burden fell most heavily on the indigenous communities.

Would-be employers routinely applied for larger or more repartimiento drafts than they needed, hoping in this way both to obtain an adequate number of workers in the face of Indian resistance and to gain the upper hand on competitors by monopolizing the available labor in their area. Josef Gonzalez Cocio, for example, in 1784 asked for workers for his wheat and corn labor near Cuilco. He requested forty from Colotenango, forty from Ixtahuacán, sixteen from San Gaspar Ixchil, eight from Cuilco, twenty-five from Tectitán, eight from Santiago Amatenango, and twenty from San Martín Mazapas. When the Fiscal Protector questioned the need for so many Indians, Cocio responded that he had requested such a large number because half of those ordered would not appear. The governor confirmed that because the Indians were reluctant to abandon their own plantings there was a shortage of labor in the area and stiff competition among the haciendas, but the Fiscal Protector dismissed Cocio's "vague and exploitative pretensions" and instead ordered the governor to provide the landowner only with the number of repartimiento workers he could actually use; the Indians, he emphasized, must not be allowed to become accustomed to disobedience.[68] Perhaps the most notorious effort to monopolize labor was the petition from Juan Carrascosa in 1773 requesting up to 600 Indians a month for his hacienda Argueta, located north of Lake Atitlán. The Audiencia rejected the application as wildly unrealistic but did recommend the not insubstantial number of 155 workers.[69]

Repartimientos and Agriculture

The Audiencia in the years after 1761 granted repartimientos for a variety of agricultural purposes including mixed food production for the capital and the indigo districts.[70] Joseph Fernandez de Córdoba, for example, owner of the hacienda Soyate on the south coast, applied in 1768 for fifty Indians a week "for planting and cleaning": fifteen from Conguaco, ten from Tecuaco, six from Moyuta, four from Azulco, and fifteen from Jutiapa.[71] When the available population of Jutiapa proved to be fully committed to other drafts, de Córdoba in 1772 asked for and received ten Indians from Comapa.[72] Producers of commercial and export crops such as tobacco, cacao, indigo, and sugar

also received repartimientos, but there were more restrictions.[73] Because of fears that it would damage their health, for example, indigo
was prohibited work even for free Indians during most of the colonial
period. It was only as the result of an informal compromise worked out
in the 1760's in response to the industry's suddenly increased importance that planters in Guatemala were allowed to use repartimiento
drafts in the fields; they still could not employ Indians in processing the dye.[74] Applicants for indigo repartimientos regularly protested
that they did not use Indians for prohibited work, and although the
laborers complained of a variety of abuses, in Guatemala these did
not usually include ones associated with the illegal aspects of dye production. Instead, they focused on the more common complaints of
physical mistreatment of themselves and their animals by employers
and foremen, on the excessive amount of work demanded of them,
and on attempts to cheat them out of their wages.[75]

A persistent, if ultimately unsuccessful, effort to mobilize repartimiento labor for indigo was mounted by the infamous Garrote Bueno
brothers. In 1794 Manuel Garrote Bueno protested to the Audiencia
that his efforts to develop commercial production of grains, food, and
especially, indigo on the south coast were stymied by the "laziness"
of the local Indians, who refused to work for him. The Audiencia
granted him a repartimiento order, but the Indians cited demanded
two reales a day, far above what the brothers were willing to pay. Asked
to comment on the situation, the governor of Suchitepéquez reported
that in the twenty-two years during which he had been familiar with
the province, repartimientos never had been local custom. Instead,
he said, the Indians tended their own plantings or found employment as free labor on the haciendas at wages of one and a half to two
reales a day, depending on the type and amount of work. Because of
population declines and the decayed condition of most of the villages,
there were only a few local Indians in the coastal lowlands, and they
were very busy with service to their priests and cofradías and with
their plantings. Most of the population was made up of immigrants
from the highlands, from Totonicapán, Verapaz, Chimaltenango and
"towns near the ruined Guatemala," who as "outsiders" could not be
drafted to fill repartimiento orders issued against local communities.
In the particular case of Manuel Garrote Bueno, the governor added,
the Indians were angry because Manuel's brother Ponciano, the local
priest, forced men and women who were supposed to be doing church
duty to work on the hacienda. The Fiscal Protector nevertheless ruled

that the Audiencia might grant repartimientos in the area.[76] When the governor attempted to enforce an order for fifteen Indians from San Gabriel, "the alcaldes indios, justicias, principales, cofradías and others of the town presented themselves to him," saying they would not work for the brothers. They had their own plantings that needed attention, they said, and they threatened that if pressed "the entire town would flee to the woods."[77]

Although the San Gabriel Indians, under threats of jail and with a promise to raise the wages slightly, finally agreed to honor the repartimiento, they did not do so. By 1802 not only had efforts to introduce the system into Suchitepéquez failed, but the planters themselves now opposed the drafts. When the government sought forced labor to replace the food plantings that had been destroyed in the locust epidemic, local landowners protested that all the workers in the area were indebted to them and that if the state persisted in its efforts to draft the Indians "many of them will run away and their employers would lose the money they have advanced."[78]

Sugar cane was a common crop in rural Guatemala, but there were few large plantations in the style of the West Indies or Morelos. The usual custom was for Indians, castas, and hacendados who had access to hot-country land to grow cane in combination with other crops and then convert it into raw sugar or, usually illegal, alcohol. Because of Crown restrictions on the use of Indians in sugar production, the few large, specialized, and highly capitalized sugar operations in the colony such as the Dominicans' sugar mills of La Compañía and San Jeronimo had to depend on black slaves and casta free labor. After 1761 the large owners did not ask for or receive repartimiento drafts,[79] but mixed producers did.[80] When Josef García de Salas, owner of the hacienda of San Josef at Tocoy, in 1779 applied to the Audiencia for eight Indians each from Santa María Magdalena and San Agustín Acasaguastlán, he said that he planned to use them to raise sugar cane, cattle, and horses. The Audiencia granted the order, but the Fiscal reminded Salas that the Indians could not be put to work in any "sugar mill."[81] Employers sometimes promised that "those who do the grinding are ladinos," but more usually requests and orders for repartimiento drafts remained specifically, and suspiciously, innocent of mention of the problem.[82] A special case was those growers who produced sugar cane for the royal aguardiente monopoly. Most claimed and received preference in access to repartimiento Indians, but they also suffered the special attention of the Fiscal Protector, who repeatedly admonished them against the use of Indians in illegal activities.[83]

As with indigo, when the Indians complained of abuses on properties known to grow sugar cane they pointed not to prohibited work but instead to the amount of work, low wages, physical beatings, and dangerous travel or working conditions.[84] In 1773, for example, San Juan Amatitlán protested that forced labor on the plantation Anís "had been the ruin of the towns of San Juan and Palín,"[85] but there was no mention of any prohibited activities, which there certainly would have been had these occurred. It seems clear that rural landowners did not generally use Indians for the illegal work of grinding or processing of sugar cane, but rather employed them legitimately in food production, woodcutting, and the cleaning, cutting, and transporting of cane.

Apart from specifically agricultural work, the Audiencia provided repartimiento drafts for clearing land and opening roads, for artisan industry, for cutting firewood and construction timber, for carrying products to market and to and from the ports on the coasts, for mining, and for the construction of the new capital.[86] Indians particularly disliked woodcutting repartimientos, which they said entailed risking dangerous conditions in "rugged mountains . . . where it is well known that many lions and tigers lurk."[87] The carrying traffic was of various sorts. Repartimientos forced Indians and their animals to transport wheat from Chimaltenango, Totonicapán, Quezaltenango, and Sololá to the capital.[88] The Indians complained not only about the roughness of the track and the excessively heavy loads they were made to carry, but also about the time they wasted waiting for loads.[89] Forced labor and carrying drafts also subsidized their competitors, for many of the highland Indian towns were themselves major market producers of wheat. In the Oriente, inhabitants of towns such as Jalapa and San Luís Jilotepeque for centuries had been drafted to transport goods on their backs to and from north coast ports.[90] The leaders of San Luís complained in 1783 that twenty-four people had died in that town alone during the past two years as a result of such work, and many more were ill. The Fiscal Protector noted that although the law forbade the use of human carriers except where the lack of roads gave no alternative, it appeared to have been completely forgotten in Chiquimula: "The precise accounting of those who have died . . . in this service would form a truly melancholy relation."[91] Using animals did not necessarily resolve the Indians' problems. The inhabitants of nearby San

Cristóbal Jutiapa explained that in order to meet transportation drafts upon their community and because they had no horses or mules, they had to rent them at great cost from nearby haciendas.[92]

The City and the Mines

Repartimientos issued to build the new capital after the 1773 earthquake and drafts of Indians sent to mines are of interest here for the effects these had on the rural population and on agriculture. Royal orders for the construction of Nueva Guatemala de la Asunción proposed drawing labor from a radius of thirty leagues around the valley, an area that included most of central Guatemala but not the Petén, the upper Verapaz, much of Totonicapán-Huehuetenango and Quezaltenango, and some parts of the Oriente. Crown officials carried out an extensive survey and count of the population and investigated existing labor demand, customs, and availability within the prescribed area.[93] Construction drafts were to fit within that one-quarter part of the villages' tributary population available for repartimientos, and even some communities within the radius, such as those on the Pacific coast, were not called to work on the city because this would have violated the rules against sending repartimiento drafts to unfamiliar or dangerous climates. The intent was to avoid as far as possible damaging the agriculture of either the communities or the haciendas, but in fact many villages soon found themselves overburdened, struggling to satisfy both existing orders and new demands. The situation worsened as a result of the impact of famine and epidemic disease in the 1770's and 1780's.[94]

The shift of the capital and the construction this entailed prompted a general reshuffling of labor relations in the region. Particularly affected was the nearby Sierra de Canales, where landowners began to complain of labor shortages and high wages.[95] Despite the efforts of the Audiencia to separate wage scales for construction from those for agricultural labor and to ensure the availability of workers to the haciendas, competition quickly drove up the general wage rate in the central part of the colony from one to one and a half reales a day before the earthquake to two to two and a half reales. Landowners responded to this and to shortages by applying more frequently to the government for labor drafts, usually warning that there would be food problems in the capital if the Audiencia failed to give them what they wanted. This becomes clear in looking at a series of repartimiento applications in the quarter-century after 1775. In 1776 Manuel Ramos, the owner of a labor in the Sierra de Canales that produced corn, wheat, and beans for the capital, asked for a repartimiento draft; the Fiscal Protector rejected the application, remarking that all the large agriculturalists in the Sierra used free labor. In 1781 Presbiterio Miguel de Arrasola asked for 100 Indians from Santa María de Jesús and 100 from San Juan Sacatepéquez for his plantings in the Canales; again, the Audiencia noted the predominance of free labor in the area and pointed out that even Arrasola himself had depended upon it until now. The judges added, however, that the governor might grant him, and other employers in the area, temporary help with cleaning and the harvest to compensate for a lack of available voluntary workers. But the balance clearly had shifted by 1784 when Santiago Moreno applied for repartimiento labor for his hacienda San Nicolás near Petapa. Efforts to use free workers and to mobilize labor by advancing money to Indians and castas, he said, had failed. The Fiscal Protector, in denying the request, reported that because of population declines resulting from recent smallpox epidemics and because growing labor pressures had prompted many Indians to leave their communities, and also because of increased labor demands in the area, the towns that were available to Moreno already suffered repartimiento burdens totaling more than one-quarter of their population. And when in 1791 Benito Ruiz sought a repartimiento order for his corn plantings in the Sierra de Canales, investigation showed that all the Indians of the surrounding towns were assigned in repartimiento to the eighteen nearby properties.[96] Under the impacts of market conditions and the labor demands of the city, free labor in the Sierra Canales gave way to a generalization of coerced wage labor. Employers sought repartimientos to avoid competition and to offset increased free wage costs, and Indians responded by fleeing the towns for the wilderness, becoming colonos on the haciendas, or migrating to the city or the south coast. The priest of San Lucas Sacatepéquez described what had happened: "All the workers of Canales have gathered [on the haciendas] . . . and they do not recognize the authority of the towns but only that of the landowners . . . and often not even that."[97]

Even villages farther afield felt the effects of the construction of the capital in terms of the sickness and death that resulted from forced migration to La Hermita valley and in the damages done to the local economy and society by the long absences of the workers from the communities. Although the Indians earned comparatively high wages in the new capital, all this money went to support them under the expensive conditions existing there, and they returned to the villages with little except disease. The bringing together of temporary gangs of workers from various parts of the country propagated and diffused disease, and travel aggravated its effects, particularly for those compelled to move to unfamiliar environments. The curate of Cobán, for example, reported that his Indians came back from Nueva Guatemala with a "great epidemic," leaving many sick and dying on the roads. Of one hundred sent from San Pedro Carchá and San Juan Chamelco, thirty-five "arrived home dying." In their absence wild animals and weeds destroyed their subsistence plots. It was dangerous, too, the priest worried, to leave young wives alone.[98] The justicias of Rabinal and Cubulco confirmed these problems and added that as a consequence of the situation the inhabitants of the towns were fleeing, leaving the communities unable to pay their tribute.[99]

Because there were few successful mining operations in Guatemala, and none that lasted more than a few years, demands for mine labor were sporadic and concentrated on a small number of towns around the grandly named but disappointing Real Minas de Alotepeque, located in the Oriente near the present border with Honduras. Repeatedly in the years after 1750 entrepreneurs sought to revive the silver mines at Alotepeque by using repartimiento workers, chiefly from San Luís Jilotepeque and Quezaltepeque. As with indigo and sugar, laws regulated what sort of labor Indians might do in mining, and they specifically forbade below-ground work. But mine owners seem to have been less scrupulous, or perhaps simply more desperate, than the landowners and more ready to attempt to evade the law, at least to judge from the Audiencia's repeated admonitions against prohibited work. Although the Audiencia canceled the drafts of particularly egregious violators, abuses continued.[100] The town of San Luís complained in the early 1770's, for example, that despite already heavy demands for carrying to the coast and in disregard of a specific exemption from mining issued in 1740, it continued to receive repartimiento orders for work at Alotepeque. Recently some fourteen men had died "in the depths" of the mine.[101] In July 1793, the villagers of San Juan Yupiltepeque petitioned the Audiencia asking that they be relieved of the "heavy burden" of having to go to the mines. Drafts to Alotepeque required a trip of fifteen leagues and the crossing of several dangerous rivers and the pay was only eight reales for a week of very long days;

nearby haciendas offered better wages, conditions, and treatment.[102] Mine owners denied underpaying or mistreating the Indians, and the governors of the region enjoyed elaborating on the possible returns to the Crown of a successful mining operation at Alotepeque. A more immediately evident effect of mine repartimientos, however, was the flight of inhabitants of the affected communities into the hills or onto haciendas. The Indians must have been more cheered than was the governor to learn in 1801 that the mines "were abandoned."[103]

Abuse and Resistance

Whatever the nature of the work, it is clear that employers regularly cheated repartimiento laborers of their wages, lied about distances and refused to pay travel costs, failed to supply the men adequate food, tools, or shelter, gave them impossibly large or difficult tasks to complete, and verbally and physically mistreated them. These abuses were routine and are structural to any system of coerced labor. Two examples will suffice. The justicias of Mataquescuintla protested in June 1779 against yet another repartimiento order for cultivation of corn and beans on the land of Timoteo Oconor: "Because of these orders many have died and others have fled leaving their wives." Oconor reportedly made them work "sun to sun" for one and a half reales, while requiring them to provide their own tools and food. They had to travel more than fourteen leagues under dangerous conditions to reach the hacienda, and Oconor refused to pay their travel costs. A Spanish witness agreed that Oconor treated the Indians "very roughly," did not allow them to rest, and did not pay them as the law required. Many returned ill from the work. Those sent on the repartimientos could not plant their own fields, and, as a result, food was scarce and expensive in the community.[104] The Audiencia ordered Oconor to find free workers.

Across the country in Sololá, the Indians of San Antonio Palopó asked in 1799 not to be sent again to the wheat hacienda of Sucún. They elaborated a long list of complaints: the property was at a great distance from their community and located in a high and uninhabited area with a climate to which they were unaccustomed; many fell ill, and some had died as a result of the work; the owner paid only a *cuartillo* (quarter of a real) for travel and refused to provide them with food; he charged them rent for the tools he was supposed to provide and fined them if they lost or broke these; the ground was hard and covered with scrub, and the task assigned was bigger than custom dictated; the administrator mistreated them and their animals "by word and deed," made them work in the rain, and often arrived at the hacienda only two or three days after they had been ordered to appear, so that they had to eat their food and pay rent on tools but not work; and they were not paid for the time they had lost, and often they had to bribe the mayordomo to be assigned work.[105] It appears, however, that abuses of this sort, though damaging to the persons and towns involved, rarely exceeded what the Indians accepted as custom, and therefore provoked little beyond customary protest and resistance. Pressures for labor were very uneven over place and time, and the demand for workers remained generally limited, at least compared with two centuries before or a century later. For most villages outside the central part of Guatemala or south toward El Salvador–Sonsonate, repartimientos and the problems these entailed either had little importance or remained within the limits of what was expected and could be tolerated.

If the indigenous communities accepted the custom and legitimacy of forced wage labor, they nevertheless hated and sought to avoid the drafts. The town leaders of San Cristóbal Amatitlán (Palín) described the difficult and emotional process of mobilizing workers for repartimientos:

First it is necessary for the justicias and other principales themselves to go from house to house citing the individuals who are to work and to give them two or four reales of their advances, money that they receive with such repugnance that often all you can do is put the money in the house, for no one will take it. On the day indicated for the repartimiento the scene is sad. The officials with the policemen round up the men while their neighbors commiserate with them. The women, children, and all the neighbors hurl reproaches and curses on the operation, and finding no escape for their beloved husbands and sons, there are everywhere tears and hopeless cries. It seems more as if they were going to prison or to the gallows.[106]

More active resistance took several forms. Towns commonly met repartimiento orders with explanations that there were not enough tributaries available to meet the new demand, either because illness or flight had reduced the population since the last tribute count or because the town already had orders covering one-quarter or more of the available workers. This sometimes provoked the Audiencia to further investigation. If the community's claims proved accurate, the court might revoke the order and tell the applicant to find another town or towns. Village justicias also asked for and gained temporary exemptions from repartimiento to finish repairing a church or to complete some other important public works, or to harvest crops. They argued that a repartimiento at a particular moment would damage the planting process and, thus, threaten their food supply or that of the cities. Others disclaimed any wish to resist the system in general but said they feared the notorious abuses of a particular employer or the dangers of travel required for a given repartimiento.[107] The Audiencia listened to such protests and often accepted and acted on the Indians' arguments. The court served the Crown, and the Crown, although it wished to promote commercial agriculture, also had a strong interest in the economic integrity of the communities and their ability to pay their taxes. It could and did make exceptions without threatening the system as a whole.

To the individual, repartimiento meant abandoning family, community, and subsistence plantings, perhaps at the most inopportune moment, and being sent to work under unpleasant conditions for low wages. As the priest of San Agustín Acasaguastlán explained, landowners "forced the Indians to labor for them during the times these most needed to be attending to their own cultivations . . . making them abandon their professions, plantings, and homes to comply with the orders."[108] The drafts routinely exposed Indians to dangerous travel and work conditions, disease and unfamiliar climates, and physical and verbal abuse and humiliation. Repartimiento also took them out of their community and exposed them to the possibilities, dangers, and temptations of the "Spanish" world. As a result, the Indians were becoming "degenerate" and losing their customs, complained the priest of Santa Catarina Pinula.[109] San Pedro Sacatepéquez reported that "for years now the Indians have been abandoning San Pedro, taking their families to live on the haciendas, ranches, and sugar plantations where they have a life of total license without subjection to our priest or to justice."[110] Resistance to forced labor, together with patterns of slash-and-burn agriculture and the pull of clan lands and sites, was responsible for the dispersal of population that alarmed the Spanish in the late colonial period. It was a powerful force, too, in the growth of the mulatto and ladino population so often remarked upon in these years.

In many instances, forced drafts could threaten the survival of the towns as corporate entities. Repartimiento damaged subsistence agriculture by draining off labor that was needed locally, and in that way it undermined the economic viability of the community and made it difficult to feed the inhabitants or to meet tax demands.[111] Returning workers introduced disease into the village, touching off epidemics that further reduced the population and increased the labor and tax pressures on those who remained.[112] Local officials responsible for mobilizing and delivering repartimiento workers found themselves in a difficult situation. Some turned this to their advantage. It was not unknown for justicias or *gobernadores* (state-appointed local Indian governors) to collude with hacendados and state officials at the expense of their fellow villagers, whether for profit or for self-protection: "From no other reflex than the hope to protect themselves from punishment, they take unfortunate men away from their work useful to the community and send them away to the haciendas."[113] Other local officials attempted to defend the community as best they could.[114] Justicias protested and petitioned against abusive tax and labor requirements and returned again and again to the argument that these pressures had caused or would cause so many people to leave the village that the community would be unable to meet labor orders or pay tribute. In other instances they sought to have former residents of the community returned to town from the countryside or from the haciendas where they had taken refuge or where, the officials perhaps wishfully argued, they were held against their will.[115] Immoderate zeal in such efforts could provoke the Audiencia and the governors into having these authorities fined, whipped, and jailed.[116] But more generally the state sought a negotiated agreement. The survival of the colony rested on the labor and taxes of the Indians, and the mobilization of both rested on the efforts of the justicias. Local officials had to be made to deliver what the state and employers required without in the process being entirely ruined themselves or allowed to destroy the village or provoke revolt.[117] Because the state would collapse without the cooperation, however grudging, of indigenous community leaders, it had a strong stake in both supporting and successfully manipulating their authority.

Effects

Repartimiento drafts in the half-century after 1760 affected chiefly three areas of the colony: the south coast toward the boundary with

El Salvador–Sonsonate, the Oriente from Mataquescuintla to Chiquimula, and, particularly, the central region around the capital. During
the period 1760–1810 the Audiencia issued some 280 agriculture-
related orders to approximately sixty communities requiring a total of
slightly less than 4,000 laborers.[118] Some of these lapsed, allowing the
Indians to be reassigned, while an undetermined number of orders
granted before 1761 and never reviewed continued in effect. In the
absence of better information the two categories are taken here to
balance each other out. The tribute population in the 1770's of the
communities involved was approximately 30,000, one quarter of which
would be 7,500. Even if one assumes both undercounting in the tribute lists and population growth after 1780, by no means the case for
all the towns, by the early 1800's there were orders outstanding for
at least half of the population in theory available for repartimientos.
This does not take into account labor drafts issued for carrying or for
the construction of the capital or the effects of exemptions granted
many tributaries for service in town government, church, and cofradías.[119] To the extent that the population obeyed the orders, then, the
towns involved were hard pressed. Too, even within the affected area
labor demands were not evenly spread. Many smaller villages appear
to have received no repartimiento orders, and a few relatively large
towns—though this may be only an artifact of incomplete records—
also apparently escaped attention. The principal towns around the
capital, however, from Santa María de Jesús to San Lucas, San Juan,
San Pedro, and Santiago Sacatepéquez to Santa Catarina Pinula and in
adjacent areas to Mataquescuintla, generally received orders for more,
and sometimes much more, than one-quarter of their tribute population, and this on top of heavy demands for construction workers (see
Table 3.2).

Most communities beyond the central part of the colony, and even
some in areas as close in as Chimaltenango and Sololá but apart from
the concentration of ladino property that surrounded the capital, escaped much more lightly. Towns unfortunate enough to attract the
interest of one of the few large haciendas in the interior, or villages in
the Oriente located among the haciendas supplying food to the indigo
districts, might also be called upon to supply proportionately large
numbers of workers. But most of the rural Indian towns suffered few
or no agricultural repartimientos in these years. The elites had no use
for their labor.

From the hacendado's side, it must be said that even if repartimien-

TABLE 3.2
*Town Population Compared with Number of Men
Called for Repartimiento Drafts*

Town	Quarter of tribute population, 1776	Number of men called for repartimientos to appx. 1800
San Lucas Sacatepéquez	62	116
Santiago Sacatepéquez	230	258
S. Juan Sacatepéquez	313	351
S. Pedro Sacatepéquez	125	216
Sta. María Jesús	104	164 + quarter of tribute population
Mixco	116	78
S. Catarina Pinula	85	110
Guazacapán	50	50 + quarter of tribute population
Mataquescuintla	36	75
Jutiapa	58	71
Utatlán	83	quarter of tribute population
S. Antonio Palopó	22	quarter of tribute population
Conguaco	37	63
Tecuaco	20	42+
D. García	5	10

SOURCE: AGCA, A3 223-27.

tos appeared to offer cheap and readily available labor, they could involve serious problems of cost, reliability, and control. Custom required that the haciendas pay all or most of the workers' wages in advance, leaving employers the problem of actually getting the men and the work.[120] Nothing was more constant than complaints of landowners that the Indians would not come when ordered, did not work as required, and escaped at the first opportunity. Advance payments also sealed free labor agreements, but compliance in these arrangements was much more likely, not only because of the element of worker choice but also because the conditions and wages were usually better than those suffered by forced labor. Employers nevertheless complained: "Although they initially worked well to make it look as though they would be reliable and in this way got additional advances," having received more money they disappeared.[121] To arrive at their true labor costs hacendados had to include in their wage bill the value of advances lost, often a head tax of one-half or one-quarter real per worker, and the bribes extorted from him by the governors, village officials, or intrusive local casta bosses. The Crown, for example, repeatedly banned the custom of giving "presents" to state officials, apparently without much success;[122] these officials were themselves in many instances major employers of repartimiento drafts.[123] The routine requests for more, sometimes absurdly more, workers than an employer needed or could actually use tied up labor potentially available to others, created confusion between communities and among employers as to who owed what to whom, and threatened to collapse the entire system into low, and not very pleasant, comedy. It was a poor system for mobilizing labor, but as long as the indigenous population had access to sufficient resources to satisfy their "needs," and as long as labor demands from the commercial and exports sector remained limited, repartimiento was the most practical and effective means to turn out workers.

Repartimientos existed at one time or another in most areas of the Spanish empire, but in Guatemala they exhibited several important peculiarities. On the one hand, they more or less permanently assigned labor from a community to a specific property or employer, and this certainly lowered levels of gratuitous abuse and made the system generally more acceptable to the indigenous population. Also, forced wage labor persisted longer in Guatemala than in most other parts of the empire, giving it a strong legitimacy and acceptance in the late colonial period and nineteenth century. Acceptance was vital because the state had only very limited power to force upon the Indians what they would not accept, as the Bourbons' largely futile efforts to increase tribute rates or to substitute cash payments for personal service and food rations demonstrated. Forced wage labor could not function without the cooperation of the Indians. The Indians, for their part and although they hated the drafts and understood the damaging effects the drafts had on themselves and their communities, accepted the right of the state to demand labor of them, provided that this was justly, by their definition, paid and that they were not subjected to exploitation that violated custom.

Reform and Independence

In 1812 the Spanish Cortes abolished labor repartimientos.[124] This initiative applied to all the empire and derived its impetus from Enlightenment philosophy and the perceived interests of a developing Spanish mercantile bourgeoisie rather than from the specific conditions of Guatemala. Nevertheless, it did address some of the criticisms of the colony's situation detailed two years earlier by the Consulado de Comercio: "As regards the extraction of Indians from the villages for the haciendas done under the name of mandamientos, this inevitably damages the agriculture of the Indians themselves. They have their own fields to mind and when they are taken for the haciendas is precisely when they need to be tending and harvesting their own plantings."[125] When the Audiencia published the 1812 decree in the colony, another of its articles that substituted Spanish taxes for the food rations and personal service customarily supplied priests in the Indian villages provoked widespread protests among the indigenous population. The end of repartimientos went almost unremarked.[126]

No doubt in some areas the drafts continued with the momentum of custom, while in others labor shifted from direct coercion to one form or another of semi-free labor, with little or no modification of wages or conditions. When Ferdinand returned to power in 1814 he tore up the laws of the Cortes and reinstated repartimientos. The Audiencia in Guatemala issued or renewed one or two orders after 1814,[127] but the entire system of forced wage labor occasioned almost no concern or attention in the last years of the colony. Labor demand was greatly reduced on account of the depressed state of the economy, but even if there had been an interest in repartimiento workers, the colonial state was less and less able to enforce its writ in the countryside. When the 1820 Spanish Liberal revolt prompted a second abolition of the repartimiento system,[128] this occasioned even less notice than had been the case in 1812.

In the flush of freedom the new government of Central America not only did away with chattel slavery but restated the ban on mandamientos. What this meant in fact is not clear. Whereas, for example, the municipal council of Salamá reported that in view of the new law they were suspending all labor drafts immediately, three years later other towns were said to continue to be "oppressed by the misery" of mandamientos.[129] In fact, at this point forced drafts for agriculture were irrelevant. The state could not enforce coerced wage labor, and the hacendados had little need of it. With the casta population continuing to increase and Indians stripped of their minor status, there were more than enough free laborers to be had for what work was available.

When the Liberals temporarily reestablished political stability in

1829, they faced economic and fiscal disaster and set about stimulating agriculture with new land laws, prizes, and the reintroduction of forced labor for the haciendas. Any Crown administrator or colonial landowner would have agreed "that . . . it is necessary to force them to work." A new agricultural labor law specifically reestablished forced drafts for Indians and ladinos, to be allocated and controlled now at the local level: "The owners of haciendas or labores or their administrators or renters may apply to the officials of the towns for the workers they need." [130] Except in the immediate and restricted area of the new cochineal plantations developing around Amatitlán and Antigua, however, and even here to only a very limited extent, there is no evidence that this law affected the countryside in any significant ways. Probably typical was a letter from a landowner to the governor of Sacatepéquez in 1831 asking "if the mandamiento law is still in effect" and, if so, requesting half a dozen workers; there is no indication that the governor responded.[131] When the rural areas erupted in revolt in the 1830's the causes had to do chiefly with epidemic disease, land disputes, and Liberal attacks on the church, but the Legislative Assembly in 1837 nevertheless specifically repealed the forced labor statute, declaring that in the future "workers may not be made to do any sort of work they do not wish to." [132]

The Conservatives revived mandamientos in 1839 and reorganized the system in 1847 and again in 1851, giving the governors the power to issue orders.[133] There continued to be little interest in labor drafts, however, and communities were fiercely resistant to demands from a government that was in any case too weak to enforce unpopular drafts. Indians and poor ladinos were coerced into service by various competitors for power in the civil wars of the 1830's and 1840's and were harassed by the gangs of bandits that crisscrossed the countryside, but in the generally depressed economy of the time there was limited need for forced, or free, labor in commercial agriculture.[134]

Chapter 4

Cochineal

Cochineal . . . has, within the last twenty years, proved an export of considerable value and importance.

Dunlop, *Travels*

Cochineal (*grana*) is a silvery red dye obtained from the bodies of female cochineal insects (*Dactylopius coccus*) that feed on certain types of nopal cactus. It was found wild in Middle America. As a commercially produced crop, it had its origins in Oaxaca, in southern Mexico, and that area of the colony of New Spain remained the chief producer until the 1830's. In 1830, for example, the harvest in Oaxaca was over 5,000 *tercios* (tercio = 150 lbs.), while that of Guatemala had not yet reached 500.[1] But by the 1840's Guatemalan grana outsold Mexican two to one on London markets, and a decade later Guatemala regularly exported more than 10,000 tercios, whereas Oaxaca was greatly decayed.[2] A traveler described the production process of cochineal at Amatitlán in the 1840's:

At short distances from the city many of the inhabitants have cochineal plantations (*nopaleras*), to which they pay considerable attention. These consist of a certain quantity of ground carefully fenced in, and planted with parallel rows of prickly-pear plants (*cactus cochenillifer*) or common Indian fig. Directly after the rains have ceased the insects are sown upon the plant. Twelve or fourteen of these are collected from the parent with a feather, and enclosed all together in a small bag of the maize leaf, left open, and pinned with a thorn to the leaf of the cactus. Seven or eight of these bags are placed on different leaves of the same plant. In a short time the insects begin to breed in the bags, and the young ones crawl out upon the plant. As they grow, they gradually cover themselves with a mantle of white paste, which protects them from injury by the weather. In the course of three months they are ready for gathering. This is done by scraping the leaf. After a sufficient number has been reserved for seed, the rest are either placed upon tins in a large oven, or thrown into hot water. When dried, they assume the appearance of small grains, and are ready for sale. A second crop [in the Amatitlán area] is then sown, and in three months a second harvest is reaped; after which the seed is preserved by covering the plant till the rainy season is passed. After four or five years the trees decay, in consequence of the quantity of nourishment drawn by the insects, and it is then necessary to root them up and plant fresh ones.[3]

Amatitlán differed from nearby but higher and cooler Antigua, Guatemala's other major cochineal center, only in that in Antigua growers gathered but one harvest a year and, because of the slower growth, the cacti lasted longer. There was, too, more production by peasant Indian growers around the old capital, and there were fewer of the larger, ladino-owned operations characteristic of Amatitlán. Techniques for cultivation varied little between the plantations and small family plots. There were few economies of scale available to large producers, apart, perhaps, from the drying stoves that these growers could more easily afford. The chief difference between the small and large growers was the widespread use of wage labor by the latter. Because of the handicraft nature of production, however, most commentators reckoned the bigger operations less efficient than the small plots. According to one observer, "Three or four estates of a much larger size have lately been planted [at Amatitlán], and one belonging to Sen. Francisco López contains 150 manzanas; but these estates are not nearly so productive as those of a smaller size, as the immense number of people who must be employed to work them causes a confusion and a great loss of labor."[4]

Cochineal fitted easily into the existing economic and transport structures of Guatemala, and the industry had the advantage, in contrast to indigo, of being completely under local control. Given the postindependence erection of international boundaries separating the Guatemala City merchants and indigo growers of El Salvador and the frequent outbreaks of fighting between the two countries, a crop wholly within the domain of Guatemala offered obvious benefits. Because small ladino and Indian growers produced much of the crop, as they had cacao and indigo, merchants could continue to use their control of export marketing and transport to drain off much of the profits while limiting their risks. The processed dye had even higher value to weight ratio than did indigo. This allowed profitable transport to the northern ports on Guatemala's notoriously poor roads. Cochineal tended to reinforce Guatemala's existing commercial, capital, and transport structures.

The Consulado de Comercio's "Apuntamientos" in 1810 had drawn attention to the possibilities of cochineal: "The grana of Panajachel is as good as that of Oaxaca."[5] The following year the Crown exempted grana from the tithe. The Economic Society and the Audiencia brought live insects from Oaxaca and encouraged experiments with the crop, and in 1818 the government published a pamphlet of instructions written by the priest of Joyabaj-Cubulco.[6] The same year the Crown issued regulations allowing the cajas de comunidad of the Indian towns to advance money to would-be Indian and ladino growers.[7] These initial efforts were mostly ineffectual. Local landowners had little idea of how to handle the insects or process the dye, and they had yet to find the areas in which it would prosper. In addition to the Joyabaj-Cubulco region, early experiments took place near Guatemala City, in the Oriente at Chiquimula and Jalapa, at Amatitlán, and around La Antigua,[8] but interest increasingly focused on Amatitlán and Antigua. By 1824, and despite a short-lived revival of indigo, grana was said to be Guatemala's most valuable export: "Almost alone cochineal covers the value of the county's imports."[9] The governor of Sacatepéquez reported in the same year, "Given the decadence of all other branches of agriculture, grana bears our fondest hopes."[10]

Not surprisingly, the new state was assiduous in its efforts to protect and promote the dye. Late in 1824, for example, mule drivers detected several Englishmen attempting to smuggle grana insects out of the country. The government confiscated the shipment and made it a crime to sell nopal plants or live insects to foreigners or for export, "because this crop is the only one that can make everyone rich."[11] The Liberals attempted a census of production, passed measures to assure the purity of exported grana, and in 1831 exempted the dye from all taxes for twenty years.[12] But the capital city monopoly merchants represented in the Consulado de Comercio, and despite their earlier interest, paid the new crop scant attention in these years. An 1822 report issued by the Consulado on ways to improve and diversify agriculture failed even to mention the dye.[13] Traditional elites preferred to stay with what they knew and controlled, that is, indigo, which revived briefly in the early 1820's, and the import and export trade, rather than risk their scarce and valuable capital financing new and uncertain forms of production. According to the historian R. L. Woodward, "Not until cochineal became an established article of commerce, and provided a substitute for declining indigo sales, did the Consulado as an institution actively work for the production and development of the industry."[14] Instead, the early development of grana was the work of individual growers, small-scale money lenders, and merchants marginal to the capital clique. Even after it prospered, Consulado members largely limited their involvement to the international aspects of the trade. They did not themselves become growers, and they had little direct participation in financing the crop.

Unnatural and Natural Disasters

State and individual enthusiasms were small proof against the chaos and violence that swept independent Guatemala. Despite government assurances that "the cochineal growers enjoy the guarantees and all possible protection of the authorities," the many uncertainties connected with the civil war limited investment in the new crop, and the fighting wrecked plantings and equipment and carried off labor. Under these circumstances cochineal failed to expand as rapidly as many had anticipated.[15] After a brief recovery in the years 1830–36, cholera and the Carrera uprising again slowed production. The governor of Amatitlán noted in 1840 that agriculture, and especially grana, was in "decadence" owing to labor shortages, in part the result of the unhealthful climate around the lake, but above all the fault of "the frequent forced recruitments that frighten off industrious people and cause serious problems because of labor scarcity."[16] Growers had attempted grana cultivation in nearby San Miguel Petapa, he added, but there, too, the plantings now lay in ruins because of the same unavailability of workers.

The Conservatives also sought to encourage cochineal, but they had few resources with which to do this and a host of problems placing demands on these: "With so little at their disposal," remarked the historian Ignacio Solís, "what could they undertake of any importance?"[17] Worse, the end of the Carrera uprising did not bring peace, for foreign wars erupted, political revolts persisted, and banditry flourished.[18] Forced recruiting by both the government and rebellious factions continued; "Sometimes," the diplomat John Lloyd Stephens reported, "all the workmen of a hacienda are taken away for soldiers at the moment when they are most needed for . . . culture."[19] The manager of the cochineal plantation Rincon de Anís, for example, complained in 1847 that a patrol of sixty government troops had invaded the property and carried off all his men, including the foreman, making it "entirely impossible to continue to work." In response to a representation against such abuses lodged with the government by the British Consul, the Carrera regime agreed to restrain its agents: "During the times that workers were needed for grana, the government would only take de-serters."[20] It was not new policies, however, so much as an easing of factional fighting and a temporary halt to wars in the early 1850's that allowed the state to clean up the banditry and limit press-ganging, alleviating some of the difficulties of the growers and their workers.

More than most crops, cochineal suffered acutely from the effects of natural hazards. In the uncertain political atmosphere of Guatemala during the early years and given the dye's poor prospects after the mid-1850's, growers did not always do enough replanting, and aging plants could not sustain the insects well enough to fight off disease. Also, the practice of bringing the nopal plants together in plantations appears to have led to inbreeding and encouraged the growth and spread of parasites. Destructive caterpillars appeared as early as the mid-1830's; during an epidemic in the late 1840's that momentarily devastated production, growers paid Indians to pick the invaders off by hand.[21] More serious, particularly to the growers around Antigua, were the problems that the rainy season brought. The cochineal insects could easily be killed by cold temperatures and knocked off the cacti by heavy rain.[22] As an experienced planter explained, "It is nothing rare for the cochineal grower to find nearly all his labour and out-lay lost, and a great part of his crop destroyed in a few minutes."[23] The danger at Amatitlán came chiefly from late season rains. There the growers seeded the plants in October and risked having the in-sects destroyed by a storm unusually late in the year. They usually harvested the second crop well before the rains began again in April or May. In Antigua, on the other hand, where because of the cold the insects grew more slowly, planters managed only one crop a year; they seeded in January and February and harvested in May or June, putting their investment at real risk from the onset of the rains. Some-times, or so it seemed, the rains and the predators worked together: "An untimely rain storm was enough to make the infestation worse and together destroy the grower's hopes."[24] In most years cochineal was a gamble against unstable markets, disease, and unpredictable weather conditions.

Capital

Capital for grana production came from various sources, but it was always expensive and in short supply. Though Crown laws allowed communities to advance money for the crop from the cajas de la comunidad, outstanding loans and village needs already absorbed most such funds; available caja records make no mention of loans for growers. The Guatemala City Cabildo in 1821 asked to be allowed to take 10,000 pesos from the funds of the colony's towns to finance grana.[25] Apparently the Crown agreed, but the scheme failed to get under way before independence.

In the absence of investment from the Consulado merchants, other lenders took the lead. Most of the financing for cochineal from the 1830's to the 1860's came from among individuals and groups at least at first marginal to the capital's mercantile elite. None of the merchants who held the principal Consulado offices during these years, for example, appears in the notarial records lending money for grana, and a thorough review of the dozen Guatemala City notaries most active in the period reveals few cochineal contracts. Similarly, the lists of persons who were called upon to contribute to forced loans include only a few who also financed cochineal production, and by and large these were not part of the dominant Guatemala City group.[26] The two or three notaries working at any one time in La Antigua, on the other hand, did a lively local business in grana financing. Two of the most frequently mentioned names in the Antigua contracts were José María Samayoa (father) and José Tomás Larraondo, both of whom started with little and raised their initial capital in the liquor monopoly. Another was Manuel María Herrera.[27] The Liberal general Gregorio Prem and his wife were active lenders. These were people from modest, even obscure, backgrounds who made their fortunes in the cochineal years, and not until the late 1850's and 1860's did they begin to enter the capital political and mercantile inner circles. Several of them, or their sons, played important roles in the Liberal regimes after 1871. Agents of Belize merchants also lent money and bought grana directly, bypassing the capital monopoly, as did such foreign-controlled companies as Klée, Skinner.[28] Many very small-scale lenders appear in the contracts financing cochineal, perhaps one-fourth or more of them women. In addition, there were hundreds of loans of but a few pesos each to Indian producers in surrounding villages that rested only on verbal contracts and therefore do not show up in the protocolos. Some Antigua lenders may have served as subagents of the large merchants of Guatemala City, but in cases where it is possible to examine legal proceedings it is clear that most acted on their own. What the situation was at Amatitlán is unclear, for notary records covering grana activities in that area have not yet turned up.

Perhaps as the crop peaked in the 1850's and 1860's capital city merchants sought more direct control over financing, but a careful study of finance and commerce in these years does not obviously support such a conclusion.[29] Although contracts from the mid- and late 1850's indicate a somewhat greater coincidence between forced loan lists and grana financing, capital city elites were still very much in the minority. Most contented themselves with bulking and exporting the dye and supplying the imports financed by it. Production of the crop remained highly speculative, and, indeed, appeared to be getting more so by the day. But in good years the returns could be very high. Enthusiasts wrote that a grower, if possessed of all-important good luck, after the first year could expect a return of 3,000 pesos a year on a 3,000-peso investment; more typically, producers estimated costs of 75 pesos to 99 pesos per tercio against returns of 103 pesos per tercio (at 5.5 reales per pound) to 150 pesos per tercio (at 8 reales per pound). A Guatemala City newspaper in the mid-1840's estimated the value of the current crop at 1,035,937 pesos, against costs, according to a group of Antigua growers, of 847,875 pesos, which amounted to a not insubstantial profit of 22 percent.[30] Such calculations did not allow for the years of crop losses or flooded markets. The risk involved and the increasingly boom-bust conditions of production provoked a high rate of circulation among lenders and growers and a constant round of bankruptcy, renegotiated contracts, and lawsuits that mediated against the concentration of control in a few hands. All evidence suggests that grana remained a crop that attracted investment by outsiders and men, and women, "on the make," whereas the more certain profits of the import and export trade continued to occupy the attentions and resources of the capital city elite.

Contracts to finance cochineal generally provided for an advance of money or seed cochineal, either at interest or, and depending on market conditions, against the promised future delivery of a certain amount of grana. Lenders made advances available several times a year, usually at the beginning of the planting season or seasons and when settling accounts at the harvest. The periods of most activity in the protocolos at Antigua were in December–January and June–July. In a typical arrangement, Andrés Dardón on December 10, 1834, lent Doroteo Vasconcelos 1,500 pesos, to be paid back in May 1835 with 1,500 pounds of cochineal. The dye was to be harvested in Antigua and stove dried, and if the borrower found that he could not supply the grana on time he was to make good the debt in silver at the price of grana as of May 31, 1835. In a margin note dated July 26, 1835, Dardon acknowledged receipt of the agreed-upon 1,500 pounds of the dye.[31] The possible permutations of such arrangements were endless. A creditor might advance seed grana said to be worth 12.5 reales a pound in return for the promise of repayment in six months at a rate of one pound of grana equaling 8 reales, effectively an annual return of more than 100 percent. The creditor might also make available funds or mercantile credit to be repaid in cochineal valued at an agreed-upon price or at a set fraction less than the market price at the time of delivery.[32] Most commonly, the lender simply required a specific amount of grana in return for the loan. Lenders attempted to juggle the various possibilities to their advantage, guessing at future prices and market trends: whereas, for example, in the 1830's and 1840's they almost always preferred repayment in cochineal, as the crop faltered after 1860 more and more contracts called for repayment in money. Real rates of interest for cochineal loans ran 1–2 percent a month on notarized contracts, and in penalty situations this escalated to 4 or 5 percent a month. After the Conservatives returned to power, the church revived its ban on usury, and contracts dropped all reference to interest rates, dealing only in specified amounts of money or grana. Much lending, too, went on at an informal level, only showing up on the written records if problems developed. As more capital flowed into grana, rates may have dropped somewhat, but they still hovered around one percent a month on well-secured loans. Interest in informal arrangements and on advances for very small amounts was higher, 5 to 10 percent a month.

For numerous reasons, borrowers did not always repay the loans or deliver the grana on schedule. Such lapses occurred both because of individual failures and dishonesty and, more broadly, in periods of general economic disruption or social unrest. Many defaulted because of labor shortages that crippled production in the wake of the 1836–37 cholera epidemic and the Carrera uprising. Fernando de Córdoba, for example, in April 1837 claimed to be unable to pay what he owed because, he said, of "the failures common as a result of the cholera epidemic last year and the political upheavals in the present year."[33] During times of generalized bad harvests or low prices for cochineal, such as the early 1840's and the 1860's, the entire economy suffered: in July 1842 the renter of a sugar plantation near Escuintla explained that she could not pay her debts because of "the decadence of all branches of commerce . . . as a result of the recent fall in the price of grana and the bad harvest this year."[34] Although loan contracts gave the creditor the right to confiscate a grower's land and equipment in event of default, few did; in most cases the lender merely extended the contract. When Mariano Palacios, for example, declared in July of 1839 that he was bankrupt and could not repay loans dating back three years, his creditors refinanced his debt and advanced him more money to work his cochineal plantings for the next season.[35] When grana prices collapsed in 1842 José María García went bankrupt owing money to Vicente Carranza; instead of foreclosing, Carranza lent García additional funds to develop three manzanas in nopal plants. For the next seven years García paid rent and developed the land but still could not repay his loans, which by the end of the decade totaled 487 pesos, plus two notes for the 1842 debts.[36] In another case, Zeferino Martinez admitted in February 1861 that he had owed Marianna Mendibelsua nine *arrobas* (arroba = 25 pounds) of cochineal since 1852 and had failed to pay her. She advanced him more seed grana, and finally in 1867 he was able to make good on the debt.[37]

Creditors did seek what guarantees they could with liens on a borrower's properties, goods, and potential future production. This might include the land used for cochineal, but many producers did not own the land but only rented from municipal ejidos, meaning that it could not be foreclosed or sold for bad debts. Most cochineal agreements therefore specified as guarantees the use rights to land, the harvest itself, improvements on the property, the nopales and similar permanent crops, commercial goods, and other items of value belonging to the borrower. Unless debts threatened to get out of hand or a creditor caught a grower attempting to sell his harvest to another buyer at a better price, the relationship was likely to continue indefinitely as long as a borrower paid regularly on the loan. Only when lenders became nervous about overdue accounts or if these became exceptionally large were they likely to move to embargo and sell a debtor's possessions. In June 1837, for example, Julian Morales acknowledged that he already owed 10,237 pesos to José Tomás Larraondo and promised to cover this with 10,237 pounds of grana by June of the following year. He secured this with a mortgage against his haciendas Matambo (in ejidos of Antigua) and Potrero de Belén. In the same month, as it later came out, he also bought a house on the plaza in Antigua on credit. When Morales failed to meet the cochineal debt, and discovering the house transaction, Larraondo obtained a court judgment against him, forcing the auction of Morales's possessions.[38] Generally speaking, though, lenders wanted grana, not land or equipment, and stood to profit more by keeping the borrower in business and paying on what was owed than by foreclosing. Few growers, even if they ended the season clearing their debts, had sufficient capital to carry forward production through the next harvest without an advance. Therefore, unless a creditor proved particularly usurious, the borrower had no incentive to end the relationship, particularly since he had little likelihood of finding markedly better terms elsewhere.

Land

Cochineal in Guatemala never involved large amounts of land. It was not a crop that could be grown widely, and market demand for the dye, competition, and a scarcity of capital kept production to a limited scale. An 1840's estimate placed the area under cultivation in nopal cacti at about 4,000 acres, and it is unlikely that at the peak of production early in the next decade there could have been more than twice this amount of land in the crop.[39] Grana had little direct effect on land tenure or use in most of rural Guatemala. Because of the survival of subsistence plantings in nearby areas, the interplanting of food crops and cochineal-bearing nopales on peasant and Indian plots, and the small labor force set to work by grana, dye production did not provide even the limited market for commercial food production and long-distance trade that indigo had furnished. But for several decades cochineal did dominate the area immediately around Antigua and, especially, Amatitlán. Most growers initially rented land in censo enfiteusis from the ejidos of these and neighboring communities; as the boom grew, they subleased this among themselves. The government encouraged these practices.[40] Because the laws kept censo rates low and the demand for the grana land was brisk, the municipalities usually were able to require an additional payment, or "gratuity," on top of censo rent. In the style of capellanías, would-be renters bid a lump sum as gratuity but actually paid only the interest on this, and when someone resold his use rights, the purchaser also assumed the gratuity debt. For example, in 1849 one grower transferred his rights to a tract of 37.5 cuerdas at Antigua to another grower for 3,000 pesos; on this parcel he paid the municipality a censo of 14 pesos, as well as 6 percent interest on a gratuity of 1,714 pesos, making the total rent some 118 pesos a year.[41] Privately owned cochineal land rented for about 10 percent of its sale price.

TABLE 4.1
Land Prices in Pesos per Manzana (with Nopal Plants)
Amatitlán and Antigua, 1835–1869

Years	Amatitlán	Antigua
1835–39	...	500
1840–44	...	400
1845–49	700	500
1850–54	600	300
1855–59	500	650
1860–64	300	500
1865–69	250	400

SOURCE: AGCA, Protocolos.

When grana land could be bought outright, it initially commanded higher prices in Amatitlán because of the possibility of two crops a year. As time went on, these values fell below those of Antigua (see Table 4.1), partly because the cooler climate of Antigua lessened the effects of the diseases that plagued the Amatitlán plantations after 1848, and also because by the early 1860's Antigua already had begun the transition from cochineal to coffee production. This new possibility kept land prices in the area up. Some sources suggest even more radical oscillations in prices: "The manzana that in 1840 was worth $100 [pesos] would have been difficult to obtain in 1860 for $1,200, and in 1865 you would find no one willing to pay $200 or $300 for it."[42] Undeveloped land thought to be suitable for cochineal sold for 60–100 pesos per manzana (= 5,000+ pesos per caballería), depending on its location and the current state of cochineal fever. By way of comparison, in these same years good land in the Sierra de Canales and at San Juan Sacatepéquez could be had for 250 pesos per caballería, and in Antigua's neighboring municipality of Sumpango for 100 pesos per caballería; in 1851 undeveloped land in the piedmont adjacent to Sacatepéquez and Amatitlán went for no more than 20 pesos a caballería.[43]

Because of escalating land values in the first decades, outsiders and local ladinos after 1830 more and more encroached on Indian ejidos and state baldíos in the cochineal areas. Competition sharpened conflicts within the villages over ownership and rights to what until then most inhabitants had thought of vaguely as "community lands." Such tensions, not surprisingly, were particularly acute in San Juan Amatitlán. The Indian justicias there complained in the early 1830's that the ladinos of the municipality were attempting to gain control of 49 caballerías of land that the indigenous population had composed with the Crown in 1751. The ladinos responded that of the community's 49 caballerías, 36 made up the ejido and as such were open to all legal residents of the town, Indian or ladino. Only what remained over and above this might be said to belong exclusively to the Indians. The ladinos then upped the ante, seeking to deny any rights or even the existence to an Indian community and arguing that the land law of 1825 awarded ejidos to the community without regard to race. The Indians' point, of course, and documents confirmed this, was that purchase by composition meant that the disputed 49 caballerías were not properly ejido but the private property of the "community of Indians" of the town that had paid for it. A remeasurement in 1834 rather conveniently found 90 caballerías in the common lands, 49 belonging to the Indians, 38 as the ejido of the town, and a few caballerías extra. This came too late for the indigenous population, however. By the middle of the decade ladinos intent on grana production controlled most of the good land in the area, and the possibilities of the dye drew more people to the region every day.

The Indians' views on these changes came through clearly in their complaint that "the ejidos produce nothing of value now because the ladinos have them fenced off into plots of grana." The records of yet another remeasurement in 1869 reveal that by then the distinction between Indian and municipal property had disappeared altogether. San Juan's community lands now were divided into hundreds of small and medium-sized, primarily ladino-owned, nopal plots. A few owners paid rent but most held their plots in de jure or de facto private property. The Indians, it was said, made their living fishing and crabbing in the lake or making salt.[44] Thus, in the affected communities, the land laws of the postindependence regimes and the influx of ladinos into the cochineal areas fatally weakened the concept of a separate, autonomous community or government of Indians with separate rights to land and a separate, subsistence agenda. Local and immigrant ladinos sold, bought, and rented among themselves land to which they had no clear rights but of which they had gained possession by trickery or collusion with local and state officials. In pursuit of development and in need of revenues the state acquiesced and even facilitated an assault that both stripped the indigenous population of power and buried it in a flood of newcomers. Unlike the coffee revolution after 1871, however, these developments remained confined to a small area and affected, or afflicted, only a tiny minority of Guatemala's indigenous population.

To the west, the municipality of Antigua attempted as early as 1824 to assert control over land in the surrounding area that growers were beginning to put into cochineal. It asked that the state declare unoccupied land in the earthquake-ruined town "abandoned" so that those who sought to use it could obtain clear title and the security to invest in commercial production.[45] The government refused, explaining that private property was "sacred," however confused the question of ownership might be, but in 1829 it did reaffirm the town's right to control those areas clearly determined to be ejido.[46] Several Antigua families attempted to claim that because land in the parish of Candelaria had remained unused since the 1773 earthquake it could be denounced as baldío. The problem with this argument, the government attorney explained, was that because of the inadequate measurements and documentation general to Guatemala, and not just in the area of Antigua, no one had an accurate idea of precisely what was or was not private property, what belonged to the towns, and what areas fell into the category of state land. In this instance, the regime ruled that the open land in Candelaria was community property, that is, part of Antigua's ejidos, and should be available to all the town's inhabitants subject to the regulations of the municipal government. So much of Antigua was still in ruins, in fact, that grana flourished in the very courtyards and patios of homes and tumbled-down buildings. Small producers predominated in the 1830's and 1840's; even by the 1850's only a few comparatively large plantations existed, many of these on rented land.[47]

The governor of Sacatepéquez reported with perhaps some exaggeration in the 1840's that for ten leagues about Antigua "there is no open land as almost all of it is occupied with cochineal plantings."[48] Some of this the neighboring villages rented to outsiders, but more generally the crop seems to have served as an adjunct to Indian subsistence agriculture in these communities. In San Felipe, the governor noted, "in the patios of their houses are plantings of nopal cacti," and in Ciudad Vieja "the house lots have little patches of nopal plantings."[49] Most of this production supplied the local textile and artisan weaving industries; what was left Antigua merchants bulked and resold in the capital. The relative importance to the total output of the region of small versus larger growers is not known, but the small producers, particularly the Indians in their communities, were much more important to the Antigua-area crop than to the industry around Lake Amatitlán.

Labor

Labor for the production of cochineal on the larger ladino holdings in and around Antigua came almost entirely from the nearby Indian villages. The municipality reported "good results" in the early 1830's "lending people" to haciendas under the 1829 labor law. A generation later the governor of Sacatepéquez elaborated regulations for forced drafts that allowed the drafting of workers from the villages to seed and harvest the grana, to cut away the weeds from the fields, and to pluck caterpillars off the plants.[50] But, overall, mandamientos played very little role in cochineal.[51] Similarly, vagrancy laws had been on the books since the late colonial period but continued to function chiefly as instruments of urban social control rather than as vehicles for the mobilization of agricultural labor.[52] Repeated decrees and orders attacking "vagrancy"—defined usually as being found drunk or drinking during normal working hours—perhaps had the effect of occasionally driving a layabout or two out of the drink shops but seldom, probably, into the fields. *El Tiempo* reported in 1840 that on Mondays the police in Antigua flushed people out of the taverns, chained them together, and sent them off to agricultural labor, but this may have been mostly wishful thinking.[53] Actual instances of this sort of recruitment were rare, at least to judge from available records, and there were no complaints from the Indians about such activities, which there certainly would have been had the practice been common. Given the Conservative regime's institutionalized attention to the concerns of the indigenous population and the Indians' vociferous complaints about roadwork in these years and about repartimientos before 1800 and mandamientos after 1871, it seems clear that drafted or forced wage labor for grana had little impact on the Indians' lives. Direct state intervention in labor mobilization was expensive, unwieldy, and, at this moment in Guatemala's economic history, unnecessary because of the availability of sufficient free labor.

Intense Spanish, creole, and casta presence in the valleys around Antigua for three centuries meant that indigenous communities already had begun to suffer land shortages well before the end of the colonial period. An 1846 survey by the governor found that many villages lacked enough land for subsistence plantings. In others, population growth and inheritance patterns had fragmented land into plots that were too tiny even for a single family. The spread of commercial cochineal production only intensified the land shortage.[54] One obvious result was that many Indians readily, and without need of force, took advances from the grana producers and went, or at least promised, to work these off at the long-established wage of one to one and a half reales a day. The governor reported of various towns: in San Pedro las Huertas, "Most of the inhabitants work as laborers on cochineal plantations . . . including the women when it comes time for seeding and harvesting the crop"; in San Miguel Escobar, "The majority occupy themselves as day laborers on the large grana plantations, while at the same time having their corn plantings and small patches of nopal plants"; in Santiago Sacatepéquez, "They suffer the necessity of seeking their subsistence in other towns and working as day laborers in Antigua, Villa Nueva, and Amatitlán where they contract grave illnesses."[55]

The impact of this labor on the towns and their inhabitants was disastrous. The governor of Sacatepéquez explained in 1847, for example, that before cochineal the residents of Santa María de Jesús and other nearby villages had enjoyed a "modest prosperity" growing corn, fruits, and vegetables and selling wood and fodder in Antigua. Although they had earned little cash, they were adequately fed, clothed, and housed and rarely had had to leave home overnight. Now the Indians could make twelve reales or more a week working in the nopal fields, but labor in the community had become scarce and expensive, food production had fallen off, and many villagers were leaving. Those who remained were "vice-ridden and corrupt."[56] A decade later the priest of Santa María painted an even grimmer picture. The villagers went to work in Antigua and Amatitlán, he said, and on the way back stopped to spend their earnings in the taverns where they fell into "prostitution, fights, woundings, and a multitude of crimes." The community was disintegrating. People preferred alcohol to marriage, parents neglected their children, no one obeyed the justicias, and it was impossible to carry out health measures.[57] In the nearby town of Ciudad Vieja conditions were so bad that local officials needed a detachment of soldiers to keep order on Sundays and Mondays.[58]

The question of labor for grana producers at Amatitlán was more serious than in Antigua because of the high cost of living and because of Amatitlán's foul reputation for disease and unhealthful working conditions.[59] Much of Amatitlán's health problem arose from its proximity to the swamp of Playón, "a terrible influence paralyzing at certain periods commerce and industry."[60] In 1841 the municipality bought the swamp with the intention of draining it, but squatters invaded the land and blocked reclamation efforts. Epidemics continued. The town lacked an adequate hospital, and workers without families "died in the plaza."[61] Food was in short supply and high prices plagued Amatitlán. Rising food costs also caused occasional hardship at Antigua,[62] but around Lake Amatitlán, owing to the greater emphasis on monoculture, the larger size of some of the plantations, and the rootlessness of much of the population, food was a matter of continuing concern. As early as 1840 the governor of Amatitlán remarked that the shift to cochineal had caused local food output to decline and prices to rise.[63] Whereas the area once had been self-sufficient, now food had to be brought in from surrounding communities to make up for falling production and to meet the needs of a rapidly increasing population. Planters offered substantially higher wages than those paid around Antigua, two and a half to three reales a day, and still they suffered shortages of workers.[64]

Cochineal labor at Amatitlán was a dangerous if relatively well paying occupation that attracted a turbulent and largely ladino labor force. Men flooded in but died of disease or violence, or fled the area when the military recruiters arrived or epidemics broke out, or left in search of better opportunities when the harvest was poor, causing employers to lose the wages they had advanced. According to Robert Dunlop, the ex-manager of an Amatitlán cochineal plantation, the best laborers were the mulatto descendants of the slaves brought in the colonial period to work Jesuit and Dominican sugar plantations. They were more active and intelligent than the castas or Indians, he claimed, but they nevertheless were ignorant and given to vice. Many of the immigrants were criminals and deserters from the various conflicts of the time. While remarking that he never actually had had to shoot anyone to keep control, Dunlop called them "the refuse of all Central America."[65] Heavy drinking aggravated both social and labor problems. After reviewing the archives of the courts, for example, a new governor remarked in the early 1840's that he had found more than 400 criminal cases, almost all of which involved alcohol. To counter this he limited taverns to two customers at a time, and the following year he issued new regulations on "good government" intended to crack down on loiterers and those found drunk in public places.[66] This apparently did little good.

Cochineal peaked as Guatemala's main cash crop and export in the

TABLE 4.2

Cochineal and Coffee Exports by Value, 1867–1871
(in pesos)

Year	Coffee	Cochineal
1867	415,878	1,068,047
1868	788,035	891,513
1869	790,227	1,266,613
1870	1,132,298	865,414
1871	1,312,129	876,025

SOURCE: Rubio Sánchez, "La grana," p. 46.

early 1850's, with some 3,000,000 pesos capital estimated to be circulating in the trade, up from 1,000,000 pesos in the 1830's.[67] By the early 1860's the boom was over, and capital had fallen to 500,000 pesos. The *Gaceta de Guatemala* whistled in the dark that Guatemala's grana could compete with the new areas of production such as the Canary Islands and with the new aniline dyes, and it assured its readers that recent disquieting news from Europe was just another maneuver by speculators to manipulate the market.[68] Others talked of moving the industry to the Verapaz, where fresh land and cheap labor promised a revival.[69] But production persisted more as a function of fixed investments and custom and for want of an obvious alternative than for any faith in the future of cochineal dye. As had been the case with indigo, growers and merchants with a vested interest in the crop were loath to risk a change without strong prospects of equal or better profitability in some other undertaking. In Amatitlán growers shifted some of their land back to sugar and experimented with cotton,[70] but the savior of the planters and the merchants, if not the general population, proved to be coffee. Although the gross value of cochineal exports actually held up better in these years than planter and merchant laments might lead one to believe, the value of coffee exports had overhauled that of the dye by the late 1860's (see Table 4.2 and Appendix B).

Coffee did not so much displace grana initially as add to the total value of Guatemala's exports. Only after a small group of pioneers had established the profitability of coffee and with the entrance of aniline scarlet on to the market in 1870 and, particularly, with the shift of government in 1871 to a Liberal regime bent on promoting coffee did the massive increases in the production of the new crop begin.

Chapter 5

The Communities

> The integration becomes a smooth blend; well stabilized, it
> has the individuality and roundness that mark any culture,
> and its continued evolution is in the form of growth out of
> itself, rather than in response to alien pressures.
>   LaFarge, "Maya Ethnology"

I n a brief essay published some fifty years ago, Oliver LaFarge argued that the years between 1800 and 1880 constituted something
of a golden age for the indigenous communities of highland Guatemala. It was in these years, he proposed, that "traditional" Indian
culture came to full fruition.[1] The opportunity for relatively autonomous development was a result both of the weakened condition of the
late colonial and independence states and of a stagnant cash and export economy that had little need of the land or labor of most of the
Indian communities. Except perhaps in the last years of the colony
when the struggle over tribute was both a cause and an effect of failing
control, the Spanish regime generally was able to enforce some measure of peace if not necessarily justice in the countryside. The newly
independent state could do neither.

Church and Community

Nowhere was the weakening of the state more evident during the
years after 1760 than in the declining role of the institutionalized
church in the communities. The church attended to its own agenda of
Christianization with a zeal and effectiveness that varied depending on
the period, the place, and the quality of its current local representatives, but it served, too, as the ideological arm of the colonial and Conservative states, preaching compliance and subservience to the man-
dates of government. Much of the time it effectively was the state in
rural areas. Even under the Liberals the church was the only national
institution that had extensive day-to-day contact with the mass of the

Indian population. These relationships were not without tensions and involved the church and agents of the secular state in persistent conflicts. The church extracted more money from the indigenous population than did any of the other branches of the Crown's government, and this was cause for considerable jealousy and carping.[2]

The Indians had their own reasons for complaint. In addition to the routine fees they paid the church for masses, confession, marriage, and burial, and the tithes and other taxes they paid to the state in the name of the church, they also faced less regular "vexations." These included the expenses resulting from the periodic visits of the archbishops or other high church officials and the costs associated with periodically rebuilding and equipping the church's properties. More personal was the abuse of the Indians by individual priests, usually connected with attempting to extract more income from them. Activities reported included beating Indians or having them whipped or put in stocks, forcing them to marry young in order to collect fees and to increase—this usually in cooperation with local justicias—the tribute population, and taking or making use of village animals or land, or renting these to outsiders.[3] Sometimes extortion took even more direct forms. In a letter to the Archbishop in 1823 the Indians of Patzicía, for example, accused the local priest of aggravating the "coughing sickness" in the community by refusing to bury the bodies of the victims until their families paid him.[4] Whether true or not in this instance, behavior of this sort was common enough to provoke frequent petitions and delegations of protest, and even riots. The governor of Sacatepéquez in 1863 summed up the state's frustrations at having to deal with such problems: "The ignorance and fears of the Indians together with the abuses and avarice of the priests are the causes of many of the disorders."[5]

Other conflicts between the towns and the church arose out of the system of rations and personal service by which the indigenous communities supported the priest. In return for reduced fees, and in acknowledgment of their poverty, Indian villages provided their priest with the basic supplies needed to run his household, including wood and water, corn, chickens and eggs, fodder for his animals, and servants.[6] A church-determined schedule and local custom supposedly set the amounts of each to be furnished, but wrangles were constant. A staple of the correspondence received by the Archbishop was complaints from the communities that their cura demanded excessive amounts of servants and food, either for resale or to support a large family. Just as routinely, the priest responded that the Indians were so occupied with drinking and practicing their pagan rituals that they did not attend church or provide him his due; they only complained because of his zealous effort to bring them to Christ. One notorious abuser of the system was said to demand, along with a variety of other items, fifty loads of firewood and ninety of fodder a day, for which the Indians "got nothing but snake bites or a soaking or a fall into a ravine."[7] Landowners and the capital city merchants tended to side with the Indians in arguments about rations and service. The church and its priests, they claimed, drew off large quantities of labor and resources better used to promote agricultural development and market commerce.

After an investigation and following on an order from the Spanish Cortes, the Audiencia of Guatemala in 1812 declared an end to personal service and rations.[8] As equal citizens under the new constitution Indians would now pay the same taxes and fees to the church as did Spaniards and ladinos. The decree touched off a storm of protest that far eclipsed complaints about the old system. Priests explained that they would not be able to live on what the Indians could pay, and the Indians flatly refused to accept the innovation, saying they could not afford Spanish charges.[9] One priest justified his failure even to read the order at Sunday service by arguing, "Replacing the system of personal service with higher fees will cause revolutions, and I would not dare to attempt it because I have no protection at all."[10] What with sporadic revolts already occurring in many of these same communities over tribute and pro-independence stirrings in the air, an indecisive Spanish state made no serious effort to enforce the reform.[11] After independence, the state reissued the law putting an end to personal service, a practice the Liberals deemed "degrading to the unfortunate Indian," but the custom continued in most rural areas throughout the nineteenth century.[12]

The persistence of personal service in the face of repeated efforts to end it highlighted the faltering hold of both church and state on the villages. The statist policies of the Bourbons hurt the church's standing in the communities, and the earthquake in 1773 and the losses in agriculture after 1800 damaged its financial situation, as did the 1804 consolidation. Independence and the disputes that followed prompted many of Guatemala's never too numerous clergy to flee, and the exile of the Archbishop and the expulsion of the regular orders in 1829 threw the hierarchy and many parishes into confusion.[13] The Liberals actively sought to limit church prerogatives by taking control of such services as marriage, birth and death registration, and the cemeteries. Revocation of the tithe and institution of the land tax in 1832 further reduced church income, a loss not recuperated until the 1840's. And the economic base of the church also suffered erosion with the confiscation of the properties of the regular orders and of exiled Spanish priests or of those priests who fled the country, and from the not inconsiderable losses of chantries and loans dissipated in the turmoil of the period.

The makeup of the clergy was gradually changing, too. Not only did a shortage of priests make it all but impossible to fill undesirable posts, but many of those available moved constantly between parishes as they looked for better livings or pursued their agricultural and commercial interests. After 1821, the shift toward a creole clergy probably increased the average size of the priest's family that a town had to support, sharpening grievances over rations and service.[14] Many of these problems surfaced in the Archbishop's frequently frustrated efforts during these years to find and keep priests in isolated Indian parishes. Late in 1856, for example, and after repeated false starts, the Archbishop managed to convince a young priest just graduated from seminary in Chiapas to take a post at Jacaltenango, high in the Cuchumatán Mountains. Upon arriving in the town, Presbítero Juan de Dios Herrera reported that local religion was in total "disorder," the church and its equipment were too filthy to use, and the capitals of the cofradías had disappeared or decayed; he worried, too, about "the many dangers to which I am exposed." Herrera was more right than he imagined, but he also soón discovered that many of his difficulties began at home. Only six months after he arrived the town rose up in a serious riot against him, an action brought on in part by the fears associated with a spreading cholera epidemic but aggravated by the activities of his own family. In particular, his brothers had availed themselves of Herrera's position to move to Jacaltenango and now monopolized local trade in "Spanish-style clothing, cacao, *petates* [woven mats], salt," and other commodities. They forced local Indians, including town officials, to carry their goods without pay, and while the young priest preached against drunkenness, they trafficked in aguardiente. By 1859 Herrera was desperate, driven to distraction by his isolation, his parishioners' recalcitrance, and his family's activities. Repeatedly he sent petitions to Guatemala City begging for a new post. The Archbishop somehow found a replacement, but on arriving the new priest surveyed the situation and left the same day. At this point Herrera, too, and without permission, abandoned Jacaltenango and took refuge in Quezaltenango. By October 1859 the Archbishop had appointed yet another priest for Jacaltenango, but already this one was complaining of the "indomitable character of these my parishioners" who had stopped his food over some disagreement.[15]

Contradictions and conflicts always had existed in Guatemala's Indian communities between orthodox Catholicism and traditional religious practices, but these seem to have surfaced more frequently with the weakening of the state after 1800.[16] The Indians of Chiquimulilla, for example, fell afoul of the state in these years by blatantly and persistently resorting to witchcraft in their efforts to control the rains upon which their crops depended ("to close the north and contain the rain or call it").[17] When a crisis threatened, local leaders met at a site "left by the ancients" where they invoked the name of Santísima Trinidad and chanted traditional formulas. Repeatedly state agents intervened in these rites, burning the ritual location, arresting the participants and having them publicly beaten, but this had little effect. When the governor's men imprisoned the leaders, the people of the community burned down the jail and released them. In defending his inability to put a stop to these activities, the departmental governor argued that a similar investigation among other towns in the highlands would reveal equal or more "ridiculous superstition" there. Probably this was true. The priest of Jacaltenango in 1815 questioned a local woman about secret religious practices. She reported that the sacristans of the church "are designated by the town council and the elders to make the prayers they are accustomed to do at the places called cuman najat during certain times of the year, taking with them a number of candles that they light before the images and a bowl of turkey or chicken blood they mix with incense; there they pray for good harvests and the health of the people." The sacristans also served as diviners, telling the future by casting colored beans, and they heard the confession of sins, because the church was "very expensive."[18] When cholera swept the altiplano in 1857 the inhabitants of San Mateo Ixtatán turned on themselves, hanging or burning alive ten or eleven villagers who they claimed had used witchcraft to bring the plague on the community. This was not a riot but carefully planned justice, arranged and sanctioned by local officials.[19]

Priests tended to ignore the deviant religious activities of the Indians, turning a more or less blind eye to all but the most blatant aberrations of their charges. Few wished to imperil their livelihood, or perhaps their life, and, in any event, there was little they could do about the Indians' unsanctioned activities, in the forest or even in the church itself. One described the daily scene in his church with distaste and fear: "They draw close to the altars, they kiss them, carrying their children in their arms, and they swing clay censers and carry on in a manner not worthy of His Sacred Holy Majesty." It did no good to attempt to correct them, he added, "because they respect only what, in their judgment, religion demands and what they feel is the proper way to please God."[20] Occasionally a priest made a stand: Presbítero Vicente Hernandez, cura of Santa Catarina Ixtahuacán in the 1850's, learned enough about the activities of the "priests of the sun," as he labeled the Indian religious leaders, to understand and use to his own advantage the Maya twenty-day calender, and he confronted the traditional religionists openly and drove them from the abandoned church they had appropriated for their rites.[21] But in the face of such attacks, a town could easily turn violent.[22] Villages also on occasion attempted to turn the table by bringing charges of witchcraft against the priest himself. In the last years of the colony, for example, the inhabitants of Chajul threatened the priest from Nebaj who served their church, claiming that "he walked abroad at night" with candles to "bewitch" the people and buried sacred objects to cast a spell and bring an epidemic on the community.[23] A half-century later another priest at Nebaj reported that recent disturbances in Chajul were merely the "fifth or sixth" such occurrence provoked by the activities of the Indian witch Xelop. "As usual," he wrote, she blamed an outbreak of disease on the priest.[24] The Indians of Comalapa made similar accusations against the assistant priest who served their town: "They accuse him of bringing death and illness with a candlestick in his hand."[25] And the people of Chiquimulilla wrote to the Archbishop that their priest "at night becomes a warlock, going out to poison the people."[26]

Cofradías

It was a measure of the weakening hold of the church on the communities that these years saw the transition of the cofradías from a state to an Indian institution. As we saw in the case of Chiquimulilla, a multi-cornered struggle not infrequently developed after 1821 for control of cofradía resources, a struggle that might pit secular Crown officials against the church, the church hierarchy against the local priest,[27] and the inhabitants of the communities against government and religious outsiders as well as against the priest. Pastoral visits by the archbishops of the late eighteenth and early nineteenth centuries regularly had taken note of the number and holdings of cofradías in each community; usually the prelate also sought to inspect the financial records of the groups, although not always with great success.[28] Popular resistance to what was seen by most Indians as prying stemmed in part from a reluctance to reveal to outsiders the extent of cofradía possessions and in part also from the fact that most of them had no license to exist, making them vulnerable to extortionate demands.[29]

By the standards of the time and place, some of the cofradías had substantial holdings in money, land, and animals. They rented out land or pasture, sold animals raised on cofradía or ejido land, and lent money at interest; some cofradías made and sold cotton thread and textiles or trafficked in illegal alcohol.[30] But the reforms of the last years of the colony and, even more seriously, the turbulence after 1821 damaged their holdings and undercut their financial condition. The consolidation of 1804 cost many cofradías loans, and the wars of the 1820's and 1830's ravaged their herds, as competing armies carried off horses and mules and slaughtered cattle.[31] The brotherhoods lost money when debtors went bankrupt or fled the country or when records disappeared in the violence. Individuals—sometimes the leaders of the cofradías themselves—and municipal corporations took advantage of the confusion to appropriate cofradía land and animals.[32] Over the course of the nineteenth century the possessions of most Indian cofradías declined dramatically (see Table 5.1). The priest of Chiquimulilla summed up the condition of many of them when he explained that "the wars, together with the mismanagement they have had, have made the cofradías disappear."[33]

Already by the 1830's the church and its parishioners were reporting that the indigenous population was "giving up" the cofradías and that more and more the Indians were refusing to serve.[34] At Sinacantán parish in the 1830's the Indians asked for a reduction or an end to cofradías. The Fiscal Protector, while admitting that they burdened the people, feared "the cofradías are the only resource that exists in those towns to maintain the Divine Cult."[35] Nevertheless, they were disappearing, or so it would seem from the correspondence of the time. The cofradías of Cuilco had been "lost"; in Mataquescuintla all was in "disarray"; Samayac, pleading poverty, asked to be allowed to

TABLE 5.1
Capitals of Cofradías in Selected Communities
(in pesos)

Town	1780's	1815	1850	1900
Santiago Atitlán	2,105	yes	"2,000"	none
Sta. Catarina Ix.	402	$ 250	?	none
Cobán	1,200	6,254	yes	none
Comalapa	711	1,911	?	none
Cubulco	1,102	638	"decayed"	?
Chichicastenango	3,046		3,731	none
Joyabaj	1,496		"little attention"	"custom"
Salamá	965	"decadent"	yes	?
Jacaltenango	853	710	yes	?
Nebaj	795		"increased"	none

SOURCE: AHA, Visitas Pastorales.

abandon its cofradías; and Atitlán protested that, under the law, "no one can be forced to serve a cofradía."[36] Even as the traditional cofradías disappeared, however, there arose increasing numbers of "illegal" organizations, sometimes also called cofradías by the Indians, or *guachivales*. Not controlled by the church, these new groups excluded the priest from all but his most necessary religious activities. "They have nothing to do with the cura," the priest of Zunil complained, and the money they raised they spent "to pay for the prayers and the hospitality of the cofradías in the houses and for fireworks, music, and alcohol, all in the name of piety."[37] "Even if you ask them, the Indians will not give an accounting," another priest protested.[38] By the second half of the century the archbishops on their visits routinely reported that there were no functioning cofradías in many of the Indian towns, and community members showed little interest in joining new church-regulated lay societies.[39]

Yet anthropologists studying the same communities in the 1930's and 1940's found that effective local governance, that is, the cargo system, was rooted in very active cofradías.[40] What had happened? Over the course of the nineteenth century, the cofradías escaped what had always been less than perfect church control to become Indian institutions that served chiefly Indian purposes.[41] The wars, turbulence, and reforms of the nineteenth century stripped the cofradías of much of their material resources and reserves. The priests and the Archbishop lost interest in the day-to-day operations of these groups, expecting instead only payment for the services they were asked to provide. A weakened church with a declining number of clergy and scant funds and meeting increased resistance among the indigenous population was, in any event, in no position to assert close supervision over the villages or their institutions. It could not and dared not press unwanted attention upon the Indians.

Too, because of their losses, the cofradías could no longer pay for masses and other ritual expenses out of available funds. The emphasis shifted to raising money from donations, "from the piety of those who wish to contribute,"[42] and from members. In particular, the mayordomos personally and individually took on the responsibility (the *cargo*) of financing the required celebrations: "It is almost universally the case that the leaders suffer the costs of fulfilling the cofradía's obligations."[43] The final blow was the Liberal nationalization of church property in 1873. Most governors took this to include what remained of the possessions of the brotherhoods. The form and function of the cofradías and the system of individual cargos that anthropologists found to be widespread in Guatemala in the 1930's were a product not of the distant colonial past but of the turbulent nineteenth century. The cofradía became an Indian institution when the state and church no longer would or could assert control over it, allowing the indigenous population to convert cofradías to its own purposes.

The State and the Community

Among the indigenous population the most evident consequence of the unaccustomed autonomy afforded them by the ebbing of state and church authority was the opportunity for an enthusiastic quarrelsomeness. The Indians fought among themselves, with their neighbors, and with the agents of the new national governments. Villages disputed the activities of local officials and intrusive ladinos, the cura, and the state, particularly where it sought to alter custom or to collect taxes. Above all they disputed land, always a matter of contention between the Indian towns but the more so now under a weakened central regime. In efforts to bring the land problem under control, national governments in the 1830's and again in the 1850's appointed survey commissions charged with measuring the boundaries and the community lands of the towns of the western highlands and with settling land disputes.[44] The task was massive and success elusive. The 1830's commission, for example, reported in 1835–36 that it had resolved, or so it imagined, disputes between: "Santo Tomás Chichicastenango and Totonicapán, Sololá, Concepción, and Tecpán Guatemala; Santo Tomás Chiché and Chinique and the hacienda Tululché; Chinique and Chiché, Quiché, and Tululché; San Pedro Jocopilas and San Bartolomé Jocotenango; San Bartolomé Jocotenango and San Pedro Jocopilas and Sacapulas; San Andrés Semetabaj and Chinique and Canilla."[45] But with each shift in government the losers in the most recent round of confrontations opened the matter anew, initiating a new round of protests, measurements, and appeals for "justice." The 1850's commission found the situation in the countryside little improved. A bewildered chief engineer reported a farrago of conflict in the area north of Lake Atitlán precisely where the 1830's commission imagined that it had straightened things out, conflicts that set: "Sololá against S.M. Totonicapán, hacienda Argueta, Santo Tomás Chichicastenango, and Concepción Chiquirichapa; Santo Tomás Chichicastenango against Sololá, Tecpán Guatemala, Chiché, and Totonicapán; Chiché against hacienda Tululché, and Chinique; Zacualpa against Canilla, and haciendas Tululché and Chuacorral; Santa Catarina Ixtahuacán against Zunil, Cantel, Santa Clara la Laguna, and others."[46]

The disputes between Chichicastenango and San Miguel Totonicapán, between Jacaltenango and San Miguel Acatán, and between San Antonio Suchitepéquez and nearly all the other towns in the department were typical of the period. The origins of the conflict between Chichicastenango and Totonicapán were, the governor of Quiché said, "almost lost in the night of time."[47] The 1836 commission had found no evidence to support extravagant claims made by Chichicastenango and instead awarded a contested 122 caballerías to Totonicapán, a "numerous and industrious people."[48] But the maxeños refused to vacate the area, provoking armed clashes between the towns, "fire and death," and the intervention of the militia.[49] Jacaltenango similarly fought for much of the century with San Miguel Acatán and others of its neighbors over boundaries.[50] These problems, too, had deep roots, going at least as far back as the early eighteenth century. They erupted anew in 1812 when Jacaltenango asked for copies to be made of its worn and illegible "titles" and for an increase in its ejidos as promised in a recent decree of the Spanish Cortes. An examination of the papers offered showed that although Jacaltenango possessed many land documents it had no title. For the next half-century the town paid repeatedly for measurements of its común, but for one reason and another the measurements never took effect. As one result, the inhabitants repeatedly fought San Miguel Acatán "with sticks" along their mutual boundary, leaving an inheritance of death and hostility. The new state sent a surveyor to the south coast shortly after independence in hopes of resolving the many land disputes that had long been a feature of life in Suchitepéquez.[51] He met with massive resistance: neither the towns nor the haciendas would show their papers, and the priest at San Antonio Suchitepéquez, who himself profited from renting out what the town claimed was "ejido" land, confronted the surveyor, questioning his authority and stirring up the population against him. The agitation forced the engineer to quit the province with the measurements unfinished.

Open conflict and violence between communities worsened as the state retreated to the cities and to the grana-growing regions around Amatitlán and Antigua. Almost every village had its tales of armed atrocities perpetrated against it by its neighbors. Towns raided one another's fields, carrying off animals and harvesting or destroying crops, burning buildings, and moving or smashing boundary markers. The not uncommon result was large-scale confrontations and pitched battles that involved hundreds, even thousands, of Indians and resulted in dozens of dead and wounded; only the small number of firearms in the highland towns kept the toll of injuries and deaths relatively low.[52] With a weak state and without adequate documents or surveys, or a willingness to accept what these declared, the parties involved rarely were able to resolve anything definitively; and so the cycles of violence persisted. A judge explained of a battle between San Juan La Laguna and Santa Clara: "In general no one knows who participated in the attacks, and despite repeated orders it has proved impossible to capture even those that are known. As a result the legal case is sunk in confusion and obscurity and cannot be resolved, and there seems no hope of resolving it."[53]

The towns fought not only each other but also, of course, the haciendas. Because of the more pervasive presence of ladinos in the Oriente and the relative decay of the Indian towns, haciendas there tended to be larger, more aggressive, and more successful in their land conflicts with the communities than elsewhere. Mataquescuintla, for example, complained in the 1780's that the ladino Jáuregui family had usurped four caballerías of its land and then bribed the town secretary—who probably was a ladino—to provide them spurious papers that supported their claim. The Jáureguis countered that they had

legitimate title to the four caballerías and demanded that the town return the animals and corn they claimed the villagers had stolen. When
the Audiencia ruled in favor of the Jáureguis, Mataquescuintla promised to comply, but five years later the community had not vacated the
land or returned the stolen property, and now the family protested
that a subdelegate was stirring up the population against them, "to
the point of drafting" their petitions. These Indians were "the most
troublesome" in the province, they said, and sought the land only to be
able to live like "animals" far from state and church control. Besides
its argument with the Jáureguis, Mataquescuintla also disputed other
haciendas for possession of another piece of nearby property called
La Sierra. Neither the town nor the haciendas involved could produce
adequate titles, but when Mataquescuintla tried to plant the area the
landowners loosed cattle on the Indians' corn. In the 1820's the government auctioned the land in question to a private individual. He
was unable to take possession before the uprisings of the War of the
Mountain "paralyzed" the situation for a generation, leaving effective
control in the hands of the townsfolk.[54]

Another land tangle in the Oriente that went on for much of the
nineteenth century involved the "community of Indians" of Jutiapa
and the hacienda San Antonio that belonged to the wealthy Nájera
family.[55] The Indians claimed that their village had "been robbed
again and again," and several times they rioted against the reputed
abuses of the Nájeras. These included, the Indians said, using the
family's power to sway the Audiencia, bribing surveyors, and having
the Indians unfairly charged court costs and getting them jailed. Government engineers sent to resolve the conflict discovered that as a
result of confused measurements and inadequate documentation, the
community was uncertain of its rights: "Because of this ignorance
they live totally subordinated to the haciendas, and such is the damage they suffer from the ladinos' cattle that were it not for the doors
the animals would be in the church." Repeated protests and investi-
gations finally uncovered the source of the problems. At some point
during the colonial period the town had been forced to abandon an
earlier site because of flooding from the Cal and Salitre rivers. The
distances involved made it all but impossible for the community to control the ejidos that surrounded the former location, which included
much better land than where they had been forced to resettle. Ladinos moved into the ejidos, loosing their cattle on the corn plantings
and driving the Indians out. Now the ladinos were attempting to title

the land. Although the community could claim two hundred years of rights to the disputed area, the Nájeras and other hacienda owners could point to eighty years of possession. President Carrera interceded. He arranged for the Nájera family to cede 43 caballerías to the town and to sell the state an additional 100 caballerías, 50 of which he had deeded to the Indians of Jutiapa and 50 to the ladinos of the town.

Disputes in the western highlands between the few haciendas and nearby Indian towns also intensified in the years after 1800. Chichicastenango and its neighbors, for example, besides feuding with each other, disputed boundaries with the Dominicans' hacienda Chiché.[56] In 1811 Chichicastenango lost a land case against Chiché, but instead of vacating the area disputed, the Indians cleared more ground in order to establish a de facto claim. As the maxeños explained the history, the land in question had always belonged to them, but at some point in the past they had "lent" (rented?) it to "one Barrutia," who upon becoming a Dominican illegally gave it to the order. The postindependence government continued to deny Chichicastenango's claim, however, and in 1834, after the confiscations of the properties of the regular orders, the state sold the hacienda to Lucas Pérez. The unfortunate Pérez and his descendants spent the next thirty years locked in a guerrilla war with neighboring communities, hounded, a representative complained, by the Indians' "insatiable thirst for land." The hacienda armed its renters and resident laborers to resist Indians from nearby towns who stole animals and burned crops. At one point two hundred Indians from Zacualpa launched a frontal assault on the main buildings of the property in an unsuccessful effort to capture or destroy the hacienda's papers and titles. Repeatedly the state ordered the Indians to abandon disputed areas, but they refused, and the state was unable to force them to comply. In 1867, the family fortune "destroyed," Vicente Pérez sold out.

By contrast, on the south coast, San Francisco Zapotitlán's old nemesis Luís Valladares made himself the "semi-king" of the region in the years after independence: "The governors fear him because of his money and his greed, opening the way for despotism," the villages complained.[57] With a promise to help them defend their lands, Valladares convinced the officials of San Antonio Suchitepéquez to let him take temporary possession of the community's titles. Not very mysteriously these disappeared. A subsequent attempt by San Antonio in the 1850's to map its ejidos revealed many ladino haciendas in the area claimed by the town, including not only Valladares's but Rafael

Carrera's Las Animas de Sumay and the Batres family's enormous La Grande. The government rejected this measurement as inaccurate, but because the surveyor had died, San Antonio could neither recover the 500 pesos it had paid him nor title its ejidos. Farther south along the coast at Chiquimulilla, and perhaps ironically given the frequent heavy rainfall in the area, conflicts focused not just on land but also on water rights.[58] The town, together with Taxisco and Guazacapán, for decades fought hacienda Chiquiquistán for possession of "lakes, rivers, [and] waters to the sea," as well as the land or bar formed where these rivers met the Pacific. At stake was the right to fish and make salt and to have access to marsh and grazing land. The government finally worked out a compromise whereby the hacienda gained possession of fourteen caballerías on the mainland while the town received confirmation of access to the waterways and use and possession of the eighteen caballerías of bar.

Highland towns planted new settlements or colonies and resettled "extinguished" towns on the south coast. The process was haphazard, and how it occurred must have varied greatly from one instance to another, but such colonizations accelerated in the nineteenth century. By 1849, for example, most of the original inhabitants of San Francisco Zapotitlán had succumbed to the ravages of ladino-owned cattle. Outsiders from the piedmont and highlands were "repopulating" the site, as they were nearby San Pablo Jocopilas.[59] The few remaining inhabitants of San Gabriel and San Lorenzo Mazatenango to the south claimed that the invasion of the coast by highland Indians was forcing them farther toward the sea and on to poorer-quality lands.[60]

No town in the western highlands sought out new land in the hot country more aggressively than did Zunil, a village located in a valley where the Samalá River wound steeply down from the plains of Quezaltenango toward the sea. It was, the justicias explained, in the most broken part of the mountains amid "heaps of stone"; for seven leagues around there was no space to expand their plantings. The inhabitants had lost much of the ejidos they once possessed, and to which they had a right, to the "armed" aggressions of their neighbors, in particular Santa Catarina Ixtahuacán. In 1777 the town applied to the Audiencia for land in what had been the ejidos of the "extinguished" town of Santo Tomás Perdido (La Unión). The subdelegate measured Zunil 67 caballerías, part as an ejido for the new settlers of Santo Tomás and part in moderated composition to Zunil itself, indicating that the town's inhabitants must already have been cultivating the area for some time. This grant quickly ran up against the "pretensions" and "arrogant insolence" of Santa Catarina Ixtahuacán, which protested the decision but refused to produce a title to the area. They had no need of documents, the townspeople said, because they recognized as theirs what their ancestors had recognized.[61] Although the conflict dragged on through riots and court cases without a definite result, Zunil had established a legal right to the area around Santo Tomás and settlers poured in.[62] Emigrants from Zunil also colonized the decayed village of San Felipe, titling there 68 caballerías, and settled what became the towns of Zunilito and Pueblo Nuevo.[63]

A dispute over the ownership of nearby El Palmar similarly set Zunil's neighbor Santa María de Jesús against the highland town of Momostenango. The fierce momostecos protested that without access to this hot-country land they would be reduced to the "poverty" of the 53 caballerías of ejido adjacent to the town itself, land consisting of "gorges, hills, and stony ground that bears no fruit." Not only had they measured and composed the 133 caballerías in question as far back as the sixteenth century, town leaders claimed, but Momostenango also had rights in the area based on their upkeep "from time immemorial" of a bridge that crossed the Samalá River there. Santa María rejected both the validity of Momostenango's titles and the town's claims to the exclusive right to maintain the bridge. The inhabitants of the two villages fought when they met on the roads. It was undeniable, however, that by the mid-nineteenth century El Palmar was populated almost entirely by migrants from Momostenango. In 1857 Momostenango's priest blessed a chapel and cemetery for the lowland settlement, noting more than 120 huts and more people arriving every day from the highlands. "Almost all [the Indians] speak Spanish except for the most recent arrivals," he noted, but they continued to think of themselves as subject to Momostenango and recognized civil and religious officials appointed from that town. By the 1860's El Palmar had a population of several hundred families, most of whom spent part of the year there and part of it in Momostenango.[64]

Highland towns had fewer problems when they sought land in the northern hot country. Villages such as Soloma, Jacaltenango, and Santa Eulalia in the Cuchumatanes, the Ixil towns of northern Quiché, and the communities in the upper Verapaz all used tracts in the northern lowlands.[65] In 1812 the governor of the Verapaz inspected an area cultivated by Indians from San Cristóbal Cajcoj (Verapaz) eight leagues northwest of the town along the Chixoy River. "They go from place to place cultivating only the best areas," he reported, gathering three or four harvests a year. The land had the advantage, too, of being distant enough from ladino settlements to be safe from their cattle. As population pressures mounted in some highland towns during the nineteenth century, access to hot-country land in the northern or southern lowlands would become increasingly important.

Land Conflicts Within the Communities

Although struggles against neighbors and the state may in some cases have helped to create and maintain a sense of unity within communities,[66] one should not draw from this sort of functionalism a false or idealized vision of village life. Individuals, settlements, and kin-based groups within Guatemala's indigenous communities also fought each other over land and for political-religious independence quite as regularly and as energetically as they did outsiders. Political autonomy, for example, was in theory not difficult to achieve: the 1836 regulations for town government provided that any "town, hamlet, or spot that by itself or in the area has two hundred inhabitants" could qualify as a separate, self-governing municipality.[67] But because the aspirant town also had to be able to pay the costs of erecting the necessary buildings and of supporting a governing bureaucracy, municipal status in practice tended to be limited to much larger settlements than the minimum the law allowed. When the settlement of María applied in 1870 for independence from Jocotán, for example, investigation showed a population of some 2,500 scattered in the area, a number that the governor said "seemed adequate"; nevertheless, the inhabitants failed to follow through with the split.[68]

The history of nineteenth-century San Pedro Sacatepéquez (Guatemala) illustrates the breakup over time of one town into several municipalities as well as some of the difficulties this involved. Shortly after independence the priest of San Pedro noted that the town had two "estancias," or colonies, San Antonio (then Nacahuil, now Las Flores) six leagues to the northeast, and (San Pedro) Ayampuc, at nine leagues, and that beyond these were another thousand sanpedreños at the settlement of Chuarrancho. Because these people lived so far from San Pedro it was difficult for them to participate in community life, and almost impossible for them to bring to the town infants for baptism and bodies for burial, and they were unhappy with this. San Antonio therefore sought, and gained, independent municipal status in the 1830's. But during the following decade the new town complained that it did not have enough land for its population, and it disputed with San Pedro control of the settlements of San José Nacahuil and Chillani. By the 1870's San José Nacahuil in turn was asserting its independence both of San Pedro and of San Antonio, complaining that because of rivalries between these towns they had been "sacked, beaten, and mistreated in the most cruel manner" and forced to give labor and service in both communities. In 1884 Chuarrancho also gained municipal independence. San Pedro Sacatepéquez claimed that as a result of the separations it was left with the worst land. Town leaders continued to deny the legality of the new municipalities or their titles to San Pedro's former lands and demanded that they be reunited under San Pedro's control.[69] If the state regularly created and suppressed municipalities, rarely did the losers accept these innovations gracefully, and struggles, conflicts, and bad feeling commonly persisted.[70]

Very little evidence of the individual quarrels over land among families or members of the indigenous communities during the nineteenth century survives in the records, in great part because, at least until the 1920's, most problems of this sort were resolved by verbal decisions of the town's justicias. Only rarely, both because of respect for custom and because of the costs and dangers of submitting themselves to ladino law, did the Indians appeal intracommunity disputes to the inaccurately named courts of First Instance (Primera Instancia) in the department capitals. But that conflicts existed is clear. In Huehuetenango, for example, the governor complained in the early 1870's that disputes in the communities were interminable and defied resolution. As many as four different persons had "title" to a given piece of land, he said, and the handwriting and condition of the few documents that existed made them almost illegible.[71] And in Momostenango "conflicts over land arose among the different groups of Indians themselves."[72]

Testimony given in a series of cases originating at Cobán probably provides a typical picture, although the upper Verapaz remained even more isolated from contact with ladinos than did much of the rest of the country, at least until the mid-nineteenth century. In 1785 an Indian of local elite status applied to title as individual property a tract of land called Chichén located two leagues north of Cobán. Local leaders (called *chimanes* in the Alta Verapaz) and the people of Cobán strongly resisted this, claiming that Chichén was part of their common lands and was needed to support the town's large population.

Although not denying that the applicant had possessed land in the area in question "from time immemorial," no one in the municipality, they argued, "bought [land] from the king." Indeed, the cobaneros had a very attenuated sense of the legal difference between community land and state land: "They do not know what belongs to the king, [but] are accustomed to buying and selling among themselves the portions of land they have acquired through their work. He who cuts back the high brush and cultivates the land makes himself the owner of it and sells it to whomever he wishes or leaves it to his heirs."[73] To acknowledge state baldío and to title portions of this as private property would upset the established local system of "government." Of course, this "government," as the Indians themselves admitted, was one of nearly constant conflict between individuals and groups over boundaries and possession rights, but it was conflict resolved within the customary framework of their own institutions and without resort to Spanish law or the Crown's officials. Over the next half-century other local Indian elites attempted to put individual title to parcels of land in areas that most residents of Cobán considered to be part of the community's common lands. The general population persisted in opposing this and on more than one occasion took up arms to thwart the designs of the "rich."[74]

Not all justicias proved as attentive to the needs or wishes of the community as those of Cobán. Petitions from the towns detailing the abuses of village officials were almost as numerous as petitions against priests. The accusations usually had to do with taxes, labor recruitment, and repartimientos of goods and thread, but there were complaints, too, against officials who used their position to take over land and promote their agricultural interests: "They act with partiality or out of revenge, which is very common in these small towns."[75] The worst offenders by far seem to have been the gobernadores, who were appointed by the departmental governor to represent state interests in the villages. Chiquimulilla, for example, in 1799 accused their gobernador of forcing town officials to work his land without pay, of demanding a "box" and thirty or forty "nets" of corn a week from the community's plantings, and of taking all of the irrigated corn land for himself.[76] The gobernador shared power in a vaguely defined manner with the town council, the elders, and other justicias, and for reasons of prestige was supposed to be selected from among the descendants of the local hereditary elites. But by the late colonial and early national period the departmental governors made and broke these officials so casually and arbitrarily that they commanded little respect in most communities. As the state weakened, so did their power. Perhaps because they lacked the base of popular support usually enjoyed by the other justicias who had worked their way up through the cofradías and the cargo system and because their position in the local hierarchy was so vaguely defined, gobernadores in the eighteenth and early nineteenth centuries appear to have been particularly abusive and rapacious in their treatment of their fellow Indians. In the confusion after independence many found opportunities to appropriate land and animals belonging to the cofradías and the community or funds from the town caja. When a government surveyor in 1859 checked land measurements near Samayac, for example, he found—and this must have been fairly common—that the gobernador for years had claimed and used as his own large tracts of the town's common lands.[77] It can hardly be surprising that riots and uprisings against the activities of gobernadores pepper the records.[78]

The Nature of Conflict

Villages fought over land among themselves and against nearby haciendas for various reasons, including economic need and population growth, control of religious and cult sites, to subordinate or keep subordinated other settlements, and to assert control over areas vacated by the population shifts resulting from congregation, natural disasters, or the effects of disease. However, although they often complained that because of land invasions and usurpation by neighbors they no longer had sufficient land to support their populations, they almost never articulated demands or petitions for land in terms of future population growth.[79] This was logical for a people accustomed to at best slow population increases punctuated by unpredictable and sudden, sharp declines brought on by recurring local outbreaks of famine and disease (see Table 5.2). Epidemics time and again swept the countryside.[80] Because of the political revolt it helped touch off, the 1836–37 cholera outbreak is the best known of the postindependence epidemic,[81] but a second outbreak of cholera in 1857, spread by the armies returning from the campaign against William Walker, probably caused even more widespread loss of life. A comparison made by the priest at Santa Cruz Quiché, for example, showed the second epidemic to have had a much more devastating impact on several of the towns in his district than that of 1836–37 (see Table 5.3).

TABLE 5.2
Incidence of Disease in Four Areas

Santiago Atitlán	Jocotán	Totonicapán	Cuchumatanes
1797–99 typhus	1777 "many deaths"	1780–81 smallpox	1777 "pests"
1800–1855 (var.)	1801 locust plague	1795–97	1780–81
yellow fever	1802 epidemic	typhus/smallpox	smallpox
1804 smallpox	1804 famine	1804 typhus/measles	1786 typhus
1820 smallpox	1805 epidemic	1811–12 typhus	1795 smallpox
1826 measles	1819 smallpox	1826 measles	1796–99 typhus
1829 smallpox		1830–31 yellow fever	1802–7 typhus
1832–34 cholera		1841 whooping	1803–7 smallpox
1836–37 whooping		cough	1804–5 measles
cough			1811 "fever"
1857 cholera			1812 "plague"
			1812–14 typhus
			1818–19 typhus

SOURCES: Madigan, "Santiago Atitlán," p. 183; Feldman, "Disasters," p. 59, Veblen, "Forest Preservation in Totonicapán," p. 345; Lovell, *Conquest and Survival*, pp. 151–53.

TABLE 5.3
*Cholera Victims in Quiché Towns, 1837 versus 1857
as Reported by Cura of Santa Cruz del Quiché*

	Years	
Town	1837	1857
Quiché	140	239
Jocopilas	79	174
Jocotenango	181	207
Patzité	?	160
Lemoa	66	127

SOURCE: AHA, Cartas, "Estadística de Kiché," Dec. 1, 1858, no. 341.

Nevertheless, the population generally appears to have begun to grow strongly in the last years of the colony and to have continued to increase at a rate of at least one percent a year during the first half-century after independence (see Appendix A).[82] The growth was not distributed evenly over time and between communities: villages on main trade and communications routes, such as Santiago Atitlán, and those along the "royal highway" to Chiapas probably suffered more from disease than did relatively more isolated communities.[83] But because there were few population counts—as opposed to estimates— done between the end of tribute and the first national-period census taken in 1880, it is difficult to arrive at accurate population figures for these years. Also, at least until the end of the nineteenth century, it is necessary to distinguish global trends from the extreme instability likely to have been experienced in any given community.

For the same reasons of local variability, it is often difficult to understand the exact content or reasons underlying specific land disputes. This uncertainty is in part an artifact of available materials. Boundary descriptions were vague, not always by accident, and rarely was a piece of land or the uses to which it might be put described in any detail. Because the people immediately involved in most cases had an intimate knowledge of the area disputed, they saw no need to detail the obvious, to the immense frustration of judges and surveyors. Participants regularly lied, and they altered or withheld documents or information that might prejudice their claims. Claimants made their cases in apocalyptic terms, anticipating death and ruin for the community, and, in the appeal most calculated to sway the state to their side, an inability to pay taxes and fees if they were granted less than their maximum demands. The patches of good land tucked in the folds of the mountains provoked the most acute battles. The towns of Cantel, Totonicapán, and Santa Catarina Ixtahuacán, for example, had hundreds of acres of ejidos, but most of this was good only for pasture and potatoes; they fought for more than a century among themselves and with a neighboring hacienda over a few caballerías of corn land at Parrasquín.[84] Over all, though, much of the area disputed among communities in the western highlands seems to the outsider to have been so poor, rocky, and without water as to have had little obvious economic value to anyone. Surveyors routinely found the cultivations of inhabitants of nearby communities intermixed along mutual boundaries. Except where land was at a premium or where conflict developed for other reasons, neighbors did not always know, or at least did not press, exact boundaries. It may be, therefore, that some conflicts over land did have less to do with economic concerns than with the reinforcement of internal unity and the routine boundary maintenance that is part of the constitution and reaffirmation of community identity. One can easily imagine the jacaltecos confronting the inhabitants of San Miguel Acatán with "the sound of drums, marimbas and trumpets, showers of rockets, and hurrahs for the government and the authorities"[85] each time a measurement went their way.

Despite the political turbulence and violence that permeated much of the countryside, the Caste Wars of Yucatán and the War of Saint

Rose in Chiapas did not spread into the western highlands of Guatemala. Certainly the ladinos feared that they might, and they saw the
horrors of race war in every sign of Indian unrest.[86] One reason for this
relative quiescence was that the Indians of Guatemala had participated
in the apparently successful uprising in the 1830's that removed the
Liberals and the source of much of their immediate irritation. Land
disputes in the Oriente involving Indians chiefly set towns against
haciendas, but those of the western highlands more commonly pitted
indigenous communities against one another, fragmenting rather than
uniting the rural indigenous population. Intertwined with existing differences of language, costume, and custom, these conflicts created conditions that limited the possibilities for bringing the Indians together.
In both Chiapas and Yucatán a key element in breaking down similar
but perhaps less intense local differences was messianic religion, but
this failed to develop during these years in any significant way among
Guatemala's highlands populations. If messiahs appeared, they gained
no wide support. Ironically, the closest thing to a highlands-wide cult
was the folk memory of the failed Liberal rebel Serapio Cruz that grew
up after he was beheaded in 1870 and continued to fuel revolts at least
as late as the 1880's.[87] Although every report of rural unrest in the
1840's and 1850's panicked the ladinos and the state, "caste" violence
never engulfed them and the communities' attention remained largely
fixed on their immediate neighbors.

A Case Study: Santa Catarina Ixtahuacán

Situated to the west of Lake Atitlán, Santa Catarina Ixtahuacán was
a Quiché-speaking Indian town with a population of 10,000–15,000
in the mid-1850's, but the municipality was poor and not well endowed
with land: "The lands belonging to Santa Catarina measure 12 leagues
by 6 or 7 leagues but in general are broken, rocky, and inaccessible."[88]
The catarinecos rented land where they could, pressed claims against
their neighbors, and invaded and squatted on baldíos. They were a
hard-working people, and one of the few highland municipalities to
enforce a ban on alcohol sales, but they had a well-justified reputation for aggressive and bellicose behavior in their relations with other
Indian towns and with the state: "They have no respect for God or the
king or the governor or their priest or any other official," the hapless
governor of Sololá explained.[89] In the last years of the colony and for

a half-century after independence they fought incessantly with Zunil and Cantel, both of which had similar land-shortage problems, and with the owners of the hacienda Urbina, and they battled San Miguel Totonicapán and Santa María Chiquimula for the land at Patzité.[90] Santa Catarina occupied land belonging to Santa Clara La Laguna and ignored repeated government orders to leave.[91] The amounts of land involved in these disputes were small, but in each case the claimants protested that they represented a substantial part of the worthwhile land available to them.

Santa Catarina also attempted in these years to gain control of a much larger area of hot-country land at Parraché on the south coast. This ambition ranged the community against various haciendas and the towns of Zunil, Santo Tomás Perdido (La Unión), and San Francisco Zapotitlán, as well as the national government. At stake was possession of almost 200 caballerías in what had been the ejidos of the "extinguished town of [Santiago] Zambo." The catarinecos had long made use of this land for their hot-country corn plantings, occupying it both as squatters and as renters from the hacienda Chocolá. When a remeasurement in the 1830's showed that the hacienda had no right to the tract developed by the Santa Catarina migrants, ladino speculators applied to buy it from the state. They then traded these so-called "rights of denuncia," that is, the priority right of application, among themselves as if these were property titles. On this basis they attempted also to collect rent from the Indians. The inhabitants of Santa Catarina protested loudly, pointing out that they had occupied and cultivated much of the area for years and should have had the opportunity to buy it. The many evident illegalities in the earlier transactions prompted the government in the 1850's to invalidate existing claims and carry out a full remeasurement and sale of the disputed area. Santa Catarina bought most of the land, some 188.5 caballerías. The final agreement provided that out of this area the catarinecos were to turn over eighteen caballerías to Zunil to compensate that community for land Santa Catarina had earlier invaded. Santa Catarina resisted doing this, and conflict dragged on for several more decades with the state unable to end it or to force the catarinecos to comply with its orders.[92]

At the same time that it was engaged in disputes with other municipalities and the state, Santa Catarina also found it necessary to resist what the justicias and population perceived as internal threats to the integrity of the community. In 1777, Santa Catarina Ixtahuacán and the inhabitants of the "almost extinguished" town of San Miguelito to the south had successfully petitioned the Audiencia to allow the latter to become part of Santa Catarina.[93] In the years after independence the priest of Santa Catarina removed the images from the run-down church in San Miguelito and took them to Santa Catarina. Because of its isolated location, San Miguelito had become something of a refuge for criminals, and because the "bad habits" of the inhabitants made them susceptible to disease, the priest of Santa Catarina felt that the town was in irreversible decline.[94] But by the 1840's this state of affairs apparently had reversed itself, and the people of San Miguelito were increasingly unhappy at having to do service in the government and church of Santa Catarina. They talked of regaining municipal independence and control over their community lands.[95] This infuriated the catarinecos, and in 1852, led by their gobernador Manuel Tzoc, the town of Santa Catarina, together with the large settlement of Nahualá located in the northern part of the municipality, assaulted and sacked San Miguelito. The people of San Miguelito fled into exile on haciendas and in towns on the south coast. Even there the catarinecos pursued and attacked them and defied government efforts to meliorate the situation. The governor could only warn the migueleños that any attempt on their part to return to their town would almost certainly provoke more violence. Twenty years later many of the migueleños had regrouped as the town of San Miguel Panán, but they still were petitioning for the return of the religious and personal items that had been taken from them by the catarinecos.[96]

Santa Catarina and Nahualá soon put aside their cooperation and were at each other's throats. The trouble originated in a growing imbalance in the distribution of population within the municipality, a situation not uncommon in rural areas as populations increased after mid-century. By the 1860's there were three main centers of settlement in the municipality of Santa Catarina Ixtahuacán: the town itself, with 6,000–7,000 inhabitants and dominated by the "party of the center" led by Miguel Salquil; Nahualá, to the north, with 11,000–12,000 people; and on the coast, an additional 9,000–10,000 people, roughly two-thirds of whom had migrated from Nahualá. The last two together constituted the "party of the mountain." Because of the distances and the difficulty of travel and because they outnumbered the residents of Santa Catarina proper, the partisans of Nahualá increasingly resented having to go the cabecera (head town) for community service and for their religious needs, and they resisted paying taxes that did them little good. Many died without the attentions of the church, the priest agreed, because of such problems.[97] The inhabitants of Santa Catarina, long accustomed to being the principal town in the municipality, more and more felt surrounded by hostile populations that threatened their prerogatives. The conflict between the center and the "mountain" was not new; it had provoked bloody riots for much of the preceding half-century. But tensions now mounted because of the settlement of Parraché, increases in population, and Santa Catarina's growing sense of encirclement.[98]

Attention came more and more to focus on the position and person of the gobernador. By custom the post in Santa Catarina was filled by election, subject to approval of the departmental governor. This meant that as the population of the "mountain" increased, the gobernador, although he resided and carried out his functions in Santa Catarina, came to represent, or at least to be identified with, the interests of Nahualá and the coast. Repeatedly the inhabitants of Santa Catarina rose against the real or imagined abuses of these gobernadores, prompting the governadores' supporters to rush to their rescue and sometimes touching off days of riots. Things came to a head in April 1865. There had been several days of protest in February against Manuel Tzoc, whose Nahualá origins made him suspect, and fights between partisans of the two groups broke out in the town, in the countryside, and even in neighboring municipalities. Early in April the government arrested two men who were caught carrying shot and powder to Santa Catarina.[99] But beset by political turmoil in the capital and weakened by the crisis in the cochineal industry, the government could no more assert control over the municipality or end these conflicts than it could protect the rights of the ex-inhabitants of San Miguelito. On April 17 violence exploded again. The catarinecos, led by Miguel Salquil, besieged a wounded Tzoc, his son, and the parish priest in the church residence. Tzoc's supporters hurried from Nahualá and in turn encircled the town. Fighting raged off and on for several days, leaving several dead and many injured. The governor of Sololá clearly had not the least idea of what was going on. He found a number of reasons to avoid exposing himself to the undoubted dangers of Santa Catarina, blamed the governors of surrounding districts for stirring up the problems there, and cheerfully contradicted himself from dispatch to dispatch.[100]

By April 20 the state had occupied Santa Catarina with a detachment of ladino militia, but even the militia was in danger from the catarinecos, and the soldiers did little beyond conspire to smuggle alcohol into the town. Although the government arrested anyone involved in the riots that the militia could catch, including Tzoc and some of the Salquil faction, outbreaks of fighting continued in the countryside, and both sides sent large delegations to the capital to plead their cases. Symbolic of the problem and the confusion surrounding it was a human head that made the rounds of various state offices, eventually taking on a certain Flying Dutchman quality. Whose head it was, and who had cut it off, no one seemed to know. In July a government delegation directed by a Supreme Court judge and protected by a strong armed escort arrived to attempt yet again to resolve the conflict. After first excluding those involved in the earlier disturbances, it held elections and left a garrison to protect the new authorities. Apparently feeling that they had come out on top, the catarinecos formally thanked the central government, but the nahualás continued to resist.[101] By December the priest was reporting that they still were not coming to mass or taking part in the *fiesta titular* (the annual celebration of the town's patron saint). Efforts to convince Tzoc, still in jail, to aid in the reconciliation elicited an angry display of wounds and threats of vengeance.[102]

With Tzoc and many of the salquiles at least temporarily out of the way, the locus of conflict shifted to the church. Not only did the partisans of Nahualá not wish to pay fees or do service to the benefit of the church in Santa Catarina, but, they said, they did not wish to come to mass where people threatened and spat on them and where they might be attacked at any moment. They wanted their own church. The people of Santa Catarina strongly resisted this, fearing the loss of payments and labor service and also suspecting that if allowed their own church the nahualás would also want to divide the images of the saints in the main church, an anathema to the deeply religious catarinecos. Furthermore, they argued, if Nahualá were allowed a church, it might seek independent municipal status and a division of community lands. The priest found himself caught in the middle, for almost any move to accommodate one side was bound to provoke anger from the other. Finally, in July 1866, Nahualá sent a delegation to the Archbishop to ask for a church.[103] After first attempting a compromise solution using a portable altar, the Archbishop allowed consecration of a chapel at Nahualá and the foundation there of five cofradías; he appointed an assistant priest to Santa Catarina to serve Nahualá. The village thus gained religious autonomy while the parish remained intact. Although

Nahualá soon put up a cabildo building and jail and often acted as if it were independent, it did not gain municipal status until the 1890's, and the two towns continued to hold their lands in common.[104]

Just as Nahualá found itself on the verge of achieving at least de facto independence from Santa Catarina, it became embroiled in its own conflict with surrounding settlements. These split among themselves over whether to follow Nahualá or to remain loyal to Santa Catarina. Based only on limited religious autonomy and without any footing in law or custom, Nahualá now sought to appoint subordinate civil officials in the surrounding hamlets, a policy that provoked disagreement and conflict among the populations. A judge who was sent to investigate learned that a group of nahualás recently had returned from Guatemala City with a bell for the new church and, they claimed, "orders to kill those of the town [Santa Catarina]."[105] The victims of Nahualá's alleged persecutions begged the judge to help, but without troops to protect himself or the petitioners he instead beat a quick retreat to Santa Catarina. Partisans of Nahualá continued to attack the uncooperative families and settlements, capturing their animals and dispersing the population.[106]

The ways in which the folk memories of the two communities recall these events are revealing.[107] According to the catarinecos, Tzoc and Miguel Salquil had been great friends in the days when Salquil was gobernador and Tzoc supervised the church, but they fell out over a woman. With the support of Nahualá, Tzoc won election as gobernador in 1862 and began to lord it over the catarinecos, imposing cruel and bizarre punishments. When he tried to do this to Salquil's son, the town rebelled, and the partisans of Nahualá rushed to attack Santa Catarina, surrounding the village and sealing the roads so that no one could escape. Fighting lasted for eight days, with much use of firearms and with the women of the town pouring boiling water laced with chiles on the invading nahualás. The government eventually learned what had happened and separated the towns into independent municipalities.

The inhabitants of Nahualá remember the events quite differently, and, with good reason, rather less dramatically. Tzoc is the founding hero.[108] Nahualá's story relates how Manuel Tzoc began to plant corn and wheat in an unused part of the community lands. When he found it to be of excellent quality, he brought his family to settle there and soon others followed. They were very religious and went each day to mass at Santa Catarina, but this was difficult because of the distance.

For the same reason it was almost impossible to carry out their necessary business with local officials in Santa Catarina. To remedy this the inhabitants of Nahualá established a new municipality. In fact, Nahualá as an identifiable settlement long predates the mid-nineteenth century, so the story told today is a romanticized myth of origin, contrived to establish the independence of Nahualá and to underplay the historical facts of conflict and a rupture of the ideal of community.

The histories of Santa Catarina and Nahualá illuminate the nature of community in Guatemala as a dynamic and flexible process rather than a fixed structure, constantly defining and redefining its population in terms of oppositions. "Community" was situationally determined and depended on the nature and site of conflict: the boundaries of what constituted the operant or applicable community shifted to meet specific situations and the immediate enemy. That unit usually associated with community in Mesoamérica, the municipality organized by the cargo system, has functioned chiefly in opposition to neighboring municipalities and the state. Whatever its utility in uniting the population against outside threats, the cargo system, even where reinforced by language and costume, did not necessarily guarantee a smoothing out of social or economic differences or suppress conflict within the community; that it might be able to do this became even less likely or possible as the effects of world capitalism increasingly penetrated the villages after 1860. Rather, multiple conflicts proceeded simultaneously at several levels, as the population re-formed and regrouped to meet each particular situation. Over the course of the nineteenth century, although internal disputes tore apart the "closed corporate community" of Santa Catarina Ixtahuacán, they in no sense destroyed the concept or the utility of the concept of "community" for the Indians.

Part II

The Coffee Revolution, 1860's–1940

Chapter 6

The Coffee Revolution

Because coffee is one of the branches of agriculture that in
this country offers the best results, it deserves the greatest
protection.   Decree 162, September 25, 1876

In the half-century after 1860 Guatemala underwent a revolution
that forever altered rural life. By definition, revolution changes the
established balance or order, improving the conditions or life chances
of some individuals and groups and at the same time damaging those
of others. So far as they can, the opposing groups react to further or to
protect their interests. From the 1850's, and at an increasing rate in the
1860's, the new export crop of coffee revolutionized the countryside
of Guatemala. Planters, made increasingly desperate by the declining
situation and prospects of the cochineal industry, and then merchants
after the mid-1850's, experimented with a variety of new export possibilities. None proved as promising as coffee: by 1871 it amounted to
half the value of the republic's overseas sales. Although coffee eventually would engage the resources of the Guatemalan countryside as no
commodity had ever done before, production expanded erratically, in
a rhythm driven by the ups and downs of the world market and conditioned by peculiar regional circumstances and patterns of acceptance
or resistance among the rural population. Coffee made its way in different regions of Guatemala at different times and in different forms;
each part of the country had its own coffee history.

Early History of Coffee in Guatemala

The coffee plant had grown in Guatemala from at least the eighteenth century, but until the 1830's it remained largely a decorative
bush and a novelty.[1] In the late 1820's, for example, travelers reported
that coffee beans were very difficult to buy and when found were more
expensive than in Europe.[2] During the 1830's cochineal seemed the
more promising crop and absorbed most of the resources available. A

few landowners attempted to lay out large-scale coffee plantations, and the government offered prizes and published pamphlets to encourage the crop, but ignorance of proper soil selection and cultivation techniques, together with the 1837–38 uprisings, brought these to nought.[3] With the return of peace, although cochineal dominated exports for the next two decades, an interest in coffee persisted, not as a substitute for but as a complement to the dye and as a hedge against the dangers of monoculture.[4] Cochineal continued to engage most of the available capital and labor. Newspapers and the Economic Society preached the example of Costa Rica and the possibilities of coffee, but by the end of the 1840's observers reported only a few small plantings around Antigua and Amatitlán.[5] Established producers are always reluctant to abandon a still profitable commodity even in the face of price instability and market uncertainty, and even when alternatives appear. Too, as long as Guatemala lacked adequate roads and ports, would-be coffee growers would find it difficult to compete with commodities such as cochineal that enjoyed high value per weight and volume.

Because merchant capital remained tied so tightly to the cochineal trade, it seemed to some that coffee offered an opportunity for the small producer who could grow it in conjunction with other crops. The state and the Economic Society, and after initial skepticism, the Consulado de Comercio, in the 1850's stepped up propaganda in favor of coffee, publishing instructions on how to cultivate and process the crop and offering prizes for the best results. The Economic Society imported hand-operated depulping machines to assist small growers in cleaning the coffee to export standards. A clear momentum in favor of coffee was gathering by the late 1850's, but obstacles remained, even beyond those of the ignorance of the proper techniques or poor roads and ports or labor shortages. And because in good years cochineal offered higher profits than coffee, with lower production costs, less capital investment, and a shorter time to fruition, it continued to reward the small grower's close attention. For the investor who thought about rooting up existing crops or clearing baldíos to attempt large coffee plantations, the risks were high. The lessons learned in Colombia and Costa Rica did not apply well to Guatemala, and experienced planters lost heavily in their attempts to establish groves in the hot and humid lowlands of Escuintla and Suchitepéquez. Such spectacular failures discouraged others who might have tried to essay coffee.[6] The Economic Society complained that when its members went door to door in the suburbs of the capital and in Amatitlán and Santa Rosa in the early 1850's seeking persons who would be willing to plant free seedlings, they found few takers. There would be no dramatic turning point in the shift to the new crop but rather a slow accumulation of evidence and experience that revealed both the declining prospects of cochineal and the information necessary for successful coffee production in Guatemala. By the early 1860's, although "costly deceptions" and "experiments, studies, vacillations, and disasters" would continue to plague coffee for some years, the future was clear.[7]

Many of the first successful commercial coffee plantations were around Antigua and Amatitlán, where cochineal had long been a major crop and land and labor were readily available. Growers commonly undertook the new crop in conjunction with cochineal and on a relatively small scale. A rental contract, for example, might call for the interplanting of coffee with grana, the old crop serving initially as shade for the new; after several years the lessee left the tract planted entirely in coffee.[8] Overall, and not surprisingly given the hold of grana on the local economy, the transition here to coffee was incremental and, as a result, was less vulnerable to the large-scale failures common on the south coast. By 1862 the governor of Sacatepéquez could report some seventeen growers around Antigua with a total of almost 48,000 trees in place and 28,000 seedlings; certainly this overlooked many small plantings.[9] Amatitlán also was moving toward coffee, and as might be anticipated, on a grander scale. In 1862 there were said to be more than 237,000 trees in the area, including some 180,000 in San Miguel Petapa, 32,000 in Amatitlán, and 16,000 in Villa Nueva; five years later the number had more than tripled.[10] Problems with excessive rain and heat damaged many of these first plantings, however. Whereas Sacatepéquez went on to earn a reputation for high productivity and high-quality coffee, Amatitlán never became an important coffee department.

Two areas that in recent centuries had remained largely outside Guatemala's export economy, the West and the Verapaz, were being drawn into the coffee economy by the 1860's. Initial efforts showed that whereas coffee did not do well on the low coast, it flourished in the neighboring piedmont, or boca costa. The difficulty was that most of this land, and the best parts, belonged to the Indian villages of the area or the adjacent highlands. Or so they had argued from colonial days, and the Conservative state generally sustained the claims of communities.[11] Some of the towns were willing to cooperate with aspirant coffee entrepreneurs to the extent of leasing them land in long-term censo enfiteusis. The Indians of the village of Santa Lucía Cotzumalguapa, for example, readily rented land to coffee growers, although the fact that ownership of much of the tract let by Santa Lucía was disputed by the large landowner and businessman Manuel Herrera may have contributed to the community's enthusiasm for censo.[12] More generally, though, the towns resisted coffee. The reason for this was simple enough, and it was not precisely because the inhabitants lacked land for their own uses or because coffee would impinge immediately upon what they needed for subsistence. The area sought for coffee was still quite limited, but coffee was a permanent crop, and the Indians practiced shifting, slash-and-burn agriculture. Not only was it possible that they would require the land in question at some future time, but, as they repeatedly pointed out, everyone understood that to give land in censo to a permanent crop meant effectively to lose it, whatever the letter of the law.

No boca costa town resisted coffee more tenaciously, if ultimately unsuccessfully, than San Felipe, a village just south of El Palmar. As early as 1861 village officials complained of ladinos invading their ejidos, demanding censo land for coffee and then treating it as if it were their private property.[13] Explaining that they were not "irrational beings," the Indians protested to the Ministry of Government in May 1862 that ladinos had seized control of the municipal government and were using censo to take control of the community's lands. Not only had the ladinos marked off large coffee plantations, which they bought and sold among themselves, but also they were not paying censo or taxes, and they had even tried to charge the Indians rent to pasture their animals on common land. The departmental governor dismissed the Indians' complaint as the work of a "shyster from Momostenango," to which the ladinos added that as residents of the town they had rights to the use of community land. They claimed that they planted coffee only in areas shunned by the Indians because of their proximity to the settlement, where domestic animals damaged crops. The ladinos argued that it was their industry that brought prosperity to the town and higher wages to the Indians.[14] After repeated threats by the Indians to "take their machetes to" the coffee, the governor traveled to San Felipe and worked out an accommodation: the ladinos would be allowed to keep their coffee plantations if they paid rent to the town and did not attempt to expand or sell their holdings.[15]

But the truce soon broke down, and the governor returned to San Felipe to investigate new complaints. A census turned up at least sixty-three people who were growing coffee, about three-quarters of them ladinos of the town and the others ladinos "from Quezaltenango"; together they claimed to possess more than 4,500 cuerdas. Of these, valid rent contracts covered only 511 cuerdas, and only the priest was actually paying the rent. Forty-eight ladinos from Quezaltenango recently had applied for an additional 6,740 cuerdas, which, if granted, would amount to about one-quarter of the community's 38.5 caballerías of common lands. And the ladinos were demanding still more, at least half the ejidos. Seeing their power and patrimony slipping away despite laws and a state avowedly committed to protecting their interests, the indigenous population of the south coast bubbled with discontent and barely suppressed violence.[16]

In late January 1864 the governor was hearing rumors that trouble connected with land disputes might erupt into violence during the upcoming feast day celebrations at San Sebastián.[17] On checking he saw only the usual drunkenness and cofradía activities and returned to Retalhuleu. But the following day news arrived that some 200 Indians from San Felipe, San Francisco Zapotitlán, and El Palmar had congregated at San Sebastián and were conspiring to "move against Retalhuleu." Taking fifteen soldiers from the garrison, the governor went again to San Sebastián. This time he rounded up more than sixty Indians, including town officials from San Felipe, San Sebastián, El Palmar, and San Martín Sacatepéquez and packed these off to jail in Retalhuleu. News of this unleashed a riot in which the Indians burned down several houses and the San Sebastián estanco, killing seven people. Armed with knives and slings, they again threatened to attack Retalhuleu. Now truly alarmed, and fearing, as the governor said, a revival of the 1830's revolt or a local echo of the Caste War still raging in Mexico, the government quickly mobilized 200 militia to put down the violence. When the governor sought the reasons for the outbreak, the "single cause" he found was coffee. The ladinos were continuing to invade the towns and to defraud the Indians of their land in order to plant coffee, and the Indians meant to stop this.

In fact, the communities had already lost and soon were in full retreat. Some of the Indian officials themselves now seized the opportunity to acquire town land and become coffee producers, and the priest of San Felipe was openly siding with "progress."[18] The ladinos demanded and got another ruling that guaranteed their right to censo land in San Felipe for coffee, and although their agreement with the Indian municipality specifically forbade the practice, notary records reveal widespread sale and resale of the use rights to this ejido land.[19] Finally, in 1871 ladinos took full control of municipal government because the Indians were "too stupid and addicted to custom" to understand progress. By the 1880's half of San Felipe's community lands had passed into the hands of primarily ladino private owners.[20]

Coffee developed more slowly in the far western department of San Marcos, not so much because of Indian resistance, for there were relatively few Indians in that part of the piedmont, but because of isolation and poor communications. Don Escolástico Ortega carried out some of the first experiments with coffee on his hacienda Montelimar beginning in the late 1850's. After losing the first harvest because of not knowing how to process it, Ortega began to sell small amounts of coffee in Quezaltenango and the capital. Other pioneers followed his example.[21] Interest in the crop accelerated after the mid-1860's. Whereas, for example, as late as 1865 the governor of San Marcos reported fewer than 3,000 cuerdas of coffee in the department, by 1871 he was asking the church to create new parishes in the piedmont to serve the great number of people now immigrating to the region to attempt the crop.[22] Would-be planters in San Marcos had little trouble gaining access to the land they needed through censo or the purchase of state lands, and the Indians from the nearby highlands worked readily for wages.[23] The more serious problem for growers here was the lack of adequate road and port facilities.[24]

Across the country, coffee sparked interest, too, in the long-isolated upper reaches of the Verapaz. Far from resisting coffee, the Indians of Cobán and nearby towns at first took it up enthusiastically as a communal crop grown on village ejidos. As early as 1854 municipal records in San Cristóbal Verapaz mentioned community coffee groves, and at the end of the decade the assistant governor of the Verapaz, who lived in Cobán, reported communal coffee plantings in Carchá, Cobán, and San Cristóbal.[25] Together with a growing investment in coffee by ladinos and foreigners, he predicted that these would end "the extreme poverty that existed before." But by 1860 conflict between communal plantings and the demands and designs of private growers was increasingly evident. The region had been attractive to private capital because of the availability of land and, above all, an abundance of labor—"humble, submissive, and religious"—for coffee cultivation and, in the near total absence of roads, for carrying the crop to market.[26] If communal coffee plantings prospered, private entrepreneurs would find it more difficult and expensive to get the land and labor they needed.

Although the Conservative state policy was to favor the Indians, its local representatives in the Verapaz in fact gave preference to the interests and concerns of the "civilized" ladinos. By the mid-1860's conditions had turned against the towns. A series of frosts in the early 1860's ruined seedlings[27] and the region's high humidity caused difficulties, but the most serious deterrent to the expansion of coffee growing by the communities was conflict over land. In April of 1867 the vicar of the Verapaz explained to the Archbishop: the governor had complained of the "lack of morals" of the populations of Cobán and San Pedro Carchá, by which he meant their tendency to live dispersed in hamlets and in the bush instead of in the town. He attributed this behavior to an insufficiency of priests and an unwillingness of the priests who were available to minister to their flocks. The vicar agreed about the "moral decline" of the local population, but he put the blame not on the priests but on the increasing sale and renting of community land to outsiders and foreigners for coffee. The governor was allowing them to take over not only the communities' ejidos but also land that belonged to the *barrios* (the Verapaz name for parcialidades) and to the cofradías, forcing the Indians to abandon their very houses and to move to the countryside. In some neighborhoods, the vicar lamented, you could now find only coffee, and, if the trend was not stopped soon, the entire town of Cobán shortly would be nothing but a coffee field. This was occurring also in Tactic and in Tucurú.[28]

In the first years, workers all over Guatemala flocked to coffee, or so enthusiasts reported. One of the early attractions of the Verapaz for growers had been a ready supply of cheap labor, and the south coast reported that "labor is not expensive; most of the Indians are workers, submissive, intelligent, and accustomed to agricultural labor in all climates. Because of their good habits they . . . come voluntarily to earn a couple of reales."[29] Many of the first coffee harvesters were women drawn on a daily basis from nearby communities.[30] But resistance grew and shortages appeared as production expanded, particularly where growers moved into less populated areas or into regions that had no recent wage labor experience, and where coffee came to be associated more and more with threats to community lands.[31] Even as the newspapers wrote of the sufficiency of workers in the Verapaz, local officials were turning to the forced wage labor of mandamientos.[32] By 1870 the Economic Society's newspaper was reporting labor shortages in Santa Rosa, Escuintla, Sololá, Suchitepéquez, Quezaltenango, and San Marcos. Two years later the governor of the Verapaz bemoaned the region's serious lack of workers.[33] The problem, he explained, developing a theme that would be repeated in innumerable letters, newspaper editorials, and government reports throughout the country over the next half-century, was not that Guatemala lacked population: there was available in the Cobán area more than three times the number of Indians needed to supply all the fincas; but they would not work. They evaded mandamiento orders and failed to honor the wage advances they received from the plantations.[34] However, when departmental governors attempted on their own to regulate local labor,[35] the Ministry of Government generally rejected their efforts as being contrary to government policy. The problem with the rules proposed, the ministry explained, was that they presumed that the Indians could or should be made to work constantly, or at least at the demand of the landowner. This was clearly what most planters and local ladino officials did think, but state policy was that the Indian was a free agent and could be compelled to work only under extraordinary circumstances.

The Economic Society in 1868 set up a commission to draft new national labor regulations more in accord with the needs of coffee. The members agreed that the present shortage of workers was due to the bad habits of the Indians, who accepted money for work, spent it on alcohol, and then thought only of how to escape their obligations. It seemed that growing numbers of "vagrants" and "swindlers" were making a joke of the law and corrupting the rest of the Indians. To remedy this the committee detailed 54 articles of a revised labor law. These divided the work force into the categories of *protejidos* (protected ones), meaning the Indians, and *independientes* (independents), the ladinos and "whites." It provided for the enforcement of voluntary labor debt agreements but rejected direct coercion: "The worker ought to be free to agree to a contract or not and to stipulate the conditions and price of his labor."[36]

When the Society debated this draft law most members accepted that the Indian was a free person and focused instead on the question of habilitaciones, the wage advances given workers against future labor. There was considerable sentiment for moving toward genuinely free labor by limiting or doing away altogether with such advances. The planter Julio Rossignon pointed out that, on the one hand, the system forced employers to tie up large, and growing, amounts of capital in advances, and on the other, because workers tended to accept more than they could repay, they were continually working off money already spent, providing little incentive to do a good job. Rossignon warned that Guatemala risked creating a "feudal" system of perpetually indebted serfs, such as characterized neighboring Tabasco and the Yucatán in Mexico.[37] Marco Aurelio Soto, soon to be an important participant in the 1871 revolution and in 1876 Liberal President of Honduras, countered with the argument that limitations of this sort would infringe artificially on the individual's right of contract: "Work must be allowed to organize itself" rather than allow "the fatal system of government intervention in individual interests."[38] The Society eventually agreed that habilitación was a "vicious custom" and that anything that worked against it should be favored, but that it could not be abandoned immediately. The members instead recommended limiting advances to no more than 25 pesos. Events overtook the debate, however, and the Revolution of 1871 put the question of a new labor law aside for almost a decade.

The first generation of coffee entrepreneurs also confronted serious problems as a result of an insufficiency of capital. To obtain needed funds "the growers had to guarantee the loans with a bond from another capitalist or with a mortgage on urban property in the capital or one of the other important cities; the interest was high and the term short."[39] From the colonial period the financing of export agriculture in Guatemala had been keyed to a term of no more than a year or two and to crop guarantees. Neither of these conditions easily fitted coffee. Also, because of the failure of mining attempts and because trade patterns drained specie from the republic, there had long been a shortage of liquid capital, and this became more acute as coffee growers attempted to expand production. Those with funds to invest generally preferred the more rapid and accustomed returns of commerce or grana. A coffee plantation was a much more expensive operation to get going than either cochineal or indigo,[40] and it did not pay a significant return for four or five years. To lenders accustomed to periods of six months to a year, this was not an attractive prospect, particularly in view of the failures of some of the early, relatively well-financed efforts undertaken by supposedly knowledgeable growers. Investors continued, too, to be reluctant to lend against rural properties, especially only partly developed agricultural land.

Prices were still low even for good coffee tracts, limiting its potential use as collateral. For those who were growing coffee on censo land—probably a majority in the early years—borrowing against their properties was not possible. Even if the grower had title, the chaotic state of rural land measurements and the absence of any functioning central land or mortgage registry made agricultural land an unpromising basis against which to seek or make loans.[41] Stopgap measures such as taking money from community cajas to promote coffee were not successful, if only because at this point few of the villages had funds available.[42] Only persons with access to other sources of funds could move directly into coffee on a large scale. One result, noted a traveler in the early 1870's, was that it was much easier to buy a good plantation than to sell one.[43] In part because foreigners usually had access to more capital at lower rates than did Guatemalans, they quickly assumed leadership roles in coffee production.[44]

The state and the planters were not any more successful in their efforts to improve communications for coffee exports in these last years of the Conservative regime. Growers complained that poor roads and the lack of adequate port facilities on the Pacific coast hampered the development of the new crop.[45] Across the country in the Verapaz the situation was worse, but when the governor suggested that the planters put up some of the funds to build a road to the Polochíc River to ship coffee out, they angrily replied that this was the government's obligation.[46] In point of fact, it was not strictly the government's responsibility to build and maintain roads but rather that of a private corporation, the Consulado de Comercio, which was licensed by the state and charged with, among other things, the maintenance and development of roads, bridges, and ports.[47] The Consulado was dominated by large wholesale merchants of the capital whose interests, at least until the end of the 1860's, lay chiefly in the export of grana and the import of finished goods from abroad. And for such trade, the existing rudimentary trails from the north coast to the capital sufficed.[48] Completion of the Panama Railroad in 1857 and the development of coffee in the mid-1860's did draw the Consulado's attention to the Pacific coast, but a continued lack of money, unrest in the countryside as a series of uprisings tested Conservative control, and resistance from the rural population to corvée labor on the roads hampered any real progress. The inhabitants of San Martín Sacatepéquez and Concepción Chiquirichapa, for example, in 1871 objected to the departmental governor's demands for labor to open a cart road from the highlands to the adjacent piedmont, which was then in the beginning of a coffee boom: existing footpaths were adequate for their purposes, so why should they labor to build a road that would benefit only the ladino coffee growers and "capitalists" of Quezaltenango?[49]

The history of early efforts to establish coffee cultivation in Guatemala demonstrated the difficulty of putting together the proper combination of land, labor, and transport to make the crop a profitable enterprise. In the area around Antigua and Amatitlán, the transition from grana to coffee, although not without problems, was deceptively easy compared with the very serious obstacles entrepreneurs faced in the less developed parts of the country. Even with the barrage of pamphlets and newspaper articles that were supposed to instruct in successful coffee cultivation, many of those who tried failed initially. Doubly damaging were the numerous cases where would-be coffee entrepreneurs rooted up existing plantations of cacao and sugar to make way for coffee, only to see it wilt in the sun. Under these circumstances, ownership and production tended to concentrate in the hands of those who had enough capital to withstand reverses. Aggravating the tendency was the fact that Guatemala became an exporter of coffee relatively late. Competition in an already sophisticated world market demanded processing and finishing of a quality only possible with an investment in elaborate and expensive machinery. Poor communications made it unprofitable to ship unprocessed coffee any distance—it took four to five pounds of *café cereza* (beans picked from the bushes) to produce one pound of *café oro* (processed coffee). Small owners and the few communities that continued to try to make a go of coffee found themselves reduced to a marginal situation, selling small quantities of unprocessed beans to merchants and nearby finqueros.

At the root of many of the planters' difficulties, or so it seemed to a growing number of them, was the Conservative attitude toward the Indian, captured well in the sentiment, "Those poor Indians are better off the way they are."[50] The role of the government, the *Gaceta de Guatemala* admonished in 1865, was to protect the Indians and to improve their spiritual and material situation; they should be "moralized" with "kindness and prudence."[51] If the Indians were lazy and given to drunkenness, they must nevertheless be protected from themselves and others and not "abandoned," and they should not be "forced . . . to perform wage labor"[52] against their will. Of course, under the laws of 1847 and 1851, not to mention dozens of vagrancy statutes, the Indians could be forced to do precisely that, and by the 1860's mandamiento drafts had already made a considerable resurgence, suggesting some confusion of purpose and policy. If the Conservatives were hardly as obstructionist of "development" as subsequent Liberal rhetoric portrayed them, they were, from the perspective of would-be coffee entrepreneurs in the 1850's and 1860's, too concerned with the rights of Indians and not nearly enough so with the growers' need for cheap and readily available labor.

It was also bothersome to the planters that the Indian peasant communities continued in many areas to block access to coffee land, often aided in this by the state. Even where the towns allowed it, censo was no substitute for private property for those who anticipated long-term investment and deferred returns. Guatemala's lack of a central title registry and up-to-date regulations for land measurement and titling made it almost impossible to develop any system of credit based on land.[53] To many among the burgeoning coffee elites it seemed that the Conservative regime was holding the country back. More active measures were needed, as one observer explained:

Neither the mildness of the climate nor the excellence of the soil nor its aptitude for one or another sort of production nor the advantageous position of our country for maritime commerce nor the many other gifts a generous God has heaped upon our country have been enough to overcome the obstacles that to date have blocked the development of agriculture. It is a principle of political economy that the state ought to limit its involvement to removing hindrances to individual action. This, like many other doctrines, necessarily must be modified in the case of new countries such as ours, where shortages of capital, of institutions of credit, of foreign immigration, of the spirit of enterprise and other obstacles require that the government more actively assist the interests of the individual.[54]

The Neo-Liberals and Development

In 1871 a new generation of Liberals under the leadership of Miguel García Granados and Justo Rufino Barrios brought down the Conservatives and initiated a reformist regime. These Neo-Liberals were a mixed lot.[55] They included the "historic Liberals," evident in the person of the first President, Miguel García Granados, who imagined an aristocratic republic based on Enlightenment liberties and a diversified economy. They found strong support among merchants of the capital marginalized by the Consulado clique and among much of the rural population, who believed that the Liberals would give them land and relieve them of hated taxes. These Liberals anticipated that Guatemala could develop a balanced agriculture and industry, which, with good roads and adequate wages, would foster internal markets and develop local sources of supply. Although the historic Liberals and their ideas were quickly shunted to one side in the power struggle after 1871, they continued to be represented among the elites by groups such as the Economic Society, until it was suppressed in 1881, and in the activities of men like Francisco Lainfiesta and Antonio Batres Jáuregui.[56] The other Liberal faction was the so-called "radicals," who had their support among the coffee planters, particularly those of the far west and the upper Verapaz, residents of the margins and interstices of the established commercial economy. Their primary interest was to develop export agriculture, especially coffee, as rapidly and extensively as possible. For this they demanded cheap land and labor, plentiful credit, and reliable access to overseas markets and sources of supply. They believed that the future of Guatemala lay not in internally oriented production and markets but in a full-scale integration of the national economy into the developing world capitalist system, as a supplier of raw materials and buyer of manufactures. Radicals favored free enterprise but not laissez faire and agreed that because of the backward condition of the country, development required a strong state that would actively intervene in the economy to facilitate and promote export production.

Apart from a few special cases, the new Liberals did not directly attack the economic power or social position of what remained of the Conservative elites, nor did they confiscate their land or possessions. Rather, they sought to redirect national efforts toward a new vision of development that would mobilize and harness the resources of the country to an unprecedented degree.[57] The effect on the elites was less circulation than enlargement to include not only the new coffee growers but non-Consulado merchants and the owners of the country's few industries, a new group of government bureaucrats and army officers, and many of the foreigners who were drawn to Guatemala by coffee. Although this newly enlarged and unified elite continued to speak of the need for diversification, to worry in print about the dangers of export monoculture, and to call for education to raise the level of the rural masses, their immediate self-interest and the logic of the world economy of the time drove Guatemala more and more firmly into its role as a "coffee" republic.

The object of the Liberal regime was "development," which they equated with their own prosperity and with the introduction into Guatemala of many of the readily apparent material and cultural characteristics of North Atlantic civilization, be these railroads or an opera house, or modern weapons and training for the army. Infatuation with "progress" and the material evidence of progress had two important results. On the one hand, these Liberals assumed that progress and "development" were politically neutral—that is, they expected to import technology and the products of technology without in any way threatening their hold on political, social, or economic power. In the short run they were correct. More accurately, new technologies such as the railroad and the repeating rifle actually reinforced and extended their control, allowing them to build a state of unprecedented power. On the other hand, they constantly were tempted to substitute appearance for reality. But they were not stupid. The erecting of, for example, a modern capital in a country blighted by miserable roads and endemic disease had a purpose beyond simply providing a more pleasant city for the privileged to live in. It was an important part of elite Guatemala's presentation of self to representatives of the developed world as a country and a government worthy of credit and investment. If subsidizing an opera company while closing an agricultural school seems foolish, President Estrada Cabrera's program of building temples to Minerva instead of schools was perfectly logical within the perspective of the economic and political interests of the planters. Liberal development was a class project that defined itself in terms of class well-being, and by that measure it was enormously successful.

After 1871 regional jealousies and personalism provoked occasional factioning, sporadic revolts, and repeated exile invasions, but for most of the next half-century the interests of the majority of the elite were tied consciously, indeed almost exclusively, to coffee. The state served these interests well, if not always as smoothly and efficiently as its supporters might have wished. What relative autonomy the state exhibited reflected the sometimes quixotic personal ambitions of a series of caudillos that the elite only partly controlled, but the projects and passions of these national leaders, if they occasionally disrupted business and ruined individuals, did not threaten the fundamental class interest of prosperity through export agriculture. The state that the caudillos and the coffee elite constructed secured hegemony over the interior of the republic to a novel degree, but this was a hegemony based more and more on force and less and less on shared culture or ideology.

Coffee provided the motive and the means for the Guatemalan state to penetrate the indigenous community to an unprecedented degree, and it destroyed much of what remained of values shared between the elites and the mass of the population. The Liberals did little to seek a popular consensus. Despite much rhetoric about schools, education, and the uplifting of the masses, most of which, in any event, was the work of Liberal intellectuals and not of the average planter, what is striking about this new generation of Liberals is the absence of any serious attempt to indoctrinate the peasantry in its vision of development or of modern society. Whereas the Enlightenment Liberals had seen the Indian as a block to national development that should and could be overcome by means of education and integration, the Neo-Liberals looked upon the Indian as probably essentially, and certainly in the short run unalterably, inferior:

The Indian is a pariah, stretched out in his hammock and drunk on chicha, his natural beverage. His house is a pig sty; a ragged wife and six or more naked children live beneath a ceiling grimy with the smoke of a fire that burns day and night in the middle of the floor; some images of saints with the faces of demons, four chickens and a rooster and two or three skinny dogs [etc.]. Yet in this state the Indian is happy.[58]

The Indian lacked "civilized needs," needs that he could not supply himself and that would force him to work for wages and thus be drawn voluntarily into the cash economy: "They have no needs to push them to progress, to seek to escape their semi-primitive lives of atony and semi-barbarism. In his poor rancho, without even a bed or any furniture . . . the aborigine lives a life of unproductivity and monotony, unable to get on the road of progressive movement."[59] A report from the Ministry of Development concurred: "It is necessary to make the Indian work for his own good, for the good of business and for the country because as result of his apathetic and stationary character and his few needs, he is satisfied with practically nothing."[60]

Opinions differed about the causes of this apathy and of the Indians' startling lack of acquisitiveness. The older generation of Liberals and many of the intellectuals among the elites believed that the Indians' attitude reflected centuries of abuse and oppression by the Spanish colonial system and their fellow landowners:

Mistreatment of the Indians by the ladinos, who have thought themselves superior from the first times of the conquest; having considered them as beasts of burden; having viewed them with scorn and cruelty, as if they were not men; having treated them as pariahs with no help from the authorities; having made them work as if they were serfs, taking them long distances [from their homes] . . . all have contributed to snuffing out in a race worthy of better luck even the hope of elevating their level of dignity and civilization.[61]

This remained very much a minority position, however. It resulted in various laws, proposals, and provisions to "civilize"—that is, "ladinoize"—the Indian, but it made little difference in the day-to-day lives of most of the indigenous population.[62] As a traveler remarked, "People regard [the Indians] as little better than animals and fit only for cargo carrying, almost always addressing them as 'chucho,' a word used for a dog."[63] Most planters and would-be elites agreed that the Indians would have to be made to work, and to work hard, under the close supervision of ladinos: "In the past he was not civilized but 'utilized' and now cannot be civilized because he opposes it, so there is no alternative but to continue to utilize him."[64] The labor of the Indian, unless and until he could be replaced by a superior immigrant population, was an all-important ingredient for export agriculture and elite prosperity. What the Indians thought mattered far less, if it mattered at all, than that they should be readily and cheaply available for work in the coffee groves; the growers wanted their bodies more than their minds. The *Diario de Centro América* summed up this debate in November 1902 when it labeled as "patriots" those who sought to raise the Indians through schools and personal liberty, and as "*practicos*" those who believed that forced labor was good for the Indians and, in any event, necessary to preserve commercial agriculture.[65]

Alcohol continued to be a focus of concern. Wages from coffee advances and labor gave the Indians unprecedented wherewithal to drink, and their employers encouraged this, at least while attempting to sign them up. A traveler described Nebaj during the height of the recruiting season:

Above all, [there is] an unceasing coming and going of labour contractors and plantation agents getting out gangs of Indians for the Pacific coast. And there is rum. The place stinks of it. The Indians are drunk from morning till night. . . . In the days I was in Nebaj you could hardly see an Indian on the streets after nine o'clock in the morning who was not already dizzy. . . . The rum business and the coffee business work together in this country, automatically.[66]

The Liberals had abolished the monopoly estanco system, in the name of free enterprise and as a reward for its thirsty supporters in the

TABLE 6.1
Government Revenue for Selected Years, 1890–1900
(percentage by source)

Year	Import duties	Export duties	Alcohol tax
		Percentage from:	
1890	41	8	33
1892	34	11	34
1894	31	10	29
1896	51	8	23
1898	40	12	31
1899	33	10	35
1900	23	18	36

SOURCE: Ministry of the Treasury, *Memoria-1903*, chart 17 and p. 231.

western highlands.[67] Not only did this do nothing to cut down on drinking, it also proved such a blow to government revenues that the state quickly reinstated controls and enforced them much more aggressively and effectively than had the Conservatives.[68] Government and private commentators continued to deplore the "doleful results" of the sale and consumption of alcohol among the Indians, particularly the interethnic violence it was said to aggravate and the damages it caused coffee production.[69] However, during these years the income from liquor taxes was the state's second most important source of revenue after import-export duties. Moreover, it was more reliable and stable than those dependent on the vagaries of international markets, as is evident in its rise to the single most important contributor to state funds in the immediate wake of the 1898 coffee crisis (see Table 6.1). For many, there was clearly a conflict between doing good and maximizing government revenue: "The income from alcohol sales is among the most valuable to the national treasury. . . . The more the vice spreads, the more the income grows and the more depravity and vagrancy and sicknesses result, and the more the race deteriorates."[70] But revenue won.

An alternative to "civilizing" the Indian was what was sometimes referred to as the "North American" solution. This involved either physically eliminating the inferior race or "bleaching it out" with superior white immigration.[71] The first was hardly feasible for Guatemala given the overwhelming predominance of the indigenous population, and the second met with little success. What the Liberals wanted after 1871, and this was somewhat different from the goals of the 1830's, was

TABLE 6.2
Government Revenue and Expenditures, 1870–1910
(in pesos)

Year	Revenues	Expenditure	
		Min. of Gvt.	Min. of War
1870	$1,130,449	$132,816	$327,779
1880	3,844,413		
1890	7,500,142	871,534	4,389,158
1900	8,860,947	1,664,621	3,392,824
1910	51,571,441	2,812,703	3,739,657

SOURCES: The figures for 1870 and 1880 are from Solís, *Memorias*, p. 1333; those for 1890 and years after are available in the annual *Memorias* of the Ministry of the Treasury.

"white" Europeans or North Americans who were willing to work for the same wages and under the same conditions that centuries of oppression had forced upon the Indians. This was hardly a choice most whites would make, particularly in view of the other possibilities for international migration in these years.[72] A number of North Americans and Europeans did come to Guatemala with capital to invest or to take advantage of the presumption of elite status their race and culture gave them, but their presence did nothing to solve the labor problem. The one population that might have been readily available in large numbers, North American blacks burdened with a tightening Jim Crow, the Liberals rejected out of hand as inferior even to the Indians.[73] The regime issued immigration laws, created societies and commissions, contracted with brokers to bring in immigrants, and debated the possibilities endlessly, but until the state could offer at least subsidized passages and help with settling-in expenses, there was little reason for the typical European emigrant worker to choose Guatemala as a destination.[74] For those who might, the prospects were not good. Reacting to one colonization scheme, the United States consul remarked, "Should this proposition be carried out and white families be brought to the Department of the Petén in any number, the end can only be death and disaster for the colonists."[75] Small-scale private efforts at "blackbirding" from the Gilbert Islands and the importation of Asians as temporary workers foundered on costs and diplomatic complications or soon collapsed in death and disease.[76] If coffee was to expand, the necessary labor would have to be extracted from the Indian. A government survey in 1900 concluded: "The abilities of these for rough agricultural work have not been found in the group called ladinos nor in workers brought from other areas (Polynesians, negroes, and Japanese)."[77]

Certain in their racist assumptions and anxious to push forward with coffee, the Neo-Liberals made no serious effort to construct an ideological consensus in national society but instead fell back on coercion in its most bald and undisguised forms.[78] This choice was facilitated by an enormous increase in resources available to the state. Benefiting especially from coffee export taxes, income and budgets grew after 1870, as did spending on agencies and instruments of repression (see Table 6.2). New technologies of control and new bureaucratic forms of organization funded by a rapidly expanding budget made the state powerful enough not to need ideological hegemony. Force, the coffee planters reasoned, was what the Indian understood, force would do, and force was what the Indians got.

The Instruments of Control

Control of the countryside after 1871 rested on the army and the militia, mobilized when needed in the diverse geography of Guatemala by the telegraph.[79] The Conservatives had flirted with the new technology, but the Liberals installed the first telegraph line in 1873, between the Pacific port of San José and Guatemala City.[80] The events of their own successful revolt had made them acutely aware of the importance of rapid communication for political intelligence and control, and they spread the telegraph quickly to the rest of the country. Lines reached the departmental capitals of Chimaltenango, Totonicapán, and Jalapa in 1874, Chiquimula and Huehuetenango in 1875, and Cobán and Zacapa by 1876. The government ministries, the governors (called *jefes políticos* under the Liberals), and local ladino officials kept the wires alive overseeing the population. Harassed telegraph operators complained that they worked late into the night after the end of public hours, receiving official messages and *circulares* and transmitting local news to the central authorities. Government telegrams increased from an average of less than 1,000 a month in the early 1870's to 15,000 a month in 1898, and rose to more than 20,000 in the peak labor mobilization month of August; by the end of the century the system handled more than 180,000 official messages a year.[81] The telegraph played the vital role, too, in repressing disturbances such as

Julian Rubio's attempt to raise the Quiché against the government in 1877 and the riot at San Juan Ixcoy in 1898.[82] After 1893 a modest telephone network supplemented the telegraph. As the judge remarks in Miguel Angel Asturias's *El Señor Presidente*: "What was the telephone invented for? To see that orders were carried out! To arrest the enemies of the government!"[83] Given the difficulty of building adequate roads or railroads in the highlands, no innovations did more to project state control into the interior than the telegraph and telephone.

Armies and militias had existed from the colonial period, but usually they were no better than ad hoc, ragtag affairs based in the towns and commanded mostly by amateurs. In times of conflict the state filled out the ranks with press-ganged, poorly trained and armed ladino and Indian peasants.[84] Because none of the governments before 1871 could bear the expense of maintaining any substantial number of regular troops under arms for an extended period, they and their opponents put armed bands together and disbanded them as circumstances dictated. The lack of a regular military force limited state control over the countryside, as demonstrated by Santa Catarina Ixtahuacán's defiance of the central government for several decades after 1839 and by the activities of the various rebel groups and bandits that roamed the country in the 1840's and 1850's. The Liberals' own triumph in 1871 in a series of small, if hard-fought battles impressed upon them the weakness of the state's available defense and control apparatus. It was hardly surprising that among the new government's early reforms was the establishment of a military training school, the Escuela Politécnica, in 1873 to build up a professional officer class.[85]

The regime also moved to put the militia on a more or less regular footing. After 1871 it becomes possible to differentiate the regular army, which in peacetime rarely numbered more than 2,000–4,000 men, garrisoned in the urban centers and on the frontiers, from the militia. In theory the latter included all ladino males between the ages of eighteen and fifty who were not otherwise exempt.[86] Whereas the army's principal task was national defense, the militia, although it acted as a reserve for the army and might be called up in time of war, served in the absence of a regular rural police force as the state's chief instrument of control and repression in the countryside. By the turn of the century there were 173 militia detachments based throughout the country in ladino-controlled towns and settlements.[87] Though still poorly trained, the militia was at least well armed with modern repeating rifles, which for the first time gave the minority ladino population in the highlands a decisive advantage over even large masses of Indians armed only with rocks, sticks, and an ancient shotgun or two. On Sundays militia soldiers under the command of the *comandante local*, usually a retired regular army officer or non-commissioned officer, mustered conspicuously for drill in the central plaza. Militia soldiers guarded land surveyors from irate contestants, repressed community conflicts, transported recalcitrant workers to the coast, and generally intervened in any problems or disturbances in the neighborhood of interest to public authorities.[88]

The indigenous population with few exceptions abhorred service in the regular army and did all they could to avoid it.[89] To be drafted into the army meant brutal treatment under ladino officers, poor food, harsh and humiliating living conditions, and, often, years away from one's home community and interests. The Indians of San Pedro Carchá in 1872 begged, "Please exempt us from military service, for we only know the carrying trade, the machete and the ax, and we don't like being soldiers."[90] A decade later, the indigenous inhabitants of Santiago Sacatepéquez similarly protested, "We don't know how to take up arms as soldiers."[91] In contrast to the press-gang practices of the regular army, the government banned Indians from the militia in peacetime. The reason is readily apparent. In the aftermath of the general mobilization for the 1890 war with El Salvador, for example, President Barillas ordered the reorganization of the armed forces, "eliminating completely all the Indians who have become part of the military, who by their conditions of unskillfulness and ineptitude lack the capacity to understand what it is to be a soldier and the very important mission he has to fulfill in the defense of the country and *in the maintenance of internal order*."[92] Only those well on the way to becoming ladinos would be allowed to remain. The role of the army was to fight foreigners, and for this Indians would serve, but the job of the militia was to uphold ladino and state authority in the countryside. Any substantial component of Indians in the militia units might put into question its reliability for rural control.

Land

A staple of Liberal ideology was that privileged corporations posed obstacles to modern development because they served and protected the special interests of their members rather than the general good.

An example was the Consulado de Comercio, long viewed by the pioneer coffee planters in the West and the Verapaz as unsympathetic to their interests, or at least as ineffectual in pursuing policies that would aid the new crop. The new Liberal regime quickly suppressed the Consulado and replaced it with a government agency, the Ministry of Development (*Fomento*).[93] The Liberals also renewed their attack on the church, because of its supposed opposition to new or modern ideas, its control of resources said to remain underutilized and untaxed, and its support for the Conservatives. Conflict between the exuberant new regime and the church was probably inevitable, and it broke out almost immediately. Starting in September 1871 government representatives began expelling religious orders and shutting down female convents and confiscating their properties. Most of the landed property consisted of urban real estate, but the Jesuits forfeited the hacienda Las Nubes near the capital, San Felipe Neri lost El Incienso, and the Dominicans again gave up Palencia, which the government parceled out among the renters.[94] Sensing that such measures presaged a general assault on church possessions, the Archbishop attempted to protect what he could. In February 1872 he secretly approved the transfer of loans due the church and of titles to church properties into the hands of "two or three trusted individuals." At the same time he ordered the administrator of the still-functioning convent of Santa Catarina to sell the houses that belonged to the order to those among the faithful who were willing to help and to convert the mortgages owing the convent into personal loans; he was to report on this in person and commit nothing to writing.[95]

Finally, in August 1873 President Barrios ordered the consolidación or *desamortización* (nationalization) of all church property, for the standard Liberal reasons:

CONSIDERING: That one of the major obstacles to the prosperity and development of the Republic is the existence of property in dead hands which withhold capital from commerce, agriculture, and industry. . . .

That it is necessary to transfer these properties, as well as loans, into the hands of active and hardworking owners who will make them produce and increase the public wealth.[96]

The decree affected all real property and credits belonging to "churches, monasteries, convents, sanctuaries, brotherhoods, hermitages, cofradías . . . and any other ecclesiastical community, whether secular or regular." Anyone who owed debts to the church now had five years to pay them, half in currency and half in the bonds of the internal debt. The estimated one million pesos that would result from this nationalization would be used to capitalize "a mortgage bank that will lend money to agriculturalists at low interest and for long terms."[97] The church protested, and priests warned potential buyers of church sanctions, but the consolidation actually went quite smoothly.[98] It turned up, at least according to available records, relatively little landed property, almost none of which was rural: of 66 transfers notarized between 1874 and 1879, all but four involved urban houses or lots.[99] How much the state collected from the property sales and from the proceeds of calling in church loans and capellanías is uncertain, although some of the priests complained bitterly of their loss in income.[100]

The effect of nationalization on the countryside is even less clear. The original decree specifically mentioned all manner of church property including that of the cofradías, but the state allowed the jefes políticos considerable latitude in dealing with local situations. In Chimaltenango and the Baja Verapaz, for example, the jefes sold off the lands and animals of the cofradías and, so they claimed, applied the proceeds to local improvements; in Quezaltenango and Totonicapán they generally left such properties alone.[101] Usually, though not always, chantries that benefited local cofradías also escaped consolidation.[102] President Barrios and the jefes políticos on their visits to the towns sometimes made on-the-spot confiscations of church buildings and lots at the request of municipal authorities.[103] The picture that emerges of desamortización in the countryside suggests an uneven impact, but little evident effect on agriculture. The experience of Momostenango was probably typical: "The confiscation of ecclesiastical properties in the communities amounted to little more than a change in legal ownership, with little evident transfer of equipment, buildings, or lands."[104] Consolidation effected no property revolution in the communities and did little to promote the small, private property that Liberal ideology claimed to favor.

More promising than church properties for the development of commercial agriculture was the vast expanse of state-held terrenos baldíos. Although the Liberals did not issue a revised general land law until the 1890's,[105] the regime moved almost immediately to make public land more easily available to those who would produce for export. For example, decrees simplified the purchase of land in the promising piedmont area of Quezaltenango known as the Costa Cuca, set auction prices and conditions for baldíos, and offered land free or at reduced cost in marginal areas for cattle and for the growing of crops such as wheat, rubber, sarsaparilla, and henequen.[106] The Costa Cuca decree helped turn that region into one of the republic's leading coffee zones, but most of the other measures did little except encourage well-connected Liberals and foreigners to speculate in public land, as well as to claim land belonging to Indian and ladino peasant communities. In February 1894 the government issued two new laws providing for a corps of surveyors that would check owners' titles and measure and mark all state lands and for the sale of baldíos and the alienation of land in the communities' ejidos.[107] The amount of baldío a person could buy in a single transaction was reduced from thirty to fifteen caballerías, although the framers recognized that it was quite possible for someone to evade this by "presenting as applicants the parents, the children, and other family members, each asking for the maximum allowed [but] being in reality only one person seeking property." No one person was to receive more than two caballerías free of cost, and in the future no one would be allowed to title as private property more than twenty manzanas in the ejidos of a community. All public lands sold were to be disposed of at public auction, with base prices set at 250 to 500 pesos a caballería depending on the potential use value of the land.[108]

As the early history of coffee made clear, initially more important than baldío to the expansion of the new crop was the leasing of land in community ejidos. The towns had claim to much of the best area, and growers sought land close to whatever roads and resident labor supply a region offered. Under the Liberals this leasing of land for coffee and other export crops accelerated, as did the protests of the communities. Where the towns resisted, the new government was more likely than the Conservatives had been to intervene on the side of coffee. In January 1874, for example, when the Indians of Cobán refused to give more land in censo for coffee, the departmental governor made his choice clear:

To put an end to the obstacles being placed in the way of growers who wish to use land possessed by Indians . . . and keeping in mind the difficulties the Municipality of Cobán has encountered in providing land to those who wish to plant coffee because of the illegal possession of much of it by Indians: 1. the only concessions will be for the planting of coffee or sugar cane and this includes all land that from remote times has been considered to be ejidos, even if not yet measured.[109]

Increasingly, too, it became the practice to shift from the fixed scale of rents set in the 1830's to competitive bidding. This tended to push rental prices beyond the reach of local Indians and subsistence food producers and concentrate the best land in the coffee areas in the hands of large users. The Indians of Santa Lucía Cotzumalguapa, perhaps repenting their earlier enthusiasm for censo, now asked that instead of auction they be allowed to pay the accustomed 50 pesos rent because "if our land is put up for auction, undoubtedly it will go to those few well-off individuals who can better our offers."[110] At Pochuta the town leaders responded to the governor's enthusiastic explanation of the advantages of leasing community land for coffee by saying that they would do this only at the direct order of President Barrios.[111] When Barrios obliged, the surveyor brought in to mark off the lots sought by ladinos found that so many had applied that already this amounted to more than the sixty caballerías allocated for coffee. The Ministry of Government ordered him to keep measuring parcels for coffee so long as there was a demand.[112] The records of notaries by the mid-1870's were filled with sales, resales, and the subletting of the use rights to ejido land for coffee.[113] Without ready access to credit, local Indians could neither afford the rising prices for land in the coffee areas nor compete at auction with the superior resources of the ladinos. More and more, they found themselves priced out of the market for land they had always imagined was theirs.

Although leasing land reduced the initial capital costs of getting coffee production going, and under the Conservatives had been almost the only way for outsiders to gain access to ejido land, the problems with censo as a basis for export development were readily apparent: "Censo enfiteusis," the new government argued, "is an institution that is not in harmony with the economic principles of our time . . . [and] necessarily is an obstacle to the free transmission of property, . . . reducing its value and the stimulus to improve it to the benefit of agriculture."[114] It was hardly a surprise, then, when in January 1877 the government issued Decree 170 providing for the *redención* (redemption), or conversion, of land presently rented in censo into individual private property.[115] The purchase price for this land depended both on the rent paid and on when the parcel had been leased originally: for tracts rented before 1840 the state capitalized the rent at 6 percent of the land's value or price; for those let between 1840 and 1860, this was 8 percent, and for those leased since 1860, 10 percent. Given that an 1864 circular had set censo rents at 3 or 4 percent of a tract's value,

Decree 170 effectively cut the purchase price of prime land by one-half to two-thirds, and where even this was considered too high, the state could fix lower prices. Funds received from these land sales went to the National Bank, which was to pay the communities 4 percent on the amounts received. Given the quick collapse of the bank and the political and financial crises in the 1870's and 1880's, it is doubtful that the Indians ever received much for what they lost.

In the many towns where there had been little or no censo before 1877, Decree 170 also encouraged private property, arguing that the "breaking of land into small lots [will] make it more productive than land held and cultivated in common that only satisfies immediate needs." Under Article 13 of the decree anyone could apply to buy any ejido land not already privately titled. Not surprisingly, this alarmed the towns, including many far distant from the coffee frontier, and its application even confused some of the state's representatives. Although the government ruled specifically that towns did not have to redeem their community property and that unless someone bought this land they could continue to use it as they always had, some officials tried to force towns to purchase all or part of their ejidos, threatening them with the loss of this land if they should fail to do so.[116] In other instances, villages voluntarily purchased their ejidos and community lands, as many had done repeatedly in the colonial period, just to be safe, or so they hoped.[117]

Labor

As coffee production expanded, a more pressing problem for growers than land was labor. Because coffee must be picked when it is ripe or the harvest is quickly lost, the success of the new crop depended on the availability of workers when and where needed. In the immediate aftermath of the 1871 revolution a planter addressed the Ministry of Government outlining the problem:

Not the least of the complaints against the past government was that of failing to attend to the growers' repeated complaints about [the labor problem]. Whatever number of workers an employer needs, he can't get these without advancing them money, but he has to realize from the outset that they will never pay it off, because as soon as they have lowered their debt a bit they ask for more and to keep them you can't deny it. One can see that these habilitaciones represent dead capital. The best solution would be to abolish the system of advances, but it gets us nowhere to talk of the impossible. With workers who have no other ambition than to get drunk the only answer is a strong system of control: the firm help of the authorities and severe punishment for those guilty of evading their obligations is what we have called for in vain in the past.[118]

From the employers' perspective the problems varied depending on the region of the country. In the southern boca costa the chief difficulty was the absence of an adequate local population to be enticed or drafted into coffee work. Although the large landowners did settle some resident workers on their properties, and on at least one occasion proposed creating an entire village in the area to serve as a labor pool, for the most part they depended upon seasonal migrant workers from the highlands.[119] In the upper Verapaz, where the relatively large indigenous population had access to land and to trade opportunities, the problem was quite different. Since the 1850's and 1860's the forced labor of mandamientos for the carrying trade had been widely used,[120] and the government and landowners soon extended these to coffee production. In the mid-1870's the jefe político appointed several landowners to form a "Commission for the Conciliation of Questions that Arise Between Workers and Employers" and charged them with surveying the municipalities to see what labor was "available."[121] At this point, substantial coffee production existed only around Cobán and San Pedro Carchá. The commission reported that in the latter area labor supplies appeared to be adequate; at Cobán, however, workers already were in short supply, and planters were finding it necessary to draft both women and men and to go to distant towns for labor to make the harvest. Given the Indians' ample access to land, the commission could imagine no alternative to coercion "to make them receive the advances and then to make them work these off."

In fact, planters across Guatemala increasingly agreed that what they needed was a national labor mobilization scheme enforced by the state.[122] Conservative uprisings in the Oriente and foreign wars preoccupied the government until the second half of the decade, but in November 1876 President Barrios issued a circular to his governors on the labor question. Without actually mentioning mandamientos by name, he revived forced wage labor on a national scale:

Because the country has extensive areas of land that it needs to exploit by cultivation using the multitude of workers who today remain outside the movement of development of the nation's productive elements, you are to give all help to export agriculture:

1. From the Indian towns of your jurisdiction provide to the owners of

fincas of that department who ask for labor the number of workers they need, be it fifty or a hundred, according to the importance of the enterprise.[123]

In April of the following year the Liberals issued their first general agricultural labor law. In contrast to most laws of the time, and perhaps because the need and justification for it seemed self-evident, Decree 177 carried no prologue or explanation.[124] In content it closely followed the 1870 draft prepared by the Economic Society, omitting only the provisions seen as too protective of the Indians. Decree 177 identified three categories of workers: resident workers (*colonos*), seasonal workers bound by wage advances (*mozos habilitados*), and workers who did not receive advances (*mozos no habilitados*). It detailed the rights and obligations of all three. The category of colono included all those who came voluntarily to live on an owner's property or who were residing on land acquired by someone else and did not wish to vacate it, all renters (unless their contract specified otherwise), and all squatters on private property. Colonos were to receive written work contracts valid for no more than four years, but they could not leave the property without the owner's permission, whatever their contract, until they had paid off their debts; they were not to accept wage advances or work from anyone else without their employer's permission. Mozos habilitados were workers who, though not living on the property, had accepted wage advances to work on the finca at specified times of the year. Mozos no habilitados worked without advances; they were free labor and a category of Indian workers increasingly rare as coffee growers expanded their control over the countryside. All rural laborers were required to carry a workbook, or *libreta*, that was to include a copy of their contract and a record of debts and credits and days worked. Decree 177 further specified that jefes políticos and village authorities, not the regular court system, were to handle employer-worker disputes and to help employers when needed to round up contracted workers.

Articles 31–37 of Decree 177 systematized mandamientos. The governors of the departments were now to grant planter requests for agricultural labor drafts from the Indian communities. The law provided that they could dispatch groups of up to sixty workers at a time, for fifteen days if the property was in the same department or thirty if outside it. Orders could be renewed if the employer requested. Apart from the absence of semipermanent assignments, the general operation of the mandamiento system erected by Decree 177 did not differ markedly from eighteenth-century repartimientos or the vestigial mandamientos more or less in effect between the 1820's and the 1860's, but article 32 introduced an important modification: "When workers in debt to another employer are included in a mandamiento draft, [the employer] has the right to ask for these back and the authorities have the obligation to give them." What this meant in practice, and keeping in mind the employers' constant struggle to mobilize labor and the jealousy with which they hoarded "their" mozos, was that a labor debt as a colono or a mozo habilitado provided, or should have provided if the drafted worker protested and his employer did not wish to see himself stripped of labor, protection against mandamiento drafts. Although this relationship was not spelled out until an 1894 revision of the labor law, from 1877 on it was clear to the Indians that debt peonage was almost the only alternative short of flight from the community if one wanted to avoid the corvée agricultural labor of mandamientos.

The coffee growers welcomed the new regulations enthusiastically: "Now the employers will not lack labor; they will not lose crops for want of workers when they need them."[125] Such expectations died aborning, however, for the problem of *brazos* ("arms" = workers) proved much more intractable than the signers of the above letter anticipated. One result was that the Liberal state continued over the next decades to issue and reissue labor-related laws, regulations, and directives— "So many that only the books of the municipal secretaries know for certain."[126] In 1881, for example, a circular reminded state officials that to ensure that Indians complied with their labor obligations, local authorities or the jefes could jail them "until they reached an agreement with their employer."[127] This order touched off a debate in the newspapers over whether Indians detained in this manner had a right to habeas corpus.[128] The conclusion was that they did and that imprisoning them in such a way was a violation of their rights; even so, the government several times reissued the 1881 circular unchanged, and the jefes enforced it.[129]

In 1893, and in the context of yet another public contest as to the best way to "civilize" the Indians,[130] a dispute erupted in the Guatemala City newspapers over, as one put it, the conflict of the personal freedom guaranteed to all Guatemalans in the Constitution as against the requirements of agriculture and the inherent and acquired vices of the Indians. Most correspondents agreed that coerced labor was unseemly for a modern country and probably uneconomic, and that mandamientos in particular should be done away with as quickly as feasible. They parted company, however, on the question of how, and how quickly, this could be accomplished without undermining exports.[131] Apparently in response, and "in order to emancipate the Indian and to bring him up to the level of his fellow citizens,"[132] President José María Reina Barrios in October 1893 announced the end to mandamientos effective March 15, 1894, approximately the end of the current harvest. This was possible, the decree argued, because the conditions that had required forced labor no longer applied: "The expansion and development that have occurred in agriculture, as well as the love of work and the desire to improve oneself awakening among all social classes, have brought to an end the reasons that dictated the law of April 3, 1877, regulating labor." Much of the press was enthusiastic: the *Diario de Centro América* agreed that forced labor was against the 1879 constitution and that the Indian was ready to be "emancipated," and *El Republicano* warmly greeted the end of "slavery" and of a "thoroughly barbarous law."[133]

In fact, however, the order abolishing mandamientos was less, or perhaps more, than it seemed. Whatever its advocates might have wished to suggest, it did not end extra-economic coercion. Article 3 stated: "Those who have been obliged to serve in mandamientos may now be drafted into the detachments of zapadores." This merely traded one form of corvée for another: persons who formerly had been liable for mandamientos now found themselves threatened with forced incorporation in the *zapadores*, labor battalions organized under military discipline that were used for work on roads and fortifications.[134] The only ways in which one could avoid this were to pay an annual tax of 10 pesos, to live as a colono, to have a debt of at least 30 pesos for labor on a rural property, or to contract for at least three months' work a year on an export plantation.[135] Now the threat of the zapadores took over from mandamientos the function of driving men into debt peonage. Reina Barrios made this clear in a circular to the departmental governors: "It has been decided that those who were obliged to serve in mandamientos may be incorporated into the Companies of Zapadores, with the object of protecting agriculture."[136] For the more dimwitted, the newspaper *La República* explained the change or lack of change: "The only indirect coercion forcing the Indian to work [is the threat] that he will be sent to the battalions of the zapadores."[137] Not surprisingly, the abuses reported in the villages and the complaints of the Indians and the planters about the zapadores echo their experience with mandamientos.[138]

The formal end to mandamientos nevertheless deleted a major section of Decree 177, prompting the government to issue a new and updated general labor law.[139] In February 1894, while the Legislative Assembly was in recess, President Reina Barrios issued Decree law 486. The new law largely repeated the provisions set out in Decree 177. Mandamientos were set aside, but the presumption of the need for coercion remained: "In a free society work should not be regulated but left to individual choice and to conditions of supply and demand, [but] in a period of transition it is necessary to issue laws that will remove difficulties and hasten the passage from coercion to independent action." When the Assembly reconvened two months later, it debated the law, made some modifications, and reissued it as Legislative Decree 243, the number under which it became known and to which it was referred for the next forty years.

It is instructive to look at the changes that the finquero-dominated Assembly made in President Reina Barrios's version and the discussion that surrounded these. The Assembly suppressed several provisions of Decree 486 with little or no debate, including article 7, which would have limited the right of a planter or his employees to punish colonos or seasonal laborers, and article 11, which provided penalties for falsely detaining or imprisoning workers. The legislators argued that these articles would only provide opportunities for "shysters to set the colono against the owner."[140] They also struck out parts of other provisions limiting legal action against workers for debts to civil rather than criminal law. But most of the discussion focused on what had been article 34 in Decree 486 and now, with the deletion of articles 7 and 11, became article 32 of Decree 243. As originally drawn, this exempted several specific categories from military service and zapadores: "(1) Seasonal workers 16 years or older owing 30 pesos or more for labor, who can prove this with a contract, and who are regularly working this off on fincas of coffee, sugar cane, cacao, or of large-scale banana cultivation; (2) colonos under the above conditions who owe 15 pesos or more; (3) Indians who can show a contract for at least three months a year labor on a finca of coffee, sugar cane, cacao, or of large-scale banana cultivation." To these, the Assembly added with little discussion exemptions for Indians who paid an annual exemption tax of 15 pesos—up from 10 pesos in the earlier zapadores decree—and Indians who owned land of sufficient value (1,000 pesos or more) to pay taxes on it, or who knew how to read and write and were giving up their Indian costumes and customs.

A heated debate broke out, however, over the first provision of the article.[141] One group in the Assembly argued for lowering the amount of debt required and raising the tax for an exemption. Smaller growers, they said, could not afford the temporary workers they needed if they had to advance each one 30 pesos or more just to keep them out of the clutches of the military and the zapadores. Their opponents, led by Antonio Batres Jáuregui and labeled the "moral opposition," responded that labor law did not exist only to "enslave" workers for the profit of the planters. Moreover, they pointed out that if the legislators made it impossible for Indians to gain exemption from the fincas, the country's food supply would suffer, or rather suffer further, for coffee already had absorbed so much labor that food production was in decline. The idea of a 15-peso exemption was precisely to allow the better-off and more productive Indians to escape forced labor so that they could raise more food for market. This sort of rhetoric in exchanges among the elites might appear to indicate more concern for the rights and condition of the Indians than other evidence has suggested. This seems evident in the following arguments, and the reaction of the Assembly to them, made in the debate about raising the cost of the exemption: "It is not just that to favor a few rich people we will sacrifice thousands of individuals. . . . Is this human, Sirs? Is it true liberalism to think only of individual interests, annulling the general interests [Bravos and applause]?" Everything we have seen so far suggests that the planters did indeed systematically put their immediate self-interests above the well-being, however defined, of the indigenous population. If, as the speaker suggested, "the majority of landowners . . . [were] to be found in this Assembly," a contradiction seems evident. Guatemalan elites held no patent on hypocrisy, of course, but the conflict between words and reality quickly became egregious: "Sirs, in the name of civilization, in the name of society, in the name of all people, I ask you not to approve [the increase] that takes away individual liberty and the rights of the majority of the inhabitants of our Republic and give them free labor [Emotion, bravos, abundant and prolonged applause]."

The speaker in this case was Batres Jáuregui and his discourse quite likely was sincere, but much of the "abundant and prolonged" applause could not have been. What were the delegates about, then? Earlier in Batres Jáuregui's speech he scolded the Assembly for seeking to take away from the Indians liberties granted them by a "dictator." José María Reina Barrios was not a popular president among the coffee planters, mainly because they suspected him of being altogether too sympathetic to the Indians and too concerned with the liberties of the general population and not enough concerned with their profits. Since article 32, and particularly item three (six in the revised version), gave ample and various opportunities to mobilize and restrain workers, it must be inferred that most of the planters were only voicing liberal platitudes about the rights of the Indians as a means to attack a "dictator" who was unwilling to give them the unquestioned support they expected. The finqueros attacked a president whose liberalism they mistrusted for not being liberal enough.

In the event, the planters found they had little to fear from Reina Barrios. Not only did the state aggressively enforce debt peonage contracts and the zapadores, but when crisis threatened Reina Barrios reinstated mandamientos. In the late 1890's attacks across from Mexico by political dissidents upset the coffee economy in the West, forcing colonos into the army and keeping temporary workers from descending from the highlands. Then news from Brazil of a record 1897 coffee harvest depressed world markets. To help counter these problems, Reina Barrios ordered the army to limit its recruiting activities and instructed the public authorities "to give [the planters] all the help the circumstances of the harvest require."[142] Several of the jefes políticos wanted to know if this meant that they were again to grant mandamientos.[143] Reina Barrios said yes: "For this one time you are to give to the planters of your department the workers they require and in proportion to the needs of each, in order to help them with the collection of the present harvest."[144] The sudden collapse of the world coffee market early in 1898, the assassination of Reina Barrios, and his replacement by Manuel Estrada Cabrera determined that the mandamientos would continue. Never again were the drafts quite respectable, and often the government and the planters denied their existence, but mandamientos persisted in Guatemala until at least 1920.[145] If there was any doubt about the role of the zapadores, shortly after the reestablishment of mandamientos President Estrada Cabrera in June of 1898 suspended the functioning of the units, and that October he abolished them altogether, "because they have served the purpose for which they were created."[146] Remnants of the labor battalions hung on in the practice of sending troublesome laborers to work off their debts on public projects and in the drafting of labor ad hoc as needed for construction. These practices were sometimes referred to as zapadores, but they were quite different from the systematic pressures the units had exerted on the Indians during the 1890's.[147]

Coffee cultivation did not implant capitalism in rural Guatemala,

TABLE 6.3

World Coffee Production vs. Prices for Guatemalan Coffee

Year	Avg. world prod. in pounds	Avg. Guat. exports in pounds	Avg. Price Guat. Coffee in German marks per half-kilo
1860–69	378,574,000		55.8
1870–79	500,671,000	191,578	79.2
1880–89	770,165,000	404,488	58.2
1889–94	777,741,000	543,223	81.6

SOURCES: *World's Coffee*, pp. 96–97; Ministry of Foreign Affairs, *Memoria-1896*, pp. 10–11.

but it did transmit the secondary effects of an expanding world capitalist economy to large areas of the countryside and to much of the indigenous population that before had had little or no part in cash or export agriculture. It absorbed enormous amounts of land and labor that formerly had been devoted to subsistence activities or had been left isolated in the wake of past booms; it paid for the construction of railroads and ports to export the new crop and bring in imports. In part these effects were the result of the ecology of coffee, for the new crop found its best conditions in areas such as the boca costa and the upper Verapaz that until then had been little exploited commercially. Even more, they were the result of the scale of coffee. Both Guatemalan and world coffee production increased dramatically after mid-century while the price held firm and even moved up, at least until the 1898 crisis (see Table 6.3). The enormous and expanding market was a product of European and North American urbanization as those economies shifted from a dominance of mercantile to industrial capital. Coffee was the classic example of an "industrial" food product, or, better put, food substitute. Not only did it benefit from the improvements in transportation and the mechanization of processing that came after 1850, but it quickly became an important element in the capitalist dynamic of raising profits by cheapening the costs of maintaining and reproducing the work force. Cheap food meant lower wages, and by the end of the nineteenth century no "food" was more vital to the functioning of the industrial working class than coffee. As urbanization and industrialization expanded, so did the market for coffee, and this market kept ahead of production until almost the end of the century.

Chapter 7

The Fincas

> There is no more beautiful sight than a coffee plantation, with its shrubs of rich dark green, bearing fragrant blossoms and bright crimson berries. . . . They usually cover many acres; have good buildings, fine avenues of trees, and large gardens nicely laid out, containing beautiful and often rare plants and shrubs. The owners are generally wealthy men, either Spaniards or Germans.
>
> Sanborn, *A Winter in Central America and Mexico*

The coffee finca was an enterprise of unprecedented scale and complexity for Guatemala, and its effects on the countryside were enormous. If few of the properties were large by the standards of Latin American latifundia, the production of coffee nevertheless drew into the circuit of national and international commercial capital wide areas of the republic that until then had been little touched. The Guatemalan coffee estate was a highly capitalized and technologically advanced enterprise tied to world markets by increasingly efficient communications, but one that at the same time continued to rely on coerced labor and the direct intervention of the state for its profit and survival. This blending of modern and retrogressive systems was characteristic of colonial economies throughout the world in the last years of the nineteenth century, but in few cases was the contrast more striking than in that of Guatemala.[1]

Land

Early in April 1909 the Hawley family of California, owners of the coffee finca Ona located in the municipality of El Quetzal, San Marcos, applied to the government for a remeasurement of the property in order to verify the boundaries and determine whether or not there was any excess over the area titled. Upon reviewing the various documents presented by the owners, the surveyor found and mapped a large coffee plantation typical of the San Marcos piedmont (Map 2). Ona had

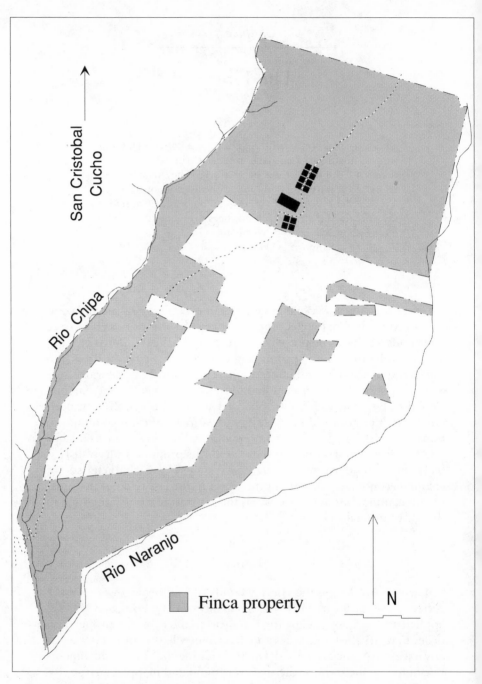

Map 2. Plantation Ona, 1909

had its origins in 1879 when Gideon Andres Hawley, in partnership with one Theodor Archibald Whitney, redeemed eight caballerías and six manzanas of land from the ejidos of the town of San Cristóbal Cucho, paying for it 405.64 pesos. Hawley soon bought out his partner, and then he, and his five children after his death in the late 1880's, developed the property into an estate that by the early 1890's had some 180,000 trees. Apparently anticipating a revival of the world coffee market once the worst effects of the 1898 crisis abated, the owners of Ona began to buy more land. In 1903 the Hawleys acquired a tract of three caballerías immediately to the north, and between 1905 and 1909 they acquired fourteen additional properties to the south, varying in size from one hundred cuerdas to one caballería. The resulting estate in 1912 measured slightly more than twenty-one caballerías (about 2,350 acres) in several noncontiguous pieces. The 1915 *Directorio oficial y guía general de la República de Guatemala* described Ona as one of the largest properties in the district, equipped with a "full set of machinery" for the processing of coffee. The family kept buying small parcels, perhaps to fill in gaps between what they owned, and by 1919 the area of Ona had increased by several more caballerías. In the same year the governor of San Marcos reported that roughly half the property was in coffee, and he noted that the owners also produced sugar for the market. Thus Ona, though more extensive than most, exhibited nearly all the characteristics of coffee properties in turn-of-century Guatemala: large-scale operation, extensive processing machinery on site, diversified cash production, foreign ownership, and a landholding accumulated over a number of years and not necessarily of a piece.[2]

The Hawleys, like other finqueros and would-be coffee entrepreneurs, acquired land above all for economic reasons, for the production or anticipated production for cash markets or for speculation, not for status or prestige. Land was a commodity readily bought and sold among the planters with none of the "artificial" restraints of precapitalist law or custom. Estates needed land not just for coffee groves and for the constant replanting necessary to maintain productivity, but also for ancillary cash or export crops such as sugar, cacao, and food for market, for pasturage of work and transport animals, and for wood for cooking, running the steam machinery and dryers, and construction. Resident workers needed land for their corn plots. Indeed, the availability of corn land was a major asset to a finca in the struggle to attract and hold both temporary and resident labor, and

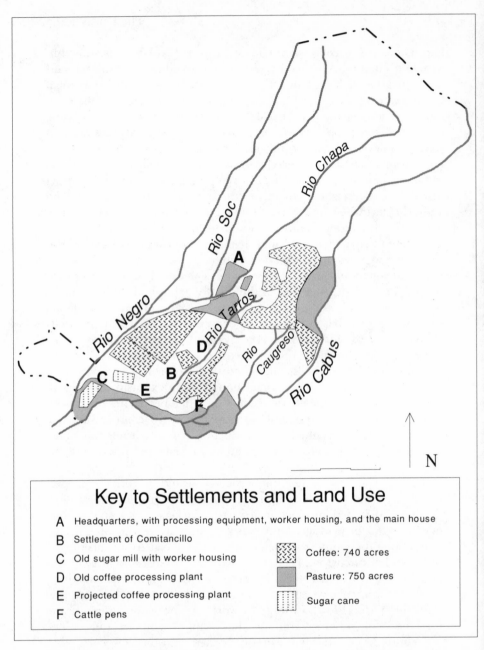

N

Key to Settlements and Land Use

A Headquarters, with processing equipment, worker housing, and the main house
B Settlement of Comitancillo
C Old sugar mill with worker housing
D Old coffee processing plant
E Projected coffee processing plant
F Cattle pens

Coffee: 740 acres
Pasture: 750 acres
Sugar cane

Map 3. Plantation El Porvenir

large landowners sometimes acquired properties solely for purposes of labor mobilization. The smaller fincas could not always manage it, but the well-administered estate attempted to have land available and in reserve for all these purposes.

Finca El Porvenir, in El Tumbador, San Marcos, was enormous by Guatemalan standards at 122 caballerías (14,000 acres), but when it was mapped in the 1920's it offered an example of the sort of land-use patterns many coffee properties followed, or sought to follow, on a more modest scale. As Map 3 shows, at the center of the estate were the houses of the administrator, the bookkeeper, and the technicians, as well as the huts and the cemetery for the resident workers, storage sheds, and the buildings housing the processing equipment. The manager allocated parcels of agricultural land for various uses: 740 acres for coffee, 750 acres of pasturage, unspecified amounts in sugar and cacao in the lowland parts of the property, land in coffee seedlings or in reserve for future plantings of coffee or other crops, land for wood (*montaña*), and land in fallow. Not marked because of the mobile slash-and-burn technology involved was land in corn production by the colonos and to feed the gangs of seasonal workers who were brought in to clean and harvest the coffee groves.[3]

Few plantations approached the size of Ona or of the huge El Porvenir. As late as 1940, after several waves of consolidation, the average coffee finca was reported to be only slightly more than 52 acres, with about 30 of that under cultivation (see Table 7.1).[4] The accuracy of such figures is impossible to know, however. Great Britain's local representative in the early 1890's explained the problem clearly:

It is not possible to give the acreage of coffee lands now under cultivation in this Republic as the Land Record Office has never published any statistics on the subject, nor is there anyone here who appears able to give any information thereon. A singular ignorance of all facts connected with this great national industry is noticeable. . . . It is equally impossible to give approximate acreage of land suitable for the cultivation of coffee . . . owing to the same cause. Coffee growers themselves are unwilling to let the real condition of their plantations be known.[5]

Leaving aside a few of the small highland departments with growing Indian populations and no direct access to the lowlands, best estimates in the first part of the century put less than 10 percent of the total area of Guatemala under cultivation of any sort.[6] This pattern resulted not just from the neglect or refusal of large holders to cultivate what they owned or from the supposed failure of Indians to

TABLE 7.1
Average Area of Coffee Fincas Circa 1940

Department	Acres under cultivation	Total acres
Suchitepéquez	107.92	140.24
Chimaltenango	68.78	109.50
Quezaltenango	68.27	88.12
San Marcos	48.12	61.32
Escuintla	36.29	65.53
Alta Verapaz	33.33	128.05
Santa Rosa	15.26	29.19
All Guatemala	30.28	52.45

SOURCE: *World's Coffee*, p. 136.

work their ejidos; it also resulted from the specific characteristics of the Guatemalan countryside, including the very uneven quality of the land itself. Such statistics also overlook a key feature of rural land use. In the highland departments such as Quiché and Huehuetenango much of the area reported as "uncultivated" was actually in the process of fallow rotation. Because of spotty rain patterns and the variable utility of land in these rural areas, at any given moment there was always a great amount of land that, although not presently in use, had been cultivated in the past and would be cultivated again when the circumstances warranted. On the coast the category "uncultivated" included an unknown amount of fallow corn land owned or used by fincas, local residents, and seasonal migrants from the highlands, as well as land held in reserve for future coffee replanting. Even with allowances for all this, however, it is still apparent that huge areas of Guatemala's countryside lay unused, either because the land was unclaimed, or because it was being held for future coffee production or speculation or for labor mobilization. Reserves of land on already established fincas that allowed the relatively rapid expansion of production when it seemed worthwhile, together with poor coffee prices and unstable world markets, helped depress the demand and price for coffee land after 1898.

Although coffee, together with bananas somewhat later and in a more restricted area, dominated the commercial economy after 1870, few areas of rural Guatemala could be characterized as entirely dominated by export monoculture. In the 1920's the Ministry of Agriculture published figures showing the area and harvest of various crops by department. These make it clear that even in the principal coffee-growing departments much of the land and labor continued to be devoted to basic food products, and several of these departments were among the most important producers of corn in the country: for example, the Alta Verapaz, Escuintla, Quezaltenango, Sacatepéquez, Santa Rosa, and Chimaltenango all produced above-average per capita amounts of corn.[7] Large-scale commercial plantations of corn in the lowlands expanded after the turn of the century to supply the fincas, urban markets, and the highland towns; the numbers and output of sugar plantations and cattle ranches also went up. Colonial, and probably precolonial, patterns of the exchange of grain between the coast and the highlands, depending upon the season of the year and the relative fortunes of the harvests in the two zones, increased after 1870, when larger numbers of people began residing all or part of the year in the piedmont and lowlands.[8] Competing with this local production were increased grain and flour imports from California facilitated by the new railroads constructed on the Pacific coast and piedmont in the 1870's and 1880's. Coffee predominated among Guatemala's exports, but coffee growing was not the main agricultural activity: in the early 1920's, for example, approximately 20 percent of the total area under cultivation was in coffee, but 50 percent was said to be in corn, and this certainly underestimated the amount in basic food crops.[9]

Finca owners also sought land as part of the process of mobilizing and controlling workers. One participant in a land dispute explained that he had acquired a particular piece of property "for the sole purpose of settling workers on it."[10] Employers with corn land available on their coffee estates rented it to poor ladinos and Indians in exchange for labor, whether as full-time resident colonos or as seasonal migrant workers. Access to such land could be a powerful draw when drought hit the highlands or for inhabitants of communities where land shortages were beginning to appear or for people who had lost access to the traditional community resources. Owners also bought land apart from the finca itself in order to set up so-called *fincas de mozos*, estates that "produced" workers. Depending on the region of the country, these might take several forms. In the Alta Verapaz where a large population and its subsistence agriculture often competed directly for land with the new export crop, finca owners generally sought control of tracts near their coffee properties. The intent was either to force the residents of these parcels to work for the planter or to clear them off and replace them with Indians who needed land and would pay labor rent for access to it.[11] Indians who lost legal possession of their lands were under no obligation to remain, but the labor laws of 1877 and 1894 required most adult male Indians to work in the export sector in any event. The only sure escape was flight into the deepest wilderness or across the border to British Honduras. Many Indians did abandon their homes for the bush or to emigrate, but most preferred to reach an accommodation with the new owners. In return for being allowed to remain, and perhaps for credit at the finca store, the Indian agreed to work one or two weeks a month as needed on the coffee plantation, work for which he was paid the going wage.[12] Much of the apparent land conflict that erupted between the indigenous population and fincas in the Alta Verapaz after 1880 had more to do with this struggle for the control of labor than with land as such.[13]

Coffee growers in the western piedmont who wished to assure themselves of more workers than could be accommodated on the property itself also sometimes set up fincas de mozos. But these were usually at some distance from the coffee estate, typically in the vicinity of the highland villages from which the planters recruited seasonal laborers.[14] Export producers bought or otherwise acquired tracts in the ejidos of the towns and then demanded labor rent from the inhabitants as a condition of remaining.[15] A typical contract was one signed in 1922 by a number of inhabitants of a property called Hato-Rejon that was located in the municipality of Sumpango but was owned by the coffee estate Osuna-Rochela of the adjacent department of Escuintla: in return for "customary" wages and the right to cultivate ten cuerdas of corn and beans on Hato-Rejon, the Indians agreed to work two periods of thirty days each on the finca during the coming year, one for cleaning and one for harvest.[16] Usually the Indians acquiesced to such changes rather than have to abandon their communities, religious sites, and the lands of their ancestors. But disputes and even violence might erupt where the municipality or previous owners had not collected rent or had required it only in cash or kind and the new proprietors now demanded that the residents work in the lowlands.[17] In another variation, the Herrera family in 1911 bought the 69-caballería hacienda Rosario Canajal in the municipality of San Martín Jilotepeque and colonized it with immigrants from El Quiché who worked as seasonal coffee workers on its piedmont properties.[18] It is not clear how many fincas de mozos existed in the late nineteenth and early twentieth centuries, since land and census records rarely identified properties as such, but there must have been dozens, perhaps a hundred. San Martín Jilotepeque alone harbored six at the turn of the century, and the properties confiscated from the Germans in the 1940's included at least a dozen.[19]

Many south coast coffee properties had had their beginnings on village censo land, but the censo system was at odds both with the nature of coffee as a permanent crop and, after 1871, with the Liberals' ideological preference for private property. When interest turned to the Costa Cuca in the late 1860's, for example, would-be planters found that most of the land there belonged to, or at least was claimed by, the few towns of the region and Indian communities in the adjacent highlands.[20] None of it had been adequately surveyed, and the governor reported that everyone offered this as an excuse to make use of what they would without buying the land or paying rent.[21] To curb growing confusion and threats of violence, as well as to promote coffee and benefit state revenues, and because "private property is to be preferred," the government in 1873 declared most of the disputed area, amounting to some 2,000 caballerías, to be baldío and put it up for auction in blocks of one to five caballerías at a base price of 500 pesos a caballería.[22] This price ensured the development of the area in large fincas rather than small or medium-sized properties. Tracts that were already under cultivation at the time of the decree could be bought by the possessor at a reduced price, but since the definition of "cultivated" included only "plantings of coffee, sugar cane, improved pasture, and cacao," the Indians tended to be shut out. Their centuries-old corn plantings gave them no special claim, and few could afford the prices set by the state. The government surveyor reported, "The Indians who are now being expelled from their plantings consider me their destroyer and executioner because I am carrying out the law that favors turning the land over to coffee cultivation."[23]

What followed was Guatemala's first coffee land rush: land applications of the Costa Cuca rose from eleven a year in 1874–75 to forty in 1878 and only declined after the mid-1880's.[24] The influx was so swift that as early as December 1874 the government authorized the jefe político of Quezaltenango to create new towns in the Costa Cuca. Colomba, for example, first put in an appearance in 1874 with an unsuccessful application for municipal independence; by 1882 the area had more than 20,000 inhabitants, and the state raised it to the level of municipality under the name of Franklin.[25] And the rush to the Costa Cuca was but the first of a series of land booms prompted by coffee. As Table 7.2 makes clear, the pattern was one of movement over time from the more accessible and readily developed areas toward the

TABLE 7.2
Land Applications by Region, 1874–1919

Years	Costa Cuca	Pamaxán[a]	Cobán/Carchá	Barillas/Uspantán
1874–75	11			
1876–79	90	7	39	
1880–84	117		59	
1885–89	60	5	68	
1890–94	14	6	54	39
1895–99	5	1	102	37
1900–1904	4		72	63
1905–9			40	39
1910–14			27	6
1915–19			15	14

SOURCE: *Indice de los expedientes.*
  [a]Pamaxán was the name given to the piedmont area south of Lake Atitlán in Sololá/(after 1934) Suchitepéquez.

periphery and less immediately promising parts of the country. Most of the applications for land in the regions of Barillas and Uspantán, for example, and except as these involved local indigenous groups of Indians seeking land for subsistence, could have had no purpose beyond speculation, since distance and the lack of roads would hinder commercial development in the reasonable future. The 1898 coffee crash confirmed this isolation. Special laws also made land available cheaply in the less settled parts of the republic for cattle or wheat or for new export products.[26] Many applied and acquired land, but few developed it for the stated or intended purposes, preferring to collect rent where they could or simply wait for prices to go up.

Most were disappointed. Although by the end of the 1880's the British Embassy in Guatemala was reporting vertiginous increases in land prices, saying that these had doubled in the past two years and tripled in the past four, such increases were for well-situated and functioning plantations, not raw land.[27] Three years later, for example, and as the 1890's boom swelled toward a crescendo, the embassy noted that undeveloped acreage for coffee could still be had for as little as U.S. $150 a caballería.[28] For those interested in coffee production rather than simply speculation, raw land was not the best investment. The auction system could drive up costs, and there were also substantial costs for the often slow process of measuring and titling a parcel. Almost inevitably, too, a new owner became embroiled in conflicts with existing inhabitants or with properties along the boundaries. Experienced planters recommended instead buying already titled fincas, preferably cleared and on the way to production.[29] The price was higher but so was the likelihood of success. Baldío prices, on the other hand, and outside of a few favored areas, remained low and the market limited.

Most of the coffee estates in the piedmont areas of Chimaltenango, Sololá, and Sacatepéquez, and many of those farther west in San Marcos, included at least a portion acquired initially under the 1877 redemption law. There were regional differences, however. In Chimaltenango and Sacatepéquez the parcels obtained under Decree 177 usually were small, averaging only one or two caballerías, and often much less.[30] Growers sometimes put larger properties together out of a number of such pieces. The finca Barberena, for example, when remeasured in the 1930's was found to contain two different lots, each of approximately two caballerías and each redeemed from the community lands of San Miguel Pochuta in 1877; Las Victorias in neighboring Acatenango consisted of parcels of four caballerías and one caballería, each of which had been redeemed originally from that municipality.[31] Guillermo Thom in 1899 titled a property within the ejidos of Tecpán Guatemala constituted by bringing together twelve lots varying in size from four manzanas to four caballerías, and all apparently initially redeemed from the community's lands.[32] Farther west in the less developed region of San Marcos the redemptions were fewer but larger, typically five caballerías or more. In 1877 this region was still sparsely settled and lacked good communications, and much of it had originally belonged to the ladino-dominated municipality of San Marcos, which was more enthusiastic about coffee than most of the Indian communities. In the Verapaz, coffee fincas based on redeemed censo land were less common, not only because of the resistance of the Indian towns but also because the new crop developed there on a large scale only a decade or so after the redemption law went into effect, when large quantities of suitable land considered by the state to be baldío still remained.

By the 1880's the market in rural private property had become quite lively. The number of transactions registered each year increased steadily from approximately 1,200 in 1886 to over 7,000 in 1900 and remained at approximately this level until the First World War. The value of these transactions measured in constant terms dropped sharply after 1895, however, soon averaging no more than 10 to 20 percent of the values registered at the height of the boom.[33] Still, as was the case in the colonial and early national periods, it would be a mistake to attempt to read too much into land prices reported to the government. In many cases it is possible to recover data on prices for individual rural properties from the land registries, but these records did not always indicate whether the currency involved in the transaction was paper or silver pesos, of considerable import as paper fell against hard money after 1900. In other cases, it is not even clear whether "$" meant pesos or U.S. dollars, both of which circulated freely in Guatemala in these years. Moreover, sellers continued the local tradition of deceptive reporting. As the head of Ministry of Development explained in 1895, "The statistics . . . leave much to be desired as regards the value of properties being alienated, which those involved in the transaction always attempt to hide in order to defraud the sales tax."[34] Nevertheless, taking together the number of sales and the values reported, there are two discernible trends, although the relation of one to the other is uncertain. One was the stagnation of the land market in the export sector after 1900, depressed by the fall in coffee prices and by reserves held on existing fincas; the other was a tendency toward an increased recording of transactions in the subsistence and petty commodity sectors and among small holders, as the commodification of land spread among the general population.

Given the ready availability and relative low cost of land for the growers, property disputes between fincas were not a serious problem. Some confusion continued to result from less than adequate mapping, but the situation was much improved over the early years of the century as the result of better techniques, improved training, and oversight of surveyors.[35] Because coffee estates were seldom as large as the old cattle ranches or colonial haciendas and the land and improvements involved were more valuable, owners tended to give these properties much closer attention. Also, by 1900 growers were enclosing their estates with wire fences and in that way preventing many of the earlier conflicts caused by squatters or casual intrusions. There were still occasional disputes, but most were relatively unimportant. The finca La Providencia, in Chicacao, for example, was on one of a series of one-caballería lots originally granted to members of the ladino militia of Totonicapán in the 1870's and later resold to coffee planters. In 1928 a surveyor employed by the owner found that instead of marking off the lots on the ground as the law required, the surveyor had simply drawn them on a map. In the process he got his lines wrong and left some lots larger than others, allowing the owners to claim as "excess" land that by rights belonged to their neighbors.[36] Across the country in the Alta Verapaz the German planter Erwin Dieseldorff became embroiled in a conflict with his neighbor Robert Hempstead that dragged on for most of the 1920's. It resulted at one point in Hempstead's throwing a rock through Dieseldorff's window in Cobán and yelling that he was, among other things, a "Jew" and the "son of a whore!"[37] But open conflict between finca owners was uncommon, genuine violence was almost unheard of, and even lawsuits were rare.[38] Indian communities, in the infrequent instances where these abutted coffee properties, probably found it more necessary to defend themselves actively, since finqueros when dealing with the villages would have felt little need to treat either boundary lines or the indigenous population with the respect they reserved for their peers. Except in the Alta Verapaz, however, communities and fincas rarely shared boundaries. On the whole, land disputes were not characteristic of coffee.

Small Property

Comparatively large units dominated Guatemalan coffee production, but there were also many small growers, some of whom raised only coffee while others cultivated the crop in conjunction with subsistence agriculture.[39] One can only guess at the number, although we know that thousands of persons redeemed small plots in the coffee piedmont in the late 1870's, and thousands more acquired land with the parceling out of community holdings (*lotificación*) and by means of so-called "supplementary titles" based on squatter's rights. Few, however, inscribed these in government land registries, and of those who did, fewer still kept up the registrations, noting sales, inheritance, divisions, and so on as the law required. For example, it is common to find in the books of the registries evidence of the breakup of a piece of land into dozens or hundreds of lots, each duly registered at the time, but about which there is no further information.[40] Subsequent transfers and subdivisions took place instead according to the rules of local custom.[41] Owners could not afford to travel to the city or pay registry charges. Almost all were poor and illiterate and kept few written records; in the context of the face-to-face village society in which they lived, most did not feel it necessary. Everyone knew who held what and where. If a dispute arose, the local justicias handled it in oral arguments and by the rules of custom. Only unusually important appeals went to the Courts of First Instance, which involved repeated trips, the hiring of lawyers, and other expenses quite beyond the resources of most Indians or poor ladinos. One expert summed up the situation saying, "Probably there are many small mixed plantings that raise coffee but do not provide information on their production to the Ministry of Agriculture."[42]

The Consulado and the Economic Society in the 1860's and the Liberal regime after 1871 had imported machinery, distributed seedlings, and attempted to encourage coffee among the general population. Intellectuals and those who drew up the laws, if less often the landowners, emphasized repeatedly the economic and moral advantages of "small property" for national development.[43] "Small property" in this context requires a clarification, however: the point of reference and pejorative comparisons was the extensive cattle ranches and largely uncultivated estates seen to be typical of the colony and Conservative years, and Indian community lands that were thought to be uncultivated and unused. The new national leaders opined that all these lands needed to be broken up into units that could be more efficiently and intensively exploited. "Small property" in the Liberal rhetoric of the late nineteenth century did not refer to the mixed agriculture or subsistence plots of the Indians or poor ladinos. Rather, it imagined a quantity of land and capital quite beyond what was available to the majority of the population. For example, when the Ministry of Development in 1902 published a study of local coffee production, it defined a "small" grower as one who harvested an annual crop up to one thousand quintales of coffee, an amount that required something more than twenty-five acres actively in production.[44] Furthermore, "small property" in the Liberal context always referred to private property, a concept that was fundamentally at odds with the attitude and predisposition of most of the indigenous and much of the rural ladino peasant population. Communal coffee flourished briefly in the early 1860's in the Alta Verapaz, but the cumulative effects of the redemption law, the divisions of community property in the 1880's and 1890's, and the coercive labor demands of the state and the planters wrecked whatever chance communal growing might have had as an alternative to production on large fincas.

There is no way of determining the amount of production by small growers and its relative weight in coffee exports during these years. Few small growers could afford the tanks and machinery or had access to enough water to prepare coffee to market standards, and transport costs made it prohibitively expensive to ship unprocessed coffee any distance. As late as 1940 a survey indicated that of 11,454 coffee fincas, almost 10,000 possessed little or no modern processing equipment.[45] Most of these ill-equipped small growers sold their harvest as raw beans to nearby larger properties, which then processed it and included it with their crop. In areas where there were relatively large concentrations of small producers, dealers sometimes set up buying and bulking stations and provided the growers modest advances to tie up future production.[46] Several western piedmont municipalities, including Pueblo Nuevo, Nuevo San Carlos, and San Francisco Zapotitlán, and the towns of San Cristóbal Verapaz and San Pedro Carchá in the Alta Verapaz supported only a few large properties as against hundreds of holdings in the range of one to ten manzanas that were held by persons with readily identifiable Indian names. Presumably these growers employed family labor or perhaps harvest workers drawn from their home communities to cultivate "coffee, corn, and beans" on a small scale.[47]

One finds only occasional accounts of the workings of small coffee properties. In 1892, for example, a ladino took out title to approximately thirty acres near Chicacao, of which he had about ten planted in coffee. He had obtained the land, he said, in various parcels during the 1870's by buying it from individual Indians of Atitlán. He had not registered these transactions or paid taxes because none had had a value of more than the 100 pesos the law set as the minimum for the transfer tax.[48] When Doña Virginia Enriquez de Alvarado died four years later, on her finca La Aurora, also near Chicacao, she had eight acres planted in coffee and some 300 quintales partly processed and ready to ship.[49] Even these, of course, were very substantial holdings compared with what the Indian migrants or settlers in the piedmont might produce as an adjunct to corn and beans. The countryside was, and is still today, inhabited by thousands of small coffee growers who remain unaccounted for in available records. It might be possible to recover their history by oral testimony at the local level, but anthropologists who have attempted to investigate landownership and use in the communities generally report strong resistance to their inquiries or misinformation.[50]

The Liberal political and economic policies of the late nineteenth century made profitable small-scale production of coffee very difficult. The scarcity and high cost of credit doomed the small grower to ruinous loans or to a permanent position as a dependent supplier of a raw or semifinished product to a neighboring finca or monopoly buyer, nor could most small growers bear the costs of surveying land and obtaining a title, the first document required to gain access to cheaper credit. The auction system of disposing of baldíos assured they were outbid whenever coffee land became available. Above all, though, it was the system of labor recruiting that undercut small-scale coffee producers. Few could afford the capital needed to secure mandamientos or debt peons, let alone the bribes demanded by public officials as a part of the recruitment process.[51] They had little land on which to settle colonos, and those who did found their workers, rather than those of the better-connected large finqueros, victimized for military recruiting, for road labor, and for mandamientos for other growers. The small growers themselves and their children not uncommonly were subjected to forced work, disrupting even family labor. And their larger neighbors were able to apply a variety of other pressures against which they had little defense. Small growers of San Cristóbal Verapaz, for example, complained in 1915 that the large estates in the region persecuted them relentlessly, trying to ruin their plantings and force them into colono status: finca agents harvested or burned their milpas and destroyed their coffee bushes.[52]

Capital

The experiences of the 1860's exposed the inadequacies of existing vehicles and sources of credit for financing coffee and stimulated efforts to improve the situation. In the last years of the decade, for example, and parallel with its attention to labor, the Economic Society sponsored a contest for the best proposal on how to develop a structure for long-term agricultural credit based on land to supplement or replace the existing system of short-term commercial and personal credit.[53] The 1871 Revolution swallowed these initiatives, but less than two months after the Liberals took power the Society called on the new regime to study and reform credit and mortgage laws.[54] In August 1873 the government responded by setting up a Banco Agrícola-Hipotecario, to be capitalized with funds and properties confiscated from the church and intended to make low-interest, long-term loans against agricultural properties; the following year it expanded this into a Banco Nacional de Guatemala with two million pesos capital.[55] Whether the bank made loans for coffee is unclear, but it quickly collapsed in the financial chaos surrounding the 1876 war with El Salvador.[56] The Liberals did not repeat this effort to enter directly into the financing of coffee for almost half a century, but the government did charter several private banks in the 1870's and 1880's with the hope that these would improve the availability of agricultural credit.[57] President Barrios also lifted the largely ineffectual legal limit on interest rates imposed in the 1840's at the behest of the church, and the government in 1877 set up a system of land registries intended to keep track of titles, transactions, and mortgages, and to make lending money against land easier and safer for creditors.[58]

But for all the initiatives undertaken in these years, the financing of coffee after 1871 differed little from that of grana, or coffee, before 1871. The system continued to reproduce, if now on an expanded scale, the obstacles and difficulties earlier growers had encountered. At least until the turn of the century, banks played a very limited role in coffee financing and always remained secondary to the merchant houses. For example, the pioneer Banco del Occidente, founded in 1881 and headquartered for most of its history in Quezaltenango, before 1890 probably never put more than 10 to 20 percent of its loans into agriculture.[59] There is no evidence of direct bank loans to agriculturalists at all in the Alta Verapaz before 1890.[60] This is not to say that bank funds did not enter agriculture, but they did so mainly through the intermediation of merchant capital. Banks lent money to merchant houses against goods, credits, and bills, and these houses in turn discounted funds and merchandise to the growers. Because the large merchants had greater resources and financial stability than most finqueros, they could get better credit terms from banks and other sources of funds both inside Guatemala and abroad and could in turn make these funds available to planters at attractive rates. Indeed, because the commercial houses almost always tied advances to planters to the right also to provide them the supplies they needed and to sell the coffee they harvested, merchants could, if they wished, underbid local banks on coffee loans, taking their profits elsewhere in the exchange. The grower had little choice but to deal with the merchants in a variety of transactions, and it was logical also to obtain financing from them.

There were several different types of loans used in financing coffee production. Would-be planters had the cost of getting a finca up and functioning and of carrying the operation for four or five years until it began to produce.[61] They never satisfactorily resolved the problem of a source of cheap and reliable capital for this purpose. Banks and merchant houses were never eager to lend money against a recently acquired tract of baldío that seemed unlikely to generate a profit in the foreseeable future. The risk was high, and there were other, better opportunities for their funds in a capital-short economy. This meant that the early planters, and planters entering new areas, constantly had to scramble to obtain funds wherever they could—from their families,[62] or from the profits of other crops or nonagricultural activities, by putting together and repeatedly rolling over short-term loans, or by entering into partnership with someone who had funds available. In July 1876, for example, Timoteo Barrios, priest of Cubulco, formed a company with Narciso Chavarría to grow coffee on a tract of land at San Cristóbal Verapaz; Chavarría was to contribute part of the land and his labor, and Barrios would put up funds to pay censo for additional land and for the expenses required until production got under way.[63] Also, Notary records in these years show thousands of loans to growers by private persons and commercial houses, ranging in amount from several hundred to several thousand pesos for periods of six months to two years and repayable in coffee or money at rates of 6 to 18 percent annually depending on the amount borrowed, the term of the loan, and the creditworthiness of the borrower. For those who qualified—and only the largest of the Guatemalan planters did—foreign funds could be had at considerably cheaper rates than domestic capital. Usually these loans cost only 6 to 9 percent annually, but they carried the special burden that if they were to be paid back in money rather than in coffee this had to be in the currency lent. At the other end of the scale, interest on small loans could run as high as 6 percent a month.[64] How many of these were made is unknown, because loans of less than 500 pesos did not have to be notarized, and few were.

By far the largest number of loans for coffee fell into the 9–12 percent range, and the amount of the loan tended to decline as the interest rate increased (see Table 7.3). Lacking outside sources of capital to carry their fincas in the early years, most coffee entrepreneurs found themselves deep in debt long before they brought in their first crop. Many never emerged from that condition. In fact, in good and bad years alike the pressure always was to borrow more, whether to expand production or to pay off past debts or simply to live in the style expected of a large planter.[65] Under such conditions, any reverse could destroy the grower or convert him into little more than a laborer for

TABLE 7.3
Notarized Loans by Rate of Interest and Average Loan Amount, 1886–1915
(in pesos)

Year	6–9% Interest		9–12% Interest		12–18% Interest		18+% Interest	
	No.	Avg. loan amt.	No.	Avg. loan amt.	No.	Avg. loan amt.	No.	Avg. loan amt.
1886	***	***	78	$6,629	24	$9,741	42	$5,480
1890	195	$21,861	135	11,047	38	2,321	40	8,884
1895	54	27,902	334	19,040	207	10,495	150	2,745
1900	444	14,647	425	6,399	364	12,588	585	2,374
1905	179	7,213	596	10,165	163	6,092	441	944
1910	84	8,512	872	10,526	206	3,626	540	1,829
1915	15	32,805	265	15,510	105	8,594	117	4,754
Average	162	$18,823	386	$11,331	158	$7,637	274	$3,859

SOURCE: Ministerio de Hacienda, *Memorias.*

his creditors, bearing most of the risk but reaping little of the profit. As with grana, merchants generally were not anxious to foreclose on coffee estates. They tended to carry debts for as long as borrowers kept current on the interest or there remained the possibility that they might be able to pay back what was owed. Land registry records are full of entries showing loans made for one or two years but not canceled until five or ten years later. Bankruptcies were comparatively rare, even in the wake of the 1898 and 1929 crises, although in both these cases an upward surge in the number of sales in the years immediately following may suggest an increase in forced liquidations and consolidations.

Once the planter established a finca as a going concern, credit was not difficult to obtain, although it remained expensive and usually short term. Funds might come in the form of a loan for a specified period and secured by the property, improvements, and the anticipated harvest, or as a current account (*refacción*). This was a line of credit made available by a merchant house or a bank against which the planter could draw for expenses during the year, paying interest only on what he used. Merchants tied these to the requirement that the growers sell their coffee through the house; if they chose not to do this, they had to pay a "false commission" of 1–2 percent on the quantity sold. Most planters established these ongoing relations with one or more brokerage houses, either in Guatemala or in Europe or, less commonly before the First World War, in the United States.

TABLE 7.4

Net Capital Flows to Agriculture, 1885–1916 (Five–year averages)
(new mortgages less mortgage repayments)

Years	Pesos	Pesos constant*a*	U.S. dollars	Marks	Marks constant*a*
1885–89	$1,116,773	$860,268			
1890–94	3,828,875	2,400,929			
1895–99	8,900,648	3,719,435			
1900–1904	6,990,603	895,794			
1905–9	9,471,514	770,895	U.S. $11,181	M614,295	M145,740
1910–14	9,974,291	455,465	796,024	3,666,019	837,864
1915–16	4,522,776	14,338	1,131,073	−3,465,528	−466,481

SOURCE: Ministerio de Hacienda, *Memorias.*
  *a*Converted to gold value in U.S. dollars

If the persistent high rate of interest suggests not only the risks of export monoculture but continuing scarcities of capital, it is clear that after 1880 the profits to be made from coffee attracted unprecedented amounts of capital from local and foreign sources. A rough indicator of funds being invested in agriculture can be obtained by subtracting mortgage repayments from new lending (see Table 7.4). Judging by this, during the period 1880–1920 there was a net positive flow of capital into agriculture, to finance land purchases, to expand production, to modernize processing equipment, to mobilize labor, and—though this is indeterminate—to fund the conspicuous consumption of the planter class. Inputs peaked in the boom years of the 1890's and declined after 1900 as the industry stagnated. The rise in loans in U.S. dollars after 1910 reflects less new investment from the United States than the "dollarization" of Guatemalan capital markets as the peso collapsed. German investors apparently withdrew capital during the war, perhaps fearing nationalization of their properties, and after 1918 holders of marks tended to convert these into dollars to avoid the effects of German, and Guatemalan, inflation.

By the turn of the century, borrowers and lenders were having to consider not only the vicissitudes of unstable coffee markets and prices but also the effects of a devalued and unstable local currency. The Liberals in the 1870's reformed the peso and melted down chipped and foreign coins long in circulation, but they kept Guatemala on the silver standard. Over the next two decades the value of the peso drifted gradually downward as silver depreciated against gold: it declined from 1.02 to the U.S. dollar in 1875 to 2.00 by 1895. After 1898 the fall became precipitous, both because of the poor state of the coffee economy and because the government converted bank notes into fiat currency and allowed their issue in ever greater numbers; by 1915 the peso had reached 43 to the dollar and by 1926, it was 60.[66] Paper drove silver out. A Brazilian traveler in Chiapas during the first decade of the twentieth century remarked that not only did Guatemalan workers harvest the coffee there, but they received their pay in Guatemalan silver.[67] Depreciation had obvious advantages for Guatemala's planters, who could pay their workers, and other locally incurred costs, in silver and then in paper while they earned their profits on the international market in gold. Inflation softened the blow of the 1898 crisis. Lenders skirted the problems these fluctuations entailed by keeping loans short term or by specifying repayment in metallic value or commodities. As the collapse accelerated, however, and as the dips and dives of the peso from month to month became increasingly erratic, merchants, lenders, and even many planters began to press the government to stabilize the currency. President Estrada Cabrera and his close associates resisted such a course because they profited from currency speculation and loans the banks made available to them.

Over all, the coffee industry never satisfactorily resolved the problem of credit. Planters continued to grumble about the lack of cheap capital in the same breath in which they complained of lazy Indians and unstable markets.[68] Although the coffee sector attracted enough in the way of capital to expand greatly after the mid-1880's, this was costly and uncertain short-term money that drained much of the profits from the planters. To conserve expensive capital the growers adopted labor-dependent production techniques that literally placed their success or failure in the hands of the despised and abused Indian. Wages were low but productivity was even lower, and productivity could not be raised without capital inputs that were not to be had. As a result, although Guatemala had to bear the effects of low wages and an impoverished population, it remained a high-cost producer relative to nearby competitors such as Mexico and El Salvador; for example, one estimate placed local costs at 15–20 percent above those of Mexico.[69]

Technology

Because Guatemala entered the world coffee economy relatively late, local growers found it necessary from the outset to conform to high standards of product quality.[70] Costa Rican exports, by con-

TABLE 7.5
Coffee Exports from Guatemala, 1899–1916
(five-year averages)

Years	Weight by type (in quintales)	
	Oro	Pergamino
1899–1903	365,511qq.	397,315qq.
1904–8	445,421	290,601
1909–13	607,484	189,854
1914–16	752,811	93,025

SOURCES: Bingham, "Guatemalan Agriculture," p. 121; Ministerio de Agricultura, *Memoria-1923*, p. 84.

trast, had begun in the 1830's with coffee that was "dry" processed by peasant growers using mortars and pestles, which left many of the beans broken and unattractive and often with a disagreeable odor; by the 1860's and 1870's this was no longer acceptable to consumers in Europe and North America. The German market, to which Guatemala shipped most of its coffee up to the First World War, placed particular emphasis on the appearance of the coffee bean. Almost all Guatemalan coffee for overseas sale was prepared from the outset by the so-called "wet" process, which required the construction of large vats and the diversion of considerable quantities of water to flush away the outer layers of fleshy material from around the bean. Exporters also began using a further refining process in which machines rub away the skin of "parchment" (*pergamino*) that holds together the two halves of the bean, producing "*café oro*" (golden coffee), and then polishing these halves to improve their appearance. The improvement in quality is reflected in the shifting balance of oro and pergamino exports between 1899 and 1916 (see Table 7.5).

. The level of mechanization and of capital investment in processing equipment increased dramatically in the half-century after 1880. By the 1920's and 1930's most large growers owned a wide array of capital equipment and machinery on their properties. Whereas in 1880 there were in all Guatemala only 686 depulpers and 230 rubbing machines, in 1934 there were 2,742 depulpers, and 1,005 rubbing machines, as well as 672 polishing machines, 304 dryers, and 999 separators.[71] Guatemala's large landowners were always interested in learning about improved processing techniques and constantly debated and experimented with new machinery. One of the best-known mechanical coffee dryers adopted worldwide, for example, was the Guardiola, invented by the owner of Guatemala's finca Chocolá.[72] Over all, a Brazilian agronomist remarked, techniques of processing coffee for market in Guatemala at the turn of the century "could not be improved upon."[73]

The situation was otherwise with cultivation. Most growers cultivated coffee "extensively"—that is, they planted a large number of trees relative to the labor available and gave these trees little attention.[74] Many failed even to prune, although it was well established that pruning increased yields and extended the useful life of the coffee bushes. Few made soil tests or used fertilizers other than spreading under the trees the residue left from depulping the beans. The crop depended instead on the qualities of Guatemala's volcanic soils, superb for coffee, and a near perfect distribution of rainfall, at least along the western piedmont. After the initial efforts of the Consulado, the Economic Society, and the Ministry of Development in the 1860's and 1870's, and particularly during Estrada Cabrera's long reign from 1898 to 1920, the government attempted little agricultural extension work and made few efforts to educate the planters on new or better cultivation techniques or to introduce new varieties of coffee. In the wake of the 1898 crisis growers did not have the resources to experiment on their own. The problem was not simply that planters were ignorant or lazy, for they readily adopted new processing ideas and techniques, but they faced difficulties, for example, in getting skilled workers who could prune efficiently and in overcoming the high costs of transporting fertilizer. Most Guatemalan coffee was shade-grown among overhanging trees and banana plants and was concentrated on the slopes of mountains. A few fincas used flumes, funiculars, or private rail lines to transport berries to the processing sheds, but in general the growing and harvesting of the crop were not easily adapted to mechanization. Where mechanization might be possible, again efforts ran up against the problem of the scarcity and cost of capital, obstacles that only the largest, typically foreign-owned, operations could overcome. The majority of fincas depended instead almost entirely on hand labor for cultivation, harvest, and carrying the berries at least as far as the processing sheds.

Coffee tended to prosper especially where growers had access to good communications, and particularly railroads.[75] Railroads greatly reduced the cost of transporting not only coffee but imports, such as cheap food from California, and labor. The government encouraged private companies to construct rail lines and attempted with limited success to build these where private entrepreneurs would not. By the end of the 1880's the rail network was largely complete on the Pacific side of the country, one of the reasons that the West developed a decade ahead of the Alta Verapaz. Only in the 1890's did a German-owned private company in the Alta Verapaz put together a system of carts, a rail line, and steam launches to carry coffee out of the Verapaz down the Polochic River to the Caribbean, and it was always inefficient, unreliable, and expensive.[76] Repeated government efforts to build the Northern Railroad from the capital to the Caribbean coast failed, and not until 1908 did the United Fruit Company complete, and monopolize, the line. Limited as it was, however, the railroad, much more than improved cultivation techniques or even better processing technology, was the greatest boon to Guatemala growers in the years after 1880.

Labor

Although they did not always agree on the causes for the problem, planters were one in complaining that they did not have enough workers: "Guatemala is probably the only country in the world where the coffee grower is bothered more by problems with workers than with the coffee trees."[77] The ones they could get, planters said, were expensive and lacked work discipline.[78] This was one of the costs of coerced labor. Wage advances disappeared when Indians died or fled, recruiting agents had to be paid, and officials at all levels demanded bribes. Wage costs, including the food supplied to workers, amounted to about half the production costs of coffee.[79] The real problem was indeed not so much an actual scarcity of workers as an absence of efficient mobilization and control. There were more than enough Indians available in Guatemala in the 1880's to carry out the required agricultural tasks on the fincas.[80] The difficulty was to turn them into workers at the time and under the conditions planters thought acceptable. The forced wage labor system routinized by the Liberals functioned successfully for three-quarters of a century after 1871, but coerced labor was neither easy nor cheap for the fincas.

The Liberals did not invent forced wage labor in Guatemala. Rather, the onset of large-scale coffee production prompted the codification of coercive systems, increased the level and efficiency of these exactions, and generalized forced wage labor to regions of the country and parts of the indigenous population that previously had been little affected. The new regime sanctioned and expanded the application of forced wage labor not only because planter elites, and, for that matter, the Indians, felt most comfortable with what they knew, but because co-erced labor worked. Under the existing conditions the planters and the planters' state could not imagine an alternative. Under existing conditions, there was no alternative. As long as the indigenous people had access to enough land to guarantee their economic and social reproduction, and if coffee was to be produced on large holdings con-trolled by a tiny elite, recourse to coercion was inescapable. If Liberal intellectuals anticipated that immigrant entrepreneurs from more ad-vanced countries would modernize the country's backward productive relations, most immigrants instead quickly fell in with and supported the existing system: "The Indian will not work unless forced to do so," they agreed.[81] In any event, it would have been financial suicide for the individual foreign or national planter in turn-of-the-century Guatemala to attempt to rely on free labor. Indians in the highlands would not sign contracts without advances; colonos, unless bound by debts, would make use of finca land for their milpas and then work for the highest bidder. And by 1900 there were few unbound laborers to be had anyway. More broadly, the existence of systematic coerced labor, together with the wide variety of forms of payment used by the fincas, tended to block the emergence of a free labor market.

Coffee dominated the nonsubsistence agricultural labor sector in the late nineteenth century,[82] but the growers were not without com-petitors. Chief of these was the state itself. The rural population, and apart from demands on its time and labor from within the commu-nities, was called upon by the government to build and repair roads, railroads, and telegraph lines, and to serve in the military. For ex-ample, the Liberals greatly increased the demand for road labor to service their program of modernizing transport and communications: the number of days a year required of the individual went from three in the 1870's to twelve by the 1930's.[83] Much as the finca owners wanted good roads, they hated having to release their workers for road work and tried always to have the burden shifted to some other property.[84] They could, of course, pay the exemption tax for their people, but that increased labor costs and led to conflict when the men failed to under-stand or refused to accept the adding of this expense to their debts. Officials trafficked in fraudulent exemptions, and "shysters" forged papers, but neither avenue was necessarily much cheaper than paying the tax and could too easily be found out. A neat alternative sometimes adopted by the employer was simply not to pay the tax on his colonos, effectively imprisoning them on the property.[85] Under pressure from superiors to fill road work quotas and complete needed repairs, local officials sometimes met this sort of planter resistance by sending armed commissions onto the fincas to search out workers: "They hunt them down like deer, grab them, tie them up, and take them away."[86] This provoked endless complaints and conflict and not a little violence and was a fruitful source of bribes for the officials involved.[87]

Planters also detested military recruiting and militia service for their workers.[88] Colono militia members were supposed to travel to the nearest town one Sunday a month for drill, but once there they often took to drinking and might only straggle back to the finca days later.[89] Larger estates combated this by obtaining permission for the men to pass muster on the property itself.[90] Owners could pay military exemptions for their workers, but, again, this added to labor costs. Military commanders, for their part, knew the local agricultural calendar and not surprisingly tended to make their demands when the planters most needed their workers, pushing up the price of bribes. The more direct simply jailed workers for real or imagined derelictions and then "sold" them back to their employers.[91] Military recruiters kidnapped men from the fincas, or waylaid seasonal workers on the way to the coast.[92] The threat of military and road duty served the planters as a group by providing the rural population yet another incentive to accept labor advances or to move to a finca, but military and road duty could do severe damage to the individual planter who was subjected to the attentions of the state's recruiting agents.

Mandamiento

Mandamiento was the most direct form of coerced wage labor but not necessarily the simplest or the least expensive for the planters.[93] Rarely was it the most satisfactory. It served instead to supplement debt servitude in specific situations, and, most importantly, to coerce workers into labor debt contracts. New fincas just being established and still without sufficient contracted workers or small or poorly capitalized plantations that found it difficult to compete for debt peons might turn to mandamientos.[94] Properties known for bad treatment or unsafe conditions sometimes needed forced drafts. The Indians of Santa María de Jesús and San Lucas Sacatepéquez, for example, in 1886 petitioned the President not to be sent again to the finca Mauricio in nearby Escuintla. Many of those who had gone in the past, they claimed, died in the lowlands or returned with "pernicious fevers, intermittent chills, or symptoms of fevers." Although local ladinos blamed the workers' problems on the excessive drinking of chicha on the road back, in this case the President agreed with the Indians and stopped the drafts.[95] Crises could provoke a resort to mandamiento labor. Owners of fincas damaged by a sudden ice storm or fire or those who found themselves in the midst of a harvest for which their contracted workers had failed to arrive commonly sought mandamiento workers. When the volcano Santa María erupted in 1902 spewing fire and ash over much of the West, the workers on many of the affected properties fled in terror or used the confusion to slip away and evade their debts. Those who survived demanded higher wages. The government responded by creating a special office in Quezaltenango, the Proveeduría General de Auxilios para la Agricultura, which organized the drafting of workers from the neighboring departments to assist the afflicted growers.[96]

The planter who wished to make use of drafted labor usually applied for an order to the jefe político of the department from which the workers would come.[97] Access to mandamiento labor therefore depended above all on the grower's personal and political relations with the jefe and other state agents. As one observer commented, the planter must "capture the good graces of the jefes políticos so as not to fall victim to their ruinous persecutions."[98] Powerful landowners with direct connections to the capital and the large foreign companies had little to fear from the governors, but for the average planter this official could cause at least as many labor problems as he might be able to resolve. He was, for example, often himself engaged in commercial agriculture and took first pick of available workers.[99] In other cases he sold orders or required bribes to attend to the planters' requests. One jefe, a secret report noted, "had come to the point of paying an agent to go about to the fincas offering gangs of workers to the planters, for which they paid him 20 pesos for each mandamiento laborer, it not mattering if the poor Indians lost their plantings."[100] The fictionalized description of an encounter with a governor given in the newspaper *Diario de Centro América* perhaps only slightly exaggerated what the desperate planter faced under the Estrada Cabrera regime: "Not too long ago it required a certain personal courage to confront the departmental boss and ask for a mandamiento. That terrible personage was for the planters something of a god dwelling in a sanctuary difficult and fearsome to enter and only accessible to those who made sacks of golden disks sound before the doors." [101] The extortions of the jefe políticos weighed heavily on those planters not well protected and greatly increased the costs and difficulties of using mandamiento labor.

The number of Indians available to be drafted for agricultural labor declined toward the end of the century as more and more of the indigenous population sought refuge in debt. Fewer each year remained without the labor contract that, at least according to the law, gave them protection from forced recruiting. Officials of the town of Santa Lucía Cotzumalguapa, for example, explained why they could not meet a recent mandamiento order: "The people leave the town and decide to become colonos on the fincas with the object of earning their living peacefully, because free they cannot live," and the residents of San Lucas Tolimán lamented in 1914: "As has happened in other towns, because of the frequent demands for mandamientos [the villagers] have had to abandon the land where they saw their first light to become colonos and to suffer and die there." [102] By the end of the 1890's justicias routinely reported that it was difficult or impossible to fill mandamiento orders because there were so few Indians not in debt to the fincas.[103] One official took to drafting men from among the traveling merchants who came to the local market, wreaking havoc on commerce.[104] Towns fell months and even years behind in meeting orders: finca Ceilan, for example, sent money to Comalapa in late December of 1896 to pay for a mandamiento draft that by November of the following year still had not arrived.[105] Even if Indians could be found, the employers almost never received the number for whom they had advanced wages. The jefe político and various local officials generally syphoned off much of the money, and despite armed escorts, some of the Indians caught up in the draft always managed to escape on the road. As the towns most readily accessible to the coffee areas came to be fully employed, mandamiento demands reached deeper into the hinterlands, raising the employers' travel costs and making it that much less likely that the drafted men would appear at the finca.

With President Estrada Cabrera's hold on power weakening in 1918 and 1919, newspapers in the capital began to publish planter complaints that the mandamientos were uneconomic and damaging to their interests and to the export economy, but the system held on for several more years. There were two reasons that mandamientos persisted in Guatemala long after similar forms had disappeared elsewhere in Latin America. On the one hand, they did supply labor, although it was expensive and reluctant, when no other method could. Certainly as late as 1920 the majority of Guatemala's highland Indians could have subsisted with little or no work in the coffee sector and would not have descended to the fincas unless forced to do so. But the mandamientos' most important contribution to the mobilization and control of coffee labor was to pressure Indians to accept contracts for temporary or colono labor in the export sector, and to punish those who did not. In Guatemala the state went beyond the enforcement of debt peonage contracts common to much of Latin America in these years to force Indians into debt servitude. Given the option of contracting with a finca or confronting repeated, and increasing, demands for draft labor, the choice, if unattractive, was not difficult.

Debt Servitude

The fincas employed both resident colonos and seasonal or temporary workers bound by debts.[106] There was no standard or even typical ratio of one to the other. The same property might exhibit marked differences over time depending on the availability of labor, the condition of the finca, and the specific preferences or abilities of the manager. For owners who had extra land available, colonos offered the advantage of a stable labor force, and most properties sought where possible to increase the number of permanent workers at their disposal. But colonos also saddled the estate with a population not always cheap to maintain or easy to control. The owner had to pay taxes, fees, and fines for the colonos, good year or bad, or risk seeing them carried away by the military or municipal authorities. Planters in the Pamaxán region, for example, petitioned the government in 1898 complaining that despite the recent fall in coffee prices they had to continue paying the same taxes for their colonos.[107] The finqueros also sometimes had to guarantee their workers credit at a store on the property or in a nearby town and provide them food where their contract called for this or when their milpas failed. Not to do this meant almost certainly to lose the workers to other employers. Such expenses drove up colono debts with no guarantee that the fincas would be able to recover their investment.

Colonos violated their contracts with relative impunity. For example, although they were almost always forbidden to engage in commercial production for themselves on finca land, many nevertheless sold the corn from their milpas on local markets; some sold even the food rations given them by the employer, confident that he needed their labor and would not let them starve. If the owner proved difficult, they could always find colono work elsewhere. The bolder and more ambitious among the colonos sometimes brought in relatives or hired labor to cultivate corn on a commercial scale on finca land. Others attempted to title the land as their own.[108] Colonos who refused to work or to follow the rules of the property could be expelled, but this might require the intervention of the jefe político or other authorities and, again, depended on political and personal relationships or bribes. If he was made to leave, there was, too, the problem of the colono's debt.[109]

It was far more common for a planter to lose colonos who fled owing money than to be troubled by workers he wished to be rid of. Because of their extended residence and experience on the coffee estates, colonos tended to be more at home in the ladino world than were the temporary workers, and they were the ones who found it easiest to slip away and were the hardest to catch. Employers eager for labor hid fugitive colonos, provided them false documents, and started them afresh with new advances. Although there were repeated calls for the introduction of an identity card to keep track of the population, until the 1930's the workers' only identification document was their libreta, which was easily "lost" or altered. Or the applicant for a job could always claim never to have worked before on a finca. In all but the worst years employers needed the colonos much more than the colonos needed a specific property, and the colonos used this as best they could to their advantage.

In examining systems of coercive labor mobilization, or, indeed, the operation of any mechanism of exploitation, one must be aware of the difference between the power that one class as a class exerts over another and the power that one person within that class can bring to bear on specific members of the subordinated class. Colonos both as a group and as members of Guatemala's lower orders had little opportunity to alter their status as dependent subjects of a coerced labor system that was enforced by direct state sanctions; but within that status they could sometimes exploit the contradictions of the system to their advantage. They could easily escape existing debts and start anew, if always within the same political and economic framework, and this strengthened their negotiating position. The planters were able to count on a combination of laws and state intervention to generate workers as a category, but they had limited control over the lives and activities of individuals.

They had even less control over their seasonal laborers. Had it not been for the Indian's attachment to his home community, they would have had next to none. This was a price of "cheap" labor. Because coffee required large numbers of workers only part of the year, most fincas made use of gangs of temporary workers brought down from the highlands. Seasonal workers cleared the groves of weeds in April and May and picked a harvest that extended from September to February or March depending on the altitude of the property. Some of these workers came in response to mandamiento orders, but most employers preferred the more dependable mechanism of debt peonage. If under the pressures of mandamientos and military and road recruiting most of the highland Indians by the end of the century had sought refuge in seasonal work contracts with the fincas, these pressures did not match specific workers to the needs of particular properties. The employers had to do this themselves or hire a *habilitador* to do it for them. The habilitador—so named from the habilitación or advance on wages they gave the workers to seal a work agreement—was a labor recruiter who traveled to or lived in the Indian highland towns. Most were ladinos, including a number of newly arrived foreigners without capital or skills, who advanced the finca's money to Indians against the promise of future labor, signed them to contracts, and rounded them up and dispatched them to the coast when needed.[110] Generally habilitadores combined labor recruiting with money lending, running small stores or taverns, or holding petty offices such as secretary in the municipal government or *comisionado político* (the governor's appointed local representative). They signed up workers in the village in which they lived and in the surrounding countryside and settlements, and they might make recruiting visits to other towns, particularly when there was a fiesta and the Indians sought money for alcohol, or during June and July when corn was in short supply and prices were high. At the system's peak in the years between 1915 and 1925 there were hundreds of habilitadores throughout the western highlands.[111] The governor of Quiché, for example, in the early 1920's listed 83 recruiters representing 58 different fincas working in 17 towns of his department.[112] These men, and occasionally women, usually received a small salary or a flat rate for each worker contracted and a commission based on the number of days worked by the men whom they recruited.[113] But they were responsible for any of the money of the finca that they advanced and that was not worked off. A few habilitadores prospered, but many did not, and the turnover in the occupation seems to have been quite high.[114]

Employers who did not have their own habilitadores or who needed more workers than their recruiters could supply sometimes turned to another sort of contractor, *contratistas* or *'tratistas*. Reviled by the newspapers and the planters as "modern slave traders" or "*encomenderos*," these men, again, typically local ladino officials or tavern proprietors, used their own money or credit, or that of an unsuspecting finca, to speculate in labor. The 'tratista got the Indian into debt with loans or credit at his store, forced or deceived him into signing a work contract, and then sold all or part of the contract to the highest bidder. The planters complained that the intervention of the 'tratista drove up the cost of labor with little advantage to the workers. Whereas, for example, a 'tratista might charge the landowner 25 or 30 pesos a day for a worker in the 1920's, the laborer himself would be lucky to have 5 or 6 pesos credited against what he was said to owe.[115]

Disputes between the habilitadores, or the 'tratistas, and the finqueros were endemic. Owners accused the recruiters of failing to deliver the number of workers contracted, paid for, and anticipated, either because they were lazy or incompetent and had not signed up the workers in the first place, or because they allowed other habilitadores to steal "their" workers.[116] Recruiters also sometimes promised the Indians wages and conditions to which employers had not agreed, or they would take money from one finca and deliver workers to another. Some branched out on their own to work as contratistas, perhaps taking their past employer's workers with them. In 1907, for example, the owners of finca El Faro complained to the governor of Huehuetenango that their habilitador in San Sebastián was sending their workers to other plantations; the now ex-habilitador replied that his contract with El Faro had expired, and "I am a contratista and . . . the workers belong not to the finca but to me . . . and only I have a right to them."[117] The finca Candelaria Xolguitz in 1927 sued its Soloma recruiter, claiming that his failure to deliver needed workers had cost the property thousands of pesos in lost advances and coffee not harvested. Letters from the manager to the habilitador reveal some of the finca's problems:

November 6, 1926: We need the workers and demand that you comply with your obligations. . . . We cannot believe that you are actually looking for our workers. . . . You have forgotten your promises and obligations. . . . The coffee is falling off the trees, workers are required, and all I have is your telegram.

November 16, 1926: You have let them take many workers that belong to La Candelaria, allowing the workers and the employers alike to be deceived. . . . It is the truth that no good employee would so damage the interests he is supposed to represent. . . . The harvest is being lost, and the workers are needed to save it.

February 2, 1927: You ought to defend our workers at any cost and not let them be bothered. . . . They are running away because you do nothing to protect them. . . . Given your notorious incompetence you ought to admit it and not further damage the interests of the finca. . . . You do not attempt to present complaints against [another recruiter] because he is the alcalde. . . . When you want to try to be a big shot and butter up people, do it with your own money, not that entrusted to you to recruit workers.

February 5, 1927: You need to understand that we are paying you a salary to take care of our workers and defend our interests, not to make yourself agreeable to your relatives and friends as you have been doing.[118]

The loss of the money was bad enough, but even worse was the loss of labor. The fact that Candelaria Xolguitz put up with such difficulties for several years before initiating action suggests that the situation was not unusual.

Recruiters and the fincas relied heavily on the help of ladino and Indian public authorities to round up reluctant workers and force them to go to the coast to work off their debts. The jefes políticos of the departments, for example, repeatedly instructed the local officials in the towns to cooperate with the habilitadores. It was the jefes, too, who heard disputes arising out of contracting practices, but they did not normally involve themselves in the day-to-day recruiting of indebted workers in the same manner that they did with mandamientos.[119] There were exceptions, of course. The newspaper *El Imparcial* in 1923 noted one such example when it described the jefe of Totonicapán as a "seller of workers," an ex-habilitador who now worked through his son to profit from the labor traffic.[120]

In the case of community officials, it is necessary to differentiate the representatives of the state from the justicias and principales of the indigenous population. The state representatives were typically ladinos appointed by the jefe político to offices such as comisionado político or municipal secretary or elected by the ladinos to represent their interests. They, or their relatives, often were deeply involved in labor recruiting, either directly as habilitadores and 'tratistas or by extracting bribes from the recruiters and the Indians.[121] The municipal secretary was particularly well placed to traffic in workers because he handled all the correspondence for the town government and validated all labor contracts. The Indians of San Juan Ixcoy in Huehuetenango in 1904, for example, petitioned that their secretary be made to stop interfering in "questions of workers and land."[122] Local authority figures such as doctors and teachers commonly had a sideline as labor recruiters. Such men were "*caciquillos*" (little bosses), *El Imparcial* complained, who converted the Indians into "feudal subjects."[123]

The roles of the Indian justicias and principales in the labor traffic were somewhat more ambiguous. The law required them to supply mandamientos and to assist habilitadores, but custom in the communities expected them to shield the population as best they could from abuses and outside threats, including exploitative and excessive demands for labor, and they often tried to do so. A correspondent of the *Diario de Centro América*, for example, complained in 1892 that it was impossible to get labor in Rabinal because the "authorities protected" the Indians. Planters protested that the Indian alcalde of Cahabón "always sides with the workers."[124] Another alcalde explained: "I didn't want to turn them in and I tried to figure out how to defend them. They got very clever about avoiding the authorities and about not betraying me. . . . When anyone saw the authorities coming, they sent out the word."[125] However, officials who out of a sense of duty to the community persistently resisted acceding to the labor demands of the finqueros and the state risked being jailed or fined or removed from office, or themselves impressed into service.[126] Other justicias used their position, as some had done in the colonial period, to protect themselves and their relatives and to profit at the expense of their fellow Indians, whether by taking bribes from recruiters and Indians or by becoming assistants to the habilitadores or themselves labor contractors.[127]

The Cost of Labor

The money value of agricultural wages increased after 1870 but the real value declined from the 1870's until the second decade of the twentieth century, when the earthquakes of 1917–18 and the postwar boom temporarily pushed them up; wages stabilized in the 1920's and then declined again in the early years of the Depression.[128] This did not necessarily mean, however, that the cost of labor to the employers was cheap or becoming cheaper. Fincas typically gave their workers or sold them at below market prices a weekly ration of corn and other basic food products; one agronomist estimated that at the turn of the century a quintal of processed coffee cost one paper peso and ten pounds of corn to harvest.[129] Because corn prices tended to fluctuate sharply from year to year, over the course of a given year, and between different regions of the country, finca owners found it difficult to predict or even calculate their actual labor costs.[130] Estates that could not grow all the corn they needed to feed their colonos and temporary workers—few managed this every year—had to buy corn on the open market. Much of this was imported. The fall in the gold value of the peso cheapened wages, but it also raised the price of imported and, in turn, locally produced corn. Any attempt to pass such costs on to the workers threatened to violate "custom" and risked provoking worker resistance and the loss of labor.[131]

To the wage and food given the worker, and in addition to the taxes and fees noted above, employers had to add the habilitador's salary and commissions, or the 'tratista's demands, and the expenses of bribes and whatever it cost to deliver the temporary workers to the property. And no matter what their outstanding debt, workers each year demanded an additional advance before they would leave the village for the coast. To refuse was to risk losing workers to other employers who were willing to spend more liberally. Indebted workers died or ran away, and although employers usually tried to pass the debt on to whatever relative they could find, this was illegal and by no means always successful. In many cases the employers simply had to write the debt off. Workers who ran away usually owed money, and the owner rarely could recover that. Employers paid 12 to 18 percent interest on the money they borrowed to advance to workers, whether or not they received the labor contracted and even when the worker died or fled across the border.[132] All such expenses, together with the more fundamental considerations of the productivity of coerced and indebted labor, had to be added to the worker's low wage to determine the real cost of labor.

By far the most serious factor driving up costs, however, was the ruinous "intrigues" among the fincas to steal each others' workers.[133] This competition was so fierce that finqueros would actively seek to employ a person described as "a bum, who once was imprisoned for a wounding, always has been lazy and is full of tricks!"[134] Habilitadores in the villages routinely raided each others' contracted workers. They hired marimbas—Indians claimed to lose all control of their actions when under the influence of the marimba—bought drinks and signed up laborers when they were too inebriated to know what they were doing, or so both would claim if caught.[135] Seasonal workers readily took money from several habilitadores and left the fincas to fight over which, if any, would actually have the benefit of their services. In theory this could not happen because under the law no worker could be contracted without written proof that he had cleared his debt with his past employer or had written permission, rarely given, from that employer to work for someone else. Labor contractors and Indians alike regularly ignored this provision when it suited their interests, and since all fincas needed labor at approximately the same times of the year, advances from more than one property inevitably led to disputes over the "ownership" of workers. Typical was one involving two fincas in San Marco, El Ferrol and California, during the early 1920's. El Ferrol complained to the jefe político of Huehuetenango that California's representative in Aguacatán was advancing money to people already contracted by El Ferrol and demanded an end to such activities. The administrator of California replied, in injured innocence, that it was common for the Indians to take more than one advance and that, in any event, all the Indians had denied owing money to another employer when they accepted California's habilitación. His explanation was that he and his recruiter were victims of the "trickery" and "perversity" of the Indians.[136]

Particularly aggressive recruiters invaded the fincas themselves to "seduce" workers away. In September 1905, for example, the administrator of San Andrés Osuna turned over to local authorities two men who had been caught at night in the shed that housed temporary labor. They had been attempting "to entice the workers away with money to work on other fincas."[137] Planters hid temporary workers who had fled old employers and old debts in the same manner they did fugitive colonos, spiriting them from property to property ahead of pursuers and providing them with false papers. There was, one aggrieved planter noted, a marked "lack of morality among finqueros."[138]

Employers addressed the problem of the cost of labor in a number of ways, most directly by cheating their workers. As the bitter joke of the time had it, a habilitador explained to an Indian his debt in the following manner: "Ten pesos I am giving you, ten pesos I am writing in your book, and ten pesos you owe makes a total debt of thirty pesos."[139] If such sleight of tongue did not often deceive the Indians, there usually was little they could do about it. Most were illiterate, and if they protested that "we keep our books in our heads,"[140] the state privileged written documents. But the libreta was subject to a variety of abuses and frauds by both the workers and the employers and was notoriously inaccurate: "Oh, what a story the books could tell if only they could talk," a newspaper editorial observed.[141] The finca also kept its own records. When a difference appeared between what an Indian worker remembered to be his debt or what his book recorded and what the finca claimed that he owed, the Indian inevitably charged that he had been cheated. Often this was true, but employers also pointed out that workers commonly neglected to allow for the taxes and exemptions that the finca had paid for them. They complained, too, that the Indians did not always present their libretas to have the necessary charges or credits noted. In legal cases the record that took precedence was the finca's account books, and from these, unless the abuse was obvious and the authorities disposed to note and act on it, the workers had no recourse within the system.

The fall in the value of the peso after 1900 and the rise in money wages did not lighten the worker's burden, for contracts always specified that advances and debts were to be worked off at the wage rate set in the initial agreement. Thus the various "minimum wages" announced from time to time by the government had no effect on the situation of the bulk of the workers.[142] Over time, and particularly as the value of money and of wages collapsed, a great deal of the accumulated worker debt became entirely artificial. The Indians long ago had worked off the real value of what they owed, but the obligation remained as an accounting fiction and even grew larger each year. The existence of this paper debt gave the fincas useful flexibility in dealing with their workers. In years of good coffee prices, for example, when demand for labor was high, employers paid in cash and goods but did not allow the workers to reduce their debts; in bad years they credited their debts and paid out little in money.[143] On those rare occasions when a worker ended the season with a balance due, and could prove it, he was seldom released; more likely, the employer advanced the Indian more wages, or said that he had done so, and noted the debt in the records. One recruiter explained: "If it happens that there is something owing a worker, I never pay cash."[144] The best the worker could hope for, and this commonly required the intervention of the jefe político, was a note certifying him to be without debt and free to offer his services to another finca.

Ignoring Indian protests, coffee planters regularly traded, transferred, and sold the rights to laborers among themselves.[145] Debts owed for labor constituted assets that could be included with the sale of a finca or separated and disposed of independently.[146] In the wake of a bankruptcy or a natural disaster such obligations might be one of the few things of value remaining. In 1903, for example, the owner of a property that was destroyed by the eruption of the volcano Santa María went to work for finca Patzulín, "Where, naturally, I took with me what little of value I still had"—the debts of his workers.[147] In other cases, the threat of transfer to an estate with a notoriously unhealthy climate was effective in repressing worker protest.[148] Fincas also sold the debts of laborers they no longer wanted or needed.[149] Government officials on occasion intervened to attempt to block what even many owners felt was a shameful practice, but only in 1906 did the state issue Decree 657 to put a stop to the "exchange or sale of workers."[150] In practice the law had little effect. State agents continued to accept such transfers as legitimate if the workers involved gave their "consent," a formality usually easily arranged or simply overlooked. Trafficking continued on into the 1920's and 1930's.[151] The market in some years was so brisk that debts went at a premium. In 1908, for example, the finca Helvetia bought 31 workers for the price of their debts plus 150 percent, and in 1913 finca Pantaleón paid a premium of 350 percent for 209 workers.[152] These levels of prices and the debts they entailed contributed to pushing small growers out of the labor market; when the large estates could afford to commit such quantities of money, it became extremely difficult for small growers to compete for workers.

Foreigners

The promise of coffee attracted a number of immigrants to Guatemala in the 1880's and 1890's, many of whom acquired land and set up fincas.[153] They had, or were said by envious Guatemalan growers to have, many advantages over local producers. These included access to capital at cheaper rates, recourse to diplomatic intervention, and closer and more favorable connections with the largely foreign-controlled export and import houses: "The foreigner enjoys guarantees in his person and property of which we nationals are deprived," local planters complained.[154] Foreigners often browbeat or ignored local authorities and acted with their workers as if they were above the law, but there is no evidence that they were more brutal toward the Indians than the local landowners, and they may well have been typically less so.[155] They got away with a highhanded manner in part because Liberal ideology presumed the inherent superiority of immigrants from more developed countries. This was particularly the case during the years of the notoriously arbitrary Estrada Cabrera dictatorship, when he put even the control of the secret police in foreign hands. Such privileges, naturally enough, left the immigrants a target of some carping. In September 1919, for example, the *Diario de Centro América* went so far as to lay the blame for the nation's labor problems at the door of immigrant employers: it was these foreigners, the writer claimed in a remarkable rewriting of history, who a generation before had introduced into Guatemala the practices of advancing money for labor and bribing officials.[156] *El Imparcial* protested in 1930: "A part of our difficulties is owed to the fact that the best part of our coffee production is in the strong hands of foreigners. Our principal national wealth practically is not Guatemalan. The land that was ours is passing rapidly into the hands of foreigners."[157] Another article a year later on the same theme complained that foreigners had gained their control over the Alta Verapaz, for example, largely by unfair competition.[158]

Much of the criticism was directed at Germans, who from early on constituted the largest and most prominent group of foreigners in the coffee industry.[159] By the late 1890's they held more than forty coffee fincas, with an area of some 230,252 manzanas.[160] German lenders and companies acquired more properties in the wake of the 1898 crisis,[161] and by 1913 they constituted the most important segment among the immigrant producers. In that year they held 170 properties that yielded a harvest of almost 360,000 quintales; by comparison, other foreigners owned 252 properties with a harvest of only 118,903 quintales, and though Guatemalan owners harvested 525,356 quintales, this was from 1,657 fincas.[162]

In 1918 President Estrada Cabrera under heavy pressure from the United States sequestered German-owned properties but did not, as the United States government had hoped, sell these off to North Americans.[163] Instead he put them under the care of government-appointed receivers—often the existing managers—and in 1919 he returned most of the intervened fincas to their former owners. Hoping

TABLE 7.6

Foreign-Controlled Coffee Export Companies in Guatemala, 1938–1939

Company	Number of fincas	Coffee harvest (in quintales)	Number of trees
CAPCO	9	65,000qq.	7,000,000
Nottebohm Her.	11	34,000	4,000,000
Gordon Smith Cia	7	21,000	2,500,000
Sapper y Cia.	15	11,000	1,200,000
G. Luttmann	2	11,000	1,200,000
M. H. Hempstead	8	9,000	1,000,000

SOURCE: Alvarado, *Tratado*, 2: 566.

TABLE 7.7

Guatemalan Coffee Exports by Nationality of Exporter,
1938–1939

Nationality	Exports (quintales)	Value (quetzales)
German	497,549qq.	Q4,974,719
Dutch	218,975	2,214,590
U.S.	210,921	2,083,194
Guatemalan	67,474	696,924
Spanish	12,025	115,122
English	9,100	86,718
TOTAL	1,016,044qq.	Q10,171,267

SOURCE: Montenegro, *La explotación cafetalera*, p. 107.

to strengthen their position and avoid future diplomatic problems, a dozen of the major German companies operating in Guatemala reorganized themselves in the early 1920's into the Central American Plantations Corporation (CAPCO), chartered in New York but controlled by German capital and management.[164] The Germans soon recovered from the effects of the war. By the early 1930's they controlled four of the six largest coffee operations in Guatemala, all of which belonged to foreign-controlled companies (see Table 7.6). And they dominated the export trade as well, accounting, for example, in 1938–39 for almost half the total value of coffee exports (see Table 7.7).

The presumption, shared by the immigrants and the local ladinos alike, of racial and cultural superiority, together with access to cheaper production resources and special treaty rights and diplomatic intervention,[165] gave foreigners and especially Germans tremendous advantages, which they were quite willing to exploit in order to take and hold a commanding position in coffee production and trade.[166] Although there was clearly a substratum of resentment among the planters at the advantages foreigners enjoyed, the intra-elite personal and business connections were too tight and Liberal ideology too committed both to the advantages of free trade and investment and to the natural superiority of North Atlantic culture for any real threat to foreign-owned property or place to develop before the Second World War.

Chapter 8

The Communities: Land

The Indians always have claims and distrust even their own
shadows.   AGCA-ST, Sololá, 31/6

In the thinking about the land histories of the indigenous population of Guatemala, there has been a vague and sometimes un-
spoken but nevertheless evident tendency to contrast a complex and
anxiety-ridden present, thought to be largely the result of the 1870's
Liberal reforms and coffee, to a vision of a past in which sufficient land
was available to all under the benign protection of the "community." [1]
But research has made it increasingly evident that the historical reality
was something else. At least from the Conquest, Indian societies and
economies have been crosscut by numerous different patterns of land
classification and use as well as by different interpretations of how land
should be held and the purposes to which it should be put. As a result,
they have been racked by internal and external conflicts over land.
The effects of the Reforma and of coffee were unprecedented and
merit special attention, but attempts at generalization must be paired
with the understanding that the history of each village was the result
of the interaction of its peculiar historical and ecological situation, the
class and interethnic struggles within and between it and other communities, and the conflicts that set the villages against commercial and
export agriculture and also against the state.

It is probably impossible to know what land meant to the indigenous
population of nineteenth-century Guatemala. To arrive at such an
understanding would at the very least require abandoning the Spanish
or English languages with their special thought patterns and concep-
tual structures and approaching the subject from an indigenous point
of view.[2] When Indian petitioners or litigants addressed why they
wanted or needed land, they did so in a very specific context, using
terms borrowed from a language with which they had limited familiarity and in the manner most calculated to ingratiate themselves with
their superiors. Probably, if asked in a general way, the whole question
would have struck them as absurd, for the utility of land was self-

evident and eternal; land meant everything. If called upon to think about it systematically, they very likely would have conceptualized land in terms of concentric circles.[3] At the center of the order lay those claims to land passed down directly to the individual through the clan or parcialidad.[4] These "ancestor estates"[5] had much more than economic significance: "The piece of land which a man has received from his ancestors is sacred; it has its shrine, where offerings are made; [it is] a place where one can approach the supernaturals."[6] It was disastrous to lose contact with this. Thus, and even in the absence of evident land shortages, the father, as the member of the patriclan closest to the ancestors and chief intermediary to the supernatural, wielded immense power; he was the one who decided who might have access to the land and on what conditions, and he demanded and generally received subservience from the younger males.

If a man[7] did fall out with his father and lose access to clan property, he could usually still continue to be a part of the broader community, at least while there remained open and available land in the village commons. This land constituted the second circle. With it a man could guarantee and perhaps improve his economic and social position, even if he could not be certain of his relations with the ancestors. He could marry, become an adult, and participate in local political and religious offices. However, if serious land shortages appeared, survival not only as an active participant in the life of the clan but as a member of the larger community might come to hinge more and more on the lands of the patrilineage. Economics reinforced ideology. The ancestor estates were the basis of the only security available in a world of narrowing access to land, and the right to these, or at least to a tiny piece of them, was protected and guaranteed for the dutiful child. Even access to hot-country land or land outside what was traditionally deemed part of the común—and this constituted the third circle—did not resolve the problem of continued participation in the life of the community. Without possession of at least some land in the vicinity of the village and the solid links to the ancestors and the community of origin this land provided, the emigrant risked increasing marginalization. Perhaps they now returned only for the annual fiesta and might soon be well on the way to becoming ladino. The generational struggles over land widely reported by anthropologists since the 1930's reflect a conflict probably predating the Conquest and one built into a community focused on contact with the ancestors, but the circumstances of the years after 1870 greatly intensified this conflict.[8]

Categories of Community Land

The Reforma, and particularly the emphasis after 1871 on clear measurements and legally recognized and registered titles, forced the highland indigenous communities to confront directly the question of the nature of land ownership and of the various categories of land typically lumped together in land documents and commonly referred to as "ejidos" or "común."[9] At the center of the community's possessions lay those properties often called *astillero* or *astilleros* in the late nineteenth century. Generally the municipal government managed this area directly, reserving it for everyone's use for pasturage, wood, and water, or in some cases allocating or renting parcels to the poor and landless of the community for cultivation.[10] By tradition if not always law the postindependence governments continued to guarantee all legally established communities an "ejido" of at least a square league, and this now included ladino and casta towns as well as Indian towns. With minor modifications this understanding persisted until the end of the century; surveyors in the 1880's and 1890's took it for granted that a square league was the norm. Despite law and tradition, however, not all villages possessed even the minimum of a square league, either because there was no land to be had in the vicinity of the town or because what was once ejido land had been broken up into other forms of property. Still, the idea, and the ideal, remained, and communities repeatedly appealed to it in their land requests and disputes. The Reforma state recognized the community's right to an ejido. After 1871 the state, having an interest in the survival of the villages as functioning institutions, if for different reasons from those held by the colonial government, added land to the ejidos of innumerable villages that sought or needed it.

Most of the Indian towns of the western highlands and the Alta Verapaz actually claimed and used much more than one square league of land, because a minimum ejido usually was not sufficient to support their populations. Some of this land they had purchased from the government or from private individuals or had acquired by composition from the Crown or the postindependence state. There also commonly was additional land, and often a far larger amount, that they claimed but for which they had no titles. If the state regarded this as illegally held excesos or excediente or simply as terreno baldío to which the villages had no right, the indigenous population countered that whatever the validity of their papers and regardless of the law the land in question was theirs by custom and by right of possession and use "from time immemorial." Since the colonial period, central governments, partly for fiscal reasons and also to reduce conflicts, had tried, with only limited success, to force the towns to title all the land they used or claimed.

Overlapping and intermixed, both physically and conceptually, with community property as the Indians understood it were tracts of land owned or used by various subgroups within the village such as the parcialidades, the cofradías, and hamlets apart from the main settlement. The patriclans seldom if ever clearly marked the boundaries of ancestor estates; in the absence of land shortages and disputes there was no urgent need to do so. Hamlets, units sometimes but not necessarily based on kinship links, frequently possessed specific tracts of land, which when pressured they might title, or attempt to title, either separately or in conjunction with the rest of the community.[11] Although many cofradías lost all or part of the land they owned in the 1804–7 and 1873 consolidations of church lands and in the wars of the 1820's and 1830's, others continued to make claims locally and to enforce them, even when the state failed to recognize them. The governor of Sololá, for example, reported in 1881 that "with . . . the highest intentions the government destroyed the cofradías and transferred the land to private hands," but a decade later the priest of Joyabaj was protesting that local ladino officials were attempting to steal a hacienda that belonged to an Indian cofradía.[12]

But what, after all, constituted "private" as against "community" property? At least three patterns are evident. From the colonial period, Spaniards, ladinos, and castas, and a few Indians, owned private property in the full Spanish legal sense of land as an alienable commodity. Among the indigenous population this was largely limited to hispanicized elites,[13] for private property was at odds both with the dominant ethos of land as a community or group resource available to all as needed and with the dominant production patterns in the indigenous economy. The customary form of land occupation and use among the Indians was one of more or less free movement of individuals and families across the broadly defined ejidos or común, following the cycles of slash-and-burn agriculture and migratory stock raising and subject only to the claims of subgroups within the community to certain tracts. The Indians of Santa Eulalia remembered that in the years before 1871 one only had to mark off a boundary to obtain generally recognized possession and the right to use a piece of land for subsistence agriculture.[14] Engineers surveying land in the late nineteenth century remarked on the extensive fallow land they encountered around the villages, even as they labeled these same areas "uninhabited." Community members normally enjoyed free use of the land they needed, and in most cases they could pass on these tracts to their descendants or sell the improvements they had made; but they were not supposed to sell the land itself, particularly not to outsiders. Local custom determined whether or not the distribution and use of community land was subject to the direct intervention of village officials, and whether or not those who cultivated or pastured on community land had to pay rent.

As pressures on land mounted after 1871, communities more often began seeking title from the state for the whole of what they regarded as their common lands. The effect of titles so secured was to draw a legally recognized line or boundary around the community in relation to neighboring towns or properties, but within these limits most of the villages' inhabitants still had no title beyond what was accorded in the traditional ways. With both land loss and population increases more and more putting into doubt continued ready access to land, individual claims to specific tracts within the común and the urgency with which these were defended tended to increase. Land itself, rather than simply improvements, was now more often bought and sold, but because of cost and because of the continued sense that "everyone knew" the limits of each plot, participants in such transactions still did not always include these in central government's registries. Instead, ownership guarantees rested on locally drawn bills of sale or receipts and on the testimony of neighbors or established figures. Speaking of one highland town in the 1930's, an investigator explained, "Most claims to land are still validated by the testimony of neighbors and local official 'witnesses.'"[15] Only gradually, following the example of the ladinos who moved into the towns in greater numbers after 1880, did some community members begin to take out full legal titles. Land disputes within the villages increased, as did resort to ladino courts.[16]

It is instructive at this point to reverse the image of concentric circles. Most Indians understood their village or town to have a "general title," obtained in the colonial period or from the national government, that guaranteed the overall land basis of the community.[17] Some towns, and an increasing number after 1871, did possess such titles, although the conditions these specified were rarely what the local inhabitants imagined. A surprising number did not. The jefe político of

TABLE 8.1
Community Lands and Titles, Department of Sololá, 1887

Town	Land claimed	Title?
Sololá	apx. 165 caballerías	partial
Concepción	?	no
S. José Chacaya	apx. 10 cabs.	?
S. Andrés Semetabaj	?	lost
Panajachel	apx. 30 cabs.	"unreadable old documents"
S. Antonio Palopó	apx. 11 cabs.	refuses to show
Sta. Catarina Palopó	apx. 25 cabs.	no
S. Juan La Laguna	61.5 cabs.	yes
S. Pedro La Laguna	apx. 97 cabs.	"useless old documents"
S. Juan Leprosos	apx. 38⅔ cabs.	no = rioted when requested
S. Marcos la Laguna	no size	no
Sta. Clara La Laguna	apx. 24 cabs.	no
Visitación	apx. 24 cabs.	no
S. Pablo	apx. 8 cabs.	no
Sta. Cruz La Laguna	apx. 2 cabs.	"old documents"
Santiago Atitlán	99.5 cabs.	yes = 1852
Sta. Lucia Utatlán	apx. 99 cabs.	yes = 1861
Nahualá/Sta Catarina Ix.	?	no = know boundaries
Patulul	apx. 1400 cabs.	no
Sta. Barbara	342 cabs.	yes = 1820's

SOURCE: AGCA, B100.1 3987 88705.

Sololá, for example, as late as 1887, found that nearly all the towns in his department either had no titles at all or had only outdated and useless documents (see Table 8.1). What many guarded carefully as "titles" was a collection of papers that might include measurements and lawsuits from the Colonial, Conservative, and Liberal periods, letters and decrees from the King and the Audiencia, stays from various officials, and an occasional ancient document pertaining to early and even preconquest claims and perhaps written in an aboriginal language. Most such papers had little or no legal validity in the late nineteenth century. Many could not even be deciphered. Within the boundaries marked by the claimed or registered municipal title there were shifting congeries of group and individual claims, possession recognized by occupation and tradition, and titles based on papers authenticated by the nearest judge or governor, or a letter dashed off by a passing president.

A vision of a past marked by equality and by the relative absence of internal tensions over land, or at least tensions resolved locally by traditional and accepted means, has been extremely important to the construction of the mythology, or demonology, of the Liberal Reforma. From this have resulted two widely held, if largely unexplored, assumptions. One of these has it that the Liberals "abolished" village ejidos, and that coffee was therefore responsible for widespread losses of land by the highland communities.[18] Following on this is the equally common assumptions that communities generally resisted this loss of land, as well as attendant demands for forced labor, by rising up violently against their oppressors.[19] One writer has summarized these interlocking positions neatly: "In the nineteenth century, when Ladinos were encouraged to resettle in Indian regions, and communal lands were abolished, the Indians of one town rose up and slaughtered the ladino settlers. . . . In the twentieth century labor revolts were common reactions to forced labor."[20] In part this simplified assessment of the history of rural Guatemala in the half-century after 1871 is due to the paucity of historical studies of the period, which allows easy generalizations about coffee, land, and Indians based on the laws of the period or a few isolated examples, or by analogy to countries with apparently similar histories. To some extent also the assumption of open resistance stems from a laudable desire to see the Indians, and oppressed peoples in general, as actors in their own history rather than merely as victims. But few would argue that law in present-day Guatemala accurately reflects reality, and there is no reason to suppose greater congruence one hundred years ago. Similarly, because of the many variations in the history of rural Guatemala, it is impossible to arrive at clear conclusions based on a few scattered examples. The prevailing mythology of the Reform period at the very least excessively simplifies a tangled reality. Moreover, and more importantly, it tends to overlook the very real resistance of the Indian to the tyranny of everyday life.

The Impacts of Coffee and the Reforma: Three Theses

For all the complexities, coffee and the Reforma did affect the land situation in the indigenous communities in several broadly general ways.[21] First of all, the Liberal reforms tended to strengthen the hold of most villages on whatever common land they possessed and used in the immediate vicinity of the village. Titling carried out under the

pressures of the Reforma gave the villages in most cases an unprecedented security of tenure over their ejido, at least in respect to their
immediate neighbors. Second, many communities, in effect, gave up
broad and poorly defined claims to land—and thereby also the conflicts these engendered—for reduced but much more clearly identified
landholdings that were duly titled and registered. Although in most
cases this was not a matter of choice, because if they resisted they
risked losing more land, that sort of exchange and the relative peace
it brought was not necessarily bad, at least not until rising populations
began to press up against the limits of the new boundaries. Finally,
it is clear that the highland villages did lose land as a result of the
shift to large-scale coffee production in the 1870's and 1880's; but the
way in which this occurred was a good deal more subtle and gradual
than what the term "abolition" suggests. Liberal regimes preserved
and expanded the ejido proper of many towns; but did the conversion
of part or all of the area traditionally recognized as común into one
of various forms of individual or group private property or possession necessarily constitute a loss? When, for example, ladinos or local
Indian elites titled land and then rented it back to the villagers, was
this a loss or merely a change in the conditions of access? Did a village
lose land in a relative sense as local populations grew, or did it lose
land in absolute terms, directly to export production or indirectly to
erosion and weathering brought on by increased population pressure,
decreased fallow time, and cultivation of marginal lands?

Changes in land laws under the new Liberal regime at first had little
or no impact on most Indian towns. Coffee in Guatemala grows mainly
at altitudes of 2,000–5,000 feet, and because most of the indigenous
population of the western highlands lived in villages at higher altitudes, coffee growers had little interest in their land. The effects of
Decree 170, the law of redemption, for example, depended entirely
on where the particular community was located. Outside the western
piedmont, few villages encountered an immediate, life-endangering
threat in the law. There was plenty of cheap land available for coffee without the need for immediate confrontation with most of the
highland villages.

Bearing in mind local differences, it is still useful to construct a
broad typology of Indian towns based on the relationship between the
communities, land, and coffee.

1. *Indigenous towns in the coffee piedmont.* These included communities in a band running from the El Salvador border through Escuintla

west along the slopes of the mountains through the decayed cacao towns of San Antonio Suchitepéquez, Samayac, and San Francisco Zapotitlán, the recently resettled villages of Santo Tomás Perdido (La Unión) and Zunilito, and on across the lightly settled coast of San Marcos to the Mexican border. With a few exceptions, these communities quickly found themselves overwhelmed by the new crop. Their lands were converted to large-scale coffee production in the hands of ladino elites, and their population was reduced to coffee labor. Seventy-five years after coffee arrived, the inhabitants of Pochuta remembered that "ladinos from Antigua" had come to their town "in the time of Justo Rufino Barrios" to buy land "for good prices" and put it into coffee. Now they worked as colonos and day laborers on the estates.[22] Even in this region, however, the effects of coffee varied. In areas where the soil was not suitable for the new export, such as Panán[23] or the upper and lower reaches of the boca costa, which were too cold or too hot for large-scale coffee, local residents and highland Indian immigrants titled substantial tracts and planted them not only in milpa but also in cotton, cacao, and coffee.

2. *The towns of the Alta Verapaz.* Here the confrontation between subsistence agriculture and coffee was also immediate, but the large amounts of unused land that continued to be available in the department and in the neighboring northern Quiché limited initial conflicts. Community leaders, and particularly those representing the main patriclans of the large towns of Carchá and Cobán where coffee first took root, moved aggressively to title land for their groups.[24] For example, in 1876 the leaders of the barrio of Santo Domingo of San Pedro Carchá, noting that the barrios of Santiago and San Sebastián had already made similar applications, asked to title twelve caballerías located three leagues to the east of Carchá. This was land the clan claimed to have possessed "from time immemorial" and that was said to be inhabited by many families of the barrio.[25] The state sold them the land at the base price of 50 pesos a caballería without auction competition. Similarly, the barrio of Santo Domingo of Cobán in these same years successfully disputed land with a foreign rancher north of the town, and in the early 1880's one Domingo Batzoc, described as the representative of the five barrios of Chamelco, applied for and received more than one hundred caballerías for the groups.[26] Large-scale coffee in the Alta Verapaz displaced Indian land possession and use away from the areas near the main towns and along the roads and into the less accessible and colder parts of the municipalities, but it

did not strip them of access to land. Although individuals and families often found themselves reduced to colono status on someone else's
property, this was more a function of the labor laws than a result of a
shortage of land.[27] The highland towns of the Alta Verapaz also continued the colonial practice of seasonal migration to the northern and
eastern lowlands to cultivate tropical crops, but little of the population,
and unlike that on the western boca costa, settled there.[28]

  3. *Communities adjacent to the coffee piedmont.* Again, it is possible to
identify a band of towns running along the upper edge of the western piedmont, from Cuilapa to Alotenango and Acatenango to the
towns along the southern edge of Lake Atitlán to San Martín Sacatepéquez and Concepción Chiquirichapa to San Pedro Sacatepéquez (San
Marcos), that for centuries had cultivated land seasonally in the piedmont. With the onset of coffee they struggled, with varying success, to
retain access to it. The justicias of San Martín Sacatepéquez, for example, protested in 1880 that outsiders had invaded land at Chuvá in
the adjacent Costa Cuca that belonged to the town.[29] They had hired
an engineer to measure the area, but before they could complete the
titling process the government had taken over the Costa Cuca and distributed it to planters. Although they recognized, they said, that much
of the area had been left uncultivated and that the land was good for
coffee that was important for national development, San Martín now
was in danger of being left without "a bit of land on the coast, which
is where we grow our food"; the ejidos around the town were suitable
only for sheep and potatoes.[30] Eventually San Martín managed to title
five caballerías on the upper fringes of Chuvá in an area too cold for
coffee.[31] Santa Catarina Ixtahuacán and Nahualá in 1889 lost the land
they had obtained on the coast at Parraché in the 1850's "because they
produced nothing but subsistence for the community"; the government replaced it with a less desirable tract at Panán.[32] In the northern
part of the republic the process of the alienation of the piedmont and
lowlands proceeded more slowly, not really getting under way until the
1890's, but towns facing the northern lowlands such as Nebaj, Cotzal
and Chajul, and Santa Eulalia and Uspantán, eventually suffered the
same sort of losses.[33] These communities saw fincas and private owners
move into and assert ownership over areas they had claimed and used
for centuries for subsistence agriculture.

  4. *Towns wholly in the highlands but with a tradition of access to and
use of lowland lands.* The fate of the hot-country land claims of these
towns was similar to that of the villages directly abutting the piedmont.

Where they had planted colonies in the area these sometimes became independent Indian-dominated municipalities, such as Santo Tomás Perdido (La Unión)[34] and Zunilito. Others, like El Palmar, fell under the control of the planters or became hamlets of new municipalities set up by and for ladino coffee growers—for example, Barillas and El Quetzal in northern Huehuetenango. At El Palmar not only did Momostenango lose its lowland settlement, but ladinos subsequently shut out momosteco immigrants from political power and access to land in the area. With the influx of coffee planters, El Palmar became an independent, ladino-run municipality in 1871.[35] In 1878 town leaders applied to title ten caballerías of what they claimed was public land for a community ejido.[36] The problem, the jefe político reported to the Ministry of Interior, was that "Indians of Momostenango resident in El Palmar" already occupied much of the area in question and cultivated it in small subsistence plots. The Ministry responded that the law regarding land in the Costa Cuca–El Palmar area was clear: only the cultivation of coffee, sugar cane, cacao, and improved pasture "when the plantings were of some size and not as those described by the surveyor" counted as effective occupancy.[37] The pattern, then, was for the highland municipalities to lose control over their lowland possessions or settlements and for the Indian residents of these in turn to lose control of local government and community lands. Nevertheless, some of the highland towns were able to take advantage of these same laws, and of direct appeals to the President, to title tracts in the hot country outside those areas most favored for coffee. Their success in offsetting land losses to coffee depended on their aggressiveness, their political relations with the central state, and their luck.

  5. *Towns wholly in the highlands and without active claims to hot-country land.* This group embraced most of the highland towns from San Martín Jilotepeque and Comalapa in the upper half of Chimaltenango through Chichicastenango and the towns north of Lake Atitlán and into the Cuchumatán Mountains. Although some had access to hot-country land in nearby mountain valleys, most centered their agriculture in the ejidos immediately around the village. The inhabitants went to the lowlands if at all chiefly as traders or to exchange local commodities and artisan manufactures for corn or tropical products. Land conflict among these communities was, as it had been for centuries, a social staple. In some cases Liberal efforts to measure and title land ended ancient disputes, but difficulties remained, and in spite of the efforts of the state to repress open, large-scale violence between

the towns, border skirmishes continued. Where titling fixed municipal boundaries, land problems tended to shift more and more to conflicts within the communities. The ladinos who invaded the villages to recruit labor or sell goods sometimes bought or otherwise acquired land, and this had the effect of cutting off or at least altering the conditions of access to this land for the local population. The same cash influx resulting from finca labor that attracted ladinos to the towns also allowed some Indians and communities to title baldío or to buy land from their distressed neighbors.[38] So far as the indigenous population was concerned, coffee provided new resources and new dangers that worked to alter the terms of relations within and between the towns.

The Impact of the Reforma Land Laws

There is no question that the Liberals privileged private property. As one jefe político explained: "One of the principal obstacles to the prosperity of the country, and particularly of the Indians, is the lands held in common. It is absolutely proven that these lands are never cultivated, except perhaps in small amounts . . . because no one has an interest in making improvements . . . and no one has security in their harvests."[39] And a ladino applicant was correct when he observed, "The intent of General Barrios . . . was to end, even if in a slow but effective manner, the communal lands that have so prejudiced the progress of agriculture."[40] But for this transformation to occur, specific parcels of ejido land had to be applied for, measured, purchased, and titled. The conversion of land from communal to private property in Guatemala did not come as the sudden and thoroughgoing event it apparently did in El Salvador or parts of Nicaragua during these years.[41] Rather, and to the extent that it happened at all, privatization was the result of a number of specific and uncoordinated positive acts taken by different persons over an extended period of time.

The alienation of land from the community under the redemption decree certainly caused many problems. As the inhabitants of Escuintla pointed out, even if the price was only a few reales a manzana, Indians did not have the money to redeem their land and as a result were losing it to outsiders. In this instance the jefe político responded by offering reduced prices if the Indians would plant cacao instead of subsistence crops and dress as ladinos.[42] At San Raymundo, north of the capital, the indigenous population fought for two decades over what redemption meant and how it should be applied. Leaders protested that the ejidos of the town rightfully belonged to the Indians and should not be sold to ladinos. Fearful that this line of argument might not afford sufficient protection, they also sought to buy the land in question. Borrowing 500 pesos at 3.25 percent a month and collecting another 500 pesos from among the population, the justicias applied to the state to "compose" thirty-five caballerías they claimed to have bought originally from the Crown in the eighteenth century. Local ladinos protested that the Indian officials were manipulating the people for their personal profit and argued that there was more than enough land available for all. The real problem, they said, was the Indians' "spirit of separatism and opposition . . . to progress and the improvement of this place," which was keeping the ladinos from being able to develop the commercial agriculture the country needed. When the jefe político intervened to favor the ladinos' request, the Indians raised more money by selling off cofradía cattle, and they successfully petitioned the President for a stay guaranteeing their possession.[43] For Sacapulas, in Quiché department, the potential threat was not from ladinos but from their aggressive neighbor, the overpopulated Indian municipality of Santa María Chiquimula. In March 1877 Sacapulas appealed to the Archbishop to intervene with the President on their behalf and that of Cunen and Uspantán. For years, they said, the chiquimulas had rented land from their towns, and now they worried that Santa María would seek to redeem it.[44]

Besides trying to buy the land themselves, threatened Indian communities became adept at other measures meant to thwart incursions by outsiders and coffee. Because the 1877 redemption law provided that individual plots could not be titled until the astillero was marked, some communities simply delayed doing this, tying up the entire process.[45] Or Indian municipal officials would refuse to turn over to purchasers the necessary documents. Among the most aggressive and obstinate were, as they described themselves, "the principales of the towns of Zunil, Zunilito, and Santo Tomás." A number of would-be coffee growers redeemed plots at Santo Tomás Perdido (La Unión) in 1877 and 1878, but three years later they still had not been able to obtain their papers from the officials of Zunil. Even jailing Zunil's gobernador had no effect. When one of the applicants gave up in disgust, saying he was willing to settle for compensation for the improvements he had made, Zunil responded that since they had never allowed him on to the land, he had not made any improvements, and his other costs were not their responsibility.[46] Many ladinos found that it was one thing to buy a piece of property from the government and quite another to obtain effective possession. Ultimately, of course, the success of such delaying tactics depended entirely on who it was who sought the land and how necessary or valuable the land was. The more marginal the land to coffee and the more marginal the ladino, or Indian, applicant to national economic and social elites, the more successful community resistance was likely to be.

When a community did title ejido lands after 1871, the document the government issued usually included a provision requiring that the tract be broken up into individual plots (lotificación). A provision written into an 1893 title obtained by the town of Uspantán was typical: "The land will be divided up equitably into lots, to avoid the defects of community ownership."[47] If this had been done it would have worked a revolution in the highlands, converting much of the area into mapped and legally registered small property. It rarely was. The state in most cases would not or could not follow up on these title requirements. Years or decades could elapse between the time when the community acquired the land and the time when local leaders made an effort to divide it legally. More often, towns simply continued the established patterns of possession and use under the umbrella of the new "general title" unless and until external or internal pressures forced some regularization. Various Indians of Jocotán, for example, complained in 1890 that some years before the town had titled a tract of ejido land called Lampocoy on which they lived, but now the ladino-controlled municipal government was giving it to outsiders. Town officials replied that they were distributing lots according to the amount of money each individual had contributed to the costs of measurement and purchase of the land. Whereas the Indians might wish "that the area remain community property," the government attorney agreed with the local ladinos that "not everyone wishes to live in the noxious state of community to which the petitioners aspire." He ordered the town authorities to continue giving out titles. The Indians objected without success: "If this is what is called distributing the land, it is in truth hostile and abusive plunder."[48]

At Balanya, in Chimaltenango, conditions were quite the opposite. Indian leaders there explained to the government in 1895 that some sixty years before the town's inhabitants had divided the community's lands into de facto private plots but had never legally titled them with the state. Over the years, the lots changed hands, by gift and inheritance, "without making note of these transactions, both because of the insignificant size of the lots and because we never have had the custom of wills or other documents. . . . Rural property passes from father to son and has no value in the conventional sense because we never sell it."[49] They had not redeemed the plots under Decree 170 because no one paid rent, but now ladinos were using this as an excuse to invade and steal their property. When the government asked for a detailed survey to allow the plots to be entered in the land registry, the town responded that this would be difficult: more than four hundred local residents possessed a total of slightly more than twenty-one caballerías divided into 1,181 lots, not counting town sites and "useless" land; one family's holdings, for example, might total as much as twenty-one cuerdas in seven parcels scattered in different places. At this the government threw up its hands, ordering the municipality itself to issue titles based on existing documents and information.

Although there were many reasons why the Liberals did not "abolish" community land, the most impelling was simply that there was no need to do so. In most areas there was no immediate land conflict or competition between coffee and subsistence, and the state resolved the labor problem by the use of extra-economic coercion. In places where coffee production did overlap actual or potential corn land, as, for example, in the western piedmont and around Carchá and Cobán, coffee tended to dispossess subsistence agriculture, but even in these areas there were still large parcels that either were unsuitable for coffee or were held in reserve and, in the meantime, were cultivated commercially in food crops, rented for milpa to highland Indians,[50] or worked by finca residents for subsistence or for the market.

An additional reason for not moving more forcefully against community property was a reluctance to undertake a direct assault on the communities. National leaders were well aware of the importance of the villages as food producers, and they were also mindful of provoking violent Indian resistance of the sort that had toppled the 1830's Liberals and of the effect this would have on the usefulness of the highland communities as producers of cheap, seasonal labor. At the same time, the state was clearly on the side of private property, as was evident in the Costa Cuca decree, the redención de censos, and various provisions to facilitate the sale of baldíos for favored crops, as well as the requirements for subdivision inserted in municipal land titles. The purpose of these laws was to encourage the conversion of "noxious" community property into private property. But three and a half centuries of colonial rule had made the Indian the master of "passive"—in fact, quite active but generally indirect and nonviolent—resistance. It was not a question of ignorance. Deceived on occasion and done repeated injury by corrupt lawyers and officials,[51] as the poor are always, at least the leadership among the Indians generally understood, if they did not necessarily agree with, the broad outlines of Liberal land laws. And they hired lawyers who knew the details. Village justicias used a variety of tactics, from lawsuits to petitions to personal appeals to the President to, though rarely, open violence, to press as best they could for what they and their community perceived as their interests. Whatever the young men of Santa Eulalia might think a century later, Indian elders of the Reforma were by and large not "men without tongues,"[52] but men who struggled ingeniously and tenaciously to guard and advance community well-being within the range of possibilities available to them.

Community Titling

Not without reason, communities perceived titling as a process fraught with risk, which, once initiated, might lead to unexpected and undesirable conclusions. At the very least it required the Indians to expose and sometimes give over to outsiders and the state the communities' closely held "titles." If these did not disappear in the resulting judicial processes, they might reveal the often tenuous or even unfounded legal basis of all or part of a community's claims to land. Worse, they might support, or be made to appear to support, the claims of their opponents. Not only was the measuring and titling process expensive,[53] even before the community faced the problem of how to pay for the land itself, but also the villagers well knew that even yet another title did not necessarily guarantee security. In 1894, for example, Nebaj obtained the right to some 1,400 caballerías in the surrounding area, land for which the town was to pay 10 to 36 pesos a caballería; when this proved too expensive, President Estrada Cabrera in 1902 reduced the price to a uniform 10 pesos a caballería, which Nebaj paid. However, two years later the state reversed itself, and, claiming that "community property is . . . inconvenient and anti-economic," allowed individuals, including those from outside the community, to buy land within the area recently titled by Nebaj. The price was 36 pesos a caballería, 10 pesos of which went to the municipality and the rest to the

TABLE 8.2
Community Land Titling, 1895–1914

Year	No. towns	Amount (manzanas)	Year	No. towns	Amount (manzanas)
1895	8	20,949	1906	5	21,103
1896	12	49,103	1907	10	46,147
1897	3	4,610	1908	8	96,371
1898	15	86,751	1909	9	52,508
1900	16	126,222	1910	13	82,204
1901	10	67,389	1911	15	83,609
1902	16	113,869	1912	7	7,498
1903	10	133,106	1913	8	19,383
1904	4	17,517	1914	5	7,225
1905	7	10,362			

SOURCES: Ministerio de Gobernación, *Memorias*; Mendez Montenegro, "444 años."
NOTE: These figures are not complete or fully accurate. Towns were often awarded simply "the land they possess" or "a piece of land" without details of the size. Several towns appear more than once.

central government. Local leaders resisted but to no avail, and Indians from land-short communities such as Santa María Chiquimula, San Francisco el Alto, and Momostenango, together with ladinos and local Indians, hastened to take up large tracts. The municipality was left with only its original square league.[54]

Despite the dangers, difficulties, and costs, however, the Indian communities did title land in large amounts. General statistics exist only for the years 1895–1914, in most cases a decade or two after the indigenous population had begun to respond to the impacts of coffee, but the figures are impressive, as Table 8.2 shows. The state facilitated the measurement and titling of ejidos and excesos for many communities, sometimes paying the measurement expenses and often granting the land at no cost or reduced prices and without auction competition.[55] This, rather than a state-led assault on the ejidos, was the dominant pattern. For example, the town of Santiago Chimaltenango applied to the state in 1879 saying that it needed secure possession of land but had neither an established ejido nor a title. An attempt to fix boundaries with the neighboring municipalities revealed that most of these also lacked titles and were not even sure of where the dividing lines ran. The surveyor measured Santiago a square league of ejidos plus 119 caballerías of excess, and the state granted this free of cost to "these poor Indians . . . as had been done for San Pedro Necta

[and] San Martín."[56] Similarly, Sanarate, in the department of Guatemala, by the 1880's possessed an immense number of land documents but no title. The surveyor who was sent to straighten out the situation found among the town's papers two letters of protection from President Barrios and two from governors guaranteeing the town's possession of the tracts of San Juan, Las Minas, and San Nicolás "and adjacent baldíos," eight letters and documents from various officials in guarantee of Sanarate's possession of public lands immediate to the hacienda San Nicolás of José María Estevez, a bill of sale dated 1881 in which Estevez sold the hacienda to the government, which in turn ceded it to the town, an agreement with Jutiapa from 1882 regarding boundaries, and miscellaneous papers regarding small pieces of baldío legalized in 1885 by Decree 352 that confirmed the many haphazard grants and concessions made throughout the republic by Barrios in his years as president.[57] Neighboring communities presented a similar bewildering array of documents. Although it was clear, the government's chief surveyor pointed out, that Sanarate had no acceptable legal basis for most of its claims, the government nevertheless titled one hundred caballerías to the town without cost.[58] San Antonio Palopó, in Sololá, applied in 1894 for the measurement and titling of its community lands. The village was fighting the efforts of one Miguel Amezquita— "who has made himself wealthy by applying for land and then selling it"—to take over their lands by claiming it was baldío. The surveyor pointed out that San Antonio's case was particularly strong because the tract in question "was not the ephemeral and transitory property of ejidos nor of the property called 'of the community' but rather the sort of solid property that originated in a very old contract of sale." President Reina Barrios ordered a title granted without cost.[59] Hundreds more communities secured title to their lands in a similar manner in the years after 1871.

Lowland Land Titling

The movement of coffee and of ladino settlers into the boca costa, although it disrupted age-old patterns of seasonal migration by Indians, did not end them. Rather, it tended to change the conditions under which migration and cultivation took place. Squatting and claims of use "from time immemorial" gave way to titles, purchase, and contract arrangements. As coffee settlers poured into the Costa

Cuca after 1873, the inhabitants of the adjacent town of Concepción Chiquirichapa struggled to salvage what they could from an area they had long considered an integral part of the community. In 1875 and again in 1877 the town petitioned for the remeasurement and titling of a tract called El Nil at Asintal. Together with San Martín Sacatepéquez, Concepción possessed a title to six and a half caballerías based on composition made in the early eighteenth century. When a surveyor measured the tract he actually found some nineteen caballerías within the boundaries indicated, a not uncommon discrepancy in these years, but highway robbers stole his baggage, and only two years later was he able to recover the documents. In the meantime, ladinos from nearby San Juan Ostuncalco obtained a grant of ten caballerías in the area claimed by Concepción and began to cultivate some of the land, populating the hamlet of San Juan Nil. It took another round of expensive measurements to demonstrate that the two tracts in fact were entirely separate. In 1886 Concepción received a new title to six and a half caballerías, as well as the right to buy thirteen caballerías of excess at one peso a hectare, all in the lowest, hottest part of the Costa Cuca good only for subsistence agriculture.[60]

To the east of Concepción lay Santiago Atitlán. Probably no town exhibited more persistence and ingenuity in attempting to hold on to and expand community land in the hot country than did Santiago. In 1877 the community bought some thirty caballerías in Panán and Pamaxán from the heirs of General Rafael Carrera. These had been part of the town's traditional lands from before the Conquest but were lost in the 1860's when Carrera obtained them, along with those of other towns in the region, as baldío. In 1888 members of the community gave up two caballerías for the site of the new town Chicacao, but received in recompense four caballerías to the west of the Cutzán River. As the coffee boom accelerated in the 1890's the town stepped up its own titling efforts: in 1896 village leaders bought 41 caballerías of state land, and between 1895 and 1901 they obtained more than 60 more caballerías from private owners. Santiago Atitlán by the turn of the century possessed more than 240 caballerías of land and since the late 1870's had more than doubled the area titled to the town.[61]

For communities farther distant from the piedmont, the new Liberal laws and policies may actually have improved their chances of obtaining secure access to hot-country land, access that in the past had sometimes been blocked or heavily conditioned by the broad claims of lowland and piedmont towns and haciendas. In 1876, for example, the Indians of San Miguel and San Cristóbal Totonicapán applied for land in Pamaxán, and the ladinos of nearby San Carlos Sija sought land at Xoljuitz. The government granted these requests, stipulating that the tracts be divided into lots of equal size and allocated by lottery among the inhabitants of the towns. Disputes arising out of already existing concessions and conflicting claims held up San Miguel Totonicapán's grant, and the townspeople did not settle these until 1889.[62] Sija, however, moved quickly to cultivate the twenty-five caballerías it had received, described as forest "broken only by a few corn plantings of the Indians of San Martín Sacatepéquez." Two years later Sija applied for and obtained at no cost an additional fifteen caballerías adjoining the original grant. Those who settled in this area, now organized into the settlement of Nuevo San Carlos, in turn applied for and acquired more land.[63] Towns also titled land in the northern lowlands. The municipality of Huehuetenango gained possession of more than 200 caballerías at Santa Cruz Yalmux in what traditionally had been the hot-country lands of Santa Eulalia but eventually would become the independent municipality of Barillas. The towns of San Francisco el Alto, Momostenango, and Chiantla, among others, acquired land north of Nebaj, and Cunen, San Cristóbal Verapaz, Rabinal, Cubulco, and Santa Cruz del Quiché successfully sought extensive tracts in the municipality of Uspantán.[64]

A close reading of land applications reveals that it was not always strictly the town or the community in the broad sense that applied for land, but one of the subgroups within the community. Hamlets titled land, either because the municipality could not afford a broader title or because of land disputes within the community itself, sometimes as a prelude to a move toward municipal independence. In 1902, for example, the residents of the hamlets of Majadas-Chiché and Xenachacul of Aguacatán applied to buy thirty caballerías "which we always have owned." The state's surveyor had measured more than 509 caballerías to Aguacatán, they complained, but the municipality did not have, or claimed not to have, the funds needed to pay for it. Because of this the hamlets found themselves in danger of losing their land to outsiders. On investigation, at least part of the problem proved to be that the inhabitants of these settlements had come originally from Santa María Chiquimula and were themselves considered outsiders by the aguacatecos, who were reluctant to pay for the land these groups used. The government approved the sale of the thirty caballerías directly to the settlers.[65] Clan groups titled land,[66] as did groups labeled simply *"compañeros"* (comrades). Because the documents do not usually specify the relationship or even necessarily the names of all applicants, it is in most instances impossible to reconstruct the links that formed these groups. Certainly they included not only kinship but *compadrazgo* (god parenthood) and other forms of fictive kinship, or they may simply have resulted from the congregation of land-seeking individuals around a powerful local boss. In a typical case, José and Martin Ax, Antonio Ico, "and other compañeros" from San Pedro Carchá in the 1870's applied to buy some forty caballerías located east of the town. To emphasize their interest, more than a hundred of the applicants carried the papers in person to the jefe político, their "father of minors." The tract turned out to contain more than 123 caballerías, but the government allowed the Indians to buy all of it at a reduced cost because "one cannot and should not damage the large number of families that have their milpas and other plantings there." In such instances, the new owners sometimes had documents of "co-ownership" drawn up and notarized and may subsequently have divided the land up into individual plots.[67]

Ladino militia units were also extremely active in titling land in these years. Where ladinos predominated the militia was largely synonymous with the male population of the community, and land applications did not always differentiate one from the other. They appealed to the state as a town in terms of the militia members' need, "race," and public service.[68] In villages divided between Indians and ladinos, and especially where the ladinos constituted a small minority, access to ejido land for non-Indians could be difficult. The Reforma opened new opportunities. The apparently beleaguered militia members of Soloma, for example, wrote to President Barillas in May 1888 to remind him that he recently had promised them, together with those of Huehuetenango, land in the northern lowlands. They explained that because Soloma had been entirely Indian when their ancestors arrived and because the indigenous population had resisted ladino immigration, the newcomers had found it possible to acquire only tiny plots of land in areas so cold that even potatoes and wheat would not grow. The government responded by granting them fifty caballerías in the north of the department.[69] Chiantla militia members in 1894 also applied for land in the same area, contrasting "the hard-working race of ladinos" with the "retrograde and troublesome . . . Indian race." A shortage of funds kept them from pursuing this application until 1905 when President Estrada Cabrera agreed to pay half the costs; by then the land in question had been awarded to the militia of Momostenango.[70] Only in 1912 did Chiantla militia members title 200 caballerías far to the north of Nebaj.

On the other side of the country President Barrios in 1877 gave tracts of land in the Pamaxán lowlands to the ladino militia members of several predominantly Indian municipalities in the department of Sololá, including Sololá itself, Santiago Atitlán, and Santa Lucía Utatlán. In the latter case the concession was ten caballerías, for which the recipients paid only the 200-peso measurement costs. They soon sold this land, together with an additional ten caballerías they had received, and a decade later successfully applied for seven caballerías more, citing "our poverty" and sacrifices for the country. The terms of each grant were that the town was to divide the tracts into lots of equal size and allocate them by lottery to the militia members. However, much of the land fell almost immediately into the hands of a few militia officers, who manipulated the distribution process so as to give several lots to themselves and to their underage children and deny land to others and then sold this to outsiders. When the utatecos applied for yet more land, the jefe político of Sololá lost his patience, complaining that they were nothing but land speculators who, if left to it, would destroy the Indian towns of San Juan la Laguna and Santa Clara la Laguna. The President revoked the most recent concession.[71]

Land Conflict

Disputes over land, up to and including violence, had deep historical roots in rural Guatemala. The assumption has been that these increased greatly as a result of the changes wrought by coffee and the Liberals, but probably the opposite was true. Cases brought to the Courts of First Instance indicate that intercommunity conflict peaked for the nineteenth century in the 1860's and declined sharply thereafter.[72] Although riots and armed attacks by no means disappeared after 1871, the increasing power of the state made them much less likely to occur.[73] A strong state had no need to foment conflict to "divide and rule" an already fragmented highland population and would not tolerate disruptions to the smooth flow of labor to the coffee economy. The Indians soon understood this. The "horrible punishment" visited on Momostenango by President Barrios in 1877 because of violence growing out of a land dispute with San Carlos Sija and the shooting of dozens of Indians after an attack on ladino labor recruit-ers in San Juan Ixcoy in 1898 were persuasive object lessons.[74] It was clear that in most cases violence no longer served a purpose useful to the Indians. More significantly, and except for the piedmont commu-nities crushed by coffee and in the Verapaz where resistance typically took the forms of avoidance and titling rather than open conflict, the indigenous community and the coffee finca rarely confronted each other across a common border. Even when the towns titled land in the piedmont, possession increasingly took the form of legal or de facto individual, private property. If a conflict erupted with a neigh-boring finca it was usually the individual or the subgroup rather than the community that responded. Boundary conflicts with Indians are remarkably absent from the measurements and remeasurements of coffee estates carried out in the 1890's and after the turn of the cen-tury, from the records of the court system, and from the reports of the local officials and the governors. There is little evidence of violence re-lated to land, such as assault, fence cutting, the moving or destruction of boundary markers, theft, and arson. Because the owners had little difficulty obtaining land for production, they had no motive to act ag-gressively against their smaller neighbors, Indian or ladino. Moreover, given the manner in which the state measured and distributed land in the piedmont, most small holders had parcels of little immediate use or interest to coffee producers: the tracts were mainly in areas too high or too low for coffee or lacked the communications facilities necessary for commercial production.[75] Those small holders who possessed land attractive to finqueros often were ready enough to sell out for what they considered very good prices.[76]

Conflicts did continue between the old, extensive sheep, cattle or wheat haciendas of the highlands and nearby communities, and there were still disputes among the villages themselves, but these conflicts were largely unrelated to coffee. For example, the struggle that for much of the century had pitted the enormous English-owned ha-cienda San Jeronimo (the former property of the Dominicans), in the Baja Verapaz, against neighboring towns culminated in these years. A traveler reported in the 1890's, "Quite lately the struggle became acute; Indians and half castes had squatted in the outlying portions of the property and played havoc with timber and game, incendiary fires were a constant occurrence, irrigation ditches were damaged and cattle mutilated; finally, a mob from the town wantonly burned down the sugar-mill and attacked the overseer in charge."[77] The government resolved the conflict by buying the property from its foreign owners and dividing part of it among the local inhabitants.[78] Across the country in the highlands above Chiantla, the hacienda Chancol-Moscoso remained locked in a long-running battle with its Indian neighbors. The owners of the property protested repeatedly in the 1870's and 1880's that the Indians of Aguacatán to the south and San Juan Ixcoy to the north were invading their land, moving boundary markers, stealing cattle and burning buildings, and planting and harvesting corn without permission. The villagers responded that it was the hacienda that was encroaching on their land and that Chancol guards shot at them when they attempted to use traditional religious sites.[79] Town-hacienda conflicts in the Oriente and the western highlands in these years sound very much like the town-hacienda conflicts of the 1780's and would have been quite familiar to any harassed Bourbon subdelegate.

Boundary disputes among the highland communities, and the day-to-day, low-level conflict these entailed, also persisted, but apart perhaps from the additional resources it may have provided to pursue these disputes, the coffee economy did not noticeably alter the form or the content of such traditional oppositions.[80] The five towns of the "curacy of Purificación Jacaltenango," for example, determined in the 1870's to measure the land they had long held in common. One perhaps unanticipated effect of this was to revive a century-old dispute with neighboring San Miguel Acatán. The surveyor sent to resolve this found that not only were the sanmigueleños encroaching in Jacaltenango's land, but they had moved traditional boundary markers and now smashed the crosses he put up to indicate the proper lines. He read them "in a loud voice" a settlement they had signed a decade before agreeing to the existing division, admonished them to leave the crosses alone, and threatened severe punishment if they persisted in obstructing the measurement. This ended the threat of violence if not the conflict.[81] Throughout the 1880's and 1890's the town of San Miguel Totonicapán disputed the area of Pixabaj with Solalá and fought Santa María Chiquimula over their mutual boundary.[82] But the key to understanding what had changed was a petition from the residents of Zaculapa: "The justicias," a surveyor reported, "begged me not to send for the troops."[83] The difference now was the existence of a powerful and intrusive state that was able and willing to pressure the towns and the haciendas to regularize their land conflicts, and swiftly repressed open violence when it broke out. The more accurate

260 ≈ THE COFFEE REVOLUTION

measurements and the relatively clear titles that these made possible tended to limit opportunities for disputes. More generally, because the old undercapitalized and unproductive colonial haciendas and the cold highland ejidos of the villages were of little direct importance to the elites or the state when compared with the wealth-making possibilities of coffee, they occupied little of their attention or resources.

If titling and the power of the state reduced, or at least repressed, violence between towns and between towns and haciendas, it may have increased conflict within the indigenous communities. In the above case of Jacaltenango, for example, hardly had the towns titled their ejidos than they fell to fighting among themselves and soon broke apart into independent municipalities.[84] A title not only marked a dividing line with neighboring towns and properties, it also fixed an external limit around the community that threatened to choke the town as population increased. In most areas, the old idea of an indefinite común could no longer be sustained: less state land was available, and the countryside was less open or open to dispute. Thus, although communities might still have access to hot-country land, coffee in the southern piedmont and lowlands and ladino cattle and land speculation to the north changed the conditions and raised the cost of land use. Under these circumstances, when population growth and soil exhaustion pressed against available resources, individuals and families in the communities might turn on each other. At first, those involved would have attempted to make use of traditional mechanisms—community justicias, discussion to consensus, sometimes violence. Few of the litigants would have had the papers to "go before the [ladino] law." The very existence of that law, however, and the growing consciousness of it among the population, together with the existence of an increasingly effective state to enforce it, undercut the power of the alcaldes and principales and of community mechanisms generally, even though most of the population could not or would not yet have recourse to outside agencies. One effect may have been that the inhabitants of the rural communities turned increasingly to individual solutions, perhaps to witchcraft (brujería), to resolve land, and other, conflicts.[85] Witchcraft thus may have served as a bridge between the time when the community defined its outer limits by titling its ejidos, in the process weakening the roles of the traditional local officials in defending and regulating land, and the time—the 1930's to 1960's, depending on the village[86]—when enough of the members of the community had written documents to make resort to ladino-regulated courts and the national law a common and recognized procedure.

The Coming of the *Ladinos*

Coffee impinged on the highland towns initially not through land grabbing but as part of labor recruitment, but this process over time affected land. The advances and wages associated with labor mobilization hastened the conversion of land into a commodity and drove up prices, shutting out or driving out the poor or those who clung to more traditional values and aggravating social differentiation. Further inequalities grew out of the new emphasis on written titles and the opportunities open to those who were ready to play an intermediary role between the demands of coffee and the local population. Those within the community who prospered in the new environment, usually the less scrupulous among the local Indian officials and the assistants to the ladino habilitadores, often invested part of their wealth in land. The activities of the alcalde Gaspar of Nebaj may not have been typical but they certainly were not unique: "Using the facilities of his office he systematically looked up Indians whose lands were mortgaged or who were otherwise hard up, got them into debt to himself and foreclosed on their properties. As a result . . . he [was] the largest Indian landowner in Nebaj and the surrounding country."[87] The indigenous population of Yepocapa complained that their gobernador deprived them of access to community lands. "He [said that he] was going to sell the land and that if we had the money, we could buy it and if not he would sell it to ladinos, and after taking two caballerías for himself and one for his brother, he told us that what remained was of concern of the town."[88] And the gobernador of San Pedro Sacatepéquez (Guatemala) by the 1890's had accumulated an estate of some twenty houses, town sites, and parcels of agricultural land, as well as a tavern "in the dark, by the right of force."[89] In contrast, Tiburicio Caal, alcalde of Cobán for twenty-four years and conscious of the "calvary that each sprig of coffee meant for the Indians," when he parceled out community land to his fellow Indians wrote in each title that it could not be sold to "foreigners."[90] There had always been exploitative indigenous officials, just as the majority had probably worked to defend the community from outside demands and oppressions. The two activities, of course, were not mutually exclusive. What had changed was that coffee provided new and unprecedented opportunities for those in the villages who wanted to enrich themselves at the expense of their neighbors.

The ladinos who often cooperated with rapacious local Indian officials sometimes displaced them altogether. Ladino settlement in the western highlands included a small number of predominantly ladino towns such as Sija, Chinique, Malacatán, and Huehuetenango, most of which had grown out of colonial valles and advanced to municipal status in the late eighteenth century or after independence. Most were land short, and after 1871 they became increasingly aggressive and successful in seeking it. Often this success came at the expense of their Indian neighbors.[91] There had also been small numbers of ladinos in many of the highland Indian towns for centuries. These numbers grew as the coffee boom created new opportunities for trade and employment,[92] and more and more they pressured the state for so-called "dual government,"[93] that is, the sharing of municipal office between the Indian and ladino populations. In practice this meant a ladino as the first alcalde even in many predominantly Indian towns and the alternation of ladino and Indian officeholders below him. "Dual government" positioned the minority to take control of community resources. By and large the indigenous population resisted this innovation, but the weight of the state and the presumption that "civilization" meant "ladinization" were against them. The ladino officials of Chiché, for example, in 1875 demanded greater access to the town's ejidos, and when the Indians rejected this the ladino officials jailed the indigenous justicias. The conflict simmered until planting time in the spring of 1877 when the Indians occupied the municipal building with 300 armed men "ready to spill blood." At this point the state intervened on the side of the ladinos and ordered the Indians to leave them in possession of the plots they had acquired.[94] Small-town ladinos also took advantage of redemption law to buy up land in the communities. In the 1880's, for example, the national government ordered the Indians of San Juan Sacatepéquez to sell all lands belonging to "the community, the guachivales, and the cofradías." Of ten lots auctioned off, only two went to Indians, and most came into the hands of the powerful local ladino family the Búcaros.[95]

In the 1880's labor recruiters fanned out through the western highlands looking for workers and selling alcohol and cheap goods. These activities tied Indians to local ladinos in a web of credit usually guaranteed by land, the only Indian asset, apart from labor itself, of interest to ladinos. For example, although the law expressly forbade the practice, recruiters generally required the Indians to secure labor contracts with their land. When they could not or would not work, or when the recruiters could successfully claim this to be the case, the ladinos took the land.[96] Again, the municipal secretary was the key figure in all this. Even in the towns without dual government, after 1871 the secretary was almost always a ladino, and usually an outsider who was appointed by the jefe político.[97] The secretary drew up and authorized labor contracts for the recruiters, and he also recorded the orders of forced labor received by the town and certified compliance. Since apparently few secretaries could or would live on the fees the law allowed them, they easily became involved in local commercial activities, labor recruiting, and the acquiring of land. Other ladino local officials such as the militia commander or the comisionado político exploited their positions in much the same way,[98] as did also well-connected "shysters" and local ladino bosses. The inhabitants of an unnamed Indian town in the Alta Verapaz complained to the jefe político in 1910 about the activities of one such person, called a "lawyer and notary" by the Indians but almost certainly without a degree. Taking advantage of their ignorance and "unhappy race" and exploiting them in a manner that was "coarse, brutal and insane," he had convinced the Indians that the President had revoked all land titles and that only he could issue new ones. He bullied, or perhaps conspired with, local leaders to take over much of the community's land.[99] Village ladinos resold the parcels of land they acquired, sometimes to Indians, sometimes to each other, or they rented it out, cultivated it with hired labor, or simply waited for a buyer from outside, perhaps a finca on the coast looking to acquire land for a labor reserve. Outsiders and local ladinos always found allies in the indigenous population ready to enrich themselves at the expense of their poor or less *listo* ("sharp") neighbors. There was, and is now, ethnic oppression and exploitation in rural Guatemala, but it has always made use of cross-ethnic class alliances. As a result of coffee, then, the communities did lose land, or at least found the conditions of access to this land altered to their disadvantage, but it was a slow, piecemeal, and very uneven process.

The effect of coffee on the communities was to constrain but not cut off access to land. Communities outside the coffee piedmont usually managed, unless and until the effects of the ladino intrusions began to be felt, to strengthen their hold on land immediately around the village, the heart of the ejido. At the same time they lost, or saw

severely diminished, their access to broader areas that they traditionally owned or claimed. Some towns gained land. Those that did not
might still be able to trade vague claims for clear title, whether as
a community or through groups in the community or as individuals.
Except for the few and sparsely populated towns of the western piedmont, coffee did not immediately threaten the survival of the communities or their hold on the most vital parts of their ejidos. The Liberals'
laws did fix boundaries and coffee did engross much of the fertile and
uncultivated land potentially within the reach of the Indian towns.
Coffee closed an important relief valve that could have bled off the
pressures resulting from population increases in the twentieth century. The indigenous population in the 1870's or 1880's, with a history
of three hundred years of population instability, had no way of anticipating the unprecedented increases that were to come; nor, given the
coercive power of the state and their own history of mutual hostility,
had they the means to block the expansion of coffee and the ultimate
loss of traditionally held land. Only an all-out revolt might have accomplished this, and the organizing conditions for such a possibility were
absent in these years. Given little real choice, trading vague claims for
promised security was logical. That they lost only part of their común,
and that typically marginal to the heart of the ejidos, limited the sense
of desperation the losses provoked and the degree of their willingness
to resist.

Chapter 9

The Communities: Labor

Mr. President: We the People of Chincacoj [Xenacoj] . . . im-
plore your help. For many years we have sacrificed ourselves
going to work on the estates Los Cerritos, Torola, Mauricio, El Baul, Pantaleón, Los Diamantes, and García. Many
of us have died at this labor, leaving numerous widows and
orphans among us. By what right can Indians be forced to
work for whatever a landowner wishes to pay? This is slavery
to which the government must put a stop.

AGCA, Residents of Xenacoj–President,
December 21, 1885

Forced labor for "Spanish" and ladino elites had for so long been a
part of the condition of the Guatemalan Indians that the schemes
put in place by the Liberals to mobilize workers for coffee did not immediately or obviously appear to violate established custom and did
not provoke new or unusual responses.[1] The Indians reacted as they
had always done, with acquiescence or resistance that varied in degree and form depending upon the specific circumstances. The push
of recruiters into the hinterland in search of workers after 1871 ebbed
and flowed with the condition of the world market, impinging upon
given areas and specific communities at different times. Mandamientos mattered little in the boca costa where villages either lost their land
outright to coffee or found the areas available to them so reduced that
the inhabitants had little alternative to colono status or debt contracts.
Similarly, the inhabitants of the highland villages immediately adjacent to the piedmont and also those of the Alta Verapaz close to the
main producing areas had little choice but to come quickly to terms
with the new crop. Early on, mandamiento drafts shifted from such
towns to the more remote settlements of the Cuchumatanes and the
Quiché. As demands mounted, more and more of the inhabitants of
even these distant communities came to see the advantages of taking
advances for seasonal work on the fincas, or they found their land
converted into fincas de mozos and themselves forced to pay rent with
labor on the coast. Escape was almost impossible. A traveler in the

distant upper reaches of the Quiché around the turn of the century reported: "There are people living in the woods here and there, though you do not see where until you come upon them; Indians mostly, immigrants from the settled parts of the Alta Verapaz, running away from plantation work and the oppressions of the Government or the authorities. . . . But they do not long escape vexation. Somebody buys the land and puts the inhabitants to work; or else they have to run away further."[2]

Mandamientos

The Indians did all they could to avoid mandamientos. One resident of San Pedro la Laguna remembered: "The survivors were those who hid from the persecution, only coming to their houses at night and slipping out again to hide at day break; they were like lizards hidden among the rocks, only raising their heads to spy the danger that came in search of more workers for forced labor."[3] Local authorities were pressed to draft anyone they could find: "When I was twelve the official and a number of policemen arrived at my house, forced my mother to accept 60 reales, and stuck my name in his black book, and I was sentenced." Faced with widespread resistance, the alcaldes and village policemen, as they had with colonial repartimientos, literally threw money at chance passersby or left it with the wife or in a house while the family was away in the fields.[4] Anyone who resisted was jailed. Probably only those who could bribe their way out or had the right connections could hope to escape being sent to the coast eventually. Gangs returning from mandamientos sometimes found themselves forced to accept more money and return at once to the coast. One sanpedraño remembered, "When a poor man would arrive home [from a mandamiento], he received the awful news from his wife that the officials had left another sixty reales with orders to work again, perhaps this time in an even less hospitable area." Men just back from working off advances as seasonal workers might be sent out immediately on mandamientos, although this violated the law and the exemption such contracts were supposed to provide.

Indians who were caught up in the drafts suffered hunger, illness, and abuse on the fincas. Employers seem to have reserved the most difficult or dangerous tasks for the drafted workers[5] or they used mandamientos for unhealthful properties for which they could not get other labor. The inhabitants of Santiago Sacatepéquez, and many other highland towns echoed this protest, argued that they were accustomed to the cool highlands and that for them the hot country was "deadly": "Who would believe that the Spanish monarchs of the sixteenth century were more humanitarian with a conquered people than the jefes políticos of an independent and democratic republic in the nineteenth century? We say this because we know that the Laws of the Indies prohibited taking Indians on mandamiento from cold to hot climates."[6] One Indian from San Pedro La Laguna recalled "the suffocating heat, the dehydration, the clouds of flies, the mosquitoes carrying disease that surrounded you during the day while you worked, and at night other insects appeared."[7] Workers on fincas in the Alta Verapaz complained that their overseers did not give them time to gather firewood to dry their clothing, wet from the perpetual rains, so that many of them came down with colds and chills.[8] The common practice of sweeping up mandamiento Indians without warning and without giving them time to prepare adequate food supplies to take with them worsened their situation.[9] It was hardly surprising that the inhabitants of one community would lament that mandamientos "have converted our luckless village into a wretched hospital."[10]

Another, probably worse, abuse of mandamientos was the employers' habit of forcing drafted laborers to remain on the finca longer than the time stipulated in the order. This was done mainly by the use of *tareas* (tasks). Mandamiento regulations provided that the Indians were to work a certain number of days for each order, but on the fincas owners frequently assigned work not on a daily basis but by the task or as piecework, such as picking a certain quantity of coffee or cleaning a given area of the groves.[11] "Day" and "task" were supposed to involve approximately the same amount of work, but more often than not tasks turned out to require far more than a day to complete. In the rare instances where by effort workers could complete more than one task in a day and earn more money, they readily agreed to the system, but the Indians constantly complained that the tasks assigned them on mandamiento required two or even three days to finish.[12] The leaders of San Andrés Sajcabajá explained about their work on the finca Las Carolinas: "We worked twelve days, not by day as the jefe ordered but by task as the owner made us, and he forced us to use the sack we show you, which contains more than two large boxes. Even though we are Indians we understand the difference between what is a day and what is a task."[13]

Illegally lengthening the stay of drafted workers clearly was to the growers' advantage, since it reduced the already low wages they paid drafted workers and depressed what they had to pay to seasonal workers or free labor. But the Indians caught in this situation sometimes ran out of food, and either had to buy it from the employer[14] or else have it brought from the home village. If they tried to stretch what they had to make it last for the extra time, they risked adding undernourishment to their difficulties. If they complained, the administrators told them to "eat dirt and shit."[15] When the Indians were drafted repeatedly or kept away from the village longer than they had anticipated, they could not work their milpa plantings. As early as 1875, local officials in Chamelco reported that because of the "incessant" demands for labor during the past year the town had lost much of its plantings and was suffering a food shortage; unless they received at least a month's relief now, they said, they would lose them again.[16] A group of workers from Santiago Chimaltenango in Huehuetenango that was sent on a mandamiento to the finca La Concha spent twenty days during the rainy season looking for the estate: "We searched all the towns and fincas of the department of Mazatenango [sic]." They finally returned to Santiago exhausted and sick from the rain and heat, having eaten or lost all the food they had taken and having also had to spend their wage advances on telegrams and other expenses trying to locate La Concha; once home, they found that they had lost much of their milpas because these had not been cleaned at the proper time. Now they received a telegram ordering them back to the coast![17] "We understand why mandamientos are necessary," another group pleaded, but the owners should not treat us like "beasts."[18] Indians ordered to work on the properties of William Dieseldorff summed up these problems when they protested, "Before we finish a week with one owner, another forces money on us, and because the tasks are so large or because there is not enough coffee, we often cannot complete a task in a day and fall behind, keeping us from getting to our plantings, which we have not yet been able to prepare."[19]

Debt Servitude: *Colonos*

In contrast, perhaps, to other areas of Latin America[20] in these years, colono status was not generally favored or sought after by most Guatemalan Indians. As long as the indigenous communities remained intact and the inhabitants had access to land, and even if this land was not sufficient to support them all the year, it would seem to make no sense to abandon the village and the ancestors for life on the boca costa under the thumb of a ladino employer. Yet thousands of Indians did. Between 1880 and 1920 the populations of the piedmont coffee municipalities grew two or three times faster than did those of the adjacent highlands. Colonos as a proportion of the coffee labor force increased steadily, amounting by 1940 to 50–65 percent of the work force of the departments of the West and almost 90 percent under the exceptional circumstances of the Alta Verapaz.[21] The reasons for leaving the community for the finca varied. For some of the poorest and most marginalized people in the villages, the shift to colono status was a direct result of the pressures of the mandamientos: "TWENTY YEARS ago, to escape the constant harassment of mandamientos in the time of the famous administration of Estrada Cabrera I took refuge as a colono on the finca LA CORTINA," one remembered.[22] In some villages at least, the unfortunate man who could not pay bribes or exert influence must have been sent on drafts again and again. The people who went most often could least effectively look after their plantings or other affairs in the community and would therefore have been the more likely to suffer losses that might make life as a permanent resident on a coffee estate an attractive alternative.[23] As land became scarce in some municipalities, children who had no inheritance[24] or whose portion was too small to be worth continued cultivation might seek a new life on the coast. Alcoholism, or even simply a prolonged drinking spree, could strip Indians of their possessions and leave them little alternative but full-time work on the fincas.

Employers aggressively sought to force temporary workers into colono status. Most contracts stipulated that if a seasonal laborer failed to appear and work as agreed, his status would change to that of colono. As one laborer explained, "I became a colono on the finca after failing one year to appear to work off what I owed."[25] Indians of Sacapulas protested that the finca La Florida was attempting to turn them into resident workers by claiming that they had large and overdue debts, but "because we cannot read, there appear in our libretas notations of money we did not receive."[26] In other instances habilitadores or employers kidnapped or imprisoned workers or their families to convince them of the advantages of remaining as residents. In one such case in 1906, Mateo Felipe and several other Indians complained that they had gone to do seasonal labor on the finca Africa at Barillas, but when they rebuffed the owner's efforts to convert them into colonos, he made off with their children, parents, and brothers.[27] And not just in the Alta Verapaz did owners sometimes appropriate land or destroy crops to drive workers and small farmers into dependence.

Thus, in return for security, and little of that if the owner wished to rid himself of them, men and women gave up control of their lives to become colonos subject to the "customs" of the finca. This meant that, along with routine agricultural work in the coffee fields, they could be required to perform other labor such as faena, unpaid Sunday tasks picking up trash, repairing fences, or collecting ashes for fertilizer, and there might also be recurrent physical abuse, sexual exploitation, and unjustified fines or imprisonment.[28] In a case aired in the municipal court of Chicacao in 1914, a colono of the finca Santa Rosa de Belén testified that he was often beaten and imprisoned without cause and that the administrator forced his daughter to live with a worker who was already married; when the colono protested, the administrator took his milpa.[29] But courts counted for little with owners and managers, who enforced their rules as they wished. "We know that the administrator represents no Court of Law," noted the workers of finca San Andrés Osuna-Rochela in 1920, "and that the fines he takes from us end up in his pocket, which we feel is robbery, but if we complain he throws us in jail."[30] Unlike the seasonal workers who soon returned to their home community, the colono was obliged to remain, or else flee to a different property where the situation might not be any better. It was no doubt true, as one writer has argued, that it was not always or only debts or compulsion that kept colonos on the property; but whether it was "fair work, mutual regard, and love for his employer"[31] is not so certain. Colonos tended to be drawn from the marginal members of the Indian and ladino rural poor, those with the fewest choices. They traded their freedom, such as it was—and in the case of the Indians, often their cultural integrity—for what was often only tenuous survival.

Debt Servitude: Seasonal Workers

Under the labor laws of late-nineteenth-century Guatemala, Indians had little choice but to accept advances to be worked off on the fincas.[32] But even though these laws gave the habilitador and the employer considerable advantage in negotiating contracts with prospective workers, Indians were not entirely without recourse. They understood that coffee depended on their labor and that the cycle of coffee allowed the landowners scant leeway. Particularly at harvest time, the failure to obtain needed labor threatened the loss of the entire crop and the ruin of the planters, many of whom were heavily burdened with debt and lived from harvest to harvest. In their struggle, the Indians tried constantly to improve the conditions and price for which they were forced to give their work, and the owners did all they could to beat down their costs. The labor laws of 1877 and 1894 gave the departmental governors authority to handle agricultural labor disputes, and most of these they resolved verbally, but even so, the jefes' papers were jammed with complaints, appeals, and petitions from laborers and owners alike. The jefes políticos were under real pressure from their superiors to resolve labor disputes quickly and without unnecessary cost or counterproductive violence; they had to listen both to the owners and to the Indians, and they generally found it expedient to seek compromise solutions.

The most common complaint of the indebted laborers was that the fincas did not fairly credit their work. In part the complaint grew out of misunderstandings and accidents. For example, it was common practice on many fincas to give the worker a token signifying completion of the day or task or to use a card that the foreman punched for the same purpose. Every two weeks the workers presented their tokens or cards to the bookkeeper to receive their pay or to have their debt credited.[33] Where the Indian did not understand how the system worked or if the tokens were lost or stolen or, in the case of the cards, damaged by rain, the worker might lose his pay. Opportunities for confusion and bad faith by both parties abounded. A related problem was that of the use of *vales* or script. Employers in Guatemala generally found the infamous *"tienda de raya"* (company store) unnecessary and unprofitable and avoided it if they could,[34] but some did resort to token currency on occasion. Vales usually were pieces of colored paper or cardboard that were issued by the finca in peso values and paid to the workers instead of money, the excuse being that because of the instability of the peso they could not get the denominations they needed.[35] The practice was illegal. But *Diario de Centro América* in January 1920 reported that recently vales had become common in Tumbador, San Marcos. The bills were filthy and falling apart and bore on the back comments such as, "It's a disgrace to work and be paid with these pieces of shit," or "What a calamity for the poor workers."[36] No doubt the employers hoped, the *Diario* added, that the workers would lose the bills or that they would disintegrate before the fincas were obliged to redeem them. However, although workers constantly reported problems with work tokens, their petitions rarely mentioned vales, so the practice may have been a localized one or one that did indeed result from temporary currency shortages as the peso collapsed.

Often, too, there were differences between what the workers thought they owed, what their libretas recorded, and what the finca books showed the debts to be. Some of these discrepancies were due to deceptions practiced by employers or workers, but there were ample chances for genuine error. As illiterates, and despite the claim of one that their mental accounting was "absolutely accurate" because they had nothing else to think about,[37] workers must have found it hard to keep track of their situation. The employers were certainly right when they said the Indians often failed to add to their debts not only the taxes covered for them by the finca but the costs of rounding them up and escorting them to the coast, and "the small obligations they have contracted with others and with the courts" that the habilitador paid before the worker left the village.[38] Even had the Indians known what was being charged against them, they could hardly have kept mental track of it all. Because they did not always agree with such charges or because they suspected, with reason, that the fincas manipulated their accounts to their disadvantage, the workers sometimes refused to present their libretas to have them brought up to date, or they would say that they had lost them. Some certainly had, but others hoped by this means to escape past debts. It was commonly the case, therefore, that the jefe político had to settle labor disputes and debt questions in which the Indians were firmly convinced that they owed or were owed one amount, their libretas or work tokens indicated another, and the books of the finca showed yet a different sum.[39] If the law provided that in such cases the finca's records were the final authority, to insist too aggressively on this could be disastrous. The owners' need for labor, and relatively docile and willing labor at that, together with the governor's acute awareness of the limited means of coercion available to him, almost always forced a compromise. Except in the case of obvious and notorious abuses,[40] however, only the old, the lame, and the sick or those with someone to buy them out could escape debt altogether. The best most Indians could hope for was a minor change in their debt or wage and an order that "without fail" they return to work.

Apart from fraud and confusion, most conflicts over debts for temporary laborers, as was the case with the mandamientos, grew out of the differences between day and task.[41] Seasonal labor contracts always provided that the laborer would work by day or by task at the option of the finca, and therefore there was no need for the outright fraud that some employers found useful with their mandamiento drafts. Instead, the Indians complained, owners made the tasks so impossibly large that they could never work off what they owed. Furthermore, because the common tasks of cleaning and weeding were undertaken by cuerda measurement, which could mean any one of at least half a dozen different-sized "cuerdas" depending on the region, problems and misunderstandings were bound to result. The owner of finca El Ferrol, for example, had some of his workers jailed when they complained of the use of a cuerda of 37 varas instead of what they said was the customary 25.[42] More commonly, difficulties arose when the finca sought to increase the size of the task without actually saying so, in order to squeeze more work for the same money from the laborers. A group from Santiago Sacatepéquez protested that they had agreed on the task of cleaning 20 brazas, with a braza (literally, an arm's length) measured from "the point of [the overseer's] nose to the tip of his finger," but because the overseer was "a very fat man" this actually amounted to a task to 27 of a more standard braza, and as a consequence each task took them longer.[43] Temporary workers from Quiché complained that in six years of laboring on the finca El Carmen their debts had only increased because of the size of the tasks assigned; the thirty tasks they had contracted for took them three months, and because they earned food rations according to the tasks they completed, they only received food every three days.[44] The lack of standardization of tasks, or even systems of weights and measures, led inescapably to conflict, but it also facilitated the efforts of the fincas to extract as much as possible from the work force.[45] The Indians, for their part, accepted and hewed to "custom" not because it was fair but because it was known. Experience had repeatedly demonstrated that innovation usually worked to their disadvantage.

Disputes of the same nature and for the same reasons revolved around the *caja* (box), which was the usual measure of the task for harvesting coffee.[46] Not only was there regional variation—in the West the box was usually two or three times larger than the box used in the Alta Verapaz owing to differences in productivity—but every finca had its own particular box. The idea was that the size of the box took account of local conditions, such as the steepness of the fields or the age and size of the trees, and reflected what could reasonably be expected in a day.[47] Given the tremendous variations in rural Guatemala, it was a sensible system. Managers who watched their properties closely increased the size of the box in the middle of the harvest when berries were plentiful and cut it back early and late in the year when berries were scarce. The workers accepted these variations as reasonable and recognized that they could escape the demands of a finca that set unrealistic tasks. But they sometimes complained that owners tried to cheat them even within the system they themselves had established by making the box markedly bigger than they admitted or by demanding that the workers overfill it before the checkers would accept it. Where harvesters worked by weight, administrators might rig the scales to underweigh each load. Other than stuffing his pick with rocks, twigs, and green berries, there was little the worker could do to combat this except vote with his feet, and labor disputes routinely involved claims by Indians that they had abandoned the finca because the owner was cheating them on the size of the caja or the weight.[48]

When Guatemala's adherence to the Washington Convention of 1923 threatened to curtail the use of corporal punishment for rural workers, habilitadores, owners, and administrators all warned that this would make control of the agricultural labor force impossible.[49] Ladinos on the fincas lived surrounded and outnumbered by a labor force they needed and compelled to work but about whom they understood little and with whom they often could not even communicate effectively. When the German administrator of finca Luarca, for example, admonished fieldworkers for pulling down and breaking the branches of coffee bushes instead of using the ladders that were provided, they "conspired" against him "in their barbarous dialect" and chased him out of the field.[50] The Indians were reluctant workers at best, and owners and administrators assumed, or found it convenient to act as if they assumed, that only violence or the fear of violence motivated them. Most managers went about armed and some used guns to attempt to intimidate the workers: "He threatened many times with a pistol in his hand to take our lives."[51] Managers sometimes shot, or shot at, the Indians,[52] and others used dogs to frighten them. In August 1921, a group of 130 laborers on the finca El Porvenir complained to the jefe político that even though they had agreed to the wages and rations offered, when they asked a question of the German administrator he set his dog on their spokesman and went for his rifle, saying he would shoot them.[53] More often, finca administrators and overseers simply threatened or hit workers with their fists, with sticks, or with the flat of the machete. Their employer had "pummeled, kicked, and beaten us with a machete and taken a shot at one of us," complained three workers, only because they did not carry wood quickly enough.[54] Lucas Velásquez of San Antonio Ilotenango alleged that "Don Manuel, the brother of my actual employer, beat me without motive . . . as well as my wife and our baby, with the result that they both died leaving me a widower."[55] Several workers in a revealing letter to the governor of Quiché protested that the habilitador for El Pacayal "beat us as if we were his children."[56]

In January 1919 the newspaper *Diario de Centro América* revealed the existence of an underground prison on the finca Peña de Plata near Acatenango.[57] The Indians employed on the property apparently had complained for years of this prison, and local authorities had searched for it, or so they said, without success. The comisionado político and the militia commander of Yepocapa found a cave equipped with chains for confining errant workers. The prison was not unique. Although finca owners could and did send laborers to jail in nearby municipalities, most of the larger properties maintained their own jails, with separate cells for men and women. Even the smaller estates might use a shed or an outbuilding to confine workers who fell afoul of the administrator. Owners locked up Indians "because they got drunk and beat their wives too much" or otherwise caused a disturbance, but they would also imprison them when they protested conditions, or when they attempted, or the owner thought they might attempt, to run away.[58] The finca San Jeronimo Miramar, for example, at one point locked up an entire work gang from Santiago Atitlán every night for fear they might flee.[59]

For lesser offenses the fincas used *cepos*, or stocks, which were probably more damaging than jail to the workers' health. One man from finca Buenavista explained that he had been "kicked and hung in the stocks because I asked my employers to credit my account with the work I had done in the last six months."[60] Men who were put in the stocks either "hung" exposed to weather and insect bites or lay in leg stocks "flat on your back in the dirt . . . for days and nights at a time."[61] After 1920 the new government abolished the use of stocks, but the practice persisted. In 1929 *El Imparcial* reported from Pochuta that "[planters of the area] act like slave drivers, putting the workers in inadequate jails and sometimes using stocks, which the law absolutely forbids, denying them food or blankets to cover themselves at night."[62]

Still, the purpose of the coffee estates was to make money, and excessive violence against the laborers "made no economic sense."[63] The almost absolute power of the finca owner or administrator could on occasion combine with racism and fear in those who were predisposed to brutality, but for most employers violence and threats of violence were only tools; the psychotic owner or drunken administrator who randomly shot workers or beat women and children to death was the exception. Strict control laced with violence seemed logical and necessary to an owner class that viewed the Indian as inferior and, correctly, as not always inclined to work efficiently for the wages and conditions the fincas were willing to provide.

Disease

Punishment such as exposure to the elements in stocks, the withholding of food or clothing, and beatings, as well as the typically inadequate housing on the fincas, aggravated one of the workers' most serious problems, that of disease.[64] Health conditions on the coast were such that few of those who descended to work in coffee escaped illness. Even by comparison with the rest of the country, mortality rates in that area remained high well into this century. According to *El Imparcial*, mortality rates per 1,000 circa 1925 were 31–35 in Escuintla and Retalhuleu and 26–30 in Suchitepéquez and Sacatepéquez, as against 21–25 in Guatemala, Chimaltenango, Amatitlán, Sololá, Totonicapán, Quezaltenango, the Baja Verapaz, the Petén, and Izabal, 16–20 in Huehuetenango, San Marcos, and Santa Rosa, and only 9–15 in Quiché, the Alta Verapaz, Zacapa, Chiquimula, Jalapa, and Jutiapa.[65] The chief killers were dysentery and malaria and recurrent outbreaks of epidemic diseases such as smallpox, cholera, and yellow fever.[66] Parasites flourished, and gastrointestinal complaints were general. According to one traveler, "The people are exceedingly careless of all sanitary precautions, especially in the matter of drainage and the waste products of the human body, trusting to the intervention of vultures and dogs to remove health-endangering filth."[67] It might have been possible for a dispersed population in a temperate climate to live under such conditions, but when the coffee boom crowded Indians together in temporary housing or colono huts on the lowland fincas, disease was rampant. Dysentery, the newspapers reported, "decimated the working class."[68] Few owners made a serious effort to improve conditions by providing latrines or adequate supplies of drinking water, and even where they did they often vitiated what good this might have done by failing to explain to the workers the reason or need for the changes.[69] Malaria was endemic, and the workers carried it back to their home communities: the *Diario de Centro América* in 1924, for example, reported that there was no disease at present on the south coast except the "usual" malaria, and the anthropologist Ruth Bunzel noted in the early 1930's that there was almost no "tropical disease" in the highland village Chichicastenango except malaria brought from the coast by returning coffee laborers.[70] Those who ventured into the lowlands took malaria for granted.

Measures to control smallpox, on the other hand, had been available from the last days of the colony, but inoculation and then vaccination had made only limited headway among the indigenous population even a century later. The census of 1893 revealed that few of the inhabitants of the highland communities were protected: percentages of those said to have been vaccinated ranged from an unlikely high of 90 percent for San Marcos to 13 percent in Quiché and the Alta Verapaz.[71] Although employers were urged to do all they could to combat the scourge "for humanity and for their own interests," apparently few of them took the trouble to see to it that all of their much needed workers were free of infection or had been vaccinated.[72] From time to time the authorities attempted to ban travel, as they had done during the cholera epidemic of the 1830's, to cut the spread of disease, but the coffee harvest could not wait.[73] A doctor at Tumbador in June 1909, for example, noted that a recent outbreak of smallpox on several plantations could be traced to workers who had brought it from their home communities or had picked it up along the way, and he feared that the approaching harvest, with its large influx of Indians from the highlands, might result in a "terrible epidemic."[74]

At the end of the rainy season in October 1918 the world influenza pandemic of 1918–19 burst upon Guatemala with a fury.[75] Although much of the subsequent press attention and almost all of the government's meager relief efforts centered on the capital, the effects of the epidemic were far worse among the already disease-ridden and poorly nourished rural population. Even incomplete figures reveal a much higher incidence of flu-related deaths in the coffee and the

highland Indian departments than in Guatemala City.[76] Reports from
the countryside sounded like a war: the epidemic had ravaged the
population around Patulul, on some boca costa plantations 50 to 60
percent of the workers had died, and most of the rest had fled. In the
highlands they were "dying like flies."[77] A doctor sent to inspect the
situation in Chimaltenango reported, "The mortality . . . is numerous
among the Indians who live in shacks poorly roofed, packed together,
piled three and four in the same bed on the ground and surrounded
by the mucous they have spit up."[78] When the disease hit the villages
the inhabitants dispersed into the bush, and there death found them.
Whole families succumbed, to be buried without markers or eaten
by animals and birds. The great "army" of Indian workers was being
"decimated like a battalion cut down by enemy machine guns." All but
a few skeptics anticipated a severe shortage of labor and massive crop
losses.[79]

Women and Children

From the earliest days of coffee growing in Guatemala, the fincas
contracted women and children, sometimes to handle special tasks
and to compensate for labor shortages, and also because they could
be paid lower wages. When the crop was first developing, landowners
employed women from nearby villages as day laborers to pick and sort
the crop, work that could be coordinated easily with the obligations
of the women's domestic economy. However, as the crop expanded and
the demand for labor drew more men into coffee labor, the situation
of women changed. Women continued to do the hand sorting required
to extract the damaged or withered beans, but more of them now
worked the harvest along with the men of their family, contributing to
the tasks credited to the man's account.[80] Children, too, picked what
they could and added this to the family basket. Thus, if at first coffee
provided some women a new source of income, perhaps reinforcing
their independence and value within the family, routinization and full
development of the crop subordinated women's labor power to men
in a way that traditional subsistence production did not.

Widows and single mothers, who continued to contract with the
estates on their own, either for harvest labor or to cook for the men
who came without families, encountered many of the same problems that the men did. Ignacia Pérez de Salas, for example, protested

against the finca La Esmeralda in Chuvá, saying that for four years she had been going there with her two children to harvest coffee but each year the estate "added money to her debt that [she] did not receive," and so she never escaped debt.[81] Another petitioner ruefully pointed out that in the case of coffee labor at least, women "have equal legal rights with men."[82]

But most women in rural Guatemala were members of families that were dominated by men—fathers, brothers, or husbands. Once these women entered into the wage sector not only were the wages they earned usually appropriated by these males—as happened, too, to sons subordinated to fathers—but they might also find themselves made liable for labor debts or obligations that they had not contracted. Habilitadores routinely sought to force wives or children, or any relative for that matter, to work off the debts of dead or runaway male family members.[83] This was illegal, but it was custom and very common. In one instance, when one woman's husband died on a finca, the recruiter came to her demanding that she work off what remained of his debt; when she refused he shot up the patio in front of her house.[84] If questioned, the habilitadores always argued that the individuals had taken on the debt voluntarily. In some cases they had, whether to continue to receive advances or, and for colonos, to avoid eviction, but others resisted demands to pay back money they had never received.[85] "No human or divine law," one woman argued successfully in October 1906, "requires a poor widow with minor children to be responsible for the labor debts contracted by her husband."[86] Juana Lopez, from San Pedro Sacatepéquez, fought back even more aggressively: she not only refused to accept responsibility for the debts of her ex-husband, who, she claimed, had thrown her out, but she demanded half the property they had acquired during the marriage, protesting that "he has taken advantage of the sweat of my brow."[87]

Apart from instances in which recruiters demanded that they work off the debts of dead or missing men, women became entangled in their relatives' labor disputes in several ways. It was common for recruiters to imprison wives, sisters, and children to pressure absent or recalcitrant workers.[88] Also, and again though it was illegal, recruiters usually demanded that the men they hired include their family in their contract and libreta. Pascuala Godinez explained: "The employers are accustomed to having the workers make their wives and children also responsible for the debts, without our consent. This is what happened to me."[89] Men sometimes simply took advances to be worked off by their wives or children; in effect, they sold the labor of members of the family. Juana Domingo wrote the jefe político of Huehuetenango in December 1909 that she was in jail in San Miguel Acatán at her father's demand because she refused to go to the finca El Rosario to work off money given him to secure the release from jail of a brother charged with murder. She had been, she said, "sold by my own father, which is the custom among our race."[90] The alcalde of Todos Santos, in another case, reported that a man was threatening his ex-wife with "selling her to the recruiters."[91] Some women protested publicly and actively opposed this manner of treatment as abusive, and many more lobbied against it in private, but most accepted the custom that the men in their families would dispose of their work according to their own purposes and labored in silence.

Women on the coffee estates also had to endure sexual abuse. Administrators and caporales apparently routinely took advantage of their power to seduce or assault female workers. "The sons of the owner . . . want to rape us" protested several women from San Pedro Sacatepéquez (San Marcos) when ordered to work off a debt.[92] A male resident of finca Santa Cecilia protested that the manager invented errands to keep him away from the property so that he could press his unwanted attentions on the worker's wife.[93] Another complained that for years an administrator had harassed his wife. Because she refused, he beat him, until finally she submitted "to end the constant cruelties to which he subjected me."[94] In February 1925 the newspaper *El Imparcial* reported a "Startling Drama in Colomba." The Spanish administrator of finca Buenos Aires had been in the habit of taking advantage of young female workers, silencing the girls and their families with threats or promises. Recently, however, when he dishonored the daughter of a seventy-four-year-old colono, the man shot him to death.[95] Generally, if occasionally at some peril, owners and administrators tended to ignore or dismiss claims of "honor and shame" from their class and race inferiors unless and until these interfered with production.[96] It did not bother the owner of the estate San Ignacio, for example, that his overseer was a notorious seducer of female workers until the overseer, caught in the act of theft, fled with several women needed for the harvest.[97] The temporary worker María Mendez, for her part, must have found it difficult to understand why the finca La Soledad added the costs of capturing the man who had assaulted her to her debt.[98] It is hard to know how common problems of sexual exploitation actually may have been, but they were a staple of the complaints of female workers.

Resistance

All this abuse might well have provoked a violent response; certainly there was due cause. But premeditated violence against administrators, recruiters, or state agents was, in fact, rare, and even spontaneous attacks were not common. Though workers outnumbered the authorities on the coffee estates, the latter went about armed and mounted, and they could count on assistance from the police and militia in nearby towns and, on the large properties, from assistant alcaldes selected by the owner and appointed by the municipality. An outraged worker might threaten his supervisor with a machete over the measurement of a cuerda or a caja of coffee or in response to blows, but if he did so he usually was quickly overpowered and punished.[99] Protests by groups of workers provoked equally swift, and typically quite disproportionate, retaliation.[100] On finca Ona in July 1901 the workers "rioted," which is to say that they complained in a group because their food ration had failed to appear. The administrator called in soldiers from the nearby town of La Reforma, who quickly suffocated the protest and remanded the leaders to hard labor on public works.[101] When workers on the finca Luarca confronted the administrator and "tried to hit [him] with [his] own club," the local militia commander arrested all those who had not already fled and sentenced them to fifteen days in prison.[102] But evidence of such open and violent conflict rarely turns up in the records of the courts or the jefes políticos. Undoubtedly there were other cases of "insubordination" that were handled on the properties with beatings, jailings, or fines and never came to the attention of the authorities. For the same reasons, and as we have seen, large-scale uprisings were rare after 1880, and the state quickly and bloodily suffocated those that did occur.[103] Because it could be so easily contained and because it invited vicious repression, the workers realized that violence against finca authorities was not an effective means of combating exploitative treatment. The price was too high.

The Alta Verapaz may have been an exception. One source familiar with the region has said, "There are allusions to many . . . altercations in the late 19th century, usually led by Indian religious practition-

ers and having the aspect of nativistic movements involving gather-
ings of several different Indian groups."[104] Perhaps this was so, and
the subject merits a thorough examination, but a closer look at one
such event reveals a more pedestrian possibility. In 1897 the jefe político of the Alta Verapaz reported rumors that a conspiracy was afoot
among the Indians of Cobán aimed at local "ladinos and foreigners
and led by the elder Juan de la Cruz," who had been collecting money
among the people for an uprising that he claimed would "put an end
to [export] agriculture and attack [private] property."[105] The putative
leader fled before he could be interrogated, but the jefe confided that
rather than planning a revolt "it may very well have been that from
the beginning Juan de la Cruz had no other intent than to take money
from the unsuspecting by promising them that for which they hoped."
Indians would have liked to expel the foreigners from the area so that
they could reclaim control over their land and labor, but the possibilities of doing this successfully, even in the isolated Alta Verapaz, were
slight. In this case their dreams may simply have made them victims
of petty fraud.

This is not to say that the Indians roped up and sent on mandamientos or caught in peonage contracts did not resist, but they tried to
choose ways of resisting that would be as effective as possible without
provoking a devastating retaliation by the state. The most common of
these was the petition, thousands of which were filed with the jefes
políticos by Indians and ladinos in the late nineteenth century.[106] If
undramatic, petitions were effective. Since most of the rural poor were
illiterate, or at best could only sign their names, it was lawyers, "shysters," and professional "secretaries" who actually wrote out most of
the petitions. What resulted were documents ranging from the almost
unintelligible to elaborate presentations of law and history, moral philosophy, and current events. They do not in an absolute sense represent the Indians' "speaking for themselves," but occasionally the individual breaks through—like Martín Morales, who in 1923 protested
that through "all the flower of my youth the patron exploited my
labor," but now he was more than eighty years old, sick and crippled,
and should be released "to die slowly in the fields as do the animals
when they become old and useless."[107] More importantly, the repeti-
tion of complaints and descriptions from widely separate areas and
times make clear the population's genuine concerns.

These protests and applications for redress for the most part
adopted the familiar "good czar" form. The difficulties and suffer-

ing they experienced were not, the petitioners assured the authorities, chiefly caused by defects in the laws, and certainly until now those sufferings had remained unknown to their "father" or "grandfather" (*tata*), the jefe político or the President. They only occurred as the result of the activities of corrupt and abusive lower officials and exploitative employers, especially foreigners, who took advantage of the isolation of rural areas and of the Indians' lack of familiarity with Spanish and civil procedure to abuse their innocence. Once *tata jefe* or the President understood the situation, the petitioners were certain he could only decide for justice, that is, in their favor.

Their confidence was not entirely misplaced, for officials whose excesses threatened the smooth operation of the system were sometimes disciplined or removed. But the prevailing forms of labor recruitment were by definition abusive of even the limited rights the law granted Indians. Tinkering with their operation could do little to ameliorate the reality. If some of the rural population might have been naive enough to anticipate relief from tata presidente, their leaders were less so, and the "shysters" they hired to frame the petitions certainly knew better. Yet the documents took, or claimed to take, laws at face value. This was not ignorance. It represented a form of suspended disbelief or, perhaps better, temporarily and artificially assumed belief. To argue their case before the authorities, the Indians had to accept the rules and categories laid down by these authorities, however detached they might be from reality and however much they might disadvantage the Indians. Given the hegemony of the state, to deny validity to the laws was the bureaucratic equivalent of an uprising and simply short-circuited the process, to the obvious detriment of the petitioners. The Indians of Santa María de Jesús, for example, protested in 1904 that according to the labor laws of Guatemala they were free individuals and could not be compelled to work against their will.[108] Of course, for centuries they had been compelled to work against their will and expected nothing else, but appeal to the law provided a point from which to bargain and something of a shield from state and planter violence. Playing by the rules was the only way to gain a hearing.

Protesting workers reinforced petitions with other forms of pressure or resistance. Flight was common. Workers or families slipped away from the estates in the night or created diversions that made it possible to escape. The administrator of finca Santa Cristina angrily claimed that colonos there had set fire to various buildings in order to use the resulting confusion to get away.[109] Some escapes of this sort, particularly when they involved large numbers, could be quite dramatic and in retelling took on almost epic overtones. According to the folk history of Aguacatán, for example, around the turn of the century some five hundred people of the village lived as colonos on finca Santa Agustina. But they became increasingly angry about abuses they suffered there, particularly the excessively large tasks, and resolved to flee the property and take the measuring cord back to their home department of Huehuetenango to prove their case.[110] One of their religious specialists (*zahorín*) resident on the property selected the proper date "according to the ancient calendar" and secured the permission of the mountains and the volcanoes to pass over them during the night. To prepare for their escape the aguacatecos dug up the remains of an ancestor who had been buried some thirty-five years before in one of the coffee groves, and "in the hours before they left spread these around so that the other employees would sleep and not realize that they had left." The zahorín also "made custom" to kill the dogs that patrolled the finca grounds. At midnight the aguacatecos slipped out of their huts and climbed into the mountains. Soon they heard the alarm bell from the property, but they kept walking, and after two days they reached Aguacatán. When they showed the governor of Huehuetenango the measuring cord, he fined the owner and the administrator of Santa Agustina and allowed the Indians to work off their debts building the road from Aguacatán to Huehuetenango, or so their descendants remembered. If the state forced local leaders to aid it in supplying labor for coffee, many of these also led resistance to state demands, and they did so on the fincas as well as in the communities. Not surprisingly, the state looked for, found, and punished *cabecillas* (leaders) for most acts of group defiance. Whether the ones who were punished were those who were actually responsible, or were simply the first half-dozen Indians whom government troops came across, it is usually impossible to know.

But if they fled, where might the Indians go? Most, as the above example suggests, returned to their home communities. Because this was the first place that the administrator and recruiter looked, it is clear that the purpose of flight usually was less to evade obligations than to initiate or to stimulate negotiations. It was possible to petition the departmental governor from a finca, but doing so invited the wrath of the administrator. Workers could also go to the capital to appeal to the President, but this was expensive. The overwhelming number of petitions and complaints to the authorities protesting conditions on the fincas came instead from Indians in their home villages, whether from workers who had escaped from coffee estates or from those who threatened to flee the town if they were forced to go to the coast at that time or under the conditions the owner demanded.

Petitioning from the community had a number of advantages for the Indians. In the village they could work together better and could maintain a more unified front, certainly more so than would have been possible on a lowland estate under ladino control. The village also offered the individual or the family solidarity and support against the owner or administrator, the recruiter, and the agents of the state, who usually were outsiders and therefore operated in the highland towns at a disadvantage quite unlike the upper hand they held on the fincas. By staying in their communities while they negotiated with the finca, the Indians could take better care of their crops and other interests and were not in danger of running up debts by buying food or being forced to accept additional advances. From their community, too, they could petition the jefe of their own jurisdiction, who had a vested interest in his population and was likely to view their explanations more sympathetically than would a governor of a coastal department whose first concern was the success of the export crop. Flight and petition drew several sets of authorities into the bargaining process and helped force concessions, or at least the promise of concessions. The product of what became rather ritualized pieces was usually the granting to the complainants of a few cents' increase in wages or a small reduction in tasks or more food, together with an order that they report immediately to the finca to fulfill their obligations. Everyone concerned understood that nothing prevented the workers from initiating the whole process again after a time.

Unless they wished simply to shift to another property and hope for better conditions there, groups of colonos or temporary workers who fled the fincas generally had little real alternative to returning to their home villages, but single persons or a family sometimes could escape the system altogether, though at a cost. Some workers disappeared into remote parts of the countryside. In the 1930's the inhabitants of Nebaj warned visitors of "dangerous" Indians who lived in the bush around the village to evade road taxes and labor duty and preyed on travelers; of others it was said "they live dispersed in the hills leading an almost nomadic life." [111] But an existence on the run, cut off from family and community, was *triste* (sad/lonely). And habilitadores and village policemen, forced to meet growing labor demands, more and more pressed their search into every corner of the municipality, so that this sort of evasion became ever harder. Another possibility was to migrate to a department where there were fewer labor pressures or less strict state control. This mode of evasion was common among inhabitants of the eastern Alta Verapaz, who slipped into the uninhabited and unpoliced mountains north of Lake Izabal in the neighboring department of Izabal. During the 1890's something of a border war broke out between the two departments over this, when the jefe político of the Alta Verapaz claimed that Izabal was encouraging the emigration. The jefe of Izabal countered, blaming the migration on the heavy labor demands of coffee in the Alta Verapaz and on the ladino invasion of Indian lands, and the jefe of the Alta Verapaz had to agree that these were at least part of the problem. By the end of the decade he reported that hundreds of Indians lived in these mountains and resisted "anything like a wage advance." [112]

Planters worried even more about the emigration of the Indians to neighboring countries, mostly Mexico and British Honduras. Indians who went to Mexico readily found work in the developing coffee plantations of Chiapas and Soconusco, and they received better wages than they could earn in Guatemala. [113] Long accustomed to smuggling, inhabitants of the towns of the western departments moved back and forth across the border at will. This was a particular problem for the governor and the planters of San Marcos. They sought to enforce pass laws, reminded local officials of border municipalities to check the papers of all Indians traveling through, and jailed habilitadores thought to be recruiting Indians for Mexican employers, all to little avail. [114] An alcalde of Tajumulco, trying to explain why he could not fill a 1901 mandamiento order for fifteen workers, pointed out that when he attempted to give local people an advance, they threatened to leave for Mexico. [115] The inhabitants of Jacaltenango took mandamiento money and then went to Mexico, and in nearby San Miguel Acatán Indians who were being held for a mandamiento broke jail and escaped across the border. [116] The government itself in its more candid moments admitted that the workers had cause. Evaluating agricultural conditions at the turn of the century, for example, the Ministerio de Fomento noted that "the old laws that were meant to promote coffee production, because they infringed on the liberty of the Indians, provoked a large number of them to emigrate to the neighboring countries of Mexico and British Honduras." [117]

The attraction of British Honduras was not wages so much as land

and freedom from labor demands, and an extradition treaty that did not recognize peonage.[118] The Guatemalan government in 1902 attempted to counter this emigration by offering land at Chisec in the northern Alta Verapaz and exemptions from taxes and military or labor services "to attract our fellow nationals who have fled to neighboring countries to avoid the unnecessarily harsh work laws that forced them to labor on the fincas."[119] It is not clear whether this lured back many of the "fugitive" Indians, but in the early 1920's the governor of the Petén reported, in gross exaggeration, that there were "more than eight thousand cobaneros, sanpedranos [Carchá] y sanjuaneros [Cahabón]" living on the other side of the Sarstoon River.[120]

Even so, all forms of open opposition, from uprisings and riots to flight, were the exception to a daily norm of grudging acquiescence mixed with minor but largely anonymous resistance to the particular manifestations of the system—"the silent but inflamed hatred of the employers."[121] Owners and the state were loath to admit the existence of even such veiled opposition both because it bespoke their failure to achieve ideological hegemony and because it granted the workers an understanding and agency the employers rejected. Planters reminded themselves, and the description was applied to many colonial peoples at this time, that the Indian was stupid, lazy, brutish, and drunken. At best, or worst, he was deceitful and sly, capable of only the lowest behavior and lacking entirely the patriotism and national spirit to work enthusiastically under conditions favorable to the employers. In fact, when the Indians were at work on the finca they seem to have been remarkably honest, or else very adept at their illegal activities. There were only very scattered reports of tool breaking, sabotage, or theft, the most common forms of individual, self-help resistance.[122] The more usual tactic of indirect resistance or manipulation of the system was that of accepting multiple advances in amounts and under conditions the worker could not possibly meet. Indians did this in their own name or under various names with falsified papers; the bolder ones, a scandalized jefe of the Alta Verapaz reported in 1896, took advances in order to gain exemption from the military and the zapadores/mandamientos and then tried to give the money back.[123] The eagerness of recruiters to sign up workers and their willingness to ignore rules and the debts owed other employers greatly aided those Indians who sought to "*burlar*" (make a joke of) the law. One observer reported watching the habilitadores working the market at Aguacatán and attempting to "steal" laborers from each other; an Indian who had signed with one finca yesterday signed with another today "with the connivance of the agent."[124]

Resistance of the weak must necessarily be oblique if it is to succeed at all.[125] In the broadest sense, Indian opposition to elite and state exploitation and oppression in Guatemala from the sixteenth century to the present has taken the form of denying ladino superiority, even given that group's evident political and economic superordination. While accepting useful elements of the Conqueror's material culture and adopting a version of his religion modified to fit their needs, the Indians also perfected the "cargo system" and "closed corporate communities," the manifest functions of which were to keep the ladino and ladino culture at arm's length.[126] The expansion of coffee in the late nineteenth century brought ladinos into the highland Indian municipalities as never before, but the result was not usually ladinization of the indigenous community so much as the constitution of parallel societies that interacted as little as possible. Popular folk tales, dances, and religious ceremonies and rituals might embrace elements from ladino culture, but in most instances they were used in such a way as to define and reinforce barriers between the Indian and ladino "worlds."[127] If Indian culture and the Indian world were in large part colonial constructs, they nevertheless provided the basis for a separate Indian identity, which the Indians perceived to be morally superior to that of the ladino. But the Liberals, to repeat a point made above, cared less about what the Indians thought than that they should be available to work under conditions profitable to coffee producers. It was against this very concrete manifestation of ladino power that the Indians had to struggle on a day-to-day basis.

San Juan Ixcoy: A Case Study in Resistance

The town of San Juan Ixcoy, set high in the Cuchumatán Mountains of the Department of Huehuetenango, for a time was not much affected by the new Liberal land and labor laws.[128] Problems began to arise only in the 1890's. In 1891 and again in 1893 ladinos from the municipality of Chiantla applied to buy almost one hundred caballerías of what they defined as baldío but in an area that San Juan considered to be part of its community lands. The governor of Huehuetenango blocked the first application, dismissing it as nothing but a scheme to force the Indians of San Juan to buy the land back, but the 1893 application presented the village a much more serious challenge. Mariano García, representing 123 militia members of Chiantla, applied for land in the southern part of the municipality of San Juan Ixcoy, where it abutted on Chiantla. Moved by the seriousness of this threat, the principales of San Juan quickly entered their own claim for 250 caballerías based on "ancient titles" and use "since time immemorial" and including the area sought by García's group. Since they lacked the funds to pay for the survey and the other titling costs, community elders opted to raise money by selling community labor. They signed a contract with Fredrick Koch, a recruiter for the finca Buenos Aires, promising to send men to the coffee harvest in return for the finca's paying the costs of titling the community's land. But as the surveyor worked, tensions mounted. When it became clear that his measurements were tending to favor claims by the neighboring municipalities of Soloma and Nebaj that San Juan had disputed for centuries, the village's representatives withdrew from the survey commission. When the governor refused to send troops to protect him the surveyor fled, fearing for his life and claiming, too, that he had not been paid.

The situation, therefore, had been building for some time when it exploded one night in mid-July 1898. Ignoring the breakdown in the titling process, the agent of finca Buenos Aires had been pressing San Juan for the promised workers, but the sanjuaneros linked the two processes and refused to comply. On the evening of July 18 inhabitants of the town and those from outlying hamlets assembled in the village. They crowded in front of the town hall where various habilitadores slept, fired the building, and cut down and killed the habilitadores as they attempted to escape. Hoping to conceal their crime from outsiders, the Indians then spread through the village, killing all the ladinos they could find and threatening Indians who had worked for the recruiters. By morning, they realized that some had escaped, and they fled into the mountains. The Soloma and Chiantla militias pursued them and killed an unknown number of the villagers and sent some sixty for trial in the departmental capital.

The years immediately following the uprising witnessed an orgy of land grabbing at the Indians' expense, most of it by ladinos from nearby municipalities. In 1900, the government awarded 60 caballerías of the disputed land to Nebaj and 113 to the militia of Chiantla. The following year Isaac Cano, a labor recruiter and the ex-municipal secretary of Soloma, received the 6-caballería property Mixla, which was part of the tract ladinos had sought unsuccessfully in 1891. In 1903

Aureliano Recinos, also a Soloma ladino, acquired the 30-caballería tract called Quisil, and the next year another Recinos, Marcos, received 15 caballerías, bounded on one side by the properties of yet another Recinos, General Aurelio Recinos. Other ladinos also bought land in the area. In each case San Juan protested the sales and refused to sign the measurement documents, but its "ancient titles" remained in the hands of finca Buenos Aires, its survey was incomplete, and it had no funds with which to pursue its case.

These initial incursions were disruptive, but the real change for San Juan came when the Soloma and Chiantla ladinos began to resell their newly acquired land to the owners of lowland properties for fincas de mozos. The new owners now demanded rent not in corn but in seasonal labor on their coffee and sugar estates. A typical contract provided that a tenant might cultivate up to sixty cuerdas of corn and beans on the highland tract in return for harvest labor on the coffee estate, with the labor to be paid at or only slightly below the going rate. The "rent" was in the having to go.[129] As early as January 1904 families living at Quisil and Jolonhuitz protested: "How can we be required to pay rent when this is and has always been community land?" But the property now belonged to the fincas.

By the end of that year even President Estrada Cabrera was becoming alarmed about the potential for further violence growing out of the wholesale despoliation of San Juan Ixcoy. When a delegation from the village traveled to the capital to appeal to him in person, President Estrada Cabrera banned land grants and sales in the area until the situation could be stabilized. San Juan now moved to the offensive. Still without funds, municipal leaders again sold labor to a finca, this time El Pensamiento. With the advances they received for this they retrieved their documents from finca Buenos Aires, had their survey completed, and entered their application for title. Anxious not to lose still more land, the village accepted the boundaries already measured with Soloma and Nebaj. In September 1910, San Juan Ixcoy received official title to 419 "poor and sterile" caballerías.

The struggle was far from through, however. Over the next decades the municipality, local groups, and individuals kept up a steady, but largely nonviolent, resistance to the neighboring finca properties and to the demands of the finca owners for their labor. They never tired of repeating that, government titles or not, the land had always belonged and still rightfully did belong to them: "We don't know how it came into the hands of the fincas." The residents on the fincas de mozos resisted paying rent and fought being sent to the coast. Jailed, roped together, and sent off under guard to the lowlands, they disputed pay and working conditions endlessly and ran away at the first opportunity. Finally, in 1919 the municipality opened the whole matter afresh. They hired yet another surveyor to "rectify" the boundaries of the ejidos, arguing that the measurements made twenty years before were incorrect because they did not allot to the village land that was illegally occupied by the fincas de mozos. This touched off a decade of conflict. To pay for the remeasurement, local leaders again sold labor to a finca, this time to the Herrera family's sugar plantation Pantaleón in Escuintla. Almost immediately this transaction collapsed into chaos. According to village leaders:

That gentleman [Herrera] commissioned the habilitador José Pérez, resident in the departmental capital of Huehuetenango, to give money to the surveyor and to take charge of sending people from San Juan to the finca. Then we, the complainants, gave Pérez the gangs of workers to pay off the loan, but he, instead of sending us to Pantaleón sold our labor to another habilitador, Frederico Scheel, who sent us to other properties and did not pay the engineer. When Pérez died his widow claimed that we owed his estate 11,700 pesos and sold the debt to yet another habilitador, Santiago Molina, who attempted to send us to work on the finca El Pacayal. But we already had paid this by working for Scheel.

In the tradition of all oppressed people, the sanjuaneros relied heavily on obfuscation. Repeatedly and in the face of immediate threats they agreed to meet planter or state demands only to fall back on delay and claims of misunderstanding when the attention and power of the authorities turned elsewhere. Community leaders several times signed agreements with the Herreras that they could not or would not keep but that defused the situation for the moment. When a frustrated recruiter took the town to court and attempted to seize the Indians' animals, they hid the sheep in the mountains and appealed to the jefe político, who had the case thrown out. By the end of the 1920's the matter was still pending and the principales had spent long months in jail and had paid out, or so they claimed, some 60,000 pesos for surveys that all parties now agreed were useless. And San Juan had not regained any land.

In the 1930's the community shifted tactics. Groups and families resident on the fincas de mozos began to bargain with the owners to buy some or all of the disputed land in exchange for labor or small cash payments. With the fall in demand for workers because of the Depression and with a new vagrancy law that restructured labor recruiting, some owners found such transactions to their advantage. A group of thirty workers, for example, agreed to buy a parcel from the Notte-bohm Company in exchange for 30,000 days of labor, and another group bought the tract Candelaria Chitamil from the Gordon Smith Company with labor. Finca Helvetia sold out to a group of sanjuaneros in the late 1940's "for a few cents an acre, because it was not worth the trouble anymore." These victories ultimately were hollow. A half-century of coercion and violence, together with population growth and soil erosion, had shattered the integrity of peasant agriculture. Land and labor had been converted into commodities not bound by the restraints of traditional society, and most of the inhabitants could no longer support themselves by working only within the community. San Juan now exported labor freely to the coffee sector and sustained and reproduced it cheaply in the off-season.

Effects on the Communities

As San Juan Ixcoy's experience makes clear, the histories of the effects of coffee on land and labor and of the reactions of the indige-nous population to these effects were closely intertwined. But each village lived a peculiar reality that in most cases remains to be written. There are as yet no adequate ethnohistories of most of the indigenous communities of Guatemala, and there have been only a few efforts to combine archival materials with oral tradition to examine what coffee meant to a town.[130] "Community" is not the only or necessarily the best level or unit at which to undertake such a study. Individuals and families found themselves drawn or forced into the web of coffee pro-duction within the context of the particular community to which they belonged, but for each it was a peculiar experience, and one that de-pended upon the resources with which they began and their abilities, prudence, and "luck-destiny."[131] The best that can be done here is to suggest schematically some of the impacts of coffee on the population. For example, what effects did the land losses resulting from the ac-tivities of the fincas in the highlands have on the family? On the one hand, losing control of land to local ladinos and to the fincas de mozos may in many areas have worsened a situation that was already deterio-rating because of population growth and ecological degradation. One consequence of the threat to land was to tighten the hold of the patri-arch over his children, especially those young men who anticipated receiving the bulk of the land and needed it to establish themselves as adults. The iron grip of the father and the tense father-son and brother-brother relations commonly reported in modern ethnographies probably became more evident in the last hundred years because of coffee. At the same time, the availability of work in the piedmont and even emigration to a finca gave alienated young men a new alternative: "To the restless youth chaffing under the autocratic rule of his father, the finca offers escape and a golden lure," one anthropologist noted in the 1930's.[132] As a third variation, perhaps some such emigration followed the life cycle: young men and families who had limited access to land or too little freedom under the demands of the father may have moved to the fincas to live there until the aging or death of relatives opened opportunities for them to return to their home community.[133] The availability of work on the coffee estates injected into traditional family structures and relations an element of variability that is not present in societies where there are few or no alternatives to subsistence agriculture in the community of origin.

Coffee greatly increased problems with alcohol in the communities. An anthropologist reported of Nebaj in the 1940's:

The Indians in those days [before the 1890's] drank *comiteco* from Comitán, Mexico, a milder drink than the present day *aguardiente*, and did not drink half as much as they did later when the ladinos came and introduced the latter drink. . . . At one time (i.e., the turn of the century) there were nearly eighty of these bars or drink shops in town. That was in the days when coffee prices were high, much Indian labor went to the fincas, and large sums of money were advanced to them which was mostly spent on drink and ceremony. . . . The ladinos are responsible for increasing the amount and strength of the liquor for the purpose of enriching themselves and with the result that drunkenness has increased to such an extent that it has become chronic amongst large numbers of Indians.[134]

To be sure, the refrain of the drunken Indian was hardly a novelty, but the inhabitants of the highlands now not only had access to more and more powerful alcoholic beverages but also had the wherewithal to indulge themselves. With rum replacing chicha and more people drinking more and longer, the results were plain. If, as some suggest,[135] occasional drinking may have been good for the Indians by allowing them the release of some of the pent-up anger and frustration they felt—which is not to say that it was good for their physical or economic well-being or for the building or holding of ethnic or class consciousness—drinking to excess was not. It was unhealthy, and the state of drunkenness exposed the Indian to a variety of hazards, from fighting and violence to accidental injury or exposure to chills, insect bites, and disease or to the enticements or threats of the unscrupulous habilitador and local official.

Yet, disease and drinking and the dangers of the coast notwithstanding, the population increased dramatically in the years of the coffee revolution (see Appendix A). A voluntarist explanation of the increase would suggest that Indians purposely had more children in order to meet the new demands and opportunities resulting from the spread of coffee.[136] Families increased in size to make labor available for both migration to the coast and to maintain the milpas in the highlands. Certainly Indians could control, or at least limit, the number of children they raised, but to prove the connections between this, coffee, and population increases would require considerably more research and evidence than is presently available. An alternate explanation focuses on the contradictory effects of finca labor on food consumption. Indians complained, and local Indian and ladino officials confirmed, that because forced labor took them away from their subsistence plantings at inopportune times, crops were damaged or lost and food shortages resulted. They also protested that on the estates they received inadequate or tainted food and water. Such circumstances must have adversely affected their health. At the same time, however, the availability of employment on the estates and the ever eager habilitador provided the Indians a new, alternative resource for survival. Finca advances and wages meant money to buy food, whatever the cause of the shortage. Plantation owners imported corn and usually provided it free as part of the workers' recompense or sold it to them at a reduced price.[137] Even if the worker had to pay market price, the food was available, as was the money or credit to buy it. Finca supplies also drove down what speculators could charge in times of shortage, and money in the hands of workers broadened the cash market for food, making it more worthwhile to undertake commercial maize production. The availability of food reduced starvation and the disease-inducing effects of malnutrition in years when crops failed. In other words, the coffee economy simultaneously damaged subsistence production and provided other avenues of access to food. But the ultimate effect was to undercut even further the independence of the rural population and render it that much more dependent on the cash economy.

Chapter 10

Transition to Capitalism

> Property in money, means of subsistence, machines, and
> other means of production does not yet stamp a man as a
> capitalist if the essential complement to these things is miss-
> ing: the wage-laborer, the other man, who is compelled to
> sell himself of his own free will.   Marx, *Capital*

I f ever God had turned his face against a country, this seemed the
fate of Guatemala in the years immediately before 1920. The First
World War was a catastrophe for the republic, as it was for many
other economies dependent on the export of primary products. With
the outbreak of fighting the antagonists began to liquidate and with-
draw overseas investments, cutting back severely on one of Guatemala's
chief sources of producer and commercial capital. The diversion of
shipping by the Allies and the Central Powers to wartime demands,
together with blockades and submarine attacks, largely closed European markets to Guatemalan coffee and shut off traditional sources
of imports. Where a vessel could be found, the hazards of wartime
drove up costs and insurance rates to impossible levels. The result
was a major reorientation of Guatemalan trade away from Europe
and toward the United States. Coffee exports to Germany fell from
458,037 quintales in 1912 to 9,998 quintales in 1916 to zero in 1918;
those to England fell from 75,013 quintales in 1912 to 9,452 quintales
in 1916 to 4,261 quintales in 1918. After a year or two the U.S. market
took up much of the slack, imports rising from 184,132 quintales in
1912 to 705,121 quintales in 1916 and 700,113 quintales in 1918, but
at prices lower than Guatemalan coffee traditionally had commanded
in Europe.[1] Moreover, the North American consumer goods industry, with ready markets at home and in the warring countries, had
little time or capacity to produce for Latin America. In some Latin
American countries this abrupt cutoff generated a burst of import substitution industrialization, but industry had little potential in a market
as small as that of Guatemala, and, in any event, it ran counter to

prevailing elite ideology that presumed the comparative advantage of producing raw material for export.[2]

For a brief moment following the war, this faith seemed justified. Prices exploded upward in a burst of speculation, the famous Dance of the Millions that affected many primary products in the years 1918–20. Coffee prices on the New York market rose from 12–15 cents a pound during the war to over 26 cents a pound in 1919.[3] But they soon collapsed in a welter of world overproduction, and they did not improve again until the middle of the decade. German companies in Guatemala revived quickly, again dominating production and commerce and by 1929 taking almost as much of the coffee exports as did the United States. German investment did not similarly recover, however, which was hardly surprising given hyperinflation and political chaos in that country during the 1920's.[4] The Guatemalan peso continued to slide against hard currencies.

These crises in the export economy and gyrations in the exchange rate took place against a background of serious internal problems. In late 1917 and early 1918 a series of earthquakes destroyed much of the capital and devastated the surrounding area.[5] The government seemed almost helpless in the crisis and did little beyond shooting a few looters, patching up the aqueducts that brought water to the city, and burning the corpses exposed in the cemeteries. Following close on this disaster came a particularly vicious outbreak of yellow fever on the south coast, and then, as the rainy season ended in late 1918, the world influenza pandemic of 1918–19 erupted into Guatemala, carrying off tens of thousands from among the urban and rural population. Again, the government was paralyzed, turning over relief efforts to a citizens' committee while Estrada Cabrera retreated to his hacienda, La Palma. Opposition mounted. Encouraged by a defection of part of the elite and the diplomatic corps and aided by a split in the army, popular mobilizations in Guatemala City finally brought down the dictator early in 1920.[6]

The overthrow of Estrada Cabrera ushered in a decade without precedent in Guatemala. There was a series of relatively open and honest elections. Paralleling these was an unusual freedom of the press and the founding of Guatemala's first modern newspaper, El Imparcial, which numbered among its contributors many of the generation's literary lights, including Miguel Angel Asturias, David Vela, and Carlos Wyld Ospina. Associations, unions, and political parties flourished, although their reach remained largely limited to literate urban dwellers and the government periodically cracked down on their activities.[7] It was on the countryside, however, that the interests of the planter elite focused and where the situation seemed to them most likely to fly out of control. The rural indigenous population had displayed considerable loyalty to Estrada Cabrera at the time of his overthrow, the result of the personalist interventions of tata presidente in their land disputes or against the abuses of local officials; some fought on his side in 1920, and many remained hostile to the new regimes.[8] The political competition for state power in the wake of Estrada Cabrera's fall further weakened the government's hold on the countryside, and there were repeated outbreaks of unrest. According to the newspapers in the capital, these "uprisings" were stimulated by the activities of the former dictator's loyalists and by sinister foreign agents, as well as by long-standing ladino-Indian and land and labor conflicts.[9] The result, said El Imparcial, was a "spirit of rebellion, disorder, and senseless demands, which is inciting the childish and barbarous spirits of our rural workers."[10] Landowners and local officials fought among themselves, scrambled to be on the winning side or to mend fences with the victors, and gave less than usual attention to the routine tasks of control and repression.[11] Politicians stirred up a "rebellious spirit" among the people for their own purposes, telling them they were "free" and arming them as guerrillas in political battles.

Rural landowners were particularly horrified by the possible influences on Guatemala of events occurring in Mexico, fearing the spread of "rural bolshevism" to their properties.[12] Already by June of 1920 they were noting an "effervescence" on the fincas "that if not controlled will occasion great evil for the country." The following year a German company complained that "since [1920] one notes among the workers a marked resistance, even rebellion, against complying with the obligations they voluntarily contracted."[13] One result was a "rain" of "insolent" protests and petitions from workers claiming abuses by their employers. Political propaganda associated with the 1926 election further agitated the rural population. Agents working for the candidate General Jorge Ubico, for example, were accused of promising local workers that if the general won he would pardon their debts and divide finca land among them. Undoubtedly, the newspapers admitted, the workers had been and were being exploited in many instances, but this could not be made an excuse to reject authority. Because the Indian understood and responded only to force, the government must halt the growing disorder in the countryside.[14]

The rural population clearly did take advantage of a weakening of state control in the 1920's to press its complaints more openly and aggressively than had been possible before, but it is less clear that there was an increase in violence. If the newspapers and the elites thought there was and reported more occurrences, at least some of this was simply the result of a less fettered press discussing what would have been censored before 1920. Fifty years of Liberal titling had produced generally agreed upon boundaries between many of the communities and greatly reduced the sort of land conflict among towns that was endemic a century earlier. Nevertheless, disputes persisted, and occasionally they burst into violence. Typical, and typical too of the way the press handled such events, was the confrontation that broke out at the settlement of Ilom, in the municipality of Chajul, in June 1924.[15] Several outsiders had hired a surveyor to mark off a tract of land given by the state to the Momostenango militia in 1902 but never measured or titled. When the engineer arrived in Ilom, "the women of the town, armed with sticks, stones, and whips and led by two or three men, appeared . . . giving savage shouts and trying to strike the party." When he persisted in his task, the Indians tied him up and threw him in the local jail. The surveyor smuggled out word of his situation to the owner of nearby finca La Perla, who rode to his rescue with half a dozen dependents. As the group entered the hamlet, "suddenly from all of the streets began to sound alarm drums, such as might call together a fanatical horde on the banks of the Ganges or a tribe in the center of Africa. Innumerable groups of Indians began to issue from the huts, bearing rocks, sticks, and machetes for the attack." The would-be rescuers beat a quick retreat and notified the jefe político, who ordered militia units from Nebaj and Cunen to put down the disturbance. Although the Indians made it clear that the cause of the riot was "the fear that . . . the ladinos were going to steal all of the lands of the hamlet," the newspaper preferred to see the violence as resulting from "the racial hatred and the fanatic aggressiveness of the Indians against landowners or 'ladinos' who venture into these areas in search of honest agricultural work . . . which prompt them to commit true atrocities, in the name of race, religion, or the interests of the community." For most urban Guatemalans, the rural highlands in the 1920's remained as foreign an area as "the center of Africa." It was a region inhabited by an inferior but vicious and violent population that could only be held in check by the active intervention of a strong central government, a government the country seemingly lacked.

More commonly reported in these years than village land conflicts was unrest among the workers on the lowland fincas and in the adjacent towns. In rare instances, such activities took the form of unions or cooperatives. Early in 1927, for example, Indians of Santa Lucía Utatlán sent a representative to the urban Workers' Federation seeking direction, and in February of that year they organized a local Union of Peasants to press for improved working conditions, schools, and cooperatives.[16] The influx of Indians into the town center to attend the inauguration ceremonies of the new organization so frightened the local ladinos that they panicked and telegraphed the jefe político that an uprising was afoot. The organization functioned for several years and repeatedly won local elections, which the jefe annulled; finally, in April 1929 he imprisoned the leaders on a charge of rebellion. Town ladinos now telegraphed *El Imparcial* to express their relief that they were no longer threatened by the "insane" ideas of "rebellious Indians." By 1929, in fact, and as the first chill winds of the Depression blew across Guatemala, a general campaign against organized labor in all its manifestations was gaining headway. The attack would culminate in the repression of a nonexistent "communist plot" in 1932 and the murder or jailing of what union leadership remained.[17]

The newspapers in these years not only gave more coverage to rural conflicts than had been the case in the time of Justo Rufino Barrios or Estrada Cabrera, but they did so in the most alarming tones and vivid vocabulary. Words such as "uprising" and "revolt" and "armed threat and insubordination" filled the pages of the capital press. This excited tone was a product of ignorance and fear mingled with a sensationalist competition for readers, but the reality in the countryside was not quite what the newspapers made it appear. In November 1925, for example, *El Imparcial* reported in bold print an "insurrection" by the workers on the finca La Abundancia, Chicacao. On closer examination, however, it was clear that what the Indians sought was only an increase in pay consonant with recent minimum wage laws,[18] and that they had made their case without any evident violence. The militia nevertheless intervened and arrested the Indians' leaders, after which the employer and the remaining workers, the newspaper noted cheerfully, came to a "satisfactory" agreement.[19] The same paper on other occasions breathlessly noted "communist buddings" on various fincas, only to admit further down the column that these were but rumors.[20] A careful reading of news reports that gave attention to the workers' complaints or demands usually reveals only the familiar problems of wages and conditions. The resolution of most of the conflicts was familiar, too: the residents of fincas Peña Pobre and Viña Chuvá, for example, reportedly "rioted" in August 1929, when in fact they had only protested their contracts, sent a petition to the President, and tried to beat up an abusive supervisor, all time-honored modes of worker-owner interaction on the coffee estates.[21] But such encounters had become increasingly common, the jefes políticos avowed, because of the activities and propaganda of persons who were "interested in exploiting the Indian race" and "sowing the seeds of insurrection among previously tranquil workers."[22]

This was patent rubbish. While all sides, and even including perhaps the much talked about but never exhibited agitators from Mexico, sought to exploit the unhappiness of rural workers for their own purposes, the discontent and the reasons for it went back much further than the 1920's, and it required no homegrown or imported "bolsheviks" to give it form or voice. The more thoughtful among the planters and the state's agents realized this, and now they too were more likely to express such opinions in print. The jefe of Suchitepéquez, for example, revealed the ill-kept secret that habilitadores and owners commonly lied to the Indians and made promises they failed to honor: "This is the origin of the uprisings of workers that constantly plague agriculture, and often it is necessary to punish workers who demand their rights."[23] But by his own admission the "constant" disturbances with which he had had to deal in the previous year were four, two on the same property. Despite the alarmist prose and the undoubted fact that rural workers did agitate for their rights whenever they saw a chance of success, there was no clear evidence that actual, as opposed to perceived, violence by rural workers increased during the decade. Because they no longer felt certain of the state or of the effectiveness of state repression, however, the planters were more fearful of the consequences of indigenous protests and more ready to see their situation in apocalyptic terms.

Agriculture

Instability in the export sector, political upheavals, disturbances in the countryside, and the availability of a more than usually open press in the early 1920's prompted Guatemala's political leaders, planters, and journalists to an extended debate about the condition of the coun-

TABLE 10.1
Coffee Export Statistics, 1873–1940
(in quintales)

Year	Quantity	Year	Quantity	Year	Quantity
1873	149,069	1896	638,474	1919	896,670
1874	159,980	1897	755,000	1920	939,538
1875	161,959	1898	826,000	1921	935,260
1876	205,346	1899	739,047	1922	935,365
1877	207,885	1900	694,817	1923	956,747
1878	207,285	1901	676,213	1924	888,002
1879	249,521	1902	774,023	1925	976,064
1880	286,893	1903	578,973	1926	932,551
1881	257,794	1904	647,663	1927	1,139,937
1882	309,179	1905	810,815	1928	959,749
1883	400,068	1906	684,409	1929	954,679
1884	367,630	1907	901,994	1930	752,409 (est.)
1885	515,167	1908	569,718	1931	784,722
1886	524,506	1909	1,115,626	1932	984,731
1887	473,951	1910	664,550	1933	765,605
1888	362,770	1911	774,571	1934	1,052,014
1889	552,389	1912	723,013	1935	880,000 (est.)
1890	508,599	1913	875,337	1936	1,101,844
1891	524,495	1914	831,365	1937	1,023,621
1892	491,641	1915	775,631	1938	1,063,469
1893	592,478	1916	803,878	1939	953,502
1894	570,752	1917	939,538	1940	902,878
1895	691,480	1918	782,520		

SOURCES: Jones, *Guatemala*, p. 210; Ministerio de Hacienda, *Memorias*.

try's agriculture. Most opined that it had stagnated or declined in recent years, although they agreed that the well-known penchant of public officials to falsify statistics made it difficult to know for certain.[24] As Table 10.1 shows, coffee expansion peaked shortly after the turn of the century and exports increased only modestly and erratically after that. Similarly, the area in Guatemala under coffee cultivation showed no evident tendency to expand after the late 1890's.[25] Facing poor prices, erratic markets, the personal and political persecutions of the Estrada Cabrera period, and a shift of production into foreign hands that drained profits and capital from the country, many owners had not replaced aging trees. Most commentators believed that as a result productivity per tree had declined since the 1890's.[26] Growers continued to be plagued, too, even after 1920 by the familiar problems of inadequate communications, the depredations of local bosses, and an unstable monetary system.[27]

Yet most of those who wrote about export agriculture in these years thought the chief difficulty faced by the industry was still that of labor. Newspapers overflowed with letters, editorials, and reports on the "labor question" and with proposed solutions.[28] A few dared to suggest that local custom squandered workers: "Such is the system of making our Indians work, without getting from them the profit we should, that we are, on the one hand, wasting thousands and thousands of days' labor on each finca, and, on the other, failing to take advantage of thousands and thousands of days' labor that we could get from the workers we manage to obtain."[29] The majority, however, felt that coffee continued to suffer from shortage of available manpower. They echoed the familiar cry of "Faltan brazos" ("Workers are lacking").[30] Some writers were certain that the absolute number of Guatemalans, and particularly that of the rural Indians, had declined in recent decades, the result of alcoholism, disease, and the emigration prompted by the abuses of the Estrada Cabrera regime.[31] But because there had been no census published since 1893, no one had a clear idea of what the population really was.[32]

For others the problem was not the size of the population as such but the difficulties of organizing and controlling the work force.[33] In the wake of the overthrow of Estrada Cabrera the state had ended mandamientos.[34] Although some argued that corvée labor was an embarrassment to a modern nation and a symbol of the hated past regime,[35] most planters believed that the real problem with the drafts was the bossism that allowed state agents and local power brokers to manipulate mandamientos to their own profit and the monopolization of drafted labor by the wealthier, and especially foreign, growers.[36] The "cruelties" that the Indians had suffered in the past, one planter wrote, were caused "entirely" by the authorities and never by the employer, who equally had been abused.[37] Others confirmed that mandamientos had favored the wealthy and well connected and destroyed the small producer.[38] Most planters by the 1920's seemed to have been willing enough to see them go, as, one imagines, were the Indians. When the jefe político of San Marcos received a request in October 1920 to supply workers to a finca, he responded that the Indians would not accept "forced advances": "It would cause a tremendous effect among the Indian masses because of the Spirit of Rebellion [present] in this period of effervescence among the Indian race."[39]

Debt peonage remained, of course, as did other pressures to enter into labor contracts, especially military recruiting. The military's "hunt of men"[40] about which the planters had complained in Estrada Cabrera's time continued to disrupt agriculture in the 1920's, and it may have increased as a result of the labor conflicts, party disputes, revolts, and attempted coups attendant on the political instability of the time. A 1921 government circular reiterated that agricultural workers who had paid the exemption tax, or had had it paid for them, were not to be taken and that where drafts were necessary they were to be made in proportion to the number of workers on each finca; and a 1923 Presidential message called upon local authorities to take special care that recruiting did not prejudice the interests of agriculture.[41] Nevertheless, in many areas local commandants continued to operate like petty tyrants, extorting bribes and invading properties at night, dragooning colonos or seasonal workers without regard to exemptions or the needs of the estates.[42] The owner of finca Variedades described that sort of "recruiting" in his area: "The main road that crosses this property has become the chief field of action in this jurisdiction of the so-called patrols, groups composed of men in civilian clothing with no badge of authority. For the last year they have constantly watched the road, hidden in the thickets, the station, or under the bridges of the railway line, intent upon grabbing men who come through here on their business . . . and when they have no success on the road is when they invade my property."[43]

Labor

Increasingly in the early 1920's the solution to the brazos problem put forward in editorials and letters was *trabajo libre* (free labor). This was not capitalist free labor. Such was impossible, repeated the now familiar arguments, because the Indians still lacked the "civilized needs" that would drive them "voluntarily" into the wage labor market.[44] The opinion remained that as long as the Indians were satisfied with "a rude shack, almost without clothing, crammed together with the family in a space of two or three meters, in nauseating promiscuity, victim of a thousand superstitions, getting drunk at every opportunity," coercion would be required.[45] Of all the themes about the Indian among the elite, none was more persistent than that he was drunken and lazy and would not work because he had no need to. It was true enough that as long as the population could supply its subsistence requirements from its own resources it had little reason to labor in someone else's coffee groves. But at some point after 1900, and precisely why and when in each case invites study, the balance tipped against subsistence in community after community. Although few of the planters or the Indians realized or fully understood the situation in the early 1920's, it was becoming apparent that under pressure from a growing population and shrinking resources more and more of the inhabitants of the highland villages were not able to survive without finca wages. The much-discussed trabajo libre was envisioned to mean that work would be of free selection, but it was understood that work, and "work" as defined by the state, would be required. A person might "choose between obligatory labor on public projects, military service, or trabajo libre, which for an Indian could not be other than work on the fincas."[46] Trabajo libre would not include the right to organize or strike.[47]

Enforcement of "free" but obligatory labor would require a strong vagrancy law. Guatemala had had vagrancy laws since the colonial period, but these defined vagrants as "those who do not have a profession, trade, income, salary, occupation, or means of support by which to live."[48] This was a measure meant for urban crime control, not for the mobilization of agricultural workers, and it would have to be overhauled if it were to serve the purposes of trabajo libre. The law also would need more effective means to implement it. For example, all adult Indian males would have to be required to carry, in addition to their libreta, a registered identity card (cédula de vecindad).[49] To back up the militia and the Treasury Police (Montada) in the countryside, planters agreed that Guatemala needed a full-time rural police force similar to El Salvador's National Guard.[50]

The coffee elites, particularly those with properties along the western frontier with Mexico and in the Alta Verapaz, continued to be preoccupied also by the flight of Indians across the borders.[51] Repeatedly they proposed revising the labor laws to include restrictions or outright bans on the recruitment of Guatemalans to work outside the country. A July 1923 decree put severe curbs on such activities, but there is no reason to suppose that this was any more effective than earlier efforts had been.[52] The new governments also renewed efforts to entice emigrants to return. Immediately after the fall of Estrada Cabrera, for example, landowners and government officials in the Tacaná region of San Marcos set up a Repatriation Committee to "attempt to repatriate by prudent and persuasive means the emigrant Guatemalan Indians presently in Chiapas, Mexico, who, as is well known, emigrated because of the innumerable abuses and arbitrary actions of the past government of Estrada Cabrera against them and their families."[53] This was an interesting revision of history, for the Indians had fled from the abuses of the planters quite as much as from those of the state. And since they must have found Mexican silver even more attractive in the years 1920–24 as the Guatemalan peso plunged toward near total collapse, it was evident that the finqueros of Guatemala had little to offer them.

The conditions that prompted emigration, and even allowing for the end of mandamientos, were still much the same. The inhabitants of San Pedro Carchá protested in 1925 that estate owners and the public authorities still seized them violently and forced them to carry heavy loads to unhealthy areas of the department, while army press gangs invaded their houses and assaulted the women; it was no wonder, they concluded, that thousands of former residents of the municipality had fled to Belize.[54] In 1928 and 1929 the government again studied repatriation and colonization schemes, to little result.[55] But by this point the effects of the Depression were becoming very apparent. Worried by unemployment, Mexico in May 1929 banned the immigration of foreign workers and began to expel some of those who were already in Mexico, putting the Guatemalan government in the unlikely position of protesting the forced return of its citizens.[56]

Any talk of transition to trabajo libre also raised the question of existing debts.[57] Should these be abolished at once or worked off, and if worked off, over how long a period? Might indebted laborers pay back in money what they owed for work? Should new advances be made? In other circumstances the planters complained of the cost of carrying worker debts, but when opposing the abolition of these and of the system of debts in general they rarely brought up the losses they must inevitably suffer. (This perhaps at least partly confirms the suspicion that much worker "debt" claimed by the fincas was exaggerated.) Employers instead protested that abolishing debts would reward those workers who had failed or refused to work off what they owed.[58] Elite resistance to ending debt peonage was, it appeared, above all a moral question.

Most finqueros, to judge from comments in the newspapers, felt that debt peonage was inefficient, but they opposed an immediate end to indebted labor and rejected any suggestion that Indians be allowed to pay back labor debts in money; they found it difficult, however, to agree upon a scheme for positive reform.[59] A number of proposals for new agricultural labor laws surfaced in these years. Because most of these varied only in detail, a brief look at two will suffice. One that the newly created Ministry of Agriculture put forward in 1921 began with the statement, "All labor will be free," but left no doubt that all would be required to work. No one could be hired by a finca who could not exhibit written proof of having cleared all obligations to previous employers. Public officials were not to serve as labor recruiters, but they could grant a laborer a work release if such was due and an employer refused. Existing debts were to be worked off gradually, and future advances were to be limited to what could be earned in a given year. Laborers would be allowed to pay off in money the debts they had contracted for labor. Any person claiming to be looking for work would be punished as a vagrant if he did not find employment within a specified time.[60] In response to planter protests, the Ministry withdrew the proposal and returned it a year later with several changes. These would have made it more difficult to repay habilitaciones in money, specified and tightened the conditions under which a worker might leave an estate even if his contract had expired, and shifted responsibility for employer-worker disputes from the courts, as the original proposal indicated, to the town officials of the finca's municipality.[61]

Complaining that the government was meddling in affairs of which it was ignorant, the Asociación de Agricultores Guatemaltecos (A.G.A.) presented its own project the same year.[62] The planters' document suggested that existing debts were to be worked off over no more than two years, and future advances would be limited to the equivalent of sixty days' labor. The activities of 'tratistas and labor recruiting by public authorities were to be banned. No worker in debt to one employer might be contracted by or receive an advance from another, and only in the case of severe illness would a worker be allowed to repay in money advances made for work. Every agricultural laborer was to carry a *boleto de trabajo* (work ticket) that recorded his name, the number of days worked each month, and the property to which he was in debt. Failure to produce this would be taken as proof of vagrancy. The provisions of the A.G.A.'s proposal would have moved more aggressively than those of the Ministry of Agriculture's to cheapen the costs of labor recruiting and in the direction of trabajo libre, but there were no major or substantive conflicts between the two or between these and others seriously entertained in these years.[63]

All this was but a flurry. Coffee prices rebounded in 1924, and with these the elite's uncharacteristic self-examination faded from the press. No new labor law emerged and "custom" asserted itself. One writer described the state of things: "We Guatemalans continue to be the most disorganized in the world as regards wages and working conditions. Our caja of coffee varies from 70 to 185 pounds and hardly two fincas are the same. Wages run 10 to 60 pesos a task. On some fincas they do not provide food while on others they give without cost meat, milk, chile, beans, corn, lye, and salt. The majority of properties cajole workers with dances, clothes, alcohol, and many presents, in addition to our disastrous system of unlimited advances."[64] Only in 1928 did the doubts resurface. Although prices continued to be good in that year, dealers sold much coffee forward, and futures prices, weighted down by the enormous 1927–28 harvest in Brazil, anticipated the Depression.[65] It now became clear that planters, rather than rationalizing production during the bonanza years of the mid-1920's, had thrown themselves into frantic competition for workers, driving up production costs. Efforts to attract and hold labor took the form not so much of increasing money wages as of offering indigenous workers the much more powerful incentive of free or below market price corn.[66] Because of this competition and because levels of domestic corn production fell in the second half of the 1920's from recent highs, the importation of corn soared, from an average of slightly more than 2,000,000 kilograms a year for 1923–27, to 22,346,588 kilograms in 1928, and 18,458,424 kilograms in 1929.[67] According to *El Imparcial*, planters used this grain to secure "their" workers and to entice labor away from other employers.[68] Even with these increases and additional expenses, Guatemalan wages were below those of their competitors in neighboring countries, but persistent low productivity, the result of outdated machinery, inadequate and monopolized communications, and a reluctant, coerced labor force, kept overall production costs high.[69]

Food

Although coffee, and bananas after the turn of the century, dominated commercial agriculture in Guatemala, the pattern in the countryside was far from monoculture. Still, the availability of food preoccupied the state and the planters. Most believed that the expansion of exports over the past half-century had damaged food production and raised prices. Guatemala did suffer repeated corn shortages in the years between 1871 and the 1930's. The jefes' records are full of notes and circulares pointing out the problem—"The scarcity of grain continues to get worse"—and urging efforts to stimulate plantings.[70] A note sent to the departmental governors in 1911 was typical: "The rainy season is approaching. . . . You must give strict orders to those of your jurisdiction that they plant not just what they need for their own consumption but that they expand their production as much as possible."[71]

But periodic scarcity had been the norm since the colonial period, and despite the emphasis on coffee from the 1870's it does not appear that short falls in domestic food production became more common, more serious, or more generalized as a result. Shortages resulted above all from continuing to rely on the irregular surpluses of peasant producers to meet much of the market demand. In 1925, for example, the United States Embassy estimated that at least 75 percent of corn production in Guatemala remained in the hands of Indian subsistence farmers.[72] Too commonly they worked tiny plots of exhausted land, and because most of them lacked storage facilities, in years when they managed a good harvest they flooded the market, selling at prices so low that they drove out commercial competition. Small-scale agriculture continued to suffer also from a host of familiar perils such as attacks of locusts and unseasonable rains.[73] A typical combination of circumstances would be a scarity of rain during most of the winter months followed by very heavy rains and a series of cold waves late in the season "that produce disastrous effects on the harvest."[74] For numerous reasons, including restrictions on exports that were meant to keep domestic prices down and improve availability and also the great fluctuations in the price of corn, there was little investment in large-scale corn production. Consistent and comparable statistics for corn production become available only from 1921 on, but these show a continued pattern of wide variations from year to year rather than a marked or clear decline. The pattern is even more evident, as would be expected, if the figures are broken down for separate departments.[75] In the late 1920's *El Imparcial* summed up the chief causes of the food shortages as locust attacks, drought or early rains, the poor techniques and primitive equipment of the Indians, export prohibitions that kept prices down and capital out, transport costs, a lack of storage facilities, and price uncertainties.[76] None of these was directly the result of coffee.

Except among the main coffee-growing districts where profits from the export crop supported railroad construction, poor and expensive transport meant that even in the 1920's and 1930's it often was not easy or profitable to move large amounts of grain from one region to another within Guatemala. A good harvest in one area meant merely lower prices there. Food prices therefore tended to vary widely from year to year: for example, corn averaged 100 pesos a quintal in Guatemala City during 1920, rose to a high of 238 pesos in 1928, and had dropped to 70 pesos by 1932.[77] Prices also followed a fairly predictable pattern during the year, being at their lowest in the months November–May following the harvest and rising sometimes 50–100 percent in July–October as available corn ran out and everyone waited for the new crop.[78] Colonos and seasonal workers were somewhat shielded from this variability by their own subsistence plantings, whether in the home community or on the finca, and by the custom of partial payment in food. Fincas attempted to recover whatever losses the system of payment in food entailed by manipulating the workers' debts, but because few Indians expected or had much incentive to pay off what they owed, such machinations mattered less than the availability of food.

Major investments in capital and technology for corn agriculture might have helped to raise and stabilize output to meet demand, but landowners who attempted this found themselves squeezed between peasant production and imports from North America. Commercial growers of basic food crops often find it difficult to compete with peasants who continue to cultivate and sell these commodities when their return falls below the average rate of return to capital or even to negative rates.[79] In Guatemala, credit was expensive, and even with the ups and downs of the world market, the profits from coffee were generally higher and more reliable in these years than those to be had from corn or beans, and they were profits earned in gold or hard currencies. Imports, too, made corn growing risky. With the completion of the main railroad links along the Pacific piedmont and in the Alta Verapaz during the 1880's and 1890's and the upgrading of port facilities, coffee planters had ready access to grain and flour imports from California and the Mississippi Valley at usually favorable prices. One result was monopsony agreements, open or tacit, such as that struck by the coffee planters of El Tumbador in 1913: to keep prices down, they agreed to pay only up to a certain price for locally grown corn, and above that they threatened to import grain, whatever the cost.[80] Similarly, the government on a number of occasions cut import duties on imported corn and sold corn at or below cost to combat scarcity and high prices.[81] Such arrangements may have been a boon to the consumer, but they undercut incentives to modernize local food production. The relative weight of local output versus imports in supplying food to Guatemala's population varied widely from year to year, a result not only of irregular corn harvests but also of the effect of coffee prices and sales on the ability to import. A fall in food imports in the early 1930's, for example, resulted more from depressed coffee markets than from any wonders worked by General Jorge Ubico.

The expansion of coffee therefore did affect domestic food agriculture, but mostly in subtle ways. Coffee encroached on land formerly used by local inhabitants and seasonal migrants for food production, yet the coffee fincas themselves also brought large amounts of land into use, and much of this they and their laborers planted in corn. Communities and individuals complained constantly that the labor demands of coffee economy damaged their subsistence production. Many observers concurred. As early 1893, for example, Antonio Batres Jáuregui had argued that Guatemala's dependence on imported food was a direct result of the system of mandamientos.[82] A new governor on taking up his post in the Quiché in 1901 echoed this, arguing that "the exploitation of forced labor" was the chief cause of the department's inadequate food production.[83] Local and departmental leaders answered government circulares calling for increased food plantings by protesting that all the workers in the communities were occupied with coffee labor.[84] Certainly, village inhabitants did sometimes lose their plantings when they were forced into mandamientos or road or military service or were held too long on the fincas, but, on the other hand, population growth may have prompted more systematic cultivation of the land in the communities. The inflow of cash from coffee labor into the villages also allowed a few of the better-off individuals and communities to accumulate land, hire labor, and develop relatively large scale cultivation of food crops.

If one is to believe available statistics, food production remained more or less static from the late 1890's to the mid-1930's and then suddenly shot up, tripling from approximately three to ten million quintales in the ten years after 1930.[85] Unless one imagines that the dictator Ubico genuinely accomplished miracles, the most obvious explanation for the phenomenon is simply that his administration falsified the production figures, much as it did the infamous 1940 census. Of course, this does not explain why the sudden increases came in 1936–37 rather than earlier.[86] Too, the larger amounts fit well with those reported in the 1950 census, which is thought to be fairly accurate.[87] If Guatemala's food agriculture did stagnate in the years between the 1890's and early 1930's while the population increased 30–40 percent (see Appendix A), this would strongly suggest growing food shortages and malnutrition among the poor. Although politically attractive to those who would castigate export agriculture for its damaging effects on the subsistence economy, in this instance such a conclusion seems incorrect. What the figures more likely represent is a vast and consistent, if unsystematic, undercounting of corn output before the 1930's by the Indian population and the local officials responsible for supplying such information to the jefes políticos. The Ministerio de Fomento explained: "The Indians when they supply data on agriculture are afraid the government asks for it in order to be able to tax them," and so they "hide especially that which refers to the quantity of production."[88] Put another way, if the Guatemalan Indians in these years did accurately report their corn production, they would be one of the few known cases of a peasant population that did not seek to shield from the state at least some of what wealth it could generate. Moreover, the 1936–37 increase corresponds exactly to Ubico's appointment of intendants from outside the communities to replace locally chosen alcaldes and principales in running municipal government.[89] Far from downplaying local production, these officials were eager to emphasize the progress and development that had come about in the villages under their direction. There also probably was a genuine increase in food output in the highlands as a result of the effects of the Depression and the fall in demand for wage employment, and because of new labor laws.[90]

All this must leave us uncertain about the true state of food production during the Coffee Revolution. There is certainly evidence that the new export impinged upon the abilities of indigenous communities to continue milpa agriculture in traditional forms, but not to the extent associated with a monocultural crop that encroaches directly on main areas of food agriculture. Coffee did not so much subtract significant amounts of land from corn production as block the expansion of subsistence cultivation into new areas to help meet the needs of a growing population. It did this both by engrossing land in the lowlands into which seasonal corn production might have spread and by extracting from the communities under disadvantageous conditions enormous amounts of labor that the inhabitants might otherwise have expended on food production. On the basis of available evidence, one cannot say whether this, when balanced against access to food on the fincas or available because of finca wages, led to an overall deterioration in the diet of the mass of the population. Before coffee the inhabitants of the highlands would have suffered a much more uneven availability of food. The effects of the coffee economy were to even out this access, but probably for most at a low level and, of course, at tremendous social and economic costs to the community and the individual.

Depression

Worried as the economy turned downward after 1928, and offended by the workers' evident affluence, the Guatemalan planters again began to debate questions of labor mobilization and control.[91] State officials and 'tratistas continued to prey on them, they protested; the end of mandamientos had not stopped local bossism. Competition from the large properties, particularly from those controlled by the resurgent German companies, drove up wages and monopolized labor, squeezing out domestic growers and small producers.[92] Planters complained that ignorant, lazy Indians still deceived them and the state by taking multiple advances and by claiming to be traders to evade work. Solutions proposed included the familiar ones of free but obligatory labor, a vagrancy law requiring a minimum number of days of work a year, an end to wage advances, and the imposition of improved instruments of control.

A new element evident in the debates of the late 1920's was an awareness among the coffee planters of increases in the nation's population. A census taken in 1921, but not published until the end of 1924, revealed that the number of Indians in Guatemala, far from declining as many had seemed to think, had increased markedly since 1893.[93] It followed that in many communities the inhabitants might no longer have access to enough land or other resources to support themselves without recourse to the wage sector. A writer in *El Imparcial* drew the conclusion: "What will the worker do without an advance? . . . Where will he go? To plant corn as some employers fear? Some may; but do all or even most of them have enough land, money, tools, etc. to be able to do this? They do not. The road to the fincas will be the only road."[94] Increasingly, Indians did voluntarily seek work on the estates, work that, at least in the early years of the Depression, often was not to be had.[95] It seemed that ecological degradation, population growth, and new tastes acquired on the estates or in the cash economy had begun to create the long-elusive "civilized" needs among the inhabitants of the highland villages. For employers, the problem of brazos was coming to focus more on control than simply on numbers.

Guatemalan coffee growers weathered the Depression remarkably well.[96] The press initially reflected the apparent widespread pessimism with reports that coffee markets were "immobile and chaotic" and that the crisis was far worse than that of 1921–22 and unlikely to be resolved as quickly. Fincas were said to be valued at half of what they would have brought a few years before: "The country is worth less than ten, twenty, or thirty years ago."[97] The crash provoked a burst of panic selling in 1930 and 1931, but the market soon stabilized at levels not markedly different from those before 1929. The availability of mortgage funds to buy fincas declined much more sharply, however, suggesting considerable self-financing by sellers.[98] After a brief hesitation,[99] planters and the government responded aggressively to the fall in world coffee prices by increasing production and exports and cutting wages. The governor of Sololá, for example, put into effect a new pay schedule lowering daily rates from recent highs of 10–15 pesos to 8 pesos; in Tumbador merchants reported harvest wages down 50 percent.[100] The prominent German grower Erwin Dieseldorff addressed the Ministry of Agriculture calling for government action to reduce wages even further: "It would be helpful if the government would begin by cutting wages and salaries because . . . of economic conditions. . . . Of course there will be opposition among the agricultural workers to lowering their wages, and the landowners need the help of the government to put such cuts into effect."[101] Rather than pay even these lowered wages, some employers sought instead only to credit a worker's debt, and all tried to limit advances.[102] They also cut back on food rations. A decline in the cost of living of 50–60 percent between 1928 and 1935 helped to offset the fall in wages and advances.[103] But whether, as a result, real income for agricultural workers rose or fell in these years it is impossible to say. Indians now turned up voluntarily at the fincas, and some found no work at any wages, at least until production began to move upward in 1933.[104] Writers who two years before had worried about a shortage of workers now suggested that the government set up registry offices to find employment for the rural population.[105] In the communities, the effects of the decline in available cash income, and the extent to which many inhabitants of these towns had become dependent upon it, were evident: the inhabitants of Chichicastenango found the 1932 fiesta "sad" for lack of the money usually earned in coffee labor, and those of Santa Eulalia revived handicrafts abandoned in the salad days of the late 1920's.[106]

As the hold of the Depression tightened, planters turned instinctively to the state to rescue them: "Finqueros in this situation expect the unconditional help of the government," one noted.[107] They wanted tax relief, cheaper and more readily available credit, and, as always, help in keeping down the costs of labor.[108] Repeatedly they called for the abolition or reduction of the export tax on coffee, but the precarious fiscal health of the government soon convinced them that this was impossible.[109] They were more successful in their efforts to have the import tax on corn eliminated and to gain reductions in shipping and wharf rates.[110] Most attention, however, focused on credit. As the market contracted, commercial houses and banks became increasingly reluctant to roll over the current accounts upon which planters depended to finance their day-to-day operations. With the value of land and producing facilities falling daily, lenders had even less interest in long-term mortgages. Those who were able to secure loans paid what they felt was excessively high interest, and on mortgages borrowers faced amortization schedules of up to 20 percent a year, which few could afford.[111] The government stepped in to salvage several private banks and commercial houses that collapsed, issued a stop law to prevent foreclosure on loans where the borrower was current on interest and taxes, and several times limited or reduced legal interest rates.[112]

After months of discussion and proposals, the regime went further. The National Assembly in May 1929 issued Decree 1616 providing for the creation of an institution of agricultural credit that would make available cheap, long-term mortgages to landowners.[113] The hope was to capitalize it with up to one million quetzales raised from a foreign loan or by issuing bonds. The government contracted the well-known Costa Rican economist Tomas Soley Guell to prepare a plan; he favored private enterprise.[114] However, following a further round of debate, a government commission decided in favor of a state-controlled bank funded by a foreign loan.[115] Attention now shifted to the possibilities of obtaining such a credit.[116] After almost a year of negotiations Guatemala received a loan of $2.5 million in U.S. dollars from the Swedish Match Company, at 7 percent and in return for a monopoly on the manufacture and sale of matches in the country.[117]

Of this the government earmarked approximately $2 million for what was now being called the Crédito Hipotecario Nacional (the National Bank of Mortgage Credit). On September 2, 1930, *El Imparcial* carried huge headlines: "The Agricultural Bank Is Founded."[118]

The Crédito, as might be imagined, was immediately flooded with applications: by December 31, 1930, it had received 793 requests for a total of Q7,068,000 in loans.[119] In the first year of operation it made approximately 150 loans totaling Q1,470,140.08, most of this in the form of twenty-year mortgages at 8 percent.[120] Therein lay the problem. Because the government stop law relieved borrowers of paying amortization, and although the bank subsequently raised small amounts of capital through the issuance of bonds, the Crédito's loans in the first years paralyzed most of its available capital.[121] Few landowners could, or at least would, pay amortization, and interest alone did not provide the basis for significant additional mortgage activity. Each new long-term loan locked up that much more capital. After the first year or two the institution was unable to continue to make any appreciable number of new, long-term mortgage loans: from 1932 to the end of the decade these rarely exceeded eight to ten a year and in 1940 the number fell to exactly one. When the bank foreclosed on properties, it often could not find a buyer for the burdened finca, or if it did, it was only by offering additional credit.[122] The initial burst of mortgages, although undoubtedly helpful to those who were lucky or well connected enough to receive them, had little impact on the overall credit situation of Guatemala's planters. As the Minister of the Treasury explained, "These operations have not been nor can they be, despite the demand, either numerous or of quantitative importance."[123] The transfer of several hundred thousand quetzales in agricultural loans from the Banco Central to the Crédito after 1932 enlarged its portfolio but did nothing to improve its ability to grant new loans.[124]

Because state regulations during the Depression made it difficult for lenders to foreclose on coffee properties, the growers' most immediate problem was not mortgages but the current accounts needed to keep their operations afloat on a daily basis.[125] The government therefore authorized both the Banco Central and the Crédito to offer short-term loans.[126] The Crédito responded by shifting funds out of dead-end long-term, low-interest mortgages into short-term and more flexible and more profitable current accounts. Except to a fortunate few, the bank did not provide the cheap mortgages, or *crédito territorial,* planters had sought since the 1860's. But because they benefited from other forms of government intervention and because they themselves responded to the Depression by aggressively increasing production, the planter class and the power of the planter class survived the decade intact.

Trabajo Libre

With the Depression local elites abandoned their flirtations with electoral politics and returned to a nineteenth-century-style order and progress dictator, in the person of General Jorge Ubico.[127] Serious debate and discussion disappeared from the newspapers. It is therefore impossible to know the specific sequence of events or decisions that led up to the general overhaul of rural labor laws in May 1934. However, the reforms followed directly from the ideas voiced during the preceding ten years.[128] Decree 1995, issued on May 2, 1934, ended long-term debt servitude, and Decree 1996, issued six days later, substituted instead a new vagrancy law specifically intended for agriculture.[129] Labor debts were abolished because of "the constant conflicts between employers and workers resulting from disagreements over debts provoked by the activities of the so-called habilitadores and because advances restrict the freedom of work and convert the laborer into an object of undue exploitation by those who contract his services."[130] Decree 1995 prohibited future wage advances and allowed workers two years in which to work off existing debts, and it outlawed the activities of the infamous 'tratistas. In effect, planters gained two years of free or nearly free labor in the worst years of the Depression at the cost of the partial loss of debts of often dubious provenance. They soon discovered, however, that, law or not, the inhabitants of the highland communities would not work without advances. That prohibition came to nought. But the courts refused to uphold long-term labor debts, effectively limiting advances to what could be worked off in a single season or year.

The struggle for control of the rural population's labor power continued, transmuted but unabated. Since few of the Indians had either the cash or the desire to pay off what they were said to owe, many of them sought instead to work as little as possible or else to evade the employers' grasp altogether, until the two years stipulated by the law had elapsed. When finca owners could get their hands on Indians, they tried to force them to stay until they had worked off all their purported debt.[131] When they could not, they sometimes tried to seize the worker's property or sought to convert debts originally contracted for labor into common debts of money at interest, for which the worker would still be liable.[132] Such efforts did not always proceed smoothly. In the town of Nebaj, for example, a recruiter conspired with a local notary to rewrite labor contracts into debt notes and to deceive illiterate Indians into signing them. When a delegation of town principales at the head of a large crowd went to complain to the local comandante, he panicked and threatened them. In the scuffle that followed an Indian hit him with a broom. The crowd quickly disarmed the small garrison without injury, but, knowing what was sure to follow, most of the Indians fled to the countryside. The government rushed troops to Nebaj, arrested and shot seven of the supposed leaders of the "riot," and threatened to try 138 of the local population for sedition.[133] More typically, and for obvious reasons, the Indians adopted less confrontational means, seeking simply to stay out of sight and hand until the time ran out.

Decree 1996 labeled as a vagrant any man—women were not subject to the law—without sufficient property to provide an "adequate" income, anyone who had contracted for work on a finca but failed to comply with that agreement, and anyone without a contract for agricultural labor who did not cultivate at least three manzanas of coffee, sugar, or tobacco, four manzanas of corn, wheat, potatoes, vegetables, or other products, or three manzanas of corn on land that gave two harvests a year. By the 1930's few Indians had access to such relatively large amounts of land.[134] Subsequent clarification of the first part of the law provided that those who cultivated ten or more cuerdas of milpa, but less than the amount that gave a labor exemption, owed 100 days a year labor for wages; those with access to less than ten cuerdas had to work at least 150 days.[135] All agricultural laborers were to carry a new form of libreta, renewable each calendar year, in which employers would note the number of days worked for wages. Those convicted as vagrants might be jailed or fined.

Ubico also strengthened state control over the countryside. Besides replacing locally chosen officials with appointed intendants and putting into effect the much-discussed identity card, he stepped up the activities of the Treasury Police. Persons arrested as vagrants usually fell into the hands of the authorities at police checkpoints on the outskirts of towns or during sweeps of outlying settlements by the Montada and local police.[136] The courts took as proof of vagrancy the failure to produce a certificate of exemption or an up-to-date libreta, although they commonly released men if there remained enough time in the year to work the required number of days. Those accused of vagrancy might defend themselves by claiming never to have worked on a finca and not to have a book—a holdover excuse from the old peonage system that did not address the demands of the new vagrancy law—or by claiming a profession that gave them a living or access to enough land in their home community or elsewhere to exempt them from compulsory labor. The most ingenious, if unsuccessful, defense was that of a man who affirmed that "in his heart he did not consider himself a vagrant."[137] Others said they were "shysters," or were between employments, or that they worked as local or traveling merchants. The courts went to considerable lengths to attempt to verify such claims, telegraphing the authorities in the home community or giving the arrested person the opportunity to retrieve documents. They regularly exonerated those found not liable under the law. Local municipal judges, that is, the intendants, heard cases initially, but decisions might be appealed to the departmental Court of First Instance. As the system became routine, those who possessed the proper documents generally also had worked the required number of days; those who did not have their papers in order usually refused to produce a libreta. Arrests almost always took place between April and August, during the off-season for coffee and preceding the drive to round up harvest labor.

The most frequent complaints of the rural population against the new labor system concerned the failure of local authorities to give proper credit for the days they had worked or to provide them needed certificates of exemption for land cultivated or a trade or profession. Intendants sought to generate the maximum number of workers possible from their communities to satisfy their superiors and to curry the favor of powerful elites.[138] Villagers protested that as a result these officials ignored their work or trade or purposely undermeasured or refused to note their plantings.[139] In October 1936, for example, eighteen inhabitants of Aguacatán-Chalchitán petitioned the Ministerio de Fomento saying that, although each cultivated enough land to be exempt, the intendant put them in jail to force them to accept a labor contract. When the official denied the charge, they protested that he knowingly undermeasured their plots to force them into finca labor and for this recruiters paid him a "gratuity."[140] Some intendants, without any legal basis, refused to accept land cultivated in the village common as meeting the new requirements. Chamelco, for example, apparently to establish a firmer basis of individual possession to satisfy the vagrancy law, began for the first time to charge rent for the use of ejido land.[141]

Even efforts such as Chamelco's were no guarantee against abuses where the intendant responded first to bribes from planters and habilitadores. The inhabitants of Comitancillo complained that instead of being allowed to work on the fincas they wished, the intendant was forcing them to go to the estates he favored and from which he presumably received bribes. When they resisted, he jailed and beat them.[142] By the late 1930's and early 1940's it was common for labor recruiters to denounce as vagrants persons who had contracted to work on their employer's finca but had, or so it was claimed, failed to appear or to complete the agreed-upon tasks. The courts refused to convict a worker of vagrancy if he could show that he had worked the required number of days, even if not on the finca that had entered the case against him, but they also ordered him to fulfill any outstanding contracts.[143] Repeatedly, too, judges ruled that no one could be forced to commute his sentence, but intendants still pressured convicted Indians to take work offered by preferred labor recruiters or planters, who were only too happy to pay the Indians' fines as a labor "advance."[144] In effect, at least some intendants sold workers to the highest bidder or briber.

The rural population resisted the vagrancy law as it always had fought state and landowner demands, with appeals to tata presidente, partial compliance, evasion, fraud, and, though very rarely, violence. Resistance was muted, however, not only by the effective coercive power of the Ubico regime but also by a sense among the indigenous population that the law was much fairer than the old ones had been. As the elders of San Andrés Semetabaj explained: "When Ubico entered the government, there was a change because he created an article in the constitution which made work sacred. . . . If the patron came to bother him, and the worker retaliated, it was because the patron deserved it. Patrones obeyed this and there was no more offense."[145] Indians recognized that Decree 1966 extended trabajo libre to ladinos as well as to Indians among the rural poor, and the police swept up ladino and Indian "vagrants" alike. This was a welcome change from the petty tyrannies of the past half-century. It did not mean, of course, that the rural population submitted to labor demands willingly.[146] Those who could afford it paid off the intendant to obtain genuine or fraudulent certifications of cultivation or merchants' exemptions. "Shysters" did a lively business in forgery. And Indian and ladino employers struck deals with laborers to work for less than the required number of days for nothing or only for food, in exchange for a notation in their books of the required 100 or 150 days.[147]

The new laws had an immediate adverse effect on the ladino labor recruiters, tavern and store keepers, and local bosses who for some time had dominated the cash economy of all but the most isolated of the highland Indian towns. The new laws both reduced and made more precarious their sources of profit. The ending of indefinite labor debts weakened the network of credit by which the ladinos kept and exploited their clientele, the Depression brought scarcer and lower wages, and the vagrancy laws meant fewer and smaller advances. Because of these changes, for example, the ladino who controlled the salt works in San Mateo Ixtatán lost his workers; they had abandoned the property, he reported, and now waited for him to fail so that they "could return to exploiting the salt springs themselves as they did before I arrived."[148] Although the abolition of debts had little real economic impact on the fincas, it wiped out many shopkeepers and 'tratistas.[149] The Indians, an official noted, "only wait for the month of May to arrive without working, because that is the date Decree 1995 goes into effect."[150] The flow of ladinos into the highland villages prompted by the coffee boom began to reverse itself. Because large landowners tended to see the 'tratistas and most other village ladinos as parasites who complicated recruitment and raised labor costs, few regretted their passing. Finally, Ubico's ambitious road-building program meant that the state could rely more on full-time police and military agents for internal control and had less need of the old community-based ladino militia units.

The laws that ended long-term debts and imposed a new definition of vagrancy hastened a process of socioeconomic differentiation within the indigenous population already accelerated by forced participation in the coffee economy. Indians rich by local standards could now more easily escape finca labor, whether by owning or cultivating sufficient land, by obtaining a merchant's exemption, or by bribing the intendant.[151] Land shortages and the desire of even poor Indians to avoid having to leave their community meant that cheap labor was more available locally. The exit of the ladinos also opened new commercial opportunities. Indians moved into the formerly ladino-

TABLE 10.2
Libreta Sales, 1937–1942

	1937	1938	1939	1940	1941	1942
Indian depts.	100,597	182,875	165,084	89,270	123,308	142,029
Ladino depts.	49,828	59,948	69,142	31,671	48,550	48,932
TOTALS	150,425	242,823	234,226	120,941	171,858	190,961

SOURCE: Ministerio de Agriculture, *Memorias-1938–44.*

dominated areas of shopkeeping and mule and truck transport, and former overseers took up labor recruiting directly.[152] These opportunities, if less attractive than they had been to the ladinos, were valuable to Indians both for the profits they promised and for the exemptions they offered. Perhaps unexpectedly, the new laws also may actually have increased Indian access to land. To stabilize their labor force some fincas provided and registered plots of land of the requisite size for their workers, whether on the lowland property itself or on highland fincas de mozos.[153]

When anthropologists in the 1930's undertook the first generation of intensive field studies in highland Guatemala, they found land shortages to be widespread. One investigation of corn production in Huehuetenango calculated that villages needed one and a half acres of arable land per inhabitant to make subsistence agriculture viable.[154] Of the twenty-three towns surveyed, only three or four had ejidos adequate for community maintenance. At the same time, as Table 10.2 shows, an evident emerging balance of supply and demand, and even oversupply, of labor for the export sector could be read in government libreta figures. These figures showed the yearly availability of 150,000 to 180,000 agricultural laborers who by most calculations did not possess or have access to sufficient land to support themselves, although some earned additional income from handicrafts and trade. By contrast, the number of workers needed to make the crop in the 1930's was not more than 140,000 to 150,000 a year, based on 100 days of labor per person. State-enforced extra-economic coercion of labor was less and less necessary and less and less economic. But the planters resisted giving up their guarantees, and the vagrancy law continued in force into the 1940's.

It was in the death throes of the repressive Ubico regime that direct coercion of agricultural labor also breathed its last in Guatemala. Under rising pressure from students and the urban middle and working classes and with the country suffering the effects of a rural economy thrown into disarray by the Second World War, Ubico abandoned office in 1944 and turned the government over to a junta headed by one of his followers, General Frederico Ponce. Ponce, though he was an unlikely reformer if ever one could be imagined, "in a desire to pander to [i.e., gain the support of] the rural population arbitrarily suppressed the libreta system." [155] This by no means ended the matter, however, for Ponce soon fell to the October (1944) Revolution, which for the first time brought genuine popular reform to Guatemala and life back to the newspapers. Again the question turned to labor, and the old complaints of the "lazy" Indian and warnings that an end to coercion would mean labor shortages reappeared. But the indigenous population now found many more public defenders: "Capitalism thinks of the Indian as forever the trash collector, but many times it is the traveler [in the highlands] who feels small when confronted by the noble spirit, the high morality, and the grace of these men of the mountains, so poorly understood." [156] Intent on converting Guatemala's "feudal" agriculture to capitalist, Congress passed yet another vagrancy law in May 1945 that ended the use of libretas and omitted the requirement of a specific number of days labor per year.[157] Now the definition of "vagrant" reverted simply to those without work or a profession or without an income or property adequate to sustain themselves. The new regime wrote this into the 1945 constitution. Guatemala was the last country in the Western Hemisphere to end state-sanctioned coerced labor.

Conclusions, and
Some Questions

To the extent that the rise of trade can be expected to affect
pre-capitalist economies, it is likely to bring about not the
loosening but the tightening, of pre-capitalist forms.
Brenner, "The Social Basis of Economic Development"

Returning to the question of primitive accumulation with which
this study began, it will be useful to summarize here the history of that process in rural Guatemala. As of 1760, both land and
labor already had been partially, but incompletely, transformed into
market commodities by two and a half centuries of Spanish colonial
rule. But if land existed as private property in Spanish, creole, ladino,
and Indian hands, apart from and within Indian communities, most
of the indigenous population found their chief economic and social
safeguard in the institution and custom of community property. Similarly, free labor in the full capitalist sense of double separation from
direct coercion and the means of production could be found in late
colonial Guatemala, but the dominant forms were, on the one hand,
self-employment in subsistence and petty commodity production, and
on the other, forced integration into the wage economy through repartimientos. Indebted labor was common, but the power of the state and
the hacendados was insufficient to qualify this as debt peonage. More
properly it should be seen as a form of competition among employers
from which the workers sometimes benefited.

The most striking characteristic of Guatemalan agriculture in 1760
and for the century after was the extraordinarily low level of development of the material forces of production. This was both a cause
and an effect of severe undercapitalization. In its search for revenue
the Bourbon state pillaged the community cajas and cofradías, raised
taxes, and called in loans, and it returned little of this revenue to agriculture. The church's taxes and capellanías also drained funds from
the countryside to the cities, to commerce, and to Spain. Ladino and

Indian peasant subsistence agriculture and food production for the cities and the indigo regions, although very efficient in terms of scarce capital inputs, was dependent upon access to cheap land and labor and on the vagaries of climate. A few comparatively well-capitalized operations such as the famous hacienda San Jeronimo with ready access to markets prospered, but most rural property and populations literally and figuratively vegetated.

Coerced labor had existed in Guatemala from the first days of the colony, but, apart from the early encomiendas and black slavery, this was forced wage labor. It resulted from a compromise between a Crown that wished to preserve the indigenous population and to assure it the means to pay state and church taxes and fees and the large landowners who sought by all means to depress labor costs. More broadly, labor was coerced because the indigenous population lacked "needs" to drive it voluntarily into the labor market. While the community remained intact and in possession of enough land for subsistence, rural inhabitants preferred working their own fields to laboring in lowland commercial plantings under the conditions and for the wages landowners and the state sought to force upon them. The partial monetization of the indigenous economy resulting from centuries of colonial rule and increased by eighteenth-century changes in tribute and tax payments drove individuals and families into the labor market. This was not sufficient, however, to meet the demands of planters heartened by the possibilities of indigo and by the general economic expansion resulting from the Bourbon Reforms. Worse, the building of the new capital and competition among employers drove up free labor wages in the central part of the colony. Indian workers sought opportunities to earn higher wages, and the Audiencia supported their right to do so. It was the planters who argued for the maintenance of lower, "customary" wages in the face of evident inflation.[1] But Indians did not seek to accumulate, being satisfied to earn only what they needed for their immediate costs and then to abandon the labor market. Higher wages would have meant fewer offers of work.

The extent and severity of the coercion used to mobilize labor in Guatemala depended above all on the world economic conjuncture. When there appeared the chance for profitable production for the world market, landowners and the state sought to round up the workers they needed as quickly and as cheaply as possible. When such opportunities receded, so did the interest in Indian labor. The expansion of indigo after the mid-eighteenth century provoked new pressures on the communities in San Salvador–Sonsonate and in nearby Guatemala. A livening labor demand spread through the whole economy. Growers sought with little success to extend coerced labor into areas such as the south coast and the Verapaz, where formerly it had not existed or had been very weak. Planters who had worked with free labor sought to increase levels of exploitation and in some cases shifted to the forced drafts of repartimientos. Nominally free labor became more entwined in debts. With the collapse of indigo, however, the economy went into a general depression. For the next half-century coerced labor fell into disuse.

The Indians and the surplus they produced, not mines or plantations or even land per se, were the real wealth of late colonial Guatemala. For the Indians their ejidos were vital. They provided resources for material subsistence and the bases for their ideological structures, the syncretic Catholicism of custom focused upon the local saints and ancestors. "Indianness" was inseparable from community; deprived of community the individual became a candidate for ladinization. And community was difficult to imagine apart from community lands. Given the Crown's reliance in Guatemala on revenues derived from the Indians, it follows that the state was generally solicitous of the needs of the villages. For example, towns caught in land disputes routinely and successfully protested their inability to pay taxes if they were deprived of rights to given areas. With Independence, and as part of their drive to homogenize the population, the first generation of Liberals eliminated most taxes specific to Indians. This markedly reduced the state's stake in the survival or integrity of the communities. It was this decline in the interest of the state in the preservation of the village as a tax-paying and labor-providing entity, rather than simply creole assent to power, that threatened community survival. But as long as the political and economic elites had only limited need for the resources of the indigenous population, and this was the case in most areas for the half-century after Independence, there would be little threat to the communities. Indeed, in these years of confusion and a weakened state, many towns expanded their resources.

The Guatemalan colonial state had achieved an impressive though uneven level of control and compliance in the countryside, but genuine hegemony proved more elusive. A low ratio of priests to population and the closed and autonomous nature of the colonial Indian community meant that even the church made little more than formal headway among most of the indígenas. As a result, by the early eighteenth century rural Guatemala was characterized by a laboriously worked out, if largely unarticulated, agreement between the mass of the population and the state and elites, a "colonial compact" codified in custom. This custom, the product of centuries of struggle, defined a level of exploitation with which the communities and the rural population could live. After the collapse of cacao in the seventeenth century, the state and the landowning and officeholding elites left the rural population largely to its own devices, subject only to exploitative forms such as taxes and repartimientos mediated by the local community, and to the demand of formal adherence to ideologies of Crown and church. The Bourbons' drive to increase revenues and centralize control partly dismantled the pact, and the Liberals' reforms of the 1820's and 1830's blasted it to ruins. Thus the Bourbon and Liberal effort to strengthen the state weakened and impoverished it.

Ultimately, of course, the ability of the Indians to maintain a protective autonomy, and even allowing for indigenous mechanisms of brokerage and resistance, depended on both the demands of the political and economic elite and the condition of the cash economy. No historical actors more closely approximate Marx's axiom about the individuals' limited ability to make their own history than do Mesoamerican indigenous peasants. Pressure mounted on some Indian, and casta, villages in the late eighteenth century with the expansion of indigo. The state increased, or at least attempted to increase, taxes, the governors illegally enforced the repartimientos de efectos, and the Crown and the hacendados competed for labor repartimientos, driving the population into the bush, into debt peonage, and into the cities. With the falloff in the indigo trade after 1800, paralleled by an almost simultaneous collapse of the Bourbon state in the Napoleonic Wars, pressures eased. The policies of the postindependence Liberals and the resulting civil wars had the result of further reducing the effectiveness of state control and hegemony in the countryside while helping to mobilize an unprecedented intervention of the mass of the population into politics to restore, if imperfectly, a preferred status quo ante.

Thus, the years between 1760 and 1860 witnessed in Guatemala at once the full fruition and the failure of the colonial system. Accommodation and resistance to three hundred years of Spanish and creole rule generated among the indigenous populations a defensive "traditional" Indian culture focused on the pueblo de indios or municipalidad. The village controlled and regulated access to the resources necessary for the physical and ritual maintenance and reproduction of the community, and most still could get enough of these to ensure individual and group survival. The inhabitants had erected political and social structures that normally held outside exploitation to tolerable levels while at the same time damping tendencies toward differentiation and exploitation among the population itself. None of these worked perfectly, of course, but they did work, reinforcing ties within the community while keeping neighbors, creole elites, and the state at arm's length. A flexible idea of "community" allowed the Indians to regroup as needed to meet the most recent or serious threat. But "community" was not flexible enough to encompass an effective pan-Indian unity, whether on the basis of a shared sense of class and exploitation or on the basis of "race." Too often the perceived enemy was the next town. Villages dissipated resources and energy in border disputes that built up legacies of hatred and made cooperation unlikely. Such fratricidal disputes were possible because of the weakness of the state. While the state remained impaired and while the landowning elites had no need of the labor and land the indigenous population controlled, intervillage conflicts could continue without seriously threatening the integrity of the communities. In a similar way, the cargo system worked to level differences in the communities only as long as the material differentials to be ironed out remained small and access to and alternate uses for material surpluses were limited. It was a precarious world for all involved. The state could not control the countryside, elites could not establish a stable basis for wealth, and the independence of the Indian population depended on these failures.

Coffee dismantled this laboriously arrived-at construct. As early as the 1870's and 1880's capitalism may be said to have "taken root" in the ideological superstructure mounted by the Liberal and state elites, but it advanced much more slowly at the level of production relations. In a century-long holding action, the villages retreated first to renewed community titling and then to lotificación according to village norms; by the 1930's many Indians had found the means and the incentive to make the final transition to full private property. This was the result less of commitment to capitalism than of population pressures and the threats posed by small ladinos and the more aggressive of their fellow Indians. As land increasingly was perceived as a commodity, the vestigial restrictions that custom attached to its use and transfer less and less imposed significant barriers to its full incorporation into the market economy.

By the 1930's, too, almost all Guatemala's adult male Indian population, and many of the women, spent at least part of the year in wage labor on the fincas, or they paid a high price to avoid this. And an even more fundamental change had occurred. If the mechanisms of coerced labor persisted, clearly they were less and less necessary. Population pressures, declining availability of resources, and new needs and possibilities—and these included schools and medical care, not merely consumer baubles—both drew and pressed individuals into the wage labor market. Just as the existence of wages tended to conceal the essential element of coercion in labor relations during most of Guatemala's early history, the persistence of coercive forms helped now to conceal the growing "free laborness" of relations after 1930. Even with the abolition of vagrancy recruitment in 1944, however, most of Guatemala's rural workers were not yet fully proletarianized. Instead they were firmly in the category of the "semi–proletarians," small holders who could not, and who knew they could not, survive without finca work.

The Guatemalan coffee finca of the late nineteenth and early twentieth centuries was the product of the growing incorporation of local land and labor into a world economy dominated by North Atlantic capitalism, but it was not itself capitalist. The finca was typical of the long history of the overseas expansion of the European economy and efforts by the bearers of that economy to dominate or incorporate into it non- or precapitalist forms of production. But history schematized is history lost. The Guatemalan coffee finca developed, too, out of the peculiar historical conditions of that area. Coffee assumed the form it did because of when and where it developed. Take, for example, land. For the planters, coffee land was fully a market commodity, to be bought and sold, cultivated or not cultivated on the basis of calculations of profitability and economic utility. Planters also bought land to control labor and to supplement systems of direct coercion administered by the state. This was effective because of the indigenous population's attachment to place and its willingness, reinforced by the overarching coercive apparatus, to enter into labor arrangements in return for being allowed to remain in their community and near the ancestors. Over all, what is startling about the acquisition and use of land for coffee in Guatemala is the lack of concern and conflict it engendered, in a striking contrast to the violence that accompanied the expansion of export agriculture in many areas during the late nineteenth century.

Labor was another question. Even more than capital, scarcity of labor was the planters' nightmare. While the Indians retained access to land or other resources that guaranteed their subsistence, they would not present themselves voluntarily to work in the landowners' coffee groves. The solution was to expand existing forms of labor coercion to embrace all the republic, to enforce these with a growing, and growingly effective, system of state power, and to pass along as much of the cost of this as possible to the same Indians and poor ladinos through taxes, monopolies, road duty, and so on. It worked, but it left planters dependent on the whims and extortions of state agents. There was no alternative. The Guatemalan state in the short run did not have the power to shatter the economic and social bases of the highland communities and create the necessary conditions for capitalist free labor. Too, and though it was not always evident to the growers, seasonal labor from the communities was cheaper than free labor. The villages supported the workers in the off-season, provided "social security" services, and reproduced the labor force outside the wage circuit. Balancing this, of course, was the cost of the coercion itself. Blocking the development of a more efficient, or at least uniform, labor system was "custom." The planters had no interest in the internal market, but custom demanded that they pay their workers rather than simply drafting or compelling them to work. Any effort to subvert this tradition would have provoked massive resistance and possibly rural uprisings.

Rural employers gave their workers not a straight cash wage but a package of payments that included advances, money wages, credit, food, sometimes free, sometimes at or below market cost, other consumer goods under concessionary conditions, and services such as medical care and protection from military recruiting or past debts. The precise mix of these various forms of payment varied from property to property and among laborers. Under these circumstances, how were planters to measure or compare their true wage costs? How were Indians to calculate their income? Indians tended to evaluate their situation in terms of overall well-being, and this focused their attention on access to sufficient corn under stable and reliable conditions. For them there was little to be gained by shifting to full money wages, which threatened to leave them at the mercy of unstable grain prices. Under these conditions, and even apart from coercion, a free wage market was unlikely to develop.

Almost two hundred years after the Bourbon administrators of the 1760's described Guatemala for their new king, the countryside was in many ways changed, but unevenly. For the central valleys the dominant feature was urbanization attendant on Guatemala City. Although the decline of grana and the transition to coffee shifted the focus of commercial agriculture west and north away from the center of the republic, coffee nevertheless greatly increased the importance of Guatemala City, at the expense of rural centers and departmental capitals. New means of communications drew power and decision making to the national capital and limited the independence that departmental chiefs and local caciques had enjoyed in earlier periods. Many planters lived in the capital for much of the year, communicating with their managers by telegraph and telephone and visiting the properties only occasionally. Better roads, hospitals, and schools financed by coffee meant improved living conditions in towns such as Chiquimula or Sololá, but relative to Guatemala City these regional centers withered away after 1900. Even the towns of the coffee piedmont offered little to compare with the capital, now only a few hours away by train.

Apart from the banana enclave, the whole of the Oriente was now even more marginalized to national power and wealth than it had been at the end of the colonial period. Not for more than a hundred years had the region produced an export of value or been a major supplier of food and commodities to a thriving commercial sector. The population continued to grow, ladinoizing into a relatively homogenous mass that with each generation fragmented the available land more, but the region was of less and less importance to the national economy.

The situation of much of the Baja Verapaz was similar, although the persistence there of the Indian population was stronger, the land, if anything, poorer, and the population more desperate. As they had two hundred years before, but now in greater numbers, residents of Salamá and Rabinal migrated each year to work on commercial plantations, chiefly the coffee fincas of the western piedmont. Few went to the nearby Alta Verapaz, where planters took advantage of a local labor force. Refugees from the arid valleys of the Baja Verapaz also provided many settlers for the new Zona Reina north of the Cuchumatán Mountains.

Above all, the Baja Verapaz contrasted dramatically with its northern neighbor, the Alta Verapaz, which on the basis of coffee wealth had become an independent department in 1877. Coffee transformed the Alta Verapaz after 1821 from a "zone of refuge" for an indigenous population under the watchful eyes of the Dominicans into one of the country's leading coffee export producing regions. Nevertheless, it remained isolated. Local residents had only limited interaction with the larger Guatemalan society or economy, and the commercial economy was largely in foreign hands. It was notorious, for example, that before the Second World War many of the Germans and other foreigners in the department failed even to register with immigration authorities. Growers, in turn, obtained most of their labor force from among Indians resident in the department and often living on or near the fincas.

The south coast in these years split dramatically. Apart from commercial banana cultivation that began in the 1920's and 1930's, the coastal lowlands remained largely uninhabited and uninhabitable, ridden with disease and subject to the flooding of large areas with every rainy season. Only in the wake of the Second World War would pesticides and antibiotics open the region to commercial cotton and meat production. The boca costa from Santa Rosa to the Mexican border, on the other hand, had become Guatemala's quintessential coffee region. Trees protecting shade-grown coffee had replaced the primeval forest that so impressed travelers in the mid-nineteenth century. The expansion of coffee swept aside most of the Indian towns and settlements in the area and converted the inhabitants into resident workers on the fincas. Ladino centers such as Escuintla and Retalhuleu mushroomed. The region enjoyed the best communications in the country, but this served and reinforced coffee exports, not some broader definition of national development or integration. This was the area of the classic form of Guatemalan coffee production: large landholdings owned by ladinos and foreigners, heavily capitalized, and worked by gangs of temporary laborers brought from the adjacent highlands.

For the indigenous population concentrated in the western highland, everything, and yet very little, had changed. Most still (circa 1940) lived in their ancestral villages, cultivated plots in what had been or still were village community lands, and preserved intact the central features of their "traditional" political and social culture. However, for two generations now the state had forced them to work at least part of the year in the coffee economy. This sort of exploitation was not new, but its extent and penetration into the western highlands was unprecedented. Whereas, for example, late colonial repartimientos demanded 25 percent of the population of a limited number of towns, by the 1930's the vagrancy law required 30–40 percent of the time of all but the better-off Indians. Land shortages determined that many worked even more than the law required. The Indians of the highlands may have remained isolated in many ways—"marginal town[s] in a marginal region," in the words of one author[2]—but the demands of coffee production integrated them ever more tightly into the export economy. They were disadvantaged and exploited participants, but participants nonetheless, in a world economic system dominated by North Atlantic capitalism.

Forced labor drained the villages of huge numbers of workers who, and apart from the hazards of disease and injury, generally did not receive a wage that compensated them or their community for the loss of labor power. Frequently gone to the coast, and commonly racked by disease when at home, the Indians could not maintain village agriculture. This often spiraled downward in a crisis of decapitalization, neglect, and overcropping.[3] Although a few communities, for example Panajachel, may have been able to respond effectively to the market opportunities opened by new concentrations of population and improved communications, most found instead that labor shortages forced them to convert gradually from an economy based on intensive and diversified agriculture and handicrafts to extensive cultivation of corn and beans. The rise of milpa monoculture in the villages paralleled that of coffee on the coast.[4] Forced out of the village by state coercion and, increasingly, to meet their subsistence needs, Indians found that the ritual system that defined and held the community together threatened to collapse. New possibilities for spending surplus income where this was available, together with new ideological models such as Catholic Action and new forms of local and national politics undercut the cofradías and the civil hierarchy. Whereas in some towns the effects of coffee labor and land incursions gutted cofradías, in others the new rich poured money into them, or into other local projects and improvements that strengthened community spirit, even if not in the traditional forms.[5]

These contrasting pictures make clear coffee's uneven and contradictory effects on the rural population. Men and women, families, and villages each had their own "luck-destiny," or fate, to work out. Broadly, though, several trends are clear. Coffee and Liberal laws hastened or exacerbated socioeconomic differences within and among the indigenous population.[6] Indians presumably always had exploited other Indians, but before the 1870's the opportunities for this were limited; the availability and distribution of subsistence resources allowed considerable independence for most families and individuals. With coffee the situation changed. Some Indians, well situated by birth or uncommonly aggressive or unscrupulous, allied themselves with the state and the fincas and profited from labor recruiting and the privatization of land. Depending on their choices, they plowed these profits back into other money-making schemes and perhaps ladinization or used it to take over the cofradía–civil hierarchy system and perpetuate the form if not the content of the "closed corporate community" to their advantage. With money or connections one could escape forced work, buy the labor power of poorer compatriots cheaply, and accumulate material goods and prestige. At this point, which many communities were beginning to reach in the 1920's and 1930's, it makes sense to begin to think in terms of classes and class exploitation among the indigenous population.

Coffee probably drained more from most communities than it returned, but it did return something. That something allowed villages to survive that might otherwise have become moribund. Once coffee cut off or greatly restricted access to the lowlands, growing populations and concomitant land shortages would inevitably have forced population out of highland communities. The availability of coffee labor allowed at least some of these families to remain. By combining milpa agriculture with work on the coast, highland dwellers could earn enough income to allow them to continue to be part of the community. The result was what Pierre-Philippe Rey has described as a situation of "reproduction-destruction":[7] the villages functioned as labor reserves for the export economy, reproducing cheap labor power and maintaining it in the off-season. In contrast to the costs of employing a genuine proletariat, the coffee growers did not have to pay the full price of maintaining or reproducing labor. Wages could be depressed below costs of reproduction because the labor force was generated outside the capitalist circuit and only brought in by extra-economic coercion when required. But because of the drain on labor power, the effects of disease, socioeconomic differentiation, and population growth this was not a stable situation, and, in fact, it tended toward a gradually decreasing viability.

Why did the Indians accept the increases in levels of exploitation resulting from the expansion of coffee? To lay this simply at the door of the expanded coercive power of the state or the divisiveness of ladino domination or more generally to write it off as a response based on custom without further exploring this begs the question. To understand exploitation it is necessary always to keep in mind what a dominant or a dominated group or class can "think" at a given moment in history, what they can imagine or comprehend as possible or real. People act not on the basis of an objective reality external to themselves but on their perception of that reality. The elites and indigenous communities of Guatemala entered the coffee era with 350 years of historical experience, however imperfectly remembered. Specifically, remnants of the colonial "compact" continued to define and underpin the right and legitimacy of the elites and the elites' state to demand money, goods, and labor from the mass of the population. Exploitation was legitimate; what was contested and negotiated was the degree, extent, and the form of this exploitation. Although during the first half of the century indigo and grana producers largely left the indigenous population alone, the formal-legal system of state-run coerced labor had persisted, as had its legitimacy. Similarly, the Indians broadly accepted the right of the state to regulate land possession, at least where this did not aggressively conflict with custom. They ignored or resisted specific applications of the laws when this suited their purposes. Demands on the population resulting from coffee increased gradually over a generation after 1860, and the Liberals not only continued to respect costumbre but were careful not to push large masses of Indians into rebellion. While a population perceives an immediate space in which to survive without having to opt for violent resistance, they will tend not to revolt. The Guatemalan state generally left them this space.[8]

This raises the broader question of the role of the state in the transition to cochineal and, later on, to coffee and its part in assuring the subsequent success and profitability of these enterprises. In both cases, the weight of the state's participation in processes that were largely market-driven was limited. Governments, for example, lacked the capital to effect rapid improvements in transport or credit facilities. On the question of maintaining the productivity or profitability of the export crop once production got under way, experience diverged. With grana the state had little to do. The dye industry operated on a reduced scale with a limited number and range of production factors, and the state had no control over the more fundamental threats to the crop of foreign competition and factor substitution. With coffee the state played a very important part in its ongoing success. Although some of the necessary production factors, for example, land, were readily available or, like credit, were supplied by market mechanisms upon which state action seems to have had little effect, the state was central to the provision of labor. The whole structure of Guatemala's export production rested on the assumed availability of state-coerced "cheap" labor. This made the planters very dependent on the state and on state agents not only to obtain labor directly from drafts and to enforce the debt peonage system, but also to quickly and effectively stifle resistance and to guarantee the repression necessary to socialize losses when the economy turned down. This dependence on the state accentuated the trend toward large-scale production, for small growers typically lacked the political access necessary to guarantee themselves labor or protect their land.

Having said this, it must be admitted that we know very little about the state in nineteenth-century Guatemala. Explaining the state, in the well-known formation, as a "committee" managing political power in the interests of the dominant class is not very helpful, nor is it clear that Guatemala's planters always had the control over the direction of state policies they might have wished. If in class society the state rules for the interests, however perceived or defined, of the dominant class or class faction, what of those members or groups among the elites who fall out with the caudillo and his clique over personal or policy matters? Did the state effectively mediate the inevitable conflicts between planters and merchants or among the planters in different regions of the republic? Did the National Assembly play any significant part in this? If not, where and how were decisions made? How did the state respond to foreign interests or demands in ways that served or failed to serve domestic or immigrant elites? In part, and for the moment one can only speculate, the answers to such questions must begin by recognizing that before the turn of the century Guatemala lacked both a stable state, as opposed to a series of more or less long-lived strongmen, and a stable elite structure with clearly articulated goals. The crop, and the class, and the state were all too new to have jelled. It is indicative of both a lack of organization among the elites and the evident tensions in relations between the caudillos and even the coffee planters that not until after 1920 did large landowners form, or have the freedom to form, a national organization.

Coffee developed the way it did in Guatemala because of the unique historical relationship between land and labor. Without labor, land had essentially no commercial value. At the same time, demands for labor were tied directly to markets and to state power. The Indians of Guatemala largely rejected a shift to petty commodity production of coffee both because it offered no evident advantages over their existing combination of subsistence agriculture, handicrafts, and trade and because the permanent nature of coffee bushes ran counter to their ideas of community possession and use. For the same reasons, large-scale coffee production by the communities held few attractions. At the very least it would have made them much more dependent on outsiders and, ultimately, on an unstable world market. As long as their interests focused on guaranteeing survival rather than on the possibility of accumulation, this made no sense. Poor ladinos who might have liked to engage in commercial coffee production found the odds against them. Few could afford good coffee land, and where such land was cheap transportation problems made export production almost impossible. Credit and capital went to those who had better connections or collateral. Above all, the political nature of labor mobilization left poor ladinos at an insuperable disadvantage. Some filled precarious spaces between the larger properties and supplied unprocessed or semiprocessed berries to their neighbors, but more managed a livelihood in related jobs, as labor recruiters, foremen, managers, and petty officials. In many coffee economies, such as Brazil and Colombia, one form or another of sharecropping (*parcería*) was common, but for Guatemala's landowners this was unnecessary. Although sharecropping has the advantage of transferring some of the costs and risks from the owners to the labor force, it also requires the owners to give up substantial portions of product and control to these same workers. This had little appeal to Guatemala's elites. Labor was available to them, and, even if it was not so cheap as imagined, the cost was still less than sharecropping; it is indicative that even colonos typically were forbidden to raise coffee.

In view of the present desperate situation of many Latin American countries including Guatemala and the poverty of their populations, there is a common, if not always well-articulated, sense that the Liberal schemes of the late nineteenth century were a mistake and that better decisions would have meant more or better development today. This misses the point. There is no "national development" but only development thought to be favorable to the groups or classes that control power. More than that, export-oriented development was the only logical path open in the nineteenth century. No other form of economic activity—and the fate of Solano López and Paraguay suggests the limited political alternatives—could have generated the wealth that the export sale of coffee, and, subsequently bananas, did. The use to which the income from such activities was put was a political question and returns us to the query, Development for whom?

Local newspapers and visitors to Guatemala in the 1920's com-

plained of the "routine" and backward methods evident in local agriculture, of which coerced labor was only the most dramatic. In fact,
Guatemalan growers from the 1870's to the 1930's drew on the experiences of the colonial and early national periods to fashion a system of
export production well suited to local circumstances. The system persisted not, or at least not entirely, because of the ignorance or conservative mentality of the ruling elites but because it worked. Moreover,
it worked well from their perspective, and they could not imagine,
and there probably was not, a system to replace it. It conserved expensive capital, used cheap land extensively, and took full advantage
of seasonal Indian labor to pick and repick the bushes, keeping the
quality and the value of the product high. It also gave the owners the
flexibility to deal with changing conditions in world markets, including the benefits to them of the falling peso. Classes, like individuals,
tend to equate the general good with their own well-being and profit.
The problem in Guatemala has been that in the twentieth century the
political and economic elites consistently have refused, or at least have
been unable, to differentiate immediate profit from a more thoughtful
view of long-run best interests. As a result, they have become reflexive
supporters of the status quo and blind political reactionaries. Their
Liberal ancestors would be astonished.

Appendixes

Appendix A

Population Data

TABLE A.1
Populations of Various Towns, 1760–1950

A. Chimaltenango

Town	1760	1770	1780	1790	1800	1810	1820
Comalapa	6,308	3,855	5,931	5,382		8,154	9,069
S. Mart. Jilotepeque	2,873	3,785	3,767	418		5,684	5,997
Patzicía	3,191	3,087	3,542	3,906		5,166	
Sumpango	3,415	2,400	4,644	3,698	4,181	3,713	4,680

Town	1830	1840	1880	1893	1914	1921	1950
Comalapa	7,423	4,545	5,668	4,796	10,665	8,379	12,313
S. Mart. Jilotepeque	5,686	6,465	9,705	10,393	17,064	14,163	20,911
Patzicía	6,268	4,760	4,634	4,434	6,021	5,355	7,081
Sumpango	5,680	1,600	2,802	3,093	4,212	3,696	5,780

B. Chiquimula

Town	1760	1770	1780	1790	1800	1810	1820
Chiquimula		6,672	2,525	1,515	1,184	1,001	1,150
Jalapa	612	1,908	783	977	1,017	816	
Jocotán	6,476	2,700	4,599	4,585	5,285	3,317	2,759
Jutiapa		1,476	1,044	3,701	921	855	779
Mataquescuintla		1,000	621	784	967		

Town	1830	1840	1880	1893	1914	1921	1950
Chiquimula	3,551	4,656	10,621	12,562	25,191	19,961	23,805
Jalapa	3,512	10,656	10,051	12,246	18,927	15,488	27,537
Jocotán	2,759	4,178	9,453	12,407	15,444	14,385	17,232
Jutiapa	2,273	6,752	10,263	11,023	18,414	18,564	33,260
Mataquescuintla		2,550	3,284	5,624	11,421	8,274	11,259

TABLE A.1 (*continued*)

C. Escuintla

Town	1760	1770	1780	1790	1800	1810	1820
Chiquimula	4,567	3,150	5,256	5,051	4,354	3,862	
Escuintla	1,444	1,200	1,557	1,598	1,613	1,607	
Guazacapán	1,110	1,150	2,214	2,034	1,863	2,070	
Cotzumalguapa	344	400	239	299	264	320	

Town	1830	1840	1880	1893	1914	1921	1950
Chiquimula		3,300	3,692	4,963	8,478	7,350	3,499
Escuintla		6,476	12,343	20,574	21,840	9,746	31,114
Guazacapán		2,235	800	1,288	7,560	3,323	5,251
Cotzumalguapa		1,728	9,032	8,106	16,902	14,112	18,969

D. Quezaltenango

Town	1760	1770	1780	1790	1800	1810	1820
S. Ped. Sacatepéquez		500	810	1,193	1,374	2,643	2,505
Cantel	248	336	671	854	1,067		1,309
Tacaná	387	646	752	1,319	1,455	1,928	2,368
S. Mart. Sacatepéquez	689	750	1,341	1,119	1,196	1,118	2,695
Zunil	1,670	1,400	2,961	3,316	3,332		1,394

Town	1830	1840	1880	1893	1914	1921	1950
S. Ped. Sacatepéquez	2,890		6,774	10,412	20,736	13,088	17,539
Cantel	1,890		5,426	6,212	8,829	6,657	8,277
Tacaná	2,603		5,250	6,458	13,824	12,159	19,247
S. Mart. Sacatepéquez	3,252		1,872	733	3,463	2,940	5,501
Zunil	2,809		2,658	3,499	2,970	4,450	3,366

E. District of Amatitlán/Sacatepéquez

Town	1760	1770	1780	1790	1800	1810	1820
Acatenango	1,247	1,365	1,413	1,252		1,854	1,875
Amatitlán	342	714	189	283	342	275	2,864
S. Juan Sacatepéquez	4,964	5,507	6,359	6,731	8,589	8,820	10,300
S. Ped. Sacatepéquez	2,192	1,080	1,782	2,867	3,794	3,929	3,884
S. María de Jesús	2,066	1,170	1,616	1,813	2,386	2,273	2,600

Town	1830	1840	1880	1893	1914	1921	1950
Acatenango		1,912	1,561	3,200	5,508	5,048	6,320
Amatitlán		6,588	7,300	8,048	10,557	7,002	11,667
S. Juan Sacatepéquez	8,589	9,226	14,309	17,649	30,186	20,160	28,426
S. Ped. Sacatepéquez	3,704	2,828	4,914	5,337	5,211	4,620	5,908
S. María de Jesús	2,186		2,399	2,704	1,701	2,940	4,207

TABLE A. 1 (*continued*)

F. Sololá

Town	1760	1770	1780	1790	1800	1810	1820
Atitlán	981	1,074	1,404	1,450	1,588	1,888	
S. Cata. Ixtahuacán			3,204	4,553	5,301	5,697	
Chichicastenango	2,335	2,505	2,336	3,015	3,353	3,416	
Joyabaj		1,653	1,409	1,440	1,615	1,679	
Patulul	491	533	590	247	199	500	

Town	1830	1840	1880	1893	1914	1921	1950
Atitlán	2,496	6,380	6,164	8,624	7,452	7,675	9,513
					Chicacao 1950 = 16,895		
S. Cata. Ixtahuacán				7,639	9,774	9,200	9,355
					Nahualá 1950 = 18,511		
Chichicastenango	4,564	12,369	17,356	16,239	35,532	25,137	27,718
Joyabaj	2,616	2,342	3,218	9,201	13,041	12,180	21,381
Patulul	366	386	4,044	5,599	9,936	10,200	10,439

G. Suchitepéquez

Town	1760	1770	1780	1790	1800	1810	1820
S. Anto. Sacatepéquez	959	1,560	999	631	511	649	
S. Fran. Zapotitlán	446	330	324	102	68	68	
Mazatenango	1,474	3,110	1,539	1,453	1,117	1,581	
Samayac	2,488	3,419	2,502	1,433	1,038	1,243	

Town	1830	1840	1880	1893	1914	1921	1950
S. Anto. Sacatepéquez	994		4,453	3,928	16,605	14,028	12,614
S. Fran. Zapotitlán	97		5,691	5,224	7,776	6,400	6,520
Mazatenango	1,256		5,169	6,970	14,742	11,319	18,120
Samayac			2,429	3,058	5,940	5,525	5,669

H. Totonicapán

Town	1760	1770	1780	1790	1800	1810	1820
Cuilco	145	844	162	162	274		1,150
Jacaltenango	882	1,748	1,013	1,062	1,200		2,107
San Juan Ixcoy	981		810	981	924		559
SM Chiquimula	4,883		4,347	4,883	4,651		5,768
SM Totonicapán	4,509	5,358	4,104	4,577	5,063		
Nebaj	1,188	2,648	1,211	1,188	1,504		1,685
Sacapulas	1,584	1,727	2,196	1,584	1,424		1,873
Todos Santos	364		531	590	359		979

TABLE A.1 (*continued*)

H. Totonicapán

Town	1830	1840	1880	1893	1914	1921	1950
Cuilco	896		6,324	5,765	6,453	5,940	9,643
Jacaltenango	1,962		3,387	5,192	4,482	4,536	8,340
San Juan Ixcoy	740		3,946	2,213	3,510	2,562	5,312
SM Chiquimula	8,450		19,524	12,374	10,827	8,043	10,005
SM Totonicapán	9,482		14,073	23,849	30,888	29,970	32,751
Nebaj	1,474		4,372	5,945	12,150	10,857	13,255
Sacapulas	1,756		3,314	5,511	6,453	7,695	10,849
Todos Santos	893		4,062	4,927	5,546	4,329	6,726

I. Verapaz

Town	1760	1770	1780	1790	1800	1810	1820
Cobán	5,882	5,652	11,600	9,875	9,980	11,459	11,192
Carchá	1,973	1,969	2,615	4,106	4,353	4,595	4,671
Cubulco	2,853	3,299	4,127	3,247	2,956	3,647	3,150
S. Cris. Verapaz	1,975		1,985	2,095	2,603	2,525	2,520
Rabinal	3,372	5,361	6,084	6,831	7,110	5,395	6,405

Town	1830	1840	1880	1893	1914	1921	1950
Cobán	12,237	9,030	18,076	22,792	30,321	26,774	26,673
Carchá	5,190	15,163	24,987	31,308	53,001	55,235	54,029
Cubulco	3,738	2,800	6,461	8,166	11,610	12,792	13,974
S. Cris. Verapaz	2,277	4,304	8,630	7,818	14,553	12,056	13,738
Rabinal	6,401	4,816	8,267	4,792	16,065	12,474	11,857

SOURCES: Figures for the years 1760–1810 come primarily from community Indian tribute counts (*padrones*); where available, the number of local ladino residents is also included. The multiplier used to convert from the number of tributaries to total population is 4.5, somewhat less than the 5 Crown officials normally supposed but more than the 4.0–4.3 many towns registered in the rare instances where it is possible to compare tributaries and total population at the same point in time. All sources (e.g., Wortman, *Government*, p. 290, and Lovell, *Conquest and Survival*, chap. 9) agree on rapid but uneven population growth in the late colonial period. For the years after 1810 see AGCA, A3 246 4912; A3 913 17773; B 842 3595 82567; Piel, *Sacabaja*, p. 223; Fernandez Molina, *Los tributos*, pp. 22–23; Pineda de Mont, *Recopilación*, table following p. 472; "Guatemala . . . cien años"; Casal, *Reseña*, p. 20; Dirección General de Estadística, *Censo . . . 1921* and *Sexto censo . . . 1950*; U.S. Department of State, Records Relating to Internal Affairs of Guatemala, 1910–29, roll no. 20; Early, *Democratic Structure*, p. 31.

TABLE A.2
Population of Guatemala by Partido/Department

Partido	1770's	1780's	1800	1810	1820's	1830's	1840's
Amatitlán/							
Sacatepéquez	42,505	39,150	42,827	40,703	34,282	95,720	39,795
Guatemala					73,201	86,939	57,092
Chiquimula	41,395	36,221	32,994	32,013	42,310	65,508	36,363
Mita					36,164		34,349
Santa Rosa							16,470
Chimaltenango	43,194	33,210	35,253	42,318	49,106		34,224
Escuintla	21,861	13,419	13,253	13,527	15,986		10,320
Suchitepéquez	16,359	13,712	12,326	12,704			
Sololá	21,293	25,520	25,862	30,879		59,722	
Quezaltenango	15,757	17,735	24,849	33,161		55,088	
Totonicapán	30,265	42,701	52,533	58,514		79,169	
Verapaz	32,156	44,024	49,775	52,440	59,946	65,568	63,903
El Petén					6,327		5,163

Department	1860	1880	1893	1914	1921	1950
Guatemala	80,000*	124,642	150,059	203,176	216,807	441,085
Amatitlán	30,000*	31,072	35,387	43,824	37,705	
El Progreso					47,678	
Sacatepéquez	45,000*	36,415	42,713	51,192	46,453	59,975
Chimaltenango	30,000*	50,117	57,177	105,570	88,030	122,310
Escuintla	25,000*	30,057	32,001	64,233	58,989	123,809
Santa Rosa	25,500*	29,162	47,293	96,255	81,343	109,812
Sololá	80,000*	76,756*	70,039	117,774	104,283	82,869
Totonicapán	100,000*	147,935*	89,338	99,819	94,080	99,434
Quezaltenango	70,000*	83,674	113,972	185,112	168,754	183,588
Suchitepéquez	40,000*	32,553	34,962	74,217	64,820	125,196
Retalhuleu		22,628	27,777	41,910	37,145	66,066
San Marcos	85,000*	67,149	89,322	199,017	176,402	230,039
Huehuetenango	65,000*	118,193*	117,127	179,886	137,166	198,872
El Quiché		73,096*	92,753	150,931	138,076	174,882
Baja Verapaz	{100,000*}	42,567	54,816	66,771	68,531	66,432
Alta Verapaz		86,943	100,759	159,456	161,405	188,758
El Petén	10,000*	8,278	6,752	7,317	7,820	15,897
Izabal	5,000*	5,240	7,401	10,989	19,932	55,191
Zacapa		36,155	47,362	39,933	65,723	69,533
Chiquimula	75,000*	52,417	63,746	111,487	94,182	112,837
Jalapa		29,797	31,066	48,276	43,041	75,091

SOURCES: AGCA, A3 246 4912; A3 913 17773; B842 3595 82567; Piel, *Sajcabaja*, p. 223; Fernandez Molina, *Los tributos*, pp. 22–23; Pineda de Mont, *Recopilación*, table following p. 472; "Guatemala . . . cien años"; E. Palacios, *Reseña*, p. 20; Dirección General de Estadística, *Censo . . . 1921* and *Sexto Censo . . . 1950*; U.S. Department of State, Records Relating to Internal Affairs of Guatemala, 1910–29, roll 20; Early, *Demographic Structure*, p. 31.
    * = estimate or partial count.

TABLE A.3
Population of Guatemala, Contact to 1950

Year	Indians	Total population
at Contact:	2,000,000	
1550	427,850	
1770's	220,500	315,000
1778	248,000	355,000
1780's	265,692	
1800	289,670	417,000
1810's	316,259	
1825	416,500	595,000
1830's	469,000	670,000
1848	592,900	847,000
1860	665,700	951,000
1870	756,000	1,180,100
1880	844,384	1,224,602
1893	1,005,767	1,364,678
1914		2,183,166
1921	1,343,283	2,004,900
1940	census altered	
1950	1,611,928	2,870,272

SOURCES: Lutz, Lovell, and Sweezy, "The Indian Population of Southern Guatemala," MS.; Lovell and Lutz, "Conquest and Population," MS.; Woodward, "Crecimiento de población"; Fernandez Molina, *Los tributos*, pp. 22–23; AGCA, A3 913 17773; Direccion General de Estadistica, *Censo . . . 1921* and *Sexto censo . . . 1950*; U.S. Department of State, Records Relating to Internal Affairs of Guatemala, 1910–29, roll 20; Early, *Demographic Structure*, p. 31.

TABLE A.4
Rates of Population Growth, 1778–1950

1778–1800 = 0.73	1880–1893 = 0.86
1800–1825 = 1.43	1893–1921 = 1.64
1825–1848 = 1.55	1914–1921 = −1.209
1848–1860 = 0.97	1921–1950 = 1.245
1860–1880 = 1.27	

SOURCES: See Table A.3. The formula for calculating growth rates is found on p. 303 of M. Palacios, *Coffee in Colombia*.

Appendix B

Cochineal Exports and Export Prices

TABLE B.1
Cochineal Exports From Guatemala, 1824–1870

Year	Exports in lbs.	Value pesos	Year	Exports in lbs.	Value pesos
1824	70,000		1850	1,605,000	
1825	65,000		1851	2,041,050	1,231,780
1826	90,000		1852	680,100	568,150
1827	15,000		1853	323,450	312,850
. . .			1854	2,587,200	1,757,500
1830	70,000		1855	1,210,360	986,560
1831	90,000		1856	1,782,550	1,381,240
. . .			1857	1,470,140	1,017,270
1833	120,000–150,000		1858	2,018,440	1,407,410
1834	180,000		1859	1,786,670	1,222,680
1835	600,000–700,000	605,757	1860	1,676,160	1,274,240
. . .			1861	1,539,780	788,630
1838–39	851,007	851,007	1862	1,659,185	837,986
1840–41	665,662		1863	1,443,000	855,838
1842–43	413,257		1864	1,460,000	688,080
1843–44	721,800		1865	1,385,900	975,933
. . .			1866	1,674,800	957,132
1845–46	1,024,950		1867	1,525,782	1,068,047
. . .			1868	1,273,591	891,513
1848	1,525,800		1869	1,862,667	1,266,613
1849	1,543,900		1870	1,443,357	865,414

SOURCES: Dunn, *Guatimala*, p. 231; Wortman, *Government*, p. 259; Solís, *Memorias*, pp. 631, 871–72, 921–22; E. Palacios, *Reseña*, p. 38; Palma Murga, "Algunas relaciones," p. 72.

TABLE B.2

Cochineal Prices, Guatemala and Great Britain, 1838–1871

Year	Guatemala (in reales)	GB (in s/d)	Year	Guatemala (in reales)	GB (in s/d)
1838	8		1856	6	3/10
...			1857	5.5	4/1
1842–43	6		1858	5.5	3/10
1843–44	6		1859	5.5	3/8
1845	7		1860	6	3/4
1846	6.5	5/4	1861	5	2/8
1847		5/4	1862		2/8
1848		4/8	1863		3/1
1849		4/1	1864		3/2
1850		4/4	1865		3/5
1851	5	3/10	1866		3/6
1852	6.75	2/10	1867	5.5	3/0
1853	8	4	1868	5.5	2/11
1854	4	4	1869	5.5	2/6
1855	7	3/11	1870	5	2/4

SOURCES: Guatemala: Solís, *Memorias*, p. 636; *El Tiempo*, Oct. 19, 1839; Rubio Sánchez, "La grana," pp. 37–46; E. Palacios, *Reseña*, pp. 36–38. Great Britain: Mulhall, *Dictionary*, pp. 475–78. The prices indicated in Naylor (*Influencia británica*, pp. 213–21) were those set by the English customs service in London for the purposes of tax collection and did not reflect market prices.

TABLE B.3

Cochineal Exports, Antigua, 1851–1870

Year	Quantity (pounds)	% of total exports	Year	Quantity (pounds)	% of total exports
1851	1,168,350	57	1861	929,400	60
1852	600,000	88	1862	982,800	60
1853	178,350	55	1863	1,067,100	74
1854	720,000	28	1864	680,400	47
1855	595,950	49	1865	981,600	71
1856	933,450	52	1866	897,000	54
1857	655,550	45	1867	1,039,200	68
1858	919,500	46	1868	715,200	56
1859	1,063,350	60	1869	1,181,400	63
1860	1,981,600	59	1870	803,400	56

SOURCE: Rubio Sánchez, "La Grana," pp. 45–46.

Reference Matter

Notes

Complete authors' names, titles, and publication information are given in the Bibliography, the opening section of which consists of a discussion of archival sources consulted. The following abbreviations are used in the Notes:

AGCA   Archivo General de Centro América
AGCA-ST Archivo General de Centro América-Sección de Tierras
AGT   Archivo General de los Tribunales
AHA   Archivo Histórico Arquidiocesano "Francisco de Paula García Peláez"

Introduction

1. Warren, *Symbolism*, p. 61.
2. Inhabitants of Guatemalan communities have collective names derived from the names of their towns. Those of San Pedro La Laguna are sanpedranos, those of Aguacatán are aguacatecos, etc. But some of the forms are irregular: for example, inhabitants of Santo Tomás Chichicastenango are maxeños, and those of San Andrés Semetabaj are trixanos.
3. Marx, *Capital*, 1, Part 8, "So-Called Primitive Accumulation." It is "so-called" because according to bourgeois economists of the time the original accumulations of money capital that made capitalism possible resulted from the superior moral fiber of those who accumulated it (p. 873). Two useful and commonly overlooked efforts to apply this concept are Frank's *Dependent Accumulation* and *World Accumulation*.

4. Marx, *Capital*, 1: 874.

5. An introduction to the debate is Foster-Carter, "Can We Articulate 'Articulation'?" See also Wolpe, ed., *Articulation of Modes of Production*, especially Wolpe's Introduction, and Rey, *Las alianzas de clases*.

6. See, for example, Terray, "Historical Materialism and Segmentary Lineage-Based Societies," in his *Primitive Societies*; Bradby, "Destruction of the Natural Economy"; Palmer and Parsons, *Rural Poverty*; and Beinhart, Dellus, and Trapido, *Plough to the Ground*.

7. Stern, "Feudalism," p. 862.

8. Wolf, *Europe*, pp. 296–97.

9. On this, see Cooper, *Slavers to Squatters*, pp. 121–24.

10. Wolf makes the useful distinction between merchant "wealth" and industrial capital in *Europe*, p. 79.

11. For more optimistic views of the continued utility of these ideas, see Roseberry, *Anthropologies and Histories*, and Stern, "Feudalism," especially p. 872 n. 104.

12. For example, Post, *Arise Ye Starvlings*.

13. For an introduction to "petty commodity production" in the context of Guatemala, see C. Smith, "Does a Commodity Economy Enrich the Few?"

14. To say that capitalism "does" anything—and leaving aside for the moment the internal contradictions of capitalism—is of course incorrect, but the usage is so common that it will occasionally intrude here.

15. Few Guatemalans were actively involved in banana production before the 1930s, and the industry will receive little attention here.

16. The effort here is to extract the term "hegemony," at least for a moment, from under the accumulating weight of Gramscian scholarship, which threatens to squeeze the life from a very useful concept. This paragraph relies heavily on Bocock, *Hegemony*; Femia, *Gramsci's Political Thought*; and Scott, "Hegemony and the Peasantry" and *Weapons of the Weak*, chap. 8.

17. Bocock, *Hegemony*, pp. 33–34.

18. Femia, *Gramsci's Political Thought*, p. 32 quoting Engels.

19. Anthropologists and social historians sometimes suggest that there is a pejorative difference in the use of town versus village in the literature on Guatemala, the former meaning ladino and more developed and the latter being Indian and less civilized. In fact, the official terminology of Guatemala includes an elaborate hierarchy of city, town, village, hamlet, settlement, etc. Here the terms village and town will be used interchangeably for Indian and ladino settlements of various sizes, but smaller than cities.

20. Cancian, "Political and Religious Organizations"; Wolf, *Sons of the Shaking Earth*.

21. The other populations were: El Salvador, 146,684; Nicaragua, 106,776; Honduras, 88,143; and Costa Rica, 24,022: Woodward, "Crecimiento de población," p. 224. There is no adequate or comprehensive political history of Guatemala, but see the bibliographic essay in Woodward, *Central America*.

22. M. Rodriguez, *Cádiz Experiment*, chap. 1.

23. For an evocation of life in Guatemala in the Carrera years, see Salazar, *Tiempo viejo*.

24. There is, as yet, no adequate history of the 1944 Revolution, but see Handy, *Revolution in the Countryside*, and Gleijeses, *Shattered Hope*.

Chapter 1

1. On pre-1750 economic history, see, among others, MacLeod, *Spanish Central America*; Wortman, *Government*, part 1; Martínez Peláez, *Patria del criollo*; Solórzano, *Evolución económica*, chaps. 1–6; and the bibliographic essay in Woodward, *Central America*.

2. Wortman, *Government*, pp. 125, 201. Palma Murga, on the other hand, tends to see creole versus peninsular conflicts as secondary to struggles between extended families and networks of familial alliances: "Núcleos de poder local."

3. Martínez Peláez, *Motines de indios*, chap. 1; "Año de 1763-autos formados."

4. Wortman, *Government*, p. 146.

5. Consulado de Comercio, "Apuntamientos," pp. 343–50; García Peláez, *Memorias*, 3: 159–61; M. Rodriguez, *Cadiz Experiment*, pp. 25–27, 85–86; AGCA, A1.23 6090 55258.

6. Fernandez Molina, *Los tributos*; Wortman, *Government*, p. 175.

7. AGCA, A1.21 199 4040; B119.3 2538 58473 f. [folio] 7–9.

8. Consulado, "Apuntamientos," p. 328. On the Consulado, see Woodward, *Class Privilege*.

9. R. Smith, "Indigo Production"; Woodward, *Class Privilege*, 39; Rubio Sanchez, *Historia del añil*, 1: 147–79; Wortman, *Government*, pp. 184–91.

10. Cabot, "Consolidation of 1804"; Woodward, "Economy of Central America," pp. 126–28.

11. Contreras, *Una rebelión indígena*; Bricker, *Indian Christ*, chap. 7; McCreery, "Atanasio Tzul."

12. R. Smith, "Indigo Production," p. 195; Rubio Sanchez, *Añil*, 1: 5; Wortman, *Government*, pp. 189–90; Floyd, "Guatemalan Merchants," p. 106.

13. AGCA, A1.24 6091 55306, ff. 58, 81.

14. García Peláez, *Memorias*, 2: 228–33 and 3: 7–12; Wortman, *Government*, pp. 143–45; Menery, "Kingdom of Guatemala," chap. 7.

15. Schafer, *Economic Societies*, chaps. 10 and 11; Luque Alcaide, *Sociedad Económica*; Solano, *Tierra y sociedad*, pp. 113–14; Woodward, *Class Privilege*, pp. 35–54; Córdoba, *Utilidades*; García Redondo, *Memoria*; López, *Instrucción*.

16. Menery, "Kingdom of Guatemala," chap. 6; Wortman, *Government*, pp. 193–94.

17. Cabot, "Consolidation of 1804," p. 34; Consulado, "Apuntamientos," p. 409; Pinto Soria, *Centroamérica*, p. 83.

18. *El Indicador*, July 11, 1825. See also ibid., July 18, 1825; Rubio Sánchez, *Añil*, 1: 181–83; Dunn, *Guatimala*, pp. 216–16; Thompson, *Narrative*, pp. 481–82.

19. Solís, *Memorias*, p. 664.

20. AGCA, B119.3 2547 59638; Baily, *Central America*, p. ix.

21. Consulado, "Apuntamientos," pp. 294–96, 372, 404–8; Rubio Sánchez, *Añil*, 1: 179; Dunn, *Guatimala*, pp. 208–10; Pinto Soria, *Guatemala*, p. 32.

22. AGCA, B119.3 2547 59638.

23. *Gaceta de Guatemala*, Sept. 5, 1851; Wortman, *Government*, p. 258. Piel, *Sajcabaja*, pp. 298–99, posits a dramatic decline between the 1820's and the 1860's but bases this on highly dubious statistics for the 1820's and on an apparent misreading of those for the 1860's.

24. Dunn, *Guatimala*, p. 93.

25. M. Rodriguez, *Cadiz Experiment*, pp. 8–18; Wortman, *Government*, chap. 9, especially p. 173.

26. Bricker, *Indian Christ*, p. 78.

27. Pineda de Mont, *Recopilación*, p. 223; Dunn, *Guatimala*, pp. 276–77; AGCA, B5.7 66 1819 f. 19.

28. AGCA-ST, Department of Sololá, 1/11.

29. *El Indicador*, Jan. 15, 1827.

30. See, for example, the activities of the soon-to-be Conservative Aycinena family: Balmori, Voss, and Wortman, *Notable Family Networks*, pp. 61–68.

31. Quoted in Solís, *Memorias*, p. 661.

32. Thompson, *Narrative*, p. 478. Although this budget was for the federal government, it is indicative of the situation at the state level also.

33. M. Rodriguez, "Livingston Codes"; Williford, "Las Luces"; Ingersoll, "War of the Mountain," chap. 1.

34. Pineda de Mont, *Recopilación*, p. 239; Woodward, *Class Privilege*, pp. 50–51.

35. Solís, *Memorias*, pp. 629, 666–67; Rubio Sánchez, "La grana," p. 28.

36. *La Verdad*, Nov. 29, 1837; Woodward, *Class Privilege*, chap. 6.

37. Stephens, *Incidents of Travel*, 1: 41–43.

38. Griffith, *Empires in the Wilderness*; Fry, "Política agraria"; Miceli, "Rafael Carrera"; Woodward, "Social Revolution"; Ingersoll, "War of the Mountain," chaps. 3–7; Burns, *Poverty of Progress*, pp. 97–104.

39. *El Tiempo*, Aug. 2, 1839; also Oct. 16 and 26, 1839. See also AGCA, Juzgado de Primera Instancia Criminal, Sololá, 4/248, and Juzgado de Primera Instancia Criminal, Totonicapán, 8/65.

40. Pineda de Mont, *Recopilación*, pp. 230–35, 241–42, 244–47.

41. AGCA, B119.3 2547 59638.

42. For more on this, see Woodward, *Class Privilege*, especially chaps. 4–6.

43. Holleran, *Church and State*, part 2, chaps. 1–2.

44. Consulado, "Apuntamientos," pp. 322–33; Van Oss, *Catholic Colonialism*, chap. 3, especially pp. 85–89.

45. Compare, for example, the situation in New Spain: Costeloe, *Church Wealth*; Van Young, *Hacienda and Market*, pp. 182–91; Bauer, "Church in the Economy."

46. AHA, Gobernación Eclesiástica, Capellanías, T3 no. 74. Although this list was drawn up in the early 1870's, very few new capellanías came into existence after 1821. This compares with some 10,000 capellanías valued at approximately $35,000,000 for New Spain circa 1800: Bauer, "Church in the Economy," p. 717.

47. This was true for New Spain as well: Van Young, *Hacienda and Market*, p. 184, and Costeloe, *Church Wealth*, pp. 67–68.

48. Costeloe, *Church Wealth*, p. 88.

49. Palma Murga, "Algunas relaciones," pp. 58–68; compare this with loans made by private sources, pp. 93–95.

50. AHA, A4.10 132 5644, A4.5 67 2633 and 73 2711.

51. For example, see Van Oss, *Catholic Colonialism*, pp. 183–85.

52. Menery, "Kingdom of Guatemala," chap. 5.

53. AGCA, A1.20 824 1810, A1.43 2721 23258, A1 2999 28662; Dunn, *Guatimala*, p. 290; Fry, "Agrarian Society," pp. 168–69. See also sale and rental contracts in AGCA, "Protocolos," which often include inventories. For the comments of the U.S. Minister, see U.S. Department of State, U.S. Minister to Guatemala, National Archives microfilms M219, roll 2, Nov. 24, 1826.

54. Wortman, *Government*, p. 133; Collins, "Colonial Jacaltenango," pp. 144, 158, 169–205; Fry, "Agrarian Society," pp. 114–15; García Peláez, *Memorias*, 1: 223–25; McCreery, "Caja."

55. For examples of spending from the cajas, see Lovell, *Conquest and Survival*, p. 157; Collins, "Colonial Jacaltenango," pp. 177–205; AGCA, A3.16 2511 36659, San Lucas Tolimán; A1.73 2143 15258, Tecpán Guatemala; A1.45 5326 44887 91779, Moyuta; A1.19 421 8819, Escuintla.

56. AGCA, A1.14.23 223 5253.

57. AGCA, A1.1 219 5145.

58. AGCA, A1.14.23 223 5253.

59. Juarros, *Compendio de la historia*, pp. 58–62; Van Oss, *Catholic Colonialism*, pp. 109–15; Collins, "Jacaltenango," pp. 206–15; Piel, *Sajcabaja*, pp. 261–63. On cofradía capitals and the uses to which they were put, see, for example, the many lists in AHA Cartas, 1823–25, and the accountings in the various pastoral visits of archbishops found in AHA, Visitas Pastorales.

60. AHA, Cartas, July 1, 1843, no. 51, and Nov. 1850, no. 188.

61. Cabot, "Consolidation of 1804"; AGCA, A1.23 4573 39490; AHA, A4.10 134 5717 and A4.10 163 20. Compare Tutino, *From Insurrection to Revolution*, pp. 107–9, and Lavrin, "Execution of the Law of *Consolidación* in New Spain."

62. AHA, Gobernación Eclesiástica, Capellanías, T3 no. 74; Cabot, "Consolidation of 1804," p. 28.

63. AHA, Cartas, July 1, 1843, no. 51.

64. von Tempsky, *Mitla*, pp. 300–301.

65. AGCA, A1 2646 22150; de Valle, *Instrucción sobre la plaga de langosta*; A1.2.2.8 36 4306, A1.2.5 2835 25289, A1.11 2450 18878, A1.11.8 171 3438; AHA, Diezmos, T2 no. 46 (Suchitepéquez); AGCA, A1.1 5458 46827 (Verapaz, 1804) and A1.1 6111 56079 (Jacaltenango, 1808); A3 227 4186; Wortman, *Government*, pp. 318–19.

66. Claxton, "Weather-based Hazards," "Drought," and "Late-Season Guatemalan Rain Showers"; Feldman, "Disasters," p. 50.

67. Claxton, "Drought," p. 41.

68. See, for example, Lovell, *Conquest*, pp. 150–53. Unfortunately for the historian, once the independent government abolished tribute, there is little information available on local outbreaks.

69. AGCA, A1 169 3417. See also B119.2 2515 56637; B86.5 3605 83571; MG 28555 5; MG 28583 41; AEG, Cartas, Oct. 28, 1869, no. 512.

70. Quoted in Pinto Soria, *Estructura agraria*, p. 29. See also Rubio Sánchez, *Añil*, 1: 127–28.

71. Capital merchants blocked various attempts to create public storage facilities: Wortman, *Government*, p. 72.

72. Ibid., pp. 191–92, 245, 260, argues from at best scattered evidence that prices increased steadily and dramatically. See also the comments on food availability by parish in Cortés y Larraz, *Descripción*, summarized in Solano, *Tierra y sociedad*, following p. 74.

73. On diezmos, see AHA, "Diezmos," by district. The records of the main hospital, San Juan de Dios, record the quantities of food purchased for the patients but not the prices paid.

74. See, for example, monthly prices "in the plaza [of Guatemala City]" from March to August 1809 in AHA, Diezmos, T3 no. 52.

75. Haefkens, *Viaje a Guatemala*, pp. 43, 260. But after a decade of war, compare Stephens, *Incidents of Travel*, 1: 52.

76. AEG, Diezmos, T3 no. 52; Woodward, "Population and Development." *La Sociedad Economica*, Aug. 1, 1870, complained that food prices had doubled in the previous ten years, but solid evidence for this remains to be uncovered.

77. *La Revista*, July 23, 1847; Montufar, *Reseña historica*, 5: 305–6; AGCA, Corregidor Verapaz–Sub-Corregidor (Cobán), Jan. 23, 1862, Papers JP Alta Verapaz, 1862; *La Semana*, Aug. 23, 1868.

78. Stephens, *Incidents of Travel*, 1: 52, 79; Dunlop, *Travels*, p. 117.

79. On the historical creation of the "Indians" in Guatemala, see Martínez Peláez, *Patria del criollo*, chaps. 5 and 7; Warren, *Symbolism*; and Hawkins, *Inverse Images*.

80. On Maya resistance to Spanish colonial domination, see Fariss, *Maya Society*.

81. An interesting aspect of this struggle was the adoption by the Indians

of "ladino" names to mystify employers and state agents. See Davis, "Land of Our Ancestors;" p. 88, LaFarge, *Santa Eulalia*, p. 26; Rosales, "Aguacatán"; and Lincoln, "Ixil Indians."

82. Lutz, "Demographic Evolution" and "Non-Spanish and Non-Indian Population." On the division of Guatemala into an Indian west and a ladino east, see MacLeod, *Spanish Central America*, p. 308, and Lutz and Lovell, "Core and Periphery."

83. Cortés y Larraz, *Descripción*, 2: 200.

84. García Peláez, *Memorias*, 1: 239.

85. AGCA, A1 2646 22150.

86. Carmack, *Historia social*, pp. 201–4. On the activities of a priest's family, see AHA, Cartas, Feb. 8, 1855 [1870], no. 42, and Oct. 26, 1857. AGCA, A1 2646 22150 lists a category of non-Indians called "jornaleros y de oficios" by district, but without differentiating workers from artisans.

87. The frequency with which the authorities repeated injunctions against "vagrants" and "evildoers" suggests the ineffectiveness of the laws. See AGCA, A1.1 6087 55110, A1.22.15 2588 21081 (various bandos), A1.22.15 4565 39152, A1.24 6091 55305, A1.22.2 4566 39176 and 39181, A1.22.15 1510 f. 7, B5.7 66 1816 f. 26, B86.5 3605 83475, B107.2 1847 42362, B87.1 1190 28915, B86.5 3605 83546, B119.3 2546 59379. See also Pineda de Mont, *Recopilación*, pp. 584–86, 592–600, 603–4; Marure, *Catálogo rezonado*, pp. 215–19; and newspaper accounts in *Gaceta de Guatemala*, Aug. 21, 1847, and July 22 and Dec. 18, 1864.

88. Quoted in Pinto Soria, *Estructura agraria*, p. 10.

89. Luján Muñoz, "Fundación de villas" and "Reducción y fundación"; García Peláez, *Memorias*, 3: 152–63; AGCA-ST, Amatitlán 2/8 and Chimaltenango 1/17.

90. AGCA, A1 2646 22150.

91. Quoted in Pinto Soria, *Estructura agraria*, p. 10.

92. AGCA, A1 2646 22150.

93. García Peláez, *Memorias*, 3: 147–48, 160.

94. Martínez Peláez, *Patria del criollo*, pp. 159–66.

95. Pinto Soria, *Estructura agraria*, pp. 36–37, n. 39.

96. But see AGCA, B119.4 2551 59985 for an assertion of renters' rights according to the "laws of Castile."

97. See, for example, AGCA, B108.7 1962 45240 (Palencia).

98. Rubio Sánchez, *Añil*, 2, append. 4. On the nonapplicability of the regulations to Guatemala, see AGCA, A3 226 4112.

99. Wortman, *Government*, p. 157.

100. *Gaceta de Guatemala*, July 25, 1803, quoted in Pinto Soria, *Estructura agraria*, p. 29, n. 1.

101. Solano, *Tierra y sociedad*, pp. 13–84, contains a survey of agriculture by area and product, based on the reports compiled by Archbishop Pedro

Cortés y Larraz, only a portion of which appear in *Descripción*. For the impacts of monoculture, see Solano, *Tierra y sociedad*, pp. 50–55, and Rubio Sánchez, *Añil*, 1: 127–28.

102. Browning, *El Salvador*, pp. 141–49.

103. For details of the transfer, see Zilbermann de Luján, *Aspectos socioeconómicos*.

104. For example, see AHA, A4.10 128 5520, A4.10 125 5384, and A4.10 146 6031.

105. Woodward, "Economy of Central America," p. 128; AGCA, A1.10 58 1567–69, A1.10 63 4474, 4476–79, 4481, 4483–90, 4501.

106. Pinto Soria, "Valle central de Guatemala," p. 83.

107. AGCA-ST, Totonicapán, 2/1.

108. AHA, Diezmos, T3 no. 52; for comparison, see Lújan Muñoz, *Mercado y sociedad*. A map of the haciendas in the immediate vicinity of Guatemala City circa 1821 appears in *Revista de la Academia Guatemalteca de Estudios Geneológicas, Heráldicas e Históricos*, 7 (1979): 615–21.

109. For an inventory of the hacienda Nuestra Señora de Guadalupe in 1819, see AGCA, A1 2000 28662.

110. AHA, Diezmos, T1 no. 51; Pinto Soria, "Valle central de Guatemala," p. 81.

111. For an example of the work history, advances, and debts of renters and colonos on a large hacienda in the Sierra de Canales, see AGCA, A1.43 2753 23728.

112. Cortés y Larraz, *Descripción*, 2: 200–201.

113. Ibid., p. 227.

114. AGCA, A3.16 253 5181; A1.16 254 5209.

115. For example, see AGCA, A1.21 2357 17815 (Mataquescuintla, 1792–98).

116. Cortés y Larraz, *Descripción*, 2: 199.

117. On congregación and its effects in the case of one town, see Hill and Monaghan, *Continuities*, pp. 83–85. More generally, see Lovell, *Conquest and Survival*, pp. 76–89.

118. When J. L. Stephens traversed the area in the 1840's, for example, he reported seeing only one hacienda between Quezaltenango and "Gueguetenango," a distance of some hundred miles. Stephens, *Incidents of Travel*, 2: 225.

119. Van Oss, *Catholic Colonialism*, p. 47; Piel, *Sajcabaja*, chap. 9.

120. For Indian complaints, see AGCA, A3 225 4062 and 226 4110.

121. AGCA, A3.5 1155 20488, A3.5 352 07318, 07308, 07309. Many of these small holdings boasted only a few dozen animals and others existed on land rented from the ejidos of communities. On the development of wheat labores in one highland community, see T. Adams, "San Martín Jilotepeque," chap. 2. For a discussion of haciendas versus labores (in the Oriente), see Fry, "Agrarian Society," pp. 167–74.

122. See, for example, the case of Prudencio Tobar and his hacienda Vasquez, AGCA, A3.5 1155 20488 and A3 226 4086.

123. Luján Muñoz, "Fundación de villas" and "Reducción y fundación."

124. The eagerness with which the ladino militia pillaged the Indians of San Miguel Totonicapán after putting down the 1820 revolt makes this dramatically clear. See McCreery, "Atanasio Tzul," pp. 53–54.

125. On the formation of the pueblos de indios, see Lovell, *Conquest and Survival*, pp. 89–91. Although Eric Wolf popularized the idea of the "closed, corporate, peasant community" and the function of the "cargo system" (*Sons of the Shaking Earth*), the paradigmatic statement, together with a review of the literature to that date, is to be found in Cancian, "Political and Religious Organizations." For its application in Guatemala, see Collins, "Colonial Jacaltenango." For an extended critique, see Wasserstrom, *Class and Society*.

126. AGCA, A3.12 2897 43013, A3.12 2899 43046, A1.25 1702 10357 f. 229–31, A1.14.25 195 3953, A1.14 190 3864, A1.22.2 5372 45467. See also Solorzano Fonseca, "Comunidades indígenas," pp. 111–15. Much of the "Año de 1763–autos formados" is devoted to an explanation of how the system operated. See also García Peláez, *Memorias*, 1: 226–27.

127. Consulado, "Apuntamientos," p. 313. For Archbishop Cortés y Larraz's attacks on the repartimientos made by the alcaldes, mayores, and corregidores, see *Descripción*, 1: 243, 270, 285, and 2: 48, 133, 268.

128. MacLeod, *Spanish Central America*, chap. 5.

129. For examples, see AGCA, A1.14.25 190 3864, A3.12 2897 43013, A1.24 6935 57626, A1.22.2 45467 5372, and A1.1 6116 56541; AHA, leg. 189 no. 92.

130. AGCA, A1.14.25 190 3864 and A3.12 2897 43013.

131. Martínez Peláez, *Motines de indios*, pp. 36–38.

132. For examples of complaints against excessive demands, see AGCA, A3.12 2899 43013 and A1.22.2 5372 45467. On abuses of local officials, see Cortés y Larraz, *Descripción*, 2: 134, 139, 160.

133. AGCA, Tierras, 6022 523101, and AGCA-ST, Totonicapán, 1/12 and 2/1. See also Veblen, "Forest Preservation in Totonicapán," chap. 7.

134. Cortés y Larraz, *Descripción*, 2: 100.

135. On the equalization reforms, see Fernandez Molina, *Los tributos*; Wortman, *Government*, pp. 173–75.

136. AGCA, A1.21 199 4040.

137. On cargo, see Wolf, *Sons of the Shaking Earth*.

138. On the financing of the cofradías, see Hill, "Manteniendo el culto a los santos." For an argument that cofradías are mechanisms of exploitation, see Diener, "The Tears of St. Anthony."

139. AGCA, A3.5 352 7315, 7319, 7320.

140. On the decline of the population in the lowlands of colonial Central America, see Newson, *Indian Survival*.

141. It is worth noting that in Jutiapa, and nowhere else in Guatemala,

planters used the same system of weights as in El Salvador: AHA, Diezmos, T1 no. 50, Jalapa.

142. See, for example, AGCA, A3 224 4024, and Tierras, 6023 53109 and 6051 53463.

143. Lutz, "Non-Spanish and Non-Indian Population."

144. On the Baja Verapaz, see Bertrand, "La tierra y los hombres" and "Lucha por la tierra," and Percheron, "Producción agrícola." For the Alta Verapaz, see King, *Cobán*, chap. 4. For the western part of the region, see Piel, *Sajcabaja*, chap. 9.

145. Cortés y Larraz, *Descripción*, 1: 296.

146. Ibid., 2: 34–35. On animal and sugar production in the region, see AGCA, A3.5 352 7314.

147. AGCA, A3.5 352 7314.

148. For a map of the lower Verapaz, see Percheron, "Producción agrícola."

149. Menery, "Kingdom of Guatemala," pp. 102–3; Haefkens, *Viaje a Guatemala*, pp. 271–72; Cortés y Larraz, *Descripción*, 1: 294.

150. AGCA, Tierras, 6033 53213.

151. AHA, leg. 189 no. 92.

152. Haefkens, *Viaje a Guatemala*, p. 28.

153. Diemecke de Gonzalez, *El negro en Guatemala*, pp. 38–41; Thompson, *Narrative*, pp. 400–402.

154. On the early history of the Pacific coast, see Orellana, *Tzutujil Mayas*, and Madigan, "Santiago Atitlán."

155. Orellana, *Tzutujil Mayas*, pp. 149–57.

156. AGCA, A3.30 2578 38864, and AGCA-ST, Mazatenango 3/2.

157. AGCA-ST, Suchitepéquez, 3/2; Escuintla, 1/11. At Mazatenango the priest's cattle ruined an adobe church by licking the walls for salt: Van Oss, *Catholic Colonialism*, p. 117.

158. "Año de 1763–autos formados," p. 324.

159. AGCA, A3 227 4146.

160. "Año de 1763–autos formados," pp. 309–15.

161. Cortés y Larraz, *Descripción*, 2: 226–27.

162. "Año de 1763–autos formados," p. 324; García Redondo, *Memoria*, p. 6.

163. Cortés y Larraz, *Descripción*, 2: 263, 275, 284.

164. Consulado, "Apuntamientos," pp. 322–33.

165. AGCA, A3 226 4122, A3 227 4146 and 4166; AGCA, Suchitepéquez, 6/10.

Chapter 2

1. García Peláez, *Memorias*, 3: 156–63.

2. On the legal differentiation between the categories of *terrenos baldíos*

and *realengas*, see Fry, "Política agraria," n. 49, n. 50. In the late colonial and national period the terms were used interchangeably in Guatemala.

3. AGCA, Tierras, 5989 52675.

4. Mendez Montenegro, "444 años," p. 14.

5. Solano, *Tierra y sociedad*, pp. 356–59.

6. Ibid., p. 277.

7. For example: AGCA-ST, Suchitepéquez, 1/11.

8. AGCA, A1.2 4576 39326; Solano, *Tierra y sociedad*, pp. 367–78; Mendez Montenegro, "444 años," pp. 31–36.

9. On the incompetence and corruption of one of the officials ordered to carry out the new law, see AGCA, Tierras, 6023 53109 and A1.45.9 2792 24478.

10. Consulado de Comercio, "Apuntamientos," pp. 299–300; M. Rodriguez, *Cadiz Experiment*, pp. 25–27; Solano, *Tierra y sociedad*, pp. 388–93; AGCA, A1.23 1538 f. 28 and 136, and 1543 f. 424; Pineda de Mont, *Recopilación*, pp. 658–75.

11. Solís, *Memorias*, p. 901.

12. On resistance to the abuses of local Indian officials, see Solano, *Los Mayas*, n. 259 bis, and Martínez Peláez, *Motines de indios*, pp. 38–41. See also AGCA, A1.21 170 3427.

13. Consulado, "Apuntamientos," p. 346.

14. AGCA, A1.23 1538 f. 136.

15. AGCA, A1.23 1538 f. 28.

16. Rubio Sánchez, "Tenencia de la tierra," p. 65; AGCA, A1.23 1543 f. 424. For a largely unsuccessful effort to survey the land situation in the Independence era, see AGCA, B5.7 3478 79409.

17. A square league was the equal of a "*sitio de ganado mayor*," which was equal to 36 "old" (pre-18th century) caballerías or 38.75 "new" (18th and 19th century) caballerías.

18. AGCA, Tierras, 6022 53095. A league was equal to approximately 2.6 miles.

19. AGCA-ST, Suchitepéquez, 3/2; Retalhuleu, 1/13.

20. AGCA-ST, Quezaltenango, 1/15.

21. AGCA-ST, Totonicapán, 2/1.

22. AGCA, Tierras, 6033 53213.

23. AGCA-ST, Chimaltenango, 1/14.

24. Pineda de Mont, *Recopilación*, pp. 658–67.

25. Ibid., pp. 675–77.

26. On Liberal agrarian policy, see Pinto Soria, *Centroamérica*, pp. 142–44. More generally, see Solís, *Memorias*, chap. 40; and Williford, "Las Luces."

27. AGCA, B78 714 15935, f. 12; Pineda de Mont, *Recopilación*, pp. 668–74.

28. AGCA, B100.1 3633 85304 (less *cuerdas* and *varas*).

29. AHA, Diezmos, T7 n. 39: "Libro de ingresos de contribución territorial."

30. Ibid., T5 no. 52; Diezmos, n/n (tithes 1847–54); Diezmos, "Cuadrante de la masa decimal, 1864–67" (in fact this volume goes back to 1856); AGCA, B86.5 3605 83700, B107.5 1914 43829, B83.3 1115 25335.

31. AGCA, B86.5 3605 83564. For an example of more active resistance, see *El Tiempo*, Oct. 26, 1839.

32. Pineda de Mont, *Recopilación*, pp. 492–503.

33. Ibid., p. 677.

34. Ibid., pp. 679–80.

35. AGCA, B100.1 1418 33158. For an example of the activities of the 1836 land survey commission, see AGCA-ST, Quiché, 1/26.

36. Ingersoll, "War of the Mountain," especially chap. 2; Woodward, "Social Revolution"; Miceli, "Rafael Carrera."

37. Pineda de Mont, *Recopilación*, p. 679 n. 130; Ingersoll, "War of the Mountain," pp. 64–76; Fry, "Política agraria," p. 39, and Fry, "Agrarian Society"; Wagley, *Economics of a Guatemalan Village*, p. 60.

38. Pineda de Mont, *Recopilación*, p. 683.

39. AGCA, B100.1 1418 33221.

40. AGCA-ST, Chimaltenango, 3/6; T. Adams, "San Martín Jilotepeque," pp. 20–22.

41. AGCA-ST, Chimaltenango, 3/6.

42. Miceli, "Carrera," p. 88; Ingersoll, "War of the Mountain," pp. 277–78; AGCA, B100.1 1419 33230 and 3633 85376.

43. Pineda de Mont, *Recopilación*, pp. 686–89.

44. Ibid., p. 688.

45. AGCA, MG 28623 159.

46. AGCA, A3.30 2578 37864.

47. AGCA-ST, San Marcos, 1/15 and Amatitlán, 2/8; AGCA, Tierras, 6023 53109, 6025 53130, 6051 53463; MG 28596 135, 28631 402, 28638 195; B122.1 3942 88225 f. 5.

48. AGCA, Protocolos, Llerena, Dec. 7, 1838.

49. AGCA-ST, Suchitepéquez, 1/11 and Retalhuleu, 1/6.

50. AGCA, A1.45.9 2792 24478.

51. AGCA, Tierras, 6031 1784.

52. AGCA, B80.1 3563 81259 f. 2.

53. See, for example, AGCA-ST, Amatitlán, 2/9.

54. AGCA, Tierras, 6023 53109 and 6051 53463, and A1.45.9 2792 24478.

55. AGCA-ST, Chiquimula, 4/8.

56. AGCA-ST, Sololá, 2/5.

57. AGCA-ST, Quiché, 1/26.

58. AGCA-ST, Alta Verapaz, 75/5.

59. AGCA, B100.1 1416 33078 and 1418 33205; Ingersoll, "War of the Mountain," p. 66; Fry, "Agrarian Society," p. 144.

60. AGCA, B100.1 1418 33166 and 3633 85301. See Fry "Política agraria," n. 53 for many cases of the use of troops in land disputes.

61. AGCA-ST, Sololá, 2/8.

62. AGCA, B100.1 3633 85286.

63. AGCA-ST, Jalapa 1833 1/11; AGCA, B100.1 1422 33587; B78.24 713 15856; B5.7 66 1820; B100.1 1422 33657.

64. On congregación, see Lovell, *Conquest and Survival*, pp. 76–89, and Hill and Monaghan, *Continuities*, pp. 85–89. For examples, see AGCA, MG 28539 114, 28549, Aug. 16, 1850, 28588 122, and 28599 45, 28637 86; AGCA-ST, Sololá 1/22 and Jutiapa, 1/15, 1/19, 3/6; *Gaceta de Guatemala*, Jan. 28, 1867.

65. AGCA-ST, Sololá, 2/4, San Marcos, 1/13, and Quezaltenango, 3/3, 4/2, 5/1; AGCA, B100.1 1419 33382.

66. For the long history of Villa Nueva's land problems, see AGCA-ST, Amatitlán, 2/8 and AGCA, B5.7 66 1820.

67. AGCA-ST, Chimaltenango, 2/6, 3/11, 20/8. For other examples, see Baja Verapaz, 4/12, 5/4; Carmack, *Historia social*, pp. 207–8.

68. In *Tierra y sociedad*, Solano confuses San Juan Amatitlán with San Cristóbal Amatitlán [Palín], but in *Mayas* he has it correct. A more recent study suggests that indigenous communities during these years made up a relatively small proportion of the buyers of government land: Belzunegui Ormazábal, *Pensamiento económico*, chap. 4.

69. AGCA, Tierras, 6035 53225.

70. AGCA, Tierras, 6023 53108. Among many other examples, see AGCA, Tierras, 5989 52676, 6052 53485, 6051 53463; A1.45.1 5326 44886; AGCA-ST, Chimaltenango 1/3, Madigan, "Santiago Atitlán," p. 145.

71. Pinto Soria, *Centroamérica*, p. 143.

72. AGCA-ST, Quiché, 2/7.

73. Pineda de Mont, *Recopilación*, p. 667.

74. AGCA-ST, Quezaltenango, 2/15.

75. AGCA-ST, Quezaltenango, 3/2, Escuintla, 2/7, Jutiapa, 1/19, Baja Verapaz, 5/4, and Chimaltenango, 1/14, 2/9, and 2/11; AGCA, MG 28580 43; AHA, Cartas, Feb. 21, 1865, n. 108.

76. Pinto Soria, *Centroamérica*, p. 143; price information for 1839 from personal communication from R. L. Woodward.

77. AGCA-ST, Huehuetenango, 6/7 and Alta Verapaz, 4/8; Brintnal, *Revolt Against the Dead*; Carmack, *Historia social*. For listings of land claims of various clans in the Totonicapán region, see *Indice de los expedientes*, pp. 250–52.

78. Hill, "Social Organization," p. 177. See also Hill and Monaghan, *Continuities*, especially chap. 7.

79. AGCA-ST, Quiché, 3/1 and 11/8.

80. For examples, see AGCA-ST, Santa Rosa, 1/2, 3/4; AGCA, Tierras

6048 53408; Cortés y Larraz, *Descripción*, 2: 229; AHA, Cartas, Jan. 12, 1923, no. 13; May 18, 1837, no. 103; Sept. 1849, no. 213; Jan. 7, 1861, no. 16; Feb. 28, 1862, no. 105; July 13, 1863, no. 236; July 28, 1866, no. 329; Aug. 24, 1866, no. 361. For general comments, see Fry, "Agrarian Society," pp. 111–12; Bertrand, "Lucha por la tierra"; Collins, "Colonial Jacaltenango," chap. 8.

81. For example: AGCA, A1.45.8 2135 15187, A1 6019 53053, and Tierras, 6048 53401; AHA, Cartas, Jan. 14, 1823, no. 13, and July 22, 1861, no. 279.

82. AHA, Cofradías, 1825, no. 63 and no. 141; Cartas, 1863, no. 308.

83. AHA, Cofradías, 1825, no. 44.

84. AHA, Cartas, 1862, no. 314 and no. 257.

85. AGCA-ST, Santa Rosa, 3/1; AGCA, Tierras, 6028 53157; B100.1 1418 33192.

86. See, for example, the description of Jutiapa's ejidos in AGCA-ST, Jutiapa, 3/6, and the half-century struggle of Zacapa versus Jocotán over the montaña of Lampocoy: AGCA-ST, Chiquimula, 4/11, 4/15, 4/19.

87. AGCA-ST, Huehuetenango, 2/12.

88. AGCA-ST, Sololá 1/11 and Escuintla 2/7.

89. For comments on this situation, see AGCA-ST, Huehuetenango, 11/2; AGCA, MG 28582 194. See also Davis, "Land of Our Ancestors," chap. 2.

90. McBryde, *Cultural and Historical Geography*, pp. 5, 15–16, and map 11.

91. Luján Muñoz, "Fundación de villas," p. 55.

92. AGCA-ST, Escuintla, 1/11 and 3/4; García Peláez, *Memorias*, 3: 157.

93. AGCA-ST, Escuintla, 3/3, 3/7; García Peláez, *Memorias*, 3: 161–62.

94. Luján Muñoz, "Reducción y fundación." On the early history of land and relations with neighboring communities around Sija, see Carmack, *Historia social*, pp. 189–220; AGCA, B100.1 3633 85286.

95. AGCA-ST, Chimaltenango 1/17. See also ibid., 2/6, 2/7, 3/11, and 26/2; Gall, *Diccionario geográfico*, 4: 355.

96. AGCA, MG 28599 97 and 28600 169; AGCA-ST, Guatemala, 28/9.

97. AGCA, B108.7 1962 45240.

98. AGCA-ST, Baja Verapaz, 15A and 5/22.

99. For an extended example of the sale, with government intervention, of hacienda land to a town (Jutiapa), see AGCA-ST, Jutiapa, 1/15, 1/18, 1/19.

100. Cortés y Larraz, *Descripción*, 1: 299–300 and 2: 301–2.

101. Consulado, "Apuntamientos," p. 291. See also AGCA, Protocolos, for inventories of property sales and rentals, and Fry, "Agrarian Society," pp. 167–71.

102. Fry, "Política agraria," pp. 34–35.

103. For Lo de Pereira, see AGCA, Tierras, 6023 53109. For Sapayuca, see AGCA, Tierras, 5987 52663.

104. The document estimated livestock for Chiantla at 22,300 but this has

been halved here on the basis of late-18th-century animal censuses that give a more accurate picture.

105. On the early history of the haciendas Moscoso and Chancol, see Lovell, *Conquest and Survival*, pp. 121–26.

106. AGCA, A1.24 6096 55491 and B100.1 1416 33087.

107. AGCA, B85 1153 26707.

108. AGCA, A1.24 6096 55491; AGCA-ST, Huehuetenango, 10/4.

109. Fry, "Agrarian Society," p. 177.

110. For an example of division as a result of inheritance, see AGCA-ST, Guatemala, 2/6. More broadly, see Bertrand, "Lucha por la tierra," and Fry, "Agrarian Society," pp. 181–85.

111. AGCA, Protocolos, and Actuaciones Civiles y Criminales. See also Bertrand, "Lucha por la tierra"; Fry, "Agrarian Society," pp. 187–88; Pinto Soria, *Estructura agraria*, p. 28.

112. Consulado, "Apuntamientos," p. 292.

113. AGCA, A1.13 172 3451.

114. Van Young develops this idea in *Hacienda and Market*, p. 123.

115. See, for example, AGCA, A1.20 817 9311 f. 23v and 822 f. 165. On the seventeenth-century depression in Central America, see MacLeod, *Spanish Central America*, part 3, and Wortman, *Government*, chap. 5.

116. AGCA, A1.20 824 1810.

117. Dunn, *Guatimala*, p. 290; Haefkens, *Viaje a Guatemala*, pp. 62–63; Baily, *Central America*, p. ix; Solís, *Memorias*, p. 929. For examples of attacks on haciendas, see AGCA, MG 28599 90, and Ingersoll, "War of the Mountain," pp. 169, 175.

118. AHA, Cartas, May 11, 1832, no. 79.

119. Putting the property in the name of a wife was insurance against losing it in case of political exile. For a similar situation involving money lending, see CIRMA, Juzgado de Primera Instancia, Sacatepéquez, 1848, no. 3.

120. AGCA-ST, Suchitepéquez, 8/6. Carrera sold his share to Larraondo in 1860.

121. AGCA, MG 28609 180. According to the *Gaceta de Guatemala* of December 19, 1865, Carrera's properties at his death included five major haciendas: (1) Hacienda Lo de Batres with 6 caballerías of property plus 4.75 in censo from Guatemala City. Equipment included a sugar mill, a machine for cleaning coffee, 151 cattle and other animals, 33,623 coffee trees planted and another 54,224 in seedling, 66 suertes of cane, as well as pastures, etc. The value was put at 56,665 pesos. (In 1881 this hacienda belonged to Ernesto Klée with an area of 5 caballerías.) (2) Hacienda Buena Vista (Chiquimulilla) with an area of 387 caballerías, 507 cattle, and a value of 13,632 pesos. (3) Hacienda Punian (Escuintla) with 250–300 caballerías, 704 cattle, and a value of 19,709 pesos. (By 1881 this had become property of J. R. Barrios with an area

of 300 caballerías.) (4) Hacienda San Jorge (Escuintla) with 190 caballerías, 451 cattle, and a value of 15,368 pesos. (5) Hacienda Panán (Mazatenango) with 66.25 caballerías, 39 cattle, and a value of 7,658 pesos. There were also various additional properties for a total value of 129,799 pesos. My thanks to R. L. Woodward for this citation.

122. For example: AGCA-ST, Santa Rosa, 3/5. On the activities of Carrera's brother and other officials, see Ingersoll, "War of the Mountain," pp. 292–93.

123. AGCA, A3.5 352 07319.

124. Pinto Soria, *Estructura agraria*, p. 11. See also ibid., pp. 16–21.

125. AGCA, Tierras, 6029 53171; A3.15 2797 40439.

126. AGCA, Protocolos, Diaz G. 1791 24v; for similar examples, see A1.20 834 f.72v and A1.20 817 9311 f 23v.

127. Holleran, *Church and State*, p. 54.

128. Montúfar y Rivera Maestre, *Reseña histórica*, 5: 241–46; Holleran, *Church and State*, pp. 58–59; AGCA, A1.1.1 29 845. An AHA Cartas index includes a reference to a document listing the properties of the orders that were expelled in 1829, but it was not found.

129. Solórzano, *Evolución económica*, p. 235; Collins, "Colonial Jacaltenango," pp. 59–60. Some orders owned considerable urban real estate.

130. See, for example, AGCA-ST, Sololá, 4/12.

131. Montúfar y Rivera Maestre, *Reseña histórica* 5: 241–46.

132. Holleran, *Church and State*, p. 59.

133. Ingersoll, "War of the Mountain," pp. 256–57.

134. AHA, Cartas, 1852, no. 212.

135. AHA, Cartas, 1864, no. 409.

136. AHA, Cartas, 1847, no. 119, 1848, no. 17, 1852, no. 212; AGCA, Tierras, 5987 52663; AGCA-ST, Guatemala, 2/13.

137. AGCA, Plano, 6021 53078; AGCA-ST, Amatitlán, 1/7.

138. AGCA, B115.1 3908 88148.

139. On Garrote Bueno's activities, see AGCA, A1.11.31 2812 24794, A1.21.11 2817 24888, A1.15 2488 19713, A1.11.31 2812 24799, A1.1131 2813 24806, A1.11.31 2813 24803 and 248044, A1.11.31 2812 24798, A1.21.11 5540 47928, A1.21.11 208 4193. Whereas in the "Inventario de las causes criminales contra individuos del estado eclesiástico" (AHA, Gobierno Eclesiástico, Capellanías, T3 no. 77), compiled by the Archbishopric in 1802, few priests merited more than one or two complaints, Ponciano Garrote Bueno registered 43, and his career was not over.

140. AGCA, B100.1 1416 33098.

141. Quoted in Pinto Soria, *Estructura agraria*, p. 9.

142. AGCA, Tierras, 6052 53491.

143. See, for example, AGCA, A3.30 2578 37864, B100.1 1416 33083; AGCA-ST, Suchitepéquez, 3/2.

144. AGCA-ST, Sololá, 2/5.

145. AGCA, B100.1 1420 33421.

146. AGCA, B119.4 2551 59985.

147. Pineda de Mont, *Recopilación*, p. 868.

148. On Cerro Redondo, see Fry, "Agrarian Society," pp. 172–73. The figures for Palencia are from AGCA, B108.7 1956 44799.

149. AGCA, B100.1 1419 33251 and 33252.

150. AGCA-ST, Baja Verapaz, 5/4; AGCA, A1.11 102 2185. For other examples, see AGCA-ST, Quezaltenango, 1/15 and Sololá, 1/5, 1/8; AGCA, B100.1 3633 85353; MG 28582 145 and 28592 83; B100.1 1422 33587.

151. AGCA, A1.71 171 7266.

152. AGCA-ST, Totonicapán, 1/11, 1/12, 2/1, 2/4; AGCA, B100. 1416 33078; Veblen, "Forest Preservation in Totonicapán," p. 351. A corregidor reported that Sacapulas was threatening the chiquimulas with arms over back rent: AGCA, MG 28592 82 and 28601 209; Tierras, 6052 53491.

153. AGCA, A3.5 352 7319. See also Fry, "Agrarian Society," p. 95. On ladino penetration of communities in the Oriente, see Martínez Peláez, *Patria del criollo*, pp. 429–31.

154. AGCA, A3 224 4024.

155. AGCA-ST, Chimaltenango, 3/6. For a similar situation in Malacatán, see AGCA, MG 28569 54.

156. AGCA, B100.1 1422 33657.

157. On orders to increase cattle production among Indians, see AGCA, A1.1 6113 56218. For Indian cattle raising in general, see Wortman, *Government*, p. 44; Bertrand, "Lucha por la tierra"; Van Oss, *Catholic Colonialism*, p. 114; AGCA, B119.2 2521 56983 f. 2.

158. AGCA, A1.45.8 2769 24065, A1.45.8 173 3515, A1.45.8 2785 24427, MG 28537 41, MG 28549 3, MG 28552 30, MG 28586 219, MG 28594 18 and 28595 72, MG 28505 43, MG 28596 119; AGCA-ST, Escuintla, 1/11 and Sololá, 1/11.

159. AGCA, A1.45.7 2174 15700; A1.45.8 5539 47901; AGCA-ST, Suchitepéquez, 2/20.

Chapter 3

1. On the early labor history of the colony, see Sherman, *Forced Native Labor*, Simpson, *Repartimiento System*, and Martínez Peláez, *Patria del criollo*, chaps. 5 and 7.

2. On population trends, see Carmack, Early, and Lutz, eds., *Historical Demography*, and Lutz, Lovell, and Sweezy, "Population History."

3. Thompson, *Narrative*, p. 175.

4. Consulado de Comercio, "Apuntamientos," p. 283. For an extended essay on the question of "needs," see Córdoba, "Utilidades."

5. García Peláez, *Memorias*, 3: 146.

6. García Redondo, *Memoria*, p. 7. See also Consulado, "Apuntamientos," p. 285.

7. See AGCA, A3.12 2882 41912 for a lengthy investigation and debate about salary and conditions for Indian workers in the central part of the colony circa 1760.

8. AGCA, A3 227 4182 and 4185.

9. On this phenomenon, see Berg, "Backward-sloping Labor Supply Functions," and Arrighi, "Labor Supplies."

10. Among many other examples of drunkenness, see Cortés y Larraz, *Descripción*, 2: 79, 110, 130, 194–95; Solano, *Los Mayas*, pp. 386–87; AGCA, A1 195 3961, A3.4 49 932, A3.4 59 1150.

11. García Peláez, *Memorias*, 2: 228–33 and 3: 7–12.

12. AGCA, A1. 195 3961. On villages claiming to be indigenous communities and therefore exempt from the liquor monopoly, see B107.2 1845 42309 (Palín), B119.3 2539 58549 (Taxisco), and B107.2 1849 42578 (Sumpango). See also, Batres Jáuregui, *Los indios*, pp. 191–94 n. 3.

13. AGCA, A3.4 49 932. About the inability of Indians to control their drinking, see Bunzel, *Chichicastenango*, pp. 254–60, and Maudsley and Maudsley, *A Glimpse at Guatemala*, p. 72.

14. AGCA, B107.2 1845 42310.

15. AGCA, A3.4 49 932.

16. AGCA, A3.4 59 1150.

17. *El Tiempo*, Nov. 16, 1839.

18. Wortman, *Government*, p. 256.

19. Dunn, *Guatimala*, pp. 101–2; Haefkens, *Viaje a Guatemala*, p. 290.

20. Palma Murga, "Algunas relaciones," pp. 113–20; Montúfar y Rivera Maestre, *Reseña histórica*, 5: 353.

21. Williford, "Las Luces," pp. 143–44.

22. Skinner-Klée, *Legislación indigenista*, p. 24.

23. AGCA, B119.1 2505 56014.

24. Among many others, see Stephens, *Incidents of Travel*, 1: 284, 292, and 2: 105, 147, 165, 200, 219, 235; Dunlop, *Travels*, p. 337; von Tempsky, *Mitla*, pp. 330, 373. Regarding the dangers of drink shops set up in unregulated areas (*en despoblado*), see *La Revista*, Mar. 26, 1847, and *Gaceta de Guatemala*, Dec. 11 and 31, 1864.

25. AHA, Cartas, Correspondence of San Cristóbal Totonicapán, June 1852 [1870] no. 147, Vicar's report, June 1869.

26. Pineda de Mont, *Recopilación*, pp. 217–19.

27. Except where noted, this discussion of slavery relies on Diemecke de Gonzalez, *El negro en Guatemala*. On the fear of "mulattoes" in the mountains even after the end of slavery, see Dunn, *Guatimala*, pp. 94–95.

28. Compare, for example, Luján Muñoz, *Agricultura*, p. 80, with AGCA, A1 2999 28662.

29. See descriptions in the sales documents in AGCA, Protocolos.

30. Holleran, *Church and State*, p. 54. Cortés y Larraz, *Descripción*, 2: 212, gives populations for several sugar mills at Amatitlán without indicating the relative numbers of slaves, ladinos, or Indians.

31. AGCA, Protocolos; Diemecke, *El negro*, p. 51, indicates that the Crown paid 150 pesos each for slaves delivered to colonize Omoa, on the Caribbean coast.

32. Diemecke, *El negro*, pp. 100–104.

33. AGCA, A3.5 986 18169; Consulado, "Apuntamientos," pp. 295–96, 404–5; B78.24 712 15806; Dunn, *Guatimala*, p. 234; Haefkens, *Viaje a Guatemala*, p. 295. Stephens, *Incidents of Travel*, 1: 70, notes the difficulty "of buying anything ready made."

34. AGCA, A1.22.15 2588 21081.

35. Pineda de Mont, *Recopilación*, p. 589.

36. Ibid., p. 748.

37. *Gaceta de Guatemala*, Aug. 21, 1847.

38. AGCA, A3 227 4146.

39. AGCA, A3 226 4111; A3 228 5674.

40. AGCA, A1.21.3 163 3309.

41. Ibid.

42. AGCA, A1.14.25 207 4170.

43. See, for example, the records (1806) of the hacienda Arrasola, AGCA, A1.43 2753 23728. For conditions that drove a person into colono status, see AGCA-ST, Totonicapán, 2/1 and Chimaltenango, 1/3.

44. Cortés y Larraz, *Descripción*, 2: 105–7; AGCA, A1.11 102 2185.

45. Ibid., 2: 233, 276.

46. AGCA, A1 207 4176.

47. AGCA, A3.12 2882 41912.

48. AGCA, A1.24 6096 55491.

49. AGCA, A1 207 4176.

50. Simpson, *Repartimiento System*, pp. 129–49; Martínez Peláez, *Patria del criollo*, pp. 466–74.

51. García Peláez, *Memorias*, 3: 142.

52. AGCA, A3.12 2882 41912.

53. AGCA, A3.12 2777 41173, A1.23 1528 f. 445, A3 228 5669.

54. AGCA, A3 228 5669.

55. For example, AGCA, A3 223 4010, 224 4014 and 4033, 225 4065, and 227 4151. On taxes and paying wages in advance, see AGCA, A1.22 6114 56327.

56. AGCA, A3 225 4071 and 226 4113.

57. AGCA, A3 225 4056 and 4067. In fact, the Audiencia already had granted one quarter of the tributaries of Chichicastenango to the owner of Portuguese/Chiché (A3 228 5668, attached to 5667), but then it granted the one quarter again to Solórzano. See also A3 228 5672, A3 227 4168, A3 227 4179.

58. For example, AGCA, A3 223 4010.

59. Based on tax records, Belzunegui Ormazábal argues that the use of repartimientos did decline in the last quarter of the century, at least in the valle de Guatemala: *Pensamiento económico*, pp. 82–83. And Wortman, in *Government*, p. 180, says repartimientos ended in 1793, but he gives no evidence; it is clear that at least in Guatemala the labor drafts did not stop at this point.

60. On local variations in custom of tribute and repartimientos, see AGCA, A1.10 58 1568.

61. On the tribute system in Guatemala, see Fernandez Molina, *Los tributos*.

62. AGCA, A3 227 4160, 4161, and 4163.

63. AGCA, A3, 226 4110, 4114 and 4140, and 227 4146.

64. AGCA, A3 227 4181.

65. AGCA, A1.14.25 380 7870.

66. AGCA, A3 227 4154.

67. AGCA, A3 227 4187.

68. AGCA, A3 226 4110.

69. AGCA, A3 224 4025.

70. For typical requests, see AGCA, A3 224 4016, 4027, 4031, 4034, 4047, 4048, 4049, 4050, and dozens more through to 4183.

71. AGCA, A3 224 4038 and 228 5665.

72. AGCA, A3 224 4017.

73. On repartimientos for tobacco, see AGCA, A3 225 4083 and 226 4041; for cacao, see A3 226 4118, 227 4153, 4155, 4160, 4161, 4162, among dozens more. For a general treatment of restrictions, see García Peláez, *Memorias*, 1: 225–28.

74. The well-known labor regulations of 1784 (Rubio Sánchez, *Añil*, 2: 134–37, 365–75, and R. Smith, "Forced Labor") applied to El Salvador–Sonsonate, not to Guatemala; see AGCA, A3 226 4112.

75. AGCA, A1.14.25 170 3425, A1 169 3393.

76. AGCA, A3 227 4146.

77. AGCA, A3 227 4166.

78. AGCA, A1.14.25 207 4170.

79. Allusion is made to an "ancient" order for 100 workers from Rabinal and 100 from Salamá, but the order apparently did not obtain in the second half of the eighteenth century: AGCA, A1.10 58 1568. The Dominican's hacienda Llano Grande near Rabinal requested and received a labor reparti-

miento of 25 Indians in 1801, but this does not appear to have involved sugar production: A3 228 5676.

80. Among many others, see AGCA, A3 224 4014 and 4023, 227 4147, 4176, 4190; A3.4 52 996.

81. AGCA, A3 225 4080.

82. See AGCA, A2.2 40 830 versus, for example, A3 226 4128. Even where a hacienda proposed to produce both indigo and sugar, the question of prohibitions might not come up; see A3 227 4190.

83. AGCA, A3.4 50 950 and 52 996.

84. AGCA, A1.14.25 169 3420, A3.4 52 996, A3 224 4041.

85. AGCA, A1.21 5398 45911.

86. For road building, see AGCA, A3 226 4141 and A1.14.25 202 4094; on iron works, see A3 227 4191; for brick making, see A3 228 5667 and 5668; and for construction of the new capital, see A10 58 1568.

87. AGCA, A3 227 4180. See also A3 224 4028 and 4044, 226 4117 and 4136; A1.14 154 3052.

88. AGCA, A1.14.25 163 3294, A1.14.25 192 3925 and 3926, A1.24.25 195 3953, A1.14.25 202 4095 and 4100, A3 225 4062.

89. AGCA, A1.14.25 163 3294.

90. Cortés y Larraz, *Descripción*, 1: 244; Wortman, *Government*, p. 178; see also, AGCA, A1.14.25 163 3286.

91. AGCA, A1.14.25 379 7851.

92. AGCA, A3 224 4022.

93. AGCA, A10 58 1568. Among dozens of protests from towns against being sent to work on the city, see A1.14.25 153 3012 and 163 3303, A1.10 62 4473.

94. AGCA, A1.10 63 4476, 4477, 4479, 4481.

95. AGCA, A1.30.1 163 3292, A3 224 4033, 4034, 4044.

96. AGCA, A3 224 4046, A1.10 58 1568, A3 226 4111 and 4126.

97. AGCA, A3 226 4126.

98. AGCA, A1.10 58 1572.

99. AGCA, A1.10 58 1572 and 63 4490.

100. For restatements of these prohibitions, see AGCA, A3 224 4021, 4022, 4030, 4039, and 225 4083, 226 4099, 4100, and 4142, and 227 4177; A3.9 157 3055; A1.14.25 176 3596. See A3 224 4013 regarding a lead mine in Huehuetenango. For the subsequent history of mining at Alotepeque, see Solís, *Memorias*, chaps. 41–42, and Boddam-Whettham, *Across Central America*, pp. 157–58.

101. AGCA, A3 224 4021 and 4022.

102. AGCA, A1.14.25 176 3596.

103. AGCA, A3 227 4177.

104. AGCA, A3 225 4074.

105. AGCA, A3 227 4168.

106. AGCA, A1.14.25 158 3183.

107. For examples of protests, see AGCA, A3 225 4075, 226 4088, 4114, 4117, 4122, and 227 4164; A3 225 4077, 226 4086 and 227 4159; A3 225 4074, 4171; A3 224 4041, 4044, 226 4136, and 227 4148; A3.12 2561 37586.

108. AGCA, A3.12 2561 37586.

109. AGCA, A3 226 4126.

110. AGCA, A1.22.20 153 3036. On flight as a result of labor pressures, see A3 226 4111.

111. AGCA, A1.14.25 158 3183.

112. AGCA, A3.12 2778 40184, A3.12 2561 37586.

113. AGCA, A3.12 2561 37586. See also, A3.12 2882 41912, A3 227 4144; Solano, *Los Mayas*, pp. 370–76; Martínez Peláez, *Patria del criollo*, pp. 477–78; Cortés y Larraz, *Descripción*, 2: 139–40.

114. See, for example, the protracted struggle of the justicias of Mataquescuintla against repartimiento demands: AGCA, A3 226 4141, 4143, and 227 4145, 4147, 4148, 4156, 4158.

115. For example: AGCA, A3 4126, A1.22.20 153 3036, A3.12 2778 40184.

116. AGCA, A3 226 4108; A1.22.20 5372.

117. AGCA, A3.12 2778 40184.

118. Where a given order involved several towns, each one is counted separately.

119. See AGCA, A3 224 4035 for a detailed example.

120. For this reason, at least one employer asked that all advances be banned: AGCA, A3 228 5675.

121. AGCA, A3 226 4111.

122. AGCA, A1.22.15 3788 4221.

123. For example: AGCA, A1.10.3 76 4580, A1.14.25 170 3425, A1.21 5420 46230.

124. AGCA, A1.23 6090 55258; M. Rodriguez, *Cadiz Experiment*, pp. 86–87.

125. Consulado, "Apuntamientos," pp. 309–10.

126. AGCA, A3.12 2900, 43183–85, 43197–98, 43200, 43202.

127. AGCA, A3 227 4194.

128. AGCA, B10.77 2281, B12 438 f. 19v.

129. AGCA, B3.6 47 1019; B92.4 1394 32293. According to B78.29 1494 35806 (1825) the articles of the 1812/1820 constitution regarding personal service had not been observed in all parts of Guatemala.

130. Both quotes from Pineda de Mont, *Recopilación*, pp. 589–90.

131. AGCA, B119.9.1, Apr. 1831.

132. Pineda de Mont, *Recopilación*, p. 748.

133. Ibid., pp. 506, 851–53; Marure, *Catálogo razonado*, p. 143.

134. Given the local nature of grants in this period and the damage to

records, no doubt much evidence was lost and there may have been more use of mandamientos than appears, but it cannot have been significant. There were scattered orders of largely nonagricultural mandamientos. For example: 1836, to cut wood for new port of Iztapa: AGCA, B119.3 2540 58608; 1837, to gather cattle on hacienda La Grande: B119.3 2542 58728; 1854, to fight locusts and plant food crops in aftermath of locusts: Corregidor Sacatepéquez, July 13, 1854, Papers JP Sacatepéquez; 1854–1860's, for carrying in the Verapaz: McAfee, "Agricultural Labor," append.

Chapter 4

1. Rubio Sánchez, "La grana," p. 37.
2. Naylor, *Influencia británica*, pp. 231–32 (almost all of the cochineal labeled "British Honduras" came in fact from Guatemala); García Laguardia, *El pensamiento Liberal*, p. 23.
3. Dunn, *Guatimala*, pp. 159–61. See also Dunlop, *Travels*, pp. 112–40 for a very thorough treatment of cochineal production and an extended comparison of Amatitlán and Antigua.
4. Dunlop, *Travels*, p. 125. López failed in one of the more spectacular bankruptcies of the period: AGCA, Protocolos, Cáceres, July 10, 1850.
5. Consulado de Comercio, "Apuntamientos," p. 400.
6. AGCA, A3.27 1759 28254; Rubio Sánchez, "La grana," pp. 19–20; López, *Instrucción para los nopales*; *Gaceta de Guatemala*, Feb. 28, 1850, and July 25, 1861; Solís, *Memorias*, p. 629; *El Indicador*, July 11, 1825.
7. AGCA, A3.1 1346 22545.
8. See, for example, AGCA, Juzgado de Primera Instancia, Quiché, 3/221. Experiments extended even to the Cuchumatanes: A1.1 6116 56541.
9. Solís, *Memorias*, p. 629. See also E. Palacios, *Reseña de la situación*, pp. 36–38; *El Indicador*, July 11, 1825. Figures often given for grana production in the early period are inaccurate: for example, Solórzano Fernández, *Evolución económica*, pp. 244–45.
10. AGCA, Oct. 14, 1824, Papers JP Sacatepéquez, 1824.
11. AGCA, B107.3 1874 43309, B87.1 1188 28798, Oct. 8, 1824, Papers JP Sacatepéquez, 1824; *El Indicador*, Nov. 1, 1824.
12. AGCA, Oct. 14, 1824, Papers JP Sacatepéquez, 1824; Woodward, *Class Privilege*, p. 44; Solís, *Memorias*, p. 629.
13. Woodward, *Class Privilege*, p. 43.
14. Ibid.
15. Solís, *Memorias*, p. 629; Haefkens, *Viaje*, pp. 267, 299; *El Indicador*, July 11, 1825.
16. AGCA, B119.3 2544 58980.
17. Solís, *Memorias*, p. 832.
18. For example, see *La Gaceta Oficial*, Jan. 25, 1844; U.S. Department

of State, Dispatches from U.S. Diplomatic Representatives Abroad: Central America, M219, roll 4, Dec. 25, 1847, and Dec. 5, 1848.

19. Stephens, *Incidents of Travel*, 1: 277.

20. Chinchilla Aguilar, *Amatitlán*, pp. 122–25.

21. Solís, *Memorias*, pp. 1092–95; Dunlop, *Travels*, pp. 130–31.

22. Claxton, "Guatemalan Rain Showers." See also AGCA, French Legation in Guatemala, 4, 1857–71, no. 93231; my thanks to Richmond Brown for this citation.

23. Dunlop, *Travels*, p. 127.

24. E. Palacios, *Reseña de la situación*, p. 36.

25. AGCA, A1. 2157 15453, A1.25 3099 29952.

26. AGCA, B 2370 49195; B12.7 4941 f. 28; my thanks to Prof. R. L. Woodward for this citation.

27. On the aguardiente monopoly, see Palma Murga, "Algunas relaciones," pp. 113–20. For indicators of the dramatic rise in station of one of its prominent investors, see the last testaments of José María Samayoa (padre): AGCA, Protocolos, Andreu, 1838, f. 36, and Caceres, 1870, f. 270. Tomás Larraondo applied to the church in 1856 to legitimize his three children, the result of living with his "wife" for more than ten years: AHA, Cartas, Aug. 2, 1856, no. 247.

28. AGCA, Protocolos, Llerena, July 11, 1837, and June 19, 1841.

29. Palma Murga, "Algunas relaciones."

30. Thompson, *Narrative*, p. 281; Solís, *Memorias*, pp. 636–40.

31. AGCA, Protocolos, Llerena, Dec. 10, 1834.

32. For example: ibid., Llerena, June 19, 1837, and July 24, 1838, and Cáceres, Feb. 1, 1850.

33. Ibid., Llerena, Apr. 26, 1837.

34. Ibid., Llerena, July 7, 1842.

35. Ibid., Llerena, July 20, 1839.

36. Ibid., Llerena, Apr. 26, 1837, July 7, 1842, and June 22, 1849.

37. Ibid., Cáceres, Feb. 19, 1861.

38. Ibid., Llerena, June 9, 1837, and Dec. 7, 1838.

39. Baily, *Central America*, p. 47.

40. AGCA-ST, Amatitlán, 1/5; AGCA, B85.1 3600 82802.

41. AGCA, Protocolos, Cáceres, June 11, 1849.

42. E. Palacios, *Reseña de la situación*, p. 37.

43. AGCA-ST and AGCA, Protocolos.

44. AGCA-ST, Amatitlán 1/4, 1/5, 2/9.

45. AGCA, B10.7 185 40405.

46. AGCA, B100.1 1415 33055.

47. AGCA, June 26, 1855, Papers JP Sacatepéquez, 1855.

48. AGCA, MG 28536 145.

49. Ibid.

50. McAfee, "Agricultural Labor," pp. 41–42; AGCA, Corregidor Sacatepéquez, visita, Mar. 5, 1861, Papers JP Sacatepéquez, 1861.

51. McAfee, "Agricultural Labor," stresses the importance of vagrancy laws in mobilizing labor for grana, but her evidence does not support such a conclusion. An 1846 population study that reported "the town of Santa María . . . is in decadence; the Indians are forced to work in Amatitlán" referred to indebted labor, not mandamientos: AGCA, B8.42 3595 82567.

52. AGCA, A1.22.15 2588 21078 and 21081, A1.1 6087 55110, A1.24 6091 55306, A1.22.2 4566 39176 and 39181, A1.22.15 1510 f. 7, B86.5 3605 83474 and 83475, B107.2 1847 42362, B78.1 1190 28915, and B119.3 2544 59039. See also Pineda de Mont, *Recopilación*, pp. 584–86, 592–600, 603–4.

53. *El Tiempo*, Mar. 4, 1840.

54. AGCA, MG 28536 145; Planos, 6021 53078.

55. AGCA, MG 28536 145. See also AGCA, Protocolos, Llerena, Apr. 25, 1837, and Corregidor Sacatepéquez, visita, Mar. 3, 1864, Papers JP Sacatepéquez, 1864.

56. AGCA, MG 28558, Aug. 6, 1847.

57. AHA, Cartas, Correspondence of San Juan de Obispo, Dec. 12, 1854 [1870], no. 299, Oct. 5, 1858.

58. AGCA, May 28, 1850, Papers JP Sacatepéquez, 1850.

59. AGCA, July 1, 1845, Papers JP Sacatepéquez, 1845; B8.42 3595 82567; Dunlop, *Travels*, p. 138–39. Ironically, in the dry season Amatitlán and Escuintla were elite resorts; see Parker, *Travels*, pp. 80–82, and Baily, *Central America*, p. 38.

60. AGCA-ST, Amatitlán 2/4.

61. AGCA, B119.2 2544 58980.

62. AGCA, MG 28536 145.

63. AGCA, B119.2 2544 58980.

64. *La Revista*, May 13 and Nov. 26, 1847; *Gaceta de Guatemala*, Oct. 14, 1860.

65. Dunlop, *Travels*, pp. 122–23, 135–36.

66. AGCA, B119.3 2546 59251 and B119.3 2547 59638. See also B119.3 2544 59039.

67. U.S. Department of State, Dispatches from U.S. Representatives Abroad: Central America, M219, roll 3, June 24, 1835; Solís, *Memorias*, p. 637; E. Palacios, *Reseña de la situación*, pp. 36–37.

68. *Gaceta de Guatemala*, July 2 and Oct. 17, 1860.

69. *La Semana*, Dec. 21, 1867.

70. On sugar, see Chinchilla Aguilar, *Amatitlán*, p. 53; for cotton see Woodward, *Class Privilege*, pp. 51–52.

Chapter 5

1. LaFarge, "Maya Ethnology." Fry, "Agrarian Society," believes that the process took place some one hundred years earlier in the Oriente. On the subsequent "genealogy" of this idea, see Carmack, "Spanish-Indian Relations." Wasserstrom restates the thesis for Chiapas in *Class and Society*.

2. Wortman, *Government*, pp. 61–63.

3. AGCA, A1.23 1528 f. 277, 1530 f. 23, and A1.23 1539 f. 23; A1.11 6105 55809. Among hundreds of such abuses noted in the church archives, see AHA, Cartas, Dec. 19, 1823, no. 280, Apr. 24, 1828, no. 130, July 4, 1828, no. 208, and Nov., 1859, no. 7. For an eloquent petition from a community protesting the removal of a priest who had served them for 22 years, see AHA, Nov. 29, 1855, no. 338.

4. AHA, Cartas, Aug. 21, 1823, no. 190, and Sept. 15, 1823, no. 204.

5. AHA, Cartas, May 13, 1857 [1870], no. 144, Correspondence of parish San Lucas and Santiago Sacatepéquez, Dec. n.d., 1863.

6. Van Oss, *Catholic Colonialism*, chap. 3. For a detailed examination of one priest's income, see AGCA, A1.21 199 4040.

7. Consulado de Comércio, "Apuntamientos," pp. 324–25.

8. AGCA, A1.23 6090 55258, B10 77 2281; Van Oss, *Catholic Colonialism*, p. 202.

9. Van Oss, *Catholic Colonialism*, p. 220 n. 22; AGCA, A3.12 2900 various.

10. AGCA, A3.12 2900 43184.

11. For more on this, see McCreery, "Atanasio Tzul"; Contreras, *Una rebelión indígena*; Bricker, *Indian Christ*, chap. 7; Martínez Peláez, *Motines de indios*, part 4; AGCA, A1.1 6931 57212. See also A1.24.20 4659 39898. For evidence of some of the confusion attendant on the process, see A1.23 1539 0388.

12. AGCA, B5.7 68 1851 f. 39v, B119.3 2538 58460 and 58473, MG 28537 41, MG 28634 356; AHA, July 17, 1865, no. 308; Skinner-Klée, *Legislación indigenista*, p. 17.

13. Van Oss, "Catholic Colonialism," p. 392, indicates a decline in clergy between 1805 and 1872 from 453 to 119 priests.

14. AHA, Cartas, Nov. 13, 1862, no. 13.

15. Ibid., Feb. 8, 1855 [1870], no. 42, Correspondence parish of Jacaltenango, Mar. 16, 1857, Oct. 26, 1857, Feb. 8, 1859, and Oct. n.d., 1859.

16. Solano, *Los Mayas*, pp. 374–76; Falla, *Quiché rebelde*, chap. 4: part 5; Wortman, *Government*, pp. 182–83.

17. AGCA, A1.15 5421 46246, A1.1 6942 57805, B119.3 2538 58476. See also Cortés y Larraz, *Descripción*, 1: 239–40 on prevalence of witchcraft in this area.

18. AHA, leg. 170 no. 50, May 22, 1815. The woman was described as a "ladina" but spoke no Spanish.

19. AGCA, Juzgado de Primera Instancia, Criminal, Huehuetenango, 7/10.

20. AHA, Cartas, 1885 no. 244, Sept. 30, 1886 (*sic*).

21. Ibid., Jan. 1 and 2, 1854, no. 1, Jan. 4, 1854, no. 5, Jan. 20, 1854, no. 27, Jan. 27, 1854, no. 34; Estrada Monroy, *Datos para la historia*, 2: 628–36.

22. For mention of an attempted attack on the priest of Santa Catarina Ixtahuacán, see von Tempsky, *Mitla*, pp. 374–77, 382–84.

23. AHA, A4.13 170 51 and 54.

24. AHA, Cartas, Jan. 30, 1856 [1870], no. 34, Correspondence parish of Nebaj, Oct. 21, 1586. The same priest accused a witch in nearby Sacapulas of inducing abortions for single women: n.d., 1858.

25. AGCA, A1.21.3 163 3289.

26. AHA, Cartas, July 28, 1857, no. 15.

27. On the importance of income from the cofradías to the priests see ibid., n.d., 1825, nos. 44 and 142, Feb. 18, 1838, no. 18, June 7, 1862, no. 215. See also AGCA, A1.45.8 2135 15189; Van Oss, *Catholic Colonialism*, p. 89.

28. AHA, Visitas Pastorales. For founding dates (real or imagined) and capitals of a number of cofradías, see AHA, Cartas, 1821–25. Añoveras, *Población y estado socioreligioso*, pp. 227–33, provides an inventory of claimed capitals for cofradías in the mid-eighteenth century, based on the records of Cortes y Larraz's investigation.

29. AHA, Cartas, Sept. 9, 1855, no. 10, Oct. 8, 1832, no. 177, and n.d., 1864, nos. 54 and 57; also see, AHA, Visitas Pastorales.

30. AHA, Cartas, 1821–25, various dates and numbers, together with Oct. 8, 1832, no. 177, May 18, 1837, no. 103, and July 1, 1843, no. 51; Cofradías, leg. 189, no. 92; AGCA, Juzgado de Primera Instancia, Sololá, 21/1199; see also Fry, "Agrarian Society," pp. 111–12; Bertrand, "Lucha por la tierra"; Piel, *Sajcabaja*, p. 220; and Collins, "Colonial Jacaltenango," chap. 8. Many cofradías, of course, were quite poor: e.g., Van Oss, *Catholic Colonialism*, p. 112.

31. AHA, Gobierno Eclesiástico, Capellanías, T3 no. 74; Cartas, Sept. 9, 1855, no. 10, Oct. 8, 1832, no. 177.

32. T. Adams, "San Martín Jilotepeque," p. 21; AHA, Cartas, Feb. 1, 1825, no. 31, Sept. 9, 1855, no. 260, Oct. 25, 1863, no. 308, Feb. 18, 1864, no. 57, Feb. 7, 1855 [1870], no. 39, Correspondence parish of Mataquescuintla, various.

33. AHA, Cartas, Feb. 8, 1862, no. 54.

34. Ibid., Feb. 18, 1838, no. 18, Aug. 9, 1845, no. 128, Jan. 2, 1854, nos. 12 and 13, June 7, 1862, no. 215; AGCA, A1.11.2 173 3522.

35. AHA, Cartas, Feb. 18, 1838, no. 18.

36. Ibid., Feb. 7, 1855 [1870], no. 39, Correspondence parish of Mataquescuintla, various; Oct. 9, 1855 [1870], Correspondence parish of Cuilco and Tacaná, Oct. 29, 1855; Aug. 9, 1845, no. 128; June 7, 1862, no. 215; AGCA, MG 28626 373.

37. AHA, Cartas, Feb. 3, 1858, no. 7.

38. Ibid., Feb. 13, 1825, no. 41.

39. AHA, Visitas Pastorales, Riveiro y Jacinto, Cantel, 1915. See also

ibid., comments on Cobán, San Cristóbal Verapaz, Zunil, Momostenango, and Acatenango.

40. Bunzel, *Chichicastenango*, pp. 164–81; Oakes, *Two Crosses*, chap. 4; LaFarge, *Santa Eulalia*; Mendelson, *Los escándalos de Maximón*.

41. For more on this, see McCreery, "Caja."

42. AHA, Visitas Pastorales, Casanova y Estrada, Nebaj, 1905. See also Riveiro y Jacinto, Zunil, 1915.

43. AHA, Cartas, Feb. 18, 1838, no. 18.

44. AGCA, B100.1 3633 85312 and MG 28569 33; AGCA-ST, Sololá, 2/4.

45. AGCA, B100.1 1418 33158. See also B100.1 3633 85305, 85312, and 85335.

46. AGCA, MG 28569 33.

47. AGCA-ST, Totonicapán, 4/2.

48. AGCA-ST, Totonicapán, 2/7.

49. AGCA-ST, Quiché, 2/1.

50. AGCA-ST, Huehuetenango, 2/8, 2/11, 7/8; AGCA, A1.57 6116 56476. Until the end of the nineteenth century the "town" Jacaltenango included for landholding purposes the populations of Jacaltenango, Petatán, San Andrés Huista, Concepción, San Marcos Huista, and San Antonio Huista.

51. AGCA-ST, Suchitepéquez, 4/11, 4/19.

52. For examples of riots and violence over land see AGCA, B100 1416 33078, B100.1 3633 85301, B119.2 2509 56355 and 2510 56377; MG 28552 62, 28560 143, 28582 194, 28589 177, 28592 81, 28595 39, 28600 203, 28608 27, 28609 191 and 246, 28613 41, 42, and 79, 28615 287 and 291, and 28680 86 and 117; Juzgado de Primera Instancia, Criminal, Sololá, 2/87, 6/375, 8/492, 18/1073, 1075, 1091; AGCA-ST, Totonicapán, 2/7, and Sololá 2/2, 2/5.

53. AGCA, Juzgado de Primera Instancia, Criminal, Sololá, 18/1091.

54. AGCA, Tierras, 6023 53109, 6051 53463 6052 53485; A1.45.9 2792 24478; AGCA-ST, Santa Rosa, 1/2, 1/5, 1/11, 2/6, 3/15. See also AGCA-ST Santa Rosa, 9/17, 9/18.

55. AGCA-ST, Jutiapa, 1/15, 1/18, 1/19, 2/4, 3/3, 3/6, 3/11, 5/2.

56. Sometimes this also was called Chuacorral and/or Portuguese and/ or Tululché. Over the course of the centuries various owners combined, divided, and recombined these properties. Tululché: AGCA-ST, Quiché, 27/9; Registro de Propiedad Inmueble, Quezaltenango f. 50 T2 no. 14 and f. 44 T2 no. 13; Chuacorral: AGCA-ST, Quiché, 17/5; Registro . . . Quezaltenango, f. 218 T3 no. 182. See also AGCA, Tierras, 6052 53491; AGCA-ST, Quiché, 1/16, 1/21, 2/9; and Piel, *Sajcabaja*, pp. 296–97, 309–10.

57. AGCA-ST, Suchitepéquez, 4/11. See also ibid., 4/19.

58. AGCA, Tierras, 5995 52736, 6008 52922, 6027 53154, 6028 53157, 6047 53379, 6048 53413; B100.1 1418 33192; AGCA-ST, Santa Rosa, 2/3, 3/1.

59. AGCA-ST, Suchitepéquez, 6/10, 6/16.

60. AGCA, A3.30 2578 37864.

61. This town was also called Santa Catarina Sija in the mid-eighteenth century.

62. AGCA, A1.45.1 5326 44886, MG 28560 128 and 131, and Tierras, 6041 5331; AGCA-ST, Sololá 2/5, Quezaltenango, 2/15, Suchitepéquez, 6/16.

63. AGCA-ST, Retalhuleu, 1/2, 1/6, 1/10, Suchitepéquez, 6/9, Quezaltenango, 2/15. See also AHA, Cartas, Nov. 5, 1855 [1870], no. 315, Correspondence parish of Zunil, Nov. 5 [appx.], 1858.

64. AGCA-ST, Quezaltenango, 3/14, 4/5; AGCA, MG 28614 220, 28616 377 and 390, and 28638 154; AHA, Apr. 9, 1849 [1860], no. 71, Correspondence parish of Momostenango–Santa María Chiquimula, May 6, 1857, and July 13, 1865, no. 283. See also Carmack, *Historia social*, p. 248.

65. Cortés y Larraz, *Descripción*, 2: 22–23, 123; AGCA, MG 28582 194; AGCA-ST, Huehuetenango, 13/1; Davis, "Land of Our Ancestors," chap. 2.

66. Van Young, "Conflict and Solidarity."

67. Pineda de Mont, *Recopilación*, p. 493.

68. AGCA, MG 28623 143. See also MG 28615 302.

69. AHA, Cartas, Aug. 7, 1828, no. 227, and Nov. 1, 1845, no. 182; AGCA, B100.1 1418 33187; MG 28596 101, 28631 416, 28635 480, 28667 443; AGCA-ST, Guatemala, 1/14, 7/14.

70. AGCA, MG 28612 407, 28614 253, 28618 117; AHA, Cartas, Sept. 1, 1869, no. 410. For the foundation dates of specific municipalities, see Gall, *Diccionario geográfico*, and Morales Urrutia, *División política*.

71. AGCA, MG 28634 341.

72. Carmack, *Historia social*, p. 209. Davis stresses that before the middle of the century most land conflicts in which Santa Eulalia became involved were town versus town or, less often, town versus hacienda, whereas by the end of the century internal conflicts were more frequent and more commonly went "before the (ladino) law"; see "Land of Our Ancestors," p. 247.

73. AGCA, Tierras, 6033 53213, 6036 53239.

74. AGCA-ST, Alta Verapaz, 1/13; AHA, Cartas, Mar. 22, 1824, no. 80.

75. AGCA, MG 28573 170.

76. AGCA, A1.21 170 3427.

77. AGCA-ST, Sololá, 2/5.

78. Solano, *Los Mayas*, p. 145 n. 259 bis; Martínez Peláez, *Motines de indios*, pp. 38–41.

79. For a rare example of such a realization, see AGCA-ST, Sololá, 35/6.

80. On disease and epidemics in general during this period, see Solano, *Los Mayas*, p. 127; Wortman, *Government*, pp. 181–82, 262; Madigan, "Santiago Atitlán," pp. 176–85; Lovell, *Conquest and Survival*, chap. 9. For some specific outbreaks, see, in addition to Lovell above, Pinto Soria, *Estructura agraria*, pp. 14–15; AGCA, A1.14.25 177 3630, A3.6 5139 3834, B82.4 3588 82120 and 82141. Regarding vaccination of Indians against smallpox, see *El Tiempo*, Apr. 4, 1840; AHA, Cartas, Apr. 9, 1849 [1860], no. 71, Correspondence

parish of Momostenango, Oct. 1, 1855; A4.13 162 81; Carmack, *Historia social*, p. 261.

81. Although historians have noted the political effects of the cholera epidemic of 1836–37 (e.g., Wortman, *Government*, p. 262; Miceli, "Rafael Carrera," p. 75; Woodward, "Social Revolution," p. 53; and Ingersoll, "War of the Mountain," chap. 2), the details of the outbreak remain largely unstudied. Most material in the AGCA deals with Guatemala City, but see B82.4 1104 24545 f. 10, 3588 82120 and 82141, and 1105 24569. For the 1857 epidemic, see AHA, Cartas, 1857 various.

82. Woodward, "Population and Development." Madigan estimates a growth rate of one percent a year between 1830 and 1940: "Santiago Atitlán," p. 189.

83. See "Relaciones geográficas–1740," pp. 21–22 regarding the relation of trade routes to outbreaks of disease.

84. AGCA, Tierras, 6022 53101 and B100.1 1419 33382.

85. AGCA-ST, Huehuetenango, 7/8.

86. AGCA, MG 28549 2 and 7, B119.1 2504 55739, Juzgado de Primera Instancia, Criminal, Sololá, 4/248, and Totonicapán, 8/65. Carmack has discovered considerable unrest in Momostenango in these years: *Historia social*, pp. 221–44.

87. AEG, Cartas, May 20, 1886, no. 343.

88. AHA, Cartas, June 1, 1852 [1870], no. 147, Correspondence of parish San Cristóbal Totonicapán, Jan. 29, 1867; AGCA, Tierras, 6022 53101.

89. AGCA, A1.45.1 5326 44886.

90. AGCA, Tierras, 6022 53101, 6041 53313, A1.45.1 5326 44886; Juzgado de Primera Instancia, Criminal, Totonicapán 9/26; AGCA-ST, Sololá, 35/6.

91. AGCA-ST, Sololá, 2/6.

92. Ibid., 2/5; AGCA, MG 28634 216 and 28664 98.

93. AGCA, A1.22.4 206 4150.

94. AHA, Cartas, Oct. 20, 1853, no. 266.

95. Ibid., Jan. 2, 1854, no. 1; AGCA, MG 28586 200.

96. AGCA, MG 28579 227, 28586 200 and 28596 111; AGCA-ST, Suchitepéquez, 6/16; AHA, Cartas, Jan. 3, 1856 [1870], no. 5, Correspondence parish of San Antonio Suchitepéquez, Feb. 22 and 23, 1866, and Feb. 22, 1868.

97. AHA, Cartas, June 1, 1852 [1870], no. 147, Correspondence parish of San Miguel Totonicapán, Jan. 29, 1867.

98. For example: AGCA, A1.2 5529 47766; Juzgado de Primera Instancia, Criminal, Totonicapán, 7/1.

99. AGCA, MG 28598 16 and 28599 82; Juzgado de Primera Instancia, Criminal, Sololá, 17/1011.

100. AGCA, MG 28599 125, and 28600 184, 185, 186; AHA, Cartas,

June 1, 1852 [1870], no. 147, Correspondence parish of San Miguel Totonicapán, Jan. 29, 1867.

101. AGCA, MG 28599 127.

102. AGCA, Juzgado de Primera Instancia, Criminal, Sololá, 18/1098.

103. AHA, Cartas, June 8, 1867, no. 216; AGCA, MG 28610 351.

104. Gall, *Diccionario*, 2: 711.

105. AGCA, Juzgado de Primera Instancia, Criminal, Sololá, 18/1098.

106. AGCA, MG 28941 1305.

107. For the folk memories, see Instituto Indigenista de Guatemala, *Monografía*, no. 253 (Santa Catarina Ixtahuacán) and no. 270 (Nahualá).

108. There is today a large statue of Manuel Tzoc in front of the church of Nahualá.

Chapter 6

1. On the early history of coffee, see Solís, *Memorias*, chap. 49; Rubio Sanchez, "Breve historia" (largely based on Solís); and Cambranes, *Coffee and Peasants*, chap. 3. See also *La Revista*, Dec. 10, 1846, and *El Imparcial*, Oct. 21, 1963.

2. Haefkens, *Viaje a Guatemala*, p. 300.

3. *El Imparcial*, Mar. 23, 1979 (reproducing a note written by the priest of Villa Nueva in 1868); McAfee, "Agricultural Labor," p. 58; Solís, *Memorias*, pp. 666–67; *Boletín Oficial*, May 26, 1833.

4. Solís, *Memorias*, p. 930.

5. *Boletín Oficial*, May 26, 1833; *La Revista*, Dec. 10, 1846, and Feb. 25, 1847; Solís, *Memorias*, p. 931; Dunlop, *Travels*, pp. 95–96, 262.

6. Solís, *Memorias*, pp. 854–55, 935–36, 938, 943, 946, 1099–1104 n. 394; *El Noticioso*, Feb. 18, 1862.

7. *La Sociedad Económica*, Sept. 5, 1851, and Jan. 2, 1852; *La Revista*, Dec. 10, 1846; AGCA, MG 28555 Mar. 24, 1852; *Gaceta de Guatemala*, Sept. 5, 1851, and May 13, 1853; Solís, *Memorias*, pp. 851–59, 932, 936; Rubio Sánchez, "Breve historia"; Pineda de Mont, *Recopilación*, pp. 760–61.

8. AGCA, Protocolos, Cáceres, Jan. 3 and 18, 1865.

9. AGCA, Report by the Jefe Político Sacatepéquez, Apr. 26, 1862, Papers JP Sacatepéquez, 1862. The largest number of these plantings were on a single property.

10. AGCA, B100.1 3256 107; MG 28487 86.

11. Cambranes, *Coffee and Peasants*, pp. 90–93.

12. AGCA, MG 28595 62, 28614 253, 28631 405. Santa Lucía had title to 237 caballerías, of which it rented 64 caballerías to ladinos for coffee and cattle, including the 57 caballerías disputed with Herrera: AGCA, MG 28602 233.

13. AGCA, MG 28564 153 and 157.

14. AGCA, MG 28588 135.
15. AGCA, MG 28589 234.
16. AGCA, MG 28593 130 and 145, 28595 37 and 39.
17. AGCA, MG 28595 37.
18. AGCA, MG 28595 51 and 28596 91.
19. AGCA, MG 28608 128 and 28611 379.
20. AGCA, MG 28632 482, 28636 610, 28704 518.
21. Solís, *Memorias*, pp. 935, 1099–1104 n. 394.
22. AGCA, MG 28600 176; AHA, Cartas, Jan. 21, 1871, no. 63.
23. AGCA, MG 28597 180 and 28628 3.
24. The first Liberal law opened the port of Ocos: *Recopilación de las leyes de Guatemala*, 1: 4.
25. McAfee, "Agricultural Labor," p. 59 n. 196; AGCA, sub-Corregidor [Cobán]–Corregidor Verapaz, Dec. 2, 1859, Papers JP Alta Verapaz, 1859.
26. *Gaceta de Guatemala*, July 6 and 18, 1860; *El Noticioso*, Nov. 25, 1861.
27. AGCA, MG 28587 33.
28. AHA, Cartas, Apr. 2, 1867, no. 138. See also the complaints of the town of San Pedro Carchá on the same topic: AGCA, MG 28612 408.
29. E. Palacios, *Reseña de la situación*, p. 42. See also *Gaceta de Guatemala*, May 8, 1859, and July 6 and 18, 1860; *El Noticioso*, Nov. 25, 1861; *La Sociedad Económica*, Sept. 30, 1870.
30. See, for example, the photographs that date from the mid-1870's reproduced in Burns, *Eadward Muybridge*. See also Boddam-Whettam, *Central America*, pp. 83–84.
31. In AGCA, MG 28630 350 the towns of Acatenango and Santa Lucía Cotzumalguapa protest that the finca Apopaya "has reduced us to eternal slavery."
32. AGCA, MG 28578 139 1859; McAfee, "Agricultural Labor," append.
33. *La Sociedad Económica*, Sept. 30, 1870; *Boletín Oficial*, May 22, 1872.
34. AGCA, Sub-Corregidor [Cobán]–Corregidor Verapaz, Jan. 28, 1862, Papers JP Alta Verapaz, 1862.
35. For example: AGCA, 28619 260, 28622 21.
36. *La Sociedad Económica*, Apr. 13, 1868, and Aug. 9, 1869. The draft law appears in ibid., Sept. 30, Oct. 15 and 31, Nov. 30, Dec. 15 and 31, 1870, and Feb. 19, 1871. McAfee, "Agricultural Labor," pp. 70–77, provides a good summary and analysis of the proposed law.
37. On Mexico, see Katz, ed., *La servidumbre agraria*, chaps. 2–6.
38. *Sociedad Económica*, Sept. 30, 1870.
39. Solís, *Memorias*, p. 946.
40. *El Noticioso*, Dec. 2, 1861; McAfee, "Agricultural Labor," p. 60; Solís, *Memorias*, pp. 856–57.
41. AGCA, MG 28623 159. For examples of loans, see AGCA, Protocolos, Lara, Apr. 23, 1866, f. 51v; May 15, 1866, f. 76v; June 4, 1866, f. 94;

July 24, 1866, f. 119; Feb. 18, 1867, f. 10v; Mar. 9, 1866, f. 41v; and Aug. 22, 1868, f. 144. See also the loans recorded in the will of merchant J. M. Rio, Cuyotenango: Lara, Apr. 4, 1866, f. 206. Although the church limited the legal interest rate to 6 percent (AGCA, Protocolos, Cáceres, 1870 f. 132) lenders routinely charged at least twice that.

42. AGCA, Corregidor–Sub-corregidor, July 31, 1861, Papers JP Alta Verapaz, 1861; MG 28600 154.

43. Boddam-Whettham, *Across Central America*, p. 77.

44. Nañez Falcón, "Dieseldorff," p. 127. On the role of Germans in the economy, see Cambranes, *El imperialismo alemán*, and Wagner, "Actividades empresariales" and *Los alemanes*.

45. AGCA, MG 28600 162; MG 28615 320.

46. AGCA, MG 28614 122. By the end of the decade, however, in desperation the planters had undertaken just such a project; see McCreery, *Development and the State*, pp. 34–36.

47. Woodward, *Class Privilege*, chaps. 5–6.

48. Ibid., p. 79.

49. AGCA, MG 28628 43 and 51.

50. Monforte Toledo, *Guatemala*, p. 143.

51. *Gaceta de Guatemala*, Feb. 17, 1865.

52. From a series of articles in the *Gaceta de Guatemala*, arguing for a more aggressive approach to mobilizing Indian labor: Feb. 7, 16, 24, 1867; see also AGCA, Corregidor–Sub-Corregidor, Aug. 27, 1867, Papers JP Alta Verapaz, 1866–69.

53. Solís, *Memorias*, pp. 900–901.

54. Ibid., p. 858.

55. Except as noted, the several paragraphs that follow are based on McCreery, *Development and the State*. See also Herrick; *Desarrollo económico*; Cazali, "El desarrollo del café"; and Garlant, "Developmental Aspects."

56. S. Palmer, "La Civilización de los Indios."

57. On the elites before and immediately after the 1871 Revolution, see Palma Murga, "Algunas relaciones."

58. *Diario de Centro América*, Apr. 19, 1892.

59. Batres Jáuregui, *Los indios*, p. 188.

60. Ministerio de Fomento, *Memoria-1890*, annex 3, p. 29.

61. Batres Jáuregui, *Los indios*, p. 195. For a bit of satire on this, see *Diario de Centro América*, Aug. 3, 1892.

62. Regarding contests for ideas on how to "civilize" the Indians, see *La Sociedad Económica*, Sept. 1, 1880, and *Diario de Centro América*, Oct. 14, 1892.

63. Sanborn, *A Winter*, p. 83.

64. *Diario de Centro América*, Dec. 10, 1880. On education, compare Garlant, "Development Aspects," p. 49, with Burgess, *Justo Rufino Barrios*, p. 32.

65. *Diario de Centro América*, Nov. 19, 1902.

66. Burkitt, "Explorations," pp. 58–59.

67. Burgess, *Justo Rufino Barrios*, p. 163; *Recopilación . . . Guatemala*, 1: 31.

68. Díaz Castillo, *Legislación económica*, pp. 274–87.

69. AGCA, MG 28629 182; Juzgado de Primera Instancia, Criminal, Totonicapán, 9/43, San Marcos, 7/9; Municipality of Patulul, "Sentencias económicas, 1912–1913."

70. Batres Jáurequi, *Los indios*, p. 191.

71. McCreery, *Development and the State*, pp. 91–96. On the superior quality of European workers, see *El Progreso*, Sept. 27, 1874. For attitudes toward Asians, see *Diario de Centro América*, Dec. 19, 1893.

72. *Diario de Centro América*, Feb. 9, 1922.

73. Concerning the use of North American black labor to build the Northern Railroad, see "The Penny Manuscript," Special Collections, Tulane University Library. By the 1920's the region was considered safe enough by Guatemalans to work there: *El Imparcial*, Aug. 1, 1925.

74. Bauer País, *Catalogación de las leyes*, pp. 10–12; Ministerio de Fomento, *Memoria-1879*, pp. 58–79, and *Memoria-1880*, pp. 64–73. See also *Recopilación . . . Guatemala*, 2: 244–52; 3: 265–66, 339–40, 408; 4: 219–23; 43: 338–41. For newspaper comments, see *El Guatemalteco*, Feb. 11, 1878; *Diario de Centro América*, June 10 and Oct. 18, 1893, and Mar. 13, 1894. J. Mendez, *Guía del inmigrante*, is a useful contemporary guide.

75. U.S. Department of State, Records Relating to Internal Affairs of Guatemala, roll 30, July 1, 1910.

76. On the Gilbertese, see McCreery and Munro, "The Cargo of the Montserrat." Regarding Asian workers, see AGCA, Ministerio de Fomento, letter book no. 14855, Dec. 4, 1893; B129.2.15, Ministerio de Fomento, "Oficina de Particulares," no. 14964, Jan. 1894; *El Guatemalteco*, Jan. 20, 1898; *Recopilación . . . Guatemala*, 12: 342, 366–67, 393.

77. *Memoria de la Dirección de Agricultura-1902*, p. 40.

78. For more on this, see McCreery "Hegemony."

79. There was also a small mounted police force, the Montada, attached to the Ministerio de Hacienda and charged with the suppression of smuggling and the manufacture and sale of contraband alcohol.

80. Barreda, *Geografía e historia*, chap. 4. The Ministerio de Fomento, *Memoria-1924*, pp. 251–54, contains a list of telegraph offices with dates of establishment.

81. Ministerio de Fomento, *Memoria-1898*, pp. 159–66.

82. AGCA, MG 28663 74 and 28677 554; McCreery, "Land," p. 242.

83. Astúrias, *El Señor Presidente*, p. 91.

84. There are no historical studies of the army, but see McClintock, *American Connection*, chap. 1, and R. Adams, *Crucifixion by Power*, chap. 4.

85. *Recopilación . . . Guatemala*, 1: 157–69.

86. Brigham, *Guatemala*, p. 296; Boddam-Whettham, *Across Central America*, pp. 205–6.

87. Ministerio de Guerra, *Memoria-1905*, p. 56.

88. AGCA, MG 28638 216, 28762 1334.

89. See Carmack, *Historia social*, pp. 271–301, on the activities of the warlike momostecos.

90. AGCA, Indians of San Pedro Carchá–sub-Jefe Político Verapaz [Cobán], July 17, 1872, Papers JP Alta Verapaz, 1870–72.

91. AGCA, Indians of Santiago Sacatepéquez–President, May 1884, Papers JP Sacatepéquez, 1884.

92. AGCA, President–Jefe Políticos (circular), Oct. 13, 1890, Papers JP Sololá, 1890. (My emphasis.)

93. McCreery, *Development and the State.*

94. See Holleran, *Church and State*, chap. 3, which includes copies of laws, expulsion orders, etc. In the case of Las Nubes the income continued to be paid at least temporarily for the upkeep of La Merced church: AGCA, MG 28635 545. On El Incienso, see Miller, *La iglesia y el estado*, p. 174. On Palencia, see *Recopilación . . . Guatemala*, 1: 107; AGCA, MG 28635 546; AGCA-ST, Guatemala 2/13.

95. AHA, Cartas, Feb. 1, 1872, no. 78, June 15, 1872, no. 340, and Feb. 9, 1874, no. 74.

96. *Recopilación . . . Guatemala*, 1: 210.

97. Ibid., pp. 211–13. Subsequently, Decree 121 (ibid., p. 262) changed the name of the institution to Banco Nacional de Guatemala and extended its loan powers to "commerce and industry" as well as to agriculture.

98. AHA, Cartas, Sept. 10, 1873, no. 505, Sept. 18, 1873, no. 410, and Sept. 30, 1874, no. 422.

99. AGCA, B115.1 3908 66148, "Banco Nacional: Estractos de testimonios de escrituras." Probably additional properties passed into private hands by unofficial routes: e.g., AGCA-ST, Sololá, 4/7 and 12.

100. For scattered figures on government income from the sale of church lands, see Herrick, *Desarrollo económico*, pp. 228–31; also, AHA, Gobierno Eclesiástico, box 75 T6; AGCA, MG 28653 122. On problems with the Banco Nacional, see Lainfiesta, *Mis memorias*, pp. 148–49, 168–69.

101. AHA, Cartas, Nov. 4, 1873, no. 607, July n.d., 1876, no. 213, and July 10, 1878, no. 179.

102. Ibid., Oct. 21, 1885, no. 294.

103. Ibid., Oct. and Nov., 1885, various.

104. Carmack, *Historia social*, p. 259.

105. The laws of the 1820's and 1830's continued to apply into the 1890's: AGCA-ST, Huehuetenango, 12/2.

106. See *Recopilación de las leyes agrarias.*

107. Mendez Montenegro, "444 años," pp. 234–45.

108. This price was up from a minimum of 50 pesos a caballería set by Decree 172 issued in 1877: *El Guatemalteco*, Feb. 20, 1877.

109. AGCA, Sub-Jefe Político [Cobán]–Jefe Político, Jan. 23, 1874, and Jefe Político–sub-Jefe Político, Jan. 29, 1874, Papers JP Alta Verapaz, 1873–74; MG 28650 453.

110. AGCA, MG 28649 429 and 28651 598. See also MG 28642 26 and 28657 406.

111. AGCA, MG 28649 406.

112. AGCA, MG 28649 391 and 406 and 28653 69.

113. For example, AGCA, Protocolos, Córdoba and Cáceres Larrave.

114. Mendez Montenegro, "444 años," p. 133.

115. Ibid., pp. 133–41.

116. AGCA, MG 28668 478. But see also AGCA-ST, Huehuetenango, 15/3.

117. AHA, Cartas, Mar. 8, 1877, no. 82; AGCA, MG 28659 526, 28662 50, 28664 43, 28677 264, 28679 201 and 264, 28704 609; B100.1 1430 33927.

118. AGCA, MG 28629 23.

119. Cambranes, *Coffee and Peasants*, pp. 107–8.

120. AGCA, Juez Municipal San Cristóbal–Sub-Jefe Político, Aug. 17, 1874, and Jefe Político–Sub-Jefe Político, Aug. 24, 1874, Papers JP Alta Verapaz, 1873–74. See also Juez Municipal Santa Cruz–Sub-Jefe Político, Oct. 25, 1874, Papers JP Alta Verapaz, 1873–74.

121. AGCA, "Comición conciliadora en las cuestiones que surjan entre jornaleros y patrones," July 23, 1877, Papers JP Alta Verapaz, 1877.

122. Examples of departmental labor regulations include Zacapa, AGCA, MG 28643 218, Sacatepéquez, MG 28644 455, and Alta Verapaz, MG 28658 272. See also *Boletín Oficial*, May 22, June 3, and July 5, 1872, and *El Crepúsculo*, June 22, 1872. Specifically on mandamientos, see Jefe Político Sacatepéquez, Nov. 10, 1874, Papers JP Sacatepéquez, 1874.

123. *Recopilación . . . Guatemala*, 1: 457. The law did not apply to ladinos, and a provision restricting where Indians could be sent was not observed. The governor of the Alta Verapaz greeted the law with surprise, observing that "mandamientos have been in use here for some time": AGCA, Sub-Jefe Político–Jefe Político, Feb. 26, 1877, Papers JP Alta Verapaz, 1877.

124. *Recopilación . . . Guatemala*, 2: 69–75.

125. *El Guatemalteco*, July 13, 1877.

126. *La Nueva Era*, Apr. 21, 1893.

127. *Recopilación . . . Guatemala*, 3: 10–11.

128. *El Guatemalteco*, Sept. 6, 13, 21, 27, 1886.

129. *Recopilación . . . Guatemala*, 6: 213.

130. *Diario de Centro América*, Oct. 10, 1892. The winning entry was Batres Jáuregui's *Los indios*.

131. *Diario de Centro América*, Apr. 10 and 14 and Oct. 5, 1893; *La Nueva Era*, Apr. 14 and 21, 1893.

132. Skinner-Klée, *Legislación indigenista*, p. 49.

133. *Diario de Centro América*, Oct. 25, 1893; *El Republicano*, Oct. 31, 1893, and Apr. 1, 1894; *La Asamblea Legislativa*, Apr. 12, 1894.

134. *Recopilación . . . Guatemala*, 11: 362–63.

135. *El Republicano*, Apr. 1, 1894; *Disposiciones emitidas*, p. 231.

136. AGCA, President–Jefes Políticos (circular), Nov. 1, 1893, Papers JP Sololá, 1893.

137. *La República*, May 9, 1894.

138. AGCA, Estrada Cabrera Papers, Feb. 6 and 9, 1894, and Feb. 22 and Aug. 31, 1895, among many others.

139. *Diario de Centro América*, Feb. 22, 23, 24, 1894; *Disposiciones emitidas*, pp. 316–24. The quotes that follow are from Decree 486 unless otherwise noted.

140. *Asemblea Legislativa*, Apr. 10, 1894.

141. Ibid., Apr. 23, 1894.

142. AGCA, President–Jefes Políticos (circular), Sept. 18, 1897, Papers JP Sacatepéquez, 1897.

143. AGCA, Ministerio de Fomento, letter book no. 14943, Sept. 23, 1897.

144. AGCA, President–Jefes Políticos (circular), Oct. 8, 1897, Papers JP Sololá, 1897; see also Ministerio de Fomento–Jefes Políticos, Oct. 19, 1897, Papers JP Sololá, 1897, and reglamento, Oct. 30, 1897, Papers JP Alta Verapaz, 1897.

145. *Agricultura-1902*, pp. 7, 47; ?–Jefe Político, July 30, 1902, Papers JP San Marcos, 1902; *Recopilación . . . Guatemala*, 28: 12; McCreery, "An Odious Feudalism," pp. 107–8.

146. *El Guatemalteco*, Oct. 8, 1898. For what proved to be rather premature thanks, see dozens of letters in AGCA, Estrada Cabrera Papers, June 1898.

147. *El Guatemalteco*, Nov. 3, 1898, and Feb. 28, 1900; *Agricultura-1902*, p. 9; Ministerio de Fomento, letter book no. 14867, Nov. 16, 1898. On drafts for construction, see B119.21.0.0 47778 26.

Chapter 7

1. On this phenomenon, see M. Palacios, *Coffee in Colombia*, p. 13.

2. AGCA-ST, San Marcos, 26/4; Ministerio de Fomento, *Memoria-1891*, "Estadistica de Café"; Ministerio de Gobernación, *Memoria-1912*, p. 175; AGCA, Jefe Político San Marcos, "Estadísticas de la municipalidad de San Diego, 1919," Papers JP San Marcos, 1919; *Directorio oficial*, p. 391.

3. AGCA-ST, San Marcos, 32/1. This was unusual in its details of land allocation within a property. See Ramos, *O café*, pp. 303–4, for a description of El Porvenir at the turn of the century.

4. Figures from Alvarado (*Tratado*, 2: 567–68) suggest a somewhat

larger average size for coffee estates and a tendency for these to increase over time, but *World's Coffee* counts 11,000+ fincas, whereas Alvarado includes only about 2,000 of the largest properties (see note at bottom of p. 571).

5. Great Britain–Foreign Office, *Report on the Coffee Industry, 1892*, p. 6. The Guatemalan government confirmed this: AGCA, MG 28959, Sección de Tierras–Ministerio de Gobernación, Dec. 1, 1898.

6. Ministerio de Fomento, *Memoria-1900*, pp. 124–26; Ministerio de Agricultura, *Memoria-1923*, p. 74.

7. Ministerio de Agricultura, *Memoria-1923*; Dirección General de Estadística, *Censo de la República de Guatemala, 1921*, p. 15.

8. McBryde, *Cultural and Historical Geography*, pp. 23–24.

9. Ministerio de Agricultura, *Memoria-1923*, pp. 74–75.

10. AGCA, Ministerio de Fomento, letter book no. 14863, Aug. 27, 1896.

11. AGCA, workers of Chimilb–Jefe Político, Nov. 13, 1895, Papers JP Alta Verapaz, 1895; "Copia certificada del acta de contrato de los mozos de Chipaxche y Sacta," Don Lorenzo Argueta, Cahabón, 1906, Papers JP Alta Verapaz, 1906; Nañez Falcón, "Dieseldorff," pp. 209–10. On conditions for colonos in the Alta Verapaz, see Montenegro Rios, *Explotación cafetalera*, pp. 296–309.

12. Dieseldorff Papers, 63: 168. For the accounting records of Dieseldorff's company stores, see vols. 249–53.

13. For example: AGCA, various of Cumbre de Amalen–Jefe Político, Aug. 26, 1915, Papers JP Alta Verapaz, 1915.

14. Growers also sometimes acquired hot-country land on the north side of the mountains and made this available to workers in return for labor: AGCA, B119.21.0.0 47773 132 and 47788 12.

15. AGCA, B119.21.0.0 47811 98 and 47712 124; McCreery, "Land."

16. AGCA, Municipality of Sumpango, "Actos de compromisos de mozos-1922."

17. *El Imparcial*, May 23, 1930.

18. T. Adams, "San Martín Jilotepeque," p. 25.

19. Ibid., p. 25a. The estimate for German-owned fincas de mozos is based on a list of confiscated properties supplied me by J. C. Cambranes. See also Wagner, *Los alemanes*, pp. 375–81.

20. AGCA, MG 28708 1376; AGCA-ST, Quezaltenango, 11/18, 12/4, 29/7.

21. AGCA, MG 28617 62.

22. Mendez Montenegro, "444 años," pp. 123–24, 131–32.

23. AGCA, MG 28650 452.

24. *Indice . . . Archivo de la Escribanía del Gobierno y Sección de Tierras.* By 1884 individuals and communities had titled some 904 caballerías in the Costa Cuca: Ministerio de Fomento, *Memoria-1884*, annex no. 5.

25. An 1889 decree changed this to Colomba: AGCA, MG 28650 452,

MG 28646 164 and 722, and MG 28684 747. See also Gall, *Diccionario geográfico*, 1: 460. For similar examples, see MG 28646 164 and 722, and MG 28650 452.

26. Mendez Montenegro, "444 años," pp. 150–56.

27. Great Britain–Foreign Office, *Report . . . 1888*, p. 11, and *Report . . . 1889*, p. 3. For an earlier, less optimistic, evaluation, see *Report . . . 1883*, p. 1043.

28. Great Britain–Foreign Office, *Coffee . . . 1892*, p. 6.

29. Nañez Falcón, "Dieseldorff," pp. 84–102.

30. AGCA, Protocolos; Registro de Propiedad Inmueble, Guatemala.

31. AGCA-ST, Chimaltenango, 28/3 and 20/7.

32. Ibid., 14/5.

33. Ministerio de Hacienda, *Memorias*.

34. Ministerio de Fomento, *Memoria-1895*, p. 10.

35. Mendez Montenegro, "444 años," pp. 144–49. Surveyors were trained at the newly founded Escuela Politécnica: Samayoa Coronado, *La Escuela Politécnica*.

36. AGCA-ST, Sololá, 34/4. For a similar error by the same engineer, see ibid., 28/2.

37. Dieseldorff Papers, vol. 91, "Asuntos antes las autoridades," f. 4, 96, and 193v.

38. For example, a survey of Juzgado de Primera Instancia, Civil, Sololá, for the years 1880–1920 reveals few law suits over land, typically one or two a year and these of minor importance: e.g., 12/694, 12/733, and 14/857.

39. For an excellent general introduction to the small producer in coffee, see Gudmundson, *Costa Rica*, chap. 5.

40. See, for example, Registro de Propiedad Inmueble, Quezaltenango, Tomo 6 Quiché and Tomo 9 Sololá, and Registro de Propiedad Inmueble, Guatemala, Tomos 3–4, Alta Verapaz.

41. For example: AGCA-ST, Chimaltenango, 8/10, 9/2, 11/9; Watanabe, "The Demise of Communal Land tenure."

42. Alvarado, *Tratado*, 2: 571. In 1944 (Apr. 26) *El Imparcial* published figures (as of 1940) showing 3,722 holders of less than 2 acres in coffee, 5,722 holding 2–35 acres, 428 holding 36–85 acres, 435 holding 86–170 acres, and 1,147 holding more than 170 acres (total, 11,454 acres).

43. Mendez Montenegro, "444 años," p. 234; Batres Jáuregui, *Los indios*, pp. 192–95; *Agricultura-1902*, p. 15.

44. *Agricultura-1902*, p. 38.

45. *El Imparcial*, Apr. 26, 1944. The survey reported that 6,774 fincas had no machinery and another 3,110 used only "human power." See also *Informe cafetalero*, p. 146.

46. Nañez Falcón, "Dieseldorff," pp. 190–200; Dieseldorff Papers, 61: 44, 111, and 114, among many others.

47. Ministerio de Fomento, *Memoria-1889*, agricultural census (no title); Ministerio de Fomento, *Memoria-1891*, "Estadística de café." Quiñonez, *Directorio general*, indicates only two or three processing plants independent of fincas. Alvarado (*Tratado*, 2: 560) suggests indirectly the existence of one or more independent processing plants in several of the towns along the boca costa railroads.

48. AGCA, Juzgado de Primera Instancia, Civil, Sololá, 1892, 12/688.

49. Ibid., 1894, 17/970.

50. Useful on local land sales is Tax, *Penny Capitalism*, pp. 68–72. But also see Wagley, *Economics*, p. 65, and Reina, *Law of the Saints*, p. 42.

51. *Diario de Centro América*, Dec. 6, 1918.

52. AGCA, Petition to President by residents of San Cristóbal Verapaz, Aug. 26, 1915, Papers JP Alta Verapaz, 1915; G. Villatoro–Jefe Político, Sept. 7, 1906, Papers JP Alta Verapaz, 1906. See also Burkitt, "Explorations," p. 43.

53. Solís, *Memorias*, p. 901.

54. *La Sociedad Económica*, Aug. 1, 1871.

55. *Recopilación . . . Guatemala*, 1: 211–13, 262–69.

56. Lainfiesta, *Mis memorias*, pp. 168–69.

57. Jones, *Guatemala*, pp. 55–56.

58. AGCA, MG 28663 82 and 84.

59. *Banco del Occidente*, table 2. This is a very rough estimate based on a comparison of bank lending and registered mortgages.

60. AGCA, Protocolos, Córdoba, Nov. 1, 1890.

61. For a detailed examination of such costs, see Alvarado, *Tratado*, 2: chap. 12.

62. Nañez Falcón, "Dieseldorff," pp. 134–35.

63. AGCA, Protocolos, Córdoba, July 8, 1867, f. 5. For similar contracts, see Córdoba, Nov. 18, 1877, and Nov. 23, 1878, as well as contracts recorded in the books of the Registro de Propiedad Inmueble, Guatemala City.

64. For a record of small loans, with amounts and interest rates (4–6 percent a month), see the bankruptcy proceedings of Nicolas Yat, an Indian of Santa Lucia Utatlán, in AGCA, Juzgado de Primera Instancia, Civil, Sololá, 1898, 19/1159.

65. Goubaud, "Notes on the Indians of the finca Nueva Granada."

66. Young, *Currency*, chap. 3; Jones, *Guatemala*, chap. 17; Mosk, "Coffee Economy." See also G. Rodriguez, *Guatemala en 1919*, chap. 14.

67. Ramos, *O café*, p. 295.

68. *Diario de Centro América*, May 11 and Oct. 14, 1918.

69. Ramos, *O café*, pp. 320–21. See also *World's Coffee*, p. 445.

70. For a general treatment of coffee technology in Guatemala, see Dominguez, "Technological and Scientific Coffee Industry," and Alvarado, *Tratado*, vol. 2.

71. Alvarado, *Tratado*, 2: 545, 572.

72. Dominguez, "Coffee Industry," p. 245.

73. Ramos, *O café*, p. 320.

74. Alvarado, *Tratado*, 2: 465.

75. On railroads, see Anderson, "Export Transportation."

76. Wagner, "Actividades empresariales," pp. 110–14, and *Los alemanes*, pp. 214–27.

77. Alvarado, *Tratado*, 2: 473.

78. *Boletín Oficial*, May 22, July 5 and 27, 1872; *El Crepúsculo*, June 22, 1872; *La Sociedad Económica*, Sept. 1, 1880; *El Guatemalteco*, Sept. 13, 1886; *Diario de Centro América*, Nov. 28, 1890, Apr. 19 and 23, May 24 and Sept. 22, 1892, July 7 and Nov. 19, 1902. See also, Great Britain–Foreign Office, *Report . . . 1889*, p. 10, and *Report . . . 1890*, p. 4; Ministerio de Fomento, *Memoria-1890*, pp. 6–7 and annex 3, p. 29; Batres Jáuregui, *Los indios*, pp. 158, 188.

79. Alvarado, *Tratado*, 2: 479.

80. For calculations on labor needs and supply, see McCreery, "Debt Servitude," p. 758.

81. Simpson, *Repartimiento System*, p. 94. For a similar opinion, see Rhul, *Central Americans*, pp. 241–42.

82. The United Fruit Company recruited mostly foreigners before the 1920's: Wilson, *Empire in Green and Gold*. The lumber camps and the chicle industries in the Petén offered only very limited competition for the coffee growers of the Alta Verapaz: Papers JP Petén, 1900–1930.

83. *Recopilación . . . Guatemala*, 5: 187; 7: 100; 17: 352. See also *El Guatemalteco*, Sept. 21, 1886; AGCA, Ministerio de Fomento, letter book no. 14860, July 23, 1895; Grieb, *Guatemalan Caudillo*, pp. 128–30.

84. For example: AGCA, Tucurú–Jefe Político, Mar. 22, 1880, Papers JP Alta Verapaz, 1880; Ministerio de Fomento, letter book no. 14867, Jan. 13 and 15, 1905. Finqueros did occasionally volunteer their workers for roads that would be of immediate benefit to them: McCreery, *Development and the State*, pp. 34–35. For the Indians' attitude toward roads, see AGCA, MG 28628 13 and 51.

85. AGCA, Ministerio de Fomento, letter books no. 14852, Aug. 31, 1899.

86. G. Rodriguez, *Guatemala en 1919*, p. 104.

87. Among many other conflicts, see AGCA, Municipality San Crisóbal Verpaz–Jefe Político, Mar. 12, 1897, Papers JP Alta Verapaz; Comisionado Político San Antonio AC–Jefe Político, Feb. 3, 1897, Papers JP Sacatepéquez, 1897; petitions, Santo Tomás Chichicastenango, Feb. 22, 1895, and Cubulco and Rabinal, Aug. 31, 1895, four mozos, San Bartolo, Jan. 10, 1898, and Santo Tomás Chichicastenango, Jan. 24, 1898, Estrada Cabrera Papers.

88. *Diario de Centro América*, July 24, 1920; G. Rodriguez, *Guatemala en 1919*, pp. 68–73.

89. AGCA, Comandante Local Patulul–Jefe Político, Sept. 9, 1881, Papers JP Sololá, 1881.

90. AGCA, various growers–Jefe Político, Oct. 18, 1910, Papers JP Alta Verapaz, 1910.

91. *Agricultura-1902*, p. 7; G. Rodriguez, *Guatemala en 1919*, pp. 73, 81; *Diario de Centro América*, July 24, 1920; *Diario del Occidente*, Aug. 30, 1898; *El Imparcial*, July 13, 1922; AGCA, Ministerío de Fomento, letter book no. 14929, Oct. 31, 1901.

92. *Agricultura-1902*, p. 47; G. Rodriguez, *Guatemala en 1919*, p. 72; AGCA, Comandante Local Patulul–Jefe Político, Feb. 22, Papers JP Sololá, 1905; Sociedad Agrícola y Cia.–Jefe Político, May 9, 1920, Papers JP Sololá, 1920; Comandante de Armas Livingston–Jefe Político, Oct. 22, 1915, Papers JP Alta Verapaz, 1915; *Diario de Centro América*, July 24, 1920; Administrator of finca El Salto–President Reina Barrios, July 14 and 18, 1895, Estrada Cabrera Papers.

93. Except where noted, this section is based on McCreery, "An Odious Feudalism."

94. AGCA, Jefe Político–Sub-Jefe Político [Cobán], Sept. 3, 1874, Papers JP Alta Verapaz, 1873–74; *Diario de Centro América*, Dec. 6, 1918.

95. AGCA, petitions, Santa María de Jesús, Aug. 20 and 21, 1886, and San Lucas Sacatepéquez, May 10 and Aug. n.d., 1886, E. Lehnoff–Jefe Político, June 21, Aug. 23, and Sept. 1 and 2, 1886, and President–Jefe Político Sacatepéquez, Aug. 21, 1886, Papers JP Sacatepéquez, 1886. For similar complaints regarding health conditions, see Sumpango–Jefe Político, May 20, 1886, Santiago Sacatepéquez–Jefe Político, July n.d., 1886, Papers JP Sacatepéquez 1886, and Alotenango–Jefe Político, June 2, 1887, Papers JP Sacatepéquez 1887.

96. AGCA, A.S.–Jefe Político, Mar. 21, 1901, Papers JP Santa Rosa, 1901. On the damage done to agriculture by the eruption of Santa María, see AGCA, Ministerio de Fomento, letter book no. 14895. On the Proveeduría, see circular, President–Jefes Políticos, Nov. n.d., 1902, Papers JP Sololá, 1902; see also *Diario de Centro América*, Nov. 20 and Dec. 11, 1902, and Ministerio de Fomento, *Memoria-1903*, p. 21.

97. *El Correo de Escuintla*, May 1, 1906; AGCA, Ministerio de Fomento, letter book no. 14895, Apr. 19, 1904. After 1900, when the mandamiento no longer officially existed, the jefes políticos generally had to clear requests by telegraph with the President or the Ministry of Development.

98. Ramos, *O café*, p. 310. See also Great Britain–Foreign Office, *Report* ... *1893*, p. 4; Batres Jáuregui, *Los indios*, p. 162; G. Rodriguez, *Guatemala en 1919*, pp. 104–6; AGCA, E. Lehnoff–Jefe Político Sacatepéquez, Sep. 1, 1886, Papers JP Sacatepéquez, 1886.

99. AGCA, MG 28665, Sept. 21, 1878.

100. AGCA, Estrada Cabrera Papers, Sept. 10, 1905.

101. *Diario de Centro América*, Jan. 29, 1919. See also ibid., Feb. 1, May 3, and Sept. 20, 1919, and G. Rodriguez, *Guatemala en 1919*, pp. 80–82.

102. AGCA, aldea Socales–Municipality Santa Lucía Cotzumalguapa, Oct. 10, 1910, Papers JP Escuintla, 1910; San Lucas Tolimán–Jefe Político, Jan. 22, 1914, Papers JP Sololá, 1914. See also Comisionado Político Patulul–Jefe Político, Feb. 20, 1905, Papers JP Sololá, 1905.

103. For example: AGCA, Ministerio de Fomento, letter books no. 14856, Oct. 28, 1893, no. 14862, June 26, 1896, no. 14864, June 2, 1897, and no. 14870, Aug. 7, 1900.

104. AGCA, Comisionado Político–Jefe Político, Feb. 22, 1905, Papers JP Sololá, 1905.

105. AGCA, Ministerio de Fomento, letter book no. 14864, Nov. 26, 1897.

106. Except as noted, the following section is based on McCreery, "Debt Servitude."

107. AGCA, MG 28939, Mar. 24, 1898.

108. AGCA, Indians–Finca Primavera, Nov. 12, 1915, Papers JP Alta Verapaz, 1915, Juez Municipal San Lucas Tolimán–Jefe Político, July 9, 1923, Papers JP Sololá, 1923, various–Jefe Político, Dec. 6, 1930, Papers JP Alta Verapaz, 1930; MG 29000 2642; Estrada Cabrera Papers, Jan. 6, 1895.

109. Dieseldorff Papers, 91: 95; AGCA, Estrada Cabrera Papers, June 5, 1898; Alvarado, *Tratado*, 2: 470–71.

110. On the operation of the system in one town, see T. Adams, "San Martín Jilotepeque," pp. 27–29. See also Colby and van den Berghe, *Ixil Country*, pp. 72–73.

111. This is despite the fact that the 1921 census (Dirección General de Estadística, *Censo . . . 1921*) reported only seven persons who gave this as their occupation.

112. AGCA, Report of Jefe Político, Oct. 6, 1926, Papers JP Quiché, 1920–29. These were only the habilitadores who paid their taxes. By contrast, in 1936 the jefe político reported only 36 labor agents authorized for the department: Ministerio de Agricultura, *Memoria-1937*, p. 539.

113. For example: AGCA, B119.21.0.0 47733 nos. 5 and 30; contract, May 20, 1906, Papers JP San Marcos, 1906.

114. T. Adams, "San Martín Jilotepeque," p. 28; AGCA, Juzgado de Primera Instancia, Civil, Huehuetenango, 1898, Soc. Hamburgesa vs. Juan Herrera, and 1904, Antonio Fernandez vs. Bernardo Pérez.

115. On the operations of the contratistas, see *El Imparcial*, Nov. 21, 1922, Nov. 1, 19, and 24, 1923, and Feb. 6 and 24, 1924.

116. For example: AGCA, T.S.–Jefe Político, Nov. 17, 1895, Papers JP Quiché, 1890 (*sic*), and finca La Esterlína–Jefe Político, Jan. 6, 1926, Papers JP Sololá, 1926; S. Shitumul, June 14, 1898, Estrada Cabrera Papers; Ministerio de Fomento, letter book no. 14867, Nov. 25, 1898; B119 47743 no. 196 and 47773 no. 18.

117. AGCA, B119.21.0.0 47759 321. Similarly, finca Helvetia protested that its habilitador in San Juan Ixcoy was "seducing" company workers to go to other fincas (B119.21.0.0 47775 241), and another owner found that his recruiter had been fraudulently canceling workers' debts so that he could recontract them for other employers: B119.21.0.0 47768 36.

118. AGCA, B119.21.0.0 47782 6. Edited.

119. AGCA, Ministerio de Fomento, letter book no. 14869, July 24, 1899, and no. 14973, July 31, 1903; circular, Feb. 11, 1897, Papers JP Sololá, 1897; Estrada Cabrera Papers, Aug. 4, 1896; El Imparcial, Aug. 9, 1922.

120. El Imparcial, Aug. 16, 1923.

121. AGCA, Ministerio de Fomento, letter book, no. 14929, Oct. 31, 1901; B119.21.0.0, 47768 23, 47772 12, and 47743 161; Juez Municipal San Pablo Laguna–Jefe Político, Apr. 20, 1899, Papers JP Sololá, 1899; N.F.–Jefe Político, May 6, 1920, Papers JP Quiché, 1920–29; Diario del Occidente, Aug. 30, 1898; G. Rodriguez, Guatemala en 1919, p. 104.

122. AGCA, Juzgado de Primera Instancia, Civil, Huehuetenango, 1904, 27/40. On the activities of one local secretary, see Burkitt, "Explorations," p. 57.

123. AGCA, B119.21.0.0 47754 17; El Imparcial, Apr. 5, 1924.

124. Diario de Centro América, Apr. 19, 1892. See also AGCA, MG 28664 43; Alcalde Carchá–Jefe Político, Sept. 3, 1880, Papers JP Alta Verapaz, 1880; Comisionado Político San Lucas Sacatepéquez–JP Sacatepéquez, May 20, 1889, Papers JP Sacatepéquez, 1889; El Imparcial, Mar. 13, 1925.

125. Quoted in T. Adams, "San Martín Jilotepeque," p. 41. The quote refers specifically to the Ubico years, but resistance in this form was common throughout the period.

126. AGCA, MG 28664 43; Comisionado Político San Lucas Sacatepéquez–Jefe Político, May 20, 1889, Papers JP Sacatepéquez, 1889; Comisionado Político Santa Lucía MA–Jefe Político, Oct. 15, 1906, Papers JP Sacatepéquez, 1906; Finca La Luz–Jefe Político, Aug. 9, 1896, Papers JP Sololá, 1896; B119.21.0.0 47732 5; Ministerio de Fomento, letter book no. 14866, May 6 and Oct. 9, 1898, and no. 14968, May 23, 1898; Finca Buena Vista–Jefe Político, Aug. 29, 1906, Papers JP San Marcos, 1906.

127. AGCA, Ministerio de Fomento, letter book no. 14869, Mar. 26, 1898; Santiago Sacatepéquez–Jefe Político, Apr. 27, 1883, Papers JP Sacatepéquez, 1883; D.A.–Jefe Político, Nov. 22, 1920, Papers JP Sololá, 1920; G. Guamax–Jefe Político, Jan. 11, 1929, Papers JP Sololá, 1929; B119.21.0.0 47743 161 and 47778 1918. See also Lincoln, "Ixil Indians."

128. McCreery, "Debt Servitude," p. 749.

129. Ramos, O café, p. 306.

130. McCreery, "Debt Servitude," pp. 751–52.

131. On the problems for the planters this system entailed, see Alvarado, Tratado, 2: 465–70.

132. AGCA, B119.21.0.0 47793 no. 30; Alvarado, Tratado, 2: 470–74.

133. *El Trabajo*, Sept. 30, 1904.

134. AGCA, A.G.–Jefe Político, June 25, 1895, Papers JP Alta Verapaz, 1895.

135. For example: AGCA, B119.21.0.0 47745 330; A.C.–Jefe Político, Nov. 19, 1922, Papers JP San Marcos, 1922; D.P.–Jefe Político, Aug. 27, 1925, Papers JP Quiché 1920–29. See also Burkitt, "Explorations," pp. 58–59.

136. AGCA, B119.21.0.0 47745 330. See also 47779 5, and 47807 8; Ministerio de Fomento, letter book no. 14856, Aug. 2, 1893, no. 14868, Aug. 9, 1899, and no. 14891, June 13, 1902; Herrera–Jefe Político, June 6, 1900, Papers JP Sacatepéquez, 1900; Finca Milan–Jefe Político, Mar. 3, 1906, Papers JP Sololá, 1906; Fleischmann–Jefe Político Feb. 21 and Apr. 30, 1906, Papers JP San Marcos, 1906; various finqueros–Jefe Político, Nov. 12, 1906, and Stucken y Andersen–Jefe Político, Aug. 10, 1906, Papers JP Alta Verapaz, 1906; Kriell–Jefe Político, Oct. n.d., 1909, Papers JP San Marcos, 1909.

137. AGCA, Finca San Andrés Osuna–Comandante Local Siquinala, Sept. 10, 1905, Papers JP Escuintla, 1905. See also administrator finca ?–Jefe Político, Sept. 10, 1923, Papers JP Sololá, 1923, and various, Papers JP Alta Verapaz, 1915.

138. AGCA, Cia. Hamburgesa de Plantaciones–Jefe Político, Sept. 4, 1906, Papers JP San Marcos, 1906; various finqueros Cobán–Jefe Político, Nov. 12, 1906, Papers JP Alta Verapaz, 1906; ?–Jefe Político, Jan. 12, 1915, Papers JP San Marcos, 1915; Rivera–Jefe Político, Aug. 19, 1926, Papers JP Sololá, 1926; Finca Madrid–Jefe Político, Aug. 6, 1930, Papers JP Sololá, 1930; Ministerio de Fomento, letter book no. 14918, Nov. 24, 1913; *El Imparcial*, May 5, 1924.

139. *Diario de Centro América*, May 3, 1919.

140. AGCA, M.P.–Jefe Político, July 12, 1889, Papers JP Sacatepéquez, 1889.

141. *El Imparcial*, Aug. 24, 1922.

142. For example: AGCA, circular, Ministerio de Fomento–Jefes Políticos, Sept. 19, 1903, Papers JP Izabal, 1903.

143. AGCA, B119.21.0 47757 1, 47770 20, 47790 86 and 90.

144. AGCA, B119.21.0.0 47772 61.

145. AGCA, B119.21.0.0 47733 17, 47735 no. 43, and 47748 no. 260; N.M.–Jefe Político, Oct. 12, 1905, Papers JP Alta Verapaz, 1905; Juez Municipal Santa Lucía Utatlán–Jefe Político, Jan. 21, 1881, and D.D./P.D.–President, Aug. 27, 1881, Papers JP Sololá, 1881; 10 Indians–Jefe Político, May 17, 1890, Papers JP Sololá, 1890; various Indians–Jefe Político, Sept. 15, 1900, Papers JP Alta Verapaz, 1900.

146. See, for example, rare advertisements of fincas for sale including mozo debts in *El Progreso Nacional*, May 3 and 4, 1898.

147. AGCA, B119.21.0.0 47743 149 and 47745 342.

148. For example: AGCA, 6 mozos–Jefe Político, Apr. 7, 1896, Papers JP Sololá, 1896.

149. AGCA, B119.21.0.0 47733 17. (Note: this is the second no. 17.)

150. AGCA, Comisionado Político Patulul–finqueros, Jan. 23, 1896, Papers JP Sololá, 1896; *Diario de Centro América*, Feb. 20, 1906; Skinner-Klée, *Legislación indigenista*, p. 86; Ministerio de Fomento, *Memoria-1906*, p. 98.

151. AGCA, Finca Concepción Candelaria–Mailandia, Sept. 12, 1924, Papers JP San Marcos, 1924–25; *El Norte*, June 5, 1937.

152. AGCA, B119.21.0.0 47760 392 and 47768 36.

153. See, for example, Great Britain–Foreign Office, *Coffee . . . 1892*, pp. 3, 8.

154. G. Rodriguez, *Guatemala en 1919*, pp. 137–38. See also *Diario de Centro América*, Apr. 25, 1924; Wagner, "Actividades empresariales" and *Los alemanes*; Cambranes, *Imperialismo alemán*; AGCA, MG 28763 1436; B119.21.0.0 47749 333; Ministerio de Fomento, letter book no. 14874, Sept. 24, 1913.

155. For an angry exchange in print between the jefe político and some of the foreign planters in the Alta Verapaz in 1892, see *Diario Oficial*, Aug. 20, 1892, and *Diario de Centro América*, Sept. 22, 1892. See also AGCA, Finca Armenia vs. Santa Rosalia, Jan. 9, 1934, Papers JP San Marcos, 1934; B119.21.0.0 47735 55.

156. *Diario de Centro América*, Sept. 20, 1919.

157. *El Imparcial*, Aug. 23, 1930.

158. Ibid., Apr. 29, 1931.

159. Great Britain–Foreign Office, *Coffee . . . 1892*, p. 2.

160. Wagner, "Actividades empresariales," pp. 100–102. A Hamburg consortium also owned Trapiche Grande in Suchitepéquez with an area of almost 1,500 caballerías, but most of this remained uncultivated and none was in coffee. See also Great Britain–Foreign Office, *Report . . . 1898*, pp. 4–5.

161. Much of this had been involuntary: Ramos, *O café*, pp. 317–18.

162. Wagner, "Actividades empresariales," p. 103.

163. *Recopilación . . . Guatemala*, 37: 19; Wagner, "Actividades empresariales," pp. 119–21; Dinwoodie, "Expedient Diplomacy," pp. 153–59.

164. Wagner, "Actividades empresariales," p. 120, and *Los alemanes*, pp. 280–82.

165. *El Imparcial*, Apr. 25, 1924; Cambranes, *Imperialismo alemán*; Wagner, "Actividades empresariales," pp. 115–21.

166. *El Imparcial*, Feb. 6 and 16 and Apr. 10, 1928, and Aug. 23, 1930.

Chapter 8

1. On change and the perception of change in land tenure and use, see, among others, Wagley, *Economics*, pp. 61–63; Bunzel, *Chichicastenango*, pp. 16–25; and W. Smith, *Fiesta System*, pp. 164–65.

2. Davis, "Land of Our Ancestors," pp. 2–3 and chap. 3.

3. For this idea, see Falla, *Quiché rebelde*, p. 280.

4. Hill and Monaghan (*Continuities*) found traces in at least one community of an intermediary group, the *amaq'*, as yet little studied.

5. Davis, "Land of Our Ancestors," p. 28 and chap. 3.

6. Bunzel, *Chichicastenango*, p. 17.

7. Women may also inherit land in most communities, but more commonly they inherit animals or money or other forms of moveable property that they can take to their married household. But see, for example, Tax, *Penny Capitalism*, p. 72.

8. On generational struggles, see, for example, Bunzel, *Chichicastenango*, pp. 22–23, 139–43. On patterns of inheritance and the conflicts these entail, see Davis, "Land of Our Ancestors," chaps. 4–6, and Tax, *Penny Capitalism*, pp. 72–80.

9. Probably typically, the older Indians of Santa Eulalia remember the Reforma as the time of the "law of titles": Davis, "Land of Our Ancestors," p. 49.

10. AGCA, MG 28664 43, MG 28658 293, and MG 28683 102; Tax, *Penny Capitalism*, pp. 57–59; Wagley, *Economics*, p. 63. See also Stadelman, "Maize Cultivation."

11. See, for example, AGCA-ST, San Marcos, 20/7.

12. AGCA, MG 28681 436; AHA, Cartas, 1893, no. 181, July 2, 1893.

13. On Indian elites and their power and wealth in one town (Santiago Atitlán), see Orellana, *Tzutujil Mayas*, chap. 7, and Madigan, "Santiago Atitlán," chap. 5.

14. Davis, "Land of Our Ancestors," p. 34.

15. Bunzel, *Chichicastenango*, p. 17. See also Wagley, *Economics*, p. 64.

16. Davis, "Land of Our Ancestors," pp. 7–8 and chap. 6.

17. See, for example, ibid., pp. 42–43.

18. Jonas and Tobis, eds., *Guatemala*, p. 19; Grieshaber, "Hacienda-Indian Community Relations," p. 119; King, *Cobán*, p. 30; Nash, "Mid-Nineteenth Century Economic Change," p. 173.

19. Handy, *Gift of the Devil*, p. 72; Carmack, *Historia social*, pp. 264–69; Cambranes, *Coffee and Peasants*, pp. 270–71.

20. Warren, *Symbolism*, p. 180.

21. For more on this, see McCreery, "State Power."

22. Instituto Indigenista de Guatemala, *Monografía*, no. 264 (Pochuta).

23. Mendez Montenegro, "444 años," p. 213. But see also ibid., p. 228.

24. For example: AGCA-ST, Alta Verapaz 4/2, 4/8, 6/1, 10/4, 13/10.

25. Ibid., 4/8.

26. Ibid., 10/4. See ibid., 26/3 for detailed examples of the costs of land measurement, fraud, theft (by a member of the community), bribery, and incompetence.

27. An 1889 law (Mendez Montenegro, "444 años," pp. 216–17) provided that each of the "Indian residents of the Alta Verapaz" was to receive 200

cuerdas [of 25 varas] land in order to avoid "that a great number of them should become reduced to the condition of colonos, with no future except to be exploited by the large owners." However, there is no evidence that the law went into effect.

28. McBryde, *Cultural and Historical Geography*, pp. 24, 34. On the impact of diseases on Alta Verapaz Indians who did settle in the lowlands, see Dieseldorff Papers, vol. 91, no. 69, Apr. 23, 1926.

29. AGCA-ST, Quezaltenango 29/7.

30. Ibid., 11/18.

31. Ibid., 25/2, 25/16, 29/7. For a similar case from nearby Concepción Chiquirichapa, see ibid., 14/2.

32. Mendez Montenegro, "444 años," pp. 213–14.

33. See, for example, *Indice . . . Archivo de la Escribanía*, pp. 107–12, 153–69. For detailed examples, see Davis, "Land of Our Ancestors," pp. 52–69 (Santa Eulalia/Barillas), and AGCA, MG 28582 194, AGCA-ST, Quiché 3/6, 16/8, 18/3, and 20/3 and 5, and Registro de Propiedad Inmueble, Quezaltenango, no. 344 f. 136 tomo 4, Quiché (Nebaj).

34. McBryde, *Geography*, p. 16, indicates that in the 1930's Santo Tomás La Unión was the only large Indian-dominated town in the Pacific boca costa.

35. Saler, "Road to El Palmar," pp. 25–26.

36. AGCA, MG 28645 653.

37. AGCA, MG 28645 654.

38. Lincoln, "Ixil Indians."

39. AGCA, Ministerio de Fomento–Jefe Político, Nov. 2, 1921, Papers JP Sacatepéquez, 1921.

40. AGCA-ST, Huehuetenango, 15/3.

41. Browning, *El Salvador*, pp. 203–13; Menjivar, *Acumulación originaria*; Wheelock, *Imperialismo*, chaps. 2 and 3.

42. AGCA, MG 28658 177.

43. AGCA, B100 33713 1423 and 33758 1424; AGCA-ST, Guatemala 4/5A, 4/11, 5/5, 6/5.

44. AHA, Cartas, Mar. 8, 1877, no. 82; AGCA-ST, Quiché, 11/8.

45. See, for example, AGCA, MG 28674 143.

46. AGCA, MG 28675 353, 28678 577, 28690 371.

47. AGCA-ST, Quiché, 7/6.

48. AGCA-ST, Chiquimula 4/11, 6/11.

49. AGCA-ST, Chimaltenango, 11/9.

50. McBryde, *Geography*, p. 24; Stadelman, "Maize Cultivation," pp. 105–6.

51. For an appraisal of "justice" in Guatemala in these years, see G. Rodriguez, *Guatemala en 1919*, chap. 7.

52. Davis, "Land of Our Ancestors," p. 50.

53. Mendez Montenegro, "444 años," pp. 250–53. For the experiences

of two communities, see AGCA-ST, Alta Verapaz, 26/3 and Huehuetenango, 17/5.

54. AGCA-ST, Quiché, 16/8, 18/3, 20/3 and 5.

55. For example, see, among dozens of others, AGCA-ST, Huehuetenango 11/1, 12/2, 24/1, and 34/5; Chimaltenango 9/2 and 11/9; Chiquimula 6/11; Quiché 7/6 and 11/8; Guatemala 3/9 and 17/11; and Sololá 7/7 and 9/5.

56. AGCA-ST, Huehuetenango 12/2.

57. Mendez Montenegro, "444 años," pp. 193–94.

58. AGCA-ST, Guatemala, 17/11 and 28/9; AGCA, B100.1 1425 33840 and 1427 33882.

59. AGCA-ST, Sololá, 9/5.

60. AGCA-ST, Quezaltenango, 12/4, 14/2, 21/3, 25/1, 50/2.

61. AGCA, MG 28658 188 and 190, and 28670 266; AGCA-ST, Sololá, 6/7, 7/7, 8/5, 31/6. See also Orellana, *Tzutujil Mayas*, p. 54–56, and Madigan, "Santiago Atitlán," append. 5.

62. AGCA, MG 28658 152 and 319, 29659 380, 28665 324 and 378, 28672 431; AGCA-ST, Totonicapán, 4/10.

63. AGCA, MG 28658 108; AGCA-ST, Quezaltenango, 6/2, 9/13, 17/6, 19/19, 37/4. At the same time, the highland towns were also seeking land in their immediate areas: AGCA-ST, Totonicapán, 4/2, 4/7, 5/7, and Quezaltenango, 33/10, 37/5.

64. Registro de Propiedad Inmueble, Quezaltenango, no. 1160 f. 219 tomo 4, Huehuetenango; Davis, "Land of Our Ancestors," pp. 52–62; AGCA-ST, Quiché, 5/6, 7/2 and 7, 20/3 and 5, 22/8, 24/6.

65. AGCA-ST, Huehuetenango 23/7. For similar activities by other settlements in the municipality, see 23/10 (Manzanillo), 20/1 (Pajuil and País Pericon), and 23/3 (Chex).

66. See, for example, AGCA-ST, Totonicapán, various; Carmack, *Historia social*, pp. 285–86; Davis, "Land of Our Ancestors," chap. 3; Madigan, "Santiago Atitlán," chap. 5.

67. AGCA-ST, Alta Verapaz, 6/1. See also AGCA, Protocolos, Córdoba, Jan. 3, 1890, f. 1, May 31, 1893, f. 167v; Registro de Propiedad Inmueble, Guatemala, tomo 3 Primera Serie, no. 220 f. 15, no. 229 f. 122, and no. 298 f. 121, and tomo 4 Primera Serie, no. 250 f. 52 and no. 257 f. 62, Alta Verapaz.

68. AGCA-ST, Quiché, 26/7.

69. AGCA-ST, Huehuetenango, 11/2 and 13/1.

70. AGCA-ST, Quiché, 17/10; *El Imparcial*, July 1, 1924; Elliot, "Men of Corn."

71. AGCA-ST, Sololá, 2/21, 3/20, 4/20, 9/5, 21/7, 35/10; AGCA, MG 28939 913.

72. McCreery, "State Power," p. 109 and n. 21.

73. Most of the riots that did occur after 1871 were grouped in the early 1870's, before the new government had consolidated control of the country-

side: AGCA-ST, Huehuetenango, 7/8, Quezaltenango, 5/1, and Totonicapán, 2/7; Carmack, *Historia social*, pp. 262–69; AGCA, Juzgado Primera Instancia, Criminal, Sololá, 25/1424 and 43/2168; MG 28638 216 and 28762 1334.

74. Carmack, *Historia social*, p. 267; McCreery, "Land," p. 242.

75. For example, AGCA-ST, Quezaltenango, 11/18, 12/4, and 14/2, and Sololá 8/5.

76. Instituto Indigenista de Guatemala, *Monografía*, no. 264 (Pochuta).

77. Maudsley and Maudsley, *Glimpse at Guatemala*, p. 108; AGCA, Juzgado de Primera Instancia, Criminal, Baja Verapaz, 38/4, 39/4, 61/22, 65/12, 66A/39, 68A/10.

78. AGCA-ST, Baja Verapaz, 15A. For other similar conflicts in the same region, see AGCA, MG 28628 42, 28673 319, 28644 462, 28711 100, 28687 33; AGCA-ST, Jutiapa, 3/6 and 3/11.

79. AGCA, MG 28635 517, 28636 583, 28645 568, 28646 774; AGCA-ST, Huehuetenango, 10/4; Registro de Propiedad Inmueble, Quezaltenango, no. 27 f. 122 tomo 2, Huehuetenango.

80. AGCA, MG 28718 and MG 28719, for example, are alive with such conflicts. For two specific cases, that of San Miguel Totonicapán versus its neighbors and Santa Lucía versus Santa Cruz La Laguna, see AGCA-ST, Totonicapán, 3/16, 4/2, 4/7; AGCA, Juzgado de Primera Instancia, Criminal, Sololá, 25/1424; and AGCA, MG 28653 4 and 28698 305.

81. AGCA-ST, Huehuetenango, 7/8.

82. AGCA-ST, Totonicapán, 4/2 and 4/7.

83. AGCA-ST, Quiché, 2/12.

84. AGCA-ST, Huehuetenango, 11/5, 11/9 and 10, 12/4 and 7, 17/5, 34/3.

85. Falla, *Quiché rebelde*, chap. 4, part 5.

86. Bunzel, *Chichicastenango*, p. 19. By contrast, the first land documents in the municipal archives of Santiago Chimaltenango date from the late 1940's: Watanabe, "Demise of Communal Land Tenure"; Wagley, *Economics*, p. 65.

87. Lincoln, "Ixil Indians."

88. AGCA-ST, Chimaltenango, 4/4.

89. AGCA-ST, Guatemala, 6/8.

90. *Diario de Centro América*, May 3, 1918.

91. A typical case was that of the ladino town of Zaragosa, which obtained 50 caballerías from the neighboring Indian municipality of Chimaltenango, first in forced rental and then as property: AGCA-ST, Chimaltenango, 26/2.

92. Just how many of these there were is open to debate. Carol Smith estimates that the number doubled: "Origins of the National Question," n. 16.

93. See AGCA, MG 28632 482 for details on the rationale for this. For additional examples, see Skinner-Klée, *Legislación indigenista*, pp. 33, 46, 50, 94.

94. AGCA, MG 28650 525, 28652 21, 28654 145, 28662 39.

95. AGCA-ST, Guatemala, 4/13B.

96. AGCA, B119.21.0.0, 47768 n.n. and 47784 5; Davis, "Land of Our Ancestors," p. 213.

97. The term secretario applied also to anyone who was literate and did written work for others. They, too, were well placed to acquire land at others' expense: AGCA, MG 28940 1106. See also Paul, "Entrepreneurs."

98. AGCA, MG 28806 1328.

99. AGCA, Petition–President, Aug. 31, 1910, Papers JP Alta Verapaz, 1910.

Chapter 9

1. On the Indians' vision of working for the "Spanish," see Warren, *Symbolism*, chap. 2.

2. Burkitt, "Explorations," p. 45.

3. This and the following two quotes come from an untitled manuscript on the oral history of San Pedro La Laguna compiled by Ben Paul.

4. AGCA, Indians Carchá–Sub-Jefe Político, Mar. 16, 1875, Papers JP Alta Verapaz, 1875; Cofradías Carchá–President, Mar. n.d., 1880, Papers JP Alta Verapaz, 1880; Comisionado Político San Lucas Sacatepéquez–Jefe Político, May 20, 1889, Papers JP Sacatepéquez, 1889. Money was forced upon the municipal officials themselves: Juez Municipal San Juan Bautista–Jefe Político, Oct. 28, 1887, Papers JP Sololá, 1887.

5. Tax, *Penny Capitalism*, p. 106.

6. AGCA, Común/Principales of Santiago Sacatepéquez–President, Sept. 3, 1885, Papers JP Sacatepéquez, 1885. See also: Indians Santiago Sacatepéquez–Jefe Político, July n.d., 1886, and Indians Sumpango–Jefe Político, May 20, 1886, Papers JP Sacatepéquez, 1886; Juez Municipal Carchá–Sub-Jefe Político, Mar. 27, 1873, Papers JP Alta Verapaz, 1873–74; Alotenango–Jefe Político, June 2, 1887, Papers JP Sacatepéquez, 1887; Sumpango–Jefe Político, June 9, 1888, Papers JP Sacatepéquez, 1888; Jocopilas–Jefe Político, Oct. 15, 1889, Papers JP Quiché, 1889; San Antonio AC–Jefe Político, Aug. 4, 1902, Papers JP Sacatepéquez, 1902; B119.21.0.0 47746 75.

7. Paul, oral history of San Pedro La Laguna.

8. AGCA, Cahabón–Comisionado Político Senajú, Dec. 20, 1880, Papers JP Alta Verapaz, 1880.

9. AGCA, B119.21.0.0 47743 #179. Food brought by the mandamiento workers usually consisted of dried tortilla meal, called *totoposte*, which lasted a week or two.

10. AGCA, Indians Santa María de Jesús–President, Aug. 21, 1887, Papers JP Sacatepéquez, 1887.

11. On tasks, see Alvarado, *Tratado*, 2: part 9.

12. AGCA, Comisionado Agrícola–Jefe Político, Aug. 18, 1880, and Cahabón–Comisionado Político Senajú, Dec. 20, 1880, Papers JP Alta Verapaz, 1880; Comisionado Político Magdalena–Jefe Político Sacatepéquez, Jan. 27, 1883, and Comisionado Político San Antonio AC–Jefe Político, June 23,

1883, Papers JP Sacatepéquez, 1883; Lanquín–Jefe Político, Mar. 13, 1885, San Pedro Carchá–Jefe Político, Sept. 5, 1885, and Comisionado Agrícola Carchá–Jefe Político, Nov. 4, 1885, Papers JP Alta Verapaz, 1885; Juez Municipal Alotenango–Jefe Político, Oct. 9, 1920, Papers JP Sacatepéquez, 1920; B119.21.0.0 47757 8 and 47770 54.

13. AGCA, San Andrés Sajcabaja–Jefe Político Quiché, Dec. 3, 1890, Papers JP Quiché, 1890.

14. AGCA, Comisionado Político Sumpango–Jefe Político, Feb. 28, 1883, Papers JP Sacatepéquez, 1883.

15. AGCA, B119.21.0.0 47749 350.

16. AGCA, Juez Municipal Chamelco–Jefe Político, Apr. 15, 1875, Papers JP Alta Verapaz, 1875. See also Juez Municipal San Antonio Palopó–Jefe Político, June 24, 1902, Papers JP Sololá, 1902; Santa Cruz Quiché, Jan. 4, 1894, Estrada Cabrera Papers.

17. AGCA, B119.21.0.0 47774 186.

18. AGCA, B119.21.0.0 47770 54.

19. AGCA, various Indians (town not identified)–Jefe Político, Apr. 12, 1885, Papers JP Alta Verapaz, 1885.

20. For details on labor relations in the Bajío, see Bazant, "Peones . . . 1851–1853," and "Peones . . . 1868–1904," and Brading, *Haciendas*.

21. *Informe cafetalero.*

22. AGCA, N.Q.–Jefe Político, July 11, 1923, Papers JP Sololá, 1923. The words capitalized are capitalized in the original.

23. For the impact of repeated demands on one individual, see Tax, *Penny Capitalism*, p. 106.

24. Colby and Colby, *Daykeeper*, pp. 54, 57, 84.

25. AGCA, B119.21.0.0 47757 1; T.Y.–Jefe Político, Apr. 17, 1914, Papers JP Sololá, 1914; T.Q.–Jefe Político, n.d., 1915, Papers JP Sololá, 1915.

26. AGCA, Various individuals of Sacapulas–Jefe Político, May 18, 1914, Papers JP Quiché, 1910–14.

27. AGCA, B119.21.0.0 47750 74; Workers finca Yalpemech [E. P. Dieseldorff]–Jefe Político, Dec. 6, 1915, Papers JP Alta Verapaz, 1915.

28. AGCA, T.C.–Jefe Político, Feb. 16, 1881, Papers JP Sololá, 1881; Workers, finca San Andrés Osuna-Rochela–Jefe Político, May 10, 1920, Papers JP Escuintla, 1920; Ministerio de Fomento, letter book no. 14871, Jan. 25, 1913. For "exposés" of colono conditions, see *La Mañana*, Jan. 1, 1921, and *El Imparcial*, Apr. 28, 1923.

29. AGCA, Juez Municipal Chicacao, 23/5, 1914, Papers Municipality of Chicacao.

30. AGCA, Workers, finca San Andrés Osuna-Rochela–Jefe Político, May 10, 1920, Papers JP Escuintla, 1920.

31. Alvarado, *Tratado*, 2: 471.

32. Regarding conditions in other parts of Latin America at this time, see

Bauer, "Rural Workers," pp. 34–63; Katz, "Labor Conditions"; Katz, ed., *La servidumbre agraria*; and Blanchard, "Recruitment of Workers."

33. Examples of these work cards often turn up stapled to petitions and reports of labor conflicts. On complaints growing out of the use of such cards or tokens, see 57 workers (from Carchá)–Jefe Político, Aug. 14, 1920, Papers JP Alta Verapaz, 1920; B119.21.0.0 47757 1 and 47770 57. For a description of the system in operation, see Goubaud, "Nueva Granada."

34. For the records of a store serving several fincas, see Dieseldorff Papers, Account books 249–53.

35. AGCA, Juzgado de Primera Instancia, Civil, Sololá, 20/1143.

36. *Diario de Centro América*, Jan. 15, 1920.

37. AGCA, J.F.S.–Jefe Político, Jan. 2, 1906, Papers JP Sololá, 1906.

38. AGCA, B119.21.0.0 47733 3 and 47788 15; P.P. (Cahabón)–Jefe Político, Nov. 14, 1906, Papers JP Alta Verapaz, 1906; Workers Santiago Sacatepéquez–President, Dec. 1, 1900, Papers JP Sacatepéquez, 1901.

39. AGCA, B119.21.0.0 47752 234 and 47773 97.

40. For example: AGCA, B119.21.0.0 47779 8.

41. AGCA, B119.21.0.0, 47763 82, 47768 24, and 47770 57; various of Santiago Sacatepéquez–President, Apr. 27, 1883, Papers JP Sacatepéquez, 1883; Workers San Lucas Tolimán–Jefe Político, May 17, 1915, Papers JP Sololá, 1915; 57 workers Carchá–Jefe Político, Aug. 14, 1920, Papers JP Alta Verapaz, 1920.

42. AGCA, Workers finca El Ferrol–Jefe Político, Dec. 29, 1922, Papers JP San Marcos, 1922.

43. AGCA, Workers Santiago Sacatepéquez–Jefe Político, Apr. 27, 1883, Papers JP Sacatepéquez, 1883. For similar complaints, see San Lucas Tolimán–Jefe Político, Oct. 10, 1887, Papers JP Sololá, 1887, and B119.21.0.0 47733 3.

44. AGCA, T.A.–Jefe Político, May 11, 1920, Papers JP Quiché, 1920–29.

45. Rural inhabitants of Guatemala during the nineteenth century used, and use today, simultaneously at least four systems of weights and measures: the English, the colonial Spanish, the metric, and indigenous units.

46. For a typical case, see "Sentencias económicas," Cobán, 1889–90, Jan. 25, 1890, Papers JP Alta Verapaz, 1890.

47. On standardizing the caja, see *El Imparcial*, Nov. 13 and Dec. 9, 1922, and Jan. 10, 1923.

48. This was rarely the only complaint: AGCA, B119.21.0.0 47733 3 and 47781 9; 11 workers Santiago Sacatepéquez–President, Dec. 1, 1900, Papers JP Sacatepéquez, 1901.

49. *El Imparcial*, May 14, 1925.

50. AGCA, Comandante Local San Rafael Pie de La Cuesta–Jefe Político, Oct. 27, 1915, Papers JP San Marcos, 1915.

51. AGCA, 12 workers finca San Francisco Miramar–Jefe Político, Oct. 25, 1911, Papers JP Sololá, 1911. See also 23 workers finca Mocá–Jefe Político,

Jan. 22, 1896, and 9 workers finca Los Horizontes–Jefe Político, Nov. 16, 1896, Papers JP Sololá, 1896; B119.21.0.0 47768 37.

52. AGCA, B119.21.0.0 47733 22, 47749 333, 47761 471, 47763 110; 2 workers San Lucas Tolimán–Jefe Político, May 17, 1915, Papers JP Sololá, 1915; 3 workers [finca?]–Jefe Político, May 18, 1920, JP Sololá, 1920.

53. AGCA, 130 workers finca El Porvenir–Jefe Político, Aug. 9, 1921, Papers JP San Marcos, 1921–23; H.A. finca El Esobillo–Jefe Político, Nov. 25, 1930, Papers JP San Marcos, 1931.

54. AGCA, 3 workers [finca?]–Jefe Político, May 18, 1920, Papers JP Sololá, 1920. See also J.J.–Jefe Político, Mar. 16, 1906, Papers JP Santa Rosa, 1910 (sic); B119.21.0.0 47733 22 and 7, and 47761 471.

55. AGCA, L.V.–Jefe Político, Aug. 9, 1902, Papers JP Quiché, 1900–1909.

56. AGCA, 2 workers [finca?]–Jefe Político, Sept. 11, 1913, Papers JP Quiché, 1910–19.

57. Diario de Centro América, Jan. 14, 1919. See also 11 workers Santiago Sacatepéquez–President, Dec. 1, 1900, Papers JP Sacatepéquez, 1901; B119.21.0.0 47761 471 and 47781 9.

58. Interview with retired finca manager, Jan. 16, 1981; AGCA, S.M.–Jefe Político, Jan. 20, 1898, Papers JP Sacatepéquez, 1898.

59. AGCA, C.P.–Jefe Político, Dec. 1, 1889, Papers JP Sacatepéquez, 1889. See also 9 workers finca La Concha–Jefe Político, Feb. 13, 1911, Papers JP Sololá, 1911; Juez Municipal Atitlán–Jefe Político, Mar. 20, 1923, Papers JP Sololá, 1923; Ministerio de Fomento, letter book no. 14862, Nov. 11, 1896.

60. AGCA, A.P.–Jefe Político, Nov. 8, 1920, Papers JP Sololá, 1920.

61. El Imparcial, Sept. 24, 1924.

62. Ibid., Aug. 9, 1929.

63. AGCA, B119.21.0.0 47789 9. See also Gleijeses, "La aldea de Ubico," p. 34.

64. For a general discussion of diseases in the plantation areas of Guatemala during this period, see Shatuck, Medical Survey.

65. El Imparcial, Nov. 6, 1926. These numbers certainly represent considerable undercounting and are used here only for purposes of comparison. See also Ministerio de Fomento, Memoria-1924, pp. 299–301.

66. Ministerio de Gobernación, Memoria-1919, p. 10; El Imparcial, Oct. 4, 1922; Pitti, "Jorge Ubico," pp. 15–20.

67. Brigham, Guatemala, p. 315.

68. El Imparcial, May 12, 1925. See also the issue of July 5, 1930.

69. Diario de Centro América, Dec. 18, 1920, and Aug. 12, 1924; El Imparcial, Feb. 11, 1928. See also Skinner-Klée, Legislación indigenista, pp. 95–96; El Imparcial, May 12, 1925.

70. Diario de Centro América, Aug. 11, 1924; Bunzel, Chichicastenango, p. 143. See also Shatuck, Medical Survey, pp. 104–5.

71. Dirección General de Estadística, *Censo . . . 1893*, p. 61.
72. *Diario de Centro América*, Dec. 1, 1890; AGCA, MG 28641 390; *El Imparcial*, Jan. 20, 1928.
73. *Diario de Centro América*, June 13, 1918.
74. AGCA, L.G.–Jefe Político, June 18, 1909, Papers JP San Marcos, 1909. Bunzel (*Chichicastenango*, p. 143) notes that smallpox was common in Chichicastenango.
75. McCreery, "A Terrible Scourge."
76. Ministerio de Gobernación, *Memoria-1919*, p. 20.
77. *Diario de Centro América*, Dec. 17, 1918.
78. Ministerio de Gobernación, *Memoria-1919*, pp. 57–58.
79. *Diario de Centro América*, Dec. 27, 1918, and Feb. 4, 1919.
80. Boddam-Whettham, *Central America*, pp. 83–84; Sanborn, *A Winter*, p. 166; Maudsley and Maudsley, *Glimpse at Guatemala*, p. 100; *Memoria de la Dirección de Agricultura-1902*, p. 37. See also the photographs in Burns, *Eadweard Muybridge*.
81. AGCA, B119.21.0.0 47781 12; M.C.–Jefe Político, Sept. 23, 1920, Papers JP Quiché, 1920–29.
82. AGCA, B119.21.0.0 47811 106.
83. For example: AGCA, B119.21.0.0 47772 43 and 63, 47773 83, 47775 217 and 257, 47778 6 and 10.
84. AGCA, G.C.–Jefe Político, Nov. n.d., 1891, Papers JP Quiché, 1890.
85. AGCA, Papers Municipality of San Martín Jilotepeque, 26/28, Apr. 19, 1885; Estrada Cabrera Papers, June 8, 1896; J.P.–Jefe Político, Sept. 25, 1903, Papers JP San Marcos "administrativa," 1902–10; ?–Jefe Político, Oct. 29, 1903, Papers JP San Marcos 1903; M.P.–Jefe Político, Apr. 7, 1906, Papers JP San Marcos, 1906.
86. AGCA, D.P.–Jefe Político, Oct. 4, 1906, Papers JP Alta Verapaz, 1906.
87. AGCA, J.L.–Jefe Político, Apr. 16, 1909, Papers JP San Marcos, 1909.
88. AGCA, M.P.–Jefe Político, June 19, 1905, Papers JP Alta Verapaz, 1905; A.C.–Jefe Político, Mar. 16, 1907, Papers JP San Marcos "administratíva," 1902–10; J.C.–Jefe Político, Sept. 10, 1910, Papers JP Alta Verapaz, 1910; F.S.–Jefe Político, July 7, 1914, Papers JP Sololá, 1914; I.N.–Jefe Político, Dec. 26, 1914, Papers JP Sololá, 1914; B119.21.0.0 47775 237.
89. AGCA, B119.21.0.0 47751 119. See also F.S.–Jefe Político, Jan. 2, 1906, Papers JP Sololá, 1906; Finca El Porvenir–Jefe Político, July 10, 1930, Papers JP San Marcos, 1929–30; C.M.–Jefe Político, Nov. 14, 1935, Papers JP San Marcos, 1935; B119.21.0.0 47751 172, 47755 120, 47770 57, 47775 217, 47776 370.
90. AGCA, B119.21.0.0 47762 3. See also B119.21.0.0 no. 47768 55 and 47770 22; receipt for 350 pesos to E.F. to be worked off by son, n.d., 1915, Papers JP San Marcos, 1915; L.R.–Jefe Político, July 24, 1923, Papers JP San Marcos, 1921–23.

91. AGCA, B119.21.0.0 47778 20.

92. AGCA, 3 Indian women–Jefe Político, Sept. 21, 1900, Papers JP San Marcos, 1900. See also S.H.–Jefe Político, July 5, 1907, Papers San Marcos "administrativa" 1902–10; P.S.–Jefe Político, Feb. 28, 1910, Papers JP Alta Verapaz, 1910.

93. AGCA, F.P.–Jefe Político, June 18, 1890, Papers JP Sololá, 1890. See also P.G.–Jefe Político, May 14, 1915, and F.A.–Jefe Político, Sept. 16, 1915, Papers JP Sololá, 1915.

94. AGCA, A.G.–Jefe Político, July 16, 1923, Papers JP San Marcos, "administrativa" 1921–23.

95. El Imparcial, Feb. 3, 1925. See also AGCA, C.L.–Jefe Político, Feb. 21, 1924, Papers JP San Marcos, 1921–25.

96. For an introduction to the concept of "honor and shame" societies, see Peristiany, ed., Honour and Shame.

97. El Imparcial, Dec. 6, 1923.

98. AGCA, Certified copy of accounts of María Mendez, Jan. 1909, Papers JP San Marcos, 1906 (sic).

99. AGCA, P.A.–finca La Aurora, Nov. 25, 1936, Papers JP San Marcos, 1936, "administrativa," no. 17; Juez Municipal–Jefe Político, June 7, 1912, Papers JP San Marcos, 1912; Municipality of San Martín Jilotepeque, Juez Municipal, 40/1, June n.d., 1897; MG 28968 "Expedientes-Escuintla," no. 1, 1898.

100. AGCA, L.J.–Jefe Político, June 20, 1890, Papers JP Sololá, 1890; B.I. and compañeros–Jefe Político, Sept. 19, 1930, Papers JP Alta Verapaz, 1930; Juzgado de Primera Instancia, Criminal, San Marcos, 18/54.

101. AGCA, Juez de Paz La Reforma–Jefe Político, July 27, 1901, Papers JP San Marcos, 1901.

102. AGCA, Comisionado Político San Rafael Pie de la Cuesta–Jefe Político, Oct. 27, 1915, Papers JP San Marcos, 1915.

103. See, for example, McCreery, "Land."

104. King, Cobán, p. 34.

105. AGCA, Jefe Político–Ministerio de Gobernación, n.d., 1897, Papers JP Alta Verapaz, 1897.

106. Petitions are to be found in the AGCA in the papers of the jefes políticos. Related material also turns up in the Ministerio de Fomento letter books and in the Cartas section of the AHA.

107. AGCA, B119.21.0.0 47780 15.

108. AGCA, Santa María de Jesús–President, Mar. 14, 1904, Papers JP Sacatepéquez, 1906 (sic).

109. AGCA, Juzgado de Primera Instancia, Criminal, Sololá, 37/1904.

110. Rosales, "Aguacatán."

111. Lincoln, "Ixil Indians." See also AGCA, MG 28669 117; Comisionado Político San Pedro las Huertas–Jefe Político, June 9, 1884, Papers JP Sacatepéquez, 1884; Comisionado Político Magdalena–Jefe Político, June 11, 1886,

Papers JP Sacatepéquez, 1886; Comisionado Político San Antonio AC–Jefe Político, July 10, 1889, Papers JP Sacatepéquez, 1889; Ministerio de Fomento, letter book no. 14914, Dec. 13, 1902; Batres Jáuregui, *Los indios*, pp. 178–80.

112. AGCA, MG 28699 117, 28673 131, 28757 225; Ministerio de Fomento, letter book no. 14865, Nov. 3, 1897.

113. Ramos, *O café*, p. 295.

114. AGCA, Juez Municipal Tacaná–Jefe Político, Sept. 11, 1901, Papers JP San Marcos, 1901; Juez Municipal Comitancillo–Jefe Político, Feb. 22, 1903, Papers JP San Marcos, 1903; R.R.–Jefe Político, May 7, 1906, Papers JP San Marcos, 1906; Comisionado Político Tacaná–Jefe Político, Aug. 7, 1909, Papers JP San Marcos, 1906 (*sic*). In one instance the government brought charges of espionage against a habilitador who was seeking to recruit Indians for work in Mexico: "Contra E.P. y M.P. por espionaje," June 15, 1922, Papers JP San Marcos, 1922.

115. AGCA, Alcalde Tajumulco–Jefe Político, n.d., 1901, Papers JP San Marcos, 1901.

116. AGCA, Ministerio de Fomento, letter book no. 14895, Oct. 12, 1900; B119.21.0.0 47768 19.

117. *Agricultura-1902*, pp. 41–42.

118. AGCA, MG 28678 569 and 28700 1072.

119. *Agricultura-1902*, p. 46; Ministerio de Fomento, letter book no. 14873, June 12, 1902.

120. AGCA, Ministerio de Fomento, letter book no. 14909, May 24, 1922. Information from Michael Stone on the population of British Honduras shows these figures to be wildly out of line with the real situation, suggesting either ignorance or a political agenda on the part of the jefe. Much less common, apparently, was flight to Honduras or El Salvador: Ministerio de Fomento, letter book no. 14855, Nov. 21, 1893.

121. *El Imparcial*, Nov. 1, 1922.

122. On theft, see AGCA, "Libro de sentencias económicas," Sacatepéquez, Mar. 10 and 16, 1881, Papers JP Sacatepéquez, 1881, and "Libro de sentencias económicas," Retalhuleu, Mar. 2, 1885, Papers JP Retalhuleu, 1885A; Juez Municipal Ciudad Vieja–Jefe Político, May 15, 1902, Papers JP Sacatepéquez, 1902; MG 28759 683; AGCA, Archivo de los Tribunales, Ramo Criminal, Cuarta Sala de Apelaciones, Quezaltenango, legajo 3b, Dec. 5, 1899; Dieseldorff Papers, 63: 152. No criminal cases concerning sabotage appear in the records, although owners complained that workers broke branches because of carelessness. Because the Indians typically worked by tasks at the harvest, there was no advantage for them in slowing the pace.

123. AGCA, Ministerio de Fomento, letter book no. 14862, n.d., 1896, no. 14865, Nov. 3, 1897, and no. 14866, Jan. 28, 1898.

124. Rosales, "Aguacatán."

125. From this perspective, Scott defines resistance as "*any* act(s) by mem-

ber(s) of a subordinated class *intended* either to mitigate or deny claims . . . made on that class by superordinate classes . . . or to advance their own claims . . . vis-a-vis those superordinate classes": Scott, *Weapons of the Weak*, p. 290 (his emphasis). See also McCreery, "Hegemony and Resistance."

126. McCreery, "Caja."

127. See Warren, *Symbolism*; Hawkins, *Inverse Images*; and Mendelson, *Los escándalos de Maximón*.

128. Except where noted, the following section is based on McCreery, "Land."

129. AGCA, B119.21.0.0 47751 172.

130. Among the best recent studies of change over time in the rural communities, mostly the work of anthropologists not historians, are Davis, "Land of Our Ancestors"; Falla, *Quiché rebelde*; Madigan, "Santiago Atitlán"; Brintnal, *Revolt*; Carmack, *Historia social*; Piel, *Sajcabaja*; Warren, *Symbolism*; and W. Smith, *Fiesta System*.

131. On "luck-destiny" see Warren, *Symbolism*, p. 65.

132. Bunzel, *Chichicastenango*, p. 9. See also Wagley, *Economics*, pp. 53–54.

133. See, for example, Davis, "Land of Our Ancestors," pp. 213–20.

134. Lincoln, "Ixil Indians." On drunkenness in Chichicastenango, see Bunzel, *Chichicastenango*, pp. 254–60.

135. LaFarge, *Santa Eulalia*, p. 7.

136. W. Smith, *Fiesta System*, p. 80. On the benefits of more children to peasant families, see de Janvry, *Agrarian Question*, pp. 87–93.

137. For a breakdown on rations and food supply to workers on one estate, see Goubaud, "Nueva Granada." Compare this with Cross, "Living Standards."

Chapter 10

1. Bingham, "Guatemalan Agriculture," p. 119.

2. On the origins of industry in Guatemala, see Paul J. Dorsal, "Dependency, Revolution, and Industrial Development in Guatemala, 1821–1986," Ph.D. diss., Tulane University, 1987.

3. For prices for Guatemalan coffee for the years 1914–40, see *World's Coffee*, p. 432.

4. On foreign "domination" in the late 1920's, see *El Imparcial*, Aug. 23, 1930.

5. Ministerio de Gobernación, *Memoria-1918*, p. 5. See also *Diario de Centro América*, Nov. 17 and Dec. 7, 1917, and Jan. 1, 1920, and *El Imparcial*, Dec. 24, 1937.

6. Pitti, "Jorge Ubico," pp. 20–29.

7. Ibid., pp. 35–38; Lopez Larrave, *Breve historia*; Bauer País, *Catalogación*, p. 35.

8. Carmack, *Historia social*, pp. 292–98.

9. *Diario de Centro América*, Apr. 26, July 15, and Aug. 17, 1921; *El Imparcial*, Nov. 20, 1922, and Oct. 10, 1923; AGCA, Juez de Paz Izabal–Jefe Político, June 29, 1920, Papers JP Izabal, 1920; Ministerio de Fomento, letter book no. 14888, Jan. 16, 1921; Ministerio de Fomento, *Memoria-1921*, p. 125.

10. *El Imparcial*, Oct. 24, 1923.

11. AGCA, Ministerio de Fomento, letter book no. 14888, Jan. 16, 1921.

12. See *El Imparcial*, Nov. 1, 1922, Oct. 24, 1923, Nov. 28, 1925, and Sept. 6, 1929; AGCA, finca La Paz–Jefe Político, Nov. 16, 1926, Papers JP San Marcos, 1926.

13. AGCA, Finqueros–Jefe Político, June 12, 1920, Papers JP Sololá, 1920; Cia. de Plantaciones Concepción–Jefe Político, Aug. 9, 1921, Papers JP Sacatepéquez, 1921; Ministerio de Fomento, *Memoria-1920*, p. 125.

14. *Diario de Centro América*, July 3, 1920. See also AGCA, Finca San Luís–Jefe Político, Nov. 17, 1926 (and similar letters from managers of fincas Carolina, Nov. 18, Las Esperanzas, Nov. 15, Mundo Nuevo, Nov. 19, and Monte Rosa, Nov. 19); AGCA, Comandante Local El Tumbador–Jefe Político, Nov. 27, 1926, Papers JP San Marcos, 1926.

15. *El Imparcial*, July 1, 1924.

16. Ibid., Feb. 14, 1928, Apr. 25 and 27, and May 2, 1929.

17. Gleijeses, "La aldea de Ubico," pp. 25–27.

18. Skinner-Klée, *Legislación indigenista*, p. 94.

19. *El Imparcial*, Nov. 9, 1925.

20. Ibid., Aug. 12, 1931.

21. Ibid., Sept. 6, 1929.

22. Ibid., Oct. 26, 1928. See also issue of Nov. 29, 1922.

23. Ministerio de Agricultura, *Memoria-1932*, p. 255.

24. *El Imparcial*, May 19, 1921, Apr. 25, 1924, and a series of articles by Wyld Ospina, Jan. 23, Feb. 6 and 10, and Apr. 10, 1928; *Diario de Centro América*, Apr. 26, 1924. On falsifying statistics, see *Diario de Centro América*, July 24, 1920, and *El Imparcial*, Apr. 26, 1924.

25. In 1890 the area in production was 63,519 manzanas; this rose to 130,383 manzanas by 1900 but had declined to 92,953 manzanas in 1922–23: Dirección de Estadística, *Memoria-1892*, p. 215; Ministerio de Fomento, *Memoria-1900*, p. 124; Ministerio de Agricultura, *Memoria-1923*, p. 73.

26. *El Imparcial*, Apr. 25, 1924; Bingham, "Guatemalan Agriculture," p. 61. Early enthusiasts claimed productivity of two or more pounds per bush, but a more accurate average at the turn of the century was one pound per bush: Ramos, *O café*, p. 310, and *Memoria de la Dirección de Agricultura-1902*, p. 36. By this measure yields had not declined by the 1920's: *El Imparcial*, Apr. 25 and 26, 1924.

27. *Diario de Centro América*, July 24, 1920, and May 11, 1921; *El Imparcial*, Aug. 16, 1923, Apr. 5, 1924, and Mar. 24 and Sept. 20, 1928; Ministerio de Agricultura, *Memoria-1924*; AGCA, Comandante Local [town?]–Comandante

de Armas, Nov. 21, 1920, Papers JP Alta Verapaz, 1920. For details on the monetary situation and its effects, see Secretario de Hacienda y Crédito Público, *Iniciativas de ley para el arreglo de la situación económica: exposición de motivos* (Guatemala City, 1921). See also Young, *Currency*, pp. 25–38. On the reforms enacted, see Jones, *Guatemala*, pp. 238–39; Bulmer-Thomas, *Political Economy*, pp. 32–33.

28. Among dozens of such items, see, for example, *Diario de Centro América*, June 17 and July 3, 1920, Apr. 15, 16, 21, 25, 29, 30, May 10, 14, 18, 19, June 1, Oct. 22, 29, 1921, Mar. 14, June 19, 1923; also *El Imparcial*, Jan. 15, July 6, 7, 14, Sept. 26, Oct. 7, Nov. 25, 30, Dec. 7, 26, 1922, Mar. 17, 23, Apr. 6, 7, 9, 1923, and Jan. 15, Apr. 3, 16, 21, 25, 26, 1924.

29. *El Imparcial*, Nov. 30, 1922.

30. *Diario de Centro América*, Sept. 20, 1919; *El Imparcial*, July 6, Nov. 30, 1922, and June 9, 1923.

31. *El Imparcial*, Nov. 25, 1922 (compare ibid., Nov. 30, 1922). See also ibid., Jan. 15, 1924, and Feb. 10, 11, 1928; Ramos, *O café*, p. 351.

32. The state apparently took several counts during these years but did not publish the results because, the U.S. Embassy reported in 1916, President Estrada Cabrera considered census data a military secret: U.S. Department of State Records Relating to Internal Affairs of Guatemala, roll 20, Oct. 1, 1919.

33. See, for example, *Diario de Centro América*, June 17, 1920; *El Imparcial*, Nov. 30, 1922.

34. Because in theory mandamientos had not existed since the last decade of the past century, their official end was not generally commented upon: AGCA, various–Jefe Político, Jan. 28, 1920, Papers JP Sacatepéquez, 1920.

35. See *El Imparcial*, June 26, 1920, for an argument against mandamientos.

36. *Diario de Centro América*, Feb. 1, 4, 12, May 3, and Sept. 20, 1919; *El Imparcial*, Apr. 25, 1924; G. Rodriguez, *Guatemala en 1919*, p. 104.

37. *Diario de Centro América*, May 11, 1921.

38. *El Imparcial*, Apr. 26, 1924, and Feb. 6, 1928.

39. AGCA, Ministerio de Fomento, letter book no. 14924, Oct. 21, 1920.

40. *El Imparcial*, Apr. 6, 1927.

41. *Diario de Centro América*, Oct. 22, 1921; see also Bauer País, *Catalogación*, p. 7.

42. AGCA, Finca La Concepción–Comandante de Armas Malacatán, Dec. 25, 1922, Papers JP San Marcos, 1922; E.M.–Jefe Político, Apr. 9, 1923, Papers JP Sololá, 1923; *El Imparcial*, July 3, 7, 14, 1923, and Sept. 7, 1925.

43. AGCA, Finca Variadades–Jefe Político, n.d., 1923, Papers JP Sololá, 1923.

44. *Diario de Centro América*, June 17, 26, 1920, May 10, 18, 1921, and Mar. 14, 1923; *El Imparcial*, July 6 and Sept. 26, 1922.

45. *El Imparcial*, July 6, 1922.

46. Ibid., Mar. 18, 1926. See also issues of April 21, 30, and May 19, 1921, Oct. 7, 1922, and Jan. 15, 1924.

47. *Diario de Centro América*, July 17, 1920; *El Imparcial*, May 11, 1921.

48. *Recopilación . . . Guatemala*, 2: 201–4.

49. See, for example, *Diario de Centro América*, Apr. 21 and 29, and May 10 and 19, 1921; *El Imparcial*, Mar. 17, 1923.

50. *El Imparcial*, Oct. 7, 1922.

51. AGCA, Ministerio de Fomento, letter book no. 14928, Nov. 12, 1921. On why workers continued to flee to Mexico, see *El Imparcial*, Oct. 14, 1922.

52. Ministerio de Agricultura, *Memoria-1924*, p. 88.

53. AGCA, Ministerio de Fomento, letter book no. 14928, Nov. 12, 1921.

54. *El Imparcial*, Apr. 27, 1925. Confirming this, see ibid., Oct. 20, 1930.

55. Ibid., Jan. 20, 1928, and Sept. 27 and 28, 1929; Ministerio de Agricultura, *Memoria-1930*, p. 256.

56. *El Imparcial*, May 6, 1929, and May 30 and June 1, 1931. On continuing emigration and cross-border trafficking in labor, see AGCA, Soc. Agrícola Tumbador–Jefe Político, Oct. 14, 1932, Papers JP San Marcos, 1933; Alcalde Primero San Pablo–Jefe Político, Mar. 3, 1935, Papers JP San Marcos, 1935.

57. For example: *Diario de Centro América*, Apr. 15 and 25, 1921, and Apr. 6, 1923; *El Imparcial*, Apr. 21 and 30, 1921, and Apr. 7, 1923.

58. *El Imparcial*, Apr. 7, 1923.

59. *Diario de Centro América*, May 30, 1921.

60. Ibid., June 1, 1921. Except as they might be punished for public drunkenness, the vagrancy provisions did not apply to women.

61. Ibid., May 10, 14, and 30, 1921, and Apr. 24, 1922.

62. Ibid., Mar. 14, 1923.

63. On this, see, for example, ibid., Apr. 29, May 19, and June 1, 1921.

64. Alvarado, *Tratado*, 2: 456.

65. Bulmer-Thomas, "Central America," p. 284.

66. See Ramos, *O café*, p. 306, and Alvarado, *Tratado*, 2: 465–70 on how payment in corn favored the workers.

67. Import statistics are found in the yearly Ministerio de Hacienda, *Memorias*.

68. *El Imparcial*, June 12, 1928, and July 19, 1931.

69. On transportation problems in these years, see Grieb, *Guatemalan Caudillo*, chap. 9. For a discussion of the costs of coerced labor, see *El Imparcial*, Apr. 27, 1929, and Aug. 26, 1943, and Alvarado, *Tratado*, 2: 459–65. Ramos, writing in the early 1920's but relying on research undertaken around the turn of the century, suggested that Guatemalan production stagnated or began to decline in the first years of the century: *O café*, p. 319.

70. AGCA, circular–Jefe Político, Jan. 20, 1905, Papers JP Alta Verapaz, 1905. See also circular(s)–Jefe Político, Mar. 3 and July 6, 1915, Papers JP El Petén, 1915. Robert Claxton ("Drought") has identified droughts in the years

412 ≈ Notes to Pages 308–10

1885, 1888–89, 1891, 1895, 1899, 1902, 1907, 1912, 1914, 1919–21, and 1922. He also notes ("Rain Showers") unusually severe rain showers that damaged at least one area of the republic in the years 1877, 1879, 1881, 1886, 1887, 1893, 1896, 1900, 1902, 1904, 1907, 1909, 1915, 1923, and 1924. On efforts to stimulate food production in the years 1898–1920, see Bingham, "Guatemalan Agriculture," pp. 62–95.

71. AGCA, circular–Jefes Político(s), May 1, 1911, Papers JP Sacatepéquez, 1911. Such exhortations continued on into the 1930's. See *El Imparcial*, Apr. 15, 1932.

72. U.S. Department of State, Records Relating to Internal Affairs of Guatemala, roll 20, Nov. 1925; *El Imparcial*, June 8, 1929.

73. *El Imparcial*, Apr. 27 and June 6 and 8, 1929. See also: AGCA, MG 28661 15; Saler, "Road to El Palmar," p. 31; AGCA, Ministerio de Fomento, letter book no. 14876, n.d. On locusts, see U.S. Department of State, Records Relating to Internal Affairs of Guatemala, roll 30, Oct. 27, 1913; Finca Cubilguitz–Jefe Político, May 11, 1915, Papers JP Alta Verapaz, 1915; *El Imparcial*, Dec. 18, 1925, Sept. 18, 1929, Aug. 14, 1930, May 14, 1931, and Aug. 16, 1943; Ministerio de Agricultura, *Memoria-1927*, p. 14, *Memoria-1936*, p. 10, and *Memoria-1940*, p. 7. The shift to coffee and away from the old extensive cattle haciendas reduced problems of cattle damage, but in the Oriente where more traditional forms persisted, the problems continued: AGCA, MG 28657 414.

74. *El Imparcial*, Dec. 18, 1925.

75. Ministerio de Agricultura, *Memorias*, 1923——.

76. *El Imparcial*, Apr. 27, 1929.

77. AGCA, Papers JP de Sacatepéquez, 1920–40; *El Imparcial*, Jan. 22, 1927; Ministerio de Agricultura, *Memoria-1923*, p. 78; also, Ministerio de Fomento, *Memoria-1924*, p. 357, *Memoria-1933*, p. 246, and *Memoria-1936*, p. 309. For the experiences of one finca with problems of food costs, see Alvarado, *Tratado*, 2: 462.

78. McCreery, "Debt Servitude," p. 752.

79. *El Imparcial*, Apr. 27, June 6 and 8, 1929; de Janvry, *Agrarian Question*, chap. 4.

80. *El Trabajo*, Oct. 15, 1913.

81. Ministerio de Gobernación, *Memoria-1881*, p. 34; AGCA, M.G.–Jefe Político, Jan. 13, 1905, Papers JP Alta Verapaz, 1905; Bauer País, *Catalogación*, p. 64; Ministerio de Agricultura, *Memoria-1923*, p. 17, and *Memoria-1927*, p. 12; *El Imparcial*, July 29, 1929.

82. Batres Jáuregui, *Los indios*, p. 162.

83. AGCA, Ministerio de Fomento, letter book no. 14914, Mar. 17, 1901.

84. AGCA, Juez Municipal San Antonio Palopó–Jefe Político, July 3, 1902, and Juez Municipal San Andrés Semetabaj–Jefe Político, July 12, 1902, Papers JP Sololá; Ministerio de Fomento, letter book no. 14929, July 15, 1902.

85. Percheron, *Producción Agrícola*, p. 3; Ministerio de Agricultura, *Memorias*.

86. Grieb ties the increases to road building and the effects of the Depression (*Guatemalan Caudillo*, chap. 10) and certainly these had an effect, but they do not explain a one-year increase between 1936 and 1937 of almost 100 percent.

87. Dirección General de Estadística, *Contribución estadística*.

88. Ministerio de Fomento, *Memoria-1893*, p. 5.

89. On the intendants, see R. Adams, *Crucifixion*, pp. 176, 179.

90. Ministerio de Agricultura, *Memoria-1935*, p. 659.

91. For example: *El Imparcial*, June 12, 1928, June 13, 14, Oct. 25, Nov. 22, and Dec. 10, 1929, Jan. 7 and Feb. 12, 1930.

92. Ibid., Feb. 6, 1928, Oct. 25, 1929, and Aug. 23, 1930.

93. Dirección General de Estadística, *Censo . . . 1921*.

94. *El Imparcial*, Nov. 23, 1929.

95. Ibid., Jan. 7, Feb. 12, and Oct. 1, 1930.

96. Bulmer-Thomas, *Political Economy*, chaps. 3 and 4; Montenegro Rios, *La explotación cafetalera*.

97. *El Imparcial*, Dec. 17, 1929.

98. See sales and mortgage statistics in the Ministerio de Hacienda, *Memorias*, 1923——. Mortgages for 1920–23 are to be found in Ministerio de Fomento, *Memoria-1924*, p. 371.

99. Bunzel reports, for example, that many planters "made no attempt to pick [the 1932] crop." *Chichicastenango*, p. 11.

100. Ministerio de Agricultura, *Memoria-1933*, p. 509; *El Imparcial*, Oct. 29, 1930. See also AGCA, B119.21.0.0 47790 86; and Montenegro Rios, *La explotación cafetalera*, p. 82. The quetzal, equal to 60 pesos or one U.S. dollar, became Guatemala's official currency in 1926, although the use of pesos persisted in rural areas for another decade.

101. Dieseldorff Papers, 92: 893–94, Jan. 8, 1930.

102. *El Imparcial*, Oct. 28, 1929, and Oct. 29, 1930; AGCA, B119.21.0.0, 47790 86; Ministerio de Agricultura, *Memoria-1932*, p. 509; Bulmer-Thomas, *Political Economy*, p. 49.

103. For cost of living indexes, see Ministerio de Fomento, *Memoria-1933*, pp. 246–47, and *Memoria-1936*, pp. 218, 307–9.

104. *El Imparcial*, Jan. 7, 1930.

105. Ibid., Oct. 3, 1930.

106. Bunzel, *Chichicastenango*, p. 11; LaFarge, *Santa Eulalia*, pp. 5, 10, 36. See also Lincoln, "Ixil Indians."

107. Dieseldorff Papers, 92: 893–94, Jan. 8, 1930.

108. For a detailed "wish list" of what the government could do for them, see the report of the Asociación de Agricultores in *El Imparcial*, Jan. 8, 1930.

109. *El Imparcial*, Nov. 20, 1929, Jan. 7, Apr. 3, 25, 26, Aug. 29, and Sept. 11, 1930.

110. Ibid., Nov. 21 and Dec. 12, 1929, Jan. 15 and 24, 1930.

111. Ibid., July 22, 1929, Jan. 8 and Sept. 11, 1930, and June 14, 1932.

112. Ministerio de Hacienda, *Memorias*; Bulmer-Thomas, *Political Economy*, p. 74; Grieb, *Guatemalan Caudillo*, pp. 58–59; Crédito Hipotecario Nacional de Guatemala, *Informe-1933*, p. 45, and *Informe-1936*, pp. 39–40.

113. *El Imparcial*, May 26, Aug. 31, Sept. 15, 1928, June 1, July 4, 1929; R. Mendez, *Leyes vigentes*, pp. 46–47.

114. Soley Guell, *Proyecto*; *El Imparcial*, Aug. 23, 24, 27, 28, 29, 30, 1929.

115. *El Imparcial*, Sept. 21, 23, 24, 26, 28, and Nov. 14, 15, 16, 20, 22, 23, 1929; Ministerio de Hacienda, *Memoria-1930*, pp. 205–11.

116. *El Imparcial*, Jan. 18, Apr. 4, 8, 10, 11, 16, May 10 and 12, and Aug. 19, 1930.

117. Ministerio de Hacienda, *Memoria-1931*, p. 95; *El Imparcial*, Sept. 10, 1930; Grieb, *Guatemalan Caudillo*, p. 179.

118. Some of these funds were syphoned off to other purposes (*El Imparcial*, Dec. 24, 1930) and some may not have been received: Crédito Hipotecario Nacional, *Informe-1932*, p. 43, and *Informe-1933*, p. 54; *El Imparcial*, Sept. 2, 1930. For a short history of the Crédito, see *El Imparcial*, Mar. 21, 1931.

119. Ministerio de Hacienda, *Memoria-1931*, p. 97. By February 1931 this had increased to 984 applications for more than Q10,000,000: *El Imparcial*, Feb. 7, 1931.

120. Crédito Hipotecario Nacional, *Informe-1932*, p. 43. For subsequent years, see Ministerio de Hacienda, *Memorias*, and Crédito Hipotecario Nacional, *Informes*.

121. U.S. Department of State, Records Relating to Internal Affairs of Guatemala, roll 9, various.

122. Ministerio de Hacienda, *Memoria-1935*, p. 55, and *Memoria-1939*, pp. 33–36.

123. Ministerio de Hacienda, *Memoria-1937*, p. 53.

124. *El Imparcial*, Dec. 24, 1932; Ministerio de Hacienda, *Memoria-1935*, pp. 54–55.

125. *El Imparcial*, June 20 and 25, 1931.

126. Ibid., June 29, 1931; Ministerio de Hacienda, *Memoria-1931*, pp. 96–97.

127. Grieb, *Guatemalan Caudillo*; Pitti, "Jorge Ubico," chap. 8; Gleijeses, "La aldea de Ubico." The Depression in Central America bottomed out in 1932–34: Bulmer-Thomas, *Political Economy*, chaps. 3 and 4.

128. *El Imparcial*, May 9, 1934.

129. R. Mendez, *Leyes vigentes*, pp. 214–15, 244–47.

130. Ibid., p. 244.

131. AGCA, various Santa Eulalia–President, Jan. 13, 1936, Papers JP San Marcos, 1936.

132. AGCA, B119.21.0.0 47795 1, 47800 71, and 47808 27.

133. Lincoln, "Ixil Indians"; Colby and van den Berghe, *Ixil Country*, p. 155. For a dramatic memory of these events, see Stoll, "Evangelicals," 101.

134. Brintnal, *Revolt*, p. 112; Stadelman, "Maize Cultivation," p. 134; Wagley, *Economics*, p. 26; Tax, *Penny Capitalism*, p. 107.

135. R. Mendez, *Leyes vigentes*, p. 215; Skinner-Klée, *Legislación indigenista*, pp. 118–19.

136. Except as specifically cited, the following description of the operation of the system draws on a large amount of material in court records: Archivo General de Los Tribunales, Juez de Paz, Huehuetenango, 1932–38 and 1942–44, Quiché, 1937–40 and 1943–44, Sololá, 1938–44, and Chiquimula, 1940.

137. AGT, Juez de Paz, Quiché, Criminal, June 3, 1939.

138. AGCA, B119.21.0.0 47800 53 and 75, and 47804 19; AGT, Juez de Paz, Huehuetenango, Criminal, no. 19, 1937–38.

139. AGCA, various San Andrés Semetabaj–President, June 18, 1936, and vecinos Sololá–President, July 10, 1936, Papers JP Sololá; B119.21.0.0 47804 19.

140. AGCA, B119.21.0.0 47799 9, 47800 69 and 75, 47801 1, 47802 64.

141. Goubaud, "Chamelco."

142. AGCA, Comitancillo–President, Aug. 21, 1936, Papers JP San Marcos, administrativa no. 17, 1936.

143. AGT, Juez de Paz, Quiché, Criminal, May 20, 1940, case no. 16.

144. AGT, Huehuetenango, Criminal, 1937–38, bundle no. 6.

145. Warren, *Symbolism*, p. 149. See also ibid., pp. 150–51.

146. For ways to "beat the system," see *El Norte*, June 5, 1937, and *El Imparcial*, Aug. 13, 1943.

147. AGCA, Intendant Panzos–Jefe Político, June 8, 1940, Papers JP, 1935 (*sic*); "small agriculturalists" Nuevo Progreso–Ministerio de Agricultura, Mar. n.d., 1943, Papers JP San Marcos administrativa no. 27, 1943.

148. AGCA, B119.21.0.0 47800 61. For earlier problems, see B119.21.0.0 47788 5 and 47790 96.

149. Interview with former finca owner, Nov. 12, 1987; Simpson, *Repartimiento System*, p. 94 n. 4; T. Adams, "San Martín Jilotepeque," p. 32.

150. AGCA, Jefe Político–Ministerio de Gobernación, Apr. 13, 1936, Papers JP Sololá, 1932 (*sic*).

151. Brintnal, *Revolt*, p. 112; Warren, *Symbolism*, p. 150.

152. For the story of one person's attempts, with only limited success, to step into what traditionally had been ladino roles, see Sexton, ed., *Tecun Uman and Campesino*.

153. See, for example, AGCA, Sumpango, "Libro de acts de comprobar

datos de jornaleros y otros oficios que solicitan constancias conforme la ley de jornaleros, 1939," and "Registro de jornaleros, 1941."

154. Stadelman, "Maize Cultivation," pp. 105, 134. See also Wagley, *Economics*, p. 31, and McBryde, *Cultural and Historical Geography*, p. 74. Bunzel (*Chichicastenango*, p. 43) presents a rather different picture for the town of Chichicastenango.

155. *El Imparcial*, Jan. 22, 1945.

156. Ibid., May 22, 1945.

157. Zelaya Gil and Lucerno, eds., *Resumen de leyes*, p. 255.

Conclusions

1. AGCA, A3 227 4182 and 4185.

2. Piel, *Sajcabaja*, p. 367. Piel misses entirely the significance of Sajcabajá's integration into the Guatemalan and world economies through forced wage labor.

3. Brintnal, *Revolt*, pp. 109–10.

4. Sweatnam, "What Else Did the Indians Have to Do?"

5. W. Smith, *Fiesta System*, pp. 100–101 and chaps. 11–12.

6. Wagley, *Economics*, pp. 72–81.

7. Rey, *Las alianzas de clases*. For introductions to Rey's ideas, see Bradby, "Destruction of the Natural Economy," and Foster-Carter, "Articulate 'Articulation.'"

8. This willingness contrasts dramatically with the violence of the 1980's: Carmack, ed., *Harvest of Violence*.

Glossary

aguardiente. Rum; cane alcohol
alcalde. Member of town council
aldea. Settlement; hamlet
altiplano. Highlands
añil. Indigo
astillero. Village common lands
baldío. State-owned land
barrio. Neighborhood; in the Alta Verapaz, a patriclan
boca costa. Piedmont
brazos. "Arms"; workers
caballería. Area of land equal to approximately 112 acres
cacique. Boss
café. Coffee
café oro. Processed coffee
caja. Box; community chest; harvest measure for coffee
capellanía. Chantry
cargo system. System of linked civil and religious offices at the community level
casta(s). Mixed bloods
caudillo. Boss
caudillaje. Bossism
censo; *censo enfiteusis.* Long-term lease on community land
cofradías. Religious brotherhoods; confraternities
colono. Resident worker
comisionado militar. Representative of the national military at village level

comisionado político. Representative of the governor at the village level

composición. Regularization of land possession with the state

común. Village common lands

consolidación. Nationalization; *desamortización*

contratista; 'tratista. Free-lance labor contractor

cuerda. Measure of land area that in Guatemala varies from 18×18 *varas* (Spanish yards) to 50×50 *varas* depending upon the region and local custom

cura. Priest

denuncia. Land application

desamortización. Nationalizaion; *consolidación*

diezmo. Tithe

ejidos. Village common lands

escoteros. Casual workers

estanco. Government monopoly

excedientes. See *excesos*

excesos. Land held by owners in excess of that titled

fanega. Grain measure equal to approximately 1.6 bushels

finca. Relatively large landholding, usually for coffee

fincas de mozos. Property held for the use of labor living on it

finquero. Owner of a finca

forastero. Outsider

gobernador. The governor's representative in the community

grana. Cochineal

guachivales. Unauthorized brotherhoods or *cofradías*

habilitaciones. Wage advances

habilitadores. Labor recruiters employed by fincas

hacendado. Hacienda owner

jefe político. Name for district governor under the Liberals

justicias. Local officials in indigenous communities

labor. Medium-sized landholding, usually for food production

ladino. Person of Spanish or "national" culture

libreta. Workbook required of workers after 1877

lotificación. Division of property into lots

mandamiento. Forced or drafted wage labor

manzana. Measure of land area equal to approximately 1.7 acres; one caballería equals approximately 66 manzanas

mercancías. Goods; wares

milpa. Subsistence agriculture, usually of corn and beans

mozo. "Boy"; worker

mozo habilitado. Category of nonresident finca labor bound by debts

obras pias. Good works.

padrones. Tribute counts

parcialidades. Patriclans

peso. Spanish-Guatemala monetary unit; consists of 8 *reales*

principal; principales. Elders or "principal" men of the community

protocolos. Notary documents

pueblo. Town

quintal. Unit of weight equal to 100 pounds

realenga. State-owned land

redención de censo. "Redemption" or purchase of leased land

reducciones. Forced settlements

repartimiento. Forced or drafted wage labor

repartimiento de efectos. Forced sale of goods

tarea. Task

terreno. Land

terrenos baldíos. State-owned land; *realenga*

titulos. Titles, as in land titles

trabajo libre. Free labor, resulting from vagrancy laws of 1934

valles. Illegal ladino settlements during the colonial period

vecino. Legitimate resident and member of a community

zapadores. Sappers, i.e., forced labor for roads and public works

Bibliography

Archival Sources

Sources are arranged here roughly in order of importance to the research. For more information on archival sources in Guatemala, see various sections in K. Grieb, ed., *Research Guide to Central America and the Caribbean* (Madison, Wisc., 1985).

Archivo General de Centro América (AGCA). Most of the colonial and many of the early national period documents in the AGCA have been catalogued, if sometimes in a peculiar style, and the card catalogue is available in the AGCA. The majority of the national period documents are unclassified, an exception being the incoming correspondence of the Ministerio de Gobernación, catalogued (1860's–1900) in a separate card file in the AGCA. Among the uncatalogued materials particularly useful for this study were the papers of the departmental governors (*jefes políticos*), organized by department and by year, and the incoming and outgoing correspondence of various government ministries.

Archivo General de Centro América–Sección de Tierras (AGCA-ST). This section of the AGCA, which resulted from the incorporation into the national archive of the old Archivo de la Escribanía, deals chiefly with the measurement and titling of land. A published index exists: *Indice de los expedientes que corresponden al Archivo de la Escribanía del Gobierno y sección de Tierras*. Guatemala City, 1945.

Archivo General de Centro América–Juzgado de Primera Instancia. Typed indexes organized by department and divided into "Civil" and "Criminal" are to be found in the AGCA. Many of the cases, and despite the name, are in fact appeals from municipal courts. Also in the AGCA are indexes and cases from the several regional appeals courts that operated during the nineteenth century. The Juzgado de Primera Instancia records for Sacatepéquez are located at the Centro de Investigaciones Regionales de Mesoamérica (CIRMA) in Antigua, where the staff is organizing and computer indexing them.

Archivo General de Centro América–Protocolos (Protocolos). The AGCA card index lists notaries for the colonial period with the years in which they worked, and the staff of the AGCA has a typed list of notaries, with the number of volumes of protocolos for each, active in the nineteenth century (to 1900 only). Published lists of notaries are not accurate. There are no indexes to the protocolos themselves, although by the 1840's most notaries included a handwritten index at the beginning of each volume.

Registro(s) de Propiedad Inmueble. This archive, organized in 1877 and using quite large folio volumes, keeps track of land sales, divisions, and mortgages. To use it effectively one must know the book/folio number of the property sought; there are no indexes of these numbers, although in some cases the documents of the AGCA-ST (particularly the remeasurements after 1900) provide the appropriate numbers. There are branches of the Registro in Guatemala City and Quezaltenango.

Archivo Histórico Arqidiocesano "Francisco de Paula García Peláez" (AHA). This archive, also called the Archivo Eclesiástico or Archivo de La Curia, contains the papers of the Archbishop of Guatemala, chiefly from the late colonial period and the nineteenth century. Categories include, among others, "Cofradías," "Diezmos," "Tributo," and "Visitas Pastorales." Most useful for this study was "Cartas," correspondence received by the Archbishop; there are typed indexes for these by year.

Archivo General de los Tribunales (AGT). At the time the research for this book was carried out, this was a separate archive, but it has since been incorporated into the AGCA where it remains uncatalogued. It was particularly helpful for vagrancy cases in the 1930's.

Hemeroteca-Biblioteca Nacional and *Hemeroteca-AGCA.* These overlap in their holdings, but the researcher generally should consult both.

Instituto Indigenista de Guatemala (now part of the Ministry of Culture). Between the late 1940's and the early 1960's the institute carried out and published (in mimeograph) a number of community surveys referred to as "monografías"; copies are available in its archives.

U.S. Department of State: Consular Dispatches. Guatemala City, 1821–1904. Microfilm copies.

————: Records Relating to Internal Affairs of Guatemala, 1910–29 and 1930–44. Microfilm copies.

Special Collections, Tulane University. The Dieseldorff Papers: Records of the business and plantation activities of Erwin Paul Dieseldorff, a German planter in the Alta Verapaz from the 1880's to the 1930's.

The Penny Manuscript: Narrative memoir of a Canadian engineer who worked in Guatemala from the 1890's to the First World War.

Newspapers

(All Guatemala City except as noted)
La Asamblea Legislativa, 1893–94
Boletín Oficial, 1831–38
Boletín Oficial, 1872
El Buen Público (Quezaltenango), 1894–99
Correo de Escuintla (Escuintla), 1906
El Crepúsculo, 1872
El Diario de Centro América, 1891–1934
Diario de Occidente (Quezaltenango), 1897–98
La Gaceta de Guatemala, 1847–65
La Gaceta Oficial, 1844
El Guatemalteco, 1872–1945
El Imparcial, 1922–45 and 1979
El Indicador, 1824–25
La Mañana, 1921
El Norte (Cobán), 1937
El Noticioso, 1861–62
La Nueva Era, 1893
El Progreso, 1874
El Progreso Nacional, 1898
La República, 1893–94
El Republicano, 1893–94
La Revista, 1847
La Semana, 1865–71
La Sociedad Económica, 1866–71
El Tiempo, 1839–40
El Trabajo (Tumbador), 1904–13
La Verdad, 1837

References

Adams, Richard. Crucifixion by Power: Essays in Guatemalan Social Structure 1944–1966. Austin, Tex., 1970.

Adams, Tani. "San Martín Jilotepeque: Aspects of the Political and Socioeconomic Structures of a Guatemalan Peasant Community." MS.

Alvarado, José. Tratado de caficultura práctica. 2 vols. Guatemala City, 1936.

Anderson, Wayne Foster. "The Development of Export Transportation in Liberal Guatemala, 1871–1920." Ph.D. diss., Tulane University, 1985.

"Año de 1763–autos formados sobre la Real Cedula para que esta Real Audiencia con la brevedad y recerva posible remita una relación individual de los Corregimientos y Alcaldías Mayores de este Reyno." Boletín del Archivo General del Gobierno (Guatemala City) 3, no. 3 (Apr. 1937): 274–329.

Añoveras, Jesús María. *Población y estado socioreligioso de la diócesis de Guatemala en el último tercio del siglo XVIII.* Guatemala City, 1987.

Arevalo Martínez, Rafael. *Ecce Pericles. La tiranía de Manuel Estrada Cabrera en Guatemala.* Guatemala City, 1945.

Arrighi, G. "Labor Supplies in Historical Perspective: A Study of the Proletarianization of the African Peasantry in Rhodesia." *Journal of Development Studies* 6, no. 3 (Apr. 1970): 185–224.

Asturias, Miguel Angel. *El problema social del indio.* Guatemala City, 1923.

———. *El Señor Presidente.* Translated by Francis Partridge. New York, 1982.

Baily, John. *Central America.* London, 1850.

Balmori, Diana, Stuart Voss, and Miles Wortman. *Notable Family Networks in Latin America.* Chicago, 1984.

Banco del Occidente: Tradición de la Banca Privada. Quezaltenango, 1956.

Bancroft, Hubert Howe. *History of Central America.* 3 vols. San Francisco, 1883–87.

Barreda, Pedro. *Geografía e historia de correos y telecomunicaciones de Guatemala.* Guatemala City, 1960.

Batres Jáuregui, Antonio. *Los indios: su historia y su civilización.* Guatemala City, 1893.

Bauer, Arnold J. "The Church in the Economy of Spanish America: *Censos* and *Depositos* in the Eighteenth and Nineteenth Centuries." *Hispanic American Historical Review* 63, no. 4 (Nov. 1983): 707–33.

———. "Rural Workers in Spanish America: Problems of Peonage and Oppression." *Hispanic American Historical Review* 59, no. 1 (Feb. 1979): 34–63.

Bauer País, Alfonso, *Catalogación de las leyes y disposiciones de trabajo de Guatemala del período, 1872–1930.* Guatemala City, 1965.

Bazant, Jan. "Peones, arrendatarios y aparceros, 1851–1853." *Historia Mexicana* 23, no. 2: (Oct.–Dec. 1973): 330–57.

———. "Peones, arrendatarios y aparceros: 1868–1904." *Historia Mexicana* 24, no. 1 (July–Sept. 1974): 91–121.

Beinhart, William, Peter Delius, and Stanley Trapido. *Putting a Plough to the Ground.* Johannesburg, 1986.

Belzunegui Ormazábal, Bernardo. *Pensamiento económico y reforma agraria en el reino de Guatemala, 1792–1812.* Guatemala City, 1992.

Berg, Elliot. "Backward-sloping Labor Supply Functions in Dual Economies: The African Case." *Quarterly Journal of Economics*, Aug. 1961: 468–92.

Bergad, Laird. *Coffee and the Growth of Agrarian Capitalism in Nineteenth Century Puerto Rico.* Princeton, N.J., 1983.

Bertrand, Michel. "Lucha por la tierra en Guatemala colonial: la tenencia de la tierra en la Baja Verapaz en los siglos XVI–XIX." MS.

———. "La tierra y los hombres: la sociedad rural en Baja Verapaz durante los siglos XVI–XIX." In Steve Webre, ed., *La sociedad colonial en Guatemala: estudios regionales y locales.* Guatemala City, 1989.

Bingham, James W. "Guatemalan Agriculture During the Administration of

President Manuel Estrada Cabrera, 1898–1920." M.A. thesis, Tulane University, 1974.

Blanchard, Peter. "The Recruitment of Workers in the Peruvian Sierra at the Turn of the Century: The Enganche System." *Inter-American Economic Affairs* 33, no. 3 (Winter 1979): 63–83.

Bocock, Robert. *Hegemony*. London, 1986.

Boddam-Whettham, James. *Across Central America*. London, 1877.

Bradby, Barbara. "The Destruction of the Natural Economy." *Economy and Society* 4 (May 1975): 127–61.

Brading, David. *Haciendas and Ranchos in the Mexican Bajío, León, 1799–1860*. Cambridge, England, 1978.

Braiterman, Jared I. "A Conflict Between Modernity and Peasant Society in the 1830's." B.A. Honors thesis, Harvard University, 1986.

Brenner, Robert. "The Social Basis of Economic Development." In John Roemer, ed., *Analytical Marxism*. Cambridge, England, 1986.

Bricker, Victoria. *The Indian Christ, The Indian King: The Historical Substrata of Maya Myth and Ritual*. Austin, Tex., 1981.

Brigham, William T. *Guatemala, Land of the Quetzal*. New York, 1887. Reprinted 1965.

Brintnal, Douglas. *Revolt Against the Dead: The Modernization of a Mayan Community in the Highlands of Guatemala*. New York, 1979.

Browning, David. *El Salvador, Landscape and Society*. Oxford, 1971.

Bulmer-Thomas, Victor. "Central America in the Inter-War Period." In Rosemary Thorp, ed., *Latin America in the 1930s*. London, 1984.

———. *Political Economy of Central America Since 1920*. Cambridge, England, 1987.

Bunzel, Ruth. *Chichicastenango: A Guatemalan Village*. Seattle, 1952.

Burgess, Paul. *Justo Rufino Barrios*. New York, 1926.

Burkitt, Robert. "Explorations in the Highlands of Western Guatemala." *The Museum Journal* (University of Pennsylvania) 21, no. 1 (1930): 41–72.

Burns, E. Bradford. *Eadweard Muybridge in Guatemala, 1875: The Photographer as Social Recorder*. Berkeley, Calif., 1986.

———. *The Poverty of Progress: Latin America in the Nineteenth Century*. Berkeley, Calif., 1980.

Cabot, Geoffrey. "The Consolidation of 1804 in Guatemala." *The Americas* 28 (July 1971): 20–38.

Cambranes, J. C. *Aspectos del desarrollo económico y social de Guatemala a la luz de fuentes históricos alemanes, 1868–1885*. Guatemala City, 1975.

———. *Coffee and Peasants in Guatemala*. Stockholm, 1985.

———. *El imperialismo alemán en Guatemala*. Guatemala City, 1977.

———. *Introducción a la historia agraria de Guatemala, 1500–1900*. Guatemala City, 1986.

Cancian, Frank, "Political and Religious Organizations." In Manning Nash, ed., *Handbook of Middle American Indians*, vol. 6. Austin, Tex., 1967.

Cardoso, C. F. S. "Central America: The Liberal Era, c. 1870–1930." In L. Bethell, ed., *Cambridge History of Latin America*, vol. 5. Cambridge, England, 1986.

———. "Historia económica del café en Centroamérica (Siglo XIX): estudio comparativo." *Estudios Sociales Centroamericanos* 10 (Jan.–Apr. 1975): 3–57.

Cardoso, C. F. S., and Héctor Pérez Brignoli. *Centro América y la economia occidental (1520–1930)*. San José, Costà Rica, 1977.

Carmack, Robert. *Historia social de los Quichés*. Guatemala City, 1979.

———. "Spanish-Indian Relations in Highland Guatemala, 1800–1944." In Murdo MacLeod and Robert Wasserstrom, eds., *Spaniards and Indians in South Eastern Mesoamerica: Essays in the History of Ethnic Relations*. Lincoln, Nebr., 1983.

———. ed., *Harvest of Violence: The Maya Indians and the Guatemalan Crisis*. Norman, Okla., 1988.

Carmack, Robert, John D. Early, and Christopher Lutz, eds. *Historical Demography*. Institute of Mesoamerican Studies publication no. 6. Albany, N.Y., 1982.

Cazali, Agusto Avila. "El desarrollo del café y su influencia en el régimen de trabajo agrícola, 1871–1885." Paper presented at I Congreso Centroamericano de Historia Demográfica, Económica y Social, San José, Costa Rica, 1973.

Chinchilla Aguilar, Ernesto. *Historia y tradición de la ciudad de Amatitlán*. Guatemala City, 1961.

Claxton, Robert. "How Guatemala Responded to Drought: 1563–1922." *Food and Climate Review*, 1978: 40–45.

———. "Notable Late-season Guatemalan Rain Showers in Historical Perspective." MS.

———. "Weather-based Hazards in Colonial Guatemala." In Robert Claxton, ed., *Investigating Natural Hazards in Latin American History*. West Georgia College Studies in the Social Sciences no. 25 (1985): 139–55.

Clegern, Wayne. "Transition from Conservatism to Liberalism in Guatemala, 1865–1871." In W. Coker, ed., *Hispanic-American Essays in Honor of Max Leon Moorhead*. Pensacola, Fla., 1979.

Colby, Benjamin, and Lore Colby. *The Daykeeper: The Life and Discourse of an Ixil Diviner*. Cambridge, Mass., 1981.

Colby, Bejamin, and Pierre van den Berghe. *Ixil Country: A Plural Society in Highland Guatemala*. Berkeley, Calif., 1969.

Collins, Anne Cox. "Colonial Jacaltenango, Guatemala: The Formation of a Corporate Community." Ph.D. diss., Tulane University, 1980.

Consulado de Comercio. "Apuntamientos sobre la agricultura y comercio del Reyno de Guatemala." In José María García Laguardia, *La génesis de constitucionalismo en Guatemala*. Guatemala City, 1971.

Contreras, J. Daniel. *Una rebelión indígena en el partido de Totonicapán en 1820*. 2d printing. Guatemala City, 1968.

Cooper, Fredrick. *From Slavers to Squatters: Plantation Labor and Agriculture in Zambia and Coastal Kenya, 1890–1925.* New Haven, Conn., 1980.

Córdoba, Fr. Matias de. "Utilidades de que todos los indios y ladinos se vistan y calcen a la española." In Flavio Guillen, *Un fraile procer y una fábula poema.* 2 vols. Guatemala City, 1966.

Cortés y Larraz, Pedro. *Descripción geográfico-moral de la díocesis de Guatemala.* 2 vols. Guatemala City, 1958.

Costeloe, Michael P. *Church Wealth in Mexico: A Study of the "Juzgado de Capellanías" in the Archbishopric of Mexico, 1800–1856.* Cambridge, England, 1967.

Crédito Hipotecario Nacional de Guatemala. *Informes,* 1931–40. Guatemala City, 1931–40.

Cross, Harry. "Living Standards in Rural Nineteenth Century Mexico: Zacatecas, 1820–80." *Journal of Latin American Studies* 10 (May 1978): 1–19.

Davis, Shelton. "Land of Our Ancestors: A Study of Land Tenure and Inheritance in the Highlands of Guatemala," Ph.D. diss., Harvard University, 1970.

Dean, Warren. *Rio Claro: A Brazilian Plantation System, 1820–1920.* Stanford, Calif., 1976.

Diaz Castillo, Roberto. *Legislación económica de Guatemala durante la reforma liberal.* Guatemala City, 1973.

Diemecke de Gonzalez, Ofelia Calderón. *El negro en Guatemala durante la época colonial.* Guatemala City, 1973.

Diener, Paul. "The Tears of St. Anthony: Ritual and Revolution in Eastern Guatemala." *Latin American Perspectives* 5, no. 3 (1978): 92–116.

Dinwoodie, David. "Expedient Diplomacy: The United States and Guatemala, 1898–1920." Ph.D. diss., University of Colorado, 1972.

Dirección General de Estadística. *Censo de la República de Guatemala,* 1921. Guatemala City, 1924.

———. *Censo de la República de Guatemala levantado el ano 1880.* Guatemala City, 1881.

———. *Censo general de la República de Guatemala levantado en 26 de February de 1893.* Guatemala City, 1894.

———. *Contribución estadística para el estudio de maíz.* Guatemala City, 1951.

———. *Sexto censo de población, 1950.* Guatemala City, 1953.

Directorio oficial y guía general de la República de Guatemala. Guatemala City, 1915.

Disposiciones emitidas por el Señor Presidente de la República General de División Don José María Reyna Barrios. Guatemala City, 1894.

Dominguez, Mauricio. "The Development of a Technological and Scientific Coffee Industry in Guatemala, 1830–1930." Ph.D. diss., Tulane University, 1970.

Dorsal, Paul. "Dependency, Revolution, and Industrial Development in Guatemala, 1821–1986." Ph.D. diss., Tulane University, 1987.

Duncan, Kenneth, and Ian Rutledge. *Land and Labor in Latin America*. Cambridge, England, 1977.

Dunkerly, James. *Power on the Isthmus: A Political History of Modern Central America*. New York, 1988.

Dunlop, Robert. *Travels in Central America*. London, 1847.

Dunn, Henry. *Guatimala, or the United Provinces of Central America in 1827–8*. New York, 1828.

Early, John D. *The Demographic Structure and Evolution of a Peasant System: The Guatemalan Population*. Boca Raton, Fla., 1982.

Ebel, Roland. *Political Modernization in Three Guatemalan Indian Communities*. Middle America Research Institute publication no. 24. New Orleans, La., 1969.

Elliott, Elaine. "Feeding the Men of Corn: Ixil Land History in Ilom." MS.

Estrada Monroy, Agustín. *Datos para la historia de la iglesia en Guatemala*. 3 vols. Guatemala City, 1972–79.

Falla, Ricardo. *Quiché rebelde*. Guatemala City, 1978.

Fariss, Nancy. *Maya Society Under Colonial Rule: The Collective Enterprise of Survival*. Princeton, N.J., 1984.

Feldman, Lawrence. "Disasters Natural and Otherwise, and Their Effects upon Population Centers in the Reino de Guatemala." In Duncan Kinkaid, ed., *Estudios del reino de Guatemala*. Seville, 1985.

Femia, Joseph V. *Gramsci's Political Thought*. Oxford, 1981.

Fernandez Molina, Manuel. *Los tributos en el reino de Guatemala: 1786–1821*. Guatemala City, n.d.

Flores Alvarado, Humberto. *La proletarización del campesino de Guatemala*. Quezaltenango, 1971.

Floyd, Troy. "The Guatemalan Merchants, the Government, and the Provincianos, 1750–1800," *Hispanic American Historical Review* 41, no. 1 (Feb. 1961): 90–110.

Foster-Carter, Aidan. "Can We Articulate 'Articulation'?" In J. Clammer, ed., *The New Economic Anthropology*. New York, 1978.

Frank, Andre Gunder. *Dependent Accumulation and Underdevelopment*. New York, 1979.

———. *World Accumulation, 1492–1789*. New York, 1978.

Fry, Michael. "Agrarian Society in the Guatemalan Montaña, 1700–1840." Ph.D. diss., Tulane University, 1988.

———. "Política agraria y reacción campesina: la región de la Montaña, 1821–1838." *Mesoamérica* 15 (June 1988): 25–46.

Gall, Francisco. *Diccionario geográfico de Guatemala*. 3 vols. Guatemala City, 1976–83.

García Laguardia, José María. *El pensamiento Liberal en Guatemala. Antología*. Guatemala City, 1977.

———. *La Reforma liberal*. Guatemala City, 1972.

García Mainieri de Villeda, Amparo. "Relaciones de produción en Guatemala durante el período 1892–1898." Tesis de licenciatura, Historia, University of San Carlos, Guatemala City, 1978.

García Peláez, Francisco de Pineda. *Memorias para la historia del antiguo reino de Guatemala*. 3 vols. Guatemala City, 1851–52. Reprinted 1943–44.

García Redondo, Antonio, *Memoria sobre el fomento de las cosechas de cacaos y de otros ramos de agricultura*. Guatemala City, 1799.

Garlant, Julia. "Developmental Aspects of Barrios' Agrarian Program." M.A. thesis, Tulane University, 1968.

Gillen, John. *The Culture of Security in San Carlos: A Study of a Guatemalan Community of Indians and Ladinos*. Middle American Research Institute publication no. 16. New Orleans, La., 1951.

Glade, W. P. *The Latin American Economies: A Study of the Institutional Evolution*. New York, 1969.

Gleijeses, Piero. "La aldea de Ubico: Guatemala, 1931–1944." *Mesoamérica* 17 (June 1989): 25–59.

———. *Shattered Hopes: The Guatemalan Revolution and the United States, 1944–1954*. Princeton, N.J., 1991.

Godelier, Maurice. *Rationality and Irrationality in Economics*. New York, 1972.

Goubaud, Antonio. "Notes on San Juan Chamelco." Microfilm Collection of Manuscripts on Middle American Cultural Anthropology, University of Chicago, no. 23.

———. "Notes on the Indians of the finca Nueva Granada." Microfilm Collection of Manuscripts on Middle American Cultural Anthropology, University of Chicago, no. 21.

Great Britain–Foreign Office. *Diplomatic and Consular Reports on Trade and Finance: Guatemala*, 1856–1900. London, 1856–1900.

Grieb, Kenneth. *Guatemalan Caudillo*. Athens, Ohio, 1979.

———, ed. *Research Guide to Central America and the Caribbean*. Madison, Wisc., 1985.

Grieshaber, Edwin. "Hacienda-Indian Community Relations and Indian Acultoration." *Latin American Research Review* 14, no. 3 (1979): 107–28.

Griffith, William. *Empires in the Wilderness: Foreign Colonization and Development in Guatemala, 1834–1844*. Chapel Hill, N.C., 1965.

"Guatemala hace cien años." *Anales de la Sociedad de Geografía e Historia de Guatemala* 5, no. 3 (May 1930): 264–86.

Gudmundson, Lowell. *Costa Rica Before Coffee*. Baton Rouge, La., 1986.

Guzmán Bockler, Carlos, and Jean Louis Herbert. *Guatemala: una interpretación histórico-social*. Mexico City, 1970.

Haefkens, Jacobo. *Viaje a Guatemala y Centroamérica*. Guatemala City, 1969.

Hamnett, Brian. *Politics and Trade in Southern Mexico, 1790–1821*. Cambridge, England, 1971.

Handy, James. *Gift of the Devil: A History of Guatemala*. Boston, 1984.

———. *Revolution in the Countryside: Community, Land, and Reform in Guatemala.* Chapel Hill, N.C., forthcoming.

Hawkins, John. *Inverse Images: The Meaning of Culture, Ethnicity, and Family in Postcolonial Guatemala.* Albuquerque, N. Mex., 1984.

Herrick, Thomas. *Desarrollo económico y político de Guatemala durante el período de Justo Rufino Barrios, 1871–1885.* Guatemala City, 1974.

Hill II, Robert M. "Continuity of Guachibales in Nineteenth Century San Pedro Sacatepéquez." Paper presented at the meeting of the American Anthropological Association, Washington, D.C., November 1989.

———. "Manteniendo el culto a los santos: aspectos financieros de las instituciones religiosas en el altiplano maya." *Mesoamérica* 11 (June 1986): 61–77.

———. "Social Organization by Decree in Colonial Highland Guatemala," *Ethnohistory* 36, no. 2 (Spring 1989): 170–98.

Hill II, Robert M., and John Monaghan. *Continuities in Highland Social Organization: Ethnohistory in Sacapulas, Guatemala.* Philadelphia, 1987.

Hindess, Barry, and Paul Q. Hirst. *Pre-Capitalist Modes of Production.* New York, 1975.

Holleran, Mary. *Church and State in Guatemala.* New York, 1949.

Hoyt, Elizabeth. "The Indian Laborer on Guatemalan Coffee Fincas." *Inter-American Economic Affairs* 9, no. 1 (1955): 33–46.

Indice de los expedientes que corresponden al Archivo de la Escribanía del Gobierno y Sección de Tierras. Guatemala City, 1945.

Informe cafetalero de Guatemala de la Oficina Central del Café, Guatemala, C.A. a la Junta Interamericana del Café. Washington, D.C., 1948.

Ingersoll, H. M. B. "The War of the Mountain: A Study of a Reactionary Peasant Insurgency in Guatemala, 1837–1873." Ph.D. diss., George Washington University, 1972.

de Janvry, Alain. *The Agrarian Question and Reformism in Latin America.* Baltimore, Md., 1982.

Jonas, Susan, and David Tobis, eds. *Guatemala: Land of Eternal Struggle.* New York, 1974.

Jones, Chester Lloyd. *Guatemala, Past and Present.* Minneapolis, 1940.

Juarros, Domingo. *Compendio de la historia del reino de Guatemala.* Guatemala City, 1981.

Katz, Friedrich. "Labor Conditions on Haciendas in Porfirian Mexico: Some Trends and Tendencies." *Hispanic American Historical Review* 54 (Feb. 1974): 1–47.

———, ed. *La servidumbre agraria en México en la época porfiriano.* Mexico City, 1976.

Kerr, Derek. "The Role of the Coffee Industry in the History of El Salvador, 1840–1906." M.A. thesis, University of Alberta–Calgary, 1977.

King, Arden. *Cobán and the Verapaz: History and Cultural Process in Northern Guatemala.* Middle American Research Institute publication no. 37. New Orleans, La., 1974.

LaFarge, Oliver. "Maya Ethnology: The Sequence of Cultures." In C. L. Hay, et al., *The Maya and Their Neighbors*. New York, 1940.

──────. *Santa Eulalia: The Religion of a Cuchumatan Town*. Chicago, 1947.

Lainfiesta, Francisco. *Apuntamientos para la historia de Guatemala*. Guatemala City, 1975.

──────. *Mis memorias*. Guatemala City, 1980.

Larreinaga, Miguel. *Prontuario de todas las reales cédulas y cartas acordadas comunicadas a la Audiencia del antiguo reino de Guatemala desde el año 1600 hasta 1818*. Guatemala City, 1857.

Lavrin, Asunción. "The Execution of the Law of Consolidación in New Spain: Economic Aims and Results." *Hispanic American Historical Review* 53, no. 1 (Feb. 1973): 27–49.

Lemale, Carlos. *Guía geográfica descriptiva de los centro de población de la República de Guatemala*. Guatemala City, 1881.

Lincoln, Jackson. "An Ethnographic Study of the Ixil Indians of the Guatemalan Highlands." Microfilm Collection of Manuscripts on Middle American Cultural Anthropology, University of Chicago, no. 1.

Lindo-Fuentes, Hector. *Weak Foundations: The Economy of El Salvador in the Nineteenth Century, 1821–1898*. Berkeley, Calif., 1991.

López, Fr. Antonio. *Instrucción para los nopales y beneficiar la grana fina*. Guatemala City, 1818.

López Larrave, Mario. *Breve historia del movimiento sindical guatemalteco*. Guatemala City, 1979.

Lovell, W. George. "Conquest and Population: Maya Demography in Historical Perspective." Paper presented at the Latin American Studies Association, Los Angeles, September 1992.

──────. *Conquest and Survival in Colonial Guatemala: A Historical Geography of the Cuchumatan Mountains*. Kingston, Ont., 1985.

Luján Muñoz, Jorge. *Agricultura, mercado y sociedad en el corregimiento del valle de Guatemala 1670–80*. Guatemala City, 1988.

──────. "Fundación de villas de ladinos en Guatemala en el último tercero del siglo XVIII." *Revista de Indias* 36 (July–Dec. 1976): 51–79.

──────. "Reducción y fundación de Salcajá y San Carlos Sija (Guatemala) en 1776." *Anales de la Sociedad de Geografía e Historia* 49 (Jan.–Dec. 1976), n.p.

Luque Alcaide, Elisa. *La Sociedad Económica del País de Guatemala*. Seville, 1962.

Lutz, Christopher. "Guatemala: The Demographic Evolution of the Non-Spanish and Non-Indian Population, 1524–1700." MS.

──────. "Guatemala's Non-Spanish and Non-Indian Population: Its Spread and Demographic Evolution, 1700–1821." MS.

Lutz, Christopher, and W. George Lovell. "Core and Periphery in Colonial Guatemala." In C. Smith, ed., *Indian Communities and the State, 1540–1988*. Austin, Tex., 1990.

Lutz, Christopher, W. George Lovell, and William Sweezy. "The Population History of Spanish Central America." MS.

McAfee, Shirley. "A Study of Agricultural Labor in Guatemala, 1821–1871." M.A. thesis, Tulane University, 1955.

McBryde, Felix Webster. *Cultural and Historical Geography of Southwest Guatemala.* Washington, D.C., 1947.

McClintock, M. *The American Connection: Guatemala.* London, 1985.

McCreery, David. "Atanasio Tzul, Lucas Aguilar, and the Indian Kingdom of Totonicapán." In Judith Ewell and William Beezley, eds., *The Human Tradition in Latin America: The Nineteenth Century.* Wilmington, Del., 1989.

————. "Caja, Cofradía, and Cabildo: The Transformation of Barrier Institutions in Nineteenth Century Guatemala." MS.

————. "Debt Servitude in Rural Guatemala, 1876–1936." *Hispanic American Historical Review* 63, no. 4 (Nov. 1983): 735–59.

————. *Development and the State in Reforma Guatemala.* Athens, Ohio, 1983.

————. "Hegemony and Repression in Rural Guatemala." *Peasant Studies* 17, no. 3 (Spring 1990): 157–77.

————. "Land, Labor, and Violence in Highland Guatemala: San Juan Ixcoy (Huehuetenango), 1890–1940." *The Americas* 45, no. 2 (Oct. 1988): 237–49.

————. "An Odious Feudalism: *Mandamientos* and Commercial Agriculture in Guatemala, 1861–1920." *Latin American Perspectives* 13, no. 1 (Winter 1986): 99–117.

————. "State Power, Indigenous Communities, and Land in Nineteenth Century Guatemala." In C. Smith, ed., *Indian Communities and the State: Guatemala, 1540–1988.* Austin, Tex., 1989.

————. "A Terrible Scourge: Guatemala in the Influenza Pandemic of 1918–19." MS.

McCreery, David, and D. Munro. "The Cargo of the Montserrat: Gilbertese Labor in Guatemalan Coffee, 1890–1908." *The Americas* 49, no. 3 (Jan. 1993): 271–95.

MacLeod, Murdo. *Spanish Central America: A Socioeconomic History, 1520–1720.* Berkeley, Calif., 1973.

Madigan, Douglas. "Santiago Atitlán: A Socioeconomic History." Ph.D. diss., University of Pittsburgh, 1976.

Mallon, Florencia. *The Defense of the Community in Peru's Central Highlands.* Princeton, N.J., 1983.

Markman, Sidney. *Colonial Central America: A Bibliography.* Tempe, Ariz., 1977.

Martinez Peláez, Severo. *Motines de indios: La violencia colonial en Centroamérica i Chiapas.* Puebla, Mexico, 1985.

————. *La Patria del criollo.* Guatemala City, 1969.

Marure, Alejandro. *Catálogo razonado de las leyes de Guatemala.* Guatemala City, 1856.

Marx, Karl. *Capital,* vol. 1. Translated by Ben Fowkes. London, 1976.

Maudsley, Anne Carey, and Alfred Percival Maudsley. *A Glimpse at Guatemala, and Some Notes on the Ancient Monuments of Central America.* London, 1899.

Meillasoux, Claude. *Mujeres, graneros y capitales.* Mexico City, 1977.

Memoria de la Dirección de Agricultura. Ministerio de Fomento. Guatemala City, 1902.

Mendelson, E. Michael. *Los escándelos de Maximón.* Guatemala City, 1965.

Mendez, J. *Guía del inmigrante en la República de Guatemala.* Guatemala City, 1896.

Mendez, Rosendo. *Leyes vigentes de agricultura.* Guatemala City, 1937.

Mendez Montenegro, J. C. "444 años de legislación agraria, 1520–1957." *Revista de la Facultad de Ciencias Jurídicas y Sociales de Guatemala,* 2d series (Jan.–Dec. 1960).

Menery, Wilber Eugene. "The Kingdom of Guatemala During the Reign of Charles III, 1759–1788." Ph.D. diss., University of North Carolina, 1975.

Menjivar, Rafael. *Acumulación originaria y desarrollo del capitalismo en El Salvador.* San José, Costa Rica, 1980.

Miceli, Keith L. "Rafael Carrera: Defender and Promoter of Peasant Interests in Guatemala, 1837–1848." *The Americas* 31, no. 1 (July 1974): 72–95.

Miller, Hubert. *La iglesia y el estado en el tiempo de Justo Rufino Barrios.* Translated by Jorge Luján Muñoz. Guatemala City, 1976.

Ministerio de Agricultura (Guatemala). *Memoria(s), 1922–1945.* Guatemala City.

Ministerio de Fomento (Guatemala). *Memoria(s), 1879–1945.* Guatemala City.

Ministerio de Gobernación (Guatemala). *Memoria(s), 1879–1945.* Guatemala City.

Ministerio de Guerra (Guatemala). *Memoria-1905.* Guatemala City, 1905.

Ministerio de Hacienda (Guatemala). *Memorias(s), 1879–1945.* Guatemala City.

Ministerio de Relaciones Exteriores (Guatemala). *Memoria-1896.* Guatemala City, 1896.

Monforte Toledo, Mario. *Guatemala: Monografía sociológica.* Mexico City, 1959.

Montenegro Rios, Carlos. *La explotación cafetalera en Guatemala, 1930–40.* Guatemala City, 1972.

Montgomery, George. *Narrative of a Journey to Guatemala in Central America in 1838.* New York, 1839.

Montufar y Rivera Maestre, Lorenzo. *Reseña histórica de Centro América.* 7 vols. Guatemala City, 1878–87.

Moore, Barrington. *The Social Origins of Dictatorship and Democracy: Lord and Peasant in the Making of the Modern World.* Boston, 1966.

Morales Urrutia, Mateo. *La división política y administrativa de la República de Guatemala con sus datos históricos y de legislación.* 2 vols. Guatemala City, 1961.

Mosk, Sanford. "The Coffee Economy of Guatemala, 1850–1918." *Inter-American Economic Affairs* 9 (Winter 1955): 6–20.

Mulhall, Michael. *The Dictionary of Statistics.* London, 1903.

Nañez Falcón, Guillermo. "Erwin Paul Dieseldorff, German Entrepreneur in the Alta Verapaz of Guatemala, 1889–1937." Ph.D. diss., Tulane University, 1970.

————. "German Contributions to the Economic Development of the Alta Vera Paz of Guatemala, 1865–1900." M.A. thesis, Tulane University, 1961.

Nash, Manning. "The Impact of Mid-Nineteenth Century Economic Change on the Indians of Middle America." In Magnus Morner, ed., *Race and Class in Latin America*. New York, 1970.

Naylor, Robert. "Guatemala: Indian Attitudes Toward Land Tenure." *Journal of Inter-American Studies* 9, no. 4 (Oct. 1967): 619–29.

————. *Influencia británica en el comercio centroamericano durante las primeras décadas de la Independencia*. Guatemala City, 1988.

Newson, Linda. *Indian Survival in Colonial Nicaragua*. Norman, Okla., 1987.

Oakes, Maude. *The Two Crosses of Todos Santos: Survivals of Mayan Religious Rituals*. Princeton, N.J., 1951.

Orellana, Sandra. *The Tzutujil Mayas: Continuity and Change, 1250–1630*. Norman, Okla., 1984.

Osborn, Wayne. "Indian Land Retention in Colonial Metztitlan." *Hispanic American Historical Review* 53, no. 2 (May 1973): 103–15.

Ouweneel, Arij, and Catrien C. J. H. Bijleveld. "The Economic Cycle in Bourbon Central Mexico: A Critique of the *Recaudación del diezmo liquido en pesos*." *Hispanic American Historical Review* 69, no. 3 (Aug. 1989): 479–530.

Palacios, Enrique [Pio Casals]. *Reseña de la situación general de Guatemala, 1863*. Guatemala City, 1863. Reprinted 1981.

Palacios, Marcos. *Coffee in Colombia, 1850–1970*. Cambridge, England, 1980.

Palma Murga, Gustavo. "Algunas relaciones entre la iglesia y grupos particulares durante el período de 1860 a 1870. Su incidencia en el movimiento liberal de 1871." Tesis de Licenciatura, University of San Carlos (Guatemala City), 1977.

————. "Núcleos de poder local y relaciones familiares en la ciudad de Guatemala a fines del siglo XVIII." *Mesoamérica* 12 (Dec. 1966): 241–308.

Palmer, Robin, and Neil Parsons. *The Roots of Rural Poverty in Central and Southern Africa*. Berkeley, Calif., 1977.

Palmer, Steve. "La Civilización de los Indios." MS.

Parker, Franklin. *Travels in Central America, 1821–1840*. Gainesville, Fla., 1970.

Paul, Benjamin. "Entrepreneurs and Economic Inequality in San Pedro La Laguna, Guatemala: A Hundred Years of History." Paper presented at the Latin American Studies Association meeting, New Orleans, La., March 1988.

————. "Oral History of San Pedro La Laguna." MS.

Percheron, Nicole. "Producción agrícola y comercio de la Verapaz en la época colonial." *Mesoamérica* 20 (Dec. 1990): 231–48.

Peristiany, J. G. *Honour and Shame: The Values of Mediterranean Society*. London, 1966.

Piel, Jean. *Sajcabaja: Muerte y resurrección de un pueblo de Guatemala, 1500–1970*. Guatemala City, 1989.

Pineda de Mont, Manuel. *Recopilación de las leyes de Guatemala*. 3 vols. Guatemala City, 1869–72. Reprinted in one vol. 1979.

Pinto Soria, J. C. *Centroamérica, de la colonia al estado nacional (1800–1840)*. Guatemala City, 1986.

———. *Estructura agraria y asentamiento en la Capitanía General de Guatemala*. Guatemala City, 1981.

———. *Guatemala en la década de Independencia*. Guatemala City, 1978.

———. "El valle central de Guatemala (1524–1821): un análisis acerca del origen histórico-económico del regionalismo en Centroamérica." *Anuario de Estudios Centroamericanos* 14, nos. 1–2 (1988): 85–107.

Pitti, Joseph A. "Jorge Ubico and Guatemalan Politics in the 1920's." Ph.D. diss., University of New Mexico, 1975.

Post, Ken. *Arise Ye Starvlings: The Jamaican Labour Rebellion of 1938 and Its Aftermath*. Boston, 1978.

Quiñonez, José. *Directorio general de la República de Guatemala*. Guatemala City, 1929.

Ramos, Augusto. *O café no Brasil e no estrangeiro*. Rio de Janeiro, 1923.

Recinos, Adrian. *Monografía del Departmento de Huehuetenango*, 2d ed. Guatemala City, 1954.

Recopilación de las leyes agrarias. Guatemala City, 1890.

Recopilación de las leyes de Guatemala. Continuous volumes, 1881——. Guatemala City.

Reina, Rubén. *The Law of the Saints: A Pokomam Community Culture*. New York, 1966.

"Relaciones geográficas—1740." *Boletín del Archivo General del Gobierno* 1 (Oct. 1935): 9–28.

Rendon, M. C. "Manuel Estrada Cabrera, Guatemalan President, 1898–1920." D. Phil. thesis, Oxford University, 1987.

Revista de la Academia Guatemalteco de Estudios Genelógicas, Heráldicas e Históricos 7 (1979).

Rey, Pierre-Philippe. *Las alianzas de clases*. Mexico City, 1976.

Rhul, Arthur. *The Central Americans: Adventures and Impressions Between Mexico and Panama*. New York, 1928.

Rodriguez, Guillermo. *Guatemala en 1919*. Guatemala City, 1920.

Rodriguez, Mario. *The Cádiz Experiment in Central America, 1808–1826*. Berkeley, Calif., 1978.

———. "The Livingston Codes in the Guatemalan Crisis of 1837–8." In *Applied Enlightenment: Nineteenth Century Liberalism, 1830–1839*. Middle American Research Institute publication no. 23. New Orleans, La., 1972.

Rosales, Juan de Dios. "Notes on Aguacatán." Microfilm Collection of Manuscripts on Middle American Cultural Anthropology, University of Chicago, no. 24.

———. "Notes on San Pedro la Laguna." Microfilm Collections of Manuscripts on Middle American Cultural Anthropology, University of Chicago, no. 25.

Roseberry, William. *Anthropologies and Histories: Essays in Culture, History, and Political Economy.* New Brunswick, N.J., 1989.

Rossignon, Julio. *Manual de cultivo del añil y del nopal, o sea extracción del indigo, educación y cosecha de la cochinilla, extracción de los principios colorantes de varias plantas tintoriales.* Paris, 1859.

Rubio Sánchez, Manuel. "Apunte para el estudio de la tenencia de la tierra en Guatemala durante siglo XIX." *Antropología e Historia de Guatemala* 11, no. 1 (Jan. 1959): 59–65.

————. "Breve historia del desarrollo del cultivo del café." *El Imparcial*, Sept. 1954.

————. "El cacao." *Anales de la Sociedad de Geografía e Historia* 31 (1958): 81–129.

————. "La grana o cochinilla." *Antropología e historia de Guatemala* 13, no. 1 (Jan. 1961): 16–46.

————. *Historia del añil o xiquilite en Centro América.* 2 vols. San Salvador, 1976.

Saint-Lu, A. *Condición colonial y conciencia criolla en Guatemala (1524–1821).* Guatemala City, 1978.

Salazar, Ramon. *Tiempo viejo: recuerdos de mi juventud.* Guatemala City, 1967.

Saler, Benson. "The Road to El Palmar: Change, Continuity, and Conservatism in a Quiché Community." Ph.D. diss., University of Pennsylvania, 1960.

Samayoa Coronado, Francisco. *La Escuela Politécnica a traves de la historia.* 2 vols. Guatemala City, 1964.

Sanborn, Helen. *A Winter in Central America and Mexico.* Boston, 1886.

Secretario de Hacienda y Crédito Público. *Incentivas de ley para el arreglo de la situación económica: exposición de motivos.* Guatemala City, 1921.

Scott, James. "Hegemony and the Peasantry." *Politics and Society* 7, no. 3 (1977): 267–96.

————. *Weapons of the Weak: Everyday Forms of Peasant Resistance.* New Haven, Conn., 1985.

Sexton, James D., ed. *Campesino.* Tucson, Ariz., 1985.

————, ed. *Son of Tecun Uman.* Tucson, Ariz., 1981.

Shafer, Robert J. *The Economic Societies in the Spanish World.* Syracuse, N.Y., 1958.

Shatuck, George C. *A Medical Survey of the Republic of Guatemala.* Washington, D.C., 1938.

Sherman, William. *Forced Native Labor in Sixteenth Century Central America.* Lincoln, Nebr., 1978.

Simpson, Lesley Bird. *Studies in the Administration in New Spain, III: The Repartimiento System of Native Labor in New Spain and Guatemala.* Berkeley, Calif., 1938.

Skinner-Klée, Jorge. *Legislación indigenista de Guatemala.* Mexico City, 1954.

Smith, Carol. "Beyond Dependency Theory: National and Regional Patterns of Underdevelopment in Guatemala." *American Ethnologist* 5, no. 3 (1978): 574–617.

———. "Does a Commodity Economy Enrich the Few While Ruining the Masses?" *Journal of Peasant Studies* 11 (1984): 60–95.

———. "Local History in Global Context: Social and Economic Transitions in Western Guatemala." *Comparative Studies in Society and History* 26, no. 2 (1984): 193–228.

———. "Origins of the National Question: A Hypothesis." In C. Smith, ed., *Guatemalan Indians and the State, 1540–1988*. Austin, Tex., 1990.

Smith, Robert. "Forced Labor in the Guatemalan Indigo Works." *Hispanic American Historical Review* 36, no. 3 (Aug. 1956): 319–28.

———. "Indigo Production and Trade in Colonial Guatemala." *Hispanic American Historical Review* 39, no. 2 (May 1959): 181–211.

Smith, Waldemar. *The Fiesta System and Economic Change*. New York, 1977.

de Solano, Francisco. *Los Mayas del siglo XVIII: Pervivencia y transformación de la sociedad indígena guatemalteca durante la administración borbónica*. Madrid, 1974.

———. *Tierra y sociedad en el Reino de Guatemala*. Guatemala City, 1977.

Soley Guell, Tomás. *Proyecto presentado por don Tomás Soley Guell, al Gobierno de la República, para establecimiento del Crédito Hipotecario de Guatemala*. Guatemala City, 1929.

Solís, Ignacio. *Memoria de la Casa de Moneda de Guatemala y del desarrollo económico del país*. 6 vols. in one. Guatemala City, 1979.

Solórzano Fernández, Valentín. *Evolución económica de Guatemala*. Guatemala City, 1949.

Solórzano Fonseca, Juan Carlos. "Las comunidades indígenas de Guatemala, El Salvador y Chiapas durante el siglo XVIII: los mecanismos de la explotación económica." *Anuario de Estudios Centroamericanos* (Costa Rica) 11, no. 2 (1985): 93–130.

Stadelman, Raymond. "Maize Cultivation in Northwestern Guatemala." In Carnegie Institution of Washington publication no. 523, Washington, D.C., 1940.

Stephens, John L. *Incidents of Travel in Central America, Chiapas, and Yucatan*. 2 vols. New York, 1841. Reprinted 1969.

Stern, Steve. "Feudalism, Capitalism, and the World-System in the Perspective of Latin America and the Caribbean." *American Historical Review* 93, no. 4 (Oct. 1988): 829–72.

———. *Peru's Indian Peoples and the Challenge of Spanish Conquest*. Madison, Wisc., 1982.

Stoll, David. "Evangelicals, Guerillas, and the Army: The Ixil Triangle Under Rios Mont." In R. Carmack, ed., *Harvest of Violence: The Maya Indians and the Guatemalan Crisis*. Norman, Okla., 1988.

Sweatnam, John. "What Else Did the Indian Have to Do with His Time? Alternatives to Labor Migration in Prerevolutionary Guatemala." *Economic Development and Cultural Change* 38, no. 1 (Oct. 1989): 89–112.

Tax, Sol. *Penny Capitalism: A Guatemalan Indian Economy.* Washington, D.C., 1953.

von Tempsky, G. F. *Mitla: a Narrative of Incidents and Personal Adventures on a Journey in Mexico, Guatemala, and Salvador in the years 1853 to 1855.* London, 1858.

Terray, Emmanuel. *Marxism and Primitive Societies.* New York, 1972.

Thompson, George Alexander. *Narrative of an Official Visit to Guatemala from Mexico.* London, 1828.

Torres-Rivas, Edelberto. *Interpretación del desarrollo centroamericano.* San José, Costa Rica, 1971.

Tutino, John. *From Insurrection to Revolution in Mexico: Social Bases of Agrarian Violence, 1750–1940.* Princeton, N.J., 1986.

Ukers, William. *All About Coffee.* New York, 1935.

de Valle, José. *Instrucción sobre la plaga de langosta; medios de esterminarla, o de disminuir sus efectos; y de precaber la escasez de comestibles.* Guatemala City, 1804.

Van Oss, Adrian C. "Catholic Colonialism: A Parish History of Guatemala, 1524–1821." Ph.D. diss., University of Texas, 1982.

———. *Catholic Colonialism: A Parish History of Guatemala, 1524–1821.* Cambridge, England, 1986.

Van Young, Eric. "Conflict and Solidarity in Indian Village Life: The Guadalajara Region in the Late Colonial Period." *Hispanic American Historical Review* 64, no. 1 (Feb. 1984): 55–79.

———. *Hacienda and Market in Eighteenth Century Mexico: The Rural Economy of the Guadalajara Region, 1675–1820.* Berkeley, Calif., 1981.

Veblen, Thomas. "The Ecological, Cultural, and Historic Bases of Forest Preservation in Totonicapán, Guatemala." Ph.D. diss., University of California, Berkeley, 1975.

Villacorta Calderón, José. *Historia de la Capitanía General de Guatemala.* Guatemala City, 1942.

Wagley, Charles. *The Economics of a Guatemalan Village.* American Anthropological Association Memoir no. 58. Menosha, Wisc., 1941.

Wagner, Regina. "Actividades empresariales de los alemanes en Guatemala, 1850–1920." *Mesoamérica* 13 (June 1987): 87–123.

———. *Los alemanes en Guatemala, 1828–1944.* Guatemala City, 1991.

Warren, Kay. *The Symbolism of Subordination: Indian Identity in a Guatemalan Town.* Austin, Tex., 1978.

Wasserstrom, Robert. *Class and Society in Central Chiapas.* Berkeley, Calif., 1983.

Watanabe, John M. "The Demise of Communal Land Tenure in Santiago Chimaltenango, Guatemala, 1879–1950." MS.

———. "A Late-Nineteenth-Century Land Title from Western Guatemala."

Paper read at the American Anthropological Association 88th Annual Meeting, Washington, D.C., November 1989.

Wheelock, Jaime. *Imperialismo y dictadura.* Mexico City, 1975.

Williford, Miriam. "Las Luces y La Civilización: The Social Reforms of Mariano Gálvez." In *Applied Enlightenment: Nineteenth Century Liberalism, 1830–1839.* Middle American Research Institute publication no. 23. New Orleans, La., 1972.

Wilson, Charles M. *Empire in Green and Gold: The Story of the American Banana Trade.* New York, 1947.

Winson, Anthony. "Class Structure and Agrarian Transition in Central America." *Latin American Perspectives* 5, no. 4 (Fall 1978): 27–48.

Wolf, Eric. *Europe and the People Without History.* Berkeley, Calif., 1982.

———. *Peasants.* New York, 1966.

———. *Sons of the Shaking Earth.* Chicago, 1959.

Wolpe, Harold, ed. *The Articulation of Modes of Production.* London, 1980.

Woodward, Ralph L. *Central America: A Nation Divided.* 2d ed. New York, 1985.

———. *Class Privilege and Economic Development: The Consulado de Comercio de Guatemala, 1793–1871.* Chapel Hill, N.C., 1966.

———. "Crecimiento de población en Centro América durante la primera mitad del siglo de la independencia, investigaciónes reciente y estimados hasta la fecha." *Mesoamérica* 1, no. 1 (Jan.–June 1980): 219–31.

———. "Economic and Social Origins of the Guatemala Political Parties (1773–1823)." *Hispanic American Historical Review* 45, no. 4 (Nov. 1965): 544–66.

———. "The Economy of Central America at the Close of the Colonial Period." In Duncan Kinkead, ed., *Estudios del Reino de Guatemala.* Seville, 1985.

———. "Liberalism, Conservatism, and the Response of the campesinos de la Montaña to the Government of Guatemala, 1821–1850." *Plantation Society in the Americas* 1, no. 1 (1979): 109–29.

———. "Population and Development in Guatemala, 1840–1870." *SECOLAS Annals* 14 (1983): 5–18.

———. "Social Revolution in Guatemala: The Carrera Revolt." In *Applied Enlightenment: Nineteenth Century Liberalism, 1830–1939.* Middle American Research Institute publication no. 23. New Orleans, La., 1972.

The World's Coffee: Studies of the Principal Agricultural Products of the World Market, no. 9. Rome, 1947.

Wortman, Miles. *Government and Society in Central America.* New York, 1982.

Young, John, *Central American Currency and Finance.* Princeton, N.J., 1925.

Zelaya Gil, Agusto, and Manuel Antonio Lucerno, eds. *Resumen de leyes de la República, clasificados y anotados por secretarías.* Guatemala City, 1955.

Zilbermann de Luján, Cristina. *Aspectos socio-económicos del traslado de la ciudad de Guatemala (1773–1783).* Guatemala City, 1987.

INDEX

In this index an "f" after a number indicates a separate reference on the next page, and an "ff" indicates separate references on the next two pages. A continuous discussion over two or more pages is indicated by a span of page numbers, e.g., "57–59." *Passim* is used for a cluster of references in close but not necessarily consecutive sequence.

Library of Congress Cataloging-in-Publication Data

McCreery, David.
Rural Guatemala, 1760–1940 / David McCreery
p. cm.
Includes bibliographical references and index.
ISBN 0-8047-2318-4 (CL.) : ISBN 0-8047-2792-9 (PBK.)
1. Agriculture—Economic aspects—Guatemala—History.
2. Guatemala—Rural conditions.   3. Coffee industry—
Guatemala—History. I. Title.
HD1807.M32   1994
307.72'097281—dc20   93-27405   CIP

Original printing 1994
Last figure below indicates year of this printing:
05   04   03   02   01   00   99   98   97   96